The National Review

TREASURY
OF
CLASSIC
CHILDREN'S
LITERATURE

Volume Two

ISI Books
Wilmington, DE
2003

The National Review Treasury of Classic Children's Literature, Volume Two
© 2003 by National Review, Inc.

Library of Congress Cataloging-in-Publication Data:
The National Review treasury of classic children's literature.
— 1st ed. —New York, NY: National Review/ISI Books, 2003

   v. ; cm.
   ISBN 0-9627841-5-X (v. 1)
   0-9627841-7-6 (v. 2)

   1. Children's literature—Collections. I. National Review
Research Library (New York, N.Y.)
PZ5.N38 2003   2003101756
808.899282—dc21   0309

Jacket Design by Luba Myts

PRINTED IN THE UNITED STATES OF AMERICA

CONTENTS

had set it upon the ground, he saw that it was a porcupine, that shook the water from its quills, and said:

"Thank you, kind boy, for taking me from the well. I should surely have drowned had you not come to my rescue. Because you helped me, what can I do to help you?"

"I am glad to have aided you, but I fear there is nothing you can do to help me," replied the boy; "I am journeying far to find a certain kind of needle. This morning I shot my arrow at a tree, but it glanced, and tore a big hole in the wizard shoemaker's leather apron. I must mend this, or he will do me harm, and to do it I must have a certain kind of needle which neither man can give me, nor woman can give me; so I do not see how I am to get it."

Then the porcupine smiled. "Perhaps I can help you in that, little brother," he said. "Take hold of one of those long quills in my back, and shut your eyes, and do just as I bid you."

This the boy did, and the porcupine then said: "Pull, little brother; pull as hard as you can!" The boy pulled, and felt the quill coming out of the porcupine's back as he pulled. So he stopped pulling, not wishing to injure his friend. But the porcupine said again: "Pull as hard as you can, I tell you; never mind me!"

So again the boy pulled, and he felt the quill come out in his hands. Then the porcupine said: "Open your eyes, little brother, and let us see what we have here."

So the boy opened his eyes, but, to his astonishment, instead of a porcupine's quill in his hands he found a long, keen, steel needle that he, somehow, knew was just the thing to mend the wizard shoemaker's leather apron.

So he said to the porcupine: "Thank you, good porcupine, for giving me this splendid needle."

But the porcupine replied: "Thanks should be from me, for I surely should have drowned if you had not come to my aid. Besides, I go up and down in the world quite a bit, and I have always seen you helping someone; and I am sure that a boy who helps others will find help himself."

So the boy stuck the needle carefully under the lapel of his coat, and went on his way. He had passed many a sunny hollow and many a shady wood, when he heard a deep "Moo-oo" of distress, and ran in the direction whence the sound came. Soon, in a sunny glade, he found a big mother-cow, calling loudly and looking this way and that, while tears rolled down her cheeks.

"Why, good mother-cow!" the boy cried, "what is the matter?"

"Alas!" said the cow, "I have lost my little calf. Always he waits for me in this sunny glade, but today I came back, and he is not here. I do not dare go to hunt for him lest he come while I am gone, so I can only stand here and call."

"Be of good cheer," said the boy, "I will help you find your little calf. Wait here,

Acknowledgments

AS WITH ITS predecessor, *The National Review Treasury of Classic Children's Literature*, most of the stories in this book first appeared in *St. Nicholas Magazine*—the renowned children's monthly magazine that was published from 1874 until 1941. Three stories from Volume Two orignated in other magazines: Howard Pyle's "The Princess of the Glass Hill" is from *Harper's Young People*; Ellis Parker Butler's "Pigs Is Pigs" is from *The American Magazine*, and Mark Twain's "Tom Sawyer, Detective" is from *Harper's New Monthly Magazine*.

Mr. Twain's is one of five novel-ish—lengthy and delightful—stories in the following pages. The others are Julia Truitt Bishop's "Another Chance," Marion Ames Taggart's "The Wyndham Girls," Jack London's "The Cruise of the *Dazzler*," and Adeline Knapp's "The Boy and the Baron." Some may appeal more to girls, and others more to boys, but in truth their appeal is universal. They are wonderfully written tales, as are all the 38 entries in this book.

About how this book was made, and who helped make it: The text and pictures were scanned, processed, and reformatted from the pages of original magazine issues, some dating back nearly 125 years. Taking a large volume of aging material—much of it with smudges and on yellowing pages—and turning it into an electronic format is a long and often-tedious process. But the drudgery does bear such wonderful fruit!

Once the "conversion" phase of the project was completed, the stories were printed out for proofreading. As with the first volume, the bulk of such was done by Julie Crane, who also helped in the process of nominating stories from which Bill Buckley selected those that made our final cut. Many thanks.

Backstopping these efforts was Associate Editor Sarah A. Bramwell, who once again played an important part in the proofreading process. Her fine work is most appreciated.

As to the final phase of production, a very special thank you goes again to *NR*'s Art Director, Luba Myts, who made sense of all the electronic data and wove and caressed the bytes, her efforts resulting in this handsome volume. Luba designed the book's layout and its cover art, and handled the myriad of "pre-press" chores that are unpleasant, but unavoidable—all this in addition to her day-to-day responsibilities with the magazine. We bow to her.

Other deserving thanks are Kevin Longstreet, Assistant to *NR*'s Publisher, who helped out in many ways large and small, to *NR* Publisher Ed Capano, whose advice and direction were critical to this project's fruition, as well as to the overall progress of *National Review*'s growing book-publishing enterprise, and to *NR* Editor-at-Large William F. Buckley Jr., who read scores upon scores of *St. Nicholas* stories, graded them, and then finally selected those that are contained within volumes 1 and 2 of *The National Review Treasury of Classic Children's Literature*.

Closer to home—indeed, at home—I must thank those family members who were conscripted into helping with this project. At their father's urging, my three oldest children, James, Mary, and Andrew, read various stories and offered their opinions as to which ones truly shined in their youthful eyes. (Elizabeth liked the pretty pictures, but provided no literary reviews, while young John, a fickle three-year-old, silently protested the lack of stories about trucks.)

I won't be able to rely on their expertise much longer—as the saying goes, they do grow up so fast. Would that they could stay young forever. Alas, at least some of the joys and beauty of youth can be preserved for them in this book. I am hopeful that those children who come into possession of *The National Review Treasury of Classic Children's Literature*—no matter which volume—will, years from now, see this old friend on a bookshelf, and with a smile reach for it and leaf through the often-visited pages, stirring warm memories of reading these wonderful and inspiring stories. And then, just maybe, they will steal away to a quiet spot to once again immerse themselves in ageless tales finely told.

Happy and enjoyable reading!

Jack Fowler
NR Associate Publisher
August 2003

Introduction

BY WILLIAM F. BUCKLEY JR.

(This is an excerpt from the Introduction by Mr. Buckley for The National Review Treasury of Classic Children's Literature—*for which this volume is the sequel. "Tommy and the Meadow Mice," referred to below, appeared in a series of stories by Thornton Burgess that also included "How It Happened that Reddy Fox Gained a Friend" and "Why Peter Rabbit Has One Less Enemy"— both of which are republished in this volume.)*

THE CHILDREN'S STORIES, you will find, are extraordinarily varied. There are also the fairy tales, into which children's minds gladly slid in those days. When we read the Oz books, we had no difficulty at all in fancying ourselves as mingling with Real People. The movie made after the book, *The Wizard of Oz*, is viewed by American children over the age of ten as palpable romance. Tell-it-to-the-Marines wasn't by any means the attitude we brought to such tales.

I remember a book in the Oz series called *The Magic of Oz*. That book disclosed a word, a mastery of the correct pronunciation of which endowed the apprentice with the power to transform himself/herself into any animal on earth. I spent a great deal of time endeavoring to master that magical word. It read something on the order of PYRZQXGL. I must have tried to order the syllables and attempt their pronunciation out loud 500 times, slightly varying the accentuation in order to activate the efficacious phonemes that would permit my reincarnation as a tiger. On achieving this, I would end forever any presumption, in our household, that because I was a mere eleven, anyone older could belittle me *and hope to survive!*

The magic word never quite worked for me, but maybe I owe to that delirious obsession some sense of the enchanting mystery of the morphology of words: *Get words right.* I reflected on the misusage phenomenon when I served in the United Nations and had to sit down in my delegate's chair to listen to a speech by the ambassador from the "German Democratic Republic." There is no magical incantation, I reminded myself, that could make the man I was listening to pass himself off persuasively as either a democrat or a republican.

Some illusions, as with all of those references for fifty years to the "democratic" states of Communist Europe, are noxious, crying out to be put down. But the illusions of this volume's storytellers—many initially selected by Mary Mapes Dodge, founding editor of *St. Nicholas Magazine*, and author of the imperishable *Hans Brinker, or The Silver Skates*—stimulate awe, wonder, delight, fear, reassurance. There are no children's tales in this collection of a kind that would have stimulated base appetites. I wonder what Adolf Hitler read as a child?

Which brings me to use a much rejected word, secretly cherished by me but which I use, out of cowardice, infrequently, and mostly in the closet. It is "wholesome." In the modern age people tend to think that wholesome goes with Cream of Wheat, marshmallows, and Kool-Aid, inducing tedium soon, nausea later. It is difficult to conceive of a movie these days that would advertise itself as "wholesome." Imagine recommending to Hollywood producers a rating of PG-6.

Well, these are wholesome stories, but some of them come with bite and wit and cunning, and one is not to be thrown off by such a title as Thornton Burgess's "Tommy and the Meadow Mice." The story survives a title all but inconceivable in modern times. . . .

WFB
Stamford, Connecticut
September 2002

The Brownies at the Sea-side

WRITTEN AND ILLUSTRATED BY PALMER COX

WITHIN a forest dark and wide,
Some distance from the ocean side,
A band of Brownies played around
On mossy stone or grassy mound,
Or, climbing through the branching tree,
Performed their antics wild and free.
When one, arising in his place
With sparkling eyes and beaming face,
Soon won attention from the rest,
And thus the listening throng addressed:
"For years and years, through heat and cold,
Our home has been this forest old;
The saplings which we used to bend
Now like a schooner's masts ascend.

Yet here we live, content to ride
A springing bough with childish pride,
Content to bathe in brook or bog
Along with lizard, leech, and frog;
We're far behind the age you'll find
If once you note the human kind.
The modern youths no longer lave
Their limbs beneath the muddy wave
Of meadow pool or village pond,
But seek the ocean far beyond;
Like people wild they spend the day
In rolling surf and dashing spray!
If pleasure in the sea is found
Not offered by the streams around,
The Brownie band at once should haste
These unfamiliar joys to taste;
For we, who scale the steepest hill
And tread the softest marsh at will,
Can soon the region scamper o'er
That lies between us and the shore;
And though the moon be hid from sight
And not a star adorn the night,
No torch nor lantern's ray we'll need
To show our path o'er dewy mead,

The ponds and pitfalls in the swale,
The open ditch, the slivered rail,
The poison vine and thistle high
Are never hidden from our eye."
Next evening, as their plan they'd laid,
The Brownies gathered in the shade,
All clustered like a swarm of bees
They darted from the sheltering trees;
And straight across the country wide
Began their journey to the tide.
And when they neared the beach at last—
The stout, the lean, the slow, the fast—
'Twas hard to say, of all the lot,
Who foremost reached the famous spot.
"And now," said one with active mind,
"What proper garments can we find?
In bathing costume, as you know,
The people in the ocean go."
Another spoke, "For such demands,
The building large that yonder stands,
As one can see on passing by,
Is full of garments clean and dry.
There every fashion, loose or tight,
We may secure with labor light."

Though Brownies never carry keys,
They find an entrance where they please;
And never do they chuckle more
Than when some miser bars his door;
For well they know that, spite of locks,
Of rings and staples, bolts and blocks,
Were they inclined to play such prank
He'd find at morn an empty bank.
So now the crafty Brownie crew
Soon brought the bathing-suits to view;
Some, working on the inner side,
The waiting group without supplied—
'Twas busy work, as may be guessed,
Before the band was fully dressed;

PALMER COX

Some still had cloth enough to lend,
Though shortened up at either end:
Some ran about to find a pin,
While others rolled, and puckered in,
And made the best of what they found,
However strange it hung around.
Then, when a boat was manned with care
To watch for daring swimmers there—
Lest some should venture, over-bold,
And fall a prey to cramp and cold—
A few began from piers to leap
And plunge at once in water deep,
But more to shiver, shrink, and shout
As, step by step, they ventured out;
While others were content to stay
In shallow surf, to duck and play
Along the lines that people laid
To give the weak and timid aid.
It was a sight one should behold,
When o'er the crowd the breakers rolled—
One took a header through the wave,

One floated like a chip or stave,
While others there, at every plunge,
Were taking water like a sponge.
But while the surf they tumbled through,
They reckoned moments as they flew,
And kept in mind their homeward race
Before the sun would show his face.
For sad and painful is the fate
Of those who roam abroad too late;
And well may Brownies bear in mind
The hills and vales they leave behind,
When far from native haunts they run,
As oft they do, in quest of fun.
But, ere they turned to leave the strand,
They made a vow with lifted hand
That every year, when ripened grain
Invited forth the sighing swain,
And Autumn's sun with burning glow
Had warmed the ocean spread below,
They'd journey far from grove and glen
To sport in rolling surf again.

First published in the August 1885 edition of *St. Nicholas Magazine*

BY LOUISA MAY ALCOTT

"THERE'S PLENTY OF time for another. Let the little folk go to bed, now that they've had their story, and then please bring out the next story, Auntie," cried Min, when all had listened with more interest than they would avow to the children's tale.

So the small people trotted off, much against their will, and this most obliging of aunts drew forth another manuscript, saying, as she glanced at several of her elder nieces, brave in the new trinkets Santa Claus had sent them:

"This is a story with a moral to it which the girls will understand; the boys can take naps while I read, for it will not interest them."

"If it shows up the girls, we shall like it," answered Geoff, as he composed himself to hear and enjoy the tale of

DAISY'S JEWEL-BOX AND HOW SHE FILLED IT

"IT WOULD BE perfectly delightful, and just what I long for, but I don't see how I can go with nothing fit to wear," said Daisy, looking up from the letter in her hand, with a face full of girlish eagerness and anxiety.

Mrs. Field set every fear at rest with a reassuring smile, as she quietly made one of the sacrifices mothers think so small, when made for the dear creatures for whom they live.

"You shall go, dear; I have a little sum put by for an emergency. Twenty-five dollars will do a great deal, when tastes are simple and we do our own dress-making."

"But, Mother, that money was for your cloak. You need it so much I can't bear to have you give it up," said sober little Jane, the home-girl, who unlike her gay elder sister, never cared for visiting.

"Hush, dear; I can do very well with a shawl over my old sack. Don't say a word to spoil Daisy's pleasure. She needs a change after this dull autumn, and she must be neat and nice."

Janey said no more, and fell to thinking what she had to offer Daisy; for both took great pride in the pretty girl, who was the queen among her young friends.

Daisy heard, but was so busy re-reading the letter that she took no notice then, though she recalled the words later.

"Come and pass the holidays with us. We all wish to see you, and Laura begs you will not disappoint her."

This was the invitation that came from Laura's mother; for the two girls had struck up a great friendship during the summer the city family passed in the little country town where Daisy lived. She had ardently hoped that Laura would not forget the charming plan, and now the cordial message came just when the season would be gayest in town.

"I suppose I must have the everlasting white muslin for a party dress, as that is the cheapest thing a girl can wear. A nun's-veiling is what I long for, but I'm afraid we can't afford it," she said, with a sigh, coming back from visions of city delights to the all-important question of dress.

"Yes, we can, and new ribbons, gloves, and slippers as well. You are so small that it doesn't take much, and we can make it up ourselves. So run and collect all your little finery, while I go and do the shopping at once."

"You dearest of mothers! how you always manage to give me what I want, and smooth all my worries away. I'll be as good as gold, and bring you the best present I can find."

Daisy's grateful kiss warmed the dear woman's heart, and made her forget how shabby the old sack was, as she hastened away to spend the money carefully hoarded for the much-needed cloak.

Needles and fingers flew, and two days before Christmas, Daisy set out for the enchanted city, feeling very rich with the pretty new dress in her trunk and with five dollars for pocket money. It seemed a large sum to the country girl, and she planned to spend it all in gifts for mother and Janey, whose tired faces rather haunted her after she had caught the last glimpse of them.

Her reception was a warm one; for all the Vaughns were interested in the blooming little maiden they had found among the hills, and did their best to make her visit a pleasant one. The first day she was in a delightful sort of maze—things were so splendid, gay and new; the second, she felt awkward and countrified, and wished she had not come. A letter from her mother on Christmas morning did her good, and gave her courage to bear the little trials that afflicted her.

"My clothes do look dowdy beside Laura's elegant costumes, though they seemed very nice at home; but my hair isn't red, and that's a comfort," she said to herself, as she dressed for the party that evening.

She could not help smiling at the bonny figure she saw in the long mirror, and wishing Mother and Janey could see the work of their hands in all its glory; for the simple white dress was very becoming, and her kind host had supplied her with lovely flowers for belt and bouquet.

But the smile faded as she took up her one ornament—an antique necklace, given her by an old aunt. At home it was considered a very rare and beautiful thing, and Daisy had been rather proud of her old-fashioned chain till she saw Laura's collection of trinkets, the variety and brilliancy of which dazzled her eyes, and woke a burning desire in her to possess treasures of the same sort. It was some consolation to find that the most striking were not very expensive; and after poring over them with deep interest, Daisy privately resolved to buy as many as her five dollars would procure. These new ornaments could be worn during her visit, and serve as gifts when she went home; so the extravagance would not be so great as it seemed.

This purpose comforted her, as she put on the old necklace, which looked very dingy beside the Rhine-stones that flashed, the silver bangles that clashed, and the gilded butterflies, spiders, arrows, flowers, and daggers that shone on the young girls whom she met that evening. Their fine dresses she could not hope to imitate, but a pin and a pair of bracelets were possible, and she resolved to have them, if she had to borrow money to get home.

Her head was quite turned by this desire for the cheap trinkets which attract all feminine eyes nowadays; and when, among the pretty things that came to her from the Christmas-tree that night, she received a blue plush jewel-box, she felt that it was almost a duty to fill it as soon as possible.

"Isn't it a beauty? I never had one, and it is just what I wanted!" said Daisy, delightedly lifting the trayful of satin beds for pretty things, and pulling out the little drawer underneath, where the giver's card lay.

"I told papa a work-box or a fan would be better; but he liked this and he would buy it," explained Laura, who knew how useless it was to her friend.

"It was very kind of him, and I prefer the jewel-box to either of those. I've nothing but my old chain and a shabby little pin to put in it now, but I'll fill it in time," answered Daisy, whose eyes seemed to behold the unbought treasures already reposing on the dainty cushion.

"Real jewels are the best, my dear, for their worth and beauty are never lost. The tinsel that girls wear now is poor stuff, and money is thrown away in buying it," said Mrs. Vaughn, who overheard them and guessed the temptation which beset the young country girl.

Daisy looked conscious, but answered with a smile, and a hand on her necklace: "This old thing wouldn't look well in my pretty box, so I'll leave it empty till I can afford something better."

"But that antique chain is worth many mock diamonds; for it is genuine, and its age adds to its value. Lovers of such things would pay a good price for that and keep it carefully. So don't be ashamed of it, my dear—though this pretty throat needs no ornament," added Mrs. Vaughn, hoping the girl would not forget the little lesson she was trying to give her.

Daisy did not; but when she went to bed, she set the jewel-box on the table where it would meet her eyes on her awakening in the morning, and then she fell asleep trying to decide that she would buy no baubles, since there were better things for which to spend her money.

Nothing more was said; but as the two girls went about the gay streets on various pleasant errands, Daisy never could pass the jewelers' windows without stopping to yearn over the trays full of enchanting ornaments. More than once, when alone, she went in to inquire the prices of these much-coveted trifles, and their cheapness made the temptation harder to resist. Certain things had a sort of fascination for her, and seemed to haunt her in an uncanny way, giving her no peace. A golden rose with a diamond drop of dew on its leaves bloomed in her very dreams; an enameled butterfly flew before her as she walked, and a pair of silver bangles rattled in her ears like goblin castanets.

"I shall not be safe till I spend that money, so I might as well decide on something and be at peace," said poor Daisy, after some days of this girlish struggle; "I needn't buy anything for mother and Janey, for I can share my nice and useful presents with them; but I should like to be able to show the girls my lovely jewel-box with something pretty in it—and I will! Laura needn't know anything about it, for I'm sure she'd think it silly, and so would her mother. I'll slip in now and buy that rose; it's only three dollars, and the other two will buy one *porte-bonheur*, or the dear butterfly."

Making her way through the crowd that always stood before the brilliant window, Daisy went in and demanded the rose; then, somewhat frightened by this reckless act, she paused, and decided to look farther before buying anything else. With a pleasant little flutter of the heart, as the pretty trinket was done up, she put her hand into her pocket to pay for it, and all the color died out of her cheeks when she found no purse there. In vain she pulled out handkerchief, keys, and pin-cushion; no sign of money was found but a ten-cent piece which had fallen out at some time. She looked so pale and dismayed that the shopman guessed her misfortune before she told it; but all the comfort he offered was the useless information that the crowded corner was a great place for pickpockets.

There was nothing to be done but to return the rose and go sadly home, feeling that fate was very cruel to snatch away this long-coveted happiness when so nearly won. Like the milk-maid who upset her pail while planning which ribbons would become her best, poor Daisy's dreams of splendor came to a sudden end; for instead of a golden rose, she was left with only ten cents, and not even a purse to put it in.

She went home angry, disappointed, and ashamed, but too proud to complain, though not able to keep the loss to herself; for it was a sad affair, and her face betrayed her in spite of her efforts to be gay.

"I know you were staring at the French diamonds in that corner store, I never can get you by there without a regular tug," cried Laura, when the tale was very briefly told.

"I can't help it; I'm perfectly fascinated by those foolish things, and I know I should have bought some; so it is as well that I lost my money, perhaps," answered Daisy, looking so innocently penitent and so frankly disappointed that Mr. Vaughn said kindly:

"So it is, for now I have a chance to complete my Christmas present. I was not sure it would suit, so I gave it empty. Please use this in buying some of the 'fascinating things' you like so well."

A bright ten-dollar gold piece was slipped into Daisy's hand, and she was obliged to keep it, in spite of all her protestations that she could live without trinkets, and did not need any money, as her ticket home was already bought. Mrs. Vaughn added a nice little purse, and Laura advised her to keep the lone ten-cent piece for a good-luck penny.

"Now I can do it with a free mind, and fill my box as Mr. Vaughn wishes me to. Won't it be fun?" thought Daisy, as she skipped upstairs after dinner, a load of care lifted from her spirits.

Laura was taking a music lesson, so her guest went to the sewing-room to mend the facing of her dress, which someone had stepped on while she stood in that fatal crowd. A seamstress was there, sewing as if for a wager, and while Daisy stitched her braid, she wondered if there were any need of such haste; for the young woman's fingers seemed to fly, a feverish color was in her cheeks, and now and then she sighed as if tired or worried.

"Let me help, if you are in a hurry, Miss White. I can sew fast, and know something of dress-making. Please let me. I'd love to do anything for Mrs. Vaughn, she is so kind to me," said Daisy, when her small job was done, lingering to make the offer, though an interesting book was waiting in her room.

"Thank you, I think I can get through by dark. I do want to finish, for my Mother is sick, and needs me as well as the money," answered the needle-woman, pausing to give the girl a grateful smile, then stitching away faster than ever.

"Then I must help. Give me that sleeve to sew up, and do you rest a little. You look dreadfully tired, and you've been working all day," insisted Daisy.

"That's very kind, and it would be a great help, if you really like it," answered

Miss White, with a sigh of relief, as she handed over the sleeve, and saw how heartily and helpfully Daisy fell to work.

Of course, they talked; for the friendly act opened both hearts, and did both girls good. As the younger listened to the little story of love and labor, the gold burned in her pocket, and tinsel trinkets looked very poor beside the sacrifices so sweetly made by this good daughter for the feeble mother whose comfort and support she was.

"Our landlord has raised the rent, but I can't move now, for the cold and the worry would kill Mother; so I'm tugging away to pay the extra money, or he will turn us out, I'm afraid."

"Why don't you tell Mrs. Vaughn? She helps everyone, and loves to do it."

"So she does, bless her! She has done a deal for us, and that's why I can't ask for more. I won't beg while I can work, but worry wears on me, and if I break down, what *will* become of Mother?"

Poor Mary shook the tears out of her eyes, for daylight was going, and she had no time to cry; but Daisy stopped to wonder how it would seem to be in her place, "tugging away" day after day to keep a roof over mother. It made her heart ache to think of it, and sent her hand to her pocket with a joyful sense of power; for almsgiving was a new pleasure, and Daisy felt very rich.

"I've had a present today, and I'd love dearly to share it with you, if you wouldn't mind. I shall only waste it, so do let me send it to your mother in any shape you like," she said, in a timid, but very earnest way.

"Oh, Miss Field! I couldn't do it! you are too kind; I never thought of hinting"—began Mary, quite overcome by this unexpected proposal. Daisy settled the matter by running away to the study, where Mr. Vaughn was napping, to ask him if he would give her two fives for the gold piece.

"Ah! the fascination is at work, I see; and we can't wait till Monday to buy the pretty things. Girls will be girls, and must sow their innocent wild oats I suppose. Here, my dear; beware of pickpockets, and good luck to the shopping," said the old gentlemen, as he put two crisp bills into her hands, with a laugh.

"Pickpockets won't get this, and I *know* my shopping will prosper now," answered Daisy, in such a happy tone that Mr. Vaughn wondered what plan was in the girl's head to make her look so sweet and glad.

She went slowly upstairs, looking at the two bills, which did not seem half so precious as when in the shape of gold.

"I wonder if it would be very extravagant to give her all of it. I shall do some silly thing if I keep it. Her boots were very thin, and she coughs, and if she is sick it will be dreadful. Suppose I give her five for herself, and five for her mother. I'd love to feel rich and generous for once in my life, and give real help."

The house was very still, and Daisy paused at the head of the stairs to settle the point, little dreaming that Mrs. Vaughn had heard the talk in the sewing-room, and saw her as she stood thoughtfully staring at the two bits of paper in her hand.

"I shouldn't feel ashamed if Mrs. Vaughn found me out in this, but I should never dare to let her see my bangles and pins, if I should buy them. I know she thinks them silly, especially so for me. She said she hoped I'd set a good example to Laura, in the way of simplicity and industry. I liked that, and Mother'll like it, too. But then, my jewel-box! All empty, and such a pretty thing—Oh, dear, I wish I could be wise and silly at the same time!"

Daisy sighed, and took a few more steps, then smiled, pulled out her purse, and taking the ten-cent piece, tossed it up, saying, "Heads, Mary; tails, myself."

Up flew the bright little coin, and down it came with the goddess of liberty uppermost.

"That settles it; she shall have the ten, and I'll be content with the old chain for all my jewelry," said Daisy aloud; and looking much relieved, she danced away, leaving the unsuspected observer to smile at her girlish mode of deciding the question, and to rejoice over the generous nature unspoiled as yet.

Mrs. Vaughn watched her young guest with new interest during the next few days; for certain fine plans were in her mind, and every trifle helped the decision for or against.

Mary White went smiling home that night to rejoice with her feeble mother over the help that came so opportunely and so kindly.

Daisy looked as if her shopping *had* prospered wonderfully, though the old necklace was the only ornament she wore; and those who saw her happy face at the merry-making thought that she needed no other. She danced as if her feet were as light as her heart, and enjoyed that party more than the first; for no envy spoiled her pleasure, and a secret content brightened all the world to her.

But the next day she discovered that temptation still had power over her, and she nearly spoiled her first self-conquest by the fall which is very apt to come after a triumph, as if to show us how hard it is to stand fast, even when small allurements get in our way.

She broke the clasp of the necklace, and Mrs. Vaughn directed her to a person who mended such things. The man examined it with interest, and asked its history. Daisy very willingly told all she knew, inquiring if it was really valuable.

"I'd give twenty-five dollars for it any time. I've been trying to get one to go with a pair of ear-rings I picked up, and this is just what I want. Of course, you don't care to sell it, miss?" he asked, glancing at Daisy's simple dress and rather excited face, for his offer had fairly startled her.

She was not sufficiently worldly-wise to see that the jeweler wanted it enough to give more for it, nor to make a good bargain for herself. Twenty-five dollars seemed a vast sum, and she only paused to collect her wits before she answered eagerly:

"Yes, I *should* like to sell it; I've had it so long that I'm tired of it, and it's all out of fashion. Mrs. Vaughn told me some people would be glad to get it, because it is genuine. Do you really think it is worth twenty-five dollars?"

"It's old, and I shall have to tinker it up; but it matches the ear-rings so well, I am willing to pay well for it. Will you take the money now, Miss, or think it over and call again?" asked the man, more respectfully, after hearing Mrs. Vaughn's name.

"I'll take it now, if you please. I shall leave town in a day or two, and may not have time to call again," said Daisy, taking a half-regretful look at the chain, as the man counted out the money.

Holding it fast, she went away, feeling that this unexpected fortune was a reward for the good use she had made of her gold piece.

"Now I can buy some really valuable ornament and wear it without being ashamed. What shall it be? No tinsel for me this time;" and she walked by the attractive shop-window with an air of lofty indifference, for she really was getting over her first craze for that sort of thing.

Feeling as if she possessed the power to buy real diamonds, Daisy turned toward the great jewelers, pausing now and then to look for some pretty gift for Janey, to be bought with her own money.

"What can I get for Mother? She never owns that she needs anything, and goes shabby so I can be fine. I could get some of those fine, thick stockings; hers are all darns—but they might not fit. Flannel is useful, but it isn't a pretty present. What *does* she need most?"

As Daisy stopped before a great window, full of all manner of comfortable garments, her eye fell on a fur-lined cloak marked "$25." It seemed to answer her question like a voice, and as she looked at it she heard again the words:

"'But, Mother, that money was for your cloak. You need it so much—'"

"'Hush, dear; I can do very well with a shawl over the old sack. Don't say a word to spoil Daisy's pleasure.'"

"How could I forget that! What a selfish girl I am, to be thinking of jewelry, when that dear, good Mother hasn't a cloak to her back. Daisy Field, I'm ashamed of you! Go in and buy that nice warm one at once, and don't let me hear of that ridiculous box again."

After this little burst of remorse and self-reproach, Daisy took another look; and prudence suggested asking the advice of some more experienced shopper than herself, before making so important a purchase. As if the fates were interested in settling the matter at once, while she stood undecided Mary White came down the street, with a parcel of work in her hands.

"Just the person! The Vaughns needn't know anything about it; and Mary is a good judge."

It was pleasant to see the two faces brighten as the girls met; rather comical to watch the deep interest with which one listened and the other explained; and beautiful to hear the grateful eagerness in Mary's voice, as she answered cordially:

"Indeed, I will! You've been so kind to my Mother, there's nothing I wouldn't be glad to do for yours."

So in they went, and after due consideration, the cloak was bought and ordered home—both girls feeling that it was a little ceremony full of love and good-will; for Mary's time was money, yet she gave it gladly, and Daisy's purse was left empty of all but the good-luck penny, which was to bring still greater happiness in unsuspected ways.

Another secret was put away in the empty jewel-box, and the cloak hidden in Daisy's trunk; for she felt shy of telling her little business transactions, lest the Vaughns should consider her extravagant. But the thought of her mother's surprise and pleasure warmed her heart, and made the last days of her visit the happiest. Being a mortal girl, she did give a sigh as she tied a bit of black velvet around her white throat, instead of the necklace, which seemed really a treasure now that it was gone; and she looked with great disfavor at the shabby little pin, worn where she had fondly hoped to see the golden rose. She put a real rose in its place, and never knew that her own fresh, happy face was as lovely; for the thought of the two mothers made comfortable by her was better than all the pearls and diamonds that fell from the lips of the good girl in the fairy tale.

"Let me help you pack your trunk; I love to cram things in, and dance on the lid when it won't shut," said Laura, joining her friend next day, just as she had well hidden the cloak-box under a layer of clothes.

"Thank you, I've almost finished, and rather like to fuss over my own things in my own way. You won't mind if I give this pretty box of handkerchiefs to Mother, will you, dear? I have so many things, I must go halves with someone. The muslin apron and box of bonbons are for Janey, because she can't wear the gloves, and this lovely *jabot* is too old for her," said Daisy, surveying her new possessions with girlish satisfaction.

"Do what you like with your own. Mamma has a box of presents for your mother and sister. She is packing it now, but I don't believe you can get it in; your trunk seems to be so full. This must go in a safe place, or your heart will break," and Laura took up the jewel-box, adding with a laugh, as she opened it, "you haven't filled it, after all! What did you do with papa's gold piece?"

"That's a secret. I'll tell some day, but not yet," said Daisy, diving into her trunk to hide the color in her cheeks.

"Sly thing! I know you have silver spiders and filagree racquets, and Rhinestone moons and stars stowed away somewhere and won't confess it. I wanted to fill this box, but Mamma said you'd do it better yourself, so I let it alone; but I was afraid you'd think I was very selfish to have a pin for every day in the month and never give you one," said Laura, as she looked at the single little brooch reposing on the satin cushion. "Where's your chain?" she added, before Daisy could speak.

"It is safe enough. I'm tired of it, and don't care if I never see it again." And Daisy packed away, and laughed as she smoothed the white dress in its tray, remembering that it was paid for by the sale of the old necklace.

"Give it to me, then. I like it immensely; it's so odd. I'll exchange for anything of mine you choose. Will you?" asked Laura, who seemed bent on asking inconvenient questions.

"I shall have to tell, or she will think me ungrateful," thought Daisy, not without a pang of regret even then, for Laura's offer was a generous one.

"Well, like George Washington, 'I cannot tell a lie'; so I must confess that I sold it, and spent the money for something I wanted very much—not jewelry, but something to give away," she said.

Daisy was spared further confessions by the entrance of Mrs. Vaughn, with a box in her hand.

"I have room for something more. Give me that, Laura, it will just fit in;" and taking the little jewel-box, she added, "Mary White wishes you to try on your dress, Laura. Go at once; I will help Daisy."

Laura went, and her mother stood looking down at the kneeling girl with an expression of affectionate satisfaction which would have puzzled Daisy, had she seen it.

"Has the visit been a pleasant one, my dear?"

"Oh, very! I can't thank you enough for the good it has done me. I hope I can pay a little of the debt next summer, if you come our way again," cried Daisy, looking up with a face full of gratitude.

"We shall probably go to Europe for the summer. Laura is of a good age for it now, and we all shall enjoy it."

"How delightful! We shall miss you very much, but I'm glad you are going, and I hope Laura will find time to write me now and then. I shall want to know how she likes the 'foreign parts' we've talked about so much."

"You *shall* know. We shall not forget you, my dear," and with a caressing touch on the smiling yet wistful face upturned to hers, Mrs. Vaughn went away to pack the empty jewel-box, leaving Daisy to drop a few irrepressible tears on the new gown, over the downfall of her summer hopes, and the longings all girls feel for that enchanted world that lies beyond the sea.

"We shall see you before we go, so we won't gush now," said Laura, as she bade her friend good-bye, adding in a whisper, "Some folk can have secrets as well as other folk, and be as sly. So don't think you have all the fun to yourself, you dear, good, generous darling."

Daisy looked bewildered, and Mrs. Vaughn added to her surprise by kissing her very warmly as she said: "I wished to find a good friend for my spoiled girl, and I think I have succeeded."

There was no time for explanation, and all the way home Daisy kept wondering what they meant. But she forgot everything when she saw the dear faces beaming at the door, and ran straight into her mother's arms, while Janey hugged the trunk till her turn came for something better.

When the first raptures were over, out came the cloak; and Daisy was well repaid for her little trials and sacrifices when she was folded in it as her mother held her close, and thanked her as mothers only can. Sitting in its soft shelter, she told all about it, and coming to the end said, as she took up the jewel-box, unpacked with the other generous gifts: "I haven't a thing to put in it, but I shall value it because it taught me a lesson which I hope I never shall forget. See how pretty it is!" and opening it, Daisy gave a cry of surprise and joy, for there lay the golden rose, with Laura's name and "*Sub rosa*" on a slip of paper.

"The dear thing! she knew I wanted it, and that is what she meant by 'secrets.' I'll write and tell her mine tomorrow."

"Here is something more," said Janey, who had been lifting the tray while her sister examined the long-desired flower.

A pair of real gold bangles shone before her delighted eyes, and a card in Mr. Vaughn's hand-writing bore these words: "Handcuffs for the thief who stole the pocket-book."

Daisy hardly had time to laugh gaily at the old gentleman's joke, when Janey cried out, as she opened the little drawer, "Here's another!"

It was a note from Mrs. Vaughn, but all thought it the greatest treasure of the three, for it read:

"DEAR DAISY—
Mary told me some of your secrets, and I found out the others. Forgive me and go to Europe with Laura, in May. Your visit was a little test. You stood it well, and we wish to know more of you. The little box is not quite empty, but the best jewels are the self-denial, sweet charity, and good sense you put in yourself.

"Your friend, A.V."

First published in the September 1884 edition of *St. Nicholas Magazine*

THE BLIND LARK
By LOUISA M. ALCOTT

HIGH UP IN an old house, full of poor people, lived Lizzie, with her mother and baby Billy. The street was a narrow, noisy place, where carts rumbled and dirty children played; where the sun seldom shone, the fresh wind seldom blew, and the white snow of winter was turned at once to black mud. One bare room was Lizzie's home, and out of it she seldom went, for she was a prisoner. We all pity the poor princesses who were shut up in towers by bad fairies, the men and women in jails, and the little birds in cages, but Lizzie was a sadder prisoner than any of these.

The prince always comes to the captive princess, the jail doors open in time, and the birds find some kind hand to set them free; but there seemed no hope of escape for this poor child. Only nine years old, and condemned to life-long helplessness, loneliness, and darkness—for she was blind.

She could dimly remember the blue sky, green earth, and beautiful sun; for the light went out when she was six, and the cruel fever left her a pale little shadow to haunt that room ever since. The father was dead, the mother worked hard for daily bread, they had no friends, and the good fairies seemed to have forgotten them. Still, like the larks one sees in Brittany, the eyes of which cruel boys put out, that they may sing the sweeter, Lizzie made music in her cage, singing to baby; and when he slept, she sat by the window listening to the noise below for company, crooning to herself till she, too, fell asleep and forgot the long, long days that had no play, no school, no change for her such as other children know.

Every morning Mother gave them their porridge, locked the door, and went away to work, leaving something for the children's dinner, and Lizzie to take care of herself and Billy till night. There was no other way, for both were too helpless to be trusted elsewhere, and there was no one to look after them. But Lizzie knew her way about the room, and could find the bed, the window, and the table where the bread and milk stood. There was seldom any fire in the stove, and the window was barred, so the little prisoners were safe, and day after day they lived together a sad, solitary, unchildlike life that makes one's heart ache to think of.

Lizzie watched over Billy like a faithful little mother, and Billy did his best to bear his trials, and comfort sister, like a man. He was not a rosy, rollicking fellow, like most year-old boys, but pale and thin and quiet, with a pathetic look in his big blue eyes, as if he said, "Something is wrong; will someone kindly put it right for us?" But he seldom complained unless in pain, and would lie for hours on the old bed, watching the flies, which were his only other playmates, stretching out his little hands to the few rays of sunshine that crept in now and then, as if longing for them, like a flower in a cellar. When Lizzie sung, he hummed softly; and when he was hungry, cold, or tired, he called "Lib! Lib!" meaning "Lizzie," and nestled up to her, forgetting all his baby woes in her tender arms.

Seeing her so fond and faithful, the poor neighbors loved as well as pitied her, and did what they could for the afflicted child. The busy women would pause at the locked door to ask if all was right; the dirty children brought her dandelions from the park, and the rough workmen of the factory opposite, with a kind word would toss an apple or a cake through the open window. They had learned to look for the little wistful face behind the bars, and loved to listen to the childish voice which caught and imitated the songs they sung and whistled, like a sweet echo. They called her "the blind lark," and, though she never knew it, many were the better for the pity they gave her.

Baby slept a great deal, for life offered him few pleasures, and, like a small philosopher, he wisely tried to forget the troubles which he could not cure; so Lizzie had nothing to do but sing, and try to imagine how the world looked. She had no one to tell her, and the few memories grew dimmer and dimmer each year. She did not know how to work or to play, never having been taught, and Mother was too tired at night to do anything but get supper and go to bed.

"The child will be an idiot soon, if she does not die," people said; and it seemed as if this would be the fate of the poor little girl, since no one came to save her during those three weary years. She often said, "I'm of *some* use. I take care of Billy, and I couldn't live without him."

But even this duty and delight was taken from her, for that cold spring nipped the poor little flower, and one day Billy shut his blue eyes with a patient sigh and left her all alone.

Then Lizzie's heart seemed broken, and people thought she would soon follow him, now that her one care and comfort was gone. All day she laid with her cheek on Billy's pillow, holding the battered tin cup and a little worn-out shoe, and it was pitiful to hear her sing the old lullabies as if baby still could hear them.

"It will be a mercy if the poor thing doesn't live; blind folks are no use and a sight of trouble," said one woman to another as they gossiped in the hall after calling on the child during her mother's absence, for the door was left unlocked since she was ill.

"Yes, Mrs. Davis would get on nicely if she hadn't such a burden. Thank Heaven, my children aren't blind," answered the other, hugging her baby closer as she went away.

Lizzie heard them, and hoped with all her sad little soul that death would set her free, since she was of no use in the world. To go and be with Billy was all her desire now, and she was on her way to him, growing daily weaker and more content to be dreaming of dear baby well and happy, waiting for her somewhere in a lovely place called Heaven.

The summer vacation came, and hundreds of eager children were hurrying away to the mountains and seashore for two months of healthful pleasure. Even the dirty children in the lane felt the approach of berry-time, and rejoiced in their freedom from cold as they swarmed like flies about the corner grocery where over-ripe fruit was thrown out for them to scramble over.

Lizzie heard about good times when some of these young neighbors were chosen to go on the poor children's picnics, and came back with big sandwiches buttoned up in their jackets; pickles, peanuts, and buns in their pockets; handsfull of faded flowers, and hearts brimming over with childish delight at a day in the woods. She listened with a faint smile, enjoyed the "woodsy" smell of the green things, and wondered if they had nice picnics in Heaven, being sorry that Billy had missed them here. But she did not seem to care much, or hope for any pleasure for herself except to see baby again.

I think there were few sadder sights in that great city than this innocent prisoner waiting so patiently to be set free. Would it be by the gentle angel of death, or one of the human angels who keep these little sparrows from falling to the ground?

One hot August day, when not a breath came into the room, and the dust and noise and evil smells were almost unendurable, poor Lizzie lay on her bed singing feebly to herself about "the beautiful blue sea." She was trying to get to sleep that she might dream of a cool place, and her voice was growing fainter and fainter, when suddenly it seemed as if the dream had come, for a sweet odor was near, something damp and fresh touched her feverish cheek, and a kind voice said in her ear:

"Here is the little bird I've been following. Will you have some flowers, dear?"

"Is it Heaven? Where's Billy?" murmured Lizzie, groping about her, half awake.

"Not yet. I'm not Billy, but a friend who carries flowers to little children who

A kind voice said, "Will you have some flowers, dear?"

cannot go and get them. Don't be afraid, but let me sit and tell you about it," answered the voice, as a gentle hand took hers.

"I thought, maybe I'd died, and I was glad, for I do want to see Billy so much. He's baby, you know." And the clinging hands held the kind one fast till it filled them with a great bunch of roses that seemed to bring all summer into the close, hot room with their sweetness.

"Oh, how nice! how nice! I never had such a lot. They're bigger 'n' better 'n dandelions, aren't they? What a good lady you must be to go 'round giving folks posies like these!" cried Lizzie, trying to realize the astonishing fact.

Then, while the new friend fanned her, she lay luxuriating in her roses, and listening to the sweet story of the Flower Mission which, like many other pleasant things, she knew nothing of in her prison. Presently she told her own little tale, never guessing how pathetic it was, till, lifting her hand to touch the new face, she found it wet with tears.

"Are you sorry for me?" she asked. "Folks are very kind, but I'm a burden, you know, and I'd better die and go to Billy; I was some use to him, but I never can be to anyone else. I heard 'em say so, and poor Mother would do better if I wasn't here."

"My child, I know a little blind girl who is no burden but a great help to her mother, and a happy, useful creature, as you might be if you were taught and helped as she was," went on the voice, sounding more than ever like a good fairy's as it told fresh wonders till Lizzie was sure it *must* be all a dream.

"Who taught her? Could I do it? Where's the place?" she asked, sitting erect in her eagerness, like a bird that hears a hand at the door of its cage.

Then, with the comfortable arm around her, the roses stirring with the flutter of her heart, and the sightless eyes looking up as if they could see the face of the deliverer, Lizzie heard the wonderful story of the House Beautiful standing white and spacious on the hill, with the blue sea before it, the fresh wind always blowing, the green gardens and parks all about, and, inside, music, happy voices, shining faces, busy hands, and year after year the patient teaching by those who dedicate themselves to this noble and tender task.

"It must be better 'n Heaven!" cried Lizzie, as she heard of work and play, health and happiness, love and companionship, usefulness and independence—all the dear rights and simple joys young creatures hunger for, and perish, soul and body, without.

It was too much for her little mind to grasp at once, and she lay as if in a blissful dream long after the kind visitor had gone, promising to come again and to find some way for Lizzie to enter into that lovely place where darkness is changed to light.

That visit was like magic medicine, and the child grew better at once, for hope was born in her heart. The heavy gloom seemed to lift, discomforts were easier to bear, and solitude was peopled now with troops of happy children living in that wonderful place where blindness was not a burden. She told it all to her mother, and the poor woman tried to believe it, but said, sadly:

"Don't set your heart on it, child. It's easy to promise and to forget. Rich folks don't trouble themselves about poor folks if they can help it."

But Lizzie's faith never wavered, though the roses faded as day after day went by and no one came. The mere thought that it was possible to teach blind people to work and study and play seemed to give her strength and courage. She got up and sat at the window again, singing to herself as she watched and waited, with the dead flowers carefully arranged in Billy's mug, and a hopeful smile on the little white face behind the bars.

Everyone was glad she was better, and nodded to one another as they heard the soft crooning, like a dove's coo, in the pauses of the harsher noises that filled the street. The workmen tossed her sweeties and whistled their gayest airs, the children brought their dilapidated toys to amuse her, and one woman came every day to put her baby in Lizzie's lap, it was such a pleasure to her to feel the soft little body in the loving arms that longed for Billy.

Poor Mother went to her work in better spirits, and the long, hot days were less oppressive as she thought, while she scrubbed, of Lizzie up again; for she loved her helpless burden, heavy though she found it.

When Saturday came around, it rained hard, and no one expected "the flower lady." Even Lizzie said, with a patient sigh and a hopeful smile:

"I don't believe she'll come; but, maybe it will clear up, and then I guess she will."

It did not clear up, but the flower lady came, and as the child sat listening to the welcome sound of her steps, her quick ear caught the tread of two pairs of feet, the whisper of two voices, and presently two persons came in to fill her hands with midsummer flowers.

"This is Minna, the little girl I told you of. She wanted to see you very much, so we paddled away like a pair of ducks, and here we are," said Miss Grace gaily; and as she spoke Lizzie felt soft fingers glide over her face, and a pair of childish lips find and kiss her own. The groping touch, the hearty kiss, made the blind children friends at once, and, dropping her flowers, Lizzie hugged the new-comer, trembling with excitement and delight. Then they talked, and how the tongues went as one asked questions and the other answered them, while Miss Grace sat by enjoying the happiness of those who do *not* forget the poor, but seek them out to save and bless.

Minna had been for a year a pupil in the happy school, where she was taught to see with her hands, as one might say; and the tales she told of the good times there made Lizzie cry eagerly:

"Can I go? Oh, *can* I go?"

"Alas, no, not yet," answered Miss Grace sadly. "I find that children under ten cannot be taken, and there is no place for the little ones unless kind people care for them."

Lizzie gave a wail, and hid her face in the pillow, feeling as if she could not bear the dreadful disappointment.

Minna comforted her, and Miss Grace went on to say that generous people were trying to get another school for the small children, that all the blind children were working hard to help on the plan, that money was coming in, and soon they hoped to have a pleasant place for every child who needed help.

Lizzie's tears stopped falling as she listened, for hope was not quite gone. "I'll not be ten till next June, and I don't see how I *can* wait 'most a year. Will the little school be ready 'fore then?" she asked.

"I fear not, dear, but I will see that the long waiting is made as easy as possible, and perhaps you can help us in some way," answered Miss Grace, anxious to atone for her mistake in speaking about the school before she had made sure that Lizzie could go.

"Oh, I'd love to help; only I can't do anything," sighed the child.

"You can sing, and that is a lovely way to help. I heard of 'the blind lark,' as they call you, and when I came to find her, your little voice led me straight to the door of the cage. That door I mean to open and let you hop out into the sunshine; then, when you are well and strong, I hope you will help us get the home for other little children who else must wait years before *they* find the light. Will you?"

As Miss Grace spoke, it was beautiful to see the clouds lift from Lizzie's wondering face, till it shone with the sweetest beauty any face can wear, the happiness of helping others. She forgot her own disappointment in the new hope that came, and held on to the bed-post as if the splendid plan were almost too much for her.

"Could I help that way?" she cried. "Would anybody care to hear me sing? Oh, how I'd love to do anything for the poor little ones who will have to wait."

"You shall. I'm sure the hardest heart would be touched by your singing, if you look as you do now. We need something new for our fair and concert, and by that time you will be ready," said Miss Grace, almost afraid she had said too much; for the child looked so frail, it seemed as if even joy would hurt her.

Fortunately her mother came in just then, and, while the lady talked to her, Minna's childish chatter soothed Lizzie so well that when they left she stood at the window smiling down at them and singing like the happiest bobolink that ever tilted on a willow branch in springtime.

All the promises were kept, and soon a new life began for Lizzie. A better room and well-paid work were found for Mrs. Davis. Minna came as often as she could to cheer up her little friend, and, best of all, Miss Grace taught her to sing, that by and by the little voice might plead with its pathetic music for others less blest than she. So the winter months went by, and Lizzie grew like mayflowers underneath the snow, getting ready to look up, sweet and rosy, when spring set her free and called her to be glad. She counted the months and weeks, and when the time dwindled to days, she could hardly sleep or eat for thinking of the happy hour when she could go to be a pupil in the school where miracles were worked.

Her birthday was in June, and, thanks to Miss Grace, her coming was celebrated by one of the pretty festivals of the school, called Daisy Day. Lizzie knew nothing of this surprise, and when her friends led her up the long flight of steps she looked like a happy little soul climbing to the gates of Heaven.

Mr. Constantine, the ruler of this small kingdom, was a man whose fatherly heart had room for every suffering child in the world, and it rejoiced over every one who came, though the great house was overflowing and many waited as Lizzie had done.

He welcomed her so kindly that the strange place seemed like home at once, and Minna led her away to the little mates who proudly showed her their small possessions and filled her hands with the treasures children love, while pouring into her ears delightful tales of the study, work, and play that made their lives so happy.

Lizzie was bewildered, and held fast to Minna, whose motherly care of her was sweet to see. Kind teachers explained rules and duties with the patience that soothes fear and wins love, and soon Lizzie began to feel that she was a "truly pupil" in this wonderful school where the blind could read, sew, study, sing, run, and play.

Boys raced along the galleries and up and down the stairs as boldly as if all had eyes. Girls swept and dusted like tidy housewives; little fellows hammered and sawed in the workshop and never hurt themselves; small girls sewed on pretty work as busy as bees, and in the schoolroom lessons went on as if both teachers and pupils were blessed with eyes.

Lizzie could not understand it, and was content to sit and listen wherever she was placed, while her little fingers fumbled at the new objects near her, and her hungry mind opened like a flower to the sun. She had no tasks that day, and in the afternoon was led away with a flock of children, all chattering like magpies, on the grand expedition. Every year, when the fields were white with daisies, these poor little souls were let loose among them to enjoy the holy day of this child's flower. Ah, but wasn't it a pretty sight to see the meeting between them, when the meadows were reached and the children scattered far and wide with cries of joy as they ran and rolled in the white sea, or filled their eager hands, or softly felt for the dear daisies and kissed them like old friends! The flowers seemed to enjoy it, too, as they danced and nodded, while the wind rippled the long grass like waves of a green sea, and the sun smiled as if he said:

"Here's the sort of thing I like to see. Why don't I find more of it?"

Lizzie's face looked like a daisy, it was so full of light as she stood looking up with the wide brim of her new hat like the white petals all round it. She did not run nor shout, but went slowly wading through the grass, feeling the flowers touch her hands, yet picking none, for it was happiness enough to know that they were there. Presently she sat down and let them tap her cheeks and rustle about her ears as though telling secrets that made her smile. Then, as if weary with so much happiness, she lay back and let the daisies hide her with their pretty coverlet.

Miss Grace was watching over her, but left her alone, and by and by, like a lark from its nest in the grass, the blind girl sent up her little voice, singing so sweetly that the children gathered around to hear, while they made chains and tied up their nosegays.

This was Lizzie's first concert, and no little prima donna was ever more pelted with flowers than she; for when she had sung all her songs, new and old, a daisy crown was put upon her head, a tall flower for a scepter in her hand, and all the boys and girls danced around her as if she had been Queen of the May.

A little feast came out of the baskets, that they might be empty for the harvest to be carried home, and, while they ate, stories were told and shouts of laughter filled the air, for all were as merry as if there was no darkness, pain, or want in the world. Then they had games, and Lizzie was taught to play, for till now she never knew what a good romp meant. Her cheeks grew rosy, her sad little face waked up, she ran and tumbled with the rest, and actually screamed, to Minna's great delight.

Two or three of the children could see a little, and these were very helpful in taking care of the little ones. Miss Grace found them playing some game with Lizzie, and observed that all but she were blindfolded. When she asked why, one whispered, "We thought we should play fairer if we were all alike." And another added, "It seems somehow as if we were proud if we see better than the rest."

Lizzie was much touched by this sweet spirit, and a little later showed that she had already learned one lesson in the school, when she gathered about her some who had never seen, and told them what she could remember of green fields and daisy-balls before the light went out forever.

"Surely my little lark was worth saving, if only for this one happy day," thought Miss Grace, as she watched the awakened look in the blind faces, all leaning toward the speaker, whose childish story pleased them well.

In all her long and useful life, Lizzie never forgot that Daisy Day, for it seemed as if she were born anew, and, like a butterfly, had left the dark chrysalis all behind her then. It was the first page of the beautiful book just opening before the eyes of her little mind—a lovely page, illustrated with flowers, kind faces, sunshine, and happy hopes. The new life was so full, so free, she soon fell into her place and enjoyed it all. People worked there so heartily, so helpfully, it was no wonder things went as if by magic, and the poor little creatures who came in so afflicted went out in some years independent people, ready to help themselves and often to benefit others.

There is no need to tell all Lizzie learned and enjoyed that summer, nor how proud her mother was when she heard her read in the curious books, making eyes of the little fingers that felt their way along so fast, when she saw the neat stitches she set, the pretty clay things she modeled, the tidy way she washed dishes, swept and dusted, and helped keep her room in order. But the poor woman's heart was too full for words when she heard the child sing—not as before, in the dreary room, sad, soft lullabies to Billy—but beautiful, gay songs, with flutes and violins to lift and carry the little voice along on waves of music.

Lizzie really had a great gift, but she was never happier than when they all sang together, or when she sat quietly listening to the band as they practiced for the autumn concert. She was to have a part in it, and the thought that she could help to earn money for the Kindergarten made the shy child bold and glad to do her part.

Many people knew her now, for she was very pretty, with the healthful roses in her cheeks, curly yellow hair, and great blue eyes that seemed to see. Her mates and teachers were proud of her, for, though she was not as quick as some of the pupils, her sweet temper, grateful heart, and friendly little ways made her very dear to all, aside from the musical talent she possessed.

Everyone was busy over the fair and the concert; and fingers flew, tongues chattered, feet trotted, and hearts beat fast with hope and fear as the time drew near, for all were eager to secure a home for the poor children still waiting in darkness. It was a charity which appealed to all hearts when it was known; but, in this busy world of ours, people have so many cares of their own that they are apt to forget the wants of others unless something brings these needs very clearly before their eyes.

Much money was needed, and many ways had been tried to add to the growing fund, that all might be well done.

"We wish to interest children in this charity for children, so that they may gladly give a part of their abundance to these poor little souls who have nothing. I think Lizzie will sing some of the pennies out of their pockets, which would otherwise go for bonbons. Let us try; so make her neat and pretty, and we'll have a special song for her."

Mr. Constantine said this, and Miss Grace carried out his wish so well that, when the time came, the little prima donna did her part better even than they had hoped.

The sun shone splendidly on the opening day of the fair, and cars and carriages came rolling out from the city, full of friendly people with plump purses and the sympathetic interest we all take in such things when we take time to see, admire, and reproach ourselves that we do so little for them.

There were many children, and when they had bought the pretty handiwork of the blind needle-women, eaten cake and ices, wondered at the strange maps and books, twirled the big globe in the hall, and tried to understand how so many blind people could be so busy and so happy, they all were seated at last to hear the music, full of expectation, for "the pretty little girl was going to sing."

It was a charming concert, and everyone enjoyed it, though many eyes grew dim as they wandered from the tall youths blowing the horns so sweetly, to the small ones chirping away like so many sparrows, for the blind faces made the sight pathetic, and such music touched the hearts as no other music can.

"Now she's coming!" whispered the eager children, as a little girl climbed up the steps and stood before them, waiting to begin.

A slender little creature, in a blue gown, with sunshine falling on her pretty hair, a pleading look in the soft eyes that had no sign of blindness but their steadfastness, and a smile on the lips that trembled at first, for Lizzie's heart beat fast, and only the thought, "I'm helping the poor little ones," gave her courage for her task.

But, when the flutes and violins began to play like a whispering wind, she forgot the crowd before her, and, lifting up her face, sang in clear sweet tones

THE BLIND LARK'S SONG

We are sitting in the shadow of a long and lonely night,
Waiting till some gentle angel comes to lead us to the light.
For we know there is a magic that can give eyes to the blind.
Oh, well-filled hands, be generous! Oh, pitying hearts, be kind!
Help stumbling feet that wander, to find the upward way;
Teach hands that now lie idle the joys of work and play.
Let pity, love, and patience our tender teachers be,
That, though the eyes be blinded, the little souls may see.
Your world is large and beautiful, our prison dim and small;
We stand and wait, imploring—"Is there not room for all?
Give us our children's garden, where we may safely bloom,
Forgetting in God's sunshine our lot of grief and gloom."
A little voice comes singing, Oh, listen to its song!
A little child is pleading for those who suffer wrong.
Grant them the patient magic that gives eyes to the blind!
Oh, well-filled hands, be generous! Oh, pitying hearts, be kind!

It was a very simple little song, but it proved wonderfully effective, for Lizzie was so carried away by her own feeling that as she sang the last lines she stretched out her hands imploringly, and two great tears rolled down her cheeks. For a minute many hands were too busy fumbling for handkerchiefs to clap, but the children were quick to answer that gesture and those tears, and one impetuous little lad tossed a small purse containing his last ten cents at Lizzie's feet, the first contribution won by her innocent appeal. Then there was great applause, and many of the flowers just bought were thrown to the little Lark, who was obliged to come back and sing again and again, smiling brightly as she dropped pretty curtsies, and sang song after song with all the added sweetness of a grateful heart.

Hidden behind the organ, Miss Grace and Mr. Constantine shook hands joyfully, for this was the sort of interest they wanted, and they knew that while the children clapped and threw flowers, the wet-eyed mothers were thinking, self-reproachfully, "I must help this lovely charity," and the stout old gentlemen who pounded with their canes were resolving to go home and write some generous checks, which would be money invested in God's savings-bank.

It was a very happy time for all, and made strangers friends in the sweet way which teaches heart to speak to heart. When the concert was over, Lizzie felt many hands press hers and leave something there, many childish lips kiss her own, with promises to "help about the Kindergarten," and her ears were full of kind voices

But, when the flutes and violins began to play like a whispering wind, she forgot the crowd before her, and, lifting up her face, sang in clear sweet tones "The Blind Lark's Song."

thanking and praising her for doing her part so well. Still later, when all were gone, she proudly put the rolls of bills into Mr. Constantine's hand, and, throwing her arms about Miss Grace's neck, said, trembling with earnestness, "I'm not a burden anymore, and I can truly help! How can I ever thank you both for making me so happy?"

One can fancy what their answer was and how Lizzie helped; for, long after the Kindergarten was filled with pale little flowers blooming slowly as she had done, the Blind Lark went on singing pennies out of pockets, and sweetly reminding people not to forget this noble charity.

First published in the November 1886 edition of *St. Nicholas Magazine*

BY BENNET MUSSON

A FEW hundred years ago, in a country called Germany, there was a village known as Grosshufelten, which was on a lake. The lake is so small that I have forgotten its name, and you will not find the village on any map of the country—which is still called Germany—unless it is on the back, where I didn't look.

The people in this village were greatly annoyed by a robber baron who dwelt on a mountain near by, and who was in the habit of levying tribute on them because he didn't like to work. The last time that he told them they must pay what he called their annual dues, they refused to do so. The baron was greatly surprised—as people are usually surprised when others refuse to do things that they have been in the habit of doing whether they ought to or not—and he resolved to punish the villagers.

At first he thought of descending on them with his band and burning their houses; but this would have required effort, so he changed his mind and called before him two magicians whom he kept to do things by magic, which he found more easy than doing them by hand.

One of these magicians was a good man who stayed with the robber only because he was afraid to go away. The other was a bad man who stayed for no particular reason.

"I am resolved," said the baron, "to kill all the people in Grosshufelten, because they will not do what I decree."

"That seems very natural," said the bad magician.

"I now wish to learn the easiest way of doing it," continued the robber.

"That, also, seems very natural," said the good magician.

The bad magician suggested a number of methods, none of which the baron liked, and he finally told him that he could take a half-holiday, and he would consult with the good magician, who worked for less money, anyhow.

"If you are bound to do this thing, the best way will be to do it quickly and painlessly," began the good magician.

"You mean the best way for them," said the robber.

"Yes, and for you," answered the magician; "for then they will have no chance to conceal their treasures, and you can get as many of them as you wish."

"Who will carry the treasures back?" the baron asked anxiously.

"You might make the bad magician do that."

The good magician then proposed a plan. Leading from the mountain to the lake was a passage which was subterranean. (That is a rather long word, but it was a rather long passage.) He suggested that through this tunnel he send some poisonous gas he had invented, which he usually used for killing potato-bugs. This gas would come up through the lake, be blown into the village, and overcome the people. The good magician did not like this idea, but he knew it was more humane than anything the bad magician would suggest, and thought he might get a chance to warn the villagers before it was carried out, so that they could escape. The robber baron was delighted with the scheme, and, telling the magician to execute it as soon as he could, he proceeded to take his afternoon nap, sleeping that kind of sleep which comes to the unjust.

As soon as the good magician was sure that the baron was sound asleep, he started the gas down the passage, and then hurried to warn the villagers. This happened on Wednesday, the day on which the people of Grosshufelten made soap, and when he arrived he found a number of them on the shore of the lake, washing out their soap-kettles. Just as the magician started to warn them of their danger, the gas began to rise. The water was rather soapy, and when the vapor rose it formed an enormous bubble that covered half of the lake.

The villagers were greatly astonished, and looked at the bubble with their mouths open and their minds closed. The magician, who made his living by thinking, began to consider the matter. In the first place, he knew that if the robber baron found that he had warned the people he would be very angry, and there was no telling what he would do—there was no telling what he would do when he wasn't angry. In the next place, the wind might blow the gas away from the village when the bubble burst. At all events, the magician would have time to think, and he might devise some plan for saving the villagers without making the baron angry.

While he was considering these things, a youth named Hans Spratzieberger-and-a-few-other-syllables ran to the shore with his bow and arrow.

"What are you going to do with that?" asked the magician.

"I'm going to shoot that big bubble, out there, and see it burst," said Hans.

"Do you know what will happen if you do that?" inquired the magician. "This town will disappear from the map."

Hans, who didn't know that the town wasn't on the map, was much impressed. The villagers, many of whom didn't know what a map was, advised him not to shoot.

While they were watching the bubble, the bad magician, who was taking his half-holiday, approached. "What is that?" he asked. They told him. "Who blew it?" he added.

"'When in the course of human events,'"—said Hans, who was very fond of making fine speeches.

The bad magician looked at Hans with interest. "You are wasting your talents here," he said. "If you will come with me I will train you so that you will become an orator. What is your name?" Hans told him all of it.

"Well," said the bad magician, "if you can remember all of your name, you certainly must have a good memory; and that will be an advantage to you in your oratory."

Hans's parents, who now regarded the bubble as a good omen, did not want to have it destroyed; and when the other villagers learned that he would practice oratory somewhere else, they decided to let it remain for a time.

The good magician returned to the mountain, and told the robber baron what had taken place. The baron was far from pleased.

"This is what comes of using so much soap," he said. When the bad magician arrived with Hans, the baron was still less pleased. "Any speech-making that is to be done on this mountain I can do myself," he declared. "As for you," he added, turning to the good magician, "you had better go back to Grosshufelten and tell the villagers what that bubble is. You can take a crossbow, and if they are not willing to pay up, burst the bubble. If they are willing, burst it after they *have* paid up."

"But what will become of me?" asked the good magician.

"I will think about that tomorrow," said the robber baron.

When the good magician delivered the baron's message the villagers were offended. Instead of offering to pay their annual dues, they seized him and put him in jail. He was perplexed at this, as the baron had not told him what to do if such a thing should happen. However, as his cell window overlooked the lake and he could see the bubble, he made the best of things, and ate the meals they brought to him.

The weather was favorable for bubbles, and the next morning, when the good magician looked out of his window, the big one was still there. Large crowds of people were coming from the surrounding country to look at it, and the villagers were trying to charge them two pennies apiece. It was hard to collect the money, however, as the bubble could be seen from any spot on the shore; so that afternoon the people decided to fence in the lake.

The next morning a committee of villagers, headed by the burgomaster, called on the good magician.

"We are much shocked to find a good man like yourself associating with robbers," said the burgomaster. "We had decided to leave you in jail, but having found a way in which you can help us to make money, we will release you."

The magician was overcome by their kindness. He thanked them, but said he could not see how the money would benefit them if the bubble happened to burst.

"We will run that risk," said the burgomaster. "With that robber baron in the neighborhood, we are so used to risks that we don't mind them. We want you to put a magic fence around the lake, as it will take our people too long to build the one they began this morning."

The magician hadn't his wand with him, so he borrowed the burgomaster's cane, waved it a few times, and a fence appeared around the lake. But as most of the country folk who lived near by had already seen the bubble, this fence was of little use. The burgomaster thought for a while, and suggested that the magician turn the gas in the bubble red. He did this, and that afternoon some of the villagers went out in the country with a banner on which was printed:

See the Great Red Bubble of Grosshufelten!
Admission, 4 Pennies.
Near-sighted People Half-price.

This attracted a big crowd, and when the burgomaster thought the people had looked at the bubble long enough, he made a little speech, in which he told them that it was filled with poison, and was liable to burst at any moment. Then they all ran away. The next day the magician made the bubble green, the third day blue; and as long as the bubble and the colors held out the people kept coming back.

In the meantime the robber baron was getting impatient, not only because Hans was learning oratory, but because he heard nothing from Grosshufelten. He called the bad magician to him and told him that if he could not suggest some way to bring the villagers to terms he should be thrown into the bubble. The bad magician was greatly alarmed at the baron's threat, and thought as hard as he could, which was not very hard. At last he suggested that the baron and his band go to the opposite side of the lake, shoot the bubble, and allow the gas to float over Grosshufelten. Then, when the villagers were overcome, they could take their treasures, which he would transport to the mountain by magic. The baron thought it would be easier to do it all by magic, but the bad magician said he was not clever enough to arrange a spell for that; besides, there would be the sport for the baron of shooting the bubble.

The next day, the baron, his band, and the bad magician appeared opposite Grosshufelten, and saw nothing but a big fence. They were rather disappointed, but climbed some trees and got a view of the bubble, which was then chrome-yellow. The baron took a crossbow and prepared to shoot.

But meanwhile the good magician—who was much pleased at living

The Baron took a crossbow and prepared to shoot.

among honest people—had not been idle. He had devised an enormous bellows, and when he saw the baron aim his crossbow at the bubble, he told the villagers to get ready to blow it.

The baron fired a bolt which struck the bubble. It burst, and as the gas rose from it the villagers blew the bellows with great force, and the vapor floated over among the trees where the baron was.

So far as I know, this was the last of that robber baron and his band, and also of the bad magician; but Hans, who had stayed behind at the mountain, became a mighty orator.

First published in the November 1903 edition of *St. Nicholas Magazine*

THE WIZARD SHOEMAKER
By Winthrop Packard

THERE WAS A boy who shot an arrow at a tree. It flew swift and straight, but glanced from the tree and tore a big hole in the leather apron of a shoemaker who was standing near. Soon the boy came running up, saying, "Please excuse me for thus tearing your apron. I shot at a tree, but the arrow glanced."

But the shoemaker was very angry, and said: "I am a wizard shoemaker, and unless you mend my apron so that it is as whole as it was before, I do not know what I shall do to you, but it will be something dreadful. There is but one kind of needle that will mend a wizard shoemaker's leather apron, and neither man can give it to you, nor woman can give it to you. There is but one kind of thread that will do it, and neither man can give it to you, nor woman can give it to you; and there is but one kind of leather that will suffice, and neither man nor woman can give that to you. So, however hard you try, you will fail, and I shall have my revenge."

"These things," said the boy, "I shall try to find—by good fortune, I may do it."

So he set forth in the world, going up and down in it, by wood and field, seeking for needle, thread, and leather. He had passed many a pleasant field and many a tall forest, when, at an open space in the wood, he suddenly heard a cry for help.

"Help!" it said, "I am drowning!" Nor could he see water in which anyone could drown. But he followed the direction whence the call came, and presently he found a deep well, and heard a splash and the cry from the water below.

"Be of good cheer," he called down, "I am coming to help you." Then he began to descend, putting his fingers and toes firmly in the chinks between the stones, and taking care lest he fall. In the dark water at the bottom, he found something splashing. This he lifted carefully to his shoulder, and climbed out again. When he

and I will bring him back to you"; and off he ran as fast as he could.

He had passed many a flowering shrub and many an ancient tree, when he came to a dark space in a tall wood whence came a faint cry of "Ma-a! Ma-a!" and he knew that he heard the voice of the little calf. Out of a big box-trap it came, one that men had set to catch a bear alive. Into this the little calf had wandered, and had sprung it.

"Be of good cheer," called the boy, "I will soon let you out." And he pulled with all his might at the door of the trap. But it had been made strong enough to hold a bear, and he could not move it. So he said again: "Be of good cheer, I will find someone stronger than I am to help me pull, and we will let you out." And on he ran as fast as he could.

As he ran, he heard a sound of laughter coming from a sunny glade, and there he saw a big donkey, sitting down in the grass, his hind legs sticking straight out in front of him, his front hoofs planted between them, and his head wagging up and down, and his ears flopping. Every time he

wagged his head he laughed, "Hee ha-aw! Hee ha-aw!" and, seeing him, the boy looked about in astonishment.

"Why, good donkey," he said, "what is the joke?"

"I am," replied the donkey, "and I am laughing at myself. Every day I draw big loads and love to do it, for I am quite the strongest donkey anywhere about. But today I thought I would have a vacation and rest here in the sun, and, do you know, I am so homesick for a good load to pull, that I do not know what to do."

"Good!" said the boy, "come with me, and I will find for you the hardest pull you ever had." Whereupon the donkey leaped to his feet, and ran with the boy toward the bear trap, laughing, "Hee ha-aw! Hee ha-aw!" as he went, so glad was he that he was to find hard work once more.

At the bear trap, the boy fastened the donkey securely to the door, took hold himself, and both pulled as hard as they could. It was a strong door, but nothing could withstand the joyous pull of that donkey, and with a crash they ripped it off the trap. The calf trotted out immediately, but neither he nor the boy had time to properly thank the donkey, who went right on, up the hill and through the wood, dragging the door after him, and laughing all the way in his joy at finding such hard work to do.

But the boy and calf ran as fast as they could to the sunny glade where the big mother-cow was waiting for them. Very glad, indeed, she was to see the calf, and soon he was eating his dinner while the mother-cow cried a little still, but now for joy, and smoothed his ruffled fur with her big red tongue.

"Thank you, kind boy," she said, "for finding my little calf. I do not know what I should have done without your help. Now tell me, what can I do to help you?"

"I am glad to have aided you," replied the boy, "but I fear there is nothing you can do to help me. I am journeying far to find a certain kind of thread. This morning I shot my arrow at a tree, but it glanced, and tore a big hole in the wizard shoemaker's leather apron. I must mend this, or he will do me harm, and to do it I must have a certain kind of thread which neither man can give me, nor woman can give me; so I do not see how I am to get it."

Then the cow smiled. "Perhaps I can help you in that, little brother," she said. "Take hold of those long hairs in my tail, shut your eyes, and do just what I tell you."

This the boy did, and the cow then said: "Pull, little brother; pull as hard as you can." The boy pulled, and soon he felt the hairs coming out in his hands.

Then the cow said: "Open your eyes, little brother, and let us see what we have here." So the boy opened his eyes, but, to his astonishment, instead of hairs his hands were full of just the finest kind of brown threads, just the thing, he was sure, to mend the wizard shoemaker's leather apron.

"Thank you, kind cow," said he, "for giving me this splendid thread."

But the cow replied: "Thanks should be from me. I should never have seen my calf again without your help. Besides, I go up and down in the world quite a bit, and always I have seen you helping someone, and I am quite sure that a boy who helps others deserves help himself."

So the boy put the thread carefully in his pocket, and went on his way. He had passed many a sandy hillside and many a rocky cliff, when he again heard a cry for help. This seemed to come from a cave among big rocks, and when he ran into it, he saw there a bat that had been caught by a big snake.

"Help!" cried the bat, and the boy replied by snatching up a big stone and throwing it at the snake. It hit him—tunk—and the snake turned an inquiring eye upon the boy, who immediately caught up another, larger stone, and hit the snake with a louder tunk. Thereupon the snake turned both eyes inquiringly on the boy, and, seeing him pick up a third even larger stone, he dropped the bat, and glided with much haste far down into holes among the stones at the bottom of the cave.

"Thank you, kind boy," said the bat, "for saving me from that dreadful snake;

but I am bitten so deep that I fear now I shall die unless I can anoint my wound with some of the honey-dew bee-balm that is made at the hive of the fairy bees."

"Be of good cheer," said the boy, "I will bring this balm. Wait for me here, and I will soon be back." And away he ran as fast as he could to the hive of the fairy bees. There he saw a big working bee, pausing a moment on the door-step with a load of wax.

He was about to speak, when the busy bee said: "I know what you are after. I go everywhere for miles, and I see everything. You want balm for the injured bat up in the cave. Wait here for me a moment, and I will bring it out for you. But please keep very quiet, for within they are putting some of the baby bees to sleep."

"I will keep very quiet," said the boy, and soon he saw the busy bee coming out.

"Well!" said the bee, "I'm glad to see you again. Here is an acorn-cup full of honey-dew bee-balm for your friend up in the cave."

The boy took the balm, thanked the bee, and ran as fast as he could to the cave, where he found the bat still alive, though feeling quite weak. No sooner had they rubbed the balm on his wound, however, than he revived, and the wound healed immediately.

"Thank you, kind boy," said the bat, "for bringing me this balm, without which I should surely have died. You have been of great help to me; how can I help you?"

"I am glad to have aided you," said the boy, "but I fear there is nothing you can do to help me. I am journeying far to find a certain kind of leather. This morning I shot my arrow at a tree, but it glanced, and tore a big hole in the wizard shoemaker's leather apron. I must mend this, or he will do me harm, and to do it I must have a certain kind of leather which neither man can give me, nor woman can give me; so I do not see how I am to get it."

Then the bat smiled and said: "Perhaps I can help you in that, little brother. Take hold of my wing, shut your eyes, and do just what I tell you."

This the boy did, and the bat then said: "Pull, little brother; pull as hard as you can!" The boy did, but when he felt the bat's wing coming off in his hands, he stopped, for he did not wish to injure his friend. But the bat said again: "Pull as hard as you can, I tell you; do not mind me!"

So again the boy pulled, and soon he felt the bat's wing come off in his hands. Then the bat said: "Open your eyes, little brother, and let us see what we have here."

To the boy's astonishment, the bat still had two wings, and in his hand, instead of one of them, was the softest and finest leather he had ever seen, just the kind, he was sure, to mend the wizard shoemaker's leather apron.

"Thank you, good bat," he said, "for giving me this splendid leather."

But the bat replied: "Thanks should be from me. I should have died without your help, and besides, I go up and down in the world quite a bit, and I have always seen you helping someone; and I am very sure that a boy who helps others deserves help himself."

So the boy put the leather carefully in his other pocket, and started for the village where he knew the wizard shoemaker was waiting to see him come back unsuccessful. But, running as fast as he could, he paused at a pond where he saw three dragon-flies, one silver, one gold, and one blue in color. Driven by a sudden gust of wind into the water, they were about to drown.

"Great as is my haste," said the boy, "I cannot leave these gentle creatures to drown." So he ran to a boat that was near by, paddled to the dragon-flies, lifted them to the gunwale of the boat with his paddle, then paddled ashore and started again, leaving the dragon-flies drying their wings in the sun. But before he was gone, they called to him.

"Thank you, kind boy," they said. "We fly everywhere, and we shall surely know when you are in trouble, and come to your aid."

"So!" said the wizard shoemaker when he saw the boy, "you have come back unsuccessful. Neither man nor woman could give you that needle, so how could you expect to get it, I should like to know!"

"But I have the needle!" said the boy. "My friend the porcupine gave it to me."

The wizard was so enraged at this that he sprang high in air and came down on the floor with a bang that made the windows rattle. "The thread!" he said, "you never could get the thread! Neither man nor woman could give it to you, so how could you expect to get it?"

"But I have the thread!" said the boy. "My good friend the mother-cow gave it to me."

Thereupon the wizard sprang again in air, coming down with two bangs on the floor, making the windows rattle twice. "But the leather!" he cried, "you never could get the leather! Of that I am sure!"

"I have the leather," replied the boy. "My good friend the bat gave it to me."

This time the wizard jumped higher yet, and the bang with which he came down made the windows rattle three times. Then he smiled a cunning smile. "Oh, well!" he said, "you never can mend it, for all that."

But the boy took the apron and tried, for all that. Strange to say, he could do

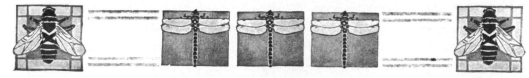

little. The needle unthreaded itself as fast as threaded, and the leather persistently curled out of place. He was almost in despair, and the wizard shoemaker was fairly dancing for joy at his ill success, when the three dragon-flies came sailing up. The silver one and the gold one took the wizard shoemaker by each ear and held his head back against the wall. He was in great fear of them, and was trembling like a leaf.

Then the blue one said gently: "Let me show you, lit-

He sprang clear to the ceiling.

tle brother. See," he said, "the needle has two ends; let us try the other end. The thread has two ends as well; let us try the other end of that."

The boy did so, and the thread fairly leaped into the eye of the needle and remained there. "Now," said the dragon-fly, "observe that a piece of leather has two sides; let us try the other side." The boy did so, whereupon the leather fairly cuddled into place, and the needle seemed to fly back and forth through it of itself, the thread making so fine a stitch that, when the work was done, which it soon was, the apron showed no patch, nor any sign of one, but was as whole as it had ever been.

When the dragon-flies released the wizard shoemaker, and he saw this, he was so enraged that he sprang clear to the ceiling, banging his head against it, and had no sooner alighted on the floor than he rushed with bowed head through the door, butting it open in his haste; rushed through his front fence in the same way, and went on across a field and through the neighboring wood, where he soon was out of sight; but he could be heard for long after, bang-butting his way along among the trees.

No one has ever seen him come back, but the people of that town, to this day, when they hear a sudden wind crashing through the forest, smile and say, "There goes the wizard shoemaker!"

As for the boy, he did not wait even a minute to see whether the wizard shoemaker came back or not, but ran home to tell his mother all about it; and I think that he ran faster then than at any other time during the day.

First published in the December 1912 edition of *St. Nicholas Magazine*

Another Chance

BY JULIA TRUITT BISHOP

CHAPTER ONE: JACK CLEARS THE WAY

HE HAD PAUSED in the post-office door long enough to tear open, with trembling fingers, a letter. It contained a note, and another letter in an unsealed envelope; and he ran his eager eyes over the note, and then went dashing down the street, joyously waving that enclosed letter. If he were making undignified haste, what did it matter? For everybody in Roseville had known him from his babyhood, and Mrs. Aldridge and Ethel knew him best of all.

He burst in at the open door of Mrs. Aldridge's kitchen, his hat on the back of his head, his eyes shining. Mrs. Aldridge, placidly sewing at the window, looked up with a questioning smile. It had been a good number of years, now, since she began making a pet of motherless Jack Carson, whose grandfather lived in the big house on the hill.

"What is it, Jack?" she asked.

"Oh, Mrs. Aldridge, such good fortune!" he cried. "Where is Ethel? Come here, Ethel; it's about you. Didn't I tell you that I would be the cause of your making your fortune some day?"

And he took off his hat with a mock-heroic flourish, and set it on the head of the girl who had come in and stood waiting, dust-brush in hand. Then he sat down and prepared to give Mrs. Aldridge the letter, but at the last minute he held it back.

"I've often told you," he said with an ingenuous blush: "that I'm 'first-class friends' with Mrs. Fairfax of Bellmont College—and I've mentioned Ethel to her—and told her about you—"

After which, finding that he was not making a very lucid explanation, he gave the letter to the astonished lady at the window, and she read it aloud:

BELLMONT COLLEGE, SPRINGFIELD
August 9

MY DEAR MRS. ALDRIDGE: Through my young friend Jack Carson I have heard of your daughter—of her capacity for learning, and of your ambitions for her. I appreciate the fact that you are unable to give her the advantages she should have. My own education was gained through the kindness of others, and it has been my pleasure to pass that kindness on to certain bright and promising girls, who will, I hope, continue the work begun by those who educated me. If you are willing to trust your daughter to my care, I will receive her as a boarding pupil; and unless she speaks of it herself no one will ever know that she is not received on the same terms as the others.

Faithfully yours,
LAURA E. FAIRFAX,
President Bellmont College

Mrs. Aldridge had turned pale before the letter was finished, and her voice had failed so that she could scarcely read. Jack barely waited for the concluding words to dance a jubilant war-dance all around the room, waving the dust-brush, which he had snatched from Ethel for that purpose.

"Now isn't that great?" he cried with boyish delight. "That's the chance of your lifetime, Ethel. Mrs. Fairfax is a regular trump, if ever there was one; and there's a great schoolful of bright girls. I say, Ethel, you'll carry off all the honors, for nine tenths of those girls are rich and don't think it necessary to study."

Ethel had forgotten that Jack's hat was still perched sidewise on her brown curls. She was standing still, with eager, parted lips and shining eyes.

"I shall have to get any amount of new clothes," she said absently. "And how am I to get them?"

"Oh, nothing of the kind," said Jack, with a

Jack danced a jubilant war-dance all around the room, waving the dust-brush.

boy's reckless disregard of clothes. "They wear a uniform at Bellmont—a—a kind of a blue sort of jacket and—and everything; all the girls just alike, you know—and it isn't anything to make, Mrs. Aldridge. I could almost make it myself, I've—I've looked at it so much. You know, sometimes they go walking past our campus," he added, with a demure twinkle in his eyes. "And then, once a month they hold receptions."

"Oh, Ethel, you're going to have a chance! You're going to have a chance!" murmured the mother, looking straight before her with quivering lips; and Jack knew she had not heard a word of his merry chatter.

"Oh, I know you can't get used to the thought of this in ten minutes," he said cheerily. "I've been working up to it by degrees ever so long, so I can hold myself down, now that it's happened. I'll go home and write to Mrs. Fairfax now, and of course you'll both write. And say, Ethel, just tell her that you've known Jack Carson all his life, and that he's the finest boy she's ever likely to meet."

He dodged the flying dust-brush which she had just rescued from him, and ran out of the door, light of heart and of foot. He had made a way for the brightest and most popular girl in Roseville to gain the thorough education for which she had longed. There was nothing meritorious in his having done so, he would have said, simply because it was the only natural thing to do. He and Ethel had been companions and friends from the mud-pie stage up to the present. When he was sent to the university at Springfield, a year before, it had seemed hard to him that Ethel must stay behind with no advantages and no hopes for the future beyond teaching some petty country school. His generous praise of her and of Mrs. Aldridge had led to this morning's triumph. No wonder that the tune Jack whistled proclaimed to his grandfather, long before he reached home, that he was in a merry mood.

The letters were duly written, and Ethel, in feverish haste, started to the post-office. The next train for Springfield would not pass through Roseville until that afternoon, but she could not wait. She was wild with excitement, and a new fire burned in her eyes and crimsoned her cheeks. This morning, only an hour or two ago, she had been sweeping and dusting, with no prospect before her but the same old hum-drum tasks every morning of her life. Now it was as though Aladdin had rubbed his lamp, and what might not come to pass? Her horizon was suddenly filled with visions of white graduating-robes, and scenes of triumph, and gay, flitting figures that were all like herself, and all happy as the day was long. She and her mother would have a sweet little cottage somewhere; and her mother would wear a black dress and a filmy white handkerchief folded across her breast, and would sit and read all day, with gold-rimmed glasses instead of those homely old steel ones; and there would be a servant to do the work—that wretched housework, which

Ethel detested with all her heart. She smiled and held up her head triumphantly at the very thought of it—and turning a corner just then, almost ran against Josie Barnes, whom she did not like. Not that she had anything against Josie Barnes, but they had been classmates and rivals in the village school from the first grade up; and then, Josie had an exasperating way of saying things.

"Mercy, Ethel! You look feverish!" said Josie, now. "Been over the stove too long this hot morning? I'm just going down to your house to get your mother to make my new dress."

"It will not be worth while to go, I am sure," said Ethel, with dignity, intensely irritated and willing to triumph a little. "I am going away to school on the first, and mama will be very busy sewing for me."

It delighted her to see Josie's start of surprise and incredulous stare, and she added complacently:

"I am going to Bellmont College to finish my course."

"My! but you are coming up!" exclaimed Josie, too astonished to be other than downright and disagreeable. "Bellmont's awfully expensive. I shouldn't think your mother could afford it."

For one swift moment an awful choice flashed before Ethel's vision. Should she tell Josie the truth, and have her bruit it abroad among all her friends? No doubt she would tell it in the least favorable way; perhaps she would even say that "Ethel Aldridge was a charity student at Bellmont." Her very soul sickened at the thought, and with a sudden access of color she replied:

"At any rate, my mother thinks she can."

And with a curt good-by she went on her way to the post-office.

Most things in our lives have their beginnings, and Ethel was wholly unconscious that this brief conversation was to be the beginning of many strange things.

"I'll stop on the way home and tell Maud Andrews all about it," she said to herself, in excuse for the little something in her conscience that troubled her.

But there were some purchases to make for her mother, because the sewing must begin at once, and she was delayed about them an hour or two. When she opened the gate at Maud's home at last, Maud came flying out to meet her.

"Oh, Ethel, Josie stopped and told us," she cried. "And isn't it good luck? I'm just as glad as though it had happened to me!"

And while Maud chattered, there was Mrs. Andrews in the door, holding out both hands and ready to hug Ethel with delight.

Well, she would tell them about it after a while.

"You know, I could scarcely believe it when Josie told me," said Maud, excitedly. "I didn't think it possible that you could be able—we've always talked over the ways and means together. But Josie said she asked you about that, and you were able—and I'll declare, I could fly, Ethel, I'm so glad. I sat right down and wrote to Will, and told him all about it."

Will was the fine young fellow who was digging a farm out of the backwoods to make a home for Maud some day. "Well," said Ethel to herself, "I'll wait, and get Maud to walk home with me, and tell her then."

But the call was over, and Maud had walked half-way home with her, and the story was not told; and now it never could the told—as Ethel imagined. Ethel Aldridge, the girl whom everyone had loved for her transparent honesty, hurried home and laid the packages on the table.

"Mama," she said, "I haven't told anyone of the terms on which I am going to Bellmont, and I've been thinking that we shouldn't let anyone know."

Mrs. Aldridge looked up in surprise.

"Why, Ethel," she cried, "we would surely tell our friends of a kindness like that—a kindness that is to give a poor girl the advantages that are enjoyed by those higher up in the world!"

"That is just it," said Ethel, eagerly. "I think her letter shows that she doesn't care to have it talked about, and you can easily see the reason. If everybody is told of it, she will be overwhelmed with applications to take other girls on the same terms—and you can understand that she can't fill the college with pupils who don't pay anything."

And the argument was such a good one that Ethel instantly let herself believe it. From that time on, it was for Mrs. Fairfax's sake that she told no one how she went to Bellmont College.

The chief difficulty was with Jack. When she made to him that evening the carefully prepared speech she had been thinking of, he looked surprised.

"Of course, Ethel, that's with you," he said. "No, I haven't mentioned it—did you think I would? But I was a little taken aback this evening when Josie Barnes told me a string of nonsense about a wonderful rise of fortune you had been telling her of—"

"Oh, Jack, I did nothing of the kind!" cried the horrified Ethel. "I said that mama was able to send me, and she *is* now. You can't go about telling all your private affairs to people like Josie Barnes. I don't mind everybody up at school knowing all about it, for they'll understand it; and after a while I'll explain it to a few intimate friends here. But you know what a gossipy little old place this is."

"I suppose you are right," replied the boy, more soberly than was his wont. "But I hadn't thought of it in that way. My way would have been just to tell it straight out to everybody that came near me, and so have done with it."

"That's very easy for you to say," said Ethel, warmly. "You've never known what poverty is."

And she ran away from him and shut herself up in her room and cried a little, notwithstanding the grand good fortune that had come into her humdrum life, and that was going to make "everything possible."

At least half the young people of the village went down to the station to see Ethel off—because she had grown up with them from her babyhood. Since Ethel's good fortune had been first announced the matter had been discussed with much excitement in every home within a radius of three miles; and many of Mrs. Aldridge's friends and acquaintances felt aggrieved because they had not been taken into her confidence. They had given her every opportunity to confide in them; they had visited her early and often, had talked about Ethel's going away, and had hinted delicately at the expense; but, remembering Ethel's "argument," she had quietly turned the subject, and they were baffled. It was evident that she had come into possession of some kind of windfall, and did not mean to tell them of it; and they thought their friendship deserved better treatment. They were not too pleased, and stood somewhat aloof, watching the little group that was gathered around Mrs. Aldridge and Ethel—and Jack Carson, for Jack was going up to the university on the same train.

"Oh, Ethel, it does seem too good to be true!" cried Maud, for the twentieth time, giving her friend's arm a delighted squeeze. "If I had been your fairy godmother, I couldn't wish better than this for you."

"Yes," added Josie Barnes, from the other side; "it must be lovely to have plenty of money and be able to go to aristocratic boarding-schools and all that. Some of the rest of us would have liked it—but we're not all rich."

A deathly silence followed the speech, and Ethel heard the slow "tick, tick, tick" of the waiting-room clock. A fierce flood of anger and humiliation sent the blood into her face and the tears to her eyes; but it was Jack who came to the rescue.

"Oh, there's nothing like an Aladdin's lamp!" he cried, with a mock-heroic air, fanning himself with his hat and using an imaginary lorgnette. You simply rub it, and, presto! off you go to boarding-school or wherever you please. You have only to look at me, now—"

And then the train-whistle sounded, and they all crowded closer, laughing with Jack. In another minute Ethel was in the car, looking out at a multitude of faces and seeing only her mother's in the midst of them, white, thin, and with eyes unnaturally large and bright because the tears were about to come.

"Good-by, Ethel! Good luck, Ethel!" Maud was crying. And so, smiling proudly back at them, Ethel went out to her new life.

CHAPTER TWO: A TANGLED WEB

THROUGH ALL JACK CARSON'S running fire of light-hearted nonsense, on the way up to Springfield, some twenty miles away, Ethel was telling herself monot-onously that now she was done with Josie Barnes, and would never again have to make equivocations that were almost falsehoods. The memory of it was a continual irritation. She had always been the soul of candor, and had even gained in her earlier years a reputation for downrightness that was not always careful to smooth things over for politeness' sake. And here had she, Ethel, the candid and truthful, been betrayed into something that was at least a misrepresentation—a something that stung and tor-tured her, and kept pace with the flying train, and was not to be left behind.

"I'll let the girls at school know all about it as soon as I get well acquainted," she told herself, dreamily. "They will understand the spirit of the thing, and how it is merely money borrowed—for of course I shall repay Mrs. Fairfax when I go to work."

Her head went up at the thought of it, and in her dreams the money was as good as paid already. How she would like to see Josie Barnes then!

"Don't curl your lip and tilt your nose at me that way, Ethel," she heard Jack saying sternly. "Really, you've said hardly a word. That's the reward I get for being entertaining. Did you know we were at the end of the journey? Yonder's Springfield around that bend—and there's the university, where they are making a doctor out o' me; and there's Bellmont, on that highest hill. Now, my dear girl, one last word of advice. It'll be a month before I'll see you—to talk to—so keep your eyes shut and your mouth open—no, turn that around; I never could get it straight!"

And he took her bundles and led the way out to the platform, where Mrs. Fairfax stood waiting.

That very evening Ethel wrote a hurried letter home. "Mrs. Fairfax is lovely," she wrote, "with the most beautiful silver-white hair you ever saw; and yet she doesn't look half old enough to be gray. She is so kind to me, and has made me feel at home already. It seems odd for poor, penniless me to be in a school like this, where there are so many rich girls. I have three room-mates, and they all are the daughters of wealthy men. One of them is Florence House; her father is the Mr. House who owns the Morrisdale factories, and he is a bank president and I don't know what all besides. I suppose they think I am rich, too."

And Ethel had meant to be frank with her schoolmates, and never again to place herself on a false footing, as she had done at home! It was not that it was her duty to tell everyone the circumstances of her admission to the school, but she had equivocated and had sent abroad a wrong impression, and the thought of it filled her with humiliation. But, again, she said to herself that the very first time there was *need* of it she would surely let the girls know how she was making her way through school, by the aid of Mrs. Fairfax's kindness.

But that first afternoon she sat in her room watching Florence and May and Elise make their hurried toilets for the daily walk. She had been ready in a very few moments, and was smiling a little as Florence jerked her jacket this way and that and tried on her college cap at many different angles.

"I'll never go to another school where there's a uniform!" she cried at last. "Think of being forced to wear this hideous blue!—and with my complexion! It's all very well for you," she added, catching Ethel's smile. "You can wear any color. But a brunette, like me! Why, I'm simply a fright!"

"But I thought the uniforms were very pretty," said Ethel, uneasily, with a sinking at her heart as she remembered how little her mother had been able to afford the money for hers.

"Oh, they are as pretty as the average uniform," said Florence, ungraciously. "But didn't it make you wretched to leave all your beautiful clothes at home and come up here to wear an old blue skirt and jacket forever?"

Once again a choice was before her. Florence had turned and was looking at her while she drew on her gloves, and the other girls stood ready. A choking something was in Ethel's throat. It seemed an age, but it was all over in a second. Then she had replied evenly:

"Oh, I didn't mind it so very much."

And then the bell sounded below, and she led the way from the room.

The walk did Ethel little good that evening, though it led past the university campus, and she caught a glimpse of Jack making a famous home run in the ball game out in front, and though the boys cheered Bellmont loud and long, Florence, who walked beside her, found Ethel a dull companion, for she was silent and absorbed. Before the walk was ended, Ethel had formed a resolution. It was not too late—she would set herself right that very evening.

But that night, as they were preparing to settle to their studies, Elise, an impulsive little madcap, said gaily:

"I'm so glad that we have Ethel this year instead of Jessie Barker. She was so disagreeable!"

"And to think of her being a charity scholar, after all we endured from her!" rejoined the haughty Florence. "We didn't find that out till the session was nearly over. Mama was astonished at Mrs. Fairfax putting her with us."

"Oh, who cares for her being a charity scholar?" retorted Elise. "Anybody may be poor, but nobody need be disagreeable."

"Well, I'm sure I don't come to Bellmont College to associate with just *any-body*," said Florence, scornfully.

And that was why Ethel never told. Her cheeks were crimson, and the pages of her book swam in an indistinct blur before her eyes. She wished herself back at home, with no prospects and no ambitions. She felt herself a coward, untruthful and dishonorable, for she had placed herself in a position to be insulted by this haughty girl who was not half so well-bred as Ethel's own poor mother, working beyond her strength that she might keep her daughter at school.

But custom reconciles one to many things. A week later Florence chanced to see the postmark on one of Ethel's letters, and exclaimed:

"Roseville! Why, I didn't know you lived there. Mama and I spent one summer with the Oliphants at Roseville. Do you know the Oliphants?"

This time she did not give herself an opportunity to choose.

"The Oliphants?" she answered readily. "Oh, yes, I know them—but not intimately. They spend most of their time in Europe, you know; and once in a long while they come down with a house-party. What a beautiful home they have! Do you remember their conservatory?"

She might have added that she knew the Oliphants as the other people of Roseville did, from meeting them as they rode or drove about the town and along the country roads; and that she had carried up to the great house some sewing which her mother had done for Mrs. Oliphant, and so had caught a glimpse of the interior of the beautiful home. But she did not tell this side of the story, and a few moments later she was singing with an untroubled conscience. On the whole, she told herself, she had adopted the only possible course. She *must* be free to study without worry and anxiety, in order to gain the education that would enable her to support herself; and if these girls learned the truth they would make her life unendurable. It did not concern them in the least whether she were rich or poor. Personally, she made herself very agreeable to them, and being their superior in thoroughness and quickness of comprehension, was always ready to help them over their little difficulties.

Before the session was two weeks old Mrs. Fairfax met Jack Carson, and said to him warmly:

"Your judgment is good, Jack. The little girl you praised so highly is going to be one of my star pupils. And she is such a sweet little lady in her manners, too. She is having a fine influence over the three girls in her room. Last year that room dragged all the session; but now they all are improving in scholarship from day to day."

"See what comes to people who put their whole confidence in me!" replied Jack, saucily.

It was at the end of the month that the pupils of Bellmont gave their first reception to the university boys, and Jack had an opportunity to shake hands with his chum and playmate of the old days. Before she had spoken half a dozen words he found himself studying Ethel with a puzzled frown, wondering if she were really changed at all, or if he had forgotten how she used to be.

"I led my class this month, Jack," she said jubilantly. "Won't that be good news for mama?"

He took her over to a window and sat down by her, while she told him that she was at last beginning to hold up her head, for here no one knew that she was poor.

"I've always known it, Ethel, and I like you just as well," said Jack, quietly. Decidedly, Ethel must have changed.

"Isn't Mrs. Fairfax lovely?" she cried, leaving the dangerous subject. "Do you know what made her hair so white? I have heard all about it. It was her son, you know—her only son; and he's broken her heart and ruined himself, and he's in prison somewhere—"

"Ethel!"

Jack's horrified eyes were fastened on her face, and he had involuntarily lifted his hand as if to stop her.

"Ethel," he went on presently, a note of sternness in his voice, "I have known Mrs. Fairfax since I was nine years old, and I have never seen the time when I would have allowed anybody to tell me anything about her private affairs."

"Oh, this is your evening to lecture, is it?" said Ethel, with rising color. "Shall I clear a place on the rostrum and ring the bell for order?"

But Jack was not easily offended.

"Don't be silly, Ethel," he said seriously and candidly. "You have been listening to gossip about the best friend you've ever had, and, worse still, you've been repeating it. No, I don't want it repeated even to me. I would have gone fifty miles out of my way to keep from hearing it!"

"You will not be troubled soon by any further speech of mine," said Ethel, rising; and with a haughty little bow she walked away. Jack made his excuses early, and went home.

He had meant to be a friend to Ethel, and now they were alienated, for the first time in their lives.

Ethel lay awake for hours that night, tingling with mortification over Jack's very decided reproof. What right had he to reprove her? Did he think that she was only a common gossip because she merely mentioned this one little incident that he should have found interesting?

Jack had certainly been very rude, and it would serve him right if she refused to be reconciled.

For by this time Ethel's point of view was wholly changed. The girls who shared her room gossiped about Mrs. Fairfax, and she had learned to join glibly in the idle talk, for she was morbidly anxious to seem in nowise different from them.

It was not long before her independence of thought and action was gone, and she was fast becoming a very servile Ethel, who followed where the silly, empty-headed Florence chose to lead.

CHAPTER THREE: ON THE WRONG ROAD

EASY IS THE descent into Avernus, says the old proverb, and Ethel was finding the truth of it. Indeed, it seemed to her that there was no other way than the downward road, when one has once started. Having committed herself to statements which carried with them the impression that she was something higher than she really was in the social scale, she had never seen a place where she could retract. True, she had told no direct falsehoods—she comforted herself with that reflection; and now her position was established among the girls, and doubtless the trouble was all over.

"Let's see!" said Elise, the evening after the reception, as the four chums sat in the moonlight near the window, indulging in one of the midnight frolics which were so carefully hidden from Mrs. Fairfax, and at which many kinds of indigestibles were devoured. "It was May's treat first, then Florence's, and this is mine. Your turn next, Ethel—and do give us something new. I am tired to death of potted chicken and chocolate creams."

The first of the stolen feasts had filled Ethel with secret dismay, but she had taken part in it, urged by her morbid fear of seeming different from other girls. With the second the sense of disloyalty to Mrs. Fairfax had grown lighter; and now her secret and only trouble was the haunting agony of spending her little store of money on midnight treats. But it must be done. There was not the smallest hesitation on her part. Her mother had sent her the sum for which she had written to buy drawing materials, and she had been very jubilant over it, for she had a real talent for art. Never mind; she would get cheaper materials than she had intended—and perhaps her mother could spare her a little more money. The home expenses were surely very light now. Doubtless there would be a little store laid up just for her expenses, and this was something she could not avoid. She would write the next morning and ask her mother to send a little more.

Somehow, that letter to her mother took a long time to write, and her face reddened as she read it over. "I am so sorry to ask you for more money already," she said, "but it does seem that there are always new expenses coming up. My gloves are looking so shabby, and I am out of stamps, and need several little things; and if you can spare me as much as two dollars I shall be so glad, and will promise not to trouble you again for a long time."

While she was reading over the letter Florence came in, and Ethel started guiltily and hastily folded the sheet and thrust it into the envelope.

"Writing home for money?" Florence asked carelessly. "Of course you are. I never write home for anything else. You've got to have plenty of money to make life bearable at a school like this. I hope you'll know how to spend it when you get it, for I'm dying for a treat that amounts to something."

Ethel thought with secret dismay of the expensive bonbons that had been spread at the other feasts, but she answered lightly:

"Oh, just leave that to me!"

Florence had gone to the mirror to arrange her hair, but she dropped her arms and cried petulantly:

"Oh, do come and help me fix my hair! Suzette always did it for me, and I can't get used to doing it myself. Isn't it awful to do without a maid when you've always been used to one?"

"It certainly is dreadful!" murmured Ethel, intent on the dark waves of hair that she was so deftly braiding.

"But you have learned how so much easier than I have," Florence went on, turning her head from side to side to admire the effect. "You do that beautifully. And see how pretty yours always is! How did you learn to do it yourself—and this your first session away from home, too?"

"Oh, mama always insisted on my learning it, so that I would never have any trouble about it," said the girl who had waited on herself from her childhood.

"Some mothers are so sensible!" purred Florence. "If it wouldn't be such an imposition I'd ask you to arrange my hair every day."

"Oh, it will be no trouble at all," said Ethel.

"How different you are from other girls!" cried Florence, smiling at her reflection in the mirror. "Jessie Barker could make my hair perfectly lovely, but when I asked her the same thing she was insulted, and said she didn't come to school to play lady's-maid to anybody; and after I had offered to pay her for it, too! I think she took a good deal on herself, considering—"

"I think so!" interrupted Ethel, hastily. "As for me, I think it a real pleasure to help the girls one likes."

"Oh, but you see, you are a lady," smiled Florence, "and that makes all the difference in the world. What a pretty color you have, Ethel! Even these wretched old uniforms look lovely on you. There's the bell; we'll have to run, or Old Lady Fairfax will have a dozen checks ready for us."

And in spite of this hot indignation that swept over Ethel like a flame at hearing such a flippant epithet applied to the lady who had befriended her, she made no protest, because—well, because they were going down the stairs the next moment, and it is difficult to talk on the stairs; and because it did not really concern her what other people said of Mrs. Fairfax, so long as she said nothing wrong herself; and because some other time would do as well; and, in short, for a multitude of good reasons. For Ethel's moral sensibilities were weakening, and she had learned how to make many ready excuses to her conscience.

The money came from her mother, with a letter that filled her with vague trouble and sharp self-reproach. "I send the money," she wrote; "but do be careful, Ethel, about spending every cent of it, and don't buy anything you are not compelled to have. Somehow, my work has fallen short lately—I think people are under the impression that I have suddenly grown independent—and most of the sewing has gone to Miss Snyder. Well, she needs it, too. I did feel hurt, though, when Mrs. Barnes put me off about paying for Josie's two dresses, and said that if I could afford to keep my daughter at Bellmont I must have a great deal more money than she had, and I could certainly afford to wait a few weeks for the money for two dresses. Worst of all, my eyes are troubling me a great deal, and I am scarcely able to go on with my work at night—and you know I can't give that up, now that the days are so short and expenses are so high."

The tears gushed to Ethel's eyes as she read these homely details. Somehow, in the midst of these new and absorbing interests, she had almost lost sight of her mother. She remembered now that she had written but three letters home since she came, and all of them had been hasty scrawls, and two of them had been requests for money. Poor, lonely, hard-working mother! She would send the money back without delay. She would ask Mrs. Fairfax if there were not some way by which she could make a little money while she was at school, and help her mother along. She would—

"Oh, your money has come!" cried all three of the girls in a breath, bursting into the room and noticing the money-order crushed up in Ethel's hand.

"That means that we have our treat promptly on time," laughed Florence. "Make it crystallized fruits, Ethel, and remember that Oliveiri's are the best, and that we shall want a quantity, for we all are half starved."

"Girls," exclaimed Elise, reflectively, laughing and dimpling at the thought, "you remember how Jessie Barker used to help eat all our treats, and then back out when her turn came, because she said it wasn't treating Mrs. Fairfax right?"

The others shrieked with laughter at the thought of it, and the speech Ethel had been going to make was never made. She even joined in the laugh, in a mirthless way, though she was very pale as she slipped the money-order into her pocketbook.

After all, now that the money had come, she might as well spend it as she had intended. Her mother would not expect it back, and of course she must be able to spare it or she would not have sent it. Besides, if the money were sent back now, her mother would naturally ask why it was asked for if it was not needed. The proper thing to do was to keep the money—she was surprised to think that had not occurred to her at first. But she would certainly make this the last. She would have nothing to do with any more of the treats, and then they would not expect anything from her. So once more Ethel mentally arranged all the future satisfactorily, and then did wrong in the present, with many good excuses for it, and, each time as she said to herself, "for the *last* time."

Saturday morning she asked and received permission to go to the post-office for stamps and to the book-store for drawing materials.

That afternoon Jack Carson, walking across the park, saw Mrs. Fairfax in a distant avenue, and leaped a hedge or two and half a dozen flower-beds to intercept her. She greeted him in the old affectionate way, but she did not begin talking of Ethel, as she had done when he met her last.

"And how is Ethel doing?" he asked presently. "Still at the head of her classes?"

"Still at the head, Jack," she answered gravely. "She is a very intelligent girl."

Was there something back of her speech, or did he only imagine so? He rattled on, trying to fill an uncomfortable pause.

"I caught a glimpse of her this morning, just coming out of Oliveiri's, but she was too far away for me to overtake her. Besides, I wouldn't talk to her here without your knowledge," he added loyally, and said good-by and went on his way. "Now what has happened?" he kept asking himself. "Has she heard some of that talk? Oh, Ethel, Ethel! to think you could be the brightest, frankest girl I ever saw until you had a chance for yourself, and then could spoil it all by such wild nonsense as that!"

There was a "treat" in Ethel's room that night, with much whispering and with convulsions of hushed merriment; and Ethel was assured over and over that her treat was the best of the series, and that they would hurry to have her time come around again. Ethel had never been so gay and witty, had never said so many sparkling things as those she whispered that night. Perhaps she had merely crossed the Rubicon, and was grown reckless. The feeling did not pass away with the night. The new spirit was still in evidence next day as she walked along the upper hall, light of foot and with head uplifted, and suddenly came face to face with Mrs. Fairfax. The principal did not pass; she stopped Ethel with a gentle hand on her shoulder, and looked gravely into her startled eyes.

"Ethel," she said, "have you anything to tell me?"

Ethel's face was white, but she did not falter.

"Anything to tell? Why, no, Mrs. Fairfax," she replied.

"Let me ask it in another way," persisted the lady. "Have you anything to confess?"

The girl turned cold to her finger-tips, but her eyes did not fall.

"How could I confess anything unless I had done something wrong?" she asked innocently.

"Nothing to tell?" repeated Mrs. Fairfax, solemnly. "I am not a hard teacher, Ethel. Think! Nothing to confess?"

"Nothing," said Ethel, a dogged resolution settling down upon her face; and Mrs. Fairfax released her and turned away.

Truly Ethel had wandered far since the summer day when Jack had opened the way to Bellmont.

CHAPTER FOUR: "WE HAVE FAILED!"

IN SPITE OF her hardihood, the moment Ethel was left alone she flew to her room, white and palpitating, and told the story of the meeting to the three girls.

"And oh, girls, she has found out something—she knows something! I don't know what it is, but she has found out."

"Who cares if she has?" cried the spoiled, foolish Florence, recklessly. "I don't doubt in the least that someone was listening at the door of our room last night. I hate a spy! Suppose she has found out? She can't do anything worse than send us home, and, so far as I am concerned, that would not trouble me much. Then mama would send me to Fair Oaks, and nothing would please me better."

The rude and angry speech would have been inexpressibly shocking to Ethel a few weeks before, but now she heard it without flinching. She, too, hated a spy, and she applauded what she called Florence's "generous spirit." It transformed things very materially, and completely altered the point of view. It was much nobler to break the rules by having a midnight treat than to eavesdrop, and, in her new state of mind, Ethel could easily persuade herself that this was what Mrs. Fairfax must have done. She felt alienated and estranged from her all at once. She tried even to think herself upon a high moral plane, and that she could criticize Mrs. Fairfax with perfect justice.

May and Elise were slower to take sides with Florence; and Elise, wild and thoughtless as she was, even suggested that it would be better for the four of them to go together to Mrs. Fairfax and confess their prank, and promise not to offend again.

"You'll do nothing of the kind, so far as I am concerned," said Florence, angrily. "You could not confess for yourself without bringing us all into trouble too, and you have no right to do that. You see how nobly Ethel protected the rest of us, even if she herself had to suffer. There is only one person meaner than a spy, and that is a telltale."

For one moment Elise's suggestion had sent an accusing pang to Ethel's conscience. She remembered it long afterward with bitterness of spirit. If that suggestion had only come from her instead of from Elise! If she could only have had this one good impulse to her credit! But instead she lifted her head proudly, elated with Florence's compliment to her faithfulness.

"I am sure I would never tell, no matter what the punishment might be," she said with the air of a martyr. "That is something one simply can't do. If I alone had been at fault, now—"

"But nobody was at fault," declared Florence. "What else can Mrs. Fairfax expect? We are compelled to indulge ourselves a little. We pay enough for our board, and look what kind of fare we get!"

The fare was quite as good as it should be, and Ethel knew it; but she made no comment.

When the girls filed into the assembly-room the next morning, Mrs. Fairfax was standing ready at her desk. As Ethel passed, going to her seat, the lady's eyes dwelt earnestly and anxiously on her face; but there was no softening in it. Ethel merely looked up with a cold and studiously polite "good morning," but there was nothing more—no contrition, no acknowledgment, no sign of a desire for reconciliation. More than that, the eyes of the principal, flashing from face to face, saw that there was an understanding among the three other girls, and that they were angry and resentful. For now, as of old, as a little leaven leaveneth the whole lump, so does the taint of evil spread.

As the days passed and Ethel met always that questioning look, she resented it more and more, and grew colder in proportion. It was a grave and sorrowful look, and it made the girl uncomfortable in spite of herself. In resistance to that uncomfortable feeling she took on a more determined air of opposition. She persuaded herself that she was the one to be offended, and that Mrs. Fairfax owed her some amends; and so she went about with her head up, and met Mrs. Fairfax's look with one as steady as her own.

It was when she chanced to be alone with Mrs. Fairfax that she suffered most. She avoided all such meetings with care, but there would come times when for a few moments she would be left alone with the principal. At such times she escaped from the room, if possible, and if this could not be done she studied intently, and saw no one. Taken altogether, these were not the happiest of times for Ethel. When the other girls were with her, numbers gave her boldness, but she had no courage to face the present condition of things without their support.

And no wonder that by this time her studies began to suffer; for she found that she could hold a book before her face and read over a lesson many times without being conscious of a word she had read.

During all the study-hours her mind went wandering over and over the incidents of the past few weeks; and at night her wide-open eyes stared into the darkness and she could not sleep. Her hand was no longer steady with the pencil, and her art teacher complained to Mrs. Fairfax that his most promising pupil seemed to be losing ground.

The ambitions with which Ethel had come to Bellmont were fading away. It had been a long time, now, since she had dreamed of the cottage she and her mother were to have, and of the pleasant freedom from care she was to bring into her mother's life when she was ready to work.

It had been agreed between herself and her mother in the summer that she would not go home for the Christmas week vacation, because she would save money and expense by remaining at the school. Most of the other pupils were going, the few who remained being those who lived at a great distance. When the gay preparations for the Christmas flitting began in her room, and Florence and Elise and May were packing their trunks days beforehand, Ethel told the girls that she would not have the week at home. She had studied over the available excuses, and, now that the time had come, gave them the one selected as she helped crowd Florence's trunk with the disordered array of garments:

"Mama wrote me that it would be better for me to stay here. She isn't very well, and I'm sure the quiet will be better for her than to have me there."

"Oh, of course, for during the holidays one is sure to have a houseful of company all the time," said Florence. "I fully expect to throw mama into nervous prostration while I'm at home. She often says that between me and the servants she never has a moment's peace."

This was but one of many heartless speeches Ethel had heard Florence make about her mother, and though shocked by them at first, now she scarcely heeded it. She was busily thinking, instead, and in a moment she added:

"And it's too bad—but mama being sick, she hasn't had an opportunity to send me any Christmas money; so if any of you are thinking of making me a present, girls, let me warn you right now—don't."

This was the speech that had given her the greatest trouble, but she found that she could make it very easily. Poor girl, all too rapidly she was growing accustomed to saying such things.

"Oh, I haven't bought the presents for you girls yet," replied Florence, carelessly. "I have something for each of the teachers; and I wish you could see the beautiful brass-and-onyx table I selected today for a peace-offering to Old Lady Fairfax!"

And again Ethel made no protest.

It was like Florence that she should propose one last grand feast before the holidays, and it was like Ethel—the new and changed Ethel—that she should seem quite ready to contribute as much as the others; for this was to be a "share-and-share-alike" feast. The little sum she had jealously guarded since the first of school to buy a Christmas present for her mother went into this feast. "Mama doesn't expect anything, anyhow," was her selfish way of quieting her conscience this time.

Just before sunset, on the night before Christmas eve, Jack came up and asked Mrs. Fairfax if he might see Ethel.

"Certainly; I will send for her," the lady replied. And when Ethel came Mrs. Fairfax left the room.

Ethel waited a little haughtily to hear what Jack might have to say. They had not met since the evening of their disagreement, and there was a burning consciousness of that evening in Ethel's face.

"I knew you were not going home, Ethel," Jack said gently, "so I came by to see how you were—for Mrs. Aldridge will want me to report to her tomorrow evening."

"You needn't trouble about it," said Ethel, stiffly. "I have written to mama today, giving her a full account of everything she would care to know."

"Oh, of course; I knew you must have written," he replied cordially, determined not to be repulsed. "But she'll want to know how you look, and everything about you—"

"She is not at all uneasy about me," replied Ethel, ungraciously.

Jack looked at his friend of the old times with wondering scrutiny.

"I scarcely know what has happened to change you so, Ethel," he said candidly. "I don't know you of late. But, at any rate, I shall go to see Mrs. Aldridge, for she's always been my friend, and is not likely to change toward me without telling me the reason. She must have had a lonely time since school began—but she'll never complain, as long as you are at the head of your classes."

He said good-by and went away, a little sore at heart; and Ethel flew upstairs and cried in secret because her world was all upside down.

Among her books was the letter she had written her mother that day, telling her that the girls were getting ready to go home for the holidays and that she would soon be left alone. "I have not come out at the head of my class this month," she had written. "Indeed, one could hardly have expected it three months in succession. And then, I have suffered with headaches a great deal. I have not said anything about it, for I did not want to worry you. I suppose it is caused by the strain on my eyes, studying so much at night."

It was a very neatly written letter, and it all sounded so plausible. What was it that made Ethel open it after Jack had gone, and write a postscript?

"How I wish I could see my darling mother, if only for a little while!" she wrote. "But we both know that it isn't best now; and we can wait and look forward to the time when your life is going to be easier. Don't worry about my eyes. The rest during Christmas week will make them all right again."

And then, in the midst of the better thoughts that were coming to her, the other girls came in and began planning for the feast, and the lonely mother down at Roseville was forgotten.

There were no lessons next day; only gay good-byes all day long, for pupils were leaving by every train. Early in the afternoon the departure of a group of girls left Ethel and her three friends standing in the wide hall together, and they walked into the assembly-room with their arms around one another and sat down.

"I wish it were evening," said Florence, discontentedly. "Think of staying here to another dinner! And then think of having to come back to eat three of those meals every day until the last of June. Honestly, Ethel, aren't you nearly starved to death?"

If Ethel could have spoken honestly she would have said that the fare was good and plentiful; but she laughed and shrugged her shoulders.

"I'm so hungry I don't know what to do with myself," she said with a doleful air.

"I certainly do pity you, here all alone all Christmas week," said Elise, cordially.

"Yes—fancy it!" cried Florence. "Less to eat than ever, and alone with the Ogress. Old Lady Fairfax will give you a lovely time after we go away. What on earth makes you stay? Write your mother you are starving and must go home to get something to eat. Get her to send you somewhere else. She could find better schools almost anywhere for the dollars and dollars a month she spends here for you; don't you think so?"

"I should think she might," said Ethel, unwaveringly, though her eyes were dropped to her hands, which were toying with a book.

"And then to think how she is going to make your life miserable about those treats! She'd be in a rage if she knew about the one last night, wouldn't she? I don't believe she would ever forgive anyone who had done a wrong thing."

The remark was made directly at Ethel, with such point and purpose that she was fired with anger, and cried hotly:

"Well, I think a woman whose own son has been disgraced should have very little to say about other people's short-comings!"

She had seen a look of wide-eyed terror on May's face directed toward the door behind her, but had been too angry to heed it. She had scarcely noticed that some one was passing her until at last, as she finished speaking, she looked up into the face of Mrs. Fairfax.

A white, drawn face, looking years older than when she had looked at it last, half an hour ago. The lady's thin hands were clasped tight together, as though to control the trembling in them. She stood there and battled for self-control, and tried to speak, and could not.

A deadly silence had settled down on the frightened group, but Ethel was no longer conscious of the others. She gazed at Mrs. Fairfax with a frightened stare, realizing at last what she had done.

"Young ladies"—the sweeping glance included only the three others—"you may go to your room."

The three fled—Ethel heard their footsteps scurrying along the hall and up the stairs; but she herself sat still, numbed and breathless.

It was a long time before Mrs. Fairfax spoke again; and when she tried to speak there was something in her throat that kept her thin hand fluttering there. But at last Ethel heard the low voice that was to pronounce her doom.

"We have tried the experiment," she said, "and it has failed. I gave you my confidence, and you have abused it. I placed you where your influence was most needed, and

As Ethel finished speaking, she looked up into the face of Mrs. Fairfax.

where you could have helped me most, and you have not been true to me, nor to yourself, and have not helped your associates. You have shown no consideration for your mother—your poor mother! Ah, I suppose a young girl can hardly know what that means! And you have shown nothing but animosity toward me. I have found nothing to build on in your character, for you have not been truthful or candid with me; and that is like building on quicksand. And at last—at last—you have stabbed me to the heart—you have dared to speak so of the great agony of my life—"

Her voice failed, and she merely sat and looked at the cowering girl. When Ethel heard the low voice again it was saying:

"You will tell the girls that it has been decided that you are to go home, after all. Tell no more than that, and no one will ever know how—how we have failed."

CHAPTER FIVE: THE GRAY DAYS AND DULL

A LONG TIME after, Ethel arose and went out of the assembly-room, feeling her way along the seats and creeping like some wounded thing. She had heard the dinner-bell hours ago, it seemed to her, but had not heeded it. Her room-mates were about to go; she heard them asking for her with subdued voices, that they might say good-by. The sound of it roused her as nothing else could have done; and she steadied herself and walked along the hall to meet them, her head erect and a smile on her white lips.

"Oh, girls, are you ready?" she cried. "I didn't think of its being so near train-time. Good-by—good-by, all of you! Merry Christmas!—though of course you'll have that!"

She wondered, long afterward, how she could have done it—how she could have stood there waving merry good-byes and uttering glib good wishes, as though hers were the lightest heart in all the world. When it was over, and they were really gone, she crept silently up the stairs and went to her room, and began throwing things into her trunk; for in less than an hour her own train would leave, and she would be speeding home—home!

The uniform she had been so proud of once, she packed away on the shelf in the closet. She no longer had any right to wear it. She put on one of the old home dresses that she had brought with her thinking it would do to wear on Saturdays—the plain, neat little old dress that her mother had fashioned with such careful handiwork.

She had never worn the dress on the school Saturdays, because it looked insignificant beside the other girls' elegant lounging-robes. Her eyes burned now with the tears that would not come, as she put it on.

She had no money for railroad fare—all her savings had gone into that last treat. Alone and friendless and beggared, she sat down on her trunk after it was packed, and looked around the desolate room, feeling that, in its emptiness and ugliness, it was a picture of the wreck she had made of her life at school.

The matron tapped at the door presently, and civilly announced that the carriage was ready, at the same time giving Ethel a ticket to Roseville. If she had only offered to shake hands with the forlorn girl—if she had only wished her a merry Christmas! But Ethel had silently acquiesced in Florence's rude treatment of the matron, and now in her extremity she was alone. The men came up after her trunk, and she silently followed them down the stairs. She lingered a moment at the last landing, to be sure that the hall was deserted, and finding everything quiet, flitted out and plunged into the waiting carriage. And this was her going away from Bellmont! And she had been so proud when she came there a little while before!

She had found a thick veil among her possessions, and had fastened it on. When Mrs. Fairfax came out and took the opposite seat in the carriage, and they drove away, the veil hid them from each other. Ethel could not see the sorrow on the pale, grave face at which she dared not more than glance; and Mrs. Fairfax could not see the miserable, dumb agony in the eyes that stared out of the window.

The day was drawing to a close when she found a seat in the car, crowded with merry Christmas travel. She had sunk down next to a window, and sat there for a little while, afraid to look out. When she did look, there was Mrs. Fairfax, standing just where she had stood to welcome her three months before. Only now it was a different Mrs. Fairfax, with a pang at her heart that Ethel had planted there; and this was a different Ethel—oh, so different!—a numb, despairing Ethel, whose little world was in ruins, whose hopes and ambitions were blighted.

The train was racing away through the fields when she found herself again, and Bellmont was miles behind; and it was then that she saw Jack.

He was two or three seats ahead of her, wholly unconscious of her, his hat off, his hands clasped behind his head, watching the other passengers with friendly interest, and whistling softly to himself.

Jack! She had not thought of him before. But now Jack would know! He had made the chance for her—he had opened the way to Bellmont; he had tried to warn her when he saw the mistake she was making; and now he would know! A cry almost burst from her lips, and she cowered and shrank down into the corner of the seat, and pressed her face against the cold glass of the window, and stared hopelessly out into the twilight. If there were only some place to hide where no one who had ever known her would see her again! But to go back among the people who had known her always—to face the curiosity, the questions, the hints, the open amusement! How Josie Barnes would go up and down and talk, and shrug her shoulders, and raise expressive eyebrows! Josie Barnes! It had all started with her. If she could only go back to that day when she had met Josie Barnes, and could start over again!

There would be a crowd at the Roseville station to see the Christmas train come in; and Ethel dwelt with agony on the recognitions. She drew the thick veil closer and folded her jacket tight around her, and as the train drew up at the station the people were only conscious that a dark little figure had slipped through the circle of light and was gone before anyone could tell who she was.

When she approached her mother's house it was by the back way; and she opened the gate and slipped stealthily in—the Ethel who had gone out so triumphantly three months before.

Something stirred in the shadows of the porch, and she almost shrieked as it came at her with a rush; but it was only old "Caesar" the dog, embracing her feet with his paws, and looking up into her face with a tremulous whine. In a moment she was down on her knees, with her arms around the old dog's neck and the tears falling on his face, for she was very desolate.

The light was shining from one of the windows, and she stood up and looked at it, and even took a few steps toward it; but then she turned and fled until the fence stopped her. She knew who was sitting in that room. How could she dare to go in there and tell her mother—her poor, toiling mother, who had been so poor ever since the daughter could remember, and who had never been ashamed of poverty, and who thought dishonor the one thing of which to be ashamed. All at once everything else faded away from Ethel's mind. During all these desolate hours she had dwelt upon her ruined hopes and her humiliation; but now she saw only her mother, her head bowed before the people who had known her all her life, bitter shame brought upon her by the girl for whom she had toiled and suffered and saved. Something had cleared Ethel's vision. She was conscious, as she had never been before, that if she had prospered in the Roseville school it was all because of the mother who had worked unceasingly that she might have a chance to study. She had grown up thinking that was a fair division of labor—that her mother should be always working while she was always studying. Her mother had never complained. Had she needed help sometimes? Ethel, crouched against the fence in the dark and looking at that lighted window through raining tears, wished that she had helped her mother once in a while, that the memory of it might make her forget how she had thrown away her great opportunity at last.

But after a while the window drew her, and she could not resist. She would look in, if only for a moment. She searched around the yard, and found a box, and placed it under the window, and climbed up on it, and saw—her mother.

She had been sewing, and was still at the machine, but had leaned her elbows on it and covered her eyes with her hands. It was because her eyes were aching, perhaps; but she was all alone, and looked so lonely—so lonely!

And then she turned a little, and Ethel saw the gleaming of tears on the cheeks that had grown so hollow since she saw them last, and a cry of anguish was wrung from the girl's heart.

The mother heard the sound, and saw the white face at the window. In another moment Ethel was stumbling up the steps and into the room, her hands outstretched as though she were feeling the way. Mrs. Aldridge had risen, and stood leaning forward, her lips parted, her hand on her heart.

"Oh, mama," cried Ethel, reaching her at last, "don't grieve so much. I'm not worth it. I'll do something to try to make a living—I will indeed! I'll help you more than I've ever done. Maybe I can get a place in a store—or somewhere. Don't look like that, mama—please don't!"

"Ethel!" whispered the mother, in a voice Ethel had never heard before, "what is it? Why have you come home—without letting me know? Has anything—happened?"

"Oh, mama!" was the girl's despairing cry, "I have been expelled from school!" And then, with a look of death in the worn face, the mother wavered and fell.

JACK CARSON'S HAND was on the latch of the gate when Ethel's agonized shriek tore the night, and in a moment he was in the room. Ethel was down on the floor, her mother's head in her arms, and she looked up with a look that he never forgot.

"I have killed mother, Jack," she cried. "I've ruined my school career—I've been sent home—and it has killed her."

It was then that Ethel learned for the first time what Jack was.

"Why, nonsense, Ethel! She isn't dead," he cried. "Help me lift her to the bed. There—that's all right. Now get some cold water. She's just fainted—and who could wonder, having you come in like a ghost, when you weren't expected, and with that forlorn face? Do get on another look by the time she comes around!"

"But you don't understand, Jack," she said desolately. "I have been expelled—*expelled* from school!"

Ethel was down on the floor, her mother's head in her arms.

But shocked as Jack was—inexpressibly shocked—he would not let her talk of it at that moment.

"I'd rather think of your mother, and of making things easier for her when she wakes," he said bluntly. "Thank Heaven, we won't have to call in anybody and make it public—not for the present, at least. And that will give us time to look over the field a little and decide what to do."

"Us!" Ah, it was the old, unselfish Jack—the Jack who had been so radiant because he had opened the way to Bellmont. Unutterably humiliated and abased and tortured with anxiety, she stood by while he bathed the white temples with cold water; and when the mother's eyes opened at last, it was Jack's bright greeting that met her first.

"Hello!" he cried, smiling down at her and caressing the worn hand affectionately. "Is that the way you receive us when we come home to give you a Christmas surprise? The next time we'll send down a herald the week before, so that you can begin to reconcile yourself to the idea of seeing us."

She passed her hands over her eyes and looked at him, bewildered.

"I thought—did I dream it?—I thought Ethel came in and told me that—that—"

"You are not a success as a dreamer," he said gaily. "Now, you are tired out—you show it in every look. We are going to sit down here and talk for a little while, and you are to lie still and rest. Don't say a word, for we won't allow it. We have taken this case in hand, you see."

And it was Jack who moved the lamp so that her face was shaded from the light, and who made Ethel sit down where her mother could not see her, while he gravely took a chair near her and waited.

The worn and exhausted mother sank into slumber almost before they were aware of it; and after a while, speaking in low tones, and choking back the sobs so that she might not disturb her mother, Ethel poured out her story to Jack.

"I didn't think of being untruthful at first," she said; "I merely thought of getting around a difficulty; and so I said things that were not exactly true, and thought that would be the end of it. But they placed me in a false position, and in order to shield myself I was constantly compelled to tell new things, and worse things, until after a while they didn't seem so very bad, and I began to excuse them to myself, and to think that I was perfectly justifiable. It seems so hard to get out of a place like that when one is once in. If only I had not started in! I know that now. I lost my independence and my self-respect at the very beginning, and then I kept going down."

"Don't cry, Ethel," said Jack. "It is something to be able to see a fault as clearly as you see yours. Lots of people don't."

Ethel's eyes were wandering around the bare rooms; she had almost forgotten the bareness of it in the midst of the comforts that had surrounded her since she went to school.

"And to think that I took mama's money to treat rich girls!" she broke out afresh. "It seemed to me that I absolutely belonged to those girls from the time I told them the first falsehood, and I didn't dare to refuse anything they suggested. I don't blame them at all—it was all my fault. It seems to me now that it would have been so easy to have told them right in the beginning that I was not able to afford any of those extra expenses; but I didn't say it then, and after that I never dared."

"Please don't cry, Ethel," said Jack, greatly moved by her repentant grief.

"And then I went on and acted so—so horribly to Mrs. Fairfax. I don't know what kind of influence was over me, for it seemed to me then it was all right, but now I can look back all along the road and see how dishonorable I was. Oh, she can never forgive me! And to speak so of her son, when her heart is broken over him! But I never understood broken-heartedness until I had trouble too. And she'll remember that always when she thinks of me."

Jack went and looked out of the window, for there was a mist in his own eyes; but when he came back he said cheerily:

"Now you've talked it all out, Ethel, keep still about it. Don't let a human being know that anything wrong has happened at Bellmont; at least, not for two or three days. And then, if we have to tell it, we can put it in some way so that we can shield your mother. And you are not to tell her, either, for the present. Naturally, you would come home at Christmas time, you know."

"But it will have to be told at last," moaned Ethel, despairingly.

"It's a bad business, Ethel," Jack said gravely. "I don't want you to think it isn't, for I believe it *would* kill your mother if she knew all about it. You see how she looks—I think she has been working too hard, to keep up with the expenses." Ethel groaned and bowed her face to the table. "And we've got to work along a few days and try to devise some means to smooth it over—for her sake, Ethel. I think she'll sleep the rest of the night; and if she wakes, just hold on to your good sense and don't let her know how things are."

And Jack slipped quietly out and walked slowly homeward, more troubled and anxious than he had ever been.

CHAPTER SIX: ANOTHER CHANCE, AND THE VALEDICTORY

THE MOTHER'S DEEP, exhausted sleep lasted all that night and far into the next morning, and when she waked a strange weakness was upon her, so that she could not stir. Ethel hung over her, and waited on her, and smoothed the soft hair that was growing white so fast, and burned her hands at the stove trying to prepare something that would tempt her mother to eat—and did not know they were burned. Mrs. Aldridge did not attempt to talk, for her strength was gone; but she followed Ethel with contented eyes, and smiled at her when she kissed the worn hands and pressed them to her cheeks.

Ethel caught herself fifty times looking out of the window for Jack, but he did not come all that day. No one came, for it was Christmas day, and people were making merry in their own homes. A lonely, desolate Christmas, Ethel thought; but there was a swift moisture in her eyes as she realized that but for her coming home her mother, weak and exhausted as she was, would have been utterly alone.

All day, whenever her mother dozed, Ethel was busy making the bare room a little more habitable—putting up the little pictures she had accumulated at school, and disposing her modest ornaments so that they would meet her mother's tired eyes when she waked. If she longed for anything more for herself that day, it was that she might give it to her mother. If she wished for wealth that day, it was only that she might make life easier for her mother. For this was another Ethel who had come home—more generous, more unselfish than she had ever been: an Ethel who had learned to love her mother.

The early night came down, and she lighted the lamps in all the rooms to make the house a little more cheerful, and sat down to her lonely vigil—anxious about her mother's continued prostration, fearing that she had killed her indeed, wishing that Jack would come and put hope and courage into her heart, as he always did, and wondering what could have kept him away all day, when he knew how she needed him. The evening train came in—the train that had brought her the night before; and she listened to its roaring; and went over that evening in memory, and felt very old and grave.

She felt very sure that she could never be happy or light-hearted again. Would she live many years like this? she wondered. Would she live long enough to atone somewhat to her mother by her devotion, and to make Jack, yes, and even Mrs. Fairfax, respect her again?

"She's asleep, is she?" whispered Jack's voice beside her, for she had been so absorbed in unhappy thought that she had not heard him come in. "That's good. I've a plan, Ethel. Come into the other room and let's talk it over."

She arose and followed him on tiptoe into the poor little parlor, and had closed the door behind her when she found herself face to face with Mrs. Fairfax!

And what would she say—the wronged and insulted principal of Bellmont who had been stabbed to the heart so cruelly? Had she come to cast her off still further? Ethel shrank back against the door, her eyes wide with terror. But Mrs. Fairfax went over to her, and put her arms around the shrinking form, and—were there tears in her eyes?—said tenderly:

"Poor little girl, did you think you were altogether forsaken? See—we have both had time to think it over. You are going to start over again, Ethel—and it will be a different start. Perhaps you and I know of a poor lad who might be a different man if he could only start over again. Some day, let us pray, he will get the new start; but I am going to give one to *you* now."

Yes, there *were* tears on her cheeks, and Ethel was clinging to her; and Jack went out and closed the door, and sat on the steps with Caesar.

Ethel shrank back against the door,
her eyes wide with terror.

"Good old doggy!" he said to that old friend. "This is a fine world, Caesar. I am glad I live in it!"

WHEN JACK WENT in, after a while, Mrs. Fairfax and Ethel sat side by side, and Ethel still held the lady's hand and clung to it. She had poured out her full heart to her teacher, and they had talked it all over.

"Do you see that boy?" Mrs. Fairfax said, smiling at Jack as he came in. "You have wondered, perhaps, why he and I are such friends, when there is such a difference in our years. It is because, from the first time I saw him, I have always thought, 'If my boy had not made his first wrong start he would have been like Jack.' I have watched Jack grow up, and have loved in him another boy who might have been like him but for the first wrong start."

When Jack spoke, after a while, it was to say:

"Your mother is saved, Ethel. She'll never know there was any trouble."

"I'll tell her some day," said Ethel, seriously. "When I have succeeded—and I *will* succeed!—I'll tell her how near I came to failure—and who saved me," she added, with a swift and eloquent glance at both.

If there was any difficulty in the road, it was Mrs. Fairfax who saw it and smoothed it away. She saw that Mrs. Aldridge needed rest and could not be left alone; and she sent down an elderly woman who longed for a country home and was willing to work for small wages. "We will merely add this to your account, Ethel," she said smilingly.

So the way was open for Ethel again, and she was to go back to Bellmont. But the day after Mrs. Fairfax's departure she left her mother sleeping, with the new "help" sitting beside her, and went out to make a visit. She walked to Mrs. Barnes's with a steady step, but her face was colorless as she stopped Josie's exclamations of surprise.

"Josie, I want to set something right," she said simply—"something I said to you once that gave you a false impression and has caused me a great deal of trouble. I told you last summer that mama felt able to send me to Bellmont, and that made you think that we must have a great deal of money, for Bellmont is such an expensive school. That was not true. We had no money. Mrs. Fairfax offered to give me my education. See, here is the letter she wrote. I am sorry I didn't show it to you then. I know you will set it right now, when people mention it to you."

Josie had given an astonished gasp at the disclosure, but she read the letter in silence. Then she looked up and said:

"Well, Ethel! I didn't think you had grit enough to own up to a thing like that, when there wasn't any particular need of it. I couldn't have done it, I'm sure."

"There was particular need of it," said Ethel, with a faint color rising in her cheeks.

"Anyhow, I'm glad you've told me," Josie responded cordially, holding out her hand. "I was very disagreeable about it, thinking you had a fortune and blaming you for not telling me more about it. What a good woman Mrs. Fairfax must be! You ought to show that letter, just to let people know there is such a woman in the world."

And Josie and Ethel parted better friends than they had ever been.

From Josie's Ethel went to Maud's and set matters right there; and then she turned her steps homeward, lighter at heart than she had been in many a day. It seemed to Ethel afterward that Jack must have visited everybody in Roseville that week, and that he must have painted her success at school in glowing colors everywhere he went. "And Ethel's going to make her mark, mind that," he said to every one. "She will pay Mrs. Fairfax for her schooling when she has finished; and, between Mrs. Fairfax up at school and Mrs. Aldridge down here, Roseville will be proud of Ethel some of these days; and then don't forget that I told you about it."

Well, if Roseville was to be proud of Ethel some day, it were as well to begin showing its appreciation now; so, again, half the town was at the station to see her go away, and this time nobody stood at a distance, and nobody wondered how she managed it. The doctor had brought Mrs. Aldridge up in his buggy, and the people were all close around her, shaking hands with her; and, in short, there was general friendliness on every side, with scores of voices wishing Ethel success and promising to look after her mother.

And so Ethel, with the happy tears on her smiling face, began life over again.

THREE YEARS WENT by.

It was graduating day at Bellmont, and the opera-house was filled to overflowing with the friends of the institution. A celebrated man had made the address to the senior class, and one after another they had read the essays that closed their school-days and sent them out into the world.

Far back among the audience was a sunburned young fellow, half concealed by a column; and when the slender, graceful valedictorian walked to the front of the stage and spoke the first clear, earnest words, he lost neither look nor tone of hers. When the applause sounded at the last, how he joined in!—for this was a day to which Jack had looked forward with a thrill at his heart. And his little playfellow of the olden time had won.

He made his way to her after the exercises were over, and she cried radiantly:

"Oh, Jack, were you here, after all? I gave you up this morning."

"I hid behind a column," he said easily. "You didn't expect me to stand the full glory of this scene? I wrote you that, in whatever part of the world I might be, I was coming home for this. Behold me, then, just from my work in the Paris hospitals."

He went with her to one of the vacant seats, and turned to look at her.

"You're all *right!*" he said smilingly. "Now tell me all about it."

But there was so much to tell, she assured him, and it was difficult to know just where to begin; only—

"See—there is mama, Jack. Doesn't she look well? Would you have known her? No, don't go to her yet—not until I have told you—"

Her voice failed a little, but she looked at him presently, a light that he had never seen in her eyes.

"We are not going back to Roseville," she said. "I have found the sweetest little cottage here, Jack—and mother and I will be together in a little home. You see, Mrs. Fairfax has given me a position, and I am going to do very well, I hope. And I am to go on with my art studies. They think I have a talent in that way, and Mrs. Fairfax is giving me the best opportunities."

Jack made an effort to speak, but thought better of it, and cleared his throat instead.

"And I have tried very hard, Jack, to undo the mischief I did in those wretched three months. As soon as I came back I told the girls how I really stood, and the next day they all went to Mrs. Fairfax and asked her pardon for the way they had acted; and they have always been my good friends. I have shared their room all this time, and we all have studied and worked together, and there has hardly ever been an inconsiderate word from any of them. You see how kind people are when you once know the best side of them."

"Yes—I see," said Jack.

"And who won the next highest honors to mine, do you think?" she asked, with laughing eyes. "Why, Josie Barnes!"

"I saw her among the graduates," he replied with an answering smile. "How did Mrs. Fairfax find her?"

"Well, Jack, I told her about Josie," she admitted with a blush. "And she said it would help me if we gave Josie a chance, too. And she had been studying at home all that time, Jack, and she went right into my classes, and has given me the hardest work of my life ever since. She was a better girl than I was, Jack; for she has been truthful and honest from the first; and no girl in the school would dare to say anything against Mrs. Fairfax in Josie's presence. One did try it once, and she said afterward that Josie was a perfect tigress."

But some one called for Ethel, and Jack lost himself in the crowd, and listened to the snatches of conversation, many of them telling what a brilliant girl the young valedictorian was.

"There she is—that is Ethel, papa," he heard a girl saying. "Isn't she a lovely girl? Oh, I am sure I would never have accomplished anything in school if it had not been for Ethel!"

"Well, Florence, let us invite her to spend the summer with you and take a trip in the yacht," suggested the portly and prosperous man, whose daughter was the pride of his life.

"Yes, invite her—but she won't come," replied the daughter. "She wouldn't leave her mother to spend the summer with a queen. I wish you could see the cottage they're going to live in, papa. It's like a doll's house. But somehow I envy Ethel."

The girl sighed as she said it, and Jack felt that his friend could have had no higher praise.

And a little later he came to Mrs. Fairfax, and, holding both his hands, she gazed into his face lovingly.

"The experiment has succeeded, Jack," she said. "Ah, how glad I have always been that you came to see me that Christmas day, and would not be denied. She has been my right hand since then, Jack. I look on that as one of the great days in my life. There has been only one greater—and that was the day you met my boy at the prison door, and took him out West, and started him in business for himself—"

"And he's doing finely!" interrupted Jack. "I found a letter from him when I reached home yesterday, and I'll bring it around—though of course you hear from him all the time."

"Yes," she murmured, with a look of peace on her face; "to have him safe, and Ethel here beside me—"

A slow red crept up into his face.

"But the day may come—when you will have to lose Ethel," he said simply.

The valedictorian

First published in the June 1902 edition of *St. Nicholas Magazine*

Richard, My King

The Story of a
Crusader Knight

BY LIVINGSTON B. MORSE

THE CRUSADES WERE holy wars undertaken by knights of old in Europe for the recovery of the sepulcher of Christ from the Saracens who then held Jerusalem and all Palestine. They were called Crusaders from the Latin word *crux*, which means cross, and because each of the soldiers wore upon his sleeve or breast or shoulder the embroidered figure of a cross to indicate the cause for which he fought. There were eight of these Crusades, or holy wars. But the story I am going to tell you belongs to the third—that one in which Richard I of England, called, for his famed strength and bravery, *Cœur de Lion*, or Lion-hearted, plays so prominent a part.

Although Richard was King of England, he had spent the greater part of his life in France; for away back in the twelfth century, when he lived, England still held many provinces in France—notably those of Normandy and Aquitaine. Those were warlike times, and Richard was no laggard, I can tell you, where blows were to be given and returned. He had quarreled with his father and with his brothers, John and Geoffrey; and to make good his possessions in Normandy against the King of France, he had built him a fortress, Château Gaillard (Saucy Castle), upon an eminence above the Seine, just where the river bends across the Norman marshes on its way to the old city of Rouen.

It was on a beautiful morning in autumn that, with a great clanging and rattling of chains, the drawbridge was lowered over the moat of Château Gaillard, and a gallant train of mounted knights and squires rode forth into the crisp, bright air, followed by the huntsmen holding their hounds in leash. At the head of the train and somewhat in advance, mounted upon a coal-black horse, rode a princely figure clothed in Lincoln green—the color of the huntsmen—who wore upon his yellow locks a cap adorned with the feather of an eagle held by a jeweled brooch. He was taller than any other by a good half head, and he sat upon his horse straight as a reed and as if the two were one. His broad shoulders and steel-blue eyes, piercing and fearless, and a certain arrogance of bearing, told more plainly than words that where'er he went Richard would be leader.

The horsemen clattered down the slope, their spurs and harnesses jingling merrily; then, putting their horses to the gallop, sped across the marshes toward the wood.

Richard still held the lead—imperiously waving back the knights who would have borne him company because they feared some accident might befall the king riding thus alone—and putting spurs to his horse, he dashed into the forest in pursuit of a noble stag which the keen hounds had already scented. Three miles and more he rode alone, following the baying hounds through beds of fern and bracken under the arching trees, when of a sudden his horse reared and shied, and then came to a standstill before a thicket.

Richard, with a start, drew rein and scanned the tangled growth. At first he could see nothing; then, as his eyes accustomed themselves to the dusk, he saw two figures prone upon the ground. In an instant he was off his steed, and, with the bridle linked in his left arm, pushed his way among the interlacing vines to where the bodies lay. One was a man of middle age, rough, unkempt, and clad in ragged garments—an outlaw or robber without doubt, one of those who infested the forest at that time. The man was dead—slain by a dagger-thrust in the breast. The other was a slender youth dressed in the simple yet elegant costume of a squire. A heavy cloak lay beside him on the grass, half covering a harp such as the troubadours, or wandering minstrels, carried. His hair was long and dark, and fell in silken curls about a face whose delicate features betokened a nature refined and sensitive; the clear white skin and long fingers told also of a life passed in the gentler pursuits of music or of literature rather than of arms.

"'Sdeath!" cried Richard. "What have we here? Robbery and murder?"

Dragging aside the fern, which half concealed the face of the youth, the king knelt beside him and laid his hand upon the heart. A slight flutter responded to his touch.

"By St. George, the boy still lives!"

He drew from his breast a silver hunting whistle and blew three long, shrill blasts, then bent his head, listening impatiently for an answer. But none responded; his companions were far behind or wandering upon other trails.

"The idle varlets!" muttered the king. "Well, since they take me at my word, and lag behind, I'll bear the lad myself."

The light burden of the youth was as nothing to the king's gigantic strength. He flung him lightly over the saddle-bow, then leaped into the saddle, and passing an arm about the body of the unconscious boy, raised him to a sitting posture, and

In the Lion's keeping

thus supporting him against his breast, turned his horse homeward.

After a little while, the rushing of the cool wind in his face revived the youth, who had been but slightly wounded.

"Where am I?" he asked—as one who wakes from sleep, but without raising himself or withdrawing his fascinated gaze from the eyes of the king, now smiling into his.

"Why, in the lion's keeping," laughed Richard, deep in his tawny beard. "Tell me, who art thou and how camest thou in the sorry plight in which I found thee?"

"My name is Blondel," said the youth, "and I am come from Arras. While journeying last evening through yonder wood I was set upon by three rough fellows who demanded of me purse or life. My answer was a dagger-thrust which did for one, I hope. But at that moment I was stricken from behind, and knew no more till now. Ah, but my harp! I had forgotten that," he cried sharply, raising himself, then falling back with weakness against the king's protecting shoulder.

"Nay, trouble not thyself with that," the king replied. "A harp thou shalt have, and a royal one, so thou provest thyself worthy of it. Thou art a minstrel, then?" he asked with interest.

"Ay, truly," said the youth; "I have a talent at that trade. I was but now upon my way to seek the English king, who, they say, is kind to minstrels, when this misfortune overtook me. Perchance thou, being, as I judge, a lord of high degree, canst tell me if I be near to him or no?"

"Nearer thou canst not well be," laughed Richard. "He who now bears thee in his arms is the king himself."

Blondel would fain have flung himself from the saddle to kneel before the Majesty of England, but Richard held him back.

"Another time," he said. "Harken, now; I admire thee, boy. When thy wound is cured, thou shalt make trial of thy skill, and if thy music pleaseth me as doth thy disposition, while Richard lives thou shalt not want a friend."

So Blondel was carried by King Richard to the castle, where his wound was dressed by the king's own physician.

By and by, when he had rested and refreshed himself, a harp was given him and he was led into the royal presence to make trial of his skill. Alone he stood there in the center of the room, a slender figure, leaning on his harp, all unabashed, yet modest, his deep, dark eyes alight with gratitude and love, raised fearlessly to the king, before whose piercing glance so many quailed. The boy drew his fingers in a soft prelude over the strings, then, joining to the music a voice of wondrous sweetness, he broke into one of those old ballads of love and war so dear to the hearts of men of all times.

Richard, with his passion for music, was enchanted; Blondel's fame was made. Henceforth the king's palace was his home; and there sprang up between the great sovereign and his humble follower a wonderful friendship. Blondel worshiped his master—his preserver—with all the fervor of his artist soul; and Richard loved the boy with that frank generosity—too seldom shown to his court, alas!—which belonged nevertheless to his better nature. Wherever he went Blondel must go also; he could not bear that the boy should be for an hour absent from his sight, and many were the songs that they composed and sang together; for the king himself was no mean musician.

Time passed, and there came the call to the Crusade. Richard, as the most warlike monarch of Christendom, promptly responded, and having gathered many men and much treasure, he left his kingdom in the hands of two archbishops and journeyed southward through France to the port of Marseilles, whence he embarked for Messina, the first stopping-place. With him, of course, went Blondel, ever by his master's side.

At the island of Cyprus the army of knights stopped awhile, and there was fighting there; but at length the long journey to Palestine was accomplished, and in the brave and noble Saladin, the leader of the Saracens, Richard found a worthy antagonist. Many are the tales told of the deeds of prowess in which the two took part, and many were the courtesies they exchanged. But, in spite of the worth of their leaders, the Crusaders won but small success, and after a little Richard was stricken with one of those devastating fevers that attack the traveler in hot climes.

The magnanimous Saladin sent to his royal enemy gifts of fruit, and snow brought at night on mule-back from the mountain tops.

During all that long and tedious illness Blondel never left his master's side, but tended him with patience and gentleness, never wearying, never murmuring. His was the hand that cooled Richard's fever-heated brow, and his the voice that, accompanied by the sweet strains of his harp, lulled the king to slumber when all other means had failed.

At length the fever broke and the king regained his health; but he was unwilling to continue longer a struggle in which neither side could claim the victory. A long truce was arranged between the Christians and the Saracens; then Richard, with a few followers, set sail for home. Blondel was not of the number. As the most faithful servant of the king, he was intrusted with an important message to the King of Cyprus, after the delivery of which he was to join his sovereign in the city of London.

Now it happened that the vessel in which Richard and his band set sail suffered shipwreck near Aquileja, on the shores of the Adriatic Sea. Fortunately few lives were lost; but being in haste to reach England, where his brother John had usurped the crown, Richard decided to take the shorter route, across Germany, rather than to risk again the perils and delays of an ocean voyage. As the Duke of Austria, with whom Richard had quarreled while in the Holy Land, was now his bitter enemy, this was a dangerous undertaking for the king. In the interests of safety, therefore, he adopted the disguise of a palmer, or wandering friar. But a man so well known and of such stature as Richard could scarcely hope to pass unchallenged; and it happened that near the city of Vienna, while halting at a little wayside inn, he was recognized and made a prisoner. The Duke of Austria, overjoyed at such good fortune, hastened to hand his royal captive over to the Holy Roman Emperor, who had him conveyed, without loss of time, to a fortress hidden in the thickness of a dark and lonely forest, the name and whereabouts of which were kept a secret.

When, after his long voyage, the faithful Blondel arrived in England, his first words were to ask for news of the king. And his heart sank as he was answered with the direful news that his beloved master, his friend and protector, was a prisoner in a foreign land.

"But where?" he asked, "and what plans are there on foot to bring about his freedom?"

They could not tell; they did not know; perchance they did not care. Perhaps they feared the wrath of Richard's broither, John, and dared not help their rightful lord. Blondel asked no aid from those false lords and traitor subjects, but, taking only his harp, set out alone to find his royal master.

All through Germany he wandered, stopping before each fortress and each castle that seemed to him likely to serve the purpose of a prison. There he would play an air familiar to the king, and wait to learn if it were heard and recognized; for in this way he hoped to discover the place of his friend's concealment, and to convey to him the information that aid was at hand. With each new tower and castle that he chanced upon hope sprang up newly in his breast. He would take the harp from its case and resting it against his knee begin to play: perchance this was the one that held the king. But, alas! his song remained unanswered, and each day he passed on with a heavier weight upon his heart—yet never discouraged.

Day succeeded day, week followed week, month slipped into month. Mile after mile of forest and of dusty road he traversed, the faithful boy, persisting in his quest. Hope never quite deserted him. The loyalty to Richard that filled his heart ever urged him onward and still onward.

One evening just before the dusk, when the slanting sunlight threw long shadows of the pines across his path, Blondel approached a somber wood into whose dark recesses it seemed that man had never penetrated. On the top-most bough of a noble spruce tree a little bird with wings and breast rosy, like flame, was caroling his evensong.

Blondel noted the bird, and suddenly, without apparent cause, there rushed through all his being a flood of joy and hope. "Rose is the color of hope," he said. "Where the bird goes, there will I follow."

As if in answer to his words, the bird left his perch and flitted farther into the wood. Now it tarried upon one tree, now upon another, Blondel always following, until it led him close to the walls of a gloomy fortress flanked by one square tower, set in the very heart of the great forest.

There was no longer doubt or hesitation in the mind of the young minstrel. The bounding joy within told him that his long search had come to a successful end. He seized his harp, and stationing himself beneath the tower, played a short prelude and began to sing a mournful little melody that he and Richard had often sung together.

Scarcely had he completed the first stanza when a voice far up in the tower, the voice he knew and loved so well, took up and repeated the tender strain. His heart overflowing with thankfulness, the minstrel fell upon his knees, and raising his eyes, dim with happy tears, to heaven, he exclaimed: "Oh, Richard, my king! Oh, my king! Found, found at last!"

He might not see his royal friend, might not have speech with him, even; for doubtless watchful eyes were on the king, and at the first indication that his place of confinement had been discovered his captors would spirit him away. Yet joy unspeakable filled the minstrel's faithful breast, for his weary search had at length

Blondel before Richard's tower

been rewarded with success. Blondel hastened back to England with the news; and presently Eleanor, the queen mother, set out with all her train and the huge ransom that the emperor demanded, to buy the freedom of her son. You may be quite sure that Blondel accompanied them, and when the tall captive, pale from his long confinement, strode out among them all, the minstrel threw himself at the feet of his sovereign, and grasping the hand of his royal and beloved friend, covered it with kisses.

Richard looked down upon the bowed head of the youth and his cold blue eyes softened. "The greatest thing in the world," he said, "is the love of a mother for her child; and after that, earth holds no more precious gem than the love of a faithful friend."

First published in the November 1903 edition of *St. Nicholas Magazine*

The Rhyme for Twelfth

BY FRANK M. BICKNELL

ONCE UPON A time there was a youth who had never learned a trade, and not knowing what else to do for a living, he resolved to be a poet. So he hung a sign over his door, and sat down in front of his cottage to wait for patrons. But the people of that country were peasants, who knew nothing about poetry, and for many days no one came near him. At last, however, the King drove by and saw his sign. Now, the King was a very stupid person, who knew little enough about anything; yet he had been sufficiently cunning to make his subjects believe he knew everything, and the way he managed it was this: He always took with him, wherever he went, an exceedingly clever young man, and when he needed any information, he would question him as a teacher catechizes a pupil who is reciting his lesson. The name of this young man was Koruhl, and he was also called the Catechized.

When the King noticed the poet's sign, he wanted to know its meaning, so he said to the Catechized:

"Attention, Koruhl! What do you see over yonder door?"

"A sign-board bearing the word 'Poet,' sire," answered the Catechized, promptly.

"Very good," said the King, approvingly; "and what does the word 'poet' signify, Koruhl?"

"One who writes poetry, sire."

"Right, Koruhl; right. And now tell me—what do we understand by the term poetry?"

"Poetry, sire, is metrical composition," returned the Catechized, and the King became silent until, noticing that the Catechized seemed to be pondering deeply, he exclaimed:

"Koruhl, what do you suppose I am thinking about?"

"Sire," answered the Catechized, slowly, "you have already a Court Orator, a Court Historian, a Court Story-teller, a Court Riddle-maker, and a Court Jester; perhaps you want to add a Court Poet."

"You have guessed my thoughts, Koruhl," returned the King, much delighted. "Let it be done."

So the poet was taken to the palace, and made Court Poet. He was given a fine apartment, where he might sit and meditate all day long, and everybody who saw him admired him, for he had a pale face, long, fair hair, and large, mournful eyes.

"How handsome and interesting he is!" they all said. "He looks as if he could write beautiful poetry." Yet no one ever knew of his writing a single word.

Every morning, the King sat in his audience chamber, after the fashion of the country, and heard the complaints and settled the disputes that his subjects brought before him; that is to say, this business was attended to with the help of the Catechized, who was always the real judge. One day, after an unusual number of decisions had been rendered, the King said, with a great yawn:

"Koruhl, I am tired, really fatigued, with so much hard thinking; do you happen to know what I am going to do for recreation?"

"Perhaps, sire, you are going to bid me send for the Court Poet, and order him to make some verses for you?"

"Exactly, Koruhl," answered the King, much pleased; "let it be done."

The Court Poet being summoned and the King's wishes made known, he bowed low and said:

"On what subject will Your Majesty have me write?"

"Koruhl," demanded the King, "on what subject do poets usually write?"

"On a variety of subjects, sire," answered the Catechized; "though in this case you will doubtless ask for a poem to be read on the twelfth birthday of the princess, which will occur next month."

The King nodded loftily to the Court Poet.

"Such is my will; let it be done."

"Your Majesty is doubtless aware," said the Court Poet, "that poetry is a work of time, and to be really good must be written in solitude."

"Certainly," returned the King, who would have been ashamed to appear ignorant in the matter; "you may go back to your apartment until the poem is done."

So the Court Poet went to his room and, taking pen and paper, be thought intently until bed-time; but he wrote nothing whatever. The next day, it was the same; he did not write because he could not think of anything to say.

"If I could only make a beginning," he exclaimed over and over again; but he could not make a beginning, so at length he threw down his pen and went to the Court Physician for help. The Court Physician was a learned man, and when the Court Poet asked him how he should begin his poem, he answered immediately:

"Oh, that is very simple; your first two lines should be something like this:

"Beautiful little princess, on your birthday—'tis the twelfth—
Permit your loving subjects to inquire about your health."

The Court Poet thanked him and went back to his work, but as he repeated the lines to himself, he noticed that *health* was not a rhyme for *twelfth* at all.

"This will not do," he said; "unless I begin my poem aright, I shall never be able to carry it through. I must find a suitable rhyme for *twelfth* before going any farther." He leaned his head on his hands, and his long hair fell down until it almost covered his face; but although he thought steadily for a long time, he could not think of any rhyme for *twelfth*.

"This is very strange," he said at last; "I did not know I should be troubled in this way. Perhaps if I go out into the open air the rhyme will come to me. I have heard that poets sometimes write their poetry while wandering in the fields."

So he left the palace and went to walk. He had not been out very long when he heard some birds singing among the trees. This led him to wonder if they ever sung in rhyme, and he listened to them patiently for nearly an hour, hoping to hear a rhyme for *twelfth*; but the birds knew nothing about *twelfth* or its rhymes, and so he was disappointed. By and by, a bright idea came to him.

"I will ask everyone I meet," he said; "surely someone must know a rhyme for *twelfth*."

The first person who chanced to pass that way was the Court Historian, who walked with hands clasped behind him and eyes fixed on the ground.

"No," said he, grandly, in answer to the question of the Court Poet, "history never uses rhymes; they are undignified," and he went his way.

Next came the Court Orator, who held his head very high and waved his hands in air majestically as he rehearsed a speech he was to give that evening at a grand dinner. He would hardly listen to the Court Poet at all.

"Rhyming is a silly amusement, unworthy a great mind," he declared, and also went his way.

Then came the Court Riddle-maker, in a great hurry.

"I am chasing an idea," he said; "do not stop me. I have something else to do beside finding rhymes for

He could not think of any rhyme for Twelfth

"He left the palace and went to walk"

other people; I have already too much trouble with my own duties," and he, too, disappeared.

As the Court Poet cast his eyes about, he saw, sitting on a stone bench under a tree, a man who was weeping bitterly; and when he went toward him he saw he was no other than the Court Jester.

"What is the matter?" he inquired, bending over him.

"Nothing," answered the Court Jester.

"Why do you weep, then?" persisted the Court Poet.

"Because the King has given me a holiday. After I have earned my bread so many years by making jokes and being merry, why may I not now enjoy a few tears undisturbed?"

"Certainly, you may; only tell me first, do you know any rhyme for *twelfth?*"

"No," replied the Court Jester, shortly.

"Alas! what shall I do? Can no one give me the information I need?"

"Have you been to the saffron-faced Carrotufti?" asked the Court Jester, taking a little pity on him.

"No, I have not," returned the Court Poet, brightening. "Who is he?"

"Do you not know?" asked the Court Jester, in surprise. "He is the wisest man in the world and he deals in language. He has a collection of many thousand words, from which he sells to those who want to buy. If there are any rhymes for *twelfth* he will surely have them."

"Can you tell me where he lives?"

"In the lower left-hand corner of the Kingdom of Kandalabara, in a stone house."

"He saw he was no other than the Court Jester"

The Court Poet thanked the Court Jester (who immediately resumed his weeping just where he had left it off) and set out for the house of the saffron-faced Carrotufti, where he arrived in about five days. This house was very large, for although only the Carrotufti lived in it, he had so many words, letters, figures, and other useful and curious things, that a great deal of room was necessary to hold them. The Carrotufti was a very old person with bright yellow skin and a long white beard, and he wore a green gown, a pair of immense round-eyed spectacles, and a pointed cap. He was exceedingly busy when the Court Poet entered his house, for there were, waiting to be served, philosophers, astronomers, priests, law-makers, orators, book-writers, and many others who had use for words. There were also dishonest persons, eager to get words with which to tell falsehoods and deceive whom they might; but the Carrotufti was too shrewd for them, and, guessing their evil designs, refused to have anything to do with them, so they were forced to get along with what words they could beg or steal from the others.

As each one made known his needs, the Carrotufti went to something that looked like a large book set up on end, and, turning one or another of its huge leaves, selected from among the little cases or drawers with which it was filled the letters, words, or figures required, laid them on the counter, and took payment according to their value.

By and by, when it was the Court Poet's turn to be waited upon, the Carrotufti nodded for him to make known his wants.

"Sir," said the Court Poet, "I have come a long distance to learn whether you have any rhymes for *twelfth*."

The Carrotufti shook his head. "There is but one rhyme for *twelfth* in the whole world, and that I sold a hundred years ago, to be used at the coronation of our good king, Sharlos Twelfth. Perhaps the rhyme is still in the royal treasury, and the young queen who is now reigning may be willing to let you have it. You might go to the palace and see her."

The Court Poet thanked the saffron-faced Carrotufti for his information, and, having taken his leave, set out for the royal palace, which he reached in something less than two days. The Queen, who was young and very beautiful, received him graciously, and directed that he should be lodged in a splendid guest-chamber and presented with a fine new suit of clothes, for his own were worn and travel-stained. After he had rested and refreshed himself he came into the Queen's presence, looking so noble and handsome in his elegant apparel that she fell in love with him straightway, and made him sit down at her side and talk with her for several hours. When he asked her about the rhyme for *twelfth*, and told her why he wanted it, she hesitated before answering, for she thought to herself:

"Although I have the rhyme among my treasures, I must not give it to him at once, lest, when he has it in his hands, he may leave me and return to his own country, which must not be, for one does not every day encounter a young man so beautiful to behold, so agreeable to converse with, and also a poet." So she presently said to him carelessly: "I think the rhyme you seek is somewhere about the palace, though I don't know exactly where. It has long been out of style, and is so cumbrous I have made no use of it whatever; therefore, I fear it has not been well taken care of, and the letters may be scattered from one end of the house to the other. I will order a search, and if it can be found you shall have it. Meanwhile, tarry with us, and I will take care that time shall pass pleasantly with you."

The Court Poet was very glad to stay and be entertained by the Queen, who, on the first day, ordered a great dinner to be prepared, and invited a brilliant company, who treated the Court Poet as if he had been a prince. At night, after this feasting had been brought to an end, the Lord Chamberlain came before the Queen and the Court Poet to make his report. He informed them that a strict search had been made through one wing of the palace, and the last letter of the rhyme for *twelfth* had been found in an old book of songs on a stone table in one of the tower chambers. He then presented the letter to the Queen, who gave it to the Court Poet, who, for safe keeping, strung it on a silken cord which he put about his neck.

On the morrow, the Queen again called together a great many illustrious people and made a grand chase, to which the Court Poet rode at her side, mounted on

He was exceedingly busy when the Court Poet entered his house.

a cream-yellow horse, and armed with a costly hunting-knife having three large diamonds in the hilt. When they returned to the palace, the Lord Chamberlain appeared as before, to say that the servants had hunted carefully through another part of the palace, and had found the next to the last letter of the rhyme for *twelfth* in a cookery book hanging on the wall near the great fire-place in the kitchen. This letter he also laid before the Queen, who handed it to the Court Poet, who put it on the silken cord with the other.

The next day, there was a grand tournament, and the next a series of games such as were peculiar to that country. Then the Queen gave a splendid ball, at which she would dance only with the Court Poet, although many nobles, and even princes, sought her as a partner.

And so each day was spent in some kind of festivity, and each night the Lord Chamberlain brought another letter of the rhyme for *twelfth*, until all but one had been given into the hands of the Court Poet and strung on the cord about his neck. This, the first and most important, the Lord Chamberlain declared, could not be found; whereupon the Queen pretended to be vexed, and ordered a continual search to be made, not only in and about the palace, but throughout the kingdom, until the missing letter should be brought to light. Meantime, she tried, by filling each day with new pleasures, to make the Court Poet's life the most agreeable that could be imagined, and to remove from his heart all desire for a return into his own country.

But, although much gratified by the attentions shown him, he could not forget that his poem was unfinished and the birthday of the little princess was approaching; so, when the Lord Chamberlain had announced for the tenth time that nothing had been found during the day, he addressed the Queen thus:

"Your Majesty, since your servants are unable to find the letter needed to complete the rhyme for *twelfth*, I am of the opinion that it must certainly have been stolen and carried out of Your Majesty's dominions. Therefore, I pray you, permit me to express my devout gratitude for all Your Majesty's gracious kindnesses—and now to go away into the world in quest of the missing letter."

At hearing these words, the Queen was very sad, for she could think of no excuse for denying his request, and she perceived he was unwilling to be detained any longer; nevertheless, she besought him to remain one more day, promising that, if the letter were not then found, she would suffer him to depart.

So he stayed, and she tried to think of a plan whereby she might forever prevent him from leaving her domains. By and by, she decided how to act, and when the sun began to go down in the western sky, she invited him to take a sail with her on a beautiful lake lying in front of the palace. When they were in the middle of this lake, which was very deep and very clear, she took from her pocket the missing first letter of the rhyme for *twelfth* and secretly dropped it into the water, where it immediately sank until it rested on the

"The Lord Chamberlin came before the Queen and the Court Poet"

bottom, far below. Then she leaned over the side of the boat and gazed at it in silence for a long time, until the Court Poet, observing her, finally asked why she did so.

"I think," answered the Queen, slowly, "that the first letter of the rhyme for *twelfth* has fallen into the lake."

He bent over to see if this were true, and as he looked down into the water, she seized a pair of scissors which she had concealed and quickly cut the silken cord on which all the other letters were hanging, so that they also fell into the lake and sank to the bottom.

At this accident—for such he thought it—the Court Poet was much dismayed, and wrung his hands with grief.

"What shall I do!" he exclaimed. "Now all are lost. I never can finish my poem without the rhyme for *twelfth*, which an unhappy mischance has now made it impossible for me ever to obtain, and I shall not dare go back to the King, who will be very angry with me, and will doubtless order me to be put to death at once. What shall I do to 'escape my fate'?"

Then the Queen looked at him kindly, and said, in her most gracious tones:

"Do not lament; why need you go back at all? Is not my country as beautiful as yours? Is not my palace as splendid as your King's? Is not my kingdom as grand and large as his? My people have asked me to choose a husband, but I have never until now cared to make a choice, for I have sworn I will wed none but a poet. But you are a great poet; can you not stay with me and share my possessions?"

It is not everyone to whom is made an offer so fine as this. The Court Poet did not hesitate long before accepting it.

"Madam," he returned, "the honor and the happiness are beyond my deserts; but to me your wishes are commands, and obedience to you is always a pleasure."

So they were married, and the Court Poet became King. He never again tried to write any poetry; the ill success of his first attempt had completely discouraged him, and, besides, he had not time for rhyming, with the affairs of a great kingdom to look after.

As for the birthday of the little princess, it came and went without any poem whatever; for the rhyme for *twelfth* lay out of reach hundreds and hundreds of feet below the surface of the lovely lake, where, if this story be true, it doubtless lies to this day.

First published in the December 1893 edition of *St. Nicholas Magazine*

The King's Ankus

BY RUDYARD KIPLING

ERE Mor the peacock flutters, ere the Monkey-people cry,
Ere Chil the kite swoops down a furlong sheer,
Through the jungle very softly flits a shadow and a sigh—
He is Fear, O Little Hunter, he is Fear!
Very softly down the glade runs a waiting, watching shade,
And the whisper spreads and widens far and near;
And the sweat is on thy brow, for he passes even now—
He is Fear, O Little Hunter, he is Fear!

Ere the moon has climbed the mountain, ere the rocks are ribbed with light,
When the downward-dipping trails are dank and drear,
Comes a breathing hard behind thee, *snuffle-snuffle* through the night—
It is Fear, O Little Hunter, it is Fear!
On thy knees and draw the bow; bid the thrilling arrow go;
In the empty, mocking thicket plunge the spear;
But thy hands are loosed and weak, and the blood has left thy cheek—
It is Fear, O Little Hunter, it is Fear!

When the heat-cloud sucks the tempest, when the slivered pine-trees fall,
When the lightning shows each littlest leaf-rib clear,
Through the trumpets of the thunder rings a voice more loud than all—
It is Fear, O Little Hunter, it is Fear!
Now the spates are banked and deep; now the footless boulders leap;
Now the blinding, lashing rain-squalls shift and veer;
But thy throat is shut and dried, and thy heart against thy side
Hammers: Fear, O Little Hunter—this is Fear!

—Song of the Little Hunter

THESE JUNGLE TALES are told the same way that Baloo left the Bee-rocks—any end first; and you must take them as they come—just as the frog took the white ants after the rains.

KAA, THE BIG rock-python, had changed his skin for exactly the hundredth time since his birth; and Mowgli, who never forgot that he owed his life to Kaa for a night's work at Cold Lairs, which you may perhaps remember, went to congratulate him. Skin-changing always makes a snake moody and depressed till the new skin begins to shine and look beautiful. Kaa never made fun of Mowgli any more, but accepted him, as the other Jungle-people did, for the Master of the Jungle, and brought him all the news that a python of his size would naturally hear. What Kaa did not know about the Middle Jungle, as they call it—the life that runs close to the earth or under it, the boulder, burrow, and the tree-bole life—might have been written upon the smallest of his scales.

That afternoon Mowgli was sitting in the circle of Kaa's great coils, fingering the flaked and broken old skin that lay all looped and twisted among the rocks just as Kaa had left it. Kaa had very courteously packed himself under Mowgli's broad, bare shoulders, so that the boy was really resting in a living arm-chair.

"Even to the scales of the eyes it is perfect," said Mowgli, under his breath, playing with the old skin. "Strange to see the covering of one's own head at one's own feet."

"Aye, but I lack feet," said Kaa; "and since this is the custom of all my people, I do not find it strange. Does thy skin never feel old and harsh?"

"Then go I and wash, Flathead; but, it is true, in the great heats I have wished I could slough my skin without pain, and run skinless."

"I wash, and *also* I take off my skin. How looks the new coat?"

Mowgli ran his hand down the diagonal checkerings of the immense back. "The turtle is harder-backed, but not so gay," he said judgmatically. "The frog, my name-bearer, is more gay, but not so hard. It is very beautiful to see—like the mottling in the mouth of a lily."

"It needs water. A new skin never comes to full color before the first bath. Let us go bathe."

"I will carry thee," said Mowgli; and he stooped down, laughing, to lift the middle section of Kaa's great body, just where the barrel was thickest. A man might just as well have tried to heave up a two-foot water-main, and Kaa lay still, puffing with quiet amusement. Then the regular evening game began—the boy in the flush of his great strength, and the python in his sumptuously painted new skin, standing up one against the other for a wrestling-match—a trial of eye and strength. Of course Kaa could have crushed a dozen Mowglis if he had let himself go; but he

Mowgli and Kaa in the pool.

played carefully, and never loosed one tenth of his power. Ever since Mowgli was strong enough to endure a little rough handling, Kaa had taught him this game, and it suppled his limbs as nothing else could. Sometimes Mowgli would stand lapped almost to his throat in Kaa's shifting coils, striving to get one arm free and catch him by the throat. Then Kaa would give way limply, and Mowgli with both quick-moving feet would try to cramp the purchase of that huge tail as it flung backward feeling for a rock or a stump. They would rock to and fro, head to head, each waiting for his chance, till the beautiful, statue-like group melted in a whirl of black-and-yellow coils and struggling legs and arms, to rise up again and again. "Now! Now! Now!" said Kaa, making feints with his head that even Mowgli's quick hand could not turn aside. "Look! I touch thee here, Little Brother! Here, and here! Are thy hands numb? Here again!"

The game always ended one way—with a straight, driving blow of the head that knocked the boy over and over. Mowgli could never learn the guard for that lightning lunge, and, as Kaa said, it was not the least use trying.

"Good hunting!" Kaa grunted at last; and Mowgli, as usual, was shot away half a dozen yards, gasping and laughing. He rose with his fingers full of grass, and followed Kaa to the wise old snake's pet bathing-place—a deep, pitchy-black pool surrounded with rocks and made interesting by sunken tree-stumps. The boy slipped in, jungle-fashion, without a sound, and dived across; rose, too, without a sound, and turned on his back, his arms behind his head, watching the moon rising above the rocks, and breaking up her reflection in the water with his toes. Kaa's diamond-shaped head cut the pool like a razor, and came out to rest on Mowgli's shoulder. They lay still, soaking luxuriously in the cool water.

"It is *very* good," said Mowgli at last, sleepily. "Now in the Man-pack, at this hour, as I remember, they laid them down upon hard pieces of wood in the inside of a mud-trap, and, having carefully shut out all the clean winds, drew foul cloth over their heavy heads, and made evil songs through their noses. It is better in the jungle."

A hurrying cobra slipped down over a rock and drank, gave them "Good hunting!" and went away.

"Sssh!" said Kaa, as though he had suddenly remembered something. "So the jungle gives thee all that thou hast ever desired, Little Brother?"

"Not all," said Mowgli, laughing; "else there would be a new and strong Shere Khan to kill once a moon. Now I could kill with my own hands, asking no help of buffaloes. And also I have wished the sun to shine in the middle of the rains, and the rains to cover the sun in the deep of summer; and also I have never gone empty but I wished that I had killed a goat; and also I have never killed a goat but I wished it had been buck; nor buck but I wished it had been nilghai. But thus do we feel, all of us."

"Thou hast no other desires?" the big snake demanded.

"What more can I wish? I have the jungle, and the love of the jungle? Is there more anywhere between sunrise and sunset?"

"Now the cobra said—" Kaa began.

"What cobra? He that went away just now said nothing. He was hunting."

"It was another."

"Hast thou many dealings with the Poison-people? I give them their own path. They carry death in the fore-tooth, and that is not good—for they are so small. But what hood is this thou hast spoken with?"

Kaa rolled slowly in the water like a steamer in a beam sea. "Three or four moons since," said he, "I hunted in Cold Lairs, which place thou hast not forgotten. And the thing I hunted fled shrieking past the tanks and to that house whose side I once broke, and ran into the ground."

"But the people of Cold Lairs do not live in burrows." Mowgli knew that Kaa was talking of the *Bandar-log* (the Monkey-people).

"This thing was not living, but seeking to live," Kaa replied, with a quiver of his tongue. "He ran into a burrow that led very far. I followed, and having killed I slept. When I waked I went forward."

"Under the earth?"

"Even so, coming at last upon a White Hood [a white cobra], who spoke of things beyond my knowledge, and showed me many things I had never before seen."

"New game? Was it good hunting?" Mowgli turned quickly on his side.

"It was no game, and would have broken all my teeth; but the White Hood said that a man—he spoke as one that knew the breed—that a man would give the breath under his ribs for only the sight of those things."

"We will look," said Mowgli. "I now remember that I was once a man."

"Slowly—slowly. It was haste killed the Yellow Snake that ate the sun. We two spoke together under the earth, and I spoke of thee, naming thee as a man. Said the White Hood, and he is indeed as old as the jungle: 'It is long since I have seen a man. Let him come, and he shall see all these things, for the least of which very many men would die.'"

"That *must* be new game. And yet the Poison-people do not tell us when game is afoot. They are an unfriendly folk."

"It is *not* game. It is—it is—I cannot say what it is."

"We will go there. I have never seen a White Hood, and I wish to see the other things. Did he kill them?"

"They are all dead things. He says he is the keeper of them all."

"Ah! As a wolf stands above meat he has taken to his own lair. Let us go."

Mowgli swam to the bank, rolled in the grass to dry himself, and the two set off for Cold Lairs, the deserted city of which you have heard. Mowgli was not the least afraid of the Monkey-people in those days, but the Monkey-people had the liveliest horror of Mowgli. Their tribes, however, were raiding in the jungle, and so Cold Lairs stood empty and silent in the moonlight. Kaa led up to the ruins of the queen's pavilion that stood on the terrace, slipped over the rubbish, and dived down the half-choked staircase that went underground from the center of the pavilion. Mowgli gave the snake-call—"We be of one blood, ye and I"—and followed on his hands and knees.

They crawled a long distance down a sloping passage that turned and twisted several times, and at last came to where the root of some great tree growing thirty feet overhead had forced out a solid stone in the wall. They crept through the gap, and found themselves in a large vault whose domed roof had been also broken away by tree-roots so that a few streaks of light dropped down into the darkness.

The Cold Lairs stood empty and silent in the moonlight.

"A safe lair," said Mowgli, rising to his firm feet, "but over far to come daily. And now what do we see?"

"Am I nothing?" said a voice in the middle of the vault; and Mowgli saw something white move till, little by little, there stood up the hugest cobra he had ever set eyes on—a creature nearly eight feet long, and bleached by being in darkness to an old ivory white. Even the spectacle-marks of his spread hood had faded to faint yellow. His eyes were as red as rubies, and altogether he was a most wonderful creature to see.

"Good hunting!" said Mowgli, who carried his manners with his knife, and that never left him.

"What of the city?" said the White Cobra, without answering the greeting. "What of the great, the walled city—the city of a hundred elephants and twenty thousand horses, and cattle past counting—the city of the king of twenty kings? I grow deaf here, and it is long since I heard their war-gongs."

"The jungle is above our heads," said Mowgli. "I know only Hathi and his sons among elephants. Bagheera has slain all the horses in one village, and—what is a king?"

"I told thee," said Kaa softly to the cobra—"I told thee, four moons ago, that thy city was not."

"The city—the great city of the forest whose gates are guarded by the king's towers—can never pass. They builded it before my father's father came from the egg, and it shall endure when my son's sons are as white as I Salomdhi, son of Chandrabija, son of Viyeja, son of Yegasuri, made it in the days of Bappa Rawal. Whose cattle are *ye?*"

"It is a lost trail," said Mowgli, turning to Kaa. "I know not his talk."

"Nor I. He is very old. Father of Cobras, there is only the jungle here, as it has been since the beginning."

"Then who is *he*," said the White Cobra, "sitting down before me, unafraid, knowing not the name of the king, talking our talk through a man's lips? Who is he with the knife and the snake's tongue?"

"Mowgli they call me," was the answer. "I am of the jungle. The wolves are my people, and Kaa here is my brother. Father of Cobras, who art thou?"

"I am the Warden of the king's treasure. Kurrun Raja built the stone above me, in the days when my skin was dark, that I might teach death to those who came to steal. Then they let down the treasure through the stone, and I heard the song of the Brahmins my masters."

"Umm!" said Mowgli to himself. "I have dealt with one Brahmin already, in the Man-pack, and—I know what I know. Evil is coming here in a little time."

"Five times since I came here has the stone been lifted, but always to let down more, and never to take away. There are no riches like these riches—the treasures of a hundred kings. But it is long and long since the stone was last moved, and I think that my city has forgotten."

"There is no city. Look up. Yonder are the roots of the great trees tearing the stones apart. Trees and men do not grow together," Kaa insisted.

"Twice and thrice have men found their way here," the White Cobra answered savagely; "but they never spoke till I came upon them groping in the dark, and then they cried only a little time. But *ye* come with lies, man and snake both, and would have me believe the city is not, and that my wardenship ends. Little do men change in the years. But *I* change never. Till the stone is lifted, and the Brahmins come down singing the songs that I know, and feed me with warm milk and take me to the light again, I—I—I, and no other, am the Warden of the king's treasure. The city is dead, ye say, and here are the roots of the trees? Stoop down, then, and take what ye will. Earth has no treasure like this. Man with the snake's tongue, if thou canst go alive by the way that thou hast entered at, the lesser kings will be thy servants!"

"Again the trail is lost," said Mowgli, coolly. "Can any jackal have burrowed so deep and bitten this great White Hood? He is surely mad. Father of Cobras, I see nothing here to take away."

"By the Gods of the Sun and Moon, it is the madness of death upon the boy!"

hissed the cobra. "Before thy eyes close I will do thee this favor. Look thou, and see what man has never seen before."

"They do not well in the jungle who speak to Mowgli of favors," said the boy, between his teeth; "but the dark changes all, as I know. I will look, if that please thee."

He stared with puckered-up eyes round the vault, and then lifted up from the floor a handful of something that glittered.

"Oho!" said he, "this is like the stuff they play with in the Man-pack, only this is yellow and the other was brown."

He let the heavy gold pieces fall, and moved forward. The floor of the vault was buried some five or six feet deep in coined gold and silver that had burst from the sacks it had been originally stored in, and, in the long years, the metal had packed and settled as sand packs at low tide. On it and in it, and rising up through it as wrecks lift through the sand, were jeweled elephant-howdahs of state, of embossed silver three fingers thick, studded with plates of hammered gold, adorned with carbuncles and turquoises. There were palanquins and litters for carrying queens, framed and braced with silver and enamel, with jade-handled poles and amber curtain-rings; there were golden candlesticks hung with pierced emeralds quivering on the branches; there were studded images, five feet high, of forgotten gods, silver with jeweled eyes; there were coats of mail, gold inlaid on steel, and fringed with rotted and blackened seed-pearls; there were helmets crested and beaded with pigeon's-blood rubies; there were shields of lacquer, of tortoise-shell and rhinoceros hide, strapped and bossed with red gold and set with emeralds at the edge; there were sheaves of diamond-hilted swords, daggers, and hunting-knives; there were golden sacrificial bowls and ladles, and portable altars of a shape that never see the light of day; there were jade cups and bracelets; there were incense-burners, combs, and pots for perfume, henna, and eye-powder, all in embossed gold; there were nose-rings, armlets, head-bands, finger-rings, and girdles past any counting; there were belts seven fingers broad, of square-cut diamonds and rubies, and wooden boxes trebly clamped with iron, from which the wood had fallen away in powder, showing the pile of uncut star-sapphires, opals, cat's-eyes, sapphires, rubies, diamonds, emeralds, and garnets within.

The White Cobra was right. No mere money would begin to pay the value of this treasure, the sifted pickings of centuries of war, plunder, trade, and taxation. The coins alone were priceless, leaving out of count all the precious stones; and the dead weight of the gold and silver alone might be two or three hundred tons. Every native ruler in India today, however poor, has a hoard to which he is always adding; and though once in a long while some enlightened prince may send off forty or fifty bullock-cart loads of silver to be exchanged for government securi-

ties, the bulk of them keep their treasure and the knowledge of it very closely to themselves.

But Mowgli naturally did not understand what these things meant. The knives interested him a little, but they did not balance as well as his own, and so he dropped them. At last he found something really interesting laid on the front of a howdah half buried in the coins. It was a four-foot ankus, or elephant-goad—something like a small boat-hook. The top was one round shining ruby, and eighteen inches of the handle below it were studded with rough turquoises close together, giving a most satisfactory grip. Below them was a rim of jade with a flower-pattern running round it—only the leaves were emeralds, and the blossoms were rubies sunk in the cool, green stone. The rest of the handle was a shaft of pure ivory, and the point—the spike and hook—was gold-inlaid steel with pictures of elephant-catching; and the pictures attracted Mowgli, who saw that they had something to do with his friend Hathi the Silent.

The White Cobra had been following him closely.

"Is it not worth dying to behold?" he said. "Have I not done thee a great favor?"

"I do not understand," said Mowgli. "The things are hard and cold, and by no means good to eat. But this"—he lifted the ankus—"I desire to take away, that I may see it in the sun. Thou sayest they are all thine. Wilt thou give it to me, and I will bring thee frogs to eat?"

The White Cobra fairly shook with evil delight. "Assuredly I will give it," he said. "All that is here I will give thee—till thou goest away."

"But I go now. This place is dark and cold, and I wish to take the thorn-pointed thing to the jungle."

"Look by thy foot! What is that there?"

Mowgli picked up something white and smooth. "It is the bone of a man's head," he said quietly. "And here are two more."

"They came to take the treasure away many years ago. I spoke to them in the dark, and they lay still."

"But what do I need of this that is called treasure? If thou wilt give me the ankus to take away, it is good hunting. If not, it is good hunting none the less. I do not fight with the Poison-people, and I was also taught the Master-word for thy tribe."

"There is but one Master-word here. It is mine!"

Kaa flung himself forward with blazing eyes. "Who bade me bring the man?" he hissed.

"I surely," the old cobra lisped. "It is long since I have seen man, and this man speaks our tongue."

"But there was no talk of killing. How can I go to the jungle and say that I have led him to his death?" said Kaa.

"I never talk of killing till the time. And as to thy going or not going, there is the hole in the wall. Peace now, thou fat monkey-killer! I have but to touch thy neck, and the jungle will know thee no longer. Never man came here that went away with the breath under his ribs. I am the Warden of the treasure of the king's city!"

"But, thou white worm of the dark, I tell thee there is neither king nor city! The jungle is all about us!" cried Kaa.

"There is still the treasure. But this can be done. Wait a while, Kaa of the Rocks, and see the boy run. There is room for great sport here. Life is good. Run to and fro a while, and make sport, boy."

Mowgli put his hand on Kaa's head quietly.

"The white thing has dealt with men of the Man-pack until now. He does not know me," he whispered. "He has asked for this hunting. Let him have it." Mowgli had been standing with the ankus held point down. He flung it from him quickly, and it dropped crossways just behind the great snake's hood, pinning him to the floor. In a flash Kaa's weight was upon the writhing body, paralyzing it from hood to tail. The red eyes burned, and the six spare inches of the head struck furiously right and left.

"Kill," said Kaa, as Mowgli's hand went to his knife.

"No," he said, as he drew the blade. "I will never kill again save for food. But look you, Kaa!" He caught the snake behind the hood, forced the mouth open with the blade of the knife, and showed the terrible poison-fangs of the upper jaw lying black and withered in the gum. The White Cobra had outlived his poison, as a snake will.

"*Thuu*" [meaning "it is dried up," but literally "a rotted out tree stump"], said Mowgli; and, motioning Kaa away, he picked up the ankus, setting the White Cobra free.

"The king's treasure needs a new warden," he said gravely. "Thuu, thou hast not done well. Run to and fro and make sport, Thuu!"

"I am ashamed. Kill me!" hissed the White Cobra.

"There has been too much talk of killing. We will go now. I take the thorn-pointed thing, Thuu, because I have fought and worsted thee."

"See then that the thing does not kill thee at last. It is death! Remember, it is death! There is enough in that thing to kill the men of all my city. Not long wilt thou hold it, jungle man, nor he who takes it from thee. They will kill and kill and kill for its sake! My strength is dried up, but the ankus will do my work. It is death! It is death! It is death!"

Mowgli crawled out through the hole into the passage again, and the last that he saw was the White Cobra striking furiously with his harmless fangs at the solid golden faces of the gods that lay on the floor, and hissing, "It is death!"

They were glad to get to the light of day once more; and when they were back in their own jungle and Mowgli made the ankus glitter in the morning light, he was almost as pleased as though he had found a bunch of new flowers to stick in his hair.

"This is brighter than Bagheera's eyes," he said delightedly, as he twirled the ruby. "I will show it to him; but what did the Thuu mean when he talked of death?"

"I cannot say. I am sorrowful to my tail's tail that he felt not thy knife. There is always evil at Cold Lairs—above ground and below. But now I am hungry. Dost thou hunt with me this dawn?" said Kaa.

"No; Bagheera must see this thing. Good hunting!" Mowgli danced off, flourishing the great ankus, and stopping from time to time to admire it, till he came to that part of the jungle Bagheera chiefly used, and found him drinking after a heavy kill. Mowgli told him all his adventures from beginning to end, and Bagheera sniffed at the ankus between whiles. When Mowgli came to the White Cobra's last words, Bagheera purred approvingly.

"Then the White Hood spoke the thing which is?" Mowgli asked quickly.

"I was born in the king's cages at Oodeypore, and it is in my stomach that I know some little of man. Very many men would kill thrice in a night for the sake of that one big red stone alone."

"But the stone makes it heavy to the hand. My little bright knife is better; and—see! the red stone is not good to eat."

"They would not kill because it is sharp, or because it is good to eat."

"Then *why* would they kill?"

"Mowgli, go thou and sleep. Thou hast lived among men, and—"

"I remember. Men kill because they are not hunting—for idleness and pleasure. Wake again, Bagheera. For what use was this thorn-pointed thing made?"

Bagheera half opened his eyes—he was very sleepy—with a malicious twinkle.

"It was made by men to thrust into the head of the sons of Hathi, so that the blood should pour out. I have seen the like in the street of Oodeypore, before our cages. That thing has tasted the blood of many such as Hathi."

"But why did they thrust into the heads of elephants?"

"To teach them Man's Law. Having neither claws nor teeth, men make these things—and worse."

"Always more blood when I come near, even to the things the Man-pack have made," said Mowgli, disgustedly. He was getting a little tired of the weight of the ankus. "If I had known this, I would not have taken it. First it was Messua's blood on the thongs, and now it is Hathi's. I will use it no more. Look!"

The ankus flew sparkling, and buried itself point down thirty yards away, between the trees. "So my hands are clean of death," said Mowgli, rubbing his palms on the fresh, moist earth. "The Thuu said death would follow me. He is old and white and mad."

"White or black, or death or life, *I* am going to sleep, Little Brother. I cannot hunt all night and howl all day, as do some folk."

Bagheera went off to a hunting-lair that he used, about two miles off. Mowgli made an easy way for himself up a convenient tree, knotted three or four creepers together, and in less time than it takes to tell was swinging in a hammock fifty feet above ground. Though he had no positive objection to strong daylight, Mowgli followed the custom of his friends, and used it as little as he could. When he waked among the very loud-voiced bird-peoples that live in the trees, it was twilight once more, and he had been dreaming of the beautiful pebbles he had thrown away.

"At least I will look at the thing again," he said, and slid down a creeper to the earth; but Bagheera was before him. Mowgli could hear the panther snuffing in the half light.

"Where is the thorn-pointed thing?" cried Mowgli. "A man has taken it. Here is his trail."

"Now we shall see whether the Thuu spoke truth. If the pointed thing is death, that man will die. Let us follow."

"Kill first," said Bagheera. "An empty-stomach makes a careless eye. Men go very slowly, and the jungle is wet enough to hold the lightest mark." They killed as soon as they could, but it was nearly three hours before they finished their meat and drink and buckled down to the trail. The Jungle-people know that nothing makes up for being hurried over your meals.

"Think you the pointed thing will turn in the man's hand and kill him?" Mowgli asked. "The Thuu said it was death."

"We shall see when we find," said Bagheera, trotting with his head low. "It is single-foot" [he meant that there was only one man], "and the weight of the thing has pressed his heel far into the ground."

"Hai! This is as clear as summer lightning," Mowgli answered; and they fell into the quick, choppy trail-trot in and out through the checkers of the moonlight, following the marks of those two bare feet.

"Now he runs swiftly," said Mowgli. "The toes are spread apart." They went on over some wet ground. "Now why does he turn aside here?"

"Wait!" said Bagheera, and flung himself forward with one superb bound as far

They fell into the quick, choppy trail-trot,
following the marks of those two bare feet.

as ever he could. The first thing to do when a trail ceases to explain itself is to cast forward without leaving your own foot-marks on the ground. Bagheera turned as he landed, and faced Mowgli, crying, "Here comes another trail to meet him. It is a smaller foot, this second trail, and the toes turn inward."

Then Mowgli ran up and looked. "It is the foot of a Gond hunter," he said. "Look!" Here he dragged his bow on the grass. "That is why the first trail turned aside so quickly. Big Foot hid from Little Foot."

"That is true," said Bagheera. "Now, lest by crossing each other's tracks we foul the signs, let each take one trail. I am Big Foot, Little Brother, and thou art Little Foot the Gond."

Bagheera leaped back to the original trail, leaving Mowgli stooping above the curious narrow track of the wild little man of the woods.

"Now," said Bagheera, moving step by step along the chain of footprints, "I, Big Foot, turn aside here. Now I hide me behind a rock and stand still, not daring to shift my feet. Cry thy trail, Little Brother."

"Now I, Little Foot, come to the rock," said Mowgli, running up his trail. "Now

I sit down under the rock, leaning upon my right hand, and resting my bow between my toes. I wait long, for the mark of my feet is deep here."

"I also," said Bagheera, hidden behind the rock. "I wait, resting the end of the thorn-pointed thing upon a stone. It slips, for here is a scratch upon the stone. Cry thy trail, Little Brother."

"One, two twigs and a big branch are broken here," said Mowgli, in an undertone. "Now how shall I cry that? Ah! It is plain now. I, Little Foot, go away making noises and tramplings that Big Foot may hear me." The boy moved away from the rock pace by pace among the trees, his voice rising in the distance as he approached a little cascade.

"I—go—far—away—to—where—the—noise—of—falling—water—covers—my—noise; and—here—I—wait. Cry thy trail, Bagheera, Big Foot!"

The panther had been casting in every direction to see how Big Foot's trail led away from behind the rock. Then he gave tongue.

"I come from behind the rock upon my knees, dragging the thorn-pointed thing. Seeing no one, I run. I, Big Foot, run swiftly. The trail is clear. Let each follow his own. I run!"

Bagheera swept on along the clearly marked trail, and Mowgli followed the steps of the Gond. For some time there was silence in the jungle.

"Where art thou, Little Foot?" cried Bagheera. Mowgli's voice answered him not fifty yards to the right.

"Um!" said the panther, with a deep cough. "The two run side by side, drawing nearer!"

They raced on another half mile, always keeping about the same distance, till Mowgli, whose head was not so close to the ground as Bagheera's, cried: "They have met. Good hunting—look! Here stood Little Foot, with his knee on a rock—and yonder is Big Foot."

Not ten yards in front of them, stretched across a pile of broken rocks, lay the body of a villager of the district, with a long, small-feathered Gond arrow through his back and breast.

"Was the Thuu so old and so mad, Little Brother?" said Bagheera, gently. "This is one death, at least."

"Follow on. But where is the drinker of elephant's blood—the red-eyed thorn?"

"Little Foot has it—perhaps. It is single-foot again now."

The single trail of a light man who had been running quickly and bearing a burden on his left shoulder, held on round a long, low spur of dried grass, on which each footfall seemed to be marked in hot iron to the sharp eyes of the trackers.

Neither spoke till the trail ran up to the ashes of a camp-fire hidden in a ravine.

"Again!" said Bagheera, checking as though he had been turned into stone.

The body of the little wizened Gond lay with its feet in the ashes, and Bagheera looked inquiringly at Mowgli.

"That was done with a bamboo," said the boy, after one glance. "I have used such a thing among the buffaloes when I served in the Man-pack. The Father of Cobras—I am sorrowful that I made a jest of him—knew the breed well, as I might have known. Said I not that men kill for idleness?"

"Indeed, they killed for the sake of the red and blue stones," Bagheera answered. "Remember, I was in the king's cages at Oodeypore."

"One, two, three, four tracks," said Mowgli, stooping over the ashes. "Four tracks of men with shod feet. They do not go so quickly as Gonds. Now, what evil had the little woodman done to them? See, they talked together all five, standing up, before they killed him. Bagheera, let us go back. My stomach is heavy in me, and yet it goes up and down like an oriole's nest at the end of a branch."

"It is not good hunting to leave the game afoot. Follow," said the panther. "Those eight shod feet have not gone far."

No more was said for fully an hour, as they looked up the broad trail of the four men with shod feet.

Bagheera flung himself forward with one superb bound.

It was clear, hot daylight now, and Bagheera said, "I smell smoke."

"Men are always more ready to eat than to run," Mowgli answered, trotting in and out between the low scrub bushes of the new jungle they were exploring. Bagheera, a little to his left, made an indescribable noise in his throat.

"Here is one that has done with feeding," said he. A tumbled bundle of gay-colored clothes lay under a bush, and round it was some spilt flour.

"That was done by the bamboo again," said Mowgli. "See! that white dust is what men eat. They have taken the kill from this one—he carried their food—and given him for a kill to Chil the kite."

"It is the third," said Bagheera.

"I will go with new, big frogs to the Father of Cobras, and feed him fat," said Mowgli to himself. "The drinker of elephants' blood is Death himself—but still I do not understand."

"Follow!" said Bagheera.

They had not gone half a mile further when they heard Ko the crow singing the death-song in the top of a tamarisk under whose shade three men were lying. A half-dead fire smoked in the center of the circle, under an iron plate which held a blackened and burned cake of unleavened bread. Close to the fire, and blazing in the sunshine, lay the ruby-and-turquoise ankus.

"The thing works quickly; all ends here," said Bagheera. "How did these die, Mowgli? There is no mark nor rub on any one."

A jungle-dweller gets to learn by experience as much as a great many doctors know of poisonous plants and berries. Mowgli sniffed the smoke that came up from the fire, broke off a morsel of the blackened bread, tasted it, and spat it out again.

"Apple of death," he coughed. "The first must have made it ready in the food for *these*, who killed him, having first killed the Gond."

"Good hunting, indeed! The kills follow close," said Bagheera.

"Apple of death" is what the Jungle call thorn-apple or dhatura, the readiest poison in all India.

"What now?" said the panther. "Shall thou and I kill each other for yonder red-eyed slayer?"

"Can it speak?" said Mowgli, in a whisper. "Did I do it a wrong when I threw it away? Between us two it can do no wrong, for we do not desire what men desire. If it be left here, it will assuredly continue to kill men one after another as fast as nuts fall in a high wind. I have no love to men, but even I would not have them die six in a night."

"What matter? They are only men. They killed one another, and were well pleased," said Bagheera. "That first little woodman hunted well."

"They are cubs none the less; and a cub will drown himself to bite the moon's light on the water. The fault was mine," said Mowgli, who spoke as though he knew all about everything. "I will never again bring into the jungle strange things—not though they be as beautiful as flowers. This"—he handled the ankus

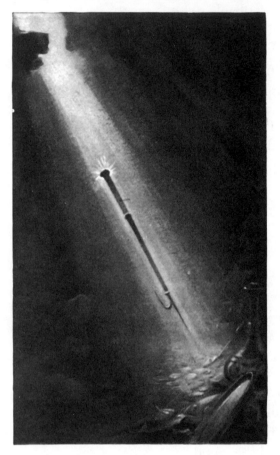

gingerly—"goes back to the Father of Cobras. But first we must sleep, and we cannot sleep near these sleepers. Also we must bury *him*, lest he run away and kill another six. Dig me a hole under that tree."

"But, Little Brother," said Bagheera, moving off to the spot, "I tell thee it is no fault of the blood-drinker. The trouble is with the men."

"All one," said Mowgli. "Dig the hole deep. When we wake I will take him up and carry him back."

* * *

TWO NIGHTS LATER, as the White Cobra sat mourning in the darkness of the vault, ashamed and robbed and alone, the turquoise ankus whirled through the hole in the wall, and clashed on the floor of golden coins.

"Father of Cobras," said Mowgli (he was careful to keep the other side of the wall), "get thee a young and ripe one of thy own people to help thee guard the king's treasure so that no man may come away alive any more."

"Ah-ha! It returns, then. I said the thing was death. How comes it that thou art still alive?" the old cobra mumbled, twining lovingly round the ankus-shaft.

"By the Bull that bought me, I do not know! That thing has killed six times in a night. Let him go out no more."

First published in the March 1895 edition of *St. Nicholas Magazine*

TOOMAI OF THE ELEPHANTS

BY

RUDYARD KIPLING

KALA NAG, WHICH means Black Snake, had served the Indian Government in every way that an elephant could serve it for forty-seven years, and as he was fully twenty years old when he was caught, that makes him nearly seventy—a ripe age for an elephant. He remembered pushing, with a big leather pad on his forehead, at a gun stuck in deep mud, and that was before the Afghan war of 1842, and he had not then come to his full strength. His mother Radha Pyari—Radha the darling—who had been caught in the same drive with Kala Nag, told him, before his little milk-tusks had dropped out, that elephants who were afraid always got hurt: and Kala Nag knew that that advice was good, for the first time that he saw a shell burst he backed, screaming, into a stand of piled rifles, and the bayonets pricked him in all his softest places. So, before he was twenty-five, he gave up being afraid, and so he was the best-loved and the best-looked-after elephant in the service of the Government of India. He had carried tents, twelve hundred pounds' weight of tents, on the march in upper India: he had been hoisted into a ship at the end of a steam-crane and taken for days across the water, and made to carry a mortar on his back in a strange and rocky country very far from India, and had seen the Emperor Theodore lying dead in Magdala, and had come back again in the steamer entitled, so the soldiers said, to the Abyssinian war medal. He had seen his fellow-elephants die of cold and epilepsy and starvation and sunstroke up at a place called Ali Musjid, ten years later; and afterward he had been sent down thousands of miles south to haul and pile big baulks of teak in the timber-yards at Moulmein. There he had half killed an insubordinate young elephant who was shirking his fair share of work.

After that he was taken off timber-hauling, and employed, with a few score other elephants who were trained to the business, in helping to catch wild elephants among the Garo hills. Elephants are very strictly preserved by the Indian Government. There is one whole department which does nothing else but hunt them, and catch them, and break them in, and send them up and down the country as they are needed for work. Kala Nag stood ten fair feet at the shoulders, and his tusks had been cut off short at five feet, and bound round the ends, to prevent them splitting, with bands of copper; but he could do more with those stumps than any untrained elephant could do with the real sharpened ones. When, after weeks and weeks of cautious driving of scattered elephants across the hills, the forty or fifty wild monsters were driven into the last stockade, and the big drop-gate, made of tree-trunks lashed together, jarred down behind them, Kala Nag, at the word of command, would go into that flaring, trumpeting pandemonium (generally at night, when the flicker of the torches made it difficult to judge distances), and, picking out the biggest and wildest tusker of the mob, would hammer him and hustle him into quiet while the men on the backs of the other elephants roped and tied the smaller ones. There was nothing in the way of fighting that Kala Nag, the old wise Black Snake, did not know, for he had stood up more than once in his time to the charge of the wounded tiger, and, curling up his soft trunk to be out of harm's way, had knocked the springing brute sideways in mid-air with a quick sickle-cut of his head, that he had invented all by himself; had knocked him over, and kneeled upon him with his huge knees till the life went out with a gasp and a howl, and there was only a fluffy striped thing on the ground for Kala Nag to pull by the tail.

"Yes," said Big Toomai, his driver, the son of Black Toomai who had taken him to Abyssinia, and grandson of Toomai of the Elephants who had seen him caught, "there is nothing that the Black Snake fears except me. He has seen three generations of us feed him and groom him, and he will live to see four."

"He is afraid of *me* also," said Little Toomai, standing up to his full height of four feet, with only one rag upon him. He was ten years old, the eldest son of Big Toomai, and, according to custom, he would take his father's place on Kala Nag's neck when he grew up, and would handle the heavy iron ankus, the elephant-goad that had been worn smooth by his father, and his grandfather, and his great-grandfather. He knew what he was talking of; for he had been born under Kala Nag's shadow, had played with the end of his trunk before he could walk, had taken him down to water as soon as he could walk, and Kala Nag would no more have dreamed of disobeying his shrill little orders than he would have dreamed of killing him on that day when Big Toomai carried the little brown baby in his arms under Kala Nag's tusks, and told him to salute his master that was to be. "Yes," said Little Toomai, "he is afraid of *me*," and he took long strides up to Kala Nag, called him a fat old pig, and made him lift up his feet, one after the other.

"Wah!" said Little Toomai, "thou art a big elephant," and he wagged his fluffy head, quoting his father. "The Government may pay for elephants, but they belong to us mahouts. When thou art old, Kala Nag, there will come some rich Rajah, and he will buy thee from the Government, on account of thy size and thy manners, and then thou wilt have nothing to do but to carry gold earrings in thy ears, and a gold howdah on thy back, and a red cloth covered with gold on thy sides, and walk at the head of the processions of the King. Then I shall sit on thy neck, O Kala Nag, with a silver ankus, and men will run before us with golden sticks, crying, 'Room for the King's elephant!' That will be good, Kala Nag, but not so good as this hunting in the jungles."

"Umph," said Big Toomai. "Thou art a boy, and as wild as a buffalo-calf. This running up and down among the hills is not the best Government service. I am get-

Little Toomia made Kala Nag lift up his feet, one after the other.

ting old, and I do not love wild elephants. Give me brick elephant-lines, one stall
to each elephant, and big stumps to tie them to safely, and flat, broad roads to exercise upon, instead of this come-and-go camping. Aha, the Cawnpore barracks were
good. There was a bazar close by, and only three hours' work a day."

Little Toomai remembered the Cawnpore elephant-lines and said nothing. He
very much preferred the camp life, and hated those broad flat roads, with the daily
grubbing for grass in the forage-reserve, and the long hours when there was nothing to do except to watch Kala Nag fidgeting in his pickets. What Little Toomai
liked was the scramble up bridle-paths that only an elephant could take; the dip
into the valley below; the glimpses of the wild elephants browsing miles away; the
rush of the frightened pig and peacock under Kala Nag's feet; the blinding warm
rains, when all the hills and valleys smoked: the beautiful misty mornings when
nobody knew where they would camp that night; the steady, cautious drive of the
wild elephants, and the mad rush, and blaze, and hullaballoo of the last night's
drive, when the elephants poured into the stockade like boulders in a landslide,
found that they could not get out, and flung themselves at the heavy posts only to
be driven back by yells and flaring torches and volleys of blank cartridge. Even a
little boy could be of use there, and Toomai was as useful as three boys. He would
get his torch and wave it, and yell with the best. But the really good time came
when the driving out began, and the Keddah, that is, the stockade, looked like a
picture of the end of the world, and men had to make signs to one another, because
they could not hear themselves speak. Then Little Toomai would climb up to the
top of one of the quivering stockade-posts, his sun-bleached brown hair flying loose
all over his shoulders, and he looking like a goblin in the torch-light; and as soon
as there was a lull you could hear his high-pitched yells of encouragement to Kala
Nag, above the trumpeting and crashing, and snapping of ropes, and groans of the
tethered elephants. "*Mail, mail, Kala Nag!* (Go on, go on, Black Snake!) *Dant do!*
(Give him the tusk!) *Somalo! Somalo!* (Careful, careful!) *Maro! Mar!* (Hit him, hit
him!) Mind the post! *Arre! Arre! Hai! Yai! Kya-a-ah!*" he would shout, and the big
fight between Kala Nag and the wild elephant would sway to and fro across the
Keddah, and the old elephant-catchers would wipe the sweat out of their eyes, and
find time to nod to Little Toomai wriggling with joy on the top of the posts. He did
more than wriggle. One night he dropped down and slipped in between the elephants, and threw up the loose end of a rope, which had dropped, to a driver who
was trying to get a purchase on the leg of a kicking young calf (calves always give
more trouble than full grown animals). Kala Nag saw him, caught him in his trunk,
and handed him up to Big Toomai, who slapped him then and there, and put him
back on the post. Next morning he gave him a scolding, and said: "Are not good
brick elephant-lines and a little tent-carrying enough for you, that you must needs

He would get his torch and wave it, and yell with the best.

go elephant-catching on your own account, little worthless? Now those foolish hunters, whose pay is less than my pay, have spoken to Petersen Sahib of the matter." Little Toomai was frightened. He did not know much of white men, but Petersen Sahib was the greatest white man in the world to him. He was the head of all the Keddah operations—the man who caught all the elephants for the Government of India, and who knew more about the ways of elephants than any living man.

"What—what will happen?" said Little Toomai.

"Happen! the worst that can happen. Petersen Sahib is a madman; else why should he go hunting these wild devils? He may even require thee to be an elephant-catcher, to sleep anywhere in these fever-filled jungles, and at last to be trampled to death in the Keddah. It is well that this nonsense ends safely. Next week the catching is over, and we of the plains are sent back to our stations. Then we will march on smooth roads, and forget all this hunting. But, son, I am angry that thou shouldst meddle in the business that belongs to these dirty Assamese jungle-folk. Kala Nag will obey none but me, so I must go with him into the Keddah, but he is only a fighting elephant, and he does not help to rope them. So I sit at my ease, as befits a mahout—not a mere hunter—a mahout, I say, and a man who gets a pension at the end of his service. Is the family of Toomai of the Elephants to be trodden underfoot in the dirt of a Keddah? Bad one! Wicked one! Worthless son! Go and wash Kala Nag and attend to his ears, and see that there are no thorns in his feet; or else Petersen Sahib will surely catch thee and make thee a wild hunter- a follower of elephant's foot-tracks, a jungle-bear. Bah! Shame! Go!"

Little Toomai went off without saying a word, but he told Kala Nag all his griev-ances while he was examining his feet. "No matter," said Little Toomai, turning up the fringe of Kala Nag's huge right ear. "They have said my name to Petersen Sahib, and perhaps—and perhaps—and perhaps—who knows? Hai! That is a big thorn that I have pulled out!"

The next few days were spent in getting the elephants together, in walking the newly caught wild elephants up and down between a couple of tame ones, to pre-vent them giving too much trouble on the downward march to the plains, and in taking stock of the blankets and ropes and things that had been worn out or lost in the forest. Petersen Sahib came in on his clever she-elephant Pudmini; he had been paying off other camps among the hills, for the season was coming to an end, and there was a native clerk sitting at a table under a tree, to pay the drivers their wages. As each man was paid he went back to his elephant, and joined the line that stood ready to start. The catchers, and hunters, and beaters, the men of the regu-lar Keddah, who stayed in the jungle year in and year out, sat on the backs of the elephants that belonged to Petersen Sahib's permanent force, or leaned against the trees with their guns across their arms, and made fun of the drivers who were going away, and laughed when the newly caught elephants broke the line and ran about. Big Toomai went up to the clerk with Little Toomai behind him, and Machua Appa, the head-tracker, said in an undertone to a friend of his, "There goes one piece of good elephant-stuff at least. 'Tis a pity to send that young jungle-cock to moult in the plains."

Now Petersen Sahib had ears all over him, as a man must have who listens to the most silent of all living things—the wild elephant. He turned where he was lying all along on Pudimni's back, and said, "What is that? I did not know of a man among the plains-drivers who had wit enough to rope even a dead elephant."

"This is not a man, but a boy. He went into the Keddah at the last drive, and threw Barmao there the rope, when we were trying to get that young calf with the blotch on his shoulder away from his mother." Machua Appa pointed at Little Toomai, and Petersen Sahib looked, and Little Toomai bowed to the earth.

"He threw a rope? He is smaller than a picket-pin. Little one, what is thy name," said Petersen Sahib. Little Toomai was too frightened to speak, but Kala Nag was behind him, and Toomai made a sign with his hand, and the elephant caught him up in his trunk and held him level with Pudmini's forehead, in front of the great Petersen Sahib. Then Little Toomai covered his face with his hands, for he was only a child, and, except where elephants were concerned, he was just as bashful as a child could be.

"Oho," said Petersen Sahib, smiling underneath his beard, "And where didst thou teach thy elephant *that* trick? Was it to help thee to steal green corn from the roofs of the houses when the ears are put out to dry?"

"Not green corn, Protector of the Poor—melons," said Little Toomai, and all the men sitting about broke into a roar of laughter. Most of them had taught their elephants that trick when they were boys. Little Toomai was hanging eight feet up in the air, and he wished very much that he was eight feet under ground.

"He is Toomai, my son, Sahib," said Big Toomai, scowling. "He is a very bad boy, and he will end in a jail, Sahib."

"Of that I have my doubts," said Petersen Sahib. "A boy who can face a full Keddah at his age does not end in jails. See, little one, here are four annas to spend in sweetmeats because thou hast a little head under

"Not green corn, Protector of the Poor—melons," said Little Toomai.

that great thatch of hair. In time thou mayest become a hunter, too." Big Toomai scowled, more than ever. "Remember, though, that Keddahs are not good for children to play in," Petersen Sahib went on.

"Must I never go there, Sahib?" asked Little Toomai, with a big gasp.

"Yes." Petersen Sahib smiled again. "When thou hast seen the elephants dance. That is the proper time. Come to me when thou hast seen the elephants dance, and then I will let thee go into all the Keddahs."

There was another roar of laughter, for that is an old joke among elephant-catchers, and it means just never. There are great cleared flat places hidden away in the forests that are called elephant's ball-rooms, but even these are only found by accident, and no man has ever seen the elephants' dance. When a driver boasts of his skill and bravery the other drivers say, "And when didst *thou* see the elephants dance?"

Kala Nag put Little Toomai down, and he bowed to the earth again and went away with his father, and gave the silver four-anna piece to his mother, who was nursing his baby brother, and they all were put up on Kala Nag's back, and the line of grunting, squealing elephants rolled down the hill path to the plains. It was a very lively march on account of the new elephants, who gave trouble at every ford, and who needed coaxing or beating every other minute.

Big Toomai prodded Kala Nag spitefully, for he was very angry, but Little Toomai was too happy to speak. Petersen Sahib had noticed him, and given him money, so he felt as a private soldier would feel if he had been called out of the ranks and praised by his commander-in-chief.

"What did Petersen Sahib mean by the elephant-dance?" he said, at last, softly to his mother.

Big Toomai heard him and grunted. "That thou shouldst never be one of these hill-buffalos of trackers. *That* was what he meant. Oh! you in front, what is blocking the way?"

An Assamese driver, two or three elephants ahead, turned round angrily, crying, "Bring up Kala Nag, and knock this youngster of mine into good behavior. Why should Petersen Sahib have chosen *me* to go down with you donkeys of the rice-fields? Lay your beast alongside, Toomai, and let him prod with his tusks. By all the Gods of the Hills, these new elephants are possessed, or else they can smell their companions in the jungle."

Kala Nag hit the new elephant in the ribs and knocked the wind out of him, as Big Toomai said, "We have swept the hills of wild elephants at the last catch. It is only your carelessness in driving. Must I keep order along the whole line?"

"Hear him!" said the Assamese. "*We* have swept the hills! Ho! Ho! You are very wise, you plains-people. Any one but a mud-head who never saw the jungle would know that *they* know that the drives are ended for the season. Therefore all the wild elephants tonight will—but why should I waste wisdom on a river-turtle?"

"What will they do?" Little Toomai called out.

"*Ohé*, little one. Art thou there? Well, I will tell thee, for thou hast a cool head. They will dance, and it behooves thy father, who has swept *all* the hills of *all* the elephants, to double-chain his pickets tonight."

"What talk is this?" said Big Toomai. "For forty years, father and son, we have tended elephants, and we have never heard such moonshine about dances."

"Yes; but a plains-man who lives in a hut knows only the four walls of his hut. Well, leave thy elephants unshackled tonight and see what comes; as for their dancing, I have seen the place where—*Bapree-Bap!* How many windings has the Dihang River? Here is another ford, and we must swim the calves. Stop still, you behind there."

And in this way, talking and wrangling and splashing through the rivers, they made their first march to a sort of receiving-camp for the new elephants; but they lost their tempers long before they got there.

Then the elephants were chained by their hind legs to their big stumps of pickets, and extra ropes were fitted to the new elephants, and the fodder was piled before them, and the hill-drivers went back to Petersen Sahib through the afternoon light, telling the plains-drivers to be extra careful that night, and laughing when the plains-drivers asked the reason.

Little Toomai attended to Kala Nag's supper, and as evening fell, wandered through the camp, unspeakably happy, in search of a tom-tom. When an Indian child's heart is full, he does not run about and make a noise in an irregular fashion. He sits down to a sort of revel all by himself. And Little Toomai had been spoken to by Petersen Sahib! If he had not found what he wanted, I believe he would have been ill. But the sweetmeat-seller in the camp lent him a little tom-tom—a drum that you beat with the flat of your hand—and he sat down, cross-legged, before Kala Nag as the stars began to come out, the tom-tom in his lap, and he thumped and he thumped and he thumped, and the more he thought of the great honor that had been done to him, the more he thumped, all alone among the elephant-fodder. There was no tune and no words, but it was the thumping that made him happy. The new elephants strained at their ropes, and squealed and trumpeted from time to time, and he could hear his mother in the camp hut putting his small brother to sleep with an old, old song about the great God Shiv, who once told all the animals what they should eat. I have forgotten the native words; but it is a very soothing lullaby, and the first verse says:

> *Shiv, who poured the harvest and made the winds to blow,*
> *Sitting at the doorways of a day of long ago,*
> *Gave to each his portion, food and toil and fate,*

From the king upon the guddee *to the beggar at the gate.*
All things made he—Shiva the preserver.
Mahadeo! Mahadeo! he made all—
Thorn for the camel, fodder for the kine,
And mother's heart for sleepy head, O little son of mine!

It goes on for ever so many verses, and Little Toomai came in with a joyous *tunk-a-tunk* at the end of each verse, till he felt sleepy and stretched himself on the fodder at Kala Nag's side. At last the elephants began to lie down one after another as is their custom, till only Kala Nag at the right of the line was left standing up; and he rocked slowly from side to side, his ears put forward to listen to the night wind as it blew very slowly across the hills. The air was full of all the night noises that, taken together, make one big silence—the click of one bamboo-stem against the other, the rustle of something alive in the undergrowth, the scratch and squawk of a half-waked bird (birds are awake in the night much more often than we imagine), and the fall of water ever so far away. Little Toomai slept for some time, and when he waked it was brilliant moonlight, and Kala Nag was still standing up with his ears cocked. Little Toomai turned, rustling in the fodder, and watched the curve of his big back against half the stars in heaven, and while he watched he heard, so far away that it sounded no more than a pinhole of noise pricked through the stillness, the "hoot-toot" of a wild elephant. All the elephants in the lines jumped up as if they had been shot, and their grunts really roused the sleeping mahouts. They came out of the huts, rubbing their eyes, and drove in the picket-pegs with big mallets, and tightened this rope and knotted that till all was quiet. One new elephant had nearly grubbed up his picket, and Big Toomai took off Kala Nag's leg-chain and shackled that elephant fore foot to hind foot, and just slipped a loop of grass string round Kala Nag's leg, and told him to stay still and remember that he was tied. He knew that he and his father and his grandfather had done the very same thing hundreds of times before. Kala Nag did not answer to the order by gurgling, as he usually did. He stayed still, looking out across the moonlight, his head a little raised and his ears spread like fans, up to the great folds of the Garo hills.

"Look after him if he grows restless in the night," said Big Toomai to Little Toomai, and he went into the hut and slept. Little Toomai was just going to sleep, too, when he heard the coir string snap with a little "ting," and Kala Nag rolled out of his pickets as slowly and as silently as a cloud rolls out of the mouth of a valley. Little Toomai pattered after him, bare-footed, down the road in the moonlight, calling under his breath, "Kala Nag! Kala Nag! Take me with you, O Kala Nag!" The elephant turned, still without a sound, took three strides back to the boy in the moonlight, put down his trunk, swung him to his neck, and almost before Little Toomai had settled his knees, slipped into the forest.

There was one blast of furious trumpeting from the lines, and then the silence shut down on everything, and Kala Nag began to move. Sometimes a tuft of high grass washed along his sides as a wave washes along the sides of a ship, and sometimes a cluster of wild-pepper vines would scrape along his back, or a bamboo would creak where his shoulder touched it; but between those times he moved absolutely without any sound, drifting through the thick Garo forest as though it had been smoke. He was going up hill, but though Little Toomai watched the stars in the rifts of the trees, he could not tell in what direction. Then Kala Nag reached the crest of the ascent and stopped for a minute, and Little Toomai could see the tops of the trees lying all speckled and furry under the moonlight for miles and miles, and the blue-white mist over the river in the hollow. Toomai leaned forward and looked, and he felt that the forest was awake below him—awake and alive and crowded. A big brown fruit-eating bat brushed past his ear; a porcupine's quills rattled in the thicket, and in the darkness between the tree-stems he heard a hog-bear digging hard in the moist warm earth, and snuffing as it digged. Then the branches closed over his head again, and Kala Nag began to go down into the valley—not quietly this time, but as a runaway gun goes down a steep bank—in one rush. The huge limbs moved as steadily as pistons, eight feet to each stride, and the wrinkled skin of the elbow-points rustled. The undergrowth on either side of him ripped with a noise like torn canvas, and the saplings that he heaved away right and left with his shoulders sprang back again, and banged him on the flank, and great trails of creepers, all matted together, hung from his tusks as he threw his head from side to side and plowed out his pathway. Then Little Toomai laid himself down close to the great neck lest a swinging bough should sweep him to the ground, and he wished that he were back in the lines again. The grass began to get squashy, and Kala Nag's feet sucked and squelched as he put them down, and the night mist at the bottom of the valley chilled Little Toomai. There was a splash and a trample, and the rush of running water, and Kala Nag strode through the bed of a river, feeling his way at each step. Above the noise of the water, as it swirled round the elephant's legs, Little Toomai could hear more splashing and some trumpeting both up-stream and down—great grunts and angry snortings, and all the mist about him seemed to be full of rolling, wavy shadows. "*Ai!*" he said, half aloud, his teeth chattering. "The elephant-folk are out tonight. It *is* the dance, then."

Kala Naga swashed out of the water, blew his trunk clear, and began another climb; but this time he was not alone, and he had not to make his path. That was made already, six feet wide, in front of him, where the bent jungle-grass was trying to recover itself and stand up. Many elephants must have gone that way only a few

Little Toomai let himself down close to the great neck.

minutes before. Little Toomai looked back, and behind him a great wild tusker with his little pig's eyes glowing like hot coals, was just lifting himself out of the misty river. Then the trees closed up again, and they went on and up, with trumpetings and crashings, and the sound of breaking branches on every side of them. At last Kala Nag stood still between two tree-trunks at the very top of the hill. They were part of a circle of trees that grew round an irregular space of some three or four acres, and in all that space, as Little Toomai could see, the ground had been trampled down as hard as a brick floor. Some trees grew in the center of the clearing, but their bark was rubbed away, and the white wood beneath showed all shiny and polished in the patches of moonlight. There were creepers hanging from the upper branches, and the bells of the flowers of the creepers, great waxy white things like convolvuluses, hung down fast asleep; but within the limits of the clearing there was not a single blade of green—nothing but the trampled earth. The moonlight showed it all iron-gray, except where some elephants stood upon it, and their shadows were inky black. Little Toomai looked, holding his breath, with his eyes starting out of his head, and as he looked, more, and more, and more elephants swung out into the open from between the tree-trunks. Little Toomai could only count up to ten, and he counted again and again on his fingers till he lost count of the tens, and his head began to swim. Outside the clearing he could hear them crashing in the undergrowth as they worked their way up the hillside; but as soon as they were within the circle of the tree-trunks they moved like ghosts.

There were white-tusked wild males, with fallen leaves and nuts and twigs lying in the wrinkles of their necks and the folds of their ears; fat, slow-footed she-elephants, with restless, little pinky-black calves only three or four feet high running under their stomachs; young elephants with their tusks just beginning to show, and very proud of them; lanky, scraggy old-maid elephants, with their hollow, anxious faces, and trunks like rough bark; savage old bull-elephants, scarred from shoulder to flank with great weals and cuts of bygone fights, and the caked dirt of their solitary mud-baths dropping from their shoulders; and there was one with a broken tusk and the marks of the full-stroke, the terrible drawing scrape, of a tiger's claws on his side. They were standing head to head, or walking to and fro across the ground in couples, or rocking and swaying all by themselves—scores and scores of elephants. Toomai knew that so long as he lay still on Kala Nag's neck nothing would happen to him; for even in the rush and scramble of a Keddah-drive a wild elephant does not reach up with his trunk and drag a man off the neck of a tame elephant; and these elephants were not thinking of men that night. Once they started and put their ears forward when they heard the chinking of a leg-iron in the forest, but it was Pudmini, Petersen Sahib's pet elephant, her chain snapped short off, grunting, snuffling up the hillside. She must have broken her pickets, and come straight from Petersen Sahib's camp; and Little Toomai saw another elephant, one that he did not know, with deep rope-galls on his back and breast. He, too, must have run away from some camp in the hills about.

At last there was no sound of any more elephants moving in the forest, and Kala Nag rolled out from his station between the trees and went into the middle of the crowd, clucking and gurgling, and all the elephants began to talk in their own tongue, and to move about. Still lying down, Little Toomai looked down upon scores and scores of broad backs, and wagging ears, and tossing trunks, and little rolling eyes. He heard the click of tusks as they crossed other tusks by accident, and the dry rustle of trunks twined together, and the chafing of enormous sides and shoulders in the crowd, and the incessant flick and *hissh* of the great tails. Then a cloud came over the moon, and he sat in black darkness; but the quiet, steady hustling and pushing and gurgling went on just the same. He knew that there were elephants all round Kala Nag, and that there was no chance of backing him out of the assembly; so he set his teeth and shivered. In a Keddah at least there was torchlight and shouting, but here he was all alone in the dark, and once a trunk came up and touched him on the knee. Then an elephant trumpeted, and they all took it up for five or ten terrible seconds. After that, he heard the dew spattering down from the trees above like rain on the unseen backs, and then a dull booming noise began, not very loud at first, and Little Toomai could not tell what it was; but it grew and grew, and Kala Nag lifted up one fore foot and then the other, and brought them down on the ground—one-two, one-two, as steadily as trip-hammers. The elephants were stamping all together now, and it sounded like a war-drum beaten at the mouth of a cave. The dew fell from the trees till there was no more left to fall, and the booming went on, and the ground rocked and shivered, and Little Toomai put his hands up to his ears to shut out the sound. But it was all one gigantic jar that ran through him—this stamp of hundreds of heavy feet on the raw earth. Once or twice he could feel Kala Nag and all the others surge forward a few strides, and for a minute or two the thumping would change to the crushing sound of juicy green things being bruised, but after the boom of feet on hard earth began again. A tree was creaking and groaning somewhere near him. He put out his arm and felt the bark, but Kala Nag moved forward, still tramping, and he could not tell where he was in the clearing. There was no sound from the elephants, except once, when two or three little calves squeaked together. Then he heard a thump and a shuffle, and the booming went on. It must have lasted fully two hours, and Little Toomai ached in every nerve; but he knew by the smell of the night air that the dawn was coming, and he would have fainted where he was sooner than have cried out.

The morning broke in one sheet of pale yellow behind the green hills, and the booming stopped with the first ray, as though the light had been an order. Before Little Toomai had got the ringing out of his head, before even he had shifted his position, there was not an elephant in sight except Kala Nag, Pudmini, and the elephant with the rope-galls, and there was no sign or rustle or whisper down the hillsides to show which way the others had taken. Little Toomai stared again and again. The clearing as he remembered it, had grown ever so much. More trees stood in the middle of it, but the undergrowth and the jungle-grass at the sides had been rolled back. Little Toomai stared once more. Now he understood the trampling. The elephants had stamped out more room—had stamped the thick grass and juicy cane to trash, the trash into slivers, the slivers into tiny fibres, and the fibres into hard earth.

"Wah!" said Little Toomai, and his eyes were very heavy. "Kala Nag, my lord, let us keep by Pudmini and go to Petersen Sahib's camp, or I shall drop from thy neck."

The third elephant watched the two go away, snorted, wheeled round, and took his own path. He may have belonged to some little native king's establishment, fifty or sixty or a hundred miles away.

Two hours later, as Petersen Sahib was eating early breakfast, his elephants, who had been doubled-chained that night, began to trumpet, and Pudmini, mired

Little Toomai would have fainted where he was sooner than have cried out.

to the shoulders, and Kala Nag, very foot-sore, shambled into the camp. Little Toomai's face was gray and pinched, and his hair was full of leaves and drenched with dew; but he tried to salute Petersen Sahib, and cried faintly: "The dance—the elephant-dance! I have seen it, and—I die!" As Kala Nag sat down, he slid off his neck in a dead faint.

But, since native children have no nerves worth speaking of, in two hours he was lying very contentedly in Petersen Sahib's hammock with Petersen Sahib's shooting-coat under his head and a glass of warm milk, a little brandy, with a dash of quinine inside of him, and while the old hairy, scarred elephant-catchers of the jungles sat three-deep before him, looking at him as though he were a spirit, he told his tale in short words, as a child will, and wound up with:

"Now, if I lie in one word send men to see, and they will find that the elephant-folk have trampled down more room in their dance-room, and they will find ten and ten, and many times ten, tracks leading to that dance-room. They made more room with their feet. I have seen it. Kala Nag took me, and I saw. Also Kala Nag is very leg-weary!"

Little Toomai lay back and slept all through the long afternoon and into the twilight, and while he slept Petersen Sahib and Machua Appa followed the track of the two elephants for fifteen miles across the hills. Petersen Sahib had spent eighteen years in catching elephants, and he had only once before seen one of their dance-places. Machua Appa had no need to look twice at the clearing to see what had been done there, or to scratch with his toe in the packed, rammed earth.

"The child speaks truth," said he. "All this was done last night, and I have counted seventy tracks crossing the river. See, Sahib, where Pudmini's leg-iron cut the bark of that tree! Yes; she was there too." They looked at one another and up and down, and they wondered; for the ways of elephants are beyond the wit of any man, black or white, to fathom.

"Forty years and five," said Machua Appa, "have I followed my lord the elephant, but never have I heard that any child of man had seen what this child has seen. By all the Gods of the Hills, it is—what can we say?" and he shook his head.

When they got back to camp it was time for the evening meal. Petersen Sahib ate alone in his tent, but he gave orders that the camp should have two sheep and some fowls, as well as a double ration of flour and rice and salt, for he knew that there would be a feast. Big Toomai had come up hot-foot from the camp in the plains to search for his son and his elephant, and now that he had found them he looked at them as though he were afraid of them both. And there was a feast by the blazing camp-fires in front of the lines of picketed elephants, and Little Toomai was the hero of it all; and the big brown elephant-catchers, the trackers and drivers and ropers, and the men who know all the secrets of breaking the wildest elephants, passed him from one to the other, and they marked his forehead with blood from the breast of a newly killed jungle-cock, to show that he was a forester, initiated and free of all the jungles.

And at last, when the flames died down, and the red light of the logs made the elephants look as though they had been dipped in blood too, Machua Appa, the head of all the drivers of all the Keddahs—Machua Appa, Petersen Sahib's other self, who had never seen a made road in forty years: Machua Appa, who was so great that he had no other name than Machua Appa—leaped to his feet, with Little Toomai held high in the air above his head, and shouted: "Listen, my brothers. Listen, too, you my lords in the lines there, for I, Machua Appa, am speaking! This little one shall no more be called Little Toomai, but Toomai of the Elephants, as his great-grandfather was called before him. What never man has seen he has seen through the long night, and the favor of the elephant-folk and of the Gods of the Jungles is with him. He shall become a great tracker; he shall become greater than I, even I, Machua Appa! He shall follow the new trail, and the stale trail, and the mixed trail, with a clear eye! He shall take no harm in the Keddah when he runs under their bellies to rope the wild tuskers; and if he slips before the feet of the charging bull-elephant, the bull-elephant shall know who he is and shall not crush him. *Aihai!* my lords in the chains"—he whirled up the line of pickets—"here is the little one that has seen your dances in your hidden places—the sight that never man saw! Give him honor, my lords! *Salaam karo*, my children. Make your salute to Toomai of the Elephants! Gunga Pershad, ahaa! Hira Guj, Birchi Guj, Kuttar Guj, ahaa! Pudmini—thou hast seen him at the dance, and thou too, Kala Nag, my pearl among elephants!—ahaa! Together! To Toomai of the Elephants. *Barrao!*"

And at that last wild yell the whole line flung up their trunks till the tips touched their foreheads, and broke out into the full salute—the crashing trumpet-peal that only the Viceroy of India hears, the Salaamut of the Keddah.

But it was all for the sake of Little Toomai, who had seen what never man had seen before—the dance of the elephants at night and alone in the heart of the Garo hills!

First published in the December 1893 edition of *St. Nicholas Magazine*

Kane and Pard

A Tale of Christmas Eve

BY ADDISON HOWARD GIBSON

"HERE WE ARE, Pard," observed Kane Osborne, looking regretfully after the receding train that had just left him at the isolated mountain station.

Pard, a bright-eyed, alert Scotch collie, glanced up intelligently into the troubled face of his companion, a slender lad of fifteen.

Kane shivered in the chill December air which swept down from the snow-clad peaks, and his somewhat pale face expressed disappointment as he looked up and down the seemingly deserted station-platform.

"No one to meet us, Pard," he said to the tail-wagging collie. "Maybe he don't want us-he didn't write that he did, but Uncle Hi was sure he'd take us in. It's Christmas eve, and we're all alone, Pard"; and Kane swallowed hard as his hand stroked the dog's head. A sympathetic whine was Pard's response.

"Looking for some one, son?" asked the station-agent, coming forward.

"Yes," answered Kane, rather bashfully; "we're looking for Mr. Jim Moreley."

Pard glanced up intelligently into the face of his companion.

"Relation of his going up to the ranch to spend Christmas?"

"No-o-o. Is his ranch near here?"

"About ten miles up Rainbow Canyon," informed the agent, eying the boy. "Moreley hasn't been down today. Going up for a vacation?"

"To live there, if he'll keep us," replied Kane.

"Haven't you any other place to go but to Moreley's ranch?" inquired the agent.

"No place. My folks are all dead, and Uncle Hi died, too, about five days ago," explained Kane, trying bravely to keep the tears back. "There's just Pard and me left. A lady offered me a home, but she wouldn't let Pard stay. Uncle Hi used to know Mr. Moreley over at Green Buttes, before he came here, so he got the doctor to write that he was sending Pard and me up to the ranch."

"If you go to live with old Moreley, he'll work you to death," declared the man. "He's changed since he lived at Green Buttes. He's drinking, these days, and he's hard on his help. He hasn't any use for any one who's not strong," scanning Kane's thin arms and legs in his worn suit.

"Oh, I'll be all right when I get to knocking about the mountains," Kane hastened to assure the agent, resenting the suggestion of physical weakness. "Uncle Hi," he continued, "was sick nearly four months, and I was shut up taking care of him, and missed my exercise. Before he died, he told me to come up to Rainbow Canyon. He was sure Mr. Moreley'd be glad to have a boy and a good dog to help with the sheep. I've worked on a sheep ranch before, and Pard knows a lot about the business."

"Well, I'm sorry for you, kid, if you're going up to old Moreley's. Wait a minute." And the agent stepped to the other end of the platform and called to an old man who was unhitching his team from a post in front of a little store near by. "Hello, Thompson! Here's a boy who wants to go up to Moreley's ranch. Can't you give him a lift as far as your place?"

"Guess so, if he's spry," the rancher called back in a crisp tone. "I'm in a hurry!" he explained, climbing into his wagon and gathering up the lines. "There's a storm brewin' in the mountains, and my sheep are scattered in the canyon."

"All right! Here's the boy," said the agent. "Good-by, kid, and a Merry Christmas to you!"

"Thank you—the same to you!" returned Kane, hurrying toward Thompson's wagon, Pard following closely at his heels.

"Here, kid!" called the agent, running after Kane with an old overcoat. "Put this on. You'll need it riding up Rainbow. You needn't mind returning it—it's too small for me now."

This unexpected kindness brought a lump in Kane's throat, but he murmured his thanks as he slipped into the overcoat. Then he climbed into the wagon. Somewhat impatiently Thompson moved over in his seat to make room for the unwelcome passenger. He puckered his brows into a frown as his sharp gray eyes ran the boy over critically.

"I'm in a rush," he asserted, starting his ponies off briskly up the mountain road. "Got a dog, I see," he remarked presently, with something like a sniff, as Pard trotted along by the wagon. "That feller's attached himself to this outfit with a mighty important air. I ain't no use for dogs ever since Bill Stevens's killed some o' my lambs. They're a right smart of a nuisance—same as boys. Boys ask too many questions, and stand around and watch the old man do the work. I had one from Denver, but he was no good, and I shipped him back. Gid ap, Pop-corn!" to one of the ponies.

"I had a boy o' my own once," his tone softening as he became reminiscent. "But pneumony took him off—pneumony goes hard up here in the Colorado Rockies. Sairy, my wife, is always at me to get a boy to live with us, but after my experience with 'Denver,' no boys for me. No, sir, never ag'in!"

Kane felt very uncomfortable as Thompson delivered himself of this speech. At first he stole only a timid, sidelong glance at the man who had no use for boys and dogs. But presently, gathering courage, he surveyed his companion's care-lined face. He decided that Thompson was not as unkindly as his words might imply.

"Moreley some connection of yours?" he asked Kane, after driving for some time in silence.

"No," answered Kane, snuggling his chin down inside the turned-up collar of his newly acquired overcoat; "Uncle Hi thought Pard and I might find a job there."

"Who's Uncle Hi?"

"A kind old man I lived with after my father and mother died."

"Why didn't you stay with him?" Thompson asked, darting a suspicious glance at Kane from under a ledge of bushy brows.

"He died, too, and it took everything to pay the funeral expenses. Dr. Bently paid my way up to Rainbow. When I earn money enough, I'll pay him back and buy a tombstone for Uncle Hi."

"Well, lad, it's a world o' trouble!" and the old man sighed deeply. "I was gittin' along tiptop till our boy died. After that I seemed to run downhill, and had to mortgage my ranch to Jim Moreley to keep goin'. But," pridefully, "I got some fine sheep, and if I've good luck winterin' 'em, I'll pay out next fall, and be independent ag'in."

As they steadily ascended, the wind grew more chilly and moaned ominously among the pines that dotted the mountain slopes. The keen air made Kane's nose and ears tingle, and he drew closer to his companion.

"Goin' to storm," observed Thompson, squinting toward the sky. "It's a sure sign when the pines screech that way. Here we are," he announced, turning off on a side trail. "That's my place," pointing to a homy-looking cottage that stood in a sheltered arm of the wide canyon.

"It's about three miles up the trail yonder to Moreley's," he explained. "You can eat a bite with Sairy and me before goin' on."

As Kane helped unhitch the ponies, a motherly looking woman called from the house that dinner was ready. She made friends with Pard at once, and brought him a plate of scraps from the kitchen.

"Some Christmas fixin's for you, Sairy," said Thompson, as he and Kane deposited on the table several packages brought from Rainbow.

In the neat, warm kitchen, Kane, seated between the old couple, ate his share of the good "boiled dinner" with a gusto caused by a keen appetite. More than once he caught Mrs. Thompson's kindly eyes fixed on his face with an almost yearning eagerness.

The meal over, Pard had another feast in the shed behind the kitchen. Then, thanking the couple for their kindness, Kane slipped into the overcoat and prepared for his climb up to Moreley's ranch.

"He reminds me so much of Harry," Kane overheard Mrs. Thompson say in an undertone to her husband. "Why can't we keep him? Moreley's will be such a rough place for him."

Thompson muttered something about boys and dogs being a great deal of bother.

"It seems as if Providence sent him to us," she persisted, "your bringing him here, and on Christmas eve, too! He's like a Christmas present," with a smile directed at Kane. Then, with a pleading quiver of the pleasant voice, "Do let's keep him-and that fine collie!"

But Thompson shook his head decisively.

"Well, we can at least keep him overnight-Christmas eve," she pleaded. "It's three o'clock now, and these short days it gets dark so early in the mountains. It's going to storm soon," looking out of the window, "and the trail being strange to him, he might miss his way."

"The trail's all right if he follows it," declared the old rancher, impatiently. "He'd best to go on, for Moreley's a crank, and might think we're tryin' to coax the boy from goin' to him."

From the foot of the steep trail Kane waved his hand to her, as she stood in the doorway watching him start.

"So much like Harry," she murmured tremulously. "God guard him!"

"Just stick to that trail, and it'll lead you straight to Moreley's," directed Thompson, calling after Kane. "Don't waste any time though. See that cloud rolling over Old Grayback?" indicating a peak, "that means a snow-storm, and my sheep are scattered somewhere in the canyon. I've got to hustle."

Kane turned to offer the services of Pard and himself to help round up the sheep, but Thompson had hurried away and disappeared down the canyon. So he went on up the trail. To reinforce his courage he began to whistle, but something in his throat choked him, and he became thoughtful.

"Pard," gently squeezing the collie's ear, "if Mr. Moreley don't want us, we'll be in a fix." A rapid movement of the tail and a low whine attested Pard's loyal sympathy.

The cloud over Old Grayback soon obscured the entire sky. Presently Kane felt fine particles of snow strike his face, and the path soon became slippery and difficult to keep.

"This is going back two steps to one forward, Pard!" he laughed, recovering from measuring his full length on an icy rock.

The wind, accompanied by a steadily falling temperature, increased in power every minute, driving the now rapidly descending snow before it. Kane pulled his cap down to protect his eyes and struggled on.

The snow soon came down in blinding sheets, entirely blotting out the trail. Pard kept close to his master, frequently whining his disapproval of the storm.

Suddenly Kane realized that he had strayed from the trail and was stumbling along half-blindly down a canyon over rocks and tangled bushes. Here the trees broke the fierce, biting force of the wind. But he had no idea which way to turn to find the path that he had lost. All around and enwrapping him was a mass of roaring, smothering whiteness.

Kane had lived most of his years among the Rockies, but he had never before been lost in one of their wild winter storms. He knew, however, that his situation was one of great danger. Unless he could find shelter, he might become buried under the snow, or stumble over a ledge into an unseen gorge. Then there might be a terrible snow-slide from the overladen heights above. He could see scarcely ten yards in any direction, and in spite of the overcoat, he began to feel chilled. He was presently so leg-weary that he felt inclined to crawl under the shelving rocks and lie down.

Realizing how fatal such a step might prove, Kane fought his way across the snow-clad canyon, followed by Pard.

All at once the collie gave a sharp bark and darted away through the trees, reappearing almost immediately and barking up at Kane as if insisting on his following.

"All right, Pard. Lead on!" directed Kane.

Only a short distance farther, a long shed loomed vague and specter-like in the wild whiteness of the evening. Pushing forward, Kane discovered that it was a rude but comfortable building for stock. It stood in an arm of the canyon with no house in sight.

Thankful for anything that promised refuge from the storm, he advanced hurriedly. At the corner of the building, he halted quickly: a herd of sheep huddled against the closed door.

Kane's appearance was greeted by a plaintive chorus of bleats. In their dumb, beseeching way they accepted him as their belated shepherd.

"All right, sheepsie-baas," he said soothingly as they crowded about him. "Wait and I'll see how things are."

Sliding back the big door, Kane revealed a warm, comfortable shed for sheep and cattle. In one of the stalls a cow stood munching hay.

Sliding back the big door, Kane revealed a warm, comfortable shed.

"Some one doesn't look after his sheep very well, Pard," said Kane. "Bring 'em in."

The well-trained collie needed no second bidding. With an assenting bark, he ran around the shivering flock, which quickly scattered among the bushes. It proved no easy task to house these sheep, for, being unused to a dog, the younger ones were frightened, and at first fled in every direction. But Kane hurried out to direct matters, and Pard, wise and careful in his part of the business, after considerable effort brought them, an obedient bunch, into their fold. Then their self-appointed shepherd filled the low racks with hay, which they began to eat gratefully.

"Well, Bossy," addressing the cow, "we've invited ourselves to spend Christmas eve with you and the sheepsie-baas. Here, Pard! Where are you?" he called, noticing that the collie had not entered the shed. Off somewhere in the bushes Pard began a spirited barking.

"Some stubborn runaways," thought Kane. "Bring 'em in, Pard," he commanded over the din of the storm.

Pard sent back a quick, answering bark. Kane repeated his order, and again the collie responded with a sharp, imperative bark. Sure that something was wrong, the boy left the shelter of the shed, and again faced the fury of the elements.

"Where are you, Pard?"

Kane bent his head to listen for the dog's bark to guide him. It came, and was instantly followed by the sound of a groan-a human groan!

Quickly Kane groped his way through the underbrush of the canyon. Guided by Pard's persistent barking, he at last reached an object lying among the rocks almost buried in snow. A nearer survey revealed to the lad a man lying prostrate and helpless in a little clump of bushes.

"I've had a fall and hurt my ankle so I can't walk in the snow!" said the unfortunate man, groaning with pain, as Kane bent solicitously over him.

"Why, it's Mr. Thompson!" cried Kane, in surprise. "How did it happen?"

"In trying to bunch my sheep, I slipped on a rock and took a bad tumble,"

"I've had a fall and hurt my ankle," said the man.

explained Mr. Thompson. "I dragged myself through the snow as far as these bushes, then my strength give out. The pain and cold together made me kind of lose my senses, I guess, till the dog roused me."

Half-leading, half-dragging the rancher, Kane managed to get him to the shed. Here, on an improvised couch of hay and empty sacks, the disabled man watched his safely sheltered flock taking their supper in calm content.

"Well, Providence works funny sometimes!" he ejaculated. "There I was, flounderin' in the snow, disablin' myself, and worryin' for fear my sheep'd all perish; and at last I thought I was a goner myself. And there you was, losin' the trail all for a purpose, to do my work, and save my life."

"It was mostly Pard," asserted Kane, stroking the collie's head. "He drove the sheep in and found you."

"It was the two of you," corrected Thompson, looking gratefully at the boy and his dog. "I'm not harborin' any more prejudices ag'in' boys and dogs—you two in particular. The storm's knocked them prejudices all out o' me. The house is jest round the bend of the canyon. The wind's fallin' now, and purty soon you can go and tell Sairy what's happened. I ain't goin' to let Jim Moreley have you! You and Pard are Christmas presents for Sairy and me!"

In silent thankfulness, Kane, too happy for words, pressed the rancher's hand. Pard only wagged his tail.

First published in the January 1913 edition of *St. Nicholas Magazine*

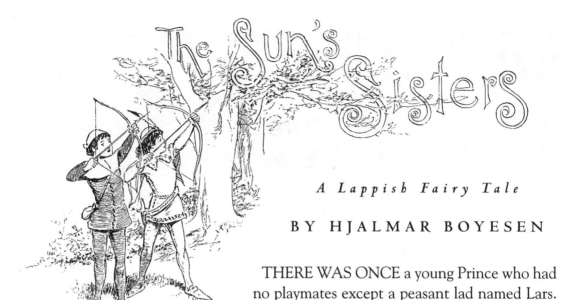

The Sun's Sisters

A Lappish Fairy Tale

BY HJALMAR BOYESEN

THERE WAS ONCE a young Prince who had no playmates except a peasant lad named Lars. The King, of course, did not like to have his son play with such a common boy; but as there were no princes or kings in the neighborhood, he had no choice but to put up with Lars. One day the Prince and Lars were shooting at a mark; and Lars hit the bull's-eye again and again, while the Prince's arrows flew rattling among the tree-trunks, and sometimes did not even hit the target. Then he grew angry and called Lars a lout and a clod-hopper. Lars did not mind that much, for he knew that princes were petted and spoiled, and could not bear to be crossed.

"Now, Prince," he said, "let us shoot up into the air and see who can shoot the highest."

The Prince, who had a beautiful gilt bow and polished steel-tipped arrows, had no doubt but that he could shoot much higher than Lars, whose bow was a juniper branch which he had himself cut and cured. So he accepted the offer.

"Let us aim at the sun," he cried, gaily.

"All right," shouted Lars; and at the same moment they let fly two arrows, which cleft the air with a whiz and vanished among the fleecy clouds.

The boys stood looking up into the sun-steeped air until their eyes ached; and after a moment or two, the Prince's arrow fell at his side, and he picked it up. Nearly fifteen minutes elapsed before Lars's arrow returned, and when he picked it up, he was astonished to find a drop of blood on the tip of it, to which clung a dazzlingly beautiful golden feather.

"Why—look at that!" cried the boy, with delight. "Isn't it wonderful?"

"Yes, but it is mine," replied the Prince; "it was my arrow."

"It was no such thing," said Lars; "I made the arrow myself and ought to know it. Yours are steel-tipped and polished."

"I tell you it is my arrow," cried the Prince in great anger; "and if you don't give me the feather, it will go ill with you."

Now, Lars would have been quite willing to part with the feather, if the Prince had asked him for it, but he was a high-spirited lad, and would not consent to be bullied.

"You know as well as I do that the arrow was mine," he said, scowling; "and the feather is mine, too, and I won't give it to anybody."

The Prince said nothing; but, pale with rage, he hurried back to the castle and told his father, the King, that his arrow had brought down a beautiful golden feather and that Lars had taken it from him.

Now, if you have any acquaintance with kings, you may perhaps imagine how the old gentleman felt when he heard that his son and heir had been thus wronged. It was to no purpose that Lars showed him the drop of blood on the rude whittled arrow; he insisted that the feather was the Prince's, and that Lars was a thief and a robber. But Lars was not to be frightened even at that. He stuck to his story and refused to give up the feather.

"Well, then," said the King, with a wicked grin, "we'll say that it is yours. But in that case you must be prepared to prove it. When you bring me the golden hen, from whose tail this feather has been shot, then I'll admit that it is yours. But if you fail, you will be burned alive in a barrel of tar."

Now, to be burned alive in a barrel of tar is not a pleasant thing; and Lars, when he heard that such a fate was in store for him, wished he had never seen the golden feather. But it would be disgraceful to back down now, so he accepted the terms, stuffed into his lunch-bag a leg of smoked mutton and a dozen loaves of bread, which the cook at the castle gave him, and started on his journey. But the question now arose, where should he go? Golden hens were not such everyday affairs that he might expect to find them in any barn-yard. And barn-yard hens, moreover, were not in the habit of flying aloft; and the golden feather had come down to him from some high region of the air. He became heavy-hearted when he thought of these things, and imagined, whenever he saw a farmer burning stumps and rubbish at the roadside, that it was the barrel of tar in which he was to end his days. For all that, he kept trudging on, and when evening came he found himself on the outskirts of a great forest. Being very tired, he put his lunch-bag under his head, and soon fell asleep. But he had not been sleeping long when he was waked up by somebody trying to pull the bag away from under him. He raised himself on his elbow, rubbed his eyes, and to his aston-ishment saw a big fox sitting on his haunches and staring at him, "Where are you going?" asked the fox.

"I wasn't going anywhere," said Lars. "I was sleeping."

"Well, I am aware of that," observed Reynard; "but when you are not sleeping, where are you then going?"

"Oh, well," said Lars, "the fact is, I am in a bad scrape. I have got to find the golden hen that has lost a tail-feather."

And he told the fox his story.

"Hum," said the fox; "that is pretty bad. Let me look at the feather."

The boy pulled out the feather from his inside vest pocket, where he kept it carefully wrapped up in birch-bark.

"Ah," said Reynard, when he had examined it; "you know I have a large acquaintance among hens. In fact, I am very fond of them. I shouldn't wonder if I might help you find the one which has lost this feather."

Lars, who had been quite down in the mouth at the prospect of the barrel of tar, was delighted to hear that.

"I wish you would bear me company," said he. "If you'll do me a good turn, I'll do you another."

The fox thought that was a fair bargain; and so they shook hands on it, and off they started together.

"Do you know where we are going? "asked Reynard, after a while.

"No," said Lars; "but I supposed you did."

"I do. We are going to the Sun's Sister. She has three golden hens. It was one of those you hit with your arrow."

"But will she be willing to part with any of them?" asked the boy.

"Leave that to me," answered Reynard; "you know I have had some experience with hens."

Day after day they walked up one hill and down another until they came to the castle of the Sun. It was a gorgeous castle, shining with silver and gold and precious stones. The boy's eyes ached when he looked at it. Even the smoke that curled up into the still air from the chimneys was radiant like clouds at sunset.

"That's a nice place," said Lars.

"So it is," said Reynard. "It is best, I think, to have me sneak into the poultry-yard, where the three golden hens are, and then I'll bring out the one that has lost its tail-feather."

Lars somehow didn't like that plan. He didn't quite trust Reynard in the matter of hens; he knew the fox had a natural weakness for poultry, but, of course, he was too polite to say so.

"No, Reynard," he began, blushing and hesitating; "I am really afraid you might come to harm. And you might make too much of a racket, you know, setting the whole poultry-yard in commotion."

"Well, then, you go yourself," said Reynard, somewhat offended; "but take heed of this warning. Look neither to the right nor to the left, and go straight to the poultry-yard, seize the hen that has lost one of the three long tail-feathers, and then hasten out as quick as you can."

Lars promised that he would obey in all particulars. The gate was wide open; the sentries, who stood dozing in their boxes, did not seem to mind him as he entered. It was high noon; the watch-dogs slept in their kennels, and a noonday drowsiness hung over the whole dazzling palace. So the boy went straight to the poultry-yard, as he had been directed, spied the three golden hens, the splendor of which nearly blinded him, grabbed the one of them that had lost a

He saw a big fox sitting on his haunches and staring at him.

tail-feather, and started again in hot haste for the gate. But as he passed by the wing of the palace he noticed a window, the shutters of which were ajar. A great curiosity to see what was behind these shutters took possession of him. "It would be a pity to leave this beautiful place without looking about a little," he thought; "I can easily catch that hen again if I let her go now, for she is as tame as a house-chicken."

So he let the hen go, opened the shutter, and peeped into the room. And what do you think he saw? Well, he could scarcely have told you himself, for he was so completely overwhelmed that he stood gazing stupidly, like a cow at a painted barn-door. But beautiful—oh, beautiful, beyond all conception, was that which he saw. That was the reason he stood speechless, with open mouth and staring eyes. Of course, now you can guess what it was. It was none other than the Sister of the Sun. She was lying upon her bed, sleeping sweetly, like a child that is taking an after-dinner nap. Goodness and kindness were shining from her features, and Lars was filled with such ineffable joy at the mere sight of her that he forgot all about the hen and the barrel of tar, and his playmate the Prince, and the fox's warning. He did not know that this was her great charm—everyone who looked upon her was instantly filled with gladness unspeakable. Sorrow, and care, and malice, and hatred instantly fled from the heart of every one who came into her presence. No wonder Lars couldn't think of hens, when he had so lovely a creature to look upon. For several minutes he stood at the window, lost in the rapturous sight. Then stealthily, and without thinking of what he was doing, he climbed over the window-sill, and step by step drew nearer.

"Oh, how beautiful! how beautiful! how beautiful!" he whispered with bated breath. "Oh, I must kiss her before I go, or I shall never have peace so long as I live."

And down he stooped and kissed the Sun's Sister. You would have supposed now that she would have wakened. But, no! She lay perfectly still; her bosom heaved gently, and the red blood went meandering busily under her soft, transparent skin, and her dazzling hair billowed in a golden stream over the silken pillow, and down upon the floor. Lars would have been content to spend all his life gazing at her. But a strange uneasiness came over him—his errand, the golden hen, the barrel of tar, and all the rest of it came back to his memory slowly, as if emerging from a golden mist, and, with a sudden determination, he covered his eyes with his hands, jumped out of the window, and started again in search of the hen. But, somehow, the whole world had now a different look to him. Everything had changed, and the golden hen, too. When he tried to catch her, this time, she flapped with her wings, gave a hoarse shriek, and ran as fast as she could. Lars plunged ahead, reaching out with both his hands to catch her, but she slipped from his grasp, and yelled and screamed worse than ever. Instantly her two companions set up a sympathetic cackle, and in another minute the entire poultry-yard—geese, ducks, peacocks, and hens—joined the chorus, making an ear-splitting racket, the like of which had scarcely been heard since the world was made. The Sun's Sister, aroused by this terrible commotion, rubbed her beautiful eyes, and started in alarm for the poultry-yard. The dogs came rushing out of their kennels, barking furiously; the sentries who had been dozing at the gates drew their swords and flourished them savagely, and everybody in the whole castle was astir.

Lars climbed over the window-sill, and step by step drew nearer.

"What are you doing here?" asked the Sun's Sister, when she saw the boy chasing her favorite golden hen.

"Oh, well," said Lars, feeling rather bashful; "I was only amusing myself."

"Well," said the Sun's Sister, gently (for she was as

good as she was beautiful), "you can't amuse yourself catching my hens unless—unless—"

"Unless what?" asked Lars.

"Unless" (and here the face of the Sun's Sister grew very sad) "unless you can rescue my sister Afterglow from the Trolds, who carried her off far behind the western mountains many years ago."

Lars scarcely knew what to answer to that; he would have liked to consult his friend Reynard before saying anything. But the Sun's Sister looked so beautiful that he had not the heart to say her nay, and so he rashly promised. Then he took his leave reluctantly, and the moment he was outside the gate and could no more see the radiant face, his heart seemed ready to break with longing and sadness.

"Well, didn't I tell you you would get into mischief?" said Reynard, when he heard the story of Lars's exploits. "So now we shall have to rescue this Afterglow too. Well, that'll be no easy matter; and if you can't behave any better than you have done today, then there's really no use in our attempting it."

Lars had to coax and beg for a full hour, and promise that his behavior should be the very pink of propriety and discretion, if Reynard would only forgive him and help him in his next enterprise. Reynard held out long, but at last took pity on Lars and gave consent.

Day after day, and night after night, they traveled toward the far mountains in the west, and at last arrived at the castle of the Trolds.

"Now," said the fox, "I shall go in alone, and when I have induced the girl to follow me, I shall hand her over to you, and then you must rush away with her as fast as you can; and leave me to detain the Trolds by my tricks, until you are so far away that they can not overtake you."

Lars thought that was a capital plan, and stationed himself outside the gate while the fox slipped in. It was early evening, and it was almost dark; but there shot up a red blaze of light from all the windows of the castle of the Trolds. Reynard, who had been there many a time before, and was an old acquaintance of the Trolds, soon perceived that something unusual was going on. So far as he could see they were having a ball; and the Trolds were all taking turns at dancing with Afterglow—for she was the only girl in the whole company. When they saw the fox one of them cried out:

"Hallo, old Reynard, you have always been a light-footed fellow. Won't you come in and have a dance?"

"Thanks," said Reynard, "I am never loath to dance."

And he placed his paw upon his breast and made his bow to Afterglow, who was darker than her sister Dawn, and more serious, but scarcely less beautiful. She filled the heart of everyone who looked upon her, not with buoyant joy and hope,

Reynard made his bow to Afterglow.

but meditation and gentle sadness. She was sad herself, too, because she hated the ugly Trolds who held her in captivity, and longed to go back to the beautiful palace of her brother, the Sun. So when Reynard asked her to dance, she scarcely looked at him, but with a weary listlessness allowed him to put his arm about her waist and swing her about to the measure of the music. And Reynard was a fine dancer. Swiftly and more swiftly he gyrated about, and every time he passed a candle he managed to blow it out. One—two—three!—before anybody knew it, it was pitch dark in the hall; and before the Trolds had recovered from their astonishment, Reynard had danced out through the door into the hall, from the hall into the court-yard, and from the court-yard into the open field, outside the gate.

"Lars," he cried to the boy, "here is Afterglow. Now take her and hurry away as fast as you can."

Lars did not have to be told that twice; but taking Afterglow by the hand ran as fast as his feet could carry him.

Reynard instantly slipped in again and pretended to help the Trolds to light the candles. But it took him a long time to strike fire with the flint, because the tinder was damp, and if the Trolds had not been as stupid as they were, they would have seen that the fox was making them trouble instead of helping them. After a long while, however, they succeeded in getting the candles lighted, and then they perceived that Afterglow was gone.

"Where is Afterglow? Where is Afterglow?" they all roared in chorus, and some of them wept with anger, while others tore their beards and hair with rage.

"Oh, you sly old fox, it is you who have let her escape," shouted one great, fat, furious Trold, "but you shall suffer for it. Just let me get hold of you, and you sha'n't have another chance to play tricks again."

Instantly they all made a rush for Reynard, yelling and weeping, and stamping and threatening. But Reynard, as you know, is no easy customer to catch; and the Trolds were no match for him in running. He led them a dance over fields, and moors, and mountains, keeping just in front of them, so that they always supposed they were on the point of catching him, but yet eluding them by his agility and unexpected turns and leaps. He took good care to lay his course in the direction opposite to that which Lars and Afterglow had taken; and thus, the farther the Trolds ran, the slighter were their chances of recovering her. After a while, however, Reynard grew tired of this game, and then he remembered that there was a big swamp near by, and thither he hastened. But while he sprang lightly from hillock to hillock, the heavy Trolds in their wrath plunged ahead, and before they knew it, they sank down in the marsh up to their very waists. The more they struggled to get out, the deeper they settled in the mud; and a chorus of angry roars and shouts and hoarse yells rose from the floundering company in that swamp and swept across the sky like a fierce, discordant storm. But shouting did not do them any good. The night passed, and when the Dawn flushed the east, the fox, sitting on his hillock, called out:

"Look, there comes the Sun's Sister."

The Trolds, supposing it was Afterglow, turned with one accord toward the east, and instantly, as the first rays of the Dawn struck them, they turned into stone. For the Trolds only go abroad in the night, and can not endure the rays of the Sun. And the huge stones, vaguely retaining their shapes, can yet be seen in the marsh in Lapland where they perished.

Now, Reynard lost no time in seeking Lars and Afterglow, and toward evening he found their tracks, and before morning came he had overtaken them. When they arrived at the castle of the Sun they were received with great delight, and Dawn and Afterglow, after their long separation, kissed and embraced each other, and wept with joy. Now Lars was at liberty to take the golden hen and depart for the King's castle; but the trouble with him now was that he did not want to depart. He could not tear himself away from Dawn's radiant presence, but sat as one bewitched, staring into her lovely face. And so it came to pass that they were engaged, and Lars promised to come back and marry her, as soon as he had made his peace with his master the King, and presented him with the golden hen. Now, that seemed to Dawn a nice arrangement, and she let him depart. Lars invited his

Reynaud leads the Trolds into the marsh.

good friend Reynard to bear him company, but when they came to the place of their first meeting Reynard refused to go any farther. So Lars fell upon his neck, thanked him for his good service, and they embraced and kissed each other. The King received Lars pretty well, and was delighted to get the golden hen. But when he heard about the Sun's Sister, whom no one could look upon without being filled with gladness, his brow became clouded, and it was easy to see that he was much displeased. So he told Lars that, unless he brought the Sun's Sister instantly to the court and gave her as a bride to the young Prince, he would have to be burned in the barrel of tar after all. Now, that was the most unpleasant thing Lars had heard for a good while, and he wished he could have had the counsel of his good friend Reynard; for otherwise he saw no way out of the scrape. Then it occurred to him that the Sun had two sisters, and that possibly he might induce Afterglow to marry the Prince. He made haste accordingly to be off on his journey, and when he saw the tar-barrels being made ready on the hill-top behind the castle, he vowed that, unless he was successful in his errand, he would be in no haste to come back again. When he arrived at the palace of the Sun, Dawn was overjoyed to see him. But when he told his story and mentioned, in passing, the tar-barrel, then she was not quite so well pleased. However, she went to consult Afterglow; and Afterglow, after her experience with the ugly Trolds, was not at all averse to marrying a handsome young Prince. So she rode away on a splendid charger with Lars, and the Prince, when he heard she was coming, rode out to meet her, and even the old King himself vowed that he had never seen anyone so beautiful. He grew so gentle, and courteous, and affectionate as he looked at her, that he forgot all about his threats; and when Afterglow asked him what that great pile of tar-barrels was for, he felt quite ashamed of himself, and answered:

"Oh, I was going to burn a wretch there; but as I suppose you don't like the smell of burnt wretch on your wedding-day, I'll give orders to have it removed."

The next day the wedding was celebrated with great magnificence; and the feasting and the dancing and rejoicing lasted for an entire week. When it was all over, Lars asked the King's permission to go on a long journey. He had no fear of a refusal, for the King had become so nice and gentle, since his daughter-in-law came into the family, that even his best friends scarcely recognized him. So he readily granted Lars's request. With a light heart and bounding steps Lars went eastward, day after day, and night after night, until he came to the palace of the Sun. And there he celebrated his wedding with Dawn, and lived with joy ineffable in her sweet presence, until the end of his days. If he is not dead, he is probably living there yet.

First published in the March 1889 edition of *St. Nicholas Magazine*

BY GEORGE HUNTINGTON

STRANGE AS IT may seem, it all came from the children's wishing. Kate wished that she was pale and thin like Aunt Elsie, with black eyes and auburn hair, and fine sets of jewelry; and Bob wished that he was six feet and an inch high, with a big mustache turned up at the ends; and little Sue, peeping shyly at Uncle Simon, wished that he would tell them a story. And so he did; and waiting until they had seated themselves, he began:

"Once on a time—oh, let me see, haven't I ever told you the story about Jack Longshort, the boy that almost ruined himself by wishing?

"Of course he hadn't, for he was making it up at that very minute. But all the children cried as with one voice, "Oh, no, no, you haven't, Uncle Simon, indeed you haven't! What was it?"

So Uncle Simon began again, and this is the story that he told them:

Once upon a time there was a little baby boy whose name was Jack Longshort—not such a *little* baby, either. In fact, so large a baby that when the nurse put on Jack's very longest baby dress, Jack's toes stuck out beneath it, and the older he grew the taller he grew. At ten he was six feet high; at twelve he was seven feet and an inch. The boys at school called him "sky-scraper," and would ask him how the weather was up there. Every day he would measure himself by the end of the long pump-handle to see how much he had grown, and every day, when he found himself taller than he had been the day before, he would wish and wish

The boys called him "sky-scraper."

Jack and the pump.

and wish: "Dear, dear, if I could only stop growing! Oh, if I could only be shorter—I don't care how little."

"Don't you?" answered the old pump, one day. Jack was very glad to find some one to whom he could confide his troubles, even if it was the pump, for Jack was an orphan, and although he had not given up his nurse, he felt it beneath his dignity to be running to her with his troubles. He was too glad to feel any surprise at the pump's speaking, and he said hotly, "No, I don't. I would rather be knee-high to a grasshopper than as tall as the obelisk. I hate being tall!"

"Well, well," screamed out the pump, "you keep on wishing and maybe you'll get your wish some day."

And—would you believe it?—at last he did. He actually began *ungrowing*, as he delightedly called it-very slowly at first, so that nobody noticed it, then so very per- ceptibly that no one could help noticing it, and everybody predicted that he would surely pine away and die. But he didn't pine away. His health was all right, and he grew fatter as he grew shorter. At sixteen he was about as tall as other boys of his age, and felt very happy, for it was exactly what he had been wishing for. But, alas! it didn't stop there. That is the worst of ungrowing, you know: it is so apt to be car- ried too far. He kept getting shorter and shorter—four feet high, three feet, two, one—until he was no taller than the cat. And now, I can tell you, he changed his tune and began to wish he was tall again. Alack! wishing seemed to be of no avail. He might as well have wished for the moon.

But at last he came to take a more cheerful view of things, and as his parents had left him a small fortune, he engaged his old nurse as his housekeeper, hired her husband, Ben, as his body-servant, dressed in the height of fashion, bought a trained rabbit for a saddle-horse, and really began to enjoy himself again.

But still he kept on ungrowing. Soon he was only four inches high and had to exchange his rabbit for a squirrel. In a little while the squirrel was too large and he tried a white mouse. But when the white mouse proved too big he was in despair. "What *shall* I try now, Ben?" he asked.

Ben suggested a caterpillar, but Jack said there was no speed in that.

"A tree-toad?"

"Don't like his gait."

"Humming-bird?"

"Well—not so bad; rather too big and hard to break. But let's try one. A small one, mind, Ben, and one with a good disposition."

So Ben caught and tamed a humming-bird, and for several weeks Jack used it as a steed until the cold weather came and it had to go South. Then Jack tried a cricket, but he "bucked," as Ben said, "worse than a mule," and after one or two pretty hard falls Jack gave up riding altogether and let Ben carry him around in a silver card-receiver.

During all this time, you will remember, Jack had little trouble about getting along, for he had more money than he could spend. But one day Ben, who had charge of his business affairs, made some unfortunate investments with all Jack's money, and the poor little fellow, now only an inch and a sixteenth high, was thrown on the cold world without a penny.
What *could* he do?

Before the "unfortunate investments."

Well, he just became a tramp—a tiny tramp, living from hand to mouth like a vagabond pigmy in a world of giants. He was rather lonely, but he was a light-hearted little fellow, and as three crumbs a day were a sufficiency, he would not have complained if only he had not kept on ungrowing. He gradually decreased to half an inch in height, and though he was as lively as a cricket, he was as small as a fly, and dared not go upon the streets in the daytime for fear of being stepped on; so he wandered about on moonlight nights, keeping a sharp lockout for cracks and holes in the sidewalk and creeping under a door-step when he heard any one coming.

On one of these moonlight nights he came to a steamship dock, and immediately he caught the tourist fever and said, "I'll go abroad." No sooner said than done. It was dusk, and none of the watchers or officers could discern the midget moving in the dim light. He climbed up the long gang-plank, hopped to the deck, up the cabin stairs, found on a bread-plate on one of the dining-tables some nice crumbs for his supper, and, stretching himself in the folds of a curtain, went sound asleep, like the happy-go-lucky little stowaway that he was.

Well, this was the beginning of his travels. I couldn't begin to tell you all his adventures: how he was a dreadfully seasick, poor little half-inch of humanity; how he got better and had ever so much fun on the ship; how he reached England, and visited all the museums and libraries and cathedrals and palaces, both there and on the Continent, without the bother of fees or tickets; for where was the need of

Jack "tries" a cricket.

those things to a manikin who could squeeze through a keyhole or crawl through the crack under a door.

And still, in all his journeyings over Europe, Asia, and Africa, in regions which no civilized man had ever reached, and on islands not down on any map or chart, on ships, on railroads, in carriages and on donkeys, on sea-gulls and on chips—still he kept on ungrowing. At last he was no bigger than a mosquito. Now he could creep into ant-holes and walk along the causeways made by the seams in the rocks; he could climb among exquisite crystals and tiny grams of sand that seemed to him as big as boulders, and sit by the side of beautiful rivers and cascades made by trickling water-drops. And then such wonderful things he saw—things not to be seen by the great coarse human eye. Oh, nobody knows what marvels may be seen by a little fellow scarcely bigger than the head of a pin.

At last, one winter, while seeking a good, warm, comfortable place in which to spend the cold months, and when he was merely a tiny brown speck which only a pair of sharp eyes could see at all, he found a delightful berth in the house of Professor von Opticon, the great naturalist. The professor had a fine microscope and made a special study of curious objects, with all of which Jack, of course, was familiar, as he had traveled among them and could see perfectly well with his little eyes.

"To think," sighed Jack, "that I know almost as much as he does, and yet the more I know the worse off I am. Oh, if I was only bigger!"

Now Professor von Opticon had a pretty daughter named Stella, who took care of his laboratory and cabinets, and assisted him in his studies.

One day, as Jack was lazily lounging on the blank slide under the microscope, Stella came in to put things in order for a meeting of the Coleoptological Society, which was to meet with her father that afternoon. As she was dusting the table, she casually stooped down and looked through the tube. Jack was exactly in focus.

"Mercy on us!" she cried. "What's that? Oh, father, father, here's a microscopic *man!*"

The professor was wonderfully excited. "What a—what a thing to show the society!" he exclaimed. "It will make me famous."

Jack enjoyed the fun immensely. He was too spry for them to catch him, and as they couldn't risk killing him or losing him, they gave up trying to catch him and took turns watching at the microscope until the Coleoptological Society assembled.

And how surprised the society was when the professor and his daughter exhibited their prize! They congratulated themselves also on their good fortune, and voted to change the name of the society to the "anthropocoleoptological" or man-beetle society, and to make Jack an honorary member.

And you may be sure Jack did his best to make the subject interesting. He lay down; he stood on his head; he walked; he danced; he turned somersaults; he gave three cheers; and at last, hopping to the inkstand and dipping his forefinger in the ink, he came back and wrote on the slide, in a good round hand and in letters the ten-thousandth of an inch high, his own name: JACK LONGSHORT.

The society was charmed. They studied and discussed poor Jack at meeting after meeting; wrote essays and learned books about him; and from that time he never lacked friends. But Stella was his best friend. The very first thing she asked him after the society's members had gone was what she could do for him.

Jack only wrote upon the glass the words, "Make me grow."

He could not have asked anything much harder. But Stella thought and thought. Suddenly an idea struck her. "I'll try father's X-ray apparatus," said she.

It was just the thing. The moment the X-rays struck him, Jack felt in his bones it was going to do him good. And it did. In a week he could be seen with the naked eye. In six he was as big as a yellow wasp. In three months he was the size of a canary-bird. And, not to make a too "long short" story, in two years from the time Stella found him under the microscope he was half a head taller than the professor himself. But he had had quite enough of growing and ungrowing. All this shrinking and stretching had worn on him terribly, but he was cheerful and happy. He found Ben, who had more than made up the losses in his unfortunate investments, and who had accumulated quite a fortune, awaiting the return of his master. Ben was delighted at seeing him, and proud to make so good an account of his stewardship.

Jack settled down to make the best of what time he had left, only regretting that he had wasted his life wishing himself into trouble and then wishing himself out again. And when he tells his singular story to the children, this is the little moral he adds to it: "Be contented, be thankful, and be yourself. Don't try to stretch yourself or shrink yourself or wriggle yourself into something else. And whether you are tall or short, thick or thin, you will be sure to find a place in the world that is of just the right size for you."

First published in the February 1904 edition of *St. Nicholas Magazine*

The Troubles of Queen Silver-bell

As Told by Queen Crosspatch

BY FRANCES HODGSON BURNETT

ILLUSTRATIONS BY HARRISON CADY

I AM A FAIRY. Now I won't be contradicted; there are such things as Fairies. I am one myself and have been one ever since the beginning of the world. What is more, I am the Queen of the Fairies. I am the Queen of millions and millions and millions and millions of lovely little people, as beautiful as flowers and butterflies. They can do all the things people want to have done, and find all the things that are lost, and turn pumpkins into golden coachmen, and anything into anything else that is nicer, and *yet* as the years have gone on, until it isn't "Once upon a Time" any more, people have grown so stupid that they don't *believe* in us; and they are so blind they cannot see us even when we are dancing before them, and they cannot hear us, even when we are singing and singing to them songs like this:

> *Why can't you see? Oh! if you knew*
> *Fairies are real—Fairies are true.*
> *Fairies are here—Fairies are there*
> *Fairies are waiting everywhere,*
> *In the house and in the street,*
> *On your shoulder, at your feet,*
> *By your fire and on your book,*
> *If you only had the sense to look.*
> *Why can't you see? Oh! if you knew*
> *Fairies are real—Fairies are true.*

But you cannot make people *believe* it. Even children don't. That is what is the matter with everything. People will believe in nasty things and they won't believe in nice things, and that has been going on so long that my great fear is that the Fairies themselves will forget their accomplishments, and then what will become of

Fairyland? Rumors have come to my palace of Fairies who were not even able to change themselves into rabbits when it was *very* important indeed, and I heard of one Fairy who was trying to turn a naughty little boy into a pussycat because he was pulling a kitten's tail, and she only got as far as the miaw and the claws and she forgot how to do the rest, and he ran away mi-a-owing and scratching his face with his sharp claws when he tried to rub his eyes because he was crying. But he could only cry like a cat—and it served him right. But it upset me very much to hear of it. If that sort of thing goes on, Fairies will be as ignorant as human beings and Fairyland will go to ruin. And I won't have it. I used to be called Queen Silver-Bell until lately—until the misfortune happened I am going to tell you about. I was called Queen Silver-Bell because I was always laughing in those good old days when it was "Once upon a Time." And all the Fairies said my laugh sounded just like tiny silver bells, tinkle—tinkle—tinkling. But now I am called Queen Crosspatch because I scold and scold and scold-and it all happened in this way:

You see, the most important thing in the world—whether you are a Fairy, or a little boy or a little girl, is never—never—never—never to lose your Temper. Most people don't know that a Temper is really a Fairy, and as long as you can keep him he is the cleverest and the delightfulest Fairy of all. He is always laughing and doing lovely things. He has little golden and silver shovels to dig dimples in your face and make you so pretty that people adore you and want to give you things and take you to the circus and the pantomime and to Christmas parties and sights and treats, and he has a tiny gold and pearl and ruby paint box full of the most heavenly colors, and tiny brushes to paint everything so that it looks beautiful and delightful, and he whispers songs and stories in your ear and makes you enjoy yourself and laugh all the time. *But* the minute he gets away and you lose him, he turns into a tiny black Imp Fairy and pinches and kicks you and tells lies to you and whispers ugly things to you until you are perfectly mizz'able and make everybody else mizz'able too. I had a lovely little Temper. There never was a cleverer one or

Temper

a prettier one. He was tiny and rosy and his face was pink and full of dimples, and I perfectly loved him. I always kept him in a tiny silver cage, or fastened to my waist by a diamond chain. I had nothing else I was as fond of and I would not have parted with him for anything. I can scarcely bear to think of him now he is gone.

One day I was in a garden where a lady was talking to a little girl. I had been sitting on roses and swinging on lilies and dancing on the very flowers they were gathering and doing everything to attract their attention. But I could not make them look at me and I began to forget I was carrying the tiny silver cage with my darling little Temper in it, and suddenly the lady said to the little girl:

"Do you like stories about Fairies?"

When I heard that, it quite cheered me up, and I jumped on to the edge of a flower and began to sing:

> *"Silver-Bell, Queen Silver-Bell!*
> *What you want to know she can always tell*
> *If you only believe in Silver-Bell."*

And what do you suppose that child said? She opened her silly blue eyes and stared like a sheep and answered:

"What is a Fairy?"

I just jumped down and screamed. I stamped my feet and shook my fist, and my golden floss silk hair flew all about, and the silver cage flew out of my hand and the door flew open and my darling little Temper burst out and darted away. And his pink face and his dimples and his silky curls and his dancing blue eyes and his tiny coat all sparkling with jewels were gone and he was changed into a vicious, ugly, black, thin little Imp with squinting steel-colored eyes it made me ill to look at.

I rushed after him as hard as I could. He hid himself in a red nasturtium and the minute I got near him he darted into a rose bush and the thorns tore his horrid little black clothes into rags and tatters but he only grinned and made faces at me; and then he ran across the lawn and into the park and jumped on to a fawn's back and it was so frightened by the horrid little thing that it galloped and galloped away, and I after it, and then he climbed an oak tree and swung on a big leaf making faces and I kept getting crosser and crosser and hotter and hotter and I began to call out:

> *"If you'll stop I'll give you a golden cage,*
> *If you'll stop I'll give you a richer wage."*

And then because I had lost my Temper, I couldn't stop, myself, and I called out:

> *"If you stop I'll give you a crack on the head."*

And he just turned round and grinned and grinned and put his tiny black thumb at the end of his tiny black nose in the most rude way imaginable and shouted back at me:

"That's not so easily done as said,
Crosspatch; Crosspatch; Crosspatch."

He jumped onto the fawn's back.

And just that second a skylark flew up out of the grass and he swung out on a leaf and sprang on to his back and was carried up and up and up and up—higher and higher and higher and higher into the very sky itself and I knew I had lost him, perhaps forever, and I flopped down on a buttercup and cried and scolded and scolded and cried as hard as ever I could. And the worst of it was that I couldn't stop scolding. When you have lost a darling sweet little Temper you can't stop. I was cross every minute and I frowned and scowled so that my face was all over wrinkles.

I scolded the grass and I scolded the flowers,
I scolded the sun and I scolded the showers,
I scolded the castles, I scolded the towers,
And I scolded the Fairies for hours and hours.
When I went to my Palace I scolded the pages,
When I sat on my throne I went into rages.
I scolded the birds as they sang in their cages,
I was afraid I should scold on for ages and ages.
The hens that were Fairies forgot how to hatch,
The Fishermen Fairies forgot how to catch,
And the little Boy Fairies all in a batch
Called after me everywhere, "Queen Crosspatch!"

That was what happened. And I should like to know if you can think of anything worse? I can't. And the very worst of it was that I knew I should never find my sweet, dear little pink Temper again, until I had done something that would make people—particularly children—believe in Fairies as they used to "Once upon a Time," and save my dear Fairyland from going to ruin and melting away. If you don't believe in things they melt away. That's what happens to them. They just *melt away*. And so many things are like the little Pig who wouldn't go over the bridge—and I knew that if I could make the children believe, the believing children would make the Fairies begin to practice turning things into something nicer, and if the Fairies began to practice turning things into something nicer, Fairyland would be saved and not go to ruin, and if Fairyland was saved and did not go to ruin, I should find my dear sweet, dimpled, pink little Temper again, and if I found my dear, sweet, dimpled, pink little Temper again, I should not be Queen Crosspatch any more but Queen Silver-bell and laugh and laugh and laugh and laugh until the other Fairies would say my laughing sounded like tiny bells of silver, tinkle—tinkle—tinkling, and everything would be lovely forever more. I wondered and wondered what I should do, and then I wondered and wondered again, and after I had wondered and wondered three times, I made up my mind that I would sit down under my hair. Of course I see you don't know what that means. Well, it means something very important. All Fairies have long, long hair—sometimes it is gold color, sometimes it is squirrel color, and sometimes it is as black as black velvet, but it is always as fine as floss silk and can either be tucked up in a knot or hidden under a pearl cap, or allowed to float and dance about—or hide you altogether if you want to be hidden. And if you want to *think*, the best thing in the world is

She shook out her hair.

to sit on the floor and shake down your hair so that it falls down to the floor, and makes a little tent all around you. I always do it when anything important is on my mind. So this time I sat down on a scarlet toadstool spotted with black, and put my head on my knees, and shook out my hair into a tent which covered me all over so that nothing but the tips of my golden shoes stuck out.

And then I sat and sat and sat, and I thought and thought and thought. And suddenly I remembered the Dormouse. Of course there was no use *my* thinking, when I could go to the Dormouse.

The Dormouse knows more than the King. Every year, when the weather grows cold, the Dormouse rolls himself into a ball and he takes his hind legs and he tucks them round his ears and he doesn't move until the Spring comes. So the people think he is asleep. But he is not asleep. He is *thinking* all the time. He can think better and faster when he is rolled up and his hind legs are tucked over his ears. Perhaps everybody could. But no one ever tries it.

He thinks of beans and he thinks of peas
He thinks of bread and he thinks of cheese
He thinks of raisins and nuts and figs
He thinks of elephants and pigs
He thinks of girls and he thinks of boys
He thinks of things that make a noise
He thinks of mice that run up-stairs
He thinks of rabbits and of hares.
He thinks cats should be taught to dance
And ferrets should be sent to France;
He thinks of cakes and steaks and chops—
He thinks for months and never stops.

And of course he is the best person to go to for advice. So I danced over a meadow and flew over a garden and floated over a lake and went

Dancing over the meadow.

to the Lord High Chief Dormouse of all the Dormice, who was rolled up for the winter in a warm nest at the root of a tree at the lakeside.

Then I picked up five round white pebbles and a shell and threw them one after another at his door.

When I threw the first pebble I said:
"This one has shaken you,"
When I threw the second I said:
"This is to waken you if you have fallen asleep,"
When I threw the third I said:
"This is to call you,"
And when I threw the fourth I said:
"This is to maul you till your eyes begin to peep."
And then I threw the fifth stone and the shell, and said quite crossly;

"Dormouse, come out of your house
Don't be proud and stiff.
Dormouse, come out of your house
Or we shall have a tiff."

And then I heard him begin to grumble and to rumble and to tumble, until he tumbled out of his house and began to unroll himself out of his ball and gradually stood up on his hind legs and laid both his hands at the front of his belt and made a polite and graceful bow.

"Your Royal Highness Queen Silver-patch," he said, "What do you want?"

He was a very polite Dormouse and he was beginning to call me Queen Silver-bell because we had been friends before I lost my darling little pink, dimpled Temper, but suddenly he remembered my new name was Queen Cross-patch so he called me Queen Silver-patch and I really liked it better.

"Can you spare me an hour from your winter thinking?" I said. "I want to ask your advice because you are so clever."

He was quite pleased and he smiled and pulled down his belt and his mouth curled up at the corners.

"Well, of course," he said, "you are very complimentary, but when a person tucks his hind legs over his ears and thinks for six months he must think something."

"Of course," I said, and I looked at him in my sweetest way and smiled. "That is why I have brought my troubles to you."

"Dear! Dear!" he said, "and a Queen too." And he sat down by me and took hold of my hand and patted it. "What a darling teensy, teenty, weenty hand!" he said, and he gave it a squeeze.

The Dormouse squeezes her teensy, teenty, weenty hand!

"Oh! if you will help me!" I said, looking at him as if he was the only Dormouse in the world.

"I will, I will," he answered and he began to settle his collar quite as if he was delighted.

And so I told him the whole story from beginning to end: how things had got worse and worse until it seemed as if Fairyland would fall to ruin and melt away, and all my Fairies would melt away because no one believed in them, and I should melt away myself if something could not be done. And I made it as bad as ever I could because I wanted to make him feel sorry and frightened.

"Well, well, well!" he said, when I had finished, and he held his chin in his hand and smoothed it. "How very profoundly interesting!"

"But you will think of a plan to help me?" I

said, and this time I gave *his* hand—or rather his paw—a squeeze. He quite started and he quite blushed. In fact I was quite sure that his paw had never been squeezed even by a common Fairy and I was a Queen, which made it much grander.

"Yes, Queen Silver-bell-patch," he said, "I really must think of a plan," and he looked embarrassed and coughed and hemmed and hawed.

"What is the matter?" I asked.

"Er—would you—er—mind—er—if I roll myself up in a ball for a few minutes and tuck my hind legs over my ears. I can think so much better that way. It is not—er—becoming—but it is—er—useful."

"Oh, do roll yourself up in a ball and tuck your hind legs over your ears!" I said. "You are mistaken about its not being becoming. It makes you look so intellectual!"

The Dormouse rolled up into a ball.

He rolled himself up like lightning—just like lightning. I never could have believed any one could roll themselves up in a ball so quickly! My Goodness Gracious! It was just like lightning—like forked lightning! And I sat on the edge of a fern leaf and waited. I think he wanted me to see how intellectual he looked, until I should be likely to remember it, for he stayed rolled up in a ball for a long time. I didn't think much of his looks myself; I must say that I would not have let him know that for the world.

At last he began to unroll. He untucked his hind legs and he untucked his front legs and he unrolled his back. Then he just gave a jump and stood on his hind legs again and made his bow, blushing and blushing.

"Did I look very intellectual?" he said.

"I shall never forget it—never," I said, "I shall think of it and think of it and think of it." And then I said in a very soft voice, "Did you find a plan?"

"Yes," he said, smiling so that his mouth spread from one ear to the other and his eyes squinched up into nothing. "I thought of a very splendid plan."

"Oh! I knew you would because you are so clever. What is it?"

"It is this," he said. "Can you write a book?"

"Certainly," I answered. "I have never written one, but of course I can if I try."

Then he rubbed his chin and looked at me out of the corners of his eyes in a very queer way.

"You are not a timid person, are you?" he said.

"No," I replied. "I am not. Besides, if I have not written books myself, I have taught other people to write them. I know a Respectable Person—*quite* a Respectable Person. She sits in a garden full of roses and any number of birds call on her and she writes books for a living, and she learned it all from me. She was apprenticed to me the minute she was born and with my help she has made quite a decent living and earned any number of roses and all sorts of flowers. And when she writes I just sit on her shoulder and whisper to her. She is really my A—manu—en—sis. Do you know what that means? It's a long word. If it's too long for you I'll explain it."

"It's a leetle too long," the Dormouse said, "though not much."

"It means a person who writes what you order him to write."

The Dormouse clapped his paws together.

"Why, that's the very thing!" he said. "You see, just now I thought in the front of my head and I thought in the back of my head and when I was thinking in the back of my head I suddenly remembered that when people who are not Fairies want to persuade any one to believe in anything they always write books about it. They write books about Lions, and books about Tigers, they write books about Africa and books about America; and why should you not write books about Fairies and Fairyland and the things the Fairies do? I once lined my nest with a leaf out of a book about Dormice—though I couldn't say I slept well that winter." He put out his paw and tapped me on the shoulder several times.

"You go to that Aman-man-sis creature of yours," he said (he couldn't pronounce the word), "and make her write thousands of books about what the Fairies are doing and about how much more sense they have than people who are just People."

"It's an excellent idea," I said.

Just for a moment he looked anxious.

"Can she spell?" he said. "You see there are quite a lot of people who will have spelling."

"I don't know whether she can spell or not," I answered. "But when I go to see her I will ask her and tell her she must speak the truth about it because I can't have my books spoiled just because of bad spelling. I must have Good Spelling. That is all she has to do with the matter; just to *spell* and I will do the rest."

"How do you know she is respectable?" asked the dormouse.

"Well, I know she is because you see she was apprenticed to me and I brought her up properly. She knows about Fairies quite well and because she knows about Fairies, Animals will associate with her, and flowers. She has a pony called Amoret and some great big horses, and when she goes into the stable in the morning they all turn round and speak to her quite as if she was an equal, besides rubbing their warm velvet noses against her. She lives in a house with a park round it and when she goes and stands on the big stone steps and calls out, 'Thistle, Thistle,' her pet donkey lifts up his head and walks slowly across the grass to her and even walks up a stone step or two just to engage in confidential conversation. No donkey would be as intimate as that with a Disrespectable person. Animals are very aristocratic. Any number of birds know her as if they had played together in their cradles, and she has a robin who follows her about the garden and is perfectly jealous of her. He flies from one tree to another and chirps

"Can she spell?"

as loud as he can to try to drown the head gardener's voice when she is talking to him. Oh, yes! she's Respectable! I wish I was as sure of her spelling as I am of her respectability."

"Well," said the Dormouse, "if, when you ask her about it, you say that you don't want to frighten her, but she *must* speak the *entire* truth about it, everything may be all right."

"There's one good thing about her," I said. "She is a Person who knows her place and keeps it. She won't be pushing and pretend she wrote the stories herself. I will explain to her that she must let every one know that I am the real author. Of course they *are* my stories and no one else's!" And just at these last words I began to be a little cross and scolding again. I knew it by the hasty way in which the Dormouse began to step backward.

"Of course! Of course! Your Royal Patch-bell-ness!" he said hurriedly. "And if you write them of course every child with any sense will understand it, and if they read story after story written by a real Fairy they will begin to believe, and if they

He flies from one tree to another,
and sings as loud as he can.

begin to believe, the other Fairies will begin to practice turning themselves into rabbits and guinea pigs and all sorts of nice things, and if the other Fairies begin to practice turning themselves into rabbits and guinea pigs and all sorts of nice things, Fairyland will be saved and will not go to ruin, and if Fairyland is saved and does not go to ruin, you will find your sweet little, pink little, plump little, dimpled little Temper again, and if you find your sweet little, pink little, plump little, dimpled little Temper again, you will not be called Queen Crosspatch but Queen Silver-bell and you will laugh and laugh and laugh until all the other Fairies think they hear tiny bells made of silver, tinkle—tinkle—tinkling, and everything will be lovely forever and evermore."

The thought of that pleased me so much that I forgot I had begun to feel cross and scolding and I jumped up and squeezed the Dormouse's paw until he blushed crimson scarlet. Then I made him a deep curtsey and walked away backward just as courtiers walk backward away from the King when they have been talking to him. And I said in my politest way:

> *"Oh, I thank you Lord High Dormouse!*
> *I thank you very much—*
> *In Spanish, French and German,*
> *In Danish and in Dutch."*

And then I whirled round and flew away as fast as I could to find the Respectable Person and ask her if she could spell, and to explain things to her.

When you see a story by me you will always see a picture of me hidden away somewhere and you had better look for it. One thing is certain, that though you may have heard of Fairies you have never read stories written by a real one. And that is what is going to happen to you.

First published in the October 1906 edition of *St. Nicholas Magazine*

The Cozy Lion

As Told by Queen Crosspatch

BY FRANCES HODGSON BURNETT

ILLUSTRATIONS BY HARRISON CADY

PART ONE

I AM VERY fond of this story of the Cozy Lion because I consider it a great credit to me. I reformed that Lion and taught him how to behave himself. The grown-up person who reads this story aloud to children *must* know how to Roar.

I shall never forget the scolding I gave him to begin with. One of the advantages of being a Fairy—even quite a common one—is that Lions can't bite you. A Fairy is too little and too light. If they snap at you it's easy to fly through their mouths, and even if they catch you, if you just get behind their teeth you can make them so uncomfortable that they will *beg* you to get out and leave them in peace.

Of course it was all the Lion's fault that I scolded him. Lions ought to live far away from people. Nobody likes Lions roaming about—particularly where there are children. But this Lion said he wanted to get into Society, and that he was very fond of children—little fat ones between three and four. So instead of living on a desert, or in a deep forest or a jungle, he took the large Cave on the Huge Green Hill, only a few miles from a village full of the fattest, rosiest little children you ever saw.

He had only been living in the Cave a few days, but even in that short time the mothers and fathers had found out he was there, and everybody who could afford it had bought a gun and snatched it up even if they saw a donkey coming down the road, because they were afraid it might turn out to be a Lion. As for the mothers, they were nearly crazy with fright and dare not let their children go out to play and had to shut them up in top rooms and cupboards and cellars, they were so afraid the Lion might be hiding behind trees to jump out at them. So everything was beginning to be quite spoiled because nobody could have any fun.

Of course if they had had any sense and believed in Fairies and had just gone out some moonlight night and all joined hands and danced slowly around in a circle and sung:

If they saw a donkey coming down the road they were afraid it might turn out to be a lion!

Fairies pink and Fairies rose,
Fairies dancing on pearly toes,
We want you, Oh! we want you!
Fairy Queens and Fairy slaves
Who are not afraid of Lions' Caves
Please to come to help us,

then it would have been all right, because we should have come in millions. Especially if they had finished with this verse:

Our troubles we can never tell,
But if you would come it would all
be well,
Par-tic-u-lar-ly Silver-Bell.

But they hadn't sense enough for that—of course they hadn't—*of course they hadn't!* Which shows what loonies some people are.

But you see I am much nicer than *un*-fairy persons, even if I have lost my nice little, pink little, sweet little Temper and if I *am* cross. So when I saw the children fretting and growing pale because they had to be shut up, and the mothers crying into their washtubs when they were washing, until the water slopped over, I made up my mind I would go and talk to that Lion myself in a way he wouldn't soon forget.

It was a beautiful morning, and the Huge Green Hill looked lovely. A shepherd who saw me thought I was a gold and purple butter-fly and threw his hat at me—the idiot! Of course he fell down on his nose—and very right and proper too.

When I got to the Cave, the Lion was sitting outside his door and he was crying. He was one of those nasty-tempered, discontented Lions who are always thinking themselves injured; large round tears were rolling down his nose and he was sniffling. But I must say he was handsome. He was big and smooth and had the most splendid mane and tail I ever saw. He would have been like a King if he had had a nicer expression. But there he sat sniffling.

"I'm so lonely," he said. "Nobody calls. Nobody pays me any attention. And I came here for the Society. No one is fonder of Society than I am."

I sat down on a flowering branch near him and shouted at him, "What's the use of Society when you eat it up?" I said.

He jumped up and lashed his tail and growled, but at first he could not see me.

"What's it for *but* to be eaten up?" he roared. "First I want it to entertain me and then I want it for dessert. Where are you? Who are you?"

"I am Queen Crosspatch—Queen Silver-Bell as was," I said. "I suppose you have heard of *me?*"

"I've heard nothing good," he growled. "A good chewing is what *you* want!"

He *had* heard something about me, but not enough. The truth was he didn't really believe in Fairies—which was what brought him into trouble.

By this time he had seen me and he was ignorant enough to think that he could catch me, so he lay down flat in the thick

The Lion was sitting outside his cave door, and he was crying.

green grass and stretched his big paws out and rested his nose on them thinking I would be taken in and imagine he was going to sleep. I burst out laughing at him and swung to and fro on my flowery branch.

"Do you want to eat me?" I said. "You'd need two or three quarts of me with sugar and cream—like strawberries."

He jumped up and ashed his tail.

That made him so angry that he sprang roaring at my tree and snapped and shook it and tore it with his claws. But I flew up into the air and buzzed all about him and he got furious—just furious. He jumped up in the air and lashed his tail and *thrashed* his tail and CRASHED his tail, and he turned round and round and tore up the grass.

"Don't be a silly," I said. "It's a nice big tufty sort of tail and you will only wear it out."

So then he opened his mouth and roared and roared. And what do you suppose *I* did? I flew right into his mouth. First I flew into his throat and buzzed about like a bee and made him cough and cough and cough—but he couldn't cough *me* up. He coughed and he houghed and he woughed; he tried to catch me with his tongue and he tried to catch me with his teeth but I simply made myself tinier and tinier and got between two big fierce white double ones and took one of my Fairy Workers' hammers out of my pocket and hammered and hammered and hammered until he began to have such a jumping toothache that he ran leaping and roaring down the Huge Green Hill and leaping and roaring down the village street to the dentist's to get some toothache drops.

You can just imagine how all the people rushed into their houses, and how the mothers screamed and clutched their children and hid under beds and tables and in coal bins, and how the fathers fumbled about for guns. As for the dentist, he locked his door and bolted it and barred it, and when he found *his* gun he poked it out of the window and fired it off as fast as ever he could until he had fired fifty times, only he was too frightened to hit anything. But the village street was so full of flashes and smoke and bullets that Mr. Lion turned with ten big roars and galloped down the street, with guns fired out of every window where the family could afford to keep a gun.

When he got to his home in the Huge Green Hill, he just laid down and cried aloud and screamed and kicked his hind legs until he scratched a hole in the floor of his cave.

"Just because I'm a Lion," he sobbed, "just because I'm a poor, sensitive, helpless orphan Lion nobody has one particle of manners. They won't even sell me a bottle of toothache drops. And I wasn't going to touch that dentist—until he had cured me and wrapped up the bottle nicely in paper. Not a touch was I going to touch him until he had done that."

Too frightened to hit anything

He opened his mouth so wide to roar with grief that I flew out of it. I had meant to give him a lesson and I'd given him one. When I flew out of his mouth of course his beautiful double teeth stopped aching. It was such a relief to him that it made quite a change in his nature and he sat up and began to smile. It was a slow smile which spread into a grin even while the teardrops hung on his whiskers.

"My word! How nice," he said. "It's stopped."

I had flown to the top of his ear and I shouted down it.

"I stopped it," I said. "And I began it. And if you don't behave yourself, I'll give you earache and that will be worse."

Before I had given him his lesson he would have jumped at me but now he knew better. He tried to touch my feelings and make me sorry for him. He put one paw before his eyes and began to sniff again.

"I am a poor sensitive, lonely orphan Lion," he said.

"You are nothing of the sort," I answered very sharply. "You are not poor, and goodness knows you are not sensitive, and you needn't be lonely. I don't know whether you are an orphan or not—and I don't care. You are a nasty, ill-tempered, selfish, biting, chewing thing."

"There's a prejudice against Lions," he wept. "People don't like them. They never

"I am a poor sensitive, lonely orphan."

invite them to children's parties—nice little fat, tender, children's parties—where they would enjoy themselves so much—and the refreshments would be just what they like best. They don't even invite them to grown-up parties. What I want to ask you is this: has *one* of those villagers called on me since I came here—even a tough one?"

"Nice stupids they would be if they did," I answered.

He lifted up his right paw and shook his head from side to side in the most mournful way.

"There," he said, "you are just as selfish as the rest. Everybody is selfish. There is no brotherly love or consideration in the world. Sometimes I can scarcely bear it. I am going to ask you another question, and it is almost like a riddle. Who did you ever see try to give pleasure to a Lion?"

I got into his ear then and shouted down it as loud as ever I could.

"Who did you ever see a *Lion* try to give pleasure to?" I said. "You just think over that. And when you find the answer, tell it to *me*."

I don't know whether it was the newness of the idea, or the suddenness of it, but he turned pale. Did you ever see a lion turn pale? I never did before and it was funny. You know people's skins turn pale but a Lion's skin is covered with hair and you can't see it, so his hair has to turn pale or else you would never know he was turning pale at all. This Lion's hair was a beautiful tawny golden color to begin with and first his whiskers turned white and then his big mane and then his paws and then his body, and last his long, splendid tail with the huge fluffy tuft on the end of it. Then he stood up and his tail hung down and he said weakly:

"I do not know the answer to that riddle. I will go and lie down in my Cave. I do not believe I have one friend in this world." And he walked into his Cave and lay down and sobbed bitterly.

He forgot I was inside his ear and that he carried me with him. But I can tell you I *had* given him something to think of and that was what he needed. This way of feeling that nothing in the World but a Lion has a right to be comfortable—just because you happen to be a Lion yourself—is *too* silly for anything.

I flew outside his ear and boxed it a little.

"Come!" I said. "Crying won't do you any good. Are you really lonely—really—really—really—so that it gives you a hollow feeling?"

"I do not know the answer to that riddle."

He sat up and shook his tears away so they splashed all about—something like rain.

"Yes," he answered, "to tell the truth I am—I *do* like Society. I want friends and neighbors—and I don't only want them for dessert. I am a sociable Lion and I am affectionate in my nature-and clinging. And people run as fast as they can the moment they hear my voice." And he quite choked with the lump in his throat.

"Well," I snapped, "what else do you expect?" That overcame him and he broke into another sob.

"I expect kindness," he said, "and invitations to afternoon teas—and g-g-garden parties"—

"Well you won't get them," I interrupted, "if you don't change your ways. If you *eat* afternoon teas and garden parties as though they were lettuce sandwiches, you can't expect to be invited to them. So you may as well go back to the desert or the jungle and live with Lions and give up Society altogether."

"But ever since I was a little tiny Lion—a tiny, tiny one—I have wanted to get into Society. I *will* change—I will! Just tell me what to do. And do sit on my ear and talk down it and stroke it. It feels so comfortable and friendly."

You see he had forgotten that he had meant to chew me up. So I began to give him advice.

"The first things you will have to do will be to change your temper and your heart and your diet, and stop growling and roaring when you are not pleased."

"I'll do that, I'll do that," he said ever so quickly. "You don't want me to cut my mane and tail off, do you?"

"No. You are a handsome Lion and beauty is much admired." Then I snuggled quite close up to his ear and said down it, "Did you ever think how *nice* a Lion would be if—if he were much nicer?"

"N-no," he faltered.

"Did you ever think how like a great big cozy lovely dog you are? And how nice your big fluffy mane would be for little girls and boys to cuddle in, and how they could play with you and pat you and hug you and go to sleep with their heads on your shoulder and love you and adore you—if you only lived on breakfast foods and things—and had a really sweet disposition?"

Kindness and afternoon teas would have made the Cozy Lion happy.

He must have been rather a nice Lion because that minute he began to look "kind of smiley round the mouth and teary round the lashes"—which is part of a piece of poetry I once read.

"Oh ! Aunt Maria!" he exclaimed a little slangily. "I never thought of that: it *would* be nice."

"A Lion could be the coziest thing in the world—if he would," I went on.

He jumped up in the air and danced and kicked his hind legs for joy.

"Could he! Could he! Could he?" he shouted out. "Oh ! let me be a Cozy Lion! Let me be a Cozy Lion! Hooray! Hooray! Hooray! I would like it better than being invited to Buckingham Palace!"

"Little children would just *flock* to see you and play with you," I said. "And then if they came, their mothers and fathers couldn't be kept away. They would flock too."

The smile of joy that spread over his face actually reached his ears and almost shook me off.

"That *would* be Society!" he grinned.

"The very best!" I answered. "Children who are *real* darlings and not imitations come first, and then mothers and fathers—the rest just straggle along anywhere."

"When could it begin? When could it begin?" he panted out.

"Not," I said very firmly, "until you have tried some Breakfast Food!"

"Where shall I get it? Oh! Where? Oh! Where?"

"*I* will get it, of course," was my answer.

Then I stood up on the very tip of his ear and put my tiny golden trumpet to my lips. (And Oh! how that Lion did roll up his eyes to try to catch a glimpse of me!) And I played this tune to call my Fairy Workers.

*"Little children would just flock to
see you and play with you."*

*I'm calling from the Huge Green Hill
Tira-lira-lira,
The Lion's Cave is cool and still,
Tira-lira-lira.
The Lion wishes to improve
And show he's filled with tender love
And NOT with Next Door Neighbor.
The Lion wishes to be good,
To fill him FULL of Breakfast Food
Will aid him in his labor.
Bring Breakfast Food from far and near
—He'll eat a dreadful lot, I fear.
Oh! Tira-lira-lira-la
And Tira-lira-ladi.
A Lion learning to be good
Needs Everybody's Breakfast Food.
You workers bring it—Tira-la
And Tira-lira-ladi.*

Then the Fairy Workers came flying in clouds. In three minutes and three quarters they were swarming all over the Huge Green Hill and into the Lion's Cave, every one of them with a little sack on his green back. They swarmed here and they swarmed there. Some were cooks and brought tiny pots and kettles and stoves and they began to cook Breakfast Foods as fast as lightning. The Lion sat up. (I forgot to say that he had turned *un*-pale long before this and was the right color again.) And his mouth fell wide open, just with surprise and amazement. What amazed him most was that not one out of all these thousands of little Workers in their green caps and smocks was the least bit afraid of him. Why, what do you think! My little Skip just jumped up and stood on the end of the Lion's nose while he asked me a question. You never saw anything as funny as that Lion looking down the bridge of his nose at him until he squinted awfully. He was so interested in him.

"Does he take it with sugar and cream, your Royal Silver-cross-bell-ness?" Skip asked me, taking off his green cap and bowing low.

"Try him with it in both ways," I said.

When the Workers had made a whole lot of all the kinds together they poured it into a hollow stone and covered it with sugar and cream.

"Ready, your Highnesses!" they all called out in chorus.

"Is that it?" said the Lion. "It looks very nice. How does one eat it? Must I bite it?"

"Dear me, no," I answered. "Lap it."

So he began. If you'll believe me, he simply reveled in it. He ate and ate and ate, and lapped and lapped and lapped and he did not stop until the hollow stone was quite clean and empty and his sides were quite swelled and puffed out. And he looked as pleased as Punch.

"I never ate anything nicer in my life," he said. "There was a Sunday School picnic I once went to—"

"A Sunday School picnic!" I shouted so fiercely that he blushed all over. The very tuft on his tail was deep rose color. "Who invited you?"

He hung his head and stammered.

"I wasn't exactly *invited*," he said, "and didn't go *with* the school to the picnic grounds—but I should have come back with it—at least some of it—but for some men with guns!"

I stamped on his ear as hard as ever I could.

"Never let me hear you mention such a subject again," I said. "Nobody in Society would speak to you if they knew of it!"

He quite shook in his shoes—only he hadn't any shoes.

"I'll never even think of it again," he said. "I see my mistake. I apologize. I do indeed!"

Now what *do* you suppose happened at that very minute? If I hadn't been a Fairy I should have been frightened to death. At

He ate and ate and ate, and lapped and lapped and lapped.

that very minute I heard little children's voices singing like skylarks farther down on the Huge Green Hill—actually little children—a whole lot of them!

PART TWO

"IT—IT SOUNDS like the Sunday School pic—" the Lion began to say—and then he remembered he must not mention the subject and stopped short.

"Has your heart changed?" I said to him. "Are you sure it has?"

"I think it has," he said meekly. "But even if it hadn't, ma'am, I'm so *full* of Breakfast Food I couldn't eat a strawberry."

It happened that I had my heart glass with me—I can examine hearts with it and see if they have properly changed or not.

"Roll over on your back," I said. "I'll examine your heart now."

And the little children on the Huge Green Hill side were coming nearer and nearer and laughing and singing and twittering more like skylarks than ever.

He rolled over on his back and I jumped off his ear on to his big chest. I thumped and listened and looked about until I could see his great heart and watch it beating—thub—thub—thub—thub. It actually had changed—almost all over except one little corner and as the children's voices came nearer and nearer and sounded like whole nests full of skylarks let loose, even the corner was changing as fast as it could. Instead of a big ugly dark red fiery heart it was a soft ivory white one with delicate pink spots on it.

"It sounds like a Sunday school pic—"

"It has changed!" I cried out. "You are going to be a great, big, nice, soft, cozy thing, and you couldn't eat a picnic if you tried—and you will never try."

He was all in a flutter with relief when he got up and stood on his feet.

And the laughing little voices came nearer and nearer and I flew to the Cave door to see what *was* happening.

It was really a picnic. And Goodness! how dangerous it would have been if it had not been for me! That's the way I am always saving people, you notice.

The little children in the village had grown so tired of being shut up indoors that about fifty of them who were too little to know any better had climbed out of win-

The little children in the village had grown tired of being shut up indoors.

dows, and slipped out of doors, and crawled under things, and hopped over them, and had all run away together to gather flowers and wild peach-straw-berines, and lovely big yellow plumri-cots which grew thick on the bushes and in the grass on the Huge Green Hill. The delicious, sweet pink and pur-ple Ice-cream-grape-juice Melons hung in clusters on trees too high for them to reach, but they thought they would just sit down under their branches and look at them and sniff and hope one would fall.

And there they came—little plump girls and boys in white frocks and with curly heads—not the least bit afraid of anything: tumbling down and laughing and picking themselves up and laugh-ing, and when they got near the Cave, one of my Working Fairies, just for fun, flew down and alighted on a little girl's fat hand. She jumped for joy when she saw him and called to the others and they came running and tumbling to see what she had found.

"Oh! look—look!" she called out.

"What is he! What is he! He isn't a bird—and he isn't a bee and he isn't a butterfly. He's a little teeny, weeny-weeny-weeny-weeny wee, and he has little green shoes on and little green stock-ings, and a little green smock and a little green hat and he's laughing and laughing."

And then a boy saw another in the grass—and another under a leaf, and he shouted out, too.

"Oh! here's another—and here's another!" And then the Workers all began to creep out of the grass and from under the leaves and fly up in swarms and light on the children's arms and hands and hats and play with them and tickle them and laugh until every child was dancing

Just for fun, a fairy flew down and alighted on a little girl's fat hand.

with fun, because they had never seen such things before in their lives.

I flew back to the Lion. He was quite nervous.

"It is a picnic," I said. "And now is your chance. Can you purr?"

"Yes, I can." And he began to make a beautiful purring which sounded like an immense velvet cat over a saucer of cream.

"Come out then," I ordered him. "Smile as sweetly as you can and don't stop purring. Try to look like a wriggling coaxing dog—I will go first and prevent the children from being frightened."

So out we went. I was riding on his ear and peeping out over the top of it. I did not let the children see me because I wanted them to look at the Lion and at nothing else.

What I did was to make them remember in a minute all the nicest Lions they had ever seen in pictures or in the circus. Many of them had never seen a Lion at all and the few who had been to a circus had only seen them in big cages behind iron bars, and with notices written up, "Don't go near the Lions!"

When my Lion came out he was smiling the biggest, sleepiest, curliest, sweetest smile you ever beheld and he was purring, and he was softly waving his fail. He stood still on the grass a moment and then lay down with his big head on his paws just like a huge, affectionate, coaxing dog waiting and begging somebody to come

The most splendid and fun picnic.

and pet him. And after staring at him for two minutes, all the children began to laugh, and then one *little* little girl who had a great mastiff for a friend at home, suddenly gave a tiny shout and ran to him and tumbled over his paws and fell against his mane and hid her face in it, chuckling and chuckling.

That was the beginning of the most splendid fun a picnic ever had. Every one of them ran laughing and shouting to the Lion. It was such a treat to them to actually have a lion to play with. They patted him, they buried their hands and faces in his big mane, they stroked him, they scrambled up on his back, and sat astride there, little boys called out "Hello, Lion! Hello, Lion!" and little girls kissed his nice tawny back and said

"Liony! Liony ! Sweet old Liony!" The Little Little Girl who had run to him first settled down right between his huge front paws, resting her back comfortably against his chest, and sucked her thumb, her blue eyes looking very round and big. She was comfy.

I kept whispering down his ear to tell him what to do. You see, he had never been in Society at all and he had to learn everything at once.

"Now, don't move suddenly," I whispered. "And be sure not to make any loud Lion noises. They don't understand Lion language yet."

"But oh! I am so happy," he whispered back, "I want to jump up and roar for joy."

"Mercy on us!" I said. "That would spoil everything. They'd be frightened to death and run away screaming and crying and never come back."

"But this little one with her head on my chest is such a *sweetie!*" he said. "Mayn't I just give her a little lick—ust a little one?"

"Your tongue is too rough. Wait a minute," I answered.

My Fairy Workers were swarming all about. They were sitting in bunches on the bushes and hanging in bunches from branches, and hopping about and giggling and laughing and nudging each other in the ribs as they looked on at the Lion and the children. They were as amused as they had been when they watched Winnie sitting on the eggs in the Rook's nest. I called Nip to come to me.

"Jump on to the Lion's tongue," I said to him, "and smooth it off with your plane until it is like satin velvet—not silk velvet, but satin velvet."

The Lion politely put out his tongue. Nip leaped up on it and began to work with his plane. He worked until he was quite hot, and he made the tongue so smooth that it was *quite* like satin velvet.

"Now you can kiss the baby," I said.

The Little Little Girl had gone to sleep by this time and she had slipped down and lay curled up on the Lion's front leg as if it was an arm and the Lion bent down and delicately licked her soft cheek, and her fat arm, and her fat leg, and purred and purred.

When the other children saw him they crowded round and were more delighted than ever.

"He's kissing her as if he was a mother

The Fairy Workers swarmed all about.

cat and she was his kitten," one called out, and she held out her hand. "Kiss me too. Kiss me, Liony," she said.

He lifted his head and licked her little hand as she asked and then all the rest wanted him to kiss them and they laughed so that the Little Little Girl woke up and laughed with them and scrambled to her feet and hugged and hugged as much of the Lion as she could put her short arms round. She felt as if he was her Lion.

"I love oo—I love oo," she said. "Tome and play wiv us."

He smiled and smiled and got up so carefully that he did not upset three or four little boys and girls who were sitting on his back. You can imagine how they shouted with glee when he began to trot gently about with them and give them a ride. Of course everybody wanted to ride. So he trotted softly over the grass, first with one load of them and then with another. When each ride was over he lay down very carefully for the children to scramble down from his back and then other ones scrambled up.

The things he did that afternoon really made me admire him. A Cozy Lion is nicer to play with than anything else in the world. He shook Ice-cream-grape-juice Melons down from the trees for them. He carried on his back, to a clear little running brook he knew, everyone who wanted a drink. He jumped for them, he played tag with them and when he caught them, he rolled them over and over on the grass as if they were kittens; he showed them how his big claws would go in and out of his velvet paws like a pussy cat's. Whatever game they played he would always be "It," if they wanted him to. When the tiniest ones got sleepy, he made grass beds under the shade of trees and picked them up daintily by their frocks or little trousers and carried them to their nests just as kittens or puppies are carried by their mothers. And when the others wanted to be carried too, he carried them as well.

The children enjoyed themselves so much that they altogether forgot about going home. And as they had laughed and run about every minute and had had *such* fun, by the time the sun began to go down they were all as sleepy as could be. But even then one little fellow in a blue sailor suit asked for something else. He went and stood by the Lion with one arm around his neck and the other under his chin, "Can you roar,

He shook the ice-cream-grape-juice melons down from the trees for them.

old Lion?" he asked him. "I am sure you can roar."

The Lion nodded slowly three times.

"He says 'Yes—Yes,'" shouted everybody. "Oh! do roar for us—as loud as ever you can. We won't be frightened the least bit."

The Lion nodded again and smiled. Then he lifted up his head and opened his mouth and roared and *roared* and ROARED. They were not the least *bit* frightened. They just shrieked and laughed and jumped up and down and made him do it over and over again.

He roared and roard *and ROARED.*

*   *   *   *

NOW I WILL tell you what had happened in the village.

At first when the children ran away the mothers and fathers were all at their work and did not miss them for several hours. It was at lunch time that the grown-ups began to find out the little folks were gone and then one mother ran out into the village street, and then another and then another, until all the mothers were there, and all of them were talking at once and wringing their hands and crying. They went and looked under beds, and tables and in cupboards, and in back gardens and in front gardens, and they rushed to the village pond to see if there were any little hats or bonnets floating on the top of the water. But all was quiet and serene and nothing was floating anywhere—and there was not one sign of the children.

When the fathers came the mothers all flew at them. You see it isn't any joke to lose fifty children all at once.

The fathers thought of the Lion the first thing but the mothers had tried *not* to think of him because they couldn't bear it.

But at last the fathers got all the guns and all the pistols and all the iron spikes and clubs and scythes and carving knives and old swords, and they armed themselves with them and began to march all together towards the Huge Green Hill. The mothers *would* go too and *they* took scissors and big needles and long hat pins and one took a big pepper pot, full of red pepper, to throw into the Lion's eyes.

They had so much to do before they were ready that when they reached the Huge Green Hill the sun was going down and what do you think they heard?

The fathers armed themselves.

They heard this—

"Ro-o-a-a-arh! Ro-o-a-a-rh! Ro-o-a-a-arrh!" almost as loud as thunder. And at the same time they heard the shouts and shrieks of the entire picnic.

But *they* did not know that the picnic was shouting and screaming for joy.

So they ran and ran and ran—and stumbled and scrambled and hurried and scurried and flurried faster and faster till they had scrambled up the Huge Green Hill to where the Lion's Cave was and then they gathered behind a big clump of bushes and the fathers began to cock their guns and the mothers to sharpen their scissors and hat pins.

But the mother with the pepper-pot had nothing to sharpen, so she peeped from behind the bushes, and suddenly she cried out, "Oh! Oh! Oh! Oh! Look! Look! And don't fire a single gun, on any account."

And they all struggled to the front to peep. And *this*—thanks to Me—*was what they saw!*

On the green places before the Lion's Cave on several soft heaps of grass, the tiniest children were sitting chuckling or sucking their thumbs. On the grass around them a lot of others were sitting or standing or rolling about with laughter and kicking up their heels—and right in front of the Cave there stood the Lion looking absolutely angelic. His tail had a beautiful blue sash on it tied just above the tuft in a lovely bow, he had a child on his head and three children on his back. The Little Little Girl who was sitting on his mane which was stuck full of flowers, was trying to place a wreath on the top of his head and couldn't get it straight, which made him look rather rakish. On one side of him stood the little boy in the sailor suit, and on the other stood a little girl, and each one held him by the end of a rope of pink and white wild roses which they were going to lead him with.

The mother of the Little Little Girl could not wait one minute longer. She ran out towards her calling out—

"Oh! Betsy-petsy! Oh! Betsy-petsy! Mam-my's Lammy-girl!"

And then the other mothers threw away their scissors and hat pins and ran after her in a crowd.

What that clever Lion did was to carefully lie down without upsetting anybody and stretch out his head on his paws as if he was a pet poodle, and purr and purr like a velvet cat.

The picnic simply shouted with glee. It was the kind of picnic which is always shouting with glee. "Oh! Mother! Mother! Father! Father!" it called out. "Look at our Lion! Look at our Lion! We found him ourselves! He's ours."

And the sailor boy shouted,

"He'll roar for me, Mother!"

And the rest cried out one after another,

"He'll sit up and beg for me!"

The children are found playing with the Cozy Lion.

"He'll carry me by my trousers!"

"He can play tag!"

"He'll show you his claws go in and out!"

"Mother, ask him to take you riding on his back to get a drink by the brook."

"May he go home and sleep with me, Mother?"

It was like a bedlam of skylarks let loose this time, and the Lion had to do so many tricks that only determination to show how Cozy he was kept up his strength. He was determined to prove to the Fathers and Mothers that he *was* Cozy.

And he did it. From that time he was the Lion of the Village. He was invited everywhere. There never was a party without him. Birthday parties, garden parties, tea parties, wedding parties—he went to them all. His life was just what he had hoped it might be—one round of gaiety.

He became *most* accomplished. He could do all the things Lions do in

Hippodromes—and a great many more. The Little Little Girl gave him a flute for a present and he learned to play on it beautifully. When he had an evening at home he would sit at his Cave door and play and sing. First he played and sang this—

"My Goodness Gracious Me!—This IS So-ci'-er-tee!
My Goodness Gracious Mercy Me!
This IS So-ci'-er-er-tee!—It IS So-ci'-er-tee!"

He had composed it himself.

First published in the February and March 1907 editions of *St. Nicholas Magazine*

The Little Maid
of the Beach

BY FLORENCE FRANCIS

IT WAS ONE of those bright, cloudless mornings in the middle of July when the sky and sea seem rivaling each other in their depth of blue, and the gleaming sand, not to be outdone by the gorgeous coloring about it, fairly flashes defiance from its dazzling whiteness.

A little girl sat on the edge of an upturned fishing-boat, carefully mending a large net, which spread around her little bare brown feet in heavy, graceful folds.

She was humming softly to herself a stray bit of a tune, gathered perhaps from an echo of the waves, and the sweet childish voice, low though it was, attracted the attention of a man who was sauntering aimlessly along the beach with a book kept open by a forefinger, his eyes turned out across the broad ocean, which he found more absorbing, in its natural greatness, than the printed pages that had failed to hold his interest.

"What a wee chick," he said half aloud, and he walked up beside her. The child raised her eyes as he approached, and gave him a little flitting, bashful smile, and then dropped them again quickly upon her work.

The young man—for he was young, young enough, at least, to feel a throb in his own heart echoing to the fresh young life beside him—seated himself on the sand, regardless of white duck trousers, and in that tone of good-fellowship which rarely fails to win its way to a child's heart he said smilingly:

"May I sit here just a little while and watch you work, if I promise to be very good and quiet?"

His tiny companion raised the downcast eyes again, and a second smile, more lingering than the first, parted the pretty red lips.

"Yes," she said graciously; "but I'm 'most done, and then I'll have to go in and get papa's dinner."

"Get papa's dinner!"—that mite of a creature, whose most serious domestic problem one would suppose to consist of providing enough little sand-pies, on tiny shells, for an assemblage of doll guests.

"Do you mean actually *cook* your papa's dinner?" was the wondering question.

"Well," she admitted, "I can't lift the heavy pot for the potatoes, or fry the fish:

but I get them all ready, and cut the bread, and papa cooks them when he gets home. There he comes now—I didn't know it was so late"; and she started up hastily.

"Will you excuse me?" she added, with an unlooked-for touch of courtesy.

She turned when a few paces distant, and called back to her visitor:

"You may come again tomorrow morning if you like. I don't generally come to the beach in the afternoons, 'cause the babies are awake then, and it's so hard to keep them from getting in the water."

On she trudged toward a row of small, unattractive houses such as one often finds along the margin of a little fishing-village, and disappeared from view.

John Wentworth smilingly watched her as far as he could distinguish the dignified little figure, and then arose and went on to the big hotel a mile farther down the beach.

"I'll come back tomorrow," he mused. "Here's more fun than watching a lot of silly girls jump up and down on a rope and call it 'bathing.'"

But the next day it rained, and so it was the second day following that he found himself almost hurrying toward the old boat and the little figure seated upon it. She was evidently expecting him, for she seemed in no wise surprised.

"I wish you'd try to get here a little earlier," she remarked, by way of greeting. "It gives us more time to visit."

Her guest laughed merrily as he threw himself at her feet.

"Tell me about the babies," he said, recalling her last remark on their previous meeting.

"Why, they're *our* babies," she answered, surprised that any one did not know—"my two little brothers, the twins; and oh! they are *so* cunning—just learning to run to the door and watch for papa and tell me when they see him coming"; and her face assumed a look of maternal pride.

"Haven't you a mother?" inquired her visitor, hesitatingly, as though fearful of bringing a memory of sorrow to the sweet little face so near his own.

"No," answered the child, sadly. "Mama has gone over the sea to God. She went in a big white ship with all the sails spread, and there was a beautiful white angel in the stern, and she had wings—" Presumably a sleeping vision was flitting through the little brain and stamping itself as a reality.

"Papa says I must be a little mother to him and the babies now," she added, after a moment; "and he says when the babies get big they will help me mend the nets and do lots of things for me, and papa says they will have a 'colloge egge-cashun,' whatever that may be."

"A college education!" Was that the aspiration of a humble and, as John had heretofore thought (if he had thought of him at all), an ignorant fisherman for his sons?

It suggested a new train of thought immediately.

"I wish I could know your papa," he said. "Don't you think you could manage it for me?"

"I don't know—my papa's very busy," responded his young hostess, demurely; "but I'll ask him if he wants to see you."

This last was more honest than flattering, but the innocent child lips knew only truth, so used it, and used it simply.

"Won't you tell me your name?" asked her guest, after silently watching her sturdy little fingers busy with their task.

"Ellen," she answered promptly. "What is yours?"

"Jack," was the reply; and then they both laughed.

"I didn't tell you the babies' names," she said, as though hurt that he omitted to ask.

"Oh! I was just going to ask the babies' names," he hastened to assure her, noting the aggrieved look.

"Teddy is one of them, and *Jack* is the other—isn't that funny?" and she laughed again as merrily as before.

"I hear them crying!" she exclaimed. "You wait here and I'll bring them." And she almost flew over the sand, scattering little showers of it behind her as she went.

A short time elapsed, and then the quaint little trio appeared, the sister in the middle, leading a sturdy two-year-old by either hand.

"Here they are!" she announced triumphantly, depositing them upon the sand, while they stared open-eyed at the stranger, "and aren't they cunning?"

"Veritable babes in the sand!" he laughed; and the youngsters, seeming to believe that his attentions toward them and their sister were friendly, gave a series of subdued chuckles.

"What's that?" Ellen asked doubtfully, not quite knowing whether the title might be considered complimentary or the reverse.

"Haven't you heard of the 'Babes in the Wood'?"

All three children brightened visibly at the prospect of a story, and the twins, a perfect bundle, or two bundles rather, of good nature, fairly gurgled with delight.

"Well, once upon a time—" A hearty laugh close at hand caused the group to turn suddenly, and three voices screamed: "Papa!"

"I beg your pardon," said the new-comer, in a rich, deep voice. "I missed the children and came out here to find 'em, and it struck me as funny to see the way they had sort o' swept over you in a tidal wave—I hope they ain't botherin' you, sir," he added with concern.

"No, indeed," was the hearty response; "we were having a royally good time. Won't you be willing to join our little band?"

The fisherman seated himself on the sand with a twin on each knee, and Ellen hovering between the two men—not allowing even her love for her father to outweigh loyalty to her new friend. She feared he might feel neglected.

This fisherman was a splendid "son of the sea"—tall without being angular, broad-shouldered, and with the muscle of an athlete. His eyes were dark and intelligent, and his browned skin and well-cut features made his face one to be studied and admired, while with his rough hand he fondled the yellow curls on the babies' heads with almost a woman's tenderness of touch.

"I trust you did not think I was trying to win away these attractive little people," John said, with something in his children-loving eyes which betokened an unspoken longing that he might be justified in so doing.

"Oh, no, sir!" answered his companion, taking the remark more seriously than it was intended. "I'm always glad when some one is kind to my wee 'mother-daughter,' as I call her. These fellows ain't old enough to feel it, but she's kind o' lonesome sometimes, I wish it wasn't so"; and he drew the little girl fondly to him.

"You see," he continued, unsolicited, "her mother slipped away from us when these two little chaps was only a week old, and she has to fill an empty space too big for even her willin' little heart," and tears stood in the strong man's eyes, which, however, he hastily brushed away with the back of his hand.

"Ellen tells me the boys are to be sent to college," John ventured, striving to turn the conversation into a happier channel.

The father smiled sadly. "Would that Ellen spoke what really may be!" he said. "You see, sir, this isn't the sort of a life—this one I'm leadin', I mean—for a boy to look forward to. It's just killin' to the soul. So I'm just givin' myself the comfort of paintin' pictures of their future, and it seems to me a man can't do his very best without a college education. It puts the right stuff in him from the beginnin' just to have it to look forward to, and I thought mebbe if I let 'em grow up expectin'—sort of expectin'," he modified his statement—"to go to college, it might be a—a sort o' somethin', I can't just think of the word—"

"An incentive, perhaps," kindly suggested his listener.

"Yes, that's it—an incentive to *be* somethin', even if we don't see the way clear to the college.

"I've read and studied some myself," he said, with a little touch of pardonable pride, "and before the little wife left me, we used to read together evenin's; she was a school-teacher before we were married," he explained, "and she always loved to have a book handy.

"I don't get much time nowadays," he continued regretfully, "for these little people keep me pretty busy. You see, when night comes, the little 'mother-daughter' is too tired to do more than tumble into her own little bed"; and he patted the mature little face nestling close to his arm.

The summer glided swiftly by, and John Wentworth had wandered many times to the humble little home beside the sea, drawn thither as much by the brave, noble character which shone through the fisherman's rough exterior as by the amusement which the children, now his sworn comrades, always afforded him.

August was drawing to its close, and John's long vacation with it. His weeks by the sea had brought him a wealth of experience sadly needed in his lonely bachelor life, and as he stood on the door-step of the fisherman's home on his last evening, and grasped the strong, hard hand extended to him, he felt himself to be, somehow, a richer man—even though, in one sense, perhaps, somewhat the poorer because of the snug little sum carefully tucked away in the savings-bank of the large neighboring town to be a beginning that would help defray the expenses of the "colloge eggecashun."

First published in the August 1902 edition of *St. Nicholas Magazine*

The Cruise of the *Dazzler*

BY JACK LONDON

CHAPTER ONE: 'FRISCO KID AND THE NEW BOY

'FRISCO KID WAS discontented—discontented and disgusted; though this would have seemed impossible to the boys who fished from the dock above and envied him mightily. He frowned, got up from where he had been sunning himself on top of the *Dazzler*'s cabin, and kicked off his heavy rubber boots. Then he stretched himself on the narrow side-deck and dangled his feet in the cool salt water.

"Now, that's freedom," thought the boys who watched him. Besides, those long sea boots, reaching the hips and buckled to the leather strap about the waist, held a strange and wonderful fascination for them. They did not know that 'Frisco Kid did not possess such things as shoes; that the boots were an old pair of Pete Le Maire's and were three sizes too large for him; nor could they guess how uncomfortable they were to wear on a hot summer day.

The cause of 'Frisco Kid's discontent was those very boys who sat on the string-piece and admired him; but his disgust was the result of quite another event. Further, the *Dazzler* was short one in its crew, and he had to do more work than was justly his share. He did not mind the cooking, nor the washing down of the decks and the pumping; but when it came to the paint-scrubbing and dish-washing, he rebelled. He felt that he had earned the right to be exempt from such scullion work. That was all the green boys were fit for; while he could make or take in sail, lift anchor, steer, and make landings.

"Stan' from un'er!" Pete Le Maire, captain of the *Dazzler* and lord and master of 'Frisco Kid, threw a bundle into the cockpit and came aboard by the starboard rigging.

"Come! Queeck!" he shouted to the boy who owned the bundle, and who now hesitated on the dock. It was a good fifteen feet to the deck of the sloop, and he could not reach the steel stay by which he must descend.

"Now! One, two, three!" the Frenchman counted good-naturedly, after the manner of all captains when their crews are short-handed. The boy swung his body into space and gripped the rigging. A moment later he struck the deck, his hands tingling warmly from the friction.

"Kid, dis is ze new sailor. I make your acquaintance." Pete smirked and bowed, and stood aside. "Mistaire Sho Bronson," he added as an afterthought.

The two boys regarded each other silently for a moment. They were evidently about the same age, though the stranger looked the heartier and the stronger of the two. 'Frisco Kid put out his hand, and they shook.

"So you're thinking of tackling the water, eh?" he asked.

Joe Bronson nodded, and glanced curiously about him before answering. "Yes; I think the Bay life will suit me for a while, and then, when I've got used to it, I'm going to sea in the forecastle."

"In the what? In the what, did you say?"

"In the forecastle—the place where the sailors live," he explained, flushing and feeling doubtful of his pronunciation.

"Oh, the fo'c'sle. Know anything about going to sea?"

"Yes—no; that is, except what I've read."

'Frisco Kid whistled, turned on his heel in lordly manner, and went into the cabin.

"Going to sea!" he remarked to himself as he built the fire and set about cooking supper; "in the 'forecastle,' too—and thinks he'll like it!"

In the meanwhile Pete Le Maire was showing the new-comer about the sloop as though he were a guest. Such affability and charm did he display that 'Frisco Kid, popping his head up through the scuttle to call them to supper, nearly choked in his effort to suppress a grin.

Joe Bronson enjoyed that supper. The food was rough but good, and the smack of the salt air and the sea-fittings around him gave zest to his appetite. The cabin was clean and snug, and, though not large, the accommodations surprised him. Every bit of space was utilized. The table swung to the centerboard-case on hinges, so that when not in use it actually occupied almost no room at all. On either side, and partly under the deck, were two

Joe eats his first meal on the Dazzler.

bunks. The blankets were rolled back, and they sat on the well-scrubbed bunk boards while they ate. A swinging sea-lamp of brightly polished brass gave them light, which in the daytime could be obtained through the four deadeyes, or small round panes of heavy glass which were fitted into the walls of the cabin. On one side of the door were the stove and wood-box, on the other the cupboard. The front end of the cabin was ornamented with a couple of rifles and a shotgun, while exposed by the rolled-back blankets of Pete's bunk was a cartridge-lined belt carrying a brace of revolvers.

It all seemed like a dream to Joe. Countless times he had imagined scenes somewhat similar to this; but here he was, right in the midst of it, and already it seemed as though he had known his two companions for years. Pete was smiling genially at him across the board. His was really a villainous countenance, but to Joe it seemed only "weather-beaten." 'Frisco Kid was describing to him, between mouthfuls, the last sou'easter the *Dazzler* had weathered, and Joe experienced an increasing awe for this boy who had lived so long upon the water and knew so much about it.

The captain, however, drank a glass of wine, and topped it off with a second and a third, and then, a vicious flush lighting his swarthy face, stretched out on top of his blankets, where he soon was snoring loudly.

"Better turn in and get a couple of hours' sleep," 'Frisco Kid said kindly, pointing Joe's bunk out to him. "We'll most likely be up the rest of the night."

Joe obeyed, but he could not fall asleep so readily as the others. He lay with his eyes wide open, watching the hands of the alarm clock that hung in the cabin, and thinking how quickly event had followed event in the last twelve hours. Only that very morning he had been a school-boy, and now he was a sailor, shipped on the *Dazzler*, and bound he knew not whither. His fifteen years increased to twenty at the thought of it, and he felt every inch a man—a sailor-man at that. He wished Charley and Fred could see him now. Well, they would hear of it quick enough. He could see them talking it over, and the other boys crowding around. "Who?" "What!—Joe Bronson?" "Yes, he's run away to sea. Used to chum with us, you know."

Joe pictured the scene proudly. Then he softened at the thought of his mother worrying, but hardened again at the recollection of his father. Not that his father was not good and kind; but he did not understand boys, Joe thought. That was where the trouble lay. Only that morning he had said that the world wasn't a play-ground, and that the boys who thought it was were liable to make sore mistakes and be glad to get home again. Well, he knew that there was plenty of hard work and rough experience in the world; but he also thought boys had some rights and should be allowed to do a lot of things without being questioned. He'd show him he could take care of himself; and, anyway, he could write home after he got settled down to his new life.

A skiff grazed the side of the *Dazzler* softly and interrupted his reveries. He wondered why he had not heard the sound of the row-locks. Then two men jumped over the cock-pit-rail and came into the cabin.

"Bli' me, if ere they ain't snoozin'," said the first of the new-comers, deftly rolling 'Frisco Kid out of his blankets with one hand and reaching for the wine-bottle with the other.

Pete put his head up on the other side of the centerboard, his eyes heavy with sleep, and made them welcome.

"'Oo's this?" asked "the Cockney," as 'Frisco Kid called him, smacking his lips over the wine and rolling Joe out upon the floor. "Passenger?"

"No, no," Pete made haste to answer. "Ze new sailor-man. Vaire good boy."

"Good boy or not, he's got to keep his tongue a-tween his teeth," growled the second new-comer, who had not yet spoken, glaring fiercely at Joe.

"I say," queried the other man, "'ow does 'e whack up on the loot? I 'ope as me an' Bill 'ave a square deal."

"Ze *Dazzler* she take one share—what you call—one third; den we split ze rest in five shares. Five men, five shares. Vaire good."

It was all Greek to Joe, except he knew that he was in some way the cause of the quarrel. In the end Pete had his way, and the newcomers gave in after much grumbling. After they had drunk their coffee all hands went on deck.

"Just stay in the cockpit an' keep out of their way," 'Frisco Kid whispered to Joe. "I'll teach you the ropes an' everything when we ain't in a hurry."

Joe's heart went out to him in sudden gratitude, for the strange feeling came to him that, of those on board, to 'Frisco Kid, and to 'Frisco Kid only, could he look for help in time of need. Already a dislike for Pete was growing up within him. Why, he could not say—he just simply felt it. A creaking of blocks for'ard, and the huge mainsail loomed above him in the night. Bill cast off the bow-line. The Cockney followed with the stern. 'Frisco Kid gave her the jib as Pete jammed up the tiller, and the *Dazzler* caught the breeze, heeling over for mid-channel. Joe heard some talking in low tones of not putting up the side-lights, and of keeping a sharp lookout, but all he could comprehend was that some law of navigation was being violated.

The water-front lights of Oakland began to slip past. Soon the stretches of docks and the shadowy ships began to be broken by dim sweeps of marsh-land, and Joe knew that they were heading out for San Francisco Bay. The wind was blowing from the north in mild squalls, and the *Dazzler* cut noiselessly through the land-locked water.

"Where are we going?" Joe asked the Cockney, in an endeavor to be friendly and at the same time satisfy his curiosity.

"Oh, my pardner 'ere, Bill—we're goin' to take a cargo from 'is factory," that worthy airily replied.

Joe thought he was rather a funny-looking individual to own a factory; but conscious that stranger things yet might be found in this new world he was entering, he said nothing. He had already exposed himself to 'Frisco Kid in the matter of his pronunciation of "fo'c'sle," and he had no desire further to show his ignorance.

A little after that he was sent in to blow out the cabin lamp. The *Dazzler* tacked about and began to work in toward the north shore. Everybody kept silent, save for occasional whispered questions and answers which passed between Bill and the captain. Finally the sloop was run into the wind and the jib and mainsail lowered cautiously.

"Short hawse, you know," Pete whispered to 'Frisco Kid, who went for'ard and dropped the anchor, paying out the slightest quantity of slack.

The *Dazzler*'s skiff was brought alongside, as was also the small boat the two strangers had come aboard in.

"See that that cub don't make a fuss," Bill commanded in an undertone, as he joined his partner in his own boat.

"Can you row?" 'Frisco Kid asked as they got into the other boat. Joe nodded his head. "Then take these oars, and don't make a racket."

'Frisco Kid took the second pair, while Pete steered. Joe noticed that the oars were muffled with sennit, and that even the rowlock sockets were protected by leather. It was impossible to make a noise except by a mis-stroke, and Joe had learned to row on Lake Merrit well enough to avoid that. They followed in the wake of the first boat, and glancing aside, he saw they were running along the length of a pier which jutted out from the land. A couple of ships, with riding-lanterns burning brightly, were moored to it, but they kept just beyond the edge of the light. He stopped rowing at the whispered command of 'Frisco Kid. Then the boats grounded like ghosts on a tiny beach, and they clambered out.

Joe followed the men, who picked their way carefully up a twenty-foot bank. At the top he found himself on a narrow railway track which ran between huge piles of rusty scrap-iron. These piles, separated by tracks, extended in every direction, he could not tell how far, though in the distance he could see the vague outlines of some great factory-like building. The men began to carry loads of the iron down to the beach, and Pete, gripping him by the arm and again warning him to not make any noise, told him to do likewise. At the beach they turned their loads over to 'Frisco Kid, who loaded them, first in one skiff and then in the other. As the boats settled under the weight, he kept pushing them farther and farther out, in order that they should keep clear of the bottom.

Joe worked away steadily, though he could not help marveling at the queerness of the whole business. Why should there be such a mystery about it, and why such care taken to maintain silence? He had just begun to ask himself these questions, and a horrible suspicion was forming itself in his mind, when he heard the hoot of an owl from the direction of the beach. Wondering at an owl being in so unlikely a place, he stooped to gather a fresh load of iron. But suddenly a man sprang out of the gloom, flashing a dark lantern full upon him. Blinded by the light, he staggered back. Then a revolver in the man's hand went off. All Joe realized was that he was being shot at, while his legs manifested an overwhelming desire to get away. Even if he had so wished, he could not very well have stayed to explain to the excited man with the smoking revolver. So he took to his heels for the beach, colliding with another man with a dark lantern who came running around the end of one of the piles of iron. This second man quickly regained his feet, and peppered away at Joe as he flew down the bank.

He dashed out into the water for the boat. Pete at the bow oars and 'Frisco Kid at the stroke had the skiff's nose pointed seaward and were calmly awaiting his arrival. They had their oars all ready for the start, but they held them quietly at rest, notwithstanding that both men on the bank had begun to fire at them. The other skiff lay closer inshore, partially aground. Bill was trying to shove it off, and was calling on the Cockney to lend a hand; but that gentleman had lost his head completely, and came floundering through the water hard after Joe. No sooner had Joe climbed in over the stern than he followed him. This extra weight on the stern of the heavily loaded craft nearly swamped them; as it was, a dangerous quantity of water was shipped. In the meantime the men on the bank had reloaded their pistols and opened fire again, this time with better aim. The alarm had spread. Voices and cries could be heard from the ships on the pier, along which men were running. In the distance a police whistle was being frantically blown.

"Get out!" 'Frisco Kid shouted. "You ain't a-going to sink us if I know it. Go and help your pardner!"

But the Cockney's teeth were chattering with fright, and he was too unnerved to move or speak.

"T'row ze crazy man out!" Pete ordered from the bow. At this moment a bullet shattered an oar in his hand, and he coolly proceeded to ship a spare one.

"Give us a hand, Joe," 'Frisco Kid commanded.

Joe understood, and together they seized the terror-stricken creature and flung him over-board. Two or three bullets splashed about him as he came to the surface just in time to be picked up by Bill, who had at last succeeded in getting clear.

"Now," Pete called, and a few strokes into the darkness quickly took them out of the zone of fire.

So much water had been shipped that the light skiff was in danger of sinking at any moment. While the other two rowed, and by the Frenchman's orders, Joe began to throw out the iron. This saved them for the time being; but just as they swept alongside the *Dazzler* the skiff lurched, shoved a side under, and turned turtle, sending the remainder of the iron to the bottom. Joe and 'Frisco Kid came up side by side, and together they clambered aboard with the skiff's painter in tow. Pete had already arrived, and now helped them out.

By the time they had canted the water out of the swamped boat, Bill and his partner appeared on the scene. All hands worked rapidly, and almost before Joe could realize, the mainsail and jib had been hoisted, the anchor broken out, and the *Dazzler* was leaping down the channel. Off a bleak piece of marshland, Bill and the Cockney said good-by and cast loose in their skiff. Pete, in the cabin, bewailed their bad luck in various languages, and sought consolation in the wine-bottle.

The wind freshened as they got clear of the land, and soon the *Dazzler* was heeling it with her lee deck buried and the water churning by half-way up the cockpit-rail. Side-lights had been hung out. 'Frisco Kid was steering, and by his side sat Joe, pondering over the events of the night.

He could no longer blind himself to the facts. His mind was in a whirl of apprehension. If he had done wrong, he reasoned, he had done it through ignorance; and he did not feel shame for the past so much as he did fear of the future. His companions were thieves and robbers—the Bay pirates of whose unlawful deeds he had heard vague tales. And here he was right in the midst of them, already possessing information which could send them to State's prison. This very fact, he knew, would force them to keep a sharp watch upon him and so lessen his chances of escape. But escape he would, at the very first opportunity.

At this point his thoughts were interrupted by a sharp squall, which hurled the *Dazzler* over till the sea rushed inboard. 'Frisco Kid luffed quickly, at the same time slacking off the main-sheet. Then, single-handed—for Pete remained below, and Joe sat still looking idly on—he proceeded to reef down.

CHAPTER TWO: JOE TRIES TAKING FRENCH LEAVE

THE SQUALL WHICH had so nearly capsized the *Dazzler* was of short duration, but it marked the rising of the wind, and soon puff after puff was shrieking down upon them out of the north. The mainsail was spilling the wind, and slapping and thrashing about till it seemed it would tear itself to pieces. The sloop was rolling wildly in the quick sea which had come up. Everything was in confusion; but even Joe's untrained eye showed him that it was an orderly confusion. He could see that 'Frisco Kid knew just what to do, and just how to do it. As he watched him he learned a lesson, the lack of which has made failures of the lives of many men—knowledge of one's own capacities. 'Frisco Kid knew what he was able to do, and because of this he had confidence in himself. He was cool and self-possessed, working hurriedly but not carelessly. There was no bungling. Every reef-point was drawn down to stay. Other accidents might occur, but the next squall, or the next forty squalls, would not carry one of these reef-knots away.

He called Joe for'ard to help stretch the mainsail by means of swinging on the peak and throat halyards. To lay out on the long bow-sprit and put a single reef in the jib was a slight task compared with what had been already accomplished; so a few moments later they were again in the cockpit. Under the other lad's directions, Joe flattened down the jib-sheet, and, going into the cabin, let down a foot or so of centerboard. The excitement of the struggle had chased all unpleasant thoughts from his mind. Patterning after the other boy, he had retained his coolness. He had executed his orders without fumbling, and at the same time without undue slowness. Together they had exerted their puny strength in the face of violent nature, and together they had outwitted her.

He came back to where his companion stood at the tiller steering, and he felt proud of him and of himself. And when he read the unspoken praise in 'Frisco Kid's eyes he blushed like a girl at her first compliment. But the next instant the thought flashed across him that this boy was a thief, a common thief, and he instinctively recoiled. His whole life had been sheltered from the harsher things of the world. His reading, which had been of the best, had laid a premium upon honesty and uprightness, and he had learned to look with abhorrence upon the criminal classes. So he drew a little away from 'Frisco Kid and remained silent. But 'Frisco Kid, devoting all his energies to the handling of the sloop, had no time in which to remark this sudden change of feeling on the part of his companion.

Yet there was one thing Joe found in himself that surprised him. While the thought of 'Frisco Kid being a thief was repulsive to him, 'Frisco Kid himself was not. Instead of feeling an honest desire to shun him, he felt drawn toward him. He could not help liking him, though he knew not why. Had he been a little older he would have understood that it was the lad's good qualities which appealed to him—his coolness and self-reliance, his manliness and bravery, and a certain kindliness and sympathy in his nature. As it was, he thought it his own natural badness which prevented him from disliking 'Frisco Kid, and while he felt shame at his own weakness, he could not smother the sort of regard which he felt growing up for this common thief, this Bay pirate.

"Take in two or three feet on the skiff's painter," commanded 'Frisco Kid, who had an eye for everything.

The skiff was lowing with too long a painter, and was behaving very badly. Every once in a while it would hold back till the tow-rope tautened, then come leaping ahead and sheering and dropping slack till it threatened to shove its nose under the huge whitecaps which roared hungrily on every hand. Joe climbed over the cockpit-rail upon the slippery after-deck, and made his way to the bitt to which the skiff was fastened.

"Be careful," 'Frisco Kid warned, as a heavy puff struck the *Dazzler* and careened her dangerously over on her side. "Keep one turn round the bitt, and heave in on it when the painter slacks."

It was ticklish work for a greenhorn. Joe threw off all the turns save the last, which he held with one hand, while with the other he attempted to bring in on the painter. But at that instant it tightened with a tremendous jerk, the boat sheering sharply into the crest of a heavy sea. The rope slipped from his hands and began to fly out over the stern. He clutched it frantically, and was dragged after it over the sloping deck.

"Let her go! Let her go!" 'Frisco Kid roared.

Joe let go just as he was on the verge of going overboard, and the skiff dropped rapidly astern. He glanced in a shamefaced way at his companion, expecting to be sharply reprimanded for his awkwardness. But 'Frisco Kid smiled good-naturedly.

"That's all right," he said. "No bones broke, and nobody overboard. Better to lose a boat than a man any day. That's what I say. Besides, I shouldn't have sent you out there. And there's no harm done. We can pick it up all right. Go in and drop some more centerboard—a couple of feet—and then come out and do what I tell you. But don't be in a hurry. Take it easy and sure."

Joe dropped the centerboard, and returned, to be stationed at the jib-sheet. "Harda-lee!" 'Frisco Kid cried, throwing the tiller down and following it with his body. "Cast off! That's right! Now lend a hand on the main-sheet!"

Together, hand over hand, they came in on the reefed mainsail. Joe began to warm up with the work. The *Dazzler* turned on her heel like a race-horse and swept into the wind, her canvas snarling and her sheets slatting like hail.

"Draw down the jib-sheet!"

Joe obeyed, and the head-sail, filling, forced her off on the other tack. This manoeuver had turned Pete's bunk from the lee to the weather side, and rolled him out on the cabin floor, where he lay in a drunken stupor.

'Frisco Kid, with his back against the tiller, and holding the sloop off that it might cover their previous course, looked at him with an expression of disgust, and muttered: "The dog! We could well go to the bottom, for all he'd care or do!"

Twice they tacked, trying to go over the same ground, and then Joe discovered the skiff bobbing to windward in the starlit darkness.

"Plenty of time," 'Frisco Kid cautioned, shooting the *Dazzler* into the wind toward it and gradually losing headway.

"Now!"

Joe leaned over the side, grasped the trailing painter, and made it fast to the bitt. Then they tacked ship again and started on their way. Joe still felt sore over the trouble he had caused, but 'Frisco Kid quickly put him at ease.

"Oh, that's nothing," he said. "Everybody does that when they're beginning. Now, some men forget all about the trouble they had in learning, and get mad when a greeny makes a mistake. I never do. Why, I remember—"

And here he told Joe of many of the mishaps which fell to him when, as a little lad, he first went on the water, and of some of the severe punishments for the same which were measured out to him. He had passed the running end of a lanyard over the tiller-neck, and, as they talked, they sat side by side and close against each other, in the shelter of the cockpit.

"What place is that?" Joe asked as they flew by a lighthouse perched on a rocky headland.

"Goat Island. They've got a naval training-station for boys over on the other side, and a torpedo magazine. There's jolly good fishing, too—rock-cod. We'll pass to the lee of it and make across and anchor in the shelter of Angel Island. There's a quarantine station there. Then, when Pete gets sober, we'll know where he wants to go. You can turn in now and get some sleep. I can manage all right."

They sat side by side in the shelter of the cockpit.

Joe shook his head. There had been too much excitement for him to feel in the least like sleeping. He could not bear to think of it, with the *Dazzler* leaping and surging along, and shattering the seas into clouds of spray on her weather bow. His clothes had half dried already, and he preferred to stay on deck and enjoy it. The lights of Oakland had dwindled till they made only a hazy flare against the sky; but to the south the San Francisco lights, topping hills and sinking into valleys, stretched miles upon miles. Starting from the great ferry building and passing on to Telegraph Hill, Joe was soon able to locate the principal places of the city. Somewhere over in that maze of light and shadow was the home of his father, and perhaps even now they were thinking and worrying about him; and over there his sister Bessie was sleeping cozily, to wake up in the morning and wonder why her brother Joe did not come down to breakfast. Joe shivered. It was almost morning. Then, slowly, his head drooped over on 'Frisco Kid's shoulder, and soon he was fast asleep.

"COME! WAKE UP! We're going into anchor."

Joe roused with a start, bewildered at the unusual scene; for sleep had banished his troubles for the time being, and he knew not where he was. Then he remembered. The wind had dropped with the night. Beyond, the heavy after-sea was still rolling, but the *Dazzler* was creeping up in the shelter of a rocky island. The sky was clear, and the air had the snap and vigor of early morning about it. The rippling water was laughing in the rays of the sun, just shouldering above the eastern sky-line. To the south lay Alcatraz Island, and from its gun-crowned heights a flourish of trumpets saluted the day. In the west the Golden Gate yawned between the Pacific Ocean and San Francisco Bay. A full-rigged ship, with her lightest canvas, even to the sky-sails, set, was coming slowly in on the flood-tide.

It was a pretty sight. Joe rubbed the sleep from his eyes and remained gazing till 'Frisco Kid told him to go for'ard and make ready for dropping the anchor.

"Overhaul about fifty fathoms of chain," he ordered, "and then stand by." He eased the sloop gently into the wind, at the same time casting off the jib-sheet. "Let go the jib-halyards and come in on the downhaul!"

Joe had seen the manoeuver performed the previous night, and so was able to carry it out with fair success.

"Now! Over with the mud-hook! Watch out for turns! Lively, now!"

The chain flew out with startling rapidity, and brought the *Dazzler* to rest. 'Frisco Kid went for'ard to help, and together they lowered the mainsail, furled it in shipshape manner, made all fast with the gaskets, and put the crutches under the main-boom.

"Here's a bucket." 'Frisco Kid passed him the article in question. "Wash down the decks, and don't be afraid of the water, nor of the dirt, neither. Here's a broom. Give it what for, and have everything shining. When you get that done, bail out the skiff; she opened her seams a little last night. I'm going below to cook breakfast."

The water was soon slushing merrily over the deck, while the smoke pouring from the cabin stove carried a promise of good things to come. Time and again Joe lifted his head from his task to take in the scene. It was one to appeal to any healthy boy, and he was no exception. The romance of it stirred him strangely, and his happiness would have been complete could he have escaped remembering who and what his companions were. But the thought of this, and of Pete in his bleary, drunken sleep below, marred the beauty of the day. He had been unused to such things, and was shocked at the harsh reality of life. But instead of hurting him, as it might a lad of weaker nature, it had the opposite effect. It strengthened his desire to be clean and strong, and to not be ashamed of himself in his own eyes. He glanced about him and sighed. Why could not men be honest and true? It seemed too bad that he must go away and leave all this; but the events of the night were strong upon him, and he knew that in order to be true to himself he must escape.

At this juncture he was called to breakfast. He discovered that 'Frisco Kid was as good a cook as he was sailor, and made haste to do justice to the fare. There were mush and condensed milk, beefsteak and fried potatoes, and all topped off with good French bread, butter, and coffee. Pete did not join them, though 'Frisco Kid attempted a couple of times to rouse him. He mumbled and grunted, half opened his bleared eyes, then went to snoring again.

"Can't tell when he's going to get those spells," 'Frisco Kid explained, when Joe, having finished washing the dishes, came on deck. "Sometimes he won't get that way for a month, and others he won't be decent for a week at a stretch. Sometimes he's good-natured, and sometimes he's dangerous. So the best thing to do is to let him alone and keep out of his way. And don't cross him, for if you do there's liable to be trouble."

"Come on; let's take a swim," he added, abruptly changing the subject to one more agreeable. "Can you swim?"

Joe nodded. "What's that place?" he asked as he poised before diving, pointing toward a sheltered beach on the island, where there were several buildings and a large number of tents.

"Quarantine station. Lots of smallpox coming in now on the China steamers, and they make them go there till the doctors say they're safe to land. I tell you, they're strict about it, too. Why—"

Splash! Had 'Frisco Kid finished his sentence just then, instead of diving overboard, much trouble might have been saved to Joe. But he did not finish it, and Joe dived after him.

"I'll tell you what," 'Frisco Kid suggested half an hour later, while they clung to the bob-stay preparatory to climbing out. "Let's catch a mess of fish for dinner, and then turn in and make up for the sleep we lost last night. What d' you say?"

They made a race to clamber aboard, but Joe was shoved over the side again. When he finally did arrive, the other lad had brought to light a pair of heavily leaded, large-hooked lines, and a mackerel-keg of salt sardines.

"Bait," he said. "Just shove a whole one on. They're not a bit partic'lar. Swallow the bait, hook and all, and go—that's their caper. The fellow that don't catch first fish has to clean 'em." Both sinkers started on their long descent together, and seventy feet of line whizzed out before they came to rest. But at the instant his sinker touched the bottom Joe felt the struggling jerks of a hooked fish. As he began to haul in he glanced at 'Frisco Kid, and saw that he, too, had evidently captured a finny prize. The race between them was exciting. Hand over hand the wet lines flashed inboard; but 'Frisco Kid was more expert, and his fish tumbled into the cockpit first. Joe's followed an instant later—a three-pound rock-cod. He was wild with joy. It was magnificent, the largest fish he had ever landed or ever seen landed. Over went the lines again, and up they came with two mates of the ones already captured. It was sport royal. Joe would have certainly continued till he had fished the Bay empty had not 'Frisco Kid persuaded him to stop.

"We've got enough for three meals now," he said, "so there's no use in having them spoil. Besides, the more you catch, the more you clean, and you'd better start in right away. I'm going to bed."

Joe did not mind. In fact, he was glad he had not caught the first fish, for it helped out a little plan which had come to him while in swimming. He threw the last cleaned fish into a bucket of water, and glanced about him. The quarantine station was a bare half-mile away, and he could make out a soldier pacing up and down at sentry duty on the beach. Going into the cabin, he listened to the heavy breathing of the sleepers. He had to pass so close to 'Frisco Kid to get his bundle of clothes that he decided not to take them. Returning outside, he carefully pulled the skiff alongside, got aboard with a pair of oars, and cast off.

At first he rowed very gently in the direction of the station, fearing the chance of noise if he made undue haste. But gradually he increased the strength of his strokes till he had settled down to the regular stride. When he had covered half the distance he glanced about. Escape was sure now, for he knew, even if he were discovered, that it would be impossible for the *Dazzler* to get under way and head him off before he made the land and the protection of that man who wore the uniform of Uncle Sam.

The report of a gun came to him from the shore, but his back was in that direction and he did not bother to turn around. A second report followed, and a bullet cut the water within a couple of feet of his oar-blade. This time he did turn around. The soldier on the beach was leveling his rifle at him for a third shot.

CHAPTER THREE: JOE LOSES LIBERTY, AND FINDS A FRIEND

JOE WAS IN a predicament, and a very tantalizing one at that. A few minutes of hard rowing would bring him to the beach and to safety; but on that beach, for some unaccountable reason, stood a United States soldier who persisted in firing at him.

When Joe saw the gun aimed at him for the third time, he backed water hastily. As a result the skiff came to a standstill, and the soldier, lowering his rifle, regarded him intently.

"I want to come ashore! Important!" Joe shouted out to him.

The man in uniform shook his head.

"But it's important, I tell you! Won't you let me come ashore?"

He took a hurried look in the direction of the *Dazzler*. The shots had evidently awakened Pete; for the mainsail had been hoisted, and as he looked he saw the anchor broken out and the jib flung to the breeze.

"Can't land here!" the soldier shouted back. "Smallpox!"

"But I must!" he cried, choking down a half-sob and preparing to row.

"Then I'll shoot," was the cheering response, and the rifle came to shoulder again.

Joe thought rapidly. The island was large. Perhaps there were no soldiers farther on, and if he only once got ashore he did not care how quickly they captured him. He might catch the smallpox, but even that was better than going back to the Bay pirates. He whirled the skiff half about to the right, and threw all his strength against the oars. The cove was quite wide, and the nearest point which he must go around a good distance away. Had he been more of a sailor he would have gone in the other direction for the opposite point, and thus had the wind on his pursuers. As it was, the *Dazzler* had a beam wind in which to overtake him.

It was nip and tuck for a while. The breeze was light and not very steady, so sometimes he gained and sometimes they. Once it freshened till the sloop was within a hundred yards of him, and then it dropped suddenly flat, the *Dazzler*'s big mainsail flapping idly from side to side.

"Ah! you steal ze skiff, eh?" Pete howled at him, running into the cabin for his rifle. "I fix you! You come back queeck, or I kill you!" But he knew the soldier was watching them from the shore, and did not dare to fire, even over the lad's head.

Joe did not think of this, for he, who had never been shot at in all his previous life, had been under fire twice in the last twenty-four hours. Once more or less couldn't amount to much. So he pulled steadily away, while Pete raved like a wild man, threatening him with all manner of punishments once he laid hands upon him again. To complicate matters, 'Frisco Kid waxed mutinous.

"Just you shoot him and I'll see you hung for it, see if I don't," he threatened. "You'd better let him go. He's a good boy and all right, and not raised for the life you and I are leading."

"You too, eh!" the Frenchman shrieked, beside himself with rage. "Den I fix you, you rat!"

He made a rush for the boy, but 'Frisco Kid led him a lively chase from cockpit to bowsprit and back again. A sharp capful of wind arriving just then, Pete abandoned the one chase for the other. Springing to the tiller and slacking away on the main-sheet—for the wind favored—he headed the sloop down upon Joe. The latter made one tremendous spurt, then gave up in despair and hauled in his oars. Pete let go the main-sheet, lost steerage-way as he rounded up alongside the motionless skiff, and dragged Joe out.

"Keep mum," 'Frisco Kid whispered to him while the irate Frenchman was busy fastening the painter. "Don't talk back. Let him say all he wants to, and keep quiet. It'll be better for you."

But Joe's blood was up and he did not heed.

"Look here, Mr. Pete, or whatever your name is," he commenced, "I give you to understand that I want to quit, and that I'm going to quit. So you'd better put me ashore at once. If you don't, I'll put you in prison, or my name's not Joe Bronson."

'Frisco Kid waited the outcome fearfully. Pete was aghast. He was being defied aboard his own vessel, and by a boy. Never had such a thing been heard of. He knew he was committing an unlawful act in detaining him, while at the same time he was afraid to let him go with the information he had gathered concerning the sloop and its occupation. The boy had spoken the unpleasant truth when he said he could send him to prison. The only thing for him to do was to bully him.

"You will, eh?" His shrill voice rose wrathfully. "Den you come too. You row ze boat last-a night—answer me dat! You steal ze iron—answer me dat! You run away—answer me dat! And den you say you put me in jail? Bah!"

"But I didn't know," Joe protested. "Ha, ha! Dat is funny. You tell dat to ze judge; mebbe him laugh, eh?"

"I say I didn't," Joe reiterated manfully. "I didn't know I'd shipped along with a lot of pirates and thieves."

'Frisco Kid winced at this epithet, and had Joe been looking at him he would have seen the red flush of shame mount to his face.

"And now that I do know," he continued, "I wish to be put ashore. I don't know anything about the law, but I do know right and wrong, and I'm willing to take my chance with any judge for whatever wrong I have done—with all the judges in the United States, for that matter. And that's more than you can say, Mr. Pete."

"You say dat, eh? Vaire good. But you are one big t'ief—"

"I'm not! Don't you dare call me that again!" Joe's face was pale, and he was trembling—but not with fear. "T'ief!" the Frenchman taunted back.

"You lie!" Joe had not been a boy among boys for nothing. He knew the penalty which attached itself to the words he had just spoken, and he expected to receive it. So he was not overmuch surprised when he picked himself up from the floor of the cockpit an instant later, his head still ringing from a stiff blow between the eyes.

"Say dat one time more," Pete bullied, his fist raised and prepared to strike.

Tears of anger stood in Joe's eyes, but he was calm and in dead earnest. "When you say I am a thief, Pete, you lie. You can kill me, but still I will say you lie."

"No, you don't!" 'Frisco Kid had darted in like a wildcat, preventing a second blow and shoving the Frenchman back across the cockpit. "You leave the boy alone," he continued, suddenly unshipping and arming himself with the heavy iron tiller, and standing between them. "This thing's gone just about as far as it's going to go. You big fool, can't you see the stuff the boy's made out of? He speaks true. He's right, and he knows it, and you could kill him and he wouldn't give in. There's my hand on it, Joe." He turned and extended his hand to Joe, who returned the grip. "You've got spunk, and you're not afraid to show it."

Pete's mouth twisted itself in a sickly smile, but the evil gleam in his eyes gave it the lie. He shrugged his shoulders and said: "Ah! So? He does not dee-sire dat I him call pet names. Ha, ha! It is only ze sailor-man play. Let us—what you call—forgive and forget, eh? Vaire good; forgive and forget."

He reached out his hand, but Joe refused to take it. 'Frisco Kid nodded approval, while Pete, still shrugging his shoulders and smiling, passed into the cabin.

"Slack off ze main-sheet," he called out, "and run down for Hunter's Point. For one time I will cook ze dinner, and den you will say dat it is ze vaire good dinner. Ah! Pete is ze great cook!"

"That's the way he always does—gets real good and cooks when he wants to make up," 'Frisco Kid hazarded, slipping the tiller into the rudder-head and obeying the order. "But even then you can't trust him."

Joe nodded his head, but did not speak. He was in no mood for conversation. He was still trembling from the excitement of the last few moments, while deep down he questioned himself on how he had behaved, and found naught to be ashamed of.

The afternoon sea-breeze had sprung up and was now rioting in from the Pacific. Angel Island was fast dropping astern, and the waterfront of San Francisco showing up, as the *Dazzler* plowed along before it. Soon they were in the midst of the shipping, passing in and out among the vessels which had come from the uttermost ends of the earth. Later they crossed the fairway, where the ferry steamers, crowded with passengers, passed backward and forward between San Francisco and

Oakland. One came so close that the passengers crowded to the side to see the gallant little sloop and the two boys in the cockpit. Joe gazed almost enviously at the row of down-turned faces. They all were going to their homes, while he—he was going he knew not whither, at the will of Pete Le Maire. He was half tempted to cry out for help; but the foolishness of such an act struck him, and he held his tongue. Turning his head, his eyes wandered along the smoky heights of the city, and he fell to musing on the strange ways of men and ships on the sea.

'Frisco Kid watched him from the corner of his eye, following his thoughts as accurately as though he spoke them aloud.

"Got a home over there somewhere?" he queried suddenly, waving his hand in the direction of the city.

Joe started, so correctly had his thought been anticipated. "Yes," he said simply.

"Tell us about it."

Joe rapidly described his home, though forced to go into greater detail because of the curious questions of his companion. 'Frisco Kid was interested in everything, especially in Mrs. Bronson and Bessie. Of the latter he could not seem to tire, and poured forth question after question concerning her. So peculiar and artless were some of them that Joe could hardly forbear to smile.

"Now tell me about your home," he said, when he at last had finished.

'Frisco Kid seemed suddenly to harden, and his face took on a stern look which the other had never seen there before. He swung his foot idly to and fro, and lifted a dull eye to the main-peak blocks, with which, by the way, there was nothing the matter.

"Go ahead," the other encouraged.

"I haven't no home."

The four words left his mouth as though they had been forcibly ejected, and his lips came together after them almost with a snap.

Joe saw he had touched a tender spot, and strove to ease the way out of it again. "Then the home you did have." He did not dream that there were lads in the world who never had known homes, or that he had only succeeded in probing deeper.

"Never had none."

"Oh!" His interest was aroused, and he now threw solicitude to the winds. "Any sisters?"

"Nope."

"Mother?"

"I was so young when she died that I don't remember her."

"Father?"

"I never saw much of him. He went to sea—anyhow, he disappeared."

"Oh!" Joe did not know what to say, and an oppressive silence, broken only by the churn of the *Dazzler*'s forefoot, fell upon them.

Just then Pete came out to relieve at the tiller, while they went in to eat. Both lads hailed his advent with feelings of relief, and the awkwardness vanished over the dinner, which was all their skipper had claimed it to be. Afterward 'Frisco Kid relieved Pete, and while he was eating, Joe washed up the dishes and put the cabin shipshape. Then they all gathered in the stern, where the captain strove to increase the general cordiality by entertaining them with descriptions of life among the pearl-divers of the South Seas.

In this fashion the afternoon wore away. They had long since left San Francisco behind, rounded Hunter's Point, and were now skirting the San Mateo shore. Joe caught a glimpse, once, of a party of cyclists rounding a cliff on the San Bruno Road, and remembered the time when he had gone over the same ground on his own wheels. That was only a month or two before, but it seemed an age to him now so much had there been to come between.

By the time supper had been eaten and the things cleared away, they were well down the Bay, off the marshes behind which Redwood City clustered. The wind had gone down with the sun, and the *Dazzler* was making but little headway, when they sighted a sloop bearing down upon them on the dying wind. 'Frisco Kid instantly named it as the *Reindeer*, to which Pete, after a deep scrutiny, agreed. He seemed greatly pleased at the meeting.

"Epont Nelson runs her," 'Frisco Kid informed Joe. "They've got something big down here, and they're always after Pete to tackle it with them. He knows more about it, whatever it is."

Joe nodded and looked at the approaching craft curiously. Though somewhat larger, it was built on about the same lines as the *Dazzler*—which meant, above everything else, that it was built for speed. The mainsail was so large that it was more like that of a racing-yacht, and it carried the points for no less than three reefs in case of rough weather. Aloft and on deck everything was in place; nothing was untidy or useless. From running-gear to standing-rigging, everything bore evidence of thorough order and smart seamanship.

The *Reindeer* came up slowly in the gathering twilight, and went to anchor not a biscuit-toss away. Pete followed suit with the *Dazzler*, and then went in the skiff to pay them a visit. The two lads stretched themselves out on top of the cabin and awaited his return.

"Do you like the life?" Joe broke silence.

The other turned on his elbow. "Well—I do, and then again I don't. The fresh air and the salt water, and all that, and the freedom—that's all right; but I don't like the—the—"

'Frisco Kid instantly named it as the Reindeer.

He paused a moment, as though his tongue had failed in its duty, and then blurted out, "the stealing."

"Then why don't you quit it?" Joe liked the lad more than he dared confess, and he felt a sudden missionary zeal come upon him.

"I will, just as soon as I can turn my hand to something else."

"But why not now?"

Now is the accepted time, was ringing in Joe's ears, and if the other wished to leave, it seemed a pity that he did not, and at once.

"Where can I go? What can I do? There's nobody in all the world to lend me a hand, just as there never has been. I tried it once, and learned my lesson too well to do it again in a hurry."

"Well, when I get out of this I'm going home. Guess my father was right, after all. And I don't see—maybe—what's the matter with you going with me?"

He said this last impulsively, without thinking, and 'Frisco Kid knew it.

"You don't know what you're talking about," he answered. "Fancy me going off with you! What'd your father say? And—and the rest? How would he think of me? And what'd he do?"

Joe felt sick at heart. He realized that in the spirit of the moment he had given an invitation which, on sober thought, he knew would be impossible to carry out. He tried to imagine his father receiving in his own house a stranger like 'Frisco Kid. No, that was not to be thought of. Then, forgetting his own plight, he fell to racking his brains for some other method by which 'Frisco Kid could get away from his present surroundings.

"He might turn me over to the police," the other went on, "and send me to a refuge. I'd die first, before I'd let that happen to me. And besides, Joe, I'm not of your kind, and you know it. Why, I'd be like a fish out of water, what with all the things I don't know. Nope; I guess I'll have to wait a little before I strike out. But there's only one thing for you to do, and that's to go straight home. First chance I get, I'll land you, and then deal with Pete—"

"No, you don't," Joe interrupted hotly. "When I leave I'm not going to leave you in trouble on my account. So don't you try anything like that. I'll get away, never fear; and if I can figure it out, I want you to come along too—come along, anyway, and figure it out afterwards. What d' you say?"

'Frisco Kid shook his head, and, gazing up at the starlit heavens, wandered off into day-dreams of the life he would like to lead, but from which he seemed inexorably shut out. The seriousness of life was striking deeper than ever into Joe's heart, and he lay silent, thinking hard. A mumble of heavy voices came to them from the *Reindeer*; from the land the solemn notes of a church bell floated across the water, while the summer night wrapped them slowly in its warm darkness.

CHAPTER FOUR: 'FRISCO KID TELLS HIS STORY

AFTER THE CONVERSATION died away, the two lads lay upon the cabin for perhaps an hour.

Then, without saying a word, 'Frisco Kid went below and struck a light. Joe could hear him fumbling about, and a little later heard his own name called softly. On going into the cabin, he saw 'Frisco Kid sitting on the edge of the bunk, a sailor's ditty-box on his knees, and in his hand a carefully folded page from a magazine.

"Does she look like this?" he asked, smoothing it out and turning it that the other might see.

It was a half-page illustration of two girls and a boy, grouped in an old-fashioned, roomy attic, and evidently holding a council of some sort. The girl who was talking faced the on-looker, while the backs of the two others were turned.

"Who?" Joe queried, glancing in perplexity from the picture to 'Frisco Kid's face.

"Like—like your sister—Bessie." The name seemed reluctant to come from his

"Does she look like this?"

lips, and he expressed it with a certain shy reverence, as though it were something unspeakably sacred.

Joe was nonplussed for the moment. He could see no bearing between the two in point, and, anyway, girls were rather silly creatures to waste one's time over. "He's actually blushing," he thought, regarding the soft glow on the other's cheeks. He felt an irresistible desire to laugh, but tried to smother it down.

"No, no; don't!" 'Frisco Kid cried, snatching the paper away and putting it back in the ditty-box with shaking fingers. Then he added more slowly: "I thought I—I kind of thought you would understand, and—and—"

His lips trembled and his eyes glistened with unwonted moistness as he turned hastily away.

The next instant Joe was by his side on the bunk, his arm around him. Prompted by some instinctive monitor, he had done it before he thought. A week before he could not have imagined himself in such an absurd situation—his arm around a boy!—but now it seemed the most natural thing in the world. He did not comprehend, but he knew that, whatever it was, it was something that seemed of deep importance to his companion.

"Go ahead and tell us," he urged. "I'll understand."

"No, you won't; you can't."

"Yes—sure. Go ahead." 'Frisco Kid choked and shook his head. "I don't think I could, anyway. It's more the things I feel, and I don't know how to put them in words." Joe's arm wrapped about him reassuringly, and he went on: "Well, it's this way. You see, I don't know much about the land, and people, and homes, and I never had no brothers, or sisters, or playmates. All the time I didn't know it, but I was lonely—sort of missed them down in here somewheres." He placed a hand over his breast to locate the seat of loss. "Did you ever feel downright hungry? Well, that's just the way I used to feel, only a different kind of hunger, and me not knowing what it was. But one day, oh, a long time back, I got a-hold of a magazine, and saw a picture—that picture, with the two girls and the boy talking together. I thought it must be fine to be like them, and I got to thinking about the things they said and did, till it came to me all of a sudden like, and I knew that it was just loneliness was the matter with me.

"But, more than anything else, I got to wondering about the girl who looks out of the picture right at you. I was thinking about her all the time, and by and by she became real to me. You see, it was making believe, and I knew it all the time; and then again I didn't. Whenever I'd think of the men, and the work, and the hard life, I'd know it was make-believe; but when I'd think of her, it wasn't. I don't know; I can't explain it."

Joe remembered all his own adventures which he had imagined on land and sea, and nodded. He at least understood that much.

"Of course it was all foolishness, but to have a girl like that for a friend seemed more like heaven to me than anything else I knew of. As I said, it was a long while back, and I was only a little kid. That's when Nelson gave me my name, and I've never been anything but 'Frisco Kid ever since. But the girl in the picture: I was always getting that picture out to look at her, and before long, if I wasn't square, why, I felt ashamed to look at her. Afterwards, when I was older, I came to look at it in another way. I thought, 'Suppose, Kid, some day you were to meet a girl like that, what would she think of you? Could she like you? Could she be even the least bit of a friend to you?' And then I'd make up my mind to be better, to try and do something with myself so that she or any of her kind of people would not be ashamed to know me.

"That's why I learned to read. That's why I ran away. Nicky Perrata, a Greek boy, taught me my letters, and it wasn't till after I learned to read that I found out there was anything really wrong in Bay-pirating. I'd been used to it ever since I could remember, and several people I knew made their living that way. But when I did find out, I ran away, thinking to quit it for good. I'll tell you about it sometime, and how I'm back at it again.

"Of course she seemed a real girl when I was a youngster, and even now she sometimes seems that way, I've thought so much about her. But while I'm talking to you it all clears up and she comes to me in this light: she stands just for—well, for a better, cleaner life than this, and one I'd like to live; and if I could live it, why, I'd come to know that kind of girls, and their kind of people—your kind, that's what I mean. So I was wondering about your sister and you, and that's why—I don't know; I guess I was just wondering. But I suppose you know lots of girls like that, don't you?"

Joe nodded his head in token that he did.

"Then tell me about them; something—anything," he added, as he noted the fleeting expression of doubt in the other's eyes.

"Oh, that's easy," Joe began valiantly. To a certain extent he did understand the lad's hunger, and it seemed a simple enough task to satisfy him. "To begin with, they're like—hem!—why, they're like—girls, just girls." He broke off with a miserable sense of failure.

'Frisco Kid waited patiently, his face a study in expectancy.

Joe struggled vainly to marshal his ideas. To his mind, in quick succession, came the girls with whom he had gone to school, the sisters of the boys he knew, and those who were his sister's friends—slim girls and plump girls, tall girls and short girls, blue-eyed and brown-eyed, curly-haired, black-haired, golden-haired; in short, a regular procession of girls of all sorts and descriptions. But, to save himself, he could say nothing about them. Anyway, he'd never been a "sissy," and why should he be expected to know anything about them? "All girls are alike," he concluded desperately. "They're just the same as the ones you know, Kid. Sure they are."

"But I don't know any."

Joe whistled. "And never did?"

"Yes, one—Carlotta Gispardi. But she couldn't speak English; and she died. I don't care; though I never knew any, I seem to know as much about them as you do."

"And I guess I know more about adventures all over the world than you do," Joe retorted.

Both boys laughed. But a moment later Joe fell into deep thought. It had come upon him quite swiftly that he had not been duly grateful for the good things of life he did possess. Already home, father, and mother had assumed a greater significance to him; but he now found himself placing a higher personal value upon his sister, his chums and friends. He never had appreciated them properly, he thought, but henceforth—well, there would be a different tale to tell.

The voice of Pete hailing them put a finish to the conversation, for they both ran on deck.

"Get up ze mainsail, and break out ze hook!" he shouted. "And den tail on to ze *Reindeer*! No side-lights!"

"Come! Cast off those gaskets! Lively!" 'Frisco Kid ordered. "Now lay onto the peak-halyards—there, that rope; cast it off the pin. And don't hoist ahead of me. There! Make fast! We'll stretch it afterwards. Run aft and come in on the main-sheet! Shove the helm up!"

Under the sudden driving power of the mainsail, the *Dazzler* strained and tugged at her anchor like an impatient horse, till the muddy iron left the bottom with a rush, and she was free.

"Let go the sheet! Come for'ard again, and lend a hand on the chain! Stand by to give her the jib!" 'Frisco Kid, the boy who mooned over a picture of a girl in a magazine, had vanished, and 'Frisco Kid the sailor, strong and dominant, was on deck. He ran aft and tacked about as the jib rattled aloft in the hands of Joe, who quickly joined him. Just then the *Reindeer*, like a monstrous bat, passed to leeward of them in the gloom.

"Ah! dose boys! Dey take all-a night!" they heard Pete exclaim; and then the gruff voice of Nelson, who said: "Never you mind, Frenchy. I learned the Kid his sailorizing, and I ain't never been ashamed of him yet."

The *Reindeer* was the faster boat, but by spilling the wind from her sails they managed so that the boys could keep them in sight. The breeze came steadily in from the west, with a promise of early increase. The stars were being blotted out by driving masses of clouds, which indicated a greater velocity in the upper strata. 'Frisco Kid surveyed the sky. "Going to have it good and stiff before morning," he prophesied, and Joe guessed so, too.

A couple of hours later both boats stood in for the land, and dropped anchor not more than a cable's-length from the shore. A little wharf ran out, the bare end of which was perceptible to them, though they could discern a small yacht lying to a buoy a short distance away.

As on the previous night, everything was in readiness for hasty departure. The anchors could be tripped and the sails flung out on a moment's notice. Both skiffs came over noiselessly from the *Reindeer*. Nelson had given one of his two men to Pete, so that each skiff was doubly manned. They were not a very prepossessing bunch of men—at least, Joe thought so, for their faces bore a savage seriousness which almost made him shiver. The captain of the *Dazzler* buckled on his pistol-belt and placed a rifle and a small double-block tackle in the boat. Nelson was also armed, while his men wore at their hips the customary sailor's sheath-knife. They were very slow and careful to avoid noise in getting into the boats, Pete pausing long enough to warn the boys to remain quietly aboard and not try any tricks.

"Now'd be your chance, Joe, if they hadn't taken the skiffs," 'Frisco Kid whispered, when the boats had vanished into the loom of the land.

"What's the matter with the *Dazzler*?" was the unexpected answer. "We could up sail and away before you could say Jack Robinson."

They crawled for'ard and began to hoist the mainsail. The anchor they could slip, if necessary, and save the time of pulling it up. But at the first rattle of the halyards on the sheaves a warning "Hist!" came to them through the darkness, followed by a loudly whispered "Drop that!"

Glancing in the direction from which these sounds proceeded, they made out a white face peering at them from over the rail of the other sloop.

"Aw, it's only the *Reindeer*'s boy," 'Frisco Kid said. "Come on."

Again they were interrupted at the first rattling of the blocks.

"I say, you fellers, you'd better let go them halyards pretty quick, I'm a-tellin' you, or I'll give you what for!"

This threat being dramatically capped by the click of a cocking pistol, 'Frisco Kid obeyed and went grumblingly back to the cockpit. "Oh, there's plenty more chances to come," he whispered consolingly to Joe. "Pete was cute, wasn't he? Kind of thought you'd be trying to make a break, and fixed it so you couldn't."

Nothing came from the shore to indicate how the pirates were faring. Not a dog barked, not a light flared; yet the air seemed quivering with an alarm about to burst forth. The night had taken on a strained feeling of intensity, as though it held in store all kinds of terrible things. The boys felt this keenly as they huddled against each other in the cockpit and waited.

"You were going to tell me about your running away," Joe ventured finally, "and why you came back again."

'Frisco Kid took up the tale at once, speaking in a muffled undertone close to the other's ear.

"You see, when I made up my mind to quit the life, there wasn't a soul to lend me a hand; but I knew that the only thing for me to do was to get ashore and find some kind of work, so I could study. Then I figured there'd be more chance in the country than in the city; so I gave Nelson the slip. I was on the *Reindeer* then—one night on the Alameda oyster beds, and headed back from the Bay. But they were all Portuguese farmers thereabouts, and none of them had work for me. Besides, it was in the wrong time of the year—winter. That shows how much I knew about the land.

"I'd saved up a couple of dollars, and I kept traveling back, deeper and deeper into the country, looking for work and buying bread and cheese, and such things, from the store-keepers. I tell you it was cold, nights, sleeping out without blankets, and I was always glad when morning came. But worse than that was the way everybody looked on me. They were all suspicious, and not a bit afraid to show it, and sometimes they'd sic their dogs on me and tell me to get along. Seemed as though there wasn't no place for me on the land. Then my money gave out, and just about the time I was good and hungry I got captured."

"Captured! What for?"

"Nothing. Living, I suppose. I crawled into a haystack to sleep one night, because it was warmer, and along comes a village constable and arrests me for being a tramp. At first they thought I was a runaway, and telegraphed my description all over. I told them I didn't have no people, but they wouldn't believe me for a long while. And then, when nobody claimed me, the judge sent me to a boy's refuge in San Francisco."

He stopped and peered intently in the direction of the shore. The darkness and the silence in which the men had been swallowed up were profound. Nothing was stirring save the rising wind.

"I thought I'd die in that refuge. Just like being in jail. You were locked up and guarded like any prisoner. Even then, if I could have liked the other boys it wouldn't have been so bad. But they were mostly street-boys of the worst sort, without one spark of manhood or one idea of square dealing and fair play. There was only one thing I did like, and that was the books. Oh, I did lots of reading, I tell you. But that couldn't make up for the rest. I wanted the freedom, and the sunlight, and the salt water. And what had I done to be kept in prison and herded with such a gang? Instead of doing wrong, I had tried to do good, to make myself better, and that's what I got for it. I wasn't old enough, you see.

"Sometimes I'd see the sunshine dancing on the water and showing white on the sails, and the *Reindeer* cutting through it just as you please, and I'd get that sick I wouldn't know hardly what I did. And then the boys would come against me with some of their meannesses, and I'd start in to lick the whole kit of them. Then the men in charge'd lock me up and punish me. After I couldn't stand it no longer, I watched my chance, and cut and run for it. Seemed as though there wasn't no place on the land for me, so I picked up with Pete and went back on the Bay. That's about all there is to it, though I'm going to try it again when I get a little older—old enough to get a square deal for myself."

"You're going to go back on the land with me," Joe said authoritatively, laying a hand on his shoulder; "that's what you're going to do. As for—"

Bang! a revolver-shot rang out from the shore. Bang! bang! More guns were speaking sharply and hurriedly. A man's voice rose wildly on the air and died away. Somebody began to cry for help. Both boys were to their feet on the instant, hoisting the mainsail and getting everything ready to run. The *Reindeer* boy was doing likewise. A man, roused from his sleep on the yacht, thrust an excited head through the skylight, but withdrew it hastily at sight of the two stranger sloops. The intensity of waiting was broken, the time for action come.

CHAPTER FIVE: PERILOUS HOURS

HEAVING IN ON the anchor-chain till it was up and down, 'Frisco Kid and Joe ceased from their exertions. Everything was in readiness to give the *Dazzler* the jib and go. They strained their eyes in the direction of the shore. The clamor had died away, but here and there lights were beginning to flash. The creaking of a block and tackle came to their ears, and they heard Nelson's voice singing out "Lower away!" and "Cast off!"

"Pete forgot to oil it," 'Frisco Kid commented, referring to the tackle.

"Takin' their time about it, ain't they?" the boy on the *Reindeer* called over to them, sitting down on the cabin and mopping his face after the exertion of hoisting the mainsail single-handed.

"Guess they're all right," 'Frisco Kid rejoined.

"Say, you," the man on the yacht cried through the skylight, not venturing to show his head. "You'd better go away."

"And you'd better stay below and keep quiet," was the response.

"We'll take care of ourselves. See you do the same," replied the boy on the *Reindeer*.

"If I was only out of this, I'd show you," the man threatened.

"Lucky for you you're not," was the response.

"Here they come!"

The two skiffs shot out of the darkness and came alongside. Some kind of an altercation was going on, as Pete's shrill voice attested.

"No, no!" he cried. "Put it on ze *Dazzler*. Ze *Reindeer* she sail too fast-a, and run away, oh, so queeck, and never more I see it. Put it on ze *Dazzler*. Eh? Wat you say?"

"All right," Nelson agreed. "We'll whack up afterwards. But hurry up. Out with you, lads, and heave her up. My arm's broke."

The men tumbled out, ropes were cast inboard, and all hands, with the exception of Joe, tailed on. The shouting of men, the sound of oars, and the rattling and slapping of blocks and sails, told that the men on shore were getting under way for the pursuit.

"Now!" Nelson commanded. "All together! Don't let her come back or you'll smash the skiff. There she takes it! A long pull and a strong pull! Once again! And yet again! Get a turn there, somebody, and take a spell."

Though the task was but half accomplished, they were exhausted by the strenuous effort, and hailed the rest eagerly. Joe glanced over the side to discover what the heavy object might be, and saw the vague outlines of a very small office safe.

"Now, all together! Take her on the run, and don't let her stop! Yo, ho! heave, ho! Once again! And another! Over with her!"

Straining and gasping, with tense muscles and heaving chests, they brought the cumbersome weight over the side, rolled it on top of the rail, and lowered it into the cockpit on the run. The cabin doors were thrown apart, and it was moved along, end for end, till it lay on the cabin floor, snug against the end of the centerboard-case. Nelson had followed it aboard to superintend. His left arm hung helpless at his side, and from the finger-tips blood dripped with monotonous regularity. He did not seem to mind it, however; nor even the mutterings of the human storm he had raised ashore, and which, to judge by the sounds, was even now threatening to break upon them.

"Lay your course for the Golden Gate," he said to Pete, as he turned to go. "I'll try to stand by you; but if you get lost in the dark, I'll meet you outside, off the Farralones, in the morning." He sprang into the skiff after the men, and, with a wave of his uninjured arm, cried heartily: "And then it's Mexico, my jolly rovers—Mexico and summer weather!"

Just as the *Dazzler*, freed from her anchor, paid off under the jib and filled away, a dark sail loomed under her stern, barely missing the skiff in tow. The cockpit of the stranger was crowded with men, who raised their voices angrily at sight of the pirates. Joe had half a mind to run for'ard and cut the halyards so that they might be captured. As he had told Pete the day before, he had done nothing to be ashamed of, and was not afraid to go before a court of justice. But the thought of 'Frisco Kid restrained him. He wished to take him ashore with him, but in so doing he did not wish to take him to jail. So he began to experience a keen interest in the escape of the *Dazzler*, after all.

The pursuing sloop rounded up hurriedly to come about after them, and in the darkness fouled the yacht which lay at anchor. The man aboard of her, thinking that at last his time had come, let out one wild yell, and ran on deck, screaming for help. In the confusion of the collision Pete and the boys slipped away into the night.

The *Reindeer* had already disappeared, and by the time Joe and 'Frisco Kid had the running-gear coiled down and everything in shape, they were standing out in open water. The wind was freshening constantly, and the *Dazzler* heeling a lively clip through the comparatively smooth water. Before an hour had passed, the lights of Hunter's Point were well on her starboard beam. 'Frisco Kid went below to make coffee, but Joe remained on deck, watching the lights of South San Francisco grow, and speculating on his destination. Mexico! They were going to sea in such a frail craft! Impossible! At least, it seemed so to him, for his conceptions of ocean travel were limited to steamers and full-rigged ships, and he did not know how the tiny fishing-boats ventured the open sea. He was beginning to feel half sorry that he had not cut the halyards, and longed to ask Pete a thousand questions; but just as the first was on his lips, that worthy ordered him to go below and get some coffee, and then to turn in. He was followed shortly afterward by 'Frisco Kid, Pete remaining at his lonely task of beating down the Bay and out to sea. Twice Pete heard the waves buffeted back from some flying forefoot, and once he saw a sail to leeward on the opposite tack, which luffed sharply and came about at sight of him. But the darkness favored, and he heard no more of it—perhaps because he worked into the wind closer by a point, and held on his way with a rebellious shaking after-leech.

Shortly after dawn the boys were called and came sleepily on deck. The day had broken cold and gray, while the wind had attained half a gale. Joe noted with astonishment the white tents of the quarantine station on Angel Island. San Francisco lay a smoky blur on the southern horizon, while the night, still lingering on the western edge of the world, slowly withdrew before their eyes. Pete was just finishing a long reach into the Raccoon Strait, and, at the same time, studiously regarding a plunging sloop-yacht half a mile astern.

"Dey t'ink to catch ze *Dazzler*, eh? Bah!" And he brought the craft in question about, laying a course straight for the Golden Gate.

The pursuing yacht followed suit. Joe watched her a few moments. She held an apparently parallel course to them, and forged ahead much faster. "Why, at this rate they'll have us in no time!" he cried.

Pete laughed. "You tink so? Bah! Dey outfoot; we outpoint. Dey are scared of ze wind; we wipe ze eye of ze wind. Ah! you wait—you see."

"They're traveling ahead faster," 'Frisco Kid explained, "but we're sailing closer to the wind. In the end we'll beat them, even if they have the nerve to cross the bar, which I don't think they have. Look! See!"

Ahead could be seen the great ocean surges, flinging themselves skyward and bursting into roaring caps of smother. In the midst of it, now rolling her dripping bottom clear, now sousing her deck-load of lumber far above the guards, a coasting steam-schooner was lumbering heavily into port. It was magnificent, this battle between man and the elements. Whatever timidity he had entertained fled away, and Joe's nostrils began to dilate and his eyes to flash at the nearness of the impending struggle.

Pete called for his oilskins and sou'wester, and Joe also was equipped with a spare suit. Then he and 'Frisco Kid were sent below to lash and cleat the safe in place. In the midst of this task Joe glanced at the firm-name gilt-lettered on the face of it, and read, "Bronson & Tate." Why, that was his father and his father's partner. That was their safe! their money! 'Frisco Kid, nailing the last retaining-cleat on the floor of the cabin, looked up and followed his fascinated gaze.

"That's rough, isn't it?" he whispered. "Your father?"

Joe nodded. He could see it all now. They had run in to San Andreas, where his father worked the big quarries, and most probably the safe contained the wages of the thousand men or so whom his firm employed. "Don't say anything," he cautioned.

'Frisco Kid agreed knowingly. "Pete can't read, anyway," he added, "and the chances are that Nelson won't know what your name is. But, just the same, it's pretty rough. They'll break it open and divide up as soon as they can, so I don't see what you're going to do about it."

"Wait and see." Joe had made up his mind that he would do his best to stand by his father's property. At the worst, it could only be lost; and that would surely be the case were he not along; while, being along, he at least held a fighting chance to save or to be in position to recover it. Responsibilities were showering upon him thick and fast. Three days before he had had but himself to consider. Then, in some subtle way, he had felt a certain accountability for 'Frisco Kid's future welfare; and after that, and still more subtly, he had become aware of duties which he owed to his position, to his sister, to his chums, and to friends. And now, by a most unexpected chain of circumstances, came the pressing need of service for his father's sake. It was a call upon his deepest strength, and he responded bravely. While the future might be doubtful, he had no doubt of himself; and this very state of mind, this self-confidence, by a generous alchemy, gave him added strength. Nor did he fail to be vaguely aware of it, and to grasp dimly at the truth that confidence breeds confidence—strength, strength.

"Now she takes it!" Pete cried. Both lads ran into the cockpit. They were on the edge of the breaking bar. A huge forty-footer reared a foam-crested head far above them, stealing their wind for the moment and threatening to crush the tiny craft like an egg-shell. Joe held his breath. It was the supreme moment. Pete luffed straight into it, and the *Dazzler* mounted the steep slope with a rush, poised a moment on the giddy summit, and fell into the yawning valley beyond. Keeping off

Pete luffed straight ahead into it, and the Dazzler *mounted the steep slope with a rush.*

in the intervals to fill the mainsail, and luffing into the combers, they worked their way across the dangerous stretch. Once they caught the tail-end of a whitecap and were well-nigh smothered in the froth; but otherwise the sloop bobbed and ducked with the happy facility of a cork.

To Joe it seemed as though he had been lifted out of himself, out of the world. Ah, this was life! This was action! Surely it could not be the old, commonplace world he had lived in so long! The sailors, grouped on the streaming deck-load of the steamer, waved their sou'westers, nor, on the bridge, was the captain above expressing his admiration for the plucky craft.

"Ah! You see! You see!" Pete pointed astern.

The sloop-yacht had been afraid to venture it, and was skirting back and forth on the inner edge of the bar. The chase was off. A pilot-boat, running for shelter from the coming storm, flew by them like a frightened bird, passing the steamer as though the latter were standing still.

Half an hour later the *Dazzler* passed beyond the last smoking sea and was sliding up and down on the long Pacific swell. The wind had increased its velocity and necessitated a reefing down of jib and mainsail. Then she laid off again, full and free on the starboard tack, for the Farralones, thirty miles away. By the time breakfast was cooked and eaten they picked up the *Reindeer*, hove to and working offshore to the south and west. The wheel was lashed down, and there was not a soul on deck.

Pete complained bitterly against such recklessness. "Dat is ze one fault of Nelson. He no care. He is afraid of not'ing. Some day he will die, oh, so vaire queeck! I know, I know."

Three times they circled about the *Reindeer*, running under her weather quarter and shouting in chorus, before they brought anybody on deck. Sail was then made at once, and together the two cockle-shells plunged away into the vastness of the Pacific. This was necessary, as 'Frisco Kid informed Joe, in order to have an offing before the whole fury of the storm broke upon them. Otherwise they would be driven on the lee shore of the California coast. "Grub and water," he said, could be obtained by running in to the land when fine weather came. He also congratulated Joe upon the fact that he was not sea-sick—which circumstance likewise brought praise from Pete, and put him in better humor with his mutinous sailor.

"I'll tell you what we'll do," 'Frisco Kid whispered, while cooking dinner. "Tonight we'll drag Pete down—"

"Drag Pete down?"

"Yes, and tie him up good and snug—as soon as it gets dark. Then put out the lights and make a run for it. Get to port anyway, anywhere, just so long as we shake loose from Nelson. You'll save your father's money, and I'll go away somewhere, over on the other side of the world, and begin all over again."

"Then we'll have to call it off, that's all."

"Call what off?"

"Tying Pete up and running for it."

"No, sir; that's decided upon."

"Now, listen here: I'll not have a thing to do with it—I'll go on to Mexico first—if you don't make me one promise."

"And what's the promise?"

"Just this: you place yourself in my hands from the moment we get ashore, and trust to me. You don't know anything about the land, anyway—you said so. And I'll fix it with my father—I know I can—so that you can get to study, and get an education, and be something else than a Bay pirate or a sailor. That's what you'd like, isn't it?"

Though he said nothing, 'Frisco Kid showed how well he liked it by the expression of his face.

"And it'll be no more than your due, either," Joe continued. "You've stood by me, and you'll have recovered my father's money. He'll owe it to you."

"But I don't do things that way. Think I do a man a favor just to be paid for it?"

"Now you keep quiet. How much do you think it'd cost my father to recover that safe? Give me your promise, that's all, and when I've got things arranged, if you don't like them you can back out. Come on; that's fair."

They shook hands on the bargain, and proceeded to map out their line of action for the night.

But the storm yelling down out of the north-west had something entirely different in store for the *Dazzler* and her crew. By the time dinner was over they were forced to put double reefs in mainsail and jib, and still the gale had not reached its height. The sea, also, had been kicked up till it was a continuous succession of water mountains, frightful and withal grand to look upon from the low deck of the sloop. It was only when the sloops were tossed up on the crests of the waves at the same time that they caught sight of each other. Occasional fragments of seas swashed into the cockpit or dashed aft clear over the cabin, and before long Joe was stationed at the small pump to keep the well dry.

At three o'clock, watching his chance, Pete motioned to the *Reindeer* that he was going to heave to and get out a sea-anchor. This latter was of the nature of a large shallow canvas bag, with the mouth held open by triangularly lashed spars. To this the towing-ropes were attached, on the kite principle, so that the greatest resisting surface was presented to the water. The sloop, drifting so much faster, would thus be held bow on to both wind and sea—the safest possible position in a storm. Nelson waved his hand in response that he understood, and to go ahead.

Pete went for'ard to launch the sea-anchor himself, leaving it to 'Frisco Kid to put the helm down at the proper moment and run into the wind.

The Frenchman poised on the slippery fore-deck, waiting an opportunity. But at this moment the *Dazzler* lifted into an unusually large sea, and, as she cleared the summit, caught a heavy snort of the gale at the very instant she was righting herself to an even keel.

Thus there was not the slightest yield to this sudden pressure coming on her sails and mast-gear.

Snap! Crash! The steel weather-rigging was carried away at the lanyards, and mast, jib, mainsail, blocks, stays, sea-anchor, Pete—everything—went over the side. Almost by a miracle, the captain clutched at the bobstay and managed to get one hand up and over the bowsprit. The boys ran for'ard to drag him into safety, and Nelson, observing the disaster, put up his helm and instantly ran the *Reindeer* down to the rescue of the imperiled crew.

CHAPTER SIX: THE END OF THE CRUISE

PETE WAS UNINJURED from the fall overboard with the *Dazzler*'s mast, but the sea-anchor which had gone with him had not escaped so easily. The gaff of the mainsail had been driven through it, and it refused to work. The wreckage, thumping alongside, held the sloop in a quartering slant to the seas—not so dangerous a position as it might be, nor as safe, either.

"Good-by, old-a *Dazzler*. Never no more you wipe ze eye of ze wind. Never no more you kick your heels at ze crack gentleman-yachts."

So the captain lamented, standing in the cockpit and surveying the ruin with wet eyes. Even Joe, who bore him great dislike, felt sorry for him at this moment. As the horse is to the Arab, so the ship is to the sailor, and Pete suffered his loss keenly. A heavier blast of the wind caught the jagged crest of a wave and buried it upon the helpless craft.

"Can't we save her?" Joe spluttered. 'Frisco Kid shook his head.

"Or the safe?"

"Impossible," he answered. "Couldn't lay another boat alongside for a United States mint. As it is, it'll keep us guessing to save ourselves."

Another sea swept over them, and the skiff, which had long since been swamped, dashed itself to pieces against the stern. Then the *Reindeer* lowered above them on a mountain of water. Joe caught himself half shrinking back, for it seemed she would fall down squarely on top of them; but the next instant she dropped into the gaping trough, and they were looking down upon her far below. It was a striking picture—one Joe was destined never to forget. The *Reindeer* was

wallowing in the snow-white smother, her rails flush with the sea, the water scud-
ding across her deck in foaming cataracts. The air was filled with flying spray,
which made the scene appear hazy and unreal. One of the men was clinging to the
perilous after-deck and striving to cast off the water-logged skiff. The boy, leaning
far over the cockpit-rail and holding on for dear life, was passing him a knife. The
second man stood at the wheel, putting it up with flying hands, and forcing the
sloop to pay off. By him, his injured arm in a sling, was Nelson, his sou'wester gone
and his fair hair plastered in wet, wind-blown ringlets about his face. His whole
attitude breathed indomitability, courage, strength. Joe looked upon him in sudden
awe, and, realizing the enormous possibilities in the man, felt sorrow for the way in
which they had been wasted. A pirate—a robber! In that flashing moment he
caught a glimpse of truth, grasped at the mystery of success and failure. Of such
stuff as Nelson were heroes made; but they possessed wherein he lacked—the
power of choice, the careful poise of mind, the sober control of soul.

These were the thoughts which came to Joe in the flight of a second. Then the
Reindeer swept skyward and hurtled across their bow to leeward on the breast of a
mighty billow.

"Ze wild man! ze wild man!" Pete shrieked, watching her in amazement. "He
t'inks he can jibe! He will die! We will all die! He must come about! Oh, ze fool!
ze fool!"

But time was precious, and Nelson ventured the chance. At the right moment
he jibed the mainsail over and hauled back on the wind.

"Here she comes! Make ready to jump for it!" 'Frisco Kid cried to Joe.

The *Reindeer* dashed by their stern, heeling over till the cabin windows were
buried, and so close that it appeared she must run them down. But a freak of the
waters lurched the two crafts apart. Nelson, seeing that the manoeuver had mis-
carried, instantly instituted another. Throwing the helm hard up, the *Reindeer*
whirled on her heel, thus swinging her overhanging main-boom closer to the
Dazzler. Pete was the nearest, and the opportunity could last no longer than a second. Like a cat he sprang, catching the foot-rope with both hands. Then the
Reindeer forged ahead, dipping him into the sea at every plunge. But he clung on,
working inboard every time he emerged, till he dropped into the cockpit, as Nelson
squared off to run down to leeward and repeat the manoeuver.

"Your turn next," 'Frisco Kid said.

"No; yours," Joe replied.

"But I know more about the water," 'Frisco Kid insisted.

"I can swim as well as you," said the other.

It would have been hard to forecast the outcome of this dispute; but, as it was,
the swift rush of events made any settlement useless. The *Reindeer* had jibed over

*Pete clung on, working inboard every time
he emerged, till he dropped into the cockpit.*

and was plowing back at breakneck speed, careening at such an angle that it seemed she must surely capsize. It was a gallant sight.

The storm burst in fury, the shouting wind flattening the ragged crests till they boiled. The *Reindeer* dipped from view behind an immense wave. The wave rolled on, but where the sloop had been the boys noted with startled eyes only the angry waters. Doubting, they looked a second time. There was no *Reindeer*. They were alone on the ocean.

"God have mercy on their souls!"

Joe was too horrified at the suddenness of the catastrophe to utter a sound.

"Sailed her clean under, and, with the ballast she carried, went straight to bottom," 'Frisco Kid gasped when he could speak. "Pete always said Nelson would drown himself that way some day! And now they're all gone. It's dreadful—dreadful. But now we've got to look out for ourselves, I tell you! The back of the storm broke in that puff, but the sea'll kick up worse yet as the wind eases down. Lend a hand, and hang on with the other. We've got to get her head-on."

Together, knives in hand, they crawled for'ard, where the pounding wreckage hampered the boat sorely. 'Frisco Kid took the lead in the ticklish work, but Joe obeyed orders like a veteran. Every minute or so the bow was swept by the sea, and they were pounded and buffeted about like a pair of shuttlecocks. First the main portion of the wreckage was securely fastened to the for'ard bitts; then, breathless and gasping, more often under the water than out, it was cut and hack at the tangle of halyards, sheets, stays, and tackles. The cockpit was taking water rapidly, and it was a race between swamping and completing the task. At last, however, everything stood clear save the lee rigging. 'Frisco Kid slashed the lanyards. The storm did the rest. The *Dazzler* drifted swiftly to leeward of the wreckage, till the strain on the line fast to the for'ard bitts jerked her bow into place, and she ducked dead into the eye of the wind and sea.

Pausing but for a cheer at the success of their undertaking, the two lads raced aft, where the cockpit was half full and the dunnage of the cabin all afloat. With a couple of buckets procured from the stern lockers, they proceeded to fling the water overboard. It was heartbreaking work, for many a barrelful was flung back upon them again; but they persevered, and when night fell, the *Dazzler*, bobbing merrily at her sea-anchor, could boast that her pumps sucked once more. As 'Frisco Kid had said, the backbone of the storm was broken, though the wind had veered to the west, where it still blew stiffly.

"If she holds," 'Frisco Kid said, referring to the breeze, "we'll drift to the California coast, somewhere along in, tomorrow. There's nothing to do now but wait."

They said little, oppressed by the loss of their comrades and overcome with exhaustion, preferring to huddle against each other for the sake of warmth and companionship. It was a miserable night, and they shivered constantly from the cold. Nothing dry was to be obtained aboard, food, blankets, everything being soaked with the salt water. Sometimes they dozed; but these intervals were short and harassing, for it seemed as if each of the two boys took turns in waking with such a sudden start as to rouse the other.

At last day broke, and they looked about. Wind and sea had dropped considerably, and there was no question as to the safety of the *Dazzler*. The coast was nearer than they had expected, its cliffs showing dark and forbidding in the gray of dawn. But with the rising of the sun they could see the yellow beaches, flanked by the white surf, and, beyond—it seemed too good to be true—the clustering houses and smoking chimneys of a town.

"It's Santa Cruz!" 'Frisco Kid cried. "And we'll run no risk of being wrecked in the surf!"

"Then you think we'll save the safe?" Joe queried.

"Yes, indeed we will! There isn't much of a sheltered harbor for large vessels, but with this breeze we'll run right up the mouth of the San Lorenzo River. Then there's a little lake like, and boat-houses. Water smooth as glass. Come on. We'll be in in time for breakfast."

Bringing to light some spare coils of rope from the lockers, he put a clove-hitch on the standing part of the sea-anchor hawser, and carried the new running-line aft, making it fast to the stern bitts. Then he cast off from the for'ard bitts. Naturally the *Dazzler* swung off into the trough, completed the evolution, and pointed her nose toward shore. A couple of spare oars from below, and as many water-soaked blankets, sufficed to make a jury-mast and sail. When this was in place Joe cast loose from the wreckage, which was now towing astern, while 'Frisco Kid took the tiller.

"How's that?" said 'Frisco Kid, as he finished making the *Dazzler* fast fore and aft, and stepped upon the stringer-piece of the tiny wharf.

"What'll we do next, captain?" Joe looked up in quick surprise.

"Why—I—what's the matter?"

"Well, aren't you captain now? Haven't we reached land? I'm crew from now on, you know. What's your orders?"

Joe caught the spirit of it. "Pipe all hands for breakfast; that is—wait a minute."

Diving below, he possessed himself of the money he had stowed away in his bundle when he came aboard. Then he locked the cabin door, and they went uptown in search of restaurants. Over the breakfast Joe planned the next move, and, when they had done, communicated it to 'Frisco Kid.

In response to his inquiry the cashier told him when the morning train started for San Francisco. He glanced at the clock.

"I've just time to catch it," he said to 'Frisco Kid. "Here is the key to the cabin door. Keep it locked, and don't let anybody come aboard. Here's money. Eat at the restaurants. Dry your blankets and sleep in the cockpit. I'll be back tomorrow. And don't let anybody into that cabin. Good-by."

With a hasty hand-grip, he sped down the street to the depot. The conductor, when he punched his ticket, looked at him with surprise. And well he might, for it was not the custom of his passengers to travel in sea-boots and sou'westers. But Joe did not mind. He did not even notice. He had bought a paper and was absorbed in its contents. Before long his eyes caught an interesting paragraph:

SUPPOSED TO HAVE BEEN LOST

The tug *Sea Queen*, chartered by Bronson & Tate, has returned from a fruitless cruise outside the heads. No news of value could be obtained concerning the pirates who so daringly carried off their safe at San Andreas last Tuesday night. The lighthouse-keeper at the Farralones mentions having sighted the two sloops Wednesday morning, clawing offshore in the teeth of the gale. It is supposed by shipping men that they perished in the storm with their ill-gotten treasure. Rumor has it that, in addition to a large sum in gold, the safe contained papers of even greater importance.

When Joe had read this he felt a great relief. It was evident no one had been killed at San Andreas on the night of the robbery, else there would have been some comment on it in the paper. Nor, if they had had any clue to his own whereabouts, would they have omitted such a striking bit of information.

At the depot in San Francisco the curious onlookers were surprised to see a boy clad conspicuously in sea-boots and sou'wester hail a cab and dash away in it. But Joe was in a hurry. He knew his father's hours, and was fearful lest he should not catch him before he went to luncheon.

The office-boy scowled at him when he pushed open the door and asked to see Mr. Bronson; nor could the head clerk, when summoned by this strange-looking intruder, recognize him.

"Don't you know me, Mr. Willis?"

Mr. Willis looked a second time.

"Why, it's Joe Bronson! Of all things under the sun, where did you drop from? Go right in. Your father's in there."

Mr. Bronson stopped dictating to his stenographer, looked up, and said: "Hello! where have you been?"

"To sea," Joe answered demurely enough, not sure of just what kind of a reception he was to get, and fingering his sou'wester nervously.

"Short trip, eh? How did you make out?"

"Oh, so-so." He had caught the twinkle in his father's eye, and knew that it was all clear sailing. "Not so bad—er—that is, considering."

"Considering?"

"Well, not exactly that; rather, it might have been worse, and, well—I don't know that it could have been better."

"You interest me; sit down." Then, turning to the stenographer, "You may go, Mr. Brown, and—hum—I sha'n't need you any more today."

It was all Joe could do to keep from crying, so kindly and naturally had his father received him—making him feel at once as if not the slightest thing uncommon had occurred. It was as if he had just returned from a vacation, or, man-grown, had come back from some business trip.

"Now go ahead, Joe. You were speaking to me a moment ago in conundrums, and have aroused my curiosity to a most uncomfortable degree."

Thereat Joe sat down and told what had happened, all that had happened, from the previous Monday night to that moment. Each little incident he related, every detail, not forgetting his conversations with 'Frisco Kid nor his plans concerning him. His face flushed and he was carried away with the excitement of the narrative, while Mr. Bronson was almost as interested, urging him on whenever he slackened his pace, but otherwise remaining silent.

"So you see," Joe said at last, "it couldn't possibly have turned out any better."

"Ah, well," Mr. Bronson deliberated judiciously, "it may be so, and then again it may not."

"I don't see it." Joe felt sharp disappointment at his father's qualified approval. It seemed to him that the return of the safe merited something stronger.

That Mr. Bronson fully comprehended the way Joe felt about it was clearly in evidence, for he went on: "As to the matter of the safe, all hail to you, Joe. Credit, and plenty of it, is your due. Mr. Tate and I have already spent five hundred dollars in attempting to recover it. So important was it that we have also offered five thousand dollars reward, and this morning were even considering the advisability of increasing the amount. But, my son"—Mr. Bronson stood up, resting a hand affectionately on his boy's shoulder—"there be certain things in this world which are of still greater importance than gold or papers which represent that which gold may buy. How about yourself? There's the point. Will you sell the best possibilities of your life right now for a million dollars?"

Joe shook his head.

"As I said, that's the point. A human life the treasure of the world cannot buy; nor can it redeem one which is misspent; nor can it make full and complete and beautiful a life which is dwarfed and warped and ugly. How about yourself? What is to be the effect of all these strange adventures on your life—your life, Joe? Are you going to pick yourself up tomorrow and try it over again? Or the next day, or the day after? Do you understand? Why, Joe, do you think for one moment that I could place against the best value of my son's life the paltry value of a safe? And can I say, until time has told me, whether this trip of yours could not possibly have been better? Such an experience is as potent for evil as for good. One dollar is exactly like another—there are many in the world; but no Joe is like my Joe, nor can there be any others in the world to take his place. Don't you see, Joe? Don't you understand?"

Mr. Bronson's voice broke slightly, and the next instant Joe was sobbing as though his heart would break. He had never understood this father of his before, and he knew now the pain he must have caused him, to say nothing of his mother and sister. But the four stirring days he had spent had given him a clearer view of the world and humanity, and he had always possessed the power of putting his thoughts into speech; so he spoke of these things and the lessons he had learned, the conclusions he had drawn from his conversations with 'Frisco Kid, from his intercourse with Pete, from the graphic picture he retained of the *Reindeer* and Nelson as they wallowed in the trough beneath him. And Mr. Bronson listened and, in turn, understood.

"But what of 'Frisco Kid, father?" Joe asked when he had finished.

"Hum! there's a great deal of promise in the boy, from what you say of him." Mr. Bronson hid the twinkle in his eye this time. "And, I must confess, he seems perfectly capable of shifting for himself."

"Sir?" Joe could not believe his ears.

"Let us see, then. He is at present entitled to the half of five thousand dollars, the other half of which belongs to you. It was you two who preserved the safe from the bottom of the Pacific, and if you only had waited a little longer, Mr. Tate and I might have increased the reward."

"Oh!" Joe caught a glimmering of the light. "Part of that is easily arranged, father. I simply refuse to take my half. As to the other—that isn't exactly what 'Frisco Kid desires. He wants friends—and—and—though you didn't say so, they are far higher than gold, nor can gold buy them. He wants friends and a chance for an education—not twenty-five hundred dollars."

"Don't you think it would be better that he choose for himself?"

"Ah, no. That's all arranged."

"Arranged?"

"Yes, sir. He's captain on sea, and I'm captain on land. So he's under my charge now."

"Then you have the power of attorney for him in the present negotiations? Good. I'll make a proposition. The twenty-five hundred dollars shall be held in trust by me, on his demand at any time. We'll settle about yours afterward. Then he shall be put on probation for, say, a year—as messenger first, and then in the office. You can either coach him in his studies, or he can attend night-school. And after that, if he comes through his period of probation with flying colors, I'll give him the same opportunities for an education that you possess. It all depends on himself. And now, Mr. Attorney, what have you to say to my offer in the interests of your client?"

"That I close with it at once—and thank you."

Father and son shook hands.

"And what are you going to do now, Joe?"

"I'm going to send a telegram to 'Frisco Kid first, and then hurry home."

"Then wait a minute till I call up San Andreas and tell Mr. Tate the good news, and I'll go with you."

"Mr. Willis," Mr. Bronson said as they left the outer office, "do you remain in charge, and kindly tell the clerks that they are free for the rest of the day.

"And I say," he called back as they entered the elevator, "don't forget the office-boy."

First published in the July 1902 edition of *St. Nicholas Magazine*

GRETCHEN WAS IN the kitchen-garden, weeding among the vegetables. "And you really want to marry me, Jacob?" she said.

"Yes, Gretchen," said Jacob.

"And for why, Jacob?"

"Well," said Jacob, "we are neighbors, and our joint property would make a farm larger than any in the country."

"No other reason, Jacob?"

"Well," said Jacob, "I think you are very beautiful, Gretchen."

"You are not the first, Jacob, to make that discovery," said Gretchen, laughing. "I count them on the fingers of my hand—Hans, the goldsmith, Fritz, the miller's son, Farmer Albrecht, Jan, the bailiff, Carl, the schoolmaster, Heinrich, the tailor, Max, the greengrocer, Parson Ludwig, and Burgomaster Wilhelm."

"Is it so?" said Jacob, and he pulled a longer face than usual, thinking of his nine rivals.

"Do you love me, Jacob?" said Gretchen.

"Humph!" said Jacob, "there are maids who would be quite content to love *me*, without asking that!"

"Let it be, then, Jacob," said Gretchen. "In spite of everything, I admire you greatly, and I will marry you on one condition: that you will come back again in seven days with at least five friends; old or young, rich or poor, wise or simple, it matters not, only that their affection for you will be such that they will not be content when separated from you, even for a moment."

"Humph!" said Jacob, crossly.

"And listen, Jacob!" said Gretchen; "leave your purse at home—promise me that! And now good-by, Jacob."

"Good-by, Gretchen," said Jacob. And he added to himself, "There are many as fair and none so impudent! Marry her indeed! She'll wait for me, that she will—I'll none of her!"

So he strode along at a great pace until he reached his own door, where he sat down under the grape-vine and smoked his pipe to soothe his feelings, which were somewhat ruffled.

Now I must tell you about Jacob. He was a worthy soul and a prosperous farmer, but one would never meet with a sourer face in a day's journey. Why, he looked at least as if he lived on pickles and sauerkraut and cider-vinegar, and a glass of sour lemonade now and then! He would have been handsome had his expression been more amiable. It was unfortunate that he had become so crabbed, for he had very little to be unhappy about. He was well-to-do, and had the finest farm in the neighborhood; he was strong and clever—in fact, he should have been quite contented. But he had become so used to flying into a temper and letting little mishaps get the better of his feelings, that he had come to be known as the sourest man in the country, and the children poked fun at him, and called him "Crab Jacob." And you may guess that that did not improve his disposition! He had scarcely a friend for miles around; in fact Gretchen seemed the only person who cared at all about him. So, you see, that condition of Gretchen's, that he should bring her five friends who loved him, rankled exceedingly.

"Gretchen indeed!" he exclaimed to himself. "I'll not be marrying her. I'm rid of a bad bargain, that I am, and easily." But he sat there in the sunshine under the grape-vine and felt a little uneasy.

Whether he would or no, he could not put her out of his mind—that bright figure in the buttercup-colored gown, and the eyes of corn-flower blue under the big garden hat. And the smile—he couldn't forget Gretchen's smile, any more than could you or I, or the ten suitors she counted on her little fingers.

"She has fine eyes, Gretchen," said Jacob, watching the smoke wreaths. Puff! puff! "She has hair like the shine on a dove's wing," he added. He knocked the ashes out of his pipe. "She smiles like the angels, for all her impertinence," he said meditatively.

Then he got up and started down the path toward the gate. When he reached the gate, he stopped, felt in his pocket, and took out his purse, heavy with gold and silver coins. He went back to the farm-house and laid the purse on the deal table. Then he strode off again, staff in hand, and out of the gate he went, closing it carefully behind him, and kicked up the dust of the king's highway. "I'm not marrying her," said Jacob. "She is the soul of impertinence!"

He plodded along, with never a glance at her farm, with its verdant acres stretching far and wide, its windmill and white barns and dove-cotes, its comfortable farm-house and garden gay with summer bloom. It was nearly noon and the sun high in the heavens, so he had hardly passed the hedge which bordered Gretchen's farm, before he sat down beneath a roadside tree to rest and meditate, for the heat tried his temper.

For a long while, he thought and thought, and at last he said: "There is something about Gretchen!" He thought of Fritz, the miller's son, and Parson Ludwig and the rest, and his heart swelled within him, for all one would have thought it of clay or stone.

"How can I go about gaining five faithful friends?" he groaned. For he had never in his memory had a friend except Gretchen, and he believed that magic itself could scarce entice five mortals to follow him for love. He was all bewildered.

As he sat there, tortured with his thoughts, an old woman appeared, seemingly from nowhere, and sat down beside him in the shadow of the tree.

"Why such a long face, lad?" she said.

Jacob, according to his usual fashion, was about to rudely reply, "Mind your own affairs, old woman!" But he checked the speech on his lips, and said: "I would marry a girl I know, but she has set a condition which I cannot meet."

"What is that condition, Jacob?" said the old woman.

"How do you know my name?" asked Jacob, astonished.

"That is neither here nor there," said the old woman. "Call me Mother Grethel, it you like, to square the bargain. But tell me what condition Gretchen sets."

"You are, indeed, a fairy!" exclaimed Jacob; "and the first, at that, that I have ever met."

"They only make themselves known to agreeable folk," said the old woman.

"Oh," said Jacob, half inclined to be angry. But he reflected, after all, that he had at last met a fairy, even though they had avoided him for more than twenty years. "If you're a fairy, Mother Grethel," he said, "you know it all without my telling you."

"That I do," said the old woman, "and if you will give me that scarlet feather in your cap, I will help you to gain all the friends you like."

"That's poor exchange, indeed, for such service," said Jacob, politely, taking the feather from his cap as he spoke. He found himself rather pleased with his own civil speeches, and the more polite he became, the more easily such speech flowed from his lips.

"Have you ever been really kind to anyone, Jacob?" said the old woman.

Jacob looked up at the sky and then down at his boots.

"Well," he said, "I once gave a beggar a silver coin."

"With a heart as cold as the silver, Jacob, I'll wager. But I'll not catechize you, Jacob. This is the secret: Be as kind as you know how to be to everybody you meet, and smile as much as you can. It's a magic talisman toward gaining affection. Whether you will or no, they'll all be fond of you."

"How do you know my name?" asked Jacob, astonished.

"That sounds like wisdom, good Mother," said Jacob, and he smiled most amiably.

"You have planted the right foot forward already, Jacob," said the old woman, "and you look as handsome as the best when you smile, too."

"And you promise me, good Mother," said Jacob, "if I follow your advice, that many will love me—as many as five, so that Gretchen will be satisfied?"

"That I promise," said Mother Grethel, "and I bid you good day and good luck. And for the scarlet feather many thanks." Then she went on her way.

So Jacob brushed the grass off his clothes, and, adjusting his featherless cap at the briskest angle, he set out at a smart pace down the highway. He murmured to himself, contentedly, "Fairies only make themselves known to agreeable folk!" He was eager to begin his collection of affectionate friends as speedily as possible, for it seemed to him that it would be a most desirable novelty. And then to be marrying Gretchen as well! No wonder that Jacob hummed and whistled!

As he gaily went along the road, kicking up the dust, he heard someone call behind him, and, looking around, saw an old woman with a basket of lettuces.

"Hi there, young Master!" said she, "you fill a body's old eyes with dust at every step you take!"

Jacob almost forgot himself for a moment, and an impertinent speech rose to his lips. But whist! in the twinkling of an eyelash he remembered, and, lifting his cap in his best manner, exclaimed: "A thousand pardons, Madam!" And he implored her to allow him the great pleasure of carrying her basket of lettuces on one arm, and offered the other that he might assist her over the rough places. So they walked, arm in arm, into the town, as gay as you please, chatting away, and the old woman thought she had never in the world met with so delightful a person as this handsome young man. Yes, he was, indeed, growing handsome, was Jacob, as fast as the time was flying, having left his long face behind him, together with his bad temper.

Now Jacob's cap was not much to boast of, especially since he had traded the scarlet feather for the old fairy's secret. As they neared the town, a crowd of small urchins eyed it mischievously. "Who would wear a cap without a feather?" cried one of them. And he picked up a clod and flung it at Jacob's cap, and knocked it off in the dust. You can imagine Jacob's old self leaped up at that!—that is, until he remembered Gretchen. Swallowing his rage, he picked up the cap, all begrimed as it was by the dust of the road, and he stuck it on one ear, and made such funny grimaces that the small urchins held their sides for laughter; and the one who had flung the clod ran up to Jacob and said: "Take me with you, sir, and I'll run your errands for as long as ever you'll have me!"

"Well," mused Jacob, "that's two already." And he whistled softly to himself, and took the urchin by the hand.

They soon reached the market-place of the town, where there was a great crowd jostling and pushing. All of a sudden, Jacob saw twenty pies and half a gross of frosted cakes go rolling in the gutter, where the dogs snatched them up.

"Alack-a-day!" cried the pastry-cook, a fat little man with one eye, "someone jostled my tray, and there's ruin for you!"

"Ho! ho!" said a rival, "none but dogs would eat your pies and cakes, One Eye!"

And everybody laughed and poked fun at the unfortunate seller of pastries—that is, everybody but Jacob. Up he strode, elbowing his way through the crowd, and said to the pastry-cook, "Could'st make a bride cake three stories high, with silver leaves, and a chime of bells, and pink Cupids, and a gross of sugar roses? For I would be married to Gretchen."

"That I can, Master," said the pastry-cook.

As for the rival pastry-cook, and all the other scoffers, they fairly gasped, for they knew that a bride cake such as Jacob described would put a pretty lot of silver coins in a pastry-cook's pocket.

"Well, then, come along," said Jacob to the pastry-cook.

But as soon as they were out of the marketing crowd, he said: "Good fellow, I would be honest with you." And he turned his pockets inside out, so that the pastry-cook could see that he had not even a copper penny.

"Is there no Gretchen, Master?" said the pastry-cook.

"Oh, yes," said Jacob; "she has eyes the color of corn-flowers."

"Gretchen is a lucky lass!" said the pastry-cook.

"Why so?" said Jacob.

"Why, to be marrying such a kind, honest, jolly fellow as you are, Master, to be sure!"

"Will you come and tell her so?" said Jacob.

"That willingly," said the pastry-cook, "and I'll make her a bride cake for a wedding gift." And he trotted along after Jacob, and the old woman, and the ragged urchin.

"That's three already," said Jacob, and he whistled a little tune all to himself. So they walked on through the town until they reached an inn, and there Jacob, and the old woman, and the urchin, and the pastry-cook sat down in the shade of the trees to rest; and the old woman, taking a lettuce from her market-basket, divided it among the four of them, and the pastry-cook cut up into equal shares the only cake he had left. Strange to relate, this meal, spiced and salted, you might say, with companionship, tasted to Jacob like a meal fit for a king. And after all the lettuce was eaten and every crumb of cake had vanished, Jacob was moved to sing a comic song which went something like this:

"Oh around and around again go,
With a ha! hal ha! and a ho!
I could dance all my life
To the whistle and fife,
With a ha! ha! ha! and a ho!"

"Sing it again, dear Jacob," said the old woman. So as soon as Jacob had got his breath again, he sang it once more. The landlord of the inn, hearing the song, came to his door. He was looking as gloomy as a thunder-cloud, for custom was poor and his purse was thin; but he found the song so irresistible, that he needs must join in, with the others. And the end of it all was that they clasped hands and danced about on the turf, and were as merry as you please.

"Well, well," said the landlord, gasping for breath, "I've not had such a frolic since I was that high! It does a man good to limber up a bit. What care I if times are bad, Jacob, my boy!" And then he urged them to accept his hospitality for the night.

"I'll tell thee now, landlord," said Jacob, "we've not a penny between us!"

"What of that, Jacob, my boy?" said the landlord, clapping him on the shoulder.

"I could dance all my life
To the whistle and fife,
With a ha! ha! ha! and a ho!"

And he danced along the corridors of the inn, and gave the old woman the very room in which the king had slept when he visited that town.

Now when Jacob and the others were about to leave the next morning, the landlord locked up the inn and threw the key down the well.

"Wherefore, landlord?" said Jacob.

"If these other folk throw in their luck with you, I'm going along, too, that I am, to dance at Gretchen's wedding, 'With a ha! ha! ha! and a ho!'" said the landlord. And he executed a few fancy steps.

Jacob whistled. "Four already," he said to himself.

So they marched along the main street of the town, Jacob, and the old woman, and the urchin, and the pastry-cook, and the landlord. As they trudged along, they came upon a crowd gathered about a vender of gold pins and rings and bangles. Jacob needs must stop and admire.

"How well this would look on Gretchen's little finger! How fine that on Gretchen's slender wrist!" and he felt reflectively in his pocket for the coins that were not there.

Now there was a man standing by looking at the fine array, and while the vender's eyes were directed at something else, he deftly extracted two rings from the tray, and no one was the wiser—except Jacob. He had sharp eyes with the best, I can tell you! He seized the thief by the ear and shouted: "Give up those rings, rascal, or I'll lead you off to jail myself!" So the man, seeing with whom he had to deal, wasted no time in returning what he had stolen, and was off before you could turn around twice.

"You have done me a good turn. Master," said the vender; "and you shall have one of my finest gold rings, that you shall!"

At that Jacob's face lighted up. "I would be marrying Gretchen," he said; "but I have no money wherewith to purchase the wedding-ring."

"How large is your Gretchen's finger?" said the peddler.

"Why," said Jacob, "it is very small and pretty, but I cannot tell you exactly."

"Well," said the peddler, "I would fain be walking along with you for the sake of your pleasant company. We will measure Gretchen's finger for the ring, and mayhap I would like to give her a gold bangle on my own account."

So Jacob whistled again as they went along, and said to himself, "Five good friends have I!" At the thought he could not forbear laughing, and he laughed and laughed until the merry tears ran down his cheeks. His amusement became so contagious that the landlord guffawed as if he would never stop, and the urchin turned a hand-spring or two for merriment, and the old woman cackled. They were standing in front of a linen-draper's shop, and he came to his door just then.

"What's all the fun about?" he cried, and forthwith joined in the laughter, without stopping for a reply.

At last Jacob could speak. "I have five good friends," he said. And then, for no reason at all, they all laughed harder than ever!

"You have six, Master," said the linen-draper, "for you do the eyes good, that you do, with your merry face!" And he asked Jacob to come into the shop and have a chair and a chat, before he went on his way.

Now when Jacob saw the linen materials in the draper's shop, he admired them exceedingly, and in his mind's eye fancied Gretchen clad in a dress of the finest, and looking her prettiest. The linen-draper read Jacob's admiration, and said: "You have an eye for my fine materials, Master, that I see easily."

"Well," said Jacob, "I would be marrying Gretchen, and cannot help thinking how fair she would look dressed in this and that!" But he turned his pockets inside out, and showed the draper that they were quite empty.

The landlord guffawed as if he would never stop.

"Look here, Master," said the draper, "I would be taking a little holiday, and will walk along with you and your merry company. So I can attend the wedding and make Gretchen a present of whatever cloth you choose."

"You are, indeed, generous!" said Jacob. And he chose a white linen cloth embroidered over with fleur-de-lis. Then the draper locked up his shop, hiding the key on top of the lintel, and marched along with Jacob, and the old woman, and the urchin, and the pastry-cook, and the landlord, and the peddler.

Now Jacob had a whole five days before Gretchen expected him to return, so he bethought himself that he would put in the time seeing the sights of the town, since he need have no uneasiness about fulfilling her condition. For, you see, he had five faithful friends and one to spare. He was quite blossoming under his popularity, moreover, and was not averse to gathering in a few more merry companions as he went along. In fact, he thought it would be quite a joke to take back with him to the farm as many as he could, just by way of a little surprise for Gretchen! So he marched along as gaily as possible, and, would you believe it?—the next day he had added to his train a jailer and a doctor, two lawyers and a parson, a carpenter and a shoemaker—and the shoemaker was possessed with a desire to measure Gretchen's foot for the neatest, prettiest little slipper in the world, and all for love of Jacob.

The urchin turned a hand-spring or two for merriment.

And on Friday, they all set out for Jacob's farm. And there were a whole hundred of them! For by this time, Jacob had become the admiration of a joiner and a conjurer, a schoolmaster, two dressmakers, and a tailor, a clock-maker and a chemist, a farmer, two huntsmen, and a scullion, a gardener and a cowherd, a hairdresser and a butcher's boy, a scissors-grinder and a mason, a goose girl and a soldier, a washerwoman and a stone-cutter, two musicians and a town crier, and ever so many more!

They started down the road, as merry a party as you'd see in a day's journey, and Jacob the merriest of them all! The town crier was ringing his bell, and the musicians were tooting on their instruments, and the landlord was singing,

> *"I could dance all my life*
> *To the whistle and fife,*
> *With a ha! ha! ha! and a ho!"*

But they had scarcely gone twenty yards beyond the town, when Jacob heard a great halloo, and, turning round, beheld the Lord Mayor coming down the road after them as fast as his legs would carry him, his ermine-bordered gown flying out in the wind, and his wig all askew.

"Hi there!" said the Lord Mayor, as soon as he could gain his breath, "what do you mean, sir, by running away with half the population of my town?"

Jacob looked at him without speaking, and then, taking a step forward, he smote the Lord Mayor on the forehead with the palm of his hand! At that the lawyer fainted away in the jailer's arms, and there was general consternation!

"What does this mean?" said the Lord Mayor, growing very red.

"Do not be hasty," said Jacob. "I stunned him."

"Stunned who?" said the Lord Mayor.

"As big a wasp as I ever saw, old chap!" said Jacob.

At that the Lord Mayor fairly fell upon Jacob's neck and embraced him. "You're the first man who ever dared to treat me as a human being," said the Lord Mayor. "I'm going along with you, that I am! I'll send in my resignation."

"Well," said Jacob, "come along." And he took the Lord Mayor by the arm, and they all started off once more down the road.

It was evening when they reached Jacob's farm. The moon was rising, and the white buildings of Gretchen's farm showed beyond Jacob's hedge.

"Friends," said Jacob, "I'll be going on to Gretchen's now, and would you kindly wait here until I return?"

"Leave us, dear Jacob!" exclaimed the pastry-cook. And his one eye filled with tears.

"Only for a half-hour," said Jacob.

"Oh, no, Jacob!" said the Lord Mayor, appealingly.

At that Jacob let his feelings get the better of him, for once.

"Am I to go a-courting with a whole hundred of you at my heels!" he exclaimed.

"Well, I'll settle the matter," said the lawyer. And he produced a paper and wrote on it, "I hereby promise to return in half an hour." So Jacob, with a patient air, affixed his signature to the document, and then off he went to see Gretchen.

Gretchen was sitting in her kitchen, industriously spinning by candle-light. Jacob knocked. Gretchen took up a candle and opened the door.

"I have come back, Gretchen," said Jacob.

"So I see," said Gretchen, and she lifted the candle high and looked at Jacob's face. She could hardly believe her eyes, he was so good-looking! His sour looks and long face had given place to merriment and kindliness. She placed the candle on the table, and then she kissed him. And you may be sure Jacob was perfectly satisfied.

"The moon is risen, Gretchen," said Jacob. "Let us take a walk, for the air is so sweet and fresh, and I smell the brier-rose in the garden."

So he led Gretchen round to his own farm, and all of a sudden, they came upon Jacob's hundred friends behind the barn.

Gretchen screamed, "Who are all these people!" for in her satisfaction at the change in Jacob's disposition, she had quite forgotten the condition she had set.

"Why, you told me I had to have five good friends before you'd marry me, Gretchen," said Jacob.

"Five!" exclaimed Gretchen; "there are twenty times five here!"

"Yes," said Jacob, "and they don't like me out of their sight, poor dears."

After the curiosity of Jacob's friends had been satisfied (and they all thought Gretchen charming), the two strolled off.

"Gretchen," said Jacob.

"Yes," said Gretchen.

"Could we be married tomorrow, do you think?"

"But I have no frock, Jacob."

"Oh, there's a linen-draper here who has whole yards of white linen embroidered in fleur-de-lis, which he has brought you for a gift."

"But, dear Jacob, there is no one to make the dress!"

"Oh, yes, two dressmakers and a tailor over yonder behind the barn!"

"What about a bride cake, Jacob?"

"Oh, there's a pastry-cook who desires no greater happiness than to bake one three stories high, with silver leaves, and a chime of bells, and pink Cupids, and a gross of sugar roses."

"But then, Jacob, a ring; we can't get married without a ring!"

"Oh, there's a man yonder would measure your finger for a ring, my dear."

"But a parson, Jacob; we can't get married without a parson!"

"Oh, there's one behind the barn, Gretchen!"

"Well then, Jacob," said Gretchen, "we may as well get married tomorrow."

So the very next day there was a fine wedding. The Lord Mayor himself gave the bride away, and she wore a white linen dress embroidered in fleur-de-lis, and little white slippers with real gold buckles; and Jacob put the most beautiful gold ring upon her finger. The musicians played "Tweedle-dum-te-dee," and everybody danced on the turf in front of the farm-house. Then Gretchen cut the bride cake, which was the largest and most wonderful confection they had ever beheld.

While all the company was still making merry, Gretchen and Jacob sat down under the grape-vine for a little chat.

"It is wonderful," said Jacob, with a contented sigh, "to have so many friends!"

"Indeed it is, Jacob," said Gretchen, "and you never told me yet how you charmed so many to follow you. Didst have a magic whistle or a fairy bell?"

"Oh, no," said Jacob, "but I met an old fairy woman who told me a secret."

"And what is the secret, Jacob?"

"Oh, just to smile at everyone and do a good deed whenever you get the opportunity."

"A great deed—like slaying a dragon, Jacob?"

"Oh, no, Gretchen, just a kind word or look as you pass along, and a helping of people over the rough places."

Gretchen smiled. "Jacob," she said.

"Yes, Gretchen?"

"I have a confession to make, Jacob."

"Yes, Gretchen?"

"That old fairy woman was myself, Jacob, in Mother's old black quilted cloak!"

You can well imagine Jacob's astonishment at that piece of news!

"*You*, Gretchen!" was all he could say.

"Yes, Jacob," said Gretchen, and taking up Jacob's old cap where it was lying on the garden seat beside them, she stuck the scarlet feather back in its place.

"It looks better," she said, twirling the cap round on her finger.

Jacob drew a long breath. Then he kissed Gretchen on both cheeks, and laughed and laughed as if he would never stop.

"I have married a clever wife, that I have!" said Jacob.

First published in the December 1912 edition of *St. Nicholas Magazine*

Why Peter Rabbit Has One Less Enemy

From "Tommy and the Wishing Stone"

BY THORNTON W. BURGESS

ILLUSTRATIONS BY HARRISON CADY

PETER RABBIT WAS happy. There was no question about that. You had only to watch him a few minutes to know it. He couldn't hide that happiness any more than the sun at midday can hide when there are no clouds in the sky. Happiness seemed to fairly shoot from his long heels as they twinkled merrily this way and that way through the Briar-patch. Peter was doing crazy things. He was so happy that he was foolish. Happiness, you know, is the only excuse for foolishness. And Peter was foolish, very, very foolish. He would suddenly jump into the air, kick his long heels, dart off to one side, change his mind and dart the other way, run in a circle, and then abruptly plump himself down under a bush and sit as still as if he couldn't move. Then, without any warning at all, he would cut up some other funny antic.

He was so foolish and so funny that finally Tommy, who, unseen by Peter, was watching him, laughed aloud. Perhaps Peter doesn't like being laughed at. Most people don't. It may be Peter was a little bit uncertain as to why he was being laughed at. Anyway, with a sudden thump of his stout hind-legs, he scampered out of sight along one of his private little paths which led into the very thickest tangle in the old Briar-patch.

"I'll have to come over here with my gun and get that rabbit for my dinner," said Tommy, as he trudged homeward. "Probably though, if I have a gun, I won't see him at all. It's funny how a fellow is forever seeing things when he hasn't got a gun, and when he goes hunting he never sees anything!"

Tommy had come to the great gray stone which was his favorite resting-place. He sat down from sheer force of habit. Somehow, he never could get past that stone without sitting down on it for a few minutes. It seemed to just beg to be sat on. He was still thinking of Peter Rabbit.

"I wonder what made him feel so frisky," thought Tommy. Then he laughed aloud once more as he remembered how comical Peter had looked. It must be fun to feel as happy as all that. Without once thinking of where he was, Tommy exclaimed aloud: "I declare, I wish I were a rabbit!"

He was. His wish had come true. Just as quick as that, he found himself a rabbit. You see, he had been sitting on the wishing-stone. If he had remembered, perhaps, he wouldn't have wished. But he had forgotten, and now here he was, looking as if he might very well be own brother to Peter Rabbit. Not only did he look like Peter, but he felt like him. Anyway, he felt a crazy impulse to run and jump and do foolish things, and he did them. He just couldn't help doing them. It was his way of showing how good he felt, just as shouting is a boy's way, and singing is the way of a bird.

But in the very midst of one of his wildest whirls, he heard a sound that brought him up short, as still as a stone. It was the sound of a heavy thump, and it came from the direction of the Briar-patch. Tommy didn't need to be told that it was a signal, a signal from Peter Rabbit to all other rabbits within hearing distance. He didn't know just the meaning of that signal, and, because he didn't, he just sat still. Now it happens that that was exactly what that signal meant—to sit tight and not move. Peter had seen something that to him looked very suspicious. So on general principles he had signaled, and then had himself sat perfectly still until he should discover if there was any real danger.

Now Tommy didn't know this, but being a rabbit now, he felt as a rabbit feels, and, from the second he heard that thump, he was as frightened as he had been happy a minute before. And being frightened, yet not knowing of what he was afraid, he sat absolutely still, listening with all his might, and looking this way and that, as best he could, without moving his head. And all the time, he worked his nose up and down, up and down, as all rabbits do, and tested the air for strange smells.

Presently Tommy heard behind him a sound that filled him with terrible fear. It was a loud sniff, sniff. Rolling his eyes back so that he could look behind without turning his head, he saw a dog sniffing and snuffing in the grass. Now that dog wasn't very big as dogs go, but he was so much bigger than even the largest rabbit, that to Tommy he looked like a giant. The terrible fear that filled him clutched at Tommy's heart until it seemed as if it would stop beating. What should he do, sit still or run? Somehow he was afraid to do either. Just then the matter was settled for him. "*Thump, thump, thump!*" the signal came along the ground from the Briar-patch, and almost anyone would have known just by the short sharp sound that those thumps meant "Run!" At just the same instant, the dog caught the scent of Tommy full and strong. With a roar of his great voice he sprang forward, his nose in Tommy's tracks.

Tommy waited no longer. With a great bound he leaped forward in the direction of the Briar-patch. How he did run! A dozen bounds brought him to the Briar-patch, and there just before him was a tiny path under the brambles. He didn't stop to question how it came there or who had made it. He dodged in and scurried along it to the very middle of the Briar-patch. Then he stopped to listen and look. The dog had just reached the edge of the briars. He knew where Tommy had gone. Of course he knew. His nose told him that. He thrust his head in at the entrance to the little path and tried to crawl in. But the sly old brambles tore his long tender ears, and he yelped with pain now instead of with the excitement of the chase. Then he backed out, whining and yelping. He ran around the edge of the Briar-patch looking for some place where he could get in more comfortably. But there was no place, and after a while he gave up and went off.

Tommy sat right where he was until he was quite sure that the dog had gone. When he was quite sure, he started to explore the Briar-patch, for he was very curious to see what it was like in there. He found little paths leading in all directions. Some of them led right through the very thickest tangles of ugly looking brambles, and Tommy found that he could run along these with never a fear of a single scratch. And as he hopped along, he knew that here he was safe, absolutely safe from most of his enemies, for no one bigger than he could possibly get through those briars without being terribly scratched.

So it was with a very comfortable feeling that Tommy peered out through the brambles and watched that annoying dog trot off in disgust. He felt that never, so long as he was within running distance of the Briar-patch, would he be afraid of a dog. Right into the midst of his pleasant thoughts broke a rude "*Thump, thump, thump!*" It wasn't a danger-signal this time. That is, it didn't mean "Run for your life." Tommy was very sure of that. And yet it might be a kind of danger-signal, too. It all depended on what Tommy decided to do. There it was again—"*Thump, thump, thump!*" It had an ugly, threatening sound. Tommy knew just as well as if there had been spoken words instead of mere thumps on the ground that he was being warned to get out of the Briar-patch—that he had no right there, because it belonged to some one else. But Tommy had no intention of leaving such a fine place, such a beautifully safe place, unless he had to, and no mere thumps on the ground could make him believe that. He could thump himself. He did. Those long hind-legs of his were just made for thumping. When he hit the ground with them, he did it with a will, and the thumps he made sounded just as ugly and threatening as the other fellow's, and he knew that the other fellow knew exactly what they meant—"I'll do as I please! Put me out if you can!"

It was very clear that this was just what the other proposed to do if his thumps meant anything at all. Presently Tommy saw a trim, neat-looking rabbit in a little open space, and it was something of a relief to find that he was about Tommy's own size. "If I can't whip him, he certainly can't whip me," thought Tommy, and straightway thumped, "I'm coming," in reply to the stranger's angry demand that he come out and fight.

Now the stranger was none other than Peter Rabbit, and he was very indignant. He considered that he owned the Briar-patch. He was perfectly willing that any other rabbit should find safety there in time of danger, but when the danger was past, they must get out. Tommy hadn't; therefore he must be driven out.

Now if Tommy had been himself, instead of a rabbit, never, never would he have dreamed of fighting as he was

Peter Rabbit was very indignant!

preparing to fight now—by biting and kicking, particularly kicking. But for a rabbit, kicking was quite the correct and proper thing. In fact, it was the only way to fight. So instead of coming together head-on, Tommy and Peter approached each other in queer little half-side-wise rushes, each watching for a chance to use his stout hind-legs. Suddenly Peter rushed, jumped, and—well, when Tommy picked himself up, he felt very much as a boy feels when he has been tackled and thrown in a football game. Certainly Peter's stout hind-legs were in good working order.

Just a minute later Tommy's chance came, and Peter was sent sprawling. Like a flash, Tommy was after him, biting and pulling out little bunches of soft fur. So they fought until at last they were so out of wind and so tired that there was no fight left in either. Then they lay and panted for breath, and quite suddenly they forgot their quarrel. Each knew that he couldn't whip the other; and, that being so, what was the use of fighting?

"I suppose the Briar-patch is big enough for both of us," said Peter, after a little.

"I'll live on one side, and you live on the other," replied Tommy. And so it was agreed.

In three things Tommy found that, as a rabbit, he was not unlike Tommy the boy. These three were appetite, curiosity, and a decided preference for pleasure rather than labor. Tommy felt as if he lived to eat instead of eating to live. He want-

Tommy and Peter made visits to a garden.

ed to eat most of the time. It seemed as if he never could get his stomach really full. There was one satisfaction, and that was that he never had to look very far for something to eat. There were clover and grass just outside the Briar-patch—all he wanted for the taking. There were certain tender-leaved plants for a change, not to mention tender bark from young trees and bushes. With Peter he made occasional visits to a not too distant garden, where they fairly reveled in goodies.

These visits were in the nature of adventure. It seemed to Tommy that not even Danny Meadow-mouse had so many enemies as he and Peter had. They used to talk it over sometimes. "It isn't fair," said Peter, in a grieved tone. "We don't hurt anybody. We don't do the least bit of harm to any-one, and yet it isn't safe for us to play two minutes outside the Briar-patch without keeping watch. No, sir, it isn't fair! There's Redtail the Hawk watching this very minute from way up there in the sky. He looks as if he were just sailing round and round for the fun of it; but he isn't. He's just watching for you or me to get one too many jumps away from these old briars. Then down he'll come like a shot. Now what harm have we ever done Redtail or any of his family? Tell me that."

Of course Tommy couldn't tell him that, and so Peter went on: "When I was a baby, I came very near to finding out just how far it is from Mr. Blacksnake's mouth to his stomach by the inside passage, and all that saved me was the interference of a boy, who set me free. Now that I'm grown, I'm not afraid of Mr. Blacksnake—though I keep out of his way—but I have to keep on the watch all the time for that boy!"

"The same one?" asked Tommy.

"The very same!" replied Peter. "He's forever setting his dog after me and trying to get a shot at me with his terrible gun. Yet I've never done *him* any harm—nor the dog either."

"It's very curious," said Tommy, not knowing what else to say.

"It seems to me there ought to be some time when it is reasonably safe for an honest rabbit to go abroad," continued Peter, who, now that he was started, seemed bound to make the worst of his troubles. "At night, I cannot even dance in the moonlight without all the time looking one way for Reddy Fox and another for Hooty the Owl."

"It's a good thing that the Briar-patch is always safe," said Tommy, because he could think of nothing else to say.

"But it isn't!" snapped Peter. "I wish to goodness it was! Now there's—listen!" Peter sat very still with his ears pricked forward. Something very like a look of fear grew and grew in his eyes. Tommy sat quite as still and listened with all his might. Presently he heard a faint rustling. It sounded as if it was in one of the little paths through the Briar-patch. Yes, it surely was, and it was drawing nearer. Tommy gathered himself together for instant flight, and a strange fear gripped his heart. "It's Billy Mink!" gasped Peter.

"If he follows you, don't run into a hole in the ground, or into a hollow log, whatever you do! Keep going! He'll get tired after a while. There he is—run!"

Peter bounded off one way and Tommy another. After a few jumps, Tommy squatted to make sure whether or not he was being followed. He saw a slim, dark form slipping through the brambles, and he knew that Billy Mink was following Peter. Tommy couldn't help a tiny sigh of relief. He was sorry for Peter; but Peter knew every path and twist and turn, while he didn't. It was a great deal better that Peter should be the one to try to fool Billy Mink.

So Tommy sat perfectly still and watched. He saw Peter twist and turn, run in a circle, criss-cross, run back on his own trail, and make a break by leaping far to one side. He saw Billy Mink follow every twist and turn, his nose in Peter's tracks. When he reached the place where Peter had broken the trail, he ran in ever widening circles until he picked it up again, and once more Peter was on the run. Tommy felt little cold shivers chase up and down his back as he watched how surely and persistently Billy Mink followed. And then—he hardly knew how it happened—Peter had jumped right over him, and there was Billy Mink coming! There was nothing to do but run, and Tommy ran. He doubled and twisted and played all the tricks he had seen Peter play, and then at last, when he was beginning to get quite tired, he played the same trick on Peter that had seemed so dreadful when Peter played it on him: He led Billy Mink straight to where Peter was sitting, and once more Peter was the hunted.

But Billy Mink was getting tired. After a little, he gave up and went in quest of something more easily caught.

Peter came back to where Tommy was sitting.

"Billy Mink's a tough customer to get rid of alone, but, with someone to change off with, it is no trick at all!" said he. "It wouldn't work so well with his cousin, Shadow the Weasel. He's the one I *am* afraid of. I think we should be safer if we had some new paths; what do you think?"

Tommy confessed that he thought so too. It would have been very much easier to have dodged Billy Mink if there had been a few more cross paths. "We'd better make them before we need them more than we did this time," said Peter; and, as this was just plain, sound, rabbit common sense, Tommy was forced to agree. And so it was that he learned that a rabbit must work if he would live long and be happy. He didn't think of it in just this way as he patiently cut paths through the brambles and tangles of bush and vine. It was fear, just plain fear, that was driving him. And even this drove him to work only by spells. Between times, when he wasn't eating, he sat squatting under a bush just lazily dreaming, but always ready to run for his life.

In the moonlight he and Peter loved to gambol and play in some open place where there was room to jump and dance; but, even in the midst of these joyous times, they must need sit up every minute or so to stop, look, and listen for danger. It was at night, too, that they wandered farthest from the Briar-patch. Once they met Bobby Coon, and Peter warned Tommy never to allow Bobby to get him cornered. And once they met Jimmy Skunk, who paid no attention to them at all, but went right on about his business. It was hard to believe that he was another to be

Meeting Bobby Coon

warned against; but so Peter said, and Peter ought to know if anybody did.

So Tommy learned to be ever on the watch. He learned to take note of his neighbors. He could tell by the sound of his voice when Sammy Jay was watching Reddy Fox, and when he saw a hunter. When Blacky the Crow was on guard, he knew that he was reasonably safe from surprise. At least once a day, but more often several times a day, he had a narrow escape. But he grew used to it, and, as soon as a fright was over, he forgot it. It was the only way to do.

As he learned more and more how to watch, and to care for himself, he grew bolder. Curiosity led him farther, and farther from the Briar-patch. And then, one day, he discovered that Reddy Fox was between him and his castle.

There was nothing for it but to run and twist and double and dodge. Every trick he had learned he tried in vain. He was in the open, and Reddy was too wise to be fooled. He was right at Tommy's heels now, and with every jump Tommy expected to feel those cruel white teeth. Just ahead was a great rock. If he could reach that, perhaps there might be a crack in it big enough for a frightened little rabbit to squeeze into, or a hole under it where he might find safety.

He was almost up to it. Would he be able to make it? One jump! He could hear Reddy panting. Two jumps! He could feel Reddy's breath. Three jumps! He was on the rock! and— slowly Tommy rubbed his eyes. Reddy Fox was nowhere to be seen. Of course

Chased by Reddy Fox

not! No fox would be foolish enough to come near a *boy* sitting in plain sight. Tommy looked over to the old Briar-patch. That at least was real. Slowly he walked over to it. Peering under the bushes, he saw Peter Rabbit squatting perfectly still, yet ready to run.

"You don't need to, Peter," said he. "You don't need to. You can cut one boy off that long list of enemies you are always watching for. You see, I know just how you feel, Peter!"

He walked around to the other side of the Briar-patch, and, stooping down, thumped the ground once with his hand. There was an answering thump from the spot where he had seen Peter Rabbit. Tommy smiled.

"We're friends, Peter," said he, "and it's all on account of the wishing-stone. I'll never hunt you again. My! I wouldn't be a rabbit for anything in the world. Being a boy is good enough for me!"

First published in the January 1915 edition of *St. Nicholas Magazine*

How It Happened That Reddy Fox Gained a Friend

From "Tommy and the Wishing Stone"

BY THORNTON W. BURGESS

ILLUSTRATIONS BY HARRISON CADY

IT WAS FUNNY that Tommy never could pass that great gray stone without sitting down on it for a few minutes. It seemed as if he just couldn't, that was all. It had been a favorite seat ever since he was big enough to drive the cows to pasture and go after them at night. It was just far enough from home for him to think that he needed a rest when he reached it. You know a growing boy needs to rest often—except when he is playing. He used to take all his troubles there to think them over. The queer part of it is he left a great many of them there, though he didn't seem to know it. If Tommy ever could have seen in one pile all the troubles he had left at that old gray stone, I am afraid that he would have called it the trouble-stone instead of the wishing-stone. It was only lately that he had begun to call it the wishing-stone.

Several times when he had been sitting on it, he had wished foolish wishes and they had come true. At least, it seemed as if they had come true. They had come as true as he ever wanted them to. He was thinking something of this kind now as he stood idly kicking at the old stone. Presently he stopped kicking at it, and, from force of habit, sat down on it. It was a bright, sunshiny day, one of those warm days that sometimes happen right in the middle of winter, as if the weather-man had somehow got mixed up and slipped a spring day into the wrong place in the calendar.

From where he sat, Tommy could look over to the Green Forest, which was green now only where the pine-trees and the hemlock-trees and the spruce-trees grew. All the rest was bare and brown, save that the ground was white with snow. He could look across the white meadow-land to the Old Pasture, where in places the brush was so thick that, in summer, he sometimes had to hunt to find the cows. Now, even from this distance, he could trace the windings of the cow-paths, each a ribbon of spotless white. It puzzled him at first. He scowled at them.

"When the whole thing is covered with snow, it ought to be harder to see those paths, but instead of that it is easier," he muttered. "'T ain't reasonable!" Tommy never *could* see any sense in grammar. He scowled harder than ever, but the scowl wasn't an unpleasant one. You know there is a difference in scowls. Some are black and heavy, like ugly thunder-heads, and from them flashes of anger are likely to dart any minute, just as the lightning darts out from the thunder-heads. Others are like the big fleecy clouds that hide the sun for a minute or two, and make it seem all the brighter by their passing. There are scowls of anger and scowls of perplexity. It was a scowl of the latter kind that wrinkled Tommy's forehead now. He was trying to understand something that seemed to him quite as much beyond common sense as the rules of the grammar he so detested.

"'T ain't reasonable!" he repeated. "I hadn't ought to be able to see 'em at all. But I do. They stick out like—"

No one will ever know just what they stuck out like, for Tommy never finished that sentence. The scowl cleared and his freckled face fairly beamed. He had made a discovery all by himself, and he felt all the joy of a discoverer. Perhaps you will think it wasn't much, but it was really important, so far as it concerned Tommy, because it proved that Tommy was learning to use his eyes and to understand what he saw. He had reasoned the thing out, and when anybody does that, it is always important.

"Why, how simple!" exclaimed Tommy. "Of course I can see those old paths! It would be funny if I couldn't. The bushes break through the snow on all sides, but where the paths are, there is nothing to break through, and so they are perfectly smooth and stand right out. Queer I never noticed that before. Hello! what's that?"

His sharp eyes had caught sight of a little spot of red up in the Old Pasture. It was moving, and, as he watched it, it gradually took shape. It was Reddy Fox, trotting along one of those little white paths. Apparently, Reddy was going to keep an engagement somewhere, for he trotted along quite as if he were bound for some particular place and had no time to waste.

"He's headed this way, and, if I keep still, perhaps he'll come close," thought Tommy.

So he sat as still as if he were a part of the old wishing-stone itself. Reddy Fox came straight on. At the edge of the Old Pasture he stopped for a minute and looked across to the Green Forest, as if to make sure that it was perfectly safe to cross the open meadows. Evidently he thought it was for he resumed his steady trot. If he kept on the way he was headed, he would pass very near to the wishing-stone and to Tommy. Just as he was half-way across the meadows, Chanticleer, Tommy's prize Plymouth Rock rooster, crowed over in the farm-yard. Instantly Reddy stopped with one black paw uplifted and turned his head in the direction of the sound. Tommy could imagine the hungry look in that sharp, crafty face. But Reddy was far too wise

Reddy Fox ran—how he ran!

to think of going up to the farm-yard in broad day-light, and in a moment resumed his journey.

Nearer and nearer he came, until he was passing not thirty feet away. How handsome he was! His beautiful red coat looked as if the coldest wind never could get through it. His great plume of a tail, black toward the end and just tipped with white, was held high to keep it out of the snow. His black stockings, white vest, and black-tipped ears gave him a wonderfully fine appearance. Quite a dandy is Reddy Fox, and he looked it.

He was almost past, when Tommy squeaked like a mouse. Like a flash Reddy turned, his sharp ears cocked forward, his yellow eyes agleam with hunger. There he stood, as motionless as Tommy himself, eagerness written in every line of his face. It was very clear that, no matter how important his business in the Green Forest was, he didn't intend knowingly to pass anything so delicious as a meadow-mouse. Once more Tommy squeaked. Instantly Reddy took several steps toward him, looking and listening intently. A look of doubt crept into his eager face. That old gray stone didn't look just as he remembered it. For a long minute he stared straight at Tommy. Then a puff of wind fluttered the bottom of Tommy's coat, and perhaps at the same time it carried to Reddy that dreaded man smell.

Reddy almost turned a back-somersault in his hurry to get away. Then he ran. How he did run! In almost no time at all he had reached the Green Forest and vanished from Tommy's sight. Quite without knowing it Tommy sighed.

"My, how handsome he is!" You know Tommy is freckle-faced and rather homely. "And gee, how he can run!" he added admiringly. "It must be fun to be able to run like that. It must be fun to be a fox anyhow. I wonder what it feels like. I wish I were a fox."

If he had remembered where he was, perhaps Tommy would have thought twice before wishing. But he had forgotten. Forgetting was one of Tommy's beset-ting sins. Hardly had the words left his mouth, when Tommy found that he was a fox, red-coated, black-stockinged—the very image of Reddy himself. And with that change in himself everything else had changed. It was summer. The Green

Meadows and the Green Forest were very beautiful. Even the Old Pasture was beautiful. But Tommy had no eyes for beauty. All that beauty meant nothing to him save that now there was plenty to eat and no great trouble to get it. Everywhere the birds were singing, but, if Tommy heeded at all, it was only to wish that some of the sweet songsters would come down on the ground where he could catch them. Those songs made him hungry. He knew of nothing he liked better, next to fat meadow-mice, than birds. That reminded him that some of them nest on the ground, Mrs. Grouse for instance. He had little hope that he could catch her, for it seemed as if she had eyes in the back of her head; but she should have a family by this time, and if he could find those youngsters—the very thought made his mouth water, and he started for the Green Forest.

Once there, he visited one place after another where he thought he might find Mrs. Grouse. He was almost ready to give up and go back to the Green Meadows to hunt for meadow-mice, when a sudden rustling in the dead leaves made him stop short and strain his ears. There was a faint *kwitt*, and then all was still. Tommy took three or four steps and then—could he believe his eyes? There was Mrs. Grouse fluttering on the ground just in front of him! One wing dragged as if broken. Tommy made a quick spring and then another. Somehow Mrs. Grouse just managed to get out of his way. But she couldn't fly. She couldn't even run as she

usually did. It was only luck that she had managed to evade him. Very stealthily he approached her as she lay fluttering among the leaves. Then, gathering himself for a long jump, he sprang. Once more he missed her, by a mere matter of inches it seemed. The same thing happened again and still again. It was maddening to have such a good dinner so near and yet not be able to get it. Then something happened that made Tommy feel so foolish that he wanted to sneak away. With a roar of wings Mrs. Grouse sailed up over the tree-tops and out of sight!

"Huh! Haven't you learned that trick yet?" said a voice.

Tommy turned. There was Reddy Fox grinning at him. "What trick?" he demanded.

Tommy took three or four steps and then—could he believe his eyes?!

"Why, that old Grouse was just fooling you!" replied Reddy. "There was nothing the matter with her. She was just pretending. She had a whole family of young ones hidden close by the place where you first saw her. My, but you are easy!"

"Let's go right back there!" cried Tommy.

"No use. Not the least bit," declared Reddy. "It's too late. Let's go over on the meadows and hunt for mice."

Together they trotted over to the Green Meadows. All through the grass were private little paths made by the mice. The grass hung over them so that they were more like tunnels than paths. Reddy crouched down by one which smelled very strong of mouse. Tommy crouched down by another. Presently there was the faint sound of tiny feet running. The grass moved ever so little over the small path Reddy was watching. Suddenly he sprang, and his two black paws came down together on something that gave a pitiful squeak. Reddy had caught a mouse without even seeing it. He had known just where to jump by the movement of the grass. Presently Tommy caught one the same way. Then, because they knew that the mice right around there were frightened, they moved on to another part of the meadows.

"I know where there are some young woodchucks," said Tommy, who had unsuccessfully tried for one of them that very morning.

"Where?" demanded Reddy.

"We'll have one of those chucks."

"Over by that old tree on the edge of the meadow," replied Tommy. "It isn't the least bit of use to try for them. They don't go far enough away from their hole, and their mother keeps watch all the time. There she is now."

Sure enough, there sat old Mrs. Chuck, looking, at that distance, for all the world like a stake driven in the ground.

"Come on," said Reddy. "We'll have one of those chucks."

But instead of going toward the woodchuck home, Reddy turned in quite the opposite direction. Tommy didn't know what to make of it, but he said nothing, and trotted along behind. When they were where Reddy knew that Mrs. Chuck could no longer see them, he stopped.

"There's no hurry," said he. "There seem to be plenty of grasshoppers here, and we may as well catch a few. When Mrs. Chuck has forgotten all about us, we'll go over there."

Tommy grinned to himself. "If he thinks we are going to get over there without being seen, he's got something to learn," thought Tommy. But he said nothing, and, for lack of anything better to do, he caught grasshoppers. After a while, Reddy said he guessed it was about time to go chuck-hunting.

"You go straight over there," said he. "When you get near, Mrs. Chuck will send all the little Chucks down into their hole and then she will follow, only she'll stay where she can peep out and watch you. Go right up to the hole so that she will go down out of sight and wait there until I come. I'll hide right back of that tree, and then you go off as if you had given up trying to catch any of them. Go hunt meadow-mice far enough away so that she won't be afraid. I'll do the rest."

Tommy didn't quite see through the plan, but he did as he was told. As he drew near Mrs. Chuck, she did just as Reddy said she would—sent her youngsters down underground. Then, as he drew nearer, she followed them. Tommy kept on right up to her door-step. The smell of those Chucks was maddening. He was tempted to try to dig them out, only somehow he just felt that it would be of no use. He was still half minded to try, however, when Reddy came trotting up and flattened himself in the long grass behind the trunk of the tree. Tommy knew then that it was time for him to do the rest of his part. He turned his back on the woodchuck home and trotted off across the meadow. He hadn't gone far when, looking back, he saw Mrs. Chuck sitting up very straight and still on her door-step, watching him. Not once did she take her eyes from him. Tommy kept on, and presently began to hunt for meadow-mice. But he kept one eye on Mrs. Chuck, and presently he saw her look this way and that, as if to make sure that all was well. Then she must have told her children that they could come out to play once more, for out they came. By this time Tommy was so excited that he almost forgot that he was supposed to be hunting mice.

Presently he saw a red flash from behind the old tree. There was a frightened scurry of little Chucks and old Mrs. Chuck dove into her hole. Reddy barked joyfully. Tommy hurried to join him. There on the ground lay two little Chucks with the life shaken out of them.

"Didn't I tell you we'd have Chuck for dinner?" said Reddy. "What one can't do, two can."

After that, Tommy and Reddy often hunted together, and Reddy taught Tommy many things. So the summer passed with plenty to eat and nothing to worry about. Not once had he known that terrible fear—the fear of being hunted—which is so large a part of the lives of Danny Meadow-mouse and Peter

Rabbit, and even Chatterer the Red Squirrel. Instead of being afraid, he was feared. He was the hunter instead of the hunted. Day and night, for he was abroad at night quite as much as by day, he went where he pleased and did as he pleased, and was happy, for there was nothing to worry him. Having plenty to eat, he kept away from the homes of men. He had been warned that there was danger there.

At last the weather grew cold. There were no more grasshoppers. There were no more foolish young rabbits or woodchucks or grouse, for those who had escaped had grown up and were wise and smart. Every day it grew harder to get enough to eat. The cold weather made him hungrier than ever, and now he had little time for sun-naps or idle play. He had to spend most of the time that he was awake hunting. He never knew where the next meal was coming from, as did thrifty Striped Chipmunk, and Happy Jack Squirrel, and Danny Meadow-mouse. It was hunt, hunt, hunt, and a meal only when his wits were sharper than the wits of those he hunted. He knew now what real hunger was. He knew what it was most of the time. So when, late one afternoon, he surprised a fat hen who had strayed away from the flock behind the barn of a lonely farm, he thought that never had he tasted anything more delicious. Thereafter he visited chicken-houses and stole many fat pullets. To him they were no more than the wild birds he hunted, only more foolish and so easily caught.

And then one morning after a successful raid on a poultry-house, he heard for the first time the voices of dogs on his trail. He, the hunter, was being hunted. At first it didn't bother him at all. He would run away and leave them far behind. So he ran, and when their voices were faint and far away, he lay down to rest. But presently he grew uneasy. Those voices were drawing nearer. Those dogs were following his every twist and turn with their noses in his tracks, just as he had so often followed a rabbit. For hours he ran, and still those dogs followed. He was almost ready to drop, when he chanced to run along in a tiny brook, and, after he left that, he heard no more of the dogs that day. So he learned that running water broke his trail.

The next day the dogs found his trail again, and, as he ran from them through a swamp, there was a sudden flash and a dreadful noise. Something stung him sharply on the shoulder. As he looked back, he caught a glimpse of a man with something in his hands that looked like a stick with smoke coming from the end of it. That night, as he lay licking his wounds, he knew that now he, who had known no fear, would never again be free from it—the fear of man.

Little by little he learned how to fool and out-wit the dogs. He learned that water destroyed his scent. He learned that dry sand did not hold it. He learned to run along stone walls and then jump far out into the field and so break his trail. He learned that, if he dashed through a flock of sheep, the foolish animals would rush around in aimless fright, and their feet would stamp out his trail. These and many other sharp tricks he learned, so that after a while he had no fear of the dogs. But his fear of man grew greater rather than less, and was with him at all times.

Surprising a fat hen

So all through the fall he hunted and was hunted. Then came the snow, the beautiful white snow. All day it fell, and when at night the moon came out, the earth was covered with a wonderful white carpet. Through the Green Forest and over the meadows Tommy hunted. One lone shivering little wood-mouse he dug out of a moldering old stump, but this was only a bite. He visited one hen-house after another, only to find each without so much as a loose board by means of which he might get in. It was dreadful to be so hungry.

As if this were not enough, the breaking of the day brought the sound of dogs on his trail. "I'll fool them in short order," thought he.

Alas! Running in the snow was a very different matter from running on the bare ground. One trick after another he tried, the very best he knew, the ones which never had failed before; but all in vain. Wherever he stepped he left a footprint plain to see. Though he might fool the noses of the dogs, he could not fool the eyes of their masters. Now one thing he had long ago learned, and this was never to seek his underground den unless he must, for then the dogs and the hunters would know where he lived. So now Tommy ran and ran, hoping to fool the dogs, but not able to. At last he realized this, and started for his den. He felt that he had got to. Running in the snow was hard work. His legs ached with weariness. His great plume of a tail, of which he was so proud, was a burden now. It had become wet with the snow and so heavy that it hampered and tired him.

A great fear, a terrible fear, filled Tommy's heart. Would he be able to reach that snug den in time? He was panting hard for breath, and his legs moved slower and slower. The voices of the dogs seemed to be in his very ears. Glancing back over his shoulder, he could see them gaining with every jump, the fierce joy of the hunt and the lust of killing in their eyes. He knew now the feeling, the terror and dreadful hopelessness, of the meadow-mice and rabbits he had so often run down. Just ahead was a great gray rock. From it he would make one last long jump in an effort to break the trail. In his fear he quite forgot that he was in plain sight now, and that his effort would be useless.

Up on the rock he leaped wearily, and—Tommy rubbed his eyes. Then he pinched himself to make quite sure that he was really himself. He shivered, for he was in a cold sweat—the sweat of fear. Before him stretched the snow-covered meadows, and away over beyond was the Old Pasture with the cow-paths showing like white ribbons. Half-way across the meadows, running toward him with their noses to the ground and making the echoes ring with the joy of the hunt, were two hounds. A dark figure moving on the edge of the Old Pasture caught his eyes and held them. It was a hunter. Reddy Fox, handsome, crafty Reddy, into whose hungry yellow eyes he had looked so short a time before, would soon be running for his life.

Hastily Tommy jumped to his feet and hurried over to the trail Reddy had made as he ran for the Green Forest. With eager feet he kicked the snow over those telltale tracks for a little way. He waited for those eager hounds, and when they reached the place where he had broken the trail, he drove them away. They and the hunter might pick up the trail again in the Green Forest, but at least Reddy would have time to get a long start of them and a good chance of getting away altogether.

Then he went back to the wishing-stone and looked down at it thoughtfully. "And I actually wished I could be a fox!" he exclaimed. "My, but I'm glad I'm not! I guess Reddy has trouble enough without one making him any more. He may kill a lot of innocent little creatures, but he has to live, and it's no more than men do." (He was thinking of the chicken dinner he would have that day.) "I'm going straight over to the Old Pasture and take up that trap I set yesterday. I guess a boy's troubles don't amount to much, after all. I'm gladder than ever that I'm a boy, and—and—well, if Reddy Fox is smart enough to get one of my chickens now and then, he's welcome. It must be awful to be hungry all the time."

First published in the February 1915 edition of *St. Nicholas Magazine*

HE PRINCESS ON THE GLASS HILL

WRITTEN AND ILLUSTRATED
BY HOWARD PYLE

ONCE UPON A time there was a King who was called to go upon a long journey. Before he went he called the Prince his son to him and said: "See, my son, here are the keys of the whole castle. You may go wherever you choose, excepting only in one room; into that you must neither step nor peep." Then the King rode away, and the Prince had the castle to himself.

For seven days he rambled up and down and hither and thither, until he had seen everything excepting what was to be found within those four walls, and he never longed for anything so much in all of his life as to know what it was they held that he was not to see.

"What harm can there be," said he, "for me to take just one little peep into the room through the crack of the door? I will let nothing either in or out, and my father will be none the wiser."

So he talked to himself, and then it was not long before he set out to do what he had been saying in his heart. Well, he opened the door the smallest crack in the world, and peeped in. There he saw a barrel, bound all round with six stout iron hoops as thick as your finger and as broad as your palm; next he saw a fountain of clear water that bubbled up into a stone basin; and last of all he saw a marble table with a silver cup upon it.

The Prince looked all about the room, and when he saw nothing more than the barrel, the fountain, and the silver cup, he opened the door and entered.

Then of a sudden he heard the sound of a weak voice coming from the barrel. "Dear Prince," said the voice, "will you not give a poor body a drink who has not had a taste of water for seventeen years?"

Now the Prince was a kind-hearted lad, and when he heard the voice in the barrel ask for nothing more than a drink of water, and that in such a poor, weak lit-

The Prince pours water into the barrel.

tle voice, his heart grew soft within him for pity. He took the silver cup from the marble slab and filled it at the fountain that bubbled up into the stone basin, and poured the water into a hole in the top of the barrel.

Then he was about to leave the room again, when the voice began speaking once more.

"Give me another drink of water!" it cried; and now it was loud and harsh, like the blare of a trumpet.

"No," said the Prince, "I will give you no more. I have done what I should not have done already."

"If you do not," cried the voice, "I will tell your father, as soon as he comes home, how you have come here to this room wherein he forbade you to enter."

When the Prince heard these words he put on his thinking-cap. "Come," said he, "I had better give the poor soul another draught of water; it can do no harm, and it will perhaps stop his mouth." So for the second time he filled the cup and poured the water into the barrel.

Crick, crack, bang! crick, crack, bang! The six iron hoops that bound the barrel tumbled to pieces, and out jumped a great creature like a man, covered all over with shaggy red hair. He said not a word, but snatching up the Prince, he jumped out of the window, and ran off faster than the wind. Across hill and valley he went, and over stock and stone, until he came to a great gloomy cave in the very midst of a dark forest; there he stopped, and set the Prince upon the ground. "Here is my home," said he, "and here you shall live with me and serve me."

And so it was as the creature said: the Prince lived with him and served him. Every day the creature went abroad into the forest, and whilst he was gone the Prince had to sweep the cave clean, and make the fire, and cook the supper until his master came home in the evening.

So passed seven years, in which time the Prince grew a great stout fellow, such as would be hard to match betwixt the four rivers; but in all that time he had seen neither a thread nor hair of any living soul like himself. But one day a great longing came upon him to get back into the world again, and to live among folk of his own kind. "Why should my master keep me here to build fires and cook food for him?" said the Prince to himself. "I will have a talk with him tonight when he comes home, and see what he has to say for himself." So saying, he cut a good stout club, and when his master came back to the cave at evening-time neither fire nor supper was ready for him, and there stood the Prince with the club in his hand.

"Why is there no fire or supper?" said the creature.

"Because," said the Prince, "I am tired of living here in the forest alone, and mean to serve you no longer."

When the Prince's master heard what the Prince said he laughed, and raising his staff he gave the lad a blow that tumbled him heels over head under the table.

But this cake was too big for him to swallow, and what he gave the Prince the Prince paid back again so soundly that his master's jacket smoked like a chimney afire.

"Stop! stop!" bawled he at last.

"And so I will," said the Prince, "if you will let me go, and show me the way out of the forest."

So off they set together, and after a while they came to the edge of the forest where the green fields began, though it was a long journey before they came there.

"Listen!" said the great creature, before they parted company; "who gives me a sprat, I give him a herring." He plucked two hairs from his head and gave them to the Prince. "Here," said he, "whenever you wish for anything, come hither and blow one of these hairs into the air. I will not be too far away to help you." Then he put his hand into his pocket and drew out an old wig full of chaff and grass-seed. "Take this also," said the wild man, "and whenever you put it on, not a soul in the world will know that you are yourself."

Thereupon the two parted company, and the one went one way, and the other the other.

The Prince put on the wig, and that moment his own mother would not have known him had she seen him, for he was no longer a tall noble hero, but a poor, lean, tattery, dusty, pale-faced lad, not fit or clean enough to sit in the kitchen corner.

Well, by-and-by, after the Prince had footed it along for a great while, he drew near to a great town, in the midst of which stood a splendid castle built all of marble, wherein the King of that country lived.

Up he went to the castle, and knocked at the door of the kitchen. And did they not want a handy lad about the place that could turn his hand to anything?—that was what he wanted to know. But such a poor, lean, tattery creature had never come to that town before, so that the cook was for clapping the door in his face, only that he happened to remember that they wanted a boy over yonder to clean out the stables and feed the pigs.

The Prince bathes.

So that was the best that the Prince could find to do. And as no one wanted to have such a looking creature about the house, he had to sleep under the kitchen steps on a litter of straw.

But early one morning, before anybody was stirring in the castle, the lad went to a cistern that stood in the court-yard back of the house, and laying aside his wig of tow, began bathing his bosom and face in the water.

Now the Princess of that country was the prettiest that ever you saw, and it happened that she also was waking just about that time, and looking out of her window she espied, not the stable-boy, but a splendid hero, with skin as white and red as milk and rose leaves, and with hair that shone like spun gold, bathing his face and neck at the cistern in the court-yard. (That was because he did not have the wig upon his head.)

But how she did look and stare, and stare and look, to be sure, for she had never seen the like of the Prince before in all her born days.

By-and-by she called one of her women, and bade her go down-stairs and fetch the lad that stood bathing at the cistern in the court-yard; and down went the woman. But when she came there she found no one but the lean, tattered, pale stable-boy, for the Prince had heard her coming, and had clapped his hat upon his head. All the same, as no one else was in the court-yard, the woman took the lad up to the Princess as she had been bidden to do.

But the Princess did not know the Prince in his ragged wig. "Why did you bring this fellow to me?" said she.

"Because," said the woman, "there was no one else in the courtyard."

Then the Princess began to put this and that together. "Why do you wear that ugly wig?" said she to the stable-lad.

"To keep my wits warm; and why else should I wear it?" said he.

Then the Princess snatched at the wig, and before the Prince knew what she was about, she had it off his head, and there he stood, the handsomest hero in the world. "Tell me who you are," said she.

"That I cannot do yet," said the Prince; "so give me my wig again, and let me go to my stables and pig-sty."

Thereupon the Princess gave him his wig, and he clapped it upon his head and ran down-stairs and away, and that was the last that she saw of him for some time to come.

NOW IN THAT country was a great fiery dragon that wasted the land and killed the folk at such a rate that all the country for three leagues about him was nothing but a staring naked desert.

So at last the King called his wisest counselors together to see whether their wits could not show him a way to get rid of the pest.

"Let it be proclaimed that whoever kills the dragon shall have the Princess for his wife, and half the country to rule over," said the oldest and the wisest counselor, "and then a hero will not be long in showing himself."

So it was done as the wise counselor advised, and the proclamation was posted on all the church doors in the town. Then, oh! what a hurly-burly there was! Nobody talked of anything but the dragon. Everyone would have liked to have the Princess for his wife, but not a soul dared face the fiery dragon.

"I would like to go and fight the dragon," said the tattery, pale-faced stable-boy.

Maybe it was five minutes before those who heard what he said could speak a word for the fit of laughing that shook them all.

"Very well," said they at last, "you may take the old lame horse that feeds up yonder on the stony hill pasture." And that was the best that the lad could get.

So off he rode, and all whom he passed turned and looked after him and laughed.

But little he cared for that. On he jogged, hoppety-clop, until he had come to the great dark forest. There he blew a hair into the air, and there stood his former master, the hairy great creature, as quick as a wink.

"And what is it that you wish for?" said he.

"I should like," said the Prince, "to have another horse and a suit of armor, so that I may kill the great fiery dragon over yonder." That was what he said, and there was what he wanted—a beautiful white horse and a suit of shining silver armor. And the best part of the business was that neither fire nor sword could harm whosoever wore that armor.

So up the Prince leaped upon his grand white horse, and off he rode to kill the dragon.

Never mind: I only wish that you could have seen the fight betwixt the Prince and the dragon, for it was better than a dance at a fair to look at. But by-and-by the end came, and there lay the dragon dead. Then the Prince cut off its head, and rode away home again.

The Prince slays the dragon.

When he came to the town, there sat the King and all his people at dinner. In walked the Prince, and nobody knew who he was. Down he flung the dragon's head, without uttering a word to a single soul, and nobody to stop him for wonder at it all.

Away he rode to the forest. There was the creature waiting for him. So he stripped off his armor and put on his tow wig, and off he rode on his old lame horse.

In the town everybody was buzzing about the hero who had killed the dragon. "Never mind," said the stable-lad; "if I had only been there in time I could have done as much myself."

Dear! dear! how they did laugh and roar at the foolish lad's words until they were half dead with their merriment, and with little breath left in their bodies!

But the King was perplexed to know who the strange knight could be. So once again he called all of his counselors together to talk the business over. "This is what you shall do," said the very oldest and wisest of all—he who had advised the King concerning the dragon—"you shall make a hill of glass, and on the top the Princess shall sit with a golden apple and a silver pear in her hand. Whoever rides up the hill and takes the one and the other from her lap is the man who killed the fiery dragon."

And so again it was done as the wise counselor said. A hill of glass was built, and on the top the Princess was to sit with the golden apple and the silver pear, and all the world was given to know that whoever could ride up the hill and fetch down the one and the other might expect great things from the King.

So every young man who could beg or borrow a bit of horseflesh to straddle rode off to the glass hill, big and little, young and old, great and small.

"I should like to go too," said the stable-boy.

"Oh yes," said the others, as well as they could for laughing, "you have done so well already that no doubt you will be able to ride up the hill and bring down the golden apple and the silver pear. Nevertheless, if you are for going, you may take the nag that is left after we have gone;" and that was the same that he had ridden before. Nevertheless he took what he could get, and off he rode to the forest, and blew the second hair into the air.

"And what is it that you want now?" said the great creature.

"I would like," said the Prince, "to have a horse with which to ride up the glass hill and fetch down the golden apple and the silver pear from the lap of the Princess, and also I should like to have a suit of armor fit for a king to wear."

"Very well," said the hairy creature, "so you shall have;" and there they were, a splendid red horse with eyes that sparkled like fire, and a suit of golden armor that shone like the sun in the morning; and the Prince put on the one and mounted the other, and off he rode.

When he came to the glass hill, there they were at it, riding and stumbling and slipping and sprawling, with their horses all of a lather. When they saw the splendid knight come riding in his golden armor they all cleared a way for him, and at the hill he went until the sparks flew.

Up he rode, as easily as though it had been a meadow, and there sat the Princess at the top with the apple and the pear in her lap.

The Prince took the one and the other, and then kissed her pretty lips.

"I know you," said she, and that is all she had the chance to say; for the Prince wheeled his horse and rode down the hill again and away, before any could lay hand on him or say a word to him. As for following after him, why, those who waited below might as well have tried to follow the March wind.

Off he rode to the forest, and there was the hairy creature waiting for him.

"Here are your horse and your armor again," said the Prince.

"You shall keep them," said the creature, "for you will need them by-and-by."

So the Prince took the old tattery rags and put them on, so that the splendid golden armor was all hidden by them. Then he mounted upon his old limping horse, and rode away to the King's castle.

"Here is the pewter penny back again," said they, and everybody had a laugh or a jeer for him. "You should have seen the splendid golden knight," said they, "that rode up the hill as easily as one can swallow a buttered egg."

"Yes—good," said the stable-boy. "But if I had been there, I could have done as well."

But the King was as far as ever from finding who it was who had done all these wonderful things. So he and all his wise counselors sat together talking the business over. Just then in came the Princess. "I can find the hero that you seek," said she.

"Very well," said the King, "and where is he?"

"Send for the lad that cleans out the stable and feeds the pigs," said the

The Prince wins the Princess.

Princess, "and then we will not be long in finding him."

So they sent for him. But when he came and stood before them, everybody began staring and snickering, for not one had ever seen such a lean, pale, tattery, dusty creature before. But the Princess knew what she was about. Up she stepped and snatched the cap and wig off from his head. Thereupon the dirty rags fell away from him, and there he stood in his golden armor that shone so that the whole room was filled with light.

The King came up to him and took him by the hand. "Are you the hero," said he, "who rode up the glass hill?"

"Yes," said the Prince, "I am he." And he thrust his hand into his bosom and drew forth the golden apple and the silver pear. "I am the son of the King of the Golden Mountain," said the Prince, "and what I wish for most of all in the world is to have the Princess for my wife."

The Princess stepped up. "I knew from the first that you were no stable-boy," said she.

After that they were married, and the King of the Golden Mountain came to the wedding; and if nobody else in the world was glad, he was, for he had long given up his son as dead.

And now if there is any more of this story to tell, you must get somebody else to tell it to you.

First published in the July 24, 1888, edition of *Harper's Young People*

The Princess and the Pirate

BY DORIS WEBB

THE PRINCESS BARBARA was sitting in her garden one day, embroidering a decorative piece of embroidery in a proper and princessy fashion, when all at once she looked up and saw standing before her—a pirate. Now, of course, we should all be surprised if we met pirates in our gardens, but Princess Barbara was particularly surprised, because pirates were never allowed in the palace grounds, by the king's ex- press orders. She knew he was a pirate, because his mustache was long and black, his hat and boots were particularly piratical, and his silk pocket-handker-chief was a miniature pirate flag.

"There are three questions I would like to ask you," he said, with a beautiful bow. "First—"

"Oh, excuse me," said the princess, "but I don't believe I'm allowed to talk to pirates."

"Oh, all right," said the pirate, quite calmly; "I thought maybe you'd like to hear the story of my life, and all about that time when I had that particularly thrilling adventure on the swimming island; but as long as you're not interested—"

"How did it swim?" asked the princess, eagerly.

So the pirate began a most thrilling tale that kept the princess breathless from beginning to end. And when he had finished, "The first of the three questions," he said—but before he had time for another word, he discovered the king standing before him, trying to look surprised and grieved and furious and dignified all at the same time.

"Begone at once!" said his majesty. "But first tell me how you came in."

"I go anon," replied the pirate, and the princess was pleased to think that he could hold his own in classical conversation.

"Anent you go," continued the king, who saw that he must summon all his court language, "inform me of your manner of ingress."

"I erstwhile came," replied the pirate, folding his arms and closing his eyes in a truly dignified manner, "by just ye route by which anon I presently depart," and opening his eyes, he seized a linden bough and climbed over the palace wall, with an agility that made even the king a little envious.

"Begone at once!" said his majesty.

"And now, my dear," continued the king, sitting down by Princess Barbara, "I must warn you not to talk to pirates again. It's quite against family tradition. And, besides, pirates are a great menace to the country, and I shall have this one seized and imprisoned at once. But, to speak of pleasanter themes, I came to tell you that Prince Goodale is coming to visit us, the most delightful of all your suitors. He is all that he should be, and he isn't all that he shouldn't be."

The princess sighed. "Is he quite, quite perfect?" she said.

"Quite!" the king assured her eagerly, and the princess sighed again.

All that day she kept sighing, and all the next. As the time for the prince's arrival drew nearer, the king was busy ordering all sorts of improvements in the palace. He introduced an extra retinue of retainers, had all the best gold and silver made ready, and engaged an itinerant painter to paint the outside of the palace.

The princess sat by her window, still occasionally sighing and thinking of the splendid stories of adventure the pirate had told her.

She idly watched the painter painting the palace, with more industry than art, and wondered if princesses were permitted to talk to painters. But she didn't need to decide the question, for just at that moment the painter raised the scaffolding, by its ropes, till he was level with her window.

"The first question," he said, leaning his arms on the window-sill, "is, do you like peppermints?"

"Oh, is it really you?" cried the princess, in delight, "I never would have dreamed it! Yes, I'm very fond of peppermints. How splendidly you are disguised!"

The pirate looked at his painter's costume with pride. "Yes," he said complacently, "I've always been very successful with disguises. There was that time when I was shipwrecked on an iceberg—" and he went

*Just at that moment the painter raised
the scaffolding by its ropes.*

on to tell such a remarkable tale that the princess scarcely breathed until she suddenly heard the king beside her.

"My dear!" he cried, "princesses must not talk to painters! You, sir," he continued, looking at the painter with an expression of doubt, indignation, and withering scorn, "had best depart with the most expeditious expediency."

"I will depart," replied the painter-pirate, with equal scorn, indignation, and doubt. "I will depart with instantaneous alacrity." And having whispered to the princess, "So do I love peppermints!" he pulled his pulley rope and let his scaffold to the ground with surprising speed.

For two days more, the princess sighed without ceasing, and then the prince's trunks began to arrive. First came all the golden hat-boxes that contained his different crowns, and then all the scepter boxes, and various other possessions, without which no prince makes a visit. The princess watched a newly engaged porter take these boxes to the suite of rooms reserved for the prince. She walked slowly downstairs, listlessly interested in the tumult, and on the stairs she met the porter, carrying three large boxes.

"The second question is, are you fond of playing parchisi?" he said, as he reached her.

"Oh, can it be you?" cried the princess, joyfully, "I thought I should never see you again! Yes, I'm very fond of parchisi. There's a parchisi board in the library. We can play a game now, if you like."

So they went to the library and played parchisi until the king discovered them there.

"What ho!" he exclaimed, really angry this time. "Be off! Begone! Depart! Don't even wait to apologize! I will not listen to your apology!"

But the porter-painter-pirate folded his arms with quiet dignity, and said: "I have nothing to apologize for! I let the princess win three games of parchisi running, and I pretended not to see when I could have sent all her men home. However, I am going by the way I came. Don't invite me to stay longer. I will not listen to your invitation!"

And with undaunted courage he walked out of the front door, and even the king could not help admiring the way he made his way through the hall and down the palace steps, without once unfolding his arms or unclosing his eyes.

At last the day came when Prince Goodale was to arrive. Everything was ready, and everything looked very well indeed, except the blotchy place on the palace wall where the pirate had started to paint. And to the princess that was the loveliest spot in the whole palace, even though the pirate's attempts at painting were somewhat amateurish.

A short while before the prince was to arrive, a wandering minstrel, with a harp, came to the palace.

"Just the thing!" cried the king. "We must have music to welcome the prince." So the minstrel, apparently something of a poet, too, began practicing some very charming songs.

The princess, who was very fond of music, stayed to listen even after the king had left to see to some final details. And as he finished an especially beautiful bar, the poet turned to her and said:

"The third question is, are you fond of picnics?"

"I love picnics!" said the princess, rapturously, "and parchisi, and peppermints, and painters, and porters, and—"

"Princes?" helpfully suggested the king, who had returned unexpectedly.

"Or pirates?" suggested the poet, softly touching his instrument.

"Oh, dear," sighed the princess. "I've been most unhappy lately."

"So have I," said the king, in a grieved tone. "You've no idea," he continued, turning to the poet, "how difficult it is to bring up a princess. Now the other day she *would* play parchisi with a porter."

"I don't mind telling you," said the poet, "that I was the porter—only *that* was a disguise."

The minstrel began practicing some very charming songs.

"You don't mean it!" exclaimed the king. "How you've changed! And before that," he went on, "she took the greatest interest in a painter."

"I don't mind telling you," said the poet, "that I was the painter—only *that* was a disguise."

"You do surprise me!" said the king. "But you haven't heard the worst. Just about a week ago, I found her deep in conversation with a pirate!"

"I don't mind telling you," said the poet, "that I was the pirate, only that"—and he struck a sweeping chord on his harp—"*that* was a disguise!"

"A disguise!" cried the princess, "then do you mean that you are *not* a pirate, after all?"

"I am no more pirate," he replied, "than I am painter or porter or poet."

"Then what are you?" cried the king and the princess, both together.

"Why, as it happens," he replied, with a smile, "I'm Prince Goodale!"

And with that there was a flourish of trumpets outside, and the palace doors were thrown open to a great retinue of Prince Goodale's followers, who advanced to the prince's right and left, and bowed low with every mark of respect and loyalty.

The prince was escorted to his apartments by the amazed king, who was trying to be cordial in court language, and the astonished princess was left alone.

But it was not long before the prince appeared again, in truly princely apparel, so dazzling that the princess could scarcely realize that she had known him as a pirate in her garden.

"Are you sure," she shyly asked, "that you *are* really Prince Goodale? This isn't a disguise, too?"

"A disguise?" said the prince, laughing, "why, yes, it is a disguise, in a way, because no one would ever recognize me now as a person who liked peppermints and parchisi and picnics. Of course I *am* Prince Goodale, but, then, that's not the important thing. Pirates, porters, painters, poets, princes, and even princesses—they're all disguises, you know—and I wanted to know what you yourself were really like—not you in the disguise of a princess. And now," he continued, "I'll take you to my kingdom, where, after our subjects have welcomed us, we can have all the peppermints and parchisi we want."

"And go on picnics every day!" whispered the princess.

First published in the July 1914 edition of *St. Nicholas Magazine*

The Brownies at School

WRITTEN AND ILLUSTRATED BY PALMER COX

AS Brownies rambled round one night,
A country school-house came in sight;
And there they paused awhile to speak
About the place, where through the week
The scholars came, with smile or whine,
Each morning, at the stroke of nine.
"This is," said one, "the place, indeed,
Where children come to write and read.
'Tis here, through rules and rods to suit,
The young idea learns to shoot;

And here the truant with a grin,
In nearest neighbor pokes the pin,
Or sighs to break his whittled slate
And spring at once to man's estate.
How oft from shades of yonder grove
I've viewed at eve the shouting drove,
As from the door they crowding broke

Like oxen from beneath the yoke,
When necks are galled and sides are sore
From treatment never known before."

Another spoke: "The teacher's chair,
The ruler, pen, and birch are there;
The blackboard hangs against the wall;
The slates at hand, the books and all.
We might go in to read and write
And master sums like scholars bright."
"I'll play," cried one, "the teacher's part;
I know some lessons quite by heart,
And every section of the land
To me is plain as open hand."

"With all respect, my friend, to you,"
Another said, "that would not do.
You're hardly fitted, sir, to rule;

Your place should be the dunce's stool.
You're not with great endowments blessed;
Besides, your temper's not the best,
And those who train the budding mind
Should own a disposition kind.
The rod looks better on the tree
Than resting by the master's knee;
I'll be the teacher, if you please;
I know the rivers, lakes, and seas,
And, like a banker's clerk, can throw
The figures nimbly in a row.
I have the patience, love, and grace,
So requisite in such a case."
The more they talked, the stronger grew
The wish to prove how much they knew.
From page to page through books to pass
And spell the words that tried the class;
So through their skill they soon obtained

Access to all the room contained.
Then desk and bench, on every side,
Without delay were occupied;
Some bent above a slate or book,
And some at blackboards station took.
They clustered round the globe with zeal,
And kept it turning like a wheel;
It seemed to yield them more delight
Than aught they found throughout the night.

Said one, "I've often heard it said,
The world is rounder than your head,
And people all about it crawl,
Like flies around a rubber ball.
And here, indeed, we find it true,
With both the poles at once in view,
With latitudes and each degree
All measured out on land and sea."

Another said, "I thought I knew
The world from Maine to Timbuctoo,
Or could, without a guide, have found
My way from Cork to Puget Sound;
But here so many things I find
That never dawned upon my mind,
On sundry points, I blush to say,
I've been a thousand miles astray."

"'Tis like an egg," another cried,
"A little longer than it's wide,
With islands scattered through the seas
Where savages may live at ease;

And buried up in Polar snows
You find the hardy Eskimos;
While here and there some scorching spots
Are set apart for Hottentots.
And see the rivers small and great,
That drain a Province or a State;
The name and shape of every nation;
Their faith, extent, and population;
And whether governed by a king,
A President, or Council ring."

While some with such expressions bold
Surveyed the globe as round it rolled,
Still others turned to ink and pen,
And, spreading like a brooding hen,
They scrawled a page to show the band

PALMER COX.

Their special "style," or "business hand."
The teacher had enough to do,
To act his part to nature true:
He lectured well the infant squad;
He rapped the desk and shook the rod,
And stood the dunce upon the stool,
A laughing-stock to all the school.
But frequent changes please the crowd,
So lengthy reign was not allowed;
And when one master had his hour,
Another took the rod of power;
And thus they changed to suit the case,
Till many filled the honored place.

So taken up was every mind
With fun and study well combined,
They noticed not the hours depart,
Until the sun commenced to dart

A sheaf of lances, long and bright,
Above the distant mountain height;
Then from the school-room, in a heap,
They jumped and tumbled, twenty-deep,
In eager haste to disappear
In deepest shade of forests near,

When next the children gathered there,
With wondering faces fresh and fair.
It took an hour of morning prime,
According to the teacher's time,
To get the books in place once more,
And order to the room restore.
So great had been the haste to hide,
The windows were left open wide;
While over slates and books and walls
Remained the pen and pencil scrawls—
And scholars knew, without a doubt,

First published in the October 1885 edition of *St. Nicholas Magazine*

The Wyndham Girls

BY MARION AMES TAGGART

CHAPTER ONE: "POOR HUMPTY-DUMPTY"

"NO PINK FOR me, please; I want that shimmering green, made up over shining white silk. It will make my glossy brown hair and eyes look like a ripe chestnut among its green leaves."

"Oh, Bab, such glistening sentences! 'Shimmering green,' 'shining white,' 'glossy hair'—you didn't mean glossy eyes, I hope! Besides, you know, chestnuts don't show among their green leaves; they stay in their burs until they drop off the trees."

"Now Phyllis, what's the use of spoiling a poetical metaphor, figure—what do you call it? Which do you like best? Have you made up your mind, Jessamy?"

"I want all white; probably this mousseline-de-soie."

The soft May wind from the distant river blew the lace curtains gently to and fro, lifting the squares of delicate fabrics scattered over the couch on which the three young girls were sitting. Jessamy, the elder of the two Wyndham sisters, was at eighteen very beautiful, with dainty elegance of motion, refinement of speech, almost stately grace, unusual to her age and generation. Barbara, a year younger, was her opposite. Life, energy, fun, were declared in every turn of her head and hands. Small in figure, with sparkling dark eyes and a saucy tilt of nose and chin, she could hardly have contrasted more sharply with her tall, gray-eyed, delicately tinted sister, and with what Bab herself called "Jessamy's Undine ways." The third girl, Phyllis, was twin in age to Jessamy, unlike either of the others in appearance and temperament. She was their cousin, the one child of their father's only brother; but as she had been brought up with them since her fourth year, Jessamy and Barbara knew no lesser kinship to her than to each other. At first glance Phyllis was not pretty; to those who had known her for even a brief time she was beautiful. Sweetness, unselfishness, content shone out from her dark blue eyes with the large pupils and dark lashes. Her lips rested together with the suggestion of a smile in their corners, and the clear pallor of her complexion was shaded by her masses of dark brown hair, which warmed into red tints under the sunlight.

Across the room from her daughters and niece, enjoying the girls' happiness, sat

Mrs. Wyndham, rocking slowly. She was a frail creature, sweet and gentle, still clad in the mourning she had worn for her husband for seven years; one felt that she had been properly placed in luxury, fortunately shielded from hardship. The Wyndhams were wealthy, and the beautiful morning-room in the house on Murray Hill was full of evidences of taste and the long possession of ample means to gratify it.

Even the samples fluttering under the girls' fingers bore the name of a French artist on Fifth Avenue, whose skill only the highly favored could command, and the consultation under way was for the selection for each young girl of gowns fit for a princess's wearing, yet intended for the use of maidens not yet "out," at the dances at the hotel at Bar Harbor in the coming summer.

"I'm afraid I'm dreadfully vain," sighed Jessamy, stroking the bits of soap-bubble-tinted gauzes as she laid them together on her knee. "I hope I love exquisite things for their own sake, not because I want them for myself; but I'm not sure my love for them is purely artistic."

"You do want them for yourself, but it's just as you want only good pictures in your room," said Phyllis, coming up flushed from the pursuit of some errant bits under the table. "You're born royal in taste. Bab and I could get on if we were beg-

Jessamy, Barbara, Phyllis, and Mrs. Wyndham

gared, but I can't imagine you shabby. Bab would revel in a sun-bonnet and driving cows home, and I could be happy in a tenement, if we were together; but you're a princess, and you can't be anything else."

"You're a bad Phyl, whose object in life is to spoil everyone by making them perfectly self-satisfied," said Jessamy. "I hope some of the excuses you find for me are true; I'm as luxurious by nature as a cat—I know that. Come to the window; I want to see this old rose in the sunlight."

Bab stopped swinging her feet, and slipped from the arm of her mother's chair, where she had perched, to follow them. "Don't you abuse cats, nor my sister Jessamy, miss," she said, putting her arms around slender Jessamy and peering over her shoulder at the sample of silk, while she rubbed Jessamy's arm with her chin, like an affectionate dog. "They're two as nice things as I know. Madrina, Mr. Hurd is crossing the street, and he's headed this way."

"Oh, dear!" sighed Mrs. Wyndham, almost fretfully. "I suppose he is coming to urge me again to withdraw our money from the business; he has tormented me all winter to do it. He says it isn't secure; but that's absurd, with Mr. Abbott at the helm, whom your dear father trusted as he did himself! It's all because they won't show the books lately—as though I wanted to see them while Mr. Abbott is managing! I can't see why Mr. Hurd is so nervous and suspicious! Mr. Abbott came expressly to see me, and explained how bad it would be for the corporation if I offered my stock in the market. I understand him much better than Mr. Hurd; he is more patient, and won't leave a point until he has made me see it as he does. I am no business woman, and I can't understand these things very well at best. You stay in the room today, children, and see if you understand. Mr. Hurd insists that I am risking beggaring you, and that distresses me unspeakably."

"Don't mind Mr. Hurd, madrina; he's an Anxious Attorney," said Barbara, with an air of lucidity, as Violet, the maid, announced the lawyer, who followed at once on the announcement.

"We are pluming, or more properly donning, our feathers for flight, Mr. Hurd," said Mrs. Wyndham, rising, and pointing to the samples on the couch, as she extended her hand.

"Yes, yes!" said the little man, shaking hands with Mrs. Wyndham without looking at her. "Good morning, Miss Jessamy; good morning, Phyllis; how do you do, little Barbara? May I interrupt your—gracious powers, dear madam, I mean I *must* interrupt your plans, Mrs. Wyndham!"

Jessamy and Phyllis clutched each other with sudden pallor. The little lawyer's voice shook with emotion. Bab flushed, and ran to her mother, putting her arms around her frail figure as though to place herself as a bulwark between her and ill.

"You will not interrupt anything more important than the selection of dancing-gowns for the children," said Mrs. Wyndham, with her soft dignity, though she turned a little paler. "Is there any special reason for your visit—kind visit always—Mr. Hurd? And may the girls hear what you have to say, since their interests are at stake?"

"Special reason, madam? Special reason, indeed! Heaven help me, I don't know how to say what must be said, but I prefer the young ladies to hear it," groaned their old friend.

"Evidently you feel that you have something unpleasant to tell me, Mr. Hurd, but I feel sure you magnify it; you know you are always more timid and pessimistic than I," said Mrs. Wyndham, dropping into the nearest chair and trying to smile.

"Mrs. Wyndham, my dear lady, it isn't a matter for self-gratulation! If I could have made you listen to me six—even two months ago, I should not be here today, the bearer of this dreadful news," burst out the lawyer, impatiently.

"Wouldn't it be better to tell us quickly, Mr. Hurd? You frighten us with hints," said Jessamy, in her silvery, even voice, but the poor child's lips were white.

Mr. Hurd glanced at her. "Yes," he said, "but it is not easy. I heard the definite news last night in Wall Street; rumors have been afloat for days. I wanted to give you one more night of untroubled sleep. It will be in the evening papers."

"What will, Mr. Hurd?" burst out Barbara, impatiently.

"The failure of the Wyndham Iron Company."

There was dead silence in the room, broken only by the low-toned French clock striking ten times.

"The company—failed?" whispered Mrs. Wyndham, trying to find her voice.

"What does that mean, Mr. Hurd?" asked Phyllis.

"It means that your mother's bonds and stocks are valueless, and as she holds everything in her own right, and has kept all that your father left in the business, it means that your inheritance has been wiped out of existence," said the lawyer, not discriminating between daughters and niece in his excitement.

"How can the company have failed? I don't believe it!" cried Mrs. Wyndham, starting to her feet with sudden strength.

"Dear Mrs. Wyndham, it is too certain," said her husband's old friend and attorney, gently. "When they refused to open up the books for inspection I knew this would come."

"Mr. Abbott—" began Mrs. Wyndham.

"Mr. Abbott is an outrageous villain," interrupted Mr. Hurd, passionately. "He has got control of the business, and ruined it by running it on a speculative basis—though justice to his business capacity compels me to add that he has secured himself against harm. Henry Wyndham was completely deceived by him."

"I never knew anyone ruined outside of books," said Jessamy, trying to smile.

"What does it mean? Going to live in an East Side tenement and working in a sweat-shop?"

"Nonsense, Jessamy!" said her mother, sharply, drying the tears which had been softly falling, while Bab wailed aloud at the picture. "Nonsense! I shall sell some stock, and I am sure we shall get on very well, perhaps economizing somewhat."

"Dear madam, you no more grasp the situation than you saw it coming," said Mr. Hurd, struggling between annoyance and pity. "The value of your stock is wiped out; practically, you have no stock. Still, I hope matters will not be as bad as Miss Jessamy pictures. This house will rent or sell for enough to give you six or eight thousand a year, and if you sell the pictures and furniture you will have a very respectable principal to live upon; bad as the case is, it might be far worse."

"Do you mean that this house will be the sole—actually the sole—source of income?" gasped Mrs. Wyndham, with more agitation than she had yet shown.

Mr. Hurd nodded.

The poor lady uttered a sharp cry, and fell back, sobbing wildly. "Then I have nothing, nothing!" she screamed. "My darlings are beggared."

Phyllis rang for Violet, and Mr. Hurd leaped to his feet, apprehending the truth. "What do you mean, Mrs. Wyndham?" he demanded.

Mrs. Wyndham rested her head on Phyllis's arm. "Last March," she said feebly, "Mr. Abbott came to me, telling me that the business was temporarily embarrassed, and asked me to let him negotiate a loan with this house as security."

Mr. Hurd, who had been pacing the floor furiously, stopped short with a fervent imprecation. Halting before the feeble creature who had been so duped, he thrust his hands deep in his pockets and gazed down at her. "And you did it?" he growled.

Mrs. Wyndham bowed her head lower, and just then Violet came back with Jessamy, who had gone to seek her, and, with her face gray from sympathy and fright, put her strong arms around her mistress's fragile body, lifting her like a baby.

"Come right along, you po' little lamb-lady," she said. "Miss Jes'my done telephone for de doctah, an' I's goin' make you comf'able in bed. Don' you cry 'nothah teah; V'ilet ain't goin' let nothin' come neah you."

Utterly prostrated in mind and body, Mrs. Wyndham found comfort in the soft voice and loving arms. She drooped her head on the tall girl's pink gingham shoulder, and let herself be carried to her chamber as if she had been a child.

Jessamy turned to Mr. Hurd. "You will not mind if we received the news rather badly?" she said. "We all shall play our parts when we have learned them. It—it—came rather suddenly, you see." Evidently Jessamy was going to be the princess her cousin called her, and meet misfortune proudly.

"You dear child!" said the lawyer, his eyes dimming as he looked in the lovely face, blanched white, and noted the lines holding the soft lips grimly set to keep them from quivering. "You and Phyllis are little heroines. Don't try to be too brave; it is better to cry, and then wipe away the tears to see what is to be done after the shipwreck."

"What are we likely to have to live on if we sell our things?" asked Jessamy, trying to thank him with a smile.

"No one can say positively; it is guesswork. But your father knew good pictures, and I should say you might have an income of two thousand a year out of the net result of the sale. We won't go into that this morning. Good-by, my dears. Try not to worry. No one knows what is best for him in this curious world. People are usually better and stronger for trying their mettle, as well as their muscle. God bless you!" Jessamy did not attempt to answer. Mr. Hurd laid his hand gently on each head, and went away.

Left to themselves, Jessamy and Phyllis looked at each other and around the pretty room still strewn with the samples of their dancing-gowns. With a sudden rush of memory they saw themselves little children playing around the kind father—father to both equally—who had given them this home, and with equal clearness saw the years stretching out before them in which this home would have no being. The necessity for self-restraint was removed; with a common impulse they threw themselves in each other's arms, and burst into passionate weeping.

Bab stirred uneasily on the floor where she had lain sobbing, dried her eyes, and said:

"Don't cry like that, girls; please don't. It doesn't matter when I cry; I always go off one way or the other: but I can't stand you being wretched."

She gathered herself up and went over to the other two, who, having controlled themselves while she cried, could not raise their heads.

Bab was mercurial; she had wept her first horror away, and now the necessity of her nature to look on the bright side asserted itself.

"I think likely two thousand a year is a lot when you are used to it," she said. "I expect to learn to manage so well that we can adopt twins on the money left over from our expenses. I'll get points from Ruth Wells; she has learned contriving. Look up; smile. 'Rise, Sally, rise; dry your weeping eyes!'"

"Don't, Bab; you haven't an idea of what has happened," said Jessamy, faintly, but at the same time she raised her head, checking her tears a little.

Bab saw it with secret triumph. "Don't I! I've as much experience as you, miss, anyway. Still, I'm willing to confess I'd rather not be poor," she said, with the air of making a generous concession. "But we'll be happy yet! It is rather hard to be thrown off your high wall, where you've sat all your life. Poor Humpty-Dumpty! I never properly felt for him before!"

And Bab was rewarded for her nonsense by a tearful smile from Jessamy and Phyllis.

CHAPTER TWO: FRIENDS, COUNSELORS, AND PLANS

THE EVENING TURNED cool and damp, with the unreliability of May. Mrs. Wyndham, too ill to rise, slept, under sedatives, the sleep of utter exhaustion. The girls had taken refuge around the grate fire in Jessamy's beautiful room, with its fine pictures, and background of moss greens and browns. They were profoundly depressed, for on taking account of their stock of accomplishments they found that, though they were talented, they were untrained to practical labor, and that Jessamy's drawing, Bab's music, Phyllis's clever stories and verses, were all too amateurish to find a place in the marts.

"I suppose there isn't much good in making plans," said Jessamy, gazing gloomily into the fire. "I think we should live quite poorly for a while, within our income, whatever it is, and fit ourselves to do something well. I don't want to rush into any kind of half-good employment, when by self-denial, hardship perhaps, at first, we might amount to something in the end."

"Hail, Minerva!" cried Phyllis. "You'll be as thoroughbred a working-girl, if you must, as you were fine lady, and that's what I love you for, Jasmine-blossom."

"My poor unfortunate children, are you sitting here in the dark?" cried a voice. "I saw that dreadful item in the *Post*; is it true?"

"How do you do, Aunt Henrietta?" said Jessamy, rising, while Bab barely stifled a groan.

"About the failure? Yes, I'm afraid it is quite true."

Mrs. Hewlett was Mr. Wyndham's aunt; he had been her favorite nephew because he bore her name. Her grand-nieces did not love her. She had a strong tendency to speak her opinions, provided they were unpleasant to the hearer, for she prided herself on her sincerity and infallibility of judgment. Jessamy, Phyllis, and Bab recognized in her coming an added hardship at the end of their hard day.

"I always knew it would end this way," said Aunt Henrietta, dropping into an easy-chair and letting her cloak slip to the floor. "Your mother has no sort of business ability. Poor Henry!"

"Mama did not ruin the Iron Company, aunt, and papa can't need pity now as much as she does," said Bab, losing her temper instantly, as she always did on encountering her whom she disrespectfully called "the drum-major."

"How are you left?" demanded Aunt Henrietta, ignoring Bab, to Jessamy's profound gratitude.

"We shall have only what the contents of this house will bring," said Jessamy. "We hope it may be two thousand a year."

Aunt Henrietta held up both hands in genuine horror, crying: "Two thousand for such a family as you are! It is practically beggary. You have been brought up in the most extravagant way—never taught the value of money. Your mother spoiled you from the cradle. I suppose you will run through what little ready money you have, and then expect to be helped by your friends."

"Really, Aunt Henrietta, I can't see why you assume us entirely to lack common sense, principles, and pride," said Jessamy, struggling to keep her voice steady. "We were just resolving to make our income suffice, investing our little capital in some safe way."

"H'm! Two thousand suffice! You're exactly like your mother—absolutely unpractical. If poor Henry—" began Mrs. Hewlett.

"Now, Aunt Henrietta, just drop mama, if you please," interrupted Barbara, hotly. "She is the dearest mother in the world, and you know how papa loved her. I don't see what pleasure there can be in trying to blame someone for this trouble, but if anyone is to blame it was dear papa himself, not mama, for he left her all his wealth, all his trust in Mr. Abbott, and never taught her one thing about business. Mama never said nor did an unkind thing in all her gentle life, and I won't have her abused. In spite of all that you say, you were very proud of her lovely face and manners always, and glad enough to point her out as your niece. You've boasted of us while we were rich, and now you talk as if this trouble was a punishment for our sins, especially mama's. And I won't let you mention her!—dear, crushed mama!—lying in there heartbroken for our sakes!"

Bab's cheeks had been getting redder, her voice higher, through this outburst, until at this point she burst into tempestuous tears.

"Highty-tighty, miss! Don't be impertinent," said the old lady, after a pause. "You'll be dependent on your friends' charity in six months, and you will be wise not to offend them."

"I won't! I'll beg from door to door, or be a cash-girl first," Bab sobbed out. "Besides, I'm not impertinent; I'm only firm."

The idea of Bab firm, on the verge of hysterics, made Jessamy and Phyllis smile faintly.

"Better not say any more, Bab," Phyllis whispered, as she stroked the hot cheek, while Jessamy said: "You must not mind Bab, aunt. We all are more or less overwrought. But I agree with her that, if you please, we will leave our mother out of the discussion."

"I don't mind that very flighty child; she never had a particle of stability, and she has had no training," said Aunt Henrietta, with what in a less dignified person would have been a sniff. "What work will you take up? For of course it is ridiculous to talk of living on two thousand a year; you must go to work."

"We have not decided anything yet, aunt; we've had only a few hours to get used to being poor," replied Phyllis.

"I've been considering your case as I drove over, and I believe there's nothing you can do decently. Your education is the thistle-down veneer girls get nowadays," said their aunt, disregarding the fact that she would have been no better armed to meet misfortune at their age.

"Veneer!" echoed Jessamy. "I hope not, though I don't know what thistle-down veneer is. I wouldn't mind being honest white pine, but I should despise the best veneer."

"I am sure you are only fit for nursery governesses. I have a place which Phyllis can take, to teach French to some girls of her own age. The mother applied to me for a teacher. They are new-rich, but that is the one thing Phyllis can do. I shall not be able to help you further," said Aunt Henrietta.

Aunt Henrietta

"We shall not need help," said Jessamy, her head up like a young racer. "Will you excuse us from more of this sort of talk, aunt? We have had a hard day."

Mrs. Hewlett rose; her eldest niece over-awed her in spite of her determination not to mind what she called "Jessamy's affected airs."

"I felt sure I should not find you chastened by misfortune," she said. "You should take your downfall in a more Christian spirit. I trust you will heed me in one point at least. Sell your best clothes and ornaments. It will be most unbecoming if, in your altered circumstances, you dress as you did when you were Henry Wyndham's daughters. People will make the most unkind comments if you do."

Barbara had recovered by this time. "Aren't we still Henry Wyndham's daughters, aunt?" she asked guilelessly. "I didn't realize parentage as well as inheritance was vested in the business. What a calamity it failed! As to unkind remarks, no mere acquaintance will make them; all but our relatives will understand that we could afford fine things when we had them, and that failure did not destroy them."

"Bab, how can you?" said Jessamy, reproachfully, as Mrs. Hewlett disappeared. "There is no use in making her worse than she is."

"I couldn't, Lady Jessamy; nature is perfect in her works," said Bab, airily, holding out her hand for a letter Violet offered her.

It was a note from a lifelong friend of her mother's, so loving, so considerate, so generously delicate in its offer of help that no better antidote to their great-aunt's trying peculiarities could have come to the poor girls, whose wounds were smarting as if salt had been dropped on them from Mrs. Hewlett's remarks.

"Dear, lovely, blessed Mrs. Van Alyn!" cried all three girls, sobbing on one another's shoulders after they had read the warm message; but this time their tears were of the sort which do good, and sent them to bed refreshed and comforted.

In the morning Bab started off early to carry out her plan of consulting Ruth Wells. Ruth was a brisk little creature of Bab's own age, who had been the Wyndhams' schoolmate for a short time, but who, meeting with misfortune also, had dropped almost entirely out of their lives; only Bab, refusing to let her go, kept up a much interrupted friendship with her.

Ruth lived with her mother in a little flat—apartment is too dignified a word—not far from the Morningside Heights. She was skilful with her needle, and earned by embroidering enough to supplement sufficiently for their needs an income hardly large enough to pay their low rent. Bab had always wondered that she was so happy. Today she resolved, if possible, to solve the secret of her content.

As she pressed the button under the speaking-tube over which the name "Wells" shone on a narrow strip of brass, the latch of the front door clicked, and pushing it open, Barbara mounted the three flights of stairs.

Ruth herself opened the door at their head, and uttered an exclamation of surprise and pleasure at the sight of Bab.

"Oh, Babbie dear, does it affect you?" she cried at once. "I saw an account of the Wyndham Iron Works' failure in this morning's *Times*."

"It affects us so much, Ruth, that I came here to get your advice. You've had experience in coming down in the world. And I want to say," Bab went on, with heightened color, "that I wish we all had been here oftener. We never realized how lonely you must have been at first." And Bab looked around the parlor with new interest.

"Oh, I was so much younger than we are now when our troubles came that they were easier to bear," said Ruth, brightly. "You've always been a good friend, Bab. People who are poor are too busy to see much of those who have all their time on their hands. It isn't possible to be intimate with people who live very differently from ourselves. But do tell me, is it as bad a failure as the paper had it?" While Ruth had talked she had gotten off Bab's outer garments, and now seated herself at her embroidery-frame, while Bab drew a chair in front of it, and shook her head.

"Quite as bad; worse, in fact," she said, and proceeded to tell Ruth the whole story. "Now, what I want to know is whether four persons can possibly live on two thousand a year—supposing we have that—until we learn to be useful?" she asked in conclusion.

"Of course," said Ruth, with cheerful decision. She did not seem to think the case very bad. Taking a pencil and paper from the table, she began to reckon.

"Do you think you could do your own work in a little flat?" she asked.

"Mercy, no!" cried Bab, in horror. "Why, we'd starve! We can't do anything. We must board."

"That's a pity, for cheap boarding is unwholesome, vulgar, and generally horrid," said Ruth. "However, if you must, you must. It won't last. Mama and I began that way, but we soon learned better. You can get two rooms, maybe, for seven dollars apiece—twenty-eight dollars a week. That's—fifty-two times—fourteen hundred and fifty-six dollars a year. That leaves five hundred for washing, clothing, possible doctor's bill, and so on."

"Can we live for that?" asked Bab, awed by Ruth's businesslike methods.

"It will be bad, but you would be foolish to spend more. Your mother is delicate, and you will have to get her dainties, no matter how you board. We ran too close to our margin once. I never forgot the lesson," said Ruth.

"You've helped me a lot, Ruth," said Bab, rising to go. "I shouldn't mind being poor if I could be like you."

"Well, I believe I've a talent for poverty. It has a good side," laughed Ruth. "I'm happy because I'm so busy I've no time to imagine troubles. I can't even stop to realize I don't feel well; so if that happens I hardly know it. I just work ahead and drive the headache off. You don't know how good it is for girls to have lots that must be done. Come see our flat," added brave Ruth, leading the way. "This is mama's room; the next one is mine. Here's the bath-room; you see, it is large, for a flat! And isn't this a nice little sunny dining-room? Here's the kitchen. Mama, this is Barbara Wyndham."

Mrs. Wells was bending over a double boiler on the gas-range. She looked sweet and well bred in her black gown, with a white apron shielding it, and held out a delicate hand to Bab, with no apology for her employment.

Bab looked at the rooms with newly perceptive eyes. Everything was of the plainest, yet so refined and dainty it could but be pretty. She began to suspect there were many things in life to learn which would prove pleasant knowledge. But she wondered, coming from the spacious Murray Hill rooms, how Ruth and her mother managed to move about in these without seriously damaging their anatomy. Ruth was so proud of it all, however, so unconscious of defects in her home, that Bab could envy her, though it was a meager box of a place, and Ruth worked hard to maintain it.

"Thank you again, Ruth," she said, as her friend hugged her at the head of the stairs, letting the pity she dared not express show in the warmth of her embrace and the tears in her eyes as she kissed her. "I'm coming often, please, for advice and courage. You've shown me already I need not fear. I suspect our first additional revenue will come from the sale of my great work, 'How to be Happy though Beggared.'"

CHAPTER THREE: WAYS AND MEANS

EVENTS MOVED SWIFTLY for the Wyndhams, impelled by the force of necessity. Mr. Wyndham had been widely known for the value of his art treasures, and collectors came from distant cities to bid for them as they hung on the walls. Everything else was to be sold by auction, and Mrs. Van Alyn, the kind friend whose loving letter had comforted the girls, persuaded Mrs. Wyndham to come to her for the final two weeks of her nominal ownership of the house. It would be less painful for the poor lady to pass its threshold for the last time, shutting the door on everything as she had loved it, than to remain through the dismal dismantling process.

Accordingly, one warm, sunny morning Mrs. Van Alyn's rotund horses drew up at the door, and Mrs. Wyndham, looking very frail, and newly widowed under her long veil, came slowly down the stairs, leaning on Jessamy's arm, and forth upon the door-steps, where for the last time the mahogany door swung close, shutting out the mistress of the house forever. Mrs. Van Alyn helped the three girls through the dreadful days of the sale, at the end of which they found themselves homeless, but with their expectation of the result of the sale realized. They had, with a little personal legacy left them by a sister of Mrs. Hewlett, thirty thousand dollars residuum of their former wealth, which, invested by Mr. Hurd, would yield them an income of two thousand a year. The first step to be made by these novices in the ungentle art of living was to find a boarding-place, and in this they were aided by Ruth, whose experience had taught what to seek and what to avoid. The limitations of their purse defined the boundaries of their search; only places where low prices obtained were open to the Wyndhams, a fact difficult to master at first, and the poor little pilgrims up Poverty Hill shrank from the mere exterior of some of the houses in their list of advertisements cut from the papers. They climbed long flights of stairs, to see repeated dingy rooms carpeted in flowery tapestry carpets, with oak or expressionless marble-topped black-walnut furniture—those furnished in mahogany or maple were beyond the Wyndhams' range of price. These days of search taught the girls more of life than their entire years had yet shown them, and the fruit of the tree of knowledge was bitter indeed.

"I tell you, you would be far better off in your own little flat, cooking your own little dinner, on your own little gas-range, in your own little spider. However, don't lose heart; there are degrees of badness," laughed Ruth, as they despondently quitted an uncommonly discouraging specimen of the typical boarding-house, impregnated with odors of the dinners of "Christmases past."

At last they found a place, in one of the "Thirty" streets, where there were two rooms adjoining, though not connected, on the very topmost floor, which they could get at their price in consideration of the fact that they were heated only by stoves, and they would be expected to look after their own fires. They were sunny, and, though plainly furnished, less ugly than others the girls had seen, and they took them, since they could do no better, proceeding to make the best of what each felt in her heart was a very bad bargain, with the courage each possessed in different forms.

There were two days intervening between engaging and taking possession of the new boarding-place, and Bab assumed the task of beautifying their unattractive quarters before her mother should see them. She would not permit any of the others to look at her improvements, but hammered her thumbs and strained her unaccustomed arms putting up curtains, shelves, casts, and photographs alone, in order, she said, "to usher her family into a bower of bliss" when it moved in.

On the afternoon before this event Barbara came down Thirty-Third Street from Sixth Avenue. Her arms were full of flower-pots—two filled them—and a boy followed with a basket containing six more. Bab had not been able to resist the temptation to invest in plants for her mother's window to make the room a little more cheerful.

She hurried down the street, and paused at the foot of the steps long enough to let her listless squire catch up with her. She had no hand for her skirt, but she sprang up the steps, regardless of tripping; and at that instant the door opened, and a cocker-spaniel rushed out, barking wildly, and throwing himself downward with that utter disregard of whether head or tail went first, and of anything which might be in his path, characteristic of a young and blissful little dog.

He flung himself down. Barbara stepped aside; her balance was uncertain and her skirts unmanageable by reason of her laden arms; she tripped—fell. Flower-pots, dog, and girl rolled crashing, and scattering dirt in all directions, into the boy and basket two steps lower, ending in a tangle on the sidewalk.

From the doorway a horrified voice cried: "Good heavens, Nixie!" and a young man dashed down the steps into the ruins.

"Are you hurt?" he cried anxiously, as he fished Barbara out of the wreck. Nixie had already slunk out from under, and was wagging his tail depreciatingly, with glances at his master of mingled shame and amazement.

"I think I am," said Barbara, raising her head and trying to state the fact cheerfully.

The young man replaced her hat—it had fallen over her eyes—and revealed a woebegone little face. Earth plastered the saucy chin; one cheek was cut; blood trickled from the bridge of the poor little tilted nose, making a paste wherever the loam from the flower-pots had spattered, and this was nearly everywhere. Barbara's hair was coming down, her hat was shapeless, and her eyes tearful from the smarting wounds.

"By Jove! you're a wreck! It's a shame!" cried the young man. "I'll whip Nixie."

"You'll do nothing of the sort," said Barbara, with spirit. "How did he know I was coming up—coming up like a flower—at that moment? You might as well whip me! Nobody is to blame, and I'll be all right when I've washed, and sewed, and plastered, and done a few other things to myself and my clothing."

"Well, you're plucky," said the youth, admiringly. "I'm a doctor in embryo, full fledged next June. I'll take you in and fix you up. Do you—you don't live here?"

"We shall tomorrow; I'm a new boarder," said Barbara. "Oh, I hope my plants aren't broken! Can they be repotted? We've become poor, and I ought not to have bought them. Why on earth doesn't that boy get up? Is he killed?" she demanded, realizing suddenly that her companion in misery was still lying with his head in the basket, under a debris of flower-pots.

"It's why *in* earth, rather," laughed the medical student. "Here, you boy, are you alive? You're buried all right! Get up."

The inert boy gathered himself slowly together. "Well, I'll be darned!" he said.

"You'll have to be," cried the doctor, sitting down to laugh, and pointing to the rent across the shoulders of the listless youngster's jacket.

"What ailed that dog? Did he have a fit?" drawled the boy, scowling at Nixie, who slunk behind Barbara self-consciously.

"He wasn't a dog, he was a cat-apult," shouted the doctor, rocking to and fro, laughing.

"Oh, please help me into the house!" cried Barbara, half laughing, half crying. Several people had paused to gaze, grinning sympathetically at the scene.

He dashed down the stairs into the ruins.

"Oh, I beg your pardon! What an idiot to keep you standing here!" cried the medical student, jumping up. "Here, hustle these plants into your basket," he added to the boy. "They're not broken; we can fix them up all right. Where's my key? There you are! Walk in. Get into the house, Nixie, you crazy pup; you've lost your walk. Leave those plants in the hall, boy, and rush back to your shop and tell your employer you want as many pots as you started out with, and a bag of loam; hurry back with them. Now, Mrs. Black—Mrs. Black, where are you?"

"Here," said the landlady, emerging from the rear. "Why, Miss Wyndham, what has happened?"

"Introduce us, please; we met on the steps," said Barbara's new acquaintance.

"Miss Wyndham, Dr. Leighton," said the bewildered Mrs. Black, automatically.

"Happy to have the honor, Miss Wyndham. There was a mix-up on the steps; there's some of it there yet. Let me have some warm water and a sponge, please. Miss Wyndham, take off your hat and have your face washed," said the unabashed boy.

"Not by you," said Barbara.

"Precisely. I'm almost a doctor, and I'm going to see that no dirt is left in your wounds to scar you. Don't be foolish, Miss Wyndham; it's not precisely a ceremonious occasion."

Barbara submitted with no further demur; and soon her face was adorned with court-plaster laid on in a plaid pattern.

"Shall I be scarred?" she asked, surveying anxiously the crisscross lines on the bridge of her nose.

"Not a bit," said Dr. Leighton, cheerfully. "Mrs. Black might give you a cup of tea, to brace you up."

"Yes," said Mrs. Black, without enthusiasm.

"No, thanks; I hate tea, and I'll be all right. There's the boy with the new pots," said Barbara.

"Let me help you to get the plants potted, and I'll settle with the boy—because it's all Nixie's fault," said the young doctor. "Not a word; get to work, Miss Wyndham."

He placed papers on the floor in the rear hall, apparently oblivious to Mrs. Black's icy disapproval, which inexperienced Barbara found oppressive.

"My father and your father were friends," said the young fellow, packing the earth around a begonia. "I knew you were coming here to board, and I know about the hard blow you've had. It's a shame, and it's all the fault of that scoundrel Abbott."

"Oh, how nice that your father knew papa! That is almost like our being friends," said Barbara, simply. "Yes, it's dreadful for mama to be poor, and for Jessamy. Phyl and I are not going to mind it so much."

"Is Phil your brother?"

"No; Phyllis, it is; she's my cousin, only she's just as much my sister as Jessamy, for she has always lived with us. I'm a year younger than they are. Jessamy's perfectly beautiful, and princessfied, and Phyllis is the most unselfish blessing in the world. I'm only Barbara."

"And I'm only Tom; I'm not a doctor yet. It's awfully jolly, your coming here. Mrs. Black gone? Yes. There isn't any one in the house I care to know; the young people aren't my sort. I hope you'll forgive Nixie and me enough to speak to us once in a while," said Tom, getting up and dusting his knees.

"Oh, we shall want to talk to you, Nixie is such a nice dog," laughed Bab.

"Only Nixie? Well, love my dog, love—oh, it's the other way about. Never mind, though; we can improve old saws. Where are your rooms?"

"First floor from the Milky Way," laughed Barbara. "We hate to have madrina climb so far, but we couldn't afford better rooms."

Tom Leighton looked down on the swollen, patched little face with brotherly kindness; respect and pity were in his voice as he said gently: "You will make any room bright and homelike. I see why you took your tumble down the steps so well; you are brave in falling, Miss Barbara."

Barbara stooped suddenly to pat Nixie, hiding her wounded face in his glossy curls. "I'm not always brave," she said huskily. "I am ashamed to think so much about my beautiful room, and home. I feel so little, and so lost, in this boarding-house."

"Poor little woman!" said Tom Leighton. "Try to feel you have one friend in it. I have two sisters, and it was lonely for me when I left home. Good-by, now; we shall meet tomorrow."

They shook hands, feeling like old friends, and Nixie sat up to shake hands too, though the dignity of his farewell was much impaired by a surreptitious lick of his quick red tongue on Bab's chin.

Tom departed, whistling, to give Nixie his postponed walk. He found himself seeing a tilted nose adorned with court-plaster, and brown eyes, wistful like Nixie's, all down the street. "She's plucky, simple, and frank; just the girl to be a fellow's good chum," he thought. "What luck they're coming to the Blackboard!"—Tom's name for his residence.

Bab finished her tasks, and returned to Mrs. Van Alyn's with glowing accounts of the jolly boy who had patched her up, and of the little dog who had undone her.

"There are two nice things in our new home," she said, "and I believe we'll be happy in spite of fate."

CHAPTER FOUR: MAKING THE BEST OF IT

"I DON'T KNOW where to put another thing," said Mrs. Wyndham, pushing aside a hat-box to get room to sit on the rocking-chair, and casting a despairing glance from the shallow closet, already full, to the floor, scattered with the hetero-geneous contents of two trunks, in the midst of which Barbara was sitting.

A scream from the next room prevented Bab replying to her mother, and Nixie bounded through the open door, triumphantly worrying a slipper. He recognized Barbara, and dropping his prize, made a leap toward the pretty face he had been the means of damaging before she, from her disadvantage-point on the floor, could stop him.

Tom Leighton appeared immediately, calling Nixie, with no result, for Bab had her arms around the wriggling black bit of enthusiasm, hugging him.

"Mama, this is the doctor who repaired me so nicely; Dr. Leighton, my moth-er," said Barbara.

"Please don't think me intrusive, Mrs. Wyndham," said Tom, stepping forward to take the delicate hand extended to him. "I am the son John Leighton, a friend of your husband, and I wanted to ask if I could be of use in getting you in order. I'm a jack-of-all-trades who has boarded long enough to have learned dodges."

"I remember your father," said Mrs. Wyndham, cordially. "It is very pleasant to find a friend among strangers. I don't see what you can do, unless you build a clos-et. This tiny cubby Bab and I must share is already over-flowing, yet just look!" And Mrs. Wyndham made a comprehensive gesture toward the littered floor.

"I suppose we've too many clothes, but we don't dare give away one thing. We may never be able to buy any more, and we're going to get paper patterns, and make over this stock until we're old and gray. I expect that to be soon, however, if I have to sew," said Bab, scrambling to her feet and tossing up Nixie's purloined slipper for him to catch.

"A dog broke and entered—entered anyway—and stole Jessamy's slipper—oh, I beg pardon," said Phyllis, stopping short in the doorway at the unexpected appari-tion of Tom.

"My niece, Miss Phyllis Wyndham. And my elder daughter, Jessamy, Dr. Leighton," added Mrs. Wyndham, as Jessamy followed Phyllis.

"I came to ask if you had any idea what Jessamy and I could do with our clothes, aunty," said Phyllis. "We haven't begun to make an impression on the room, yet the closet and bureau are full."

"Not I; Bab and I are in the same plight," said Mrs. Wyndham. "How do peo-ple manage in such narrow space!"

"You'll have to have a wigwam," said Tom.

"A wigwam! That would have no closets at all; and, besides, where could we build it in New York?" laughed Phyllis.

"In that corner. I'll make it," said Tom. "It's a corner shelf, with hooks in the under side and a curtain around it. Then you want a divan—a woven-wire cot-bed with the legs cut off, fastened by hinges to a box. We could upholster it ourselves. You would be surprised to see what it could hold. Then, if one of you were ill, it would be useful as a couch."

"There spoke the doctor," said Jessamy. "I suppose we shall have to have a trunk in each room besides," she added ruefully.

"Why not put that flat-topped trunk in the window, case it in with boards, cover it with felt, and use it as a book-stand?" suggested Tom

"Well, you are a genius!" cried Bab, in open admiration, while Phyllis sang softly under her breath, to the tune of "St. Patrick's Day in the Morning":

> *"All hail to the doctor who seems to be able*
> *To mend up a nose or to make up a table!*
> *We gladly would cheer him, but that it seems risky,*
> *For cheers in a boarding-house might be too frisky."*

"Well, I never!" laughed Tom. "Say, was that—of course it had to be improvised?"

"Oh, Phyl is a genius," said Jessamy, proudly. "One of these days her name will be in all the magazines, and at last in the encyclopedia."

"And likely in oblivion," added Phyl, while at that instant a cheery voice cried, "First aid to the injured!" and Ruth Wells "burst into the gloom like an arc-light," Barbara said, jumping up to hug her rapturously.

"No, don't; I've tacks and a hammer here," said Ruth, struggling free. "I knew you had no closets, or none worth calling one, so I came down to show you how to make a charity."

"A what?" asked Jessamy.

"A charity; it covers a multitude of things, you see," laughed Ruth. "You take a board—we can get one downstairs probably—saw it to the right length, and nail it in a corner. Then you screw hooks—"

"In the under side; we know," Phyllis interrupted. "Only Dr. Leighton says it's a 'wig-wam.' This is Dr. Leighton, and Nixie—Miss Ruth Wells," she added.

In five minutes the little room was ringing with fun. The "charitable wigwam"—Phyllis's compromise on its name—could not be made at once, for lack of boards, but the young people managed to cover up their dismal first impressions of the bleak side of life, and this was making a real "charity," as Jessamy pointed out in bidding Ruth good night.

The wigwam was made, in the end, the divan too, and the Wyndhams began to learn to adjust themselves to the new conditions. Tom had become almost one of themselves, Nixie a necessity and no longer a luxury, as Bab noted. Tom was such a bright, honest, boyish creature that no greater piece of good fortune could well have befallen the girls in their trouble than his friendship, a fact their mother recognized gratefully. As to Tom himself, the motherly kindness of Mrs. Wyndham, the sweet, frank companionship of the girls, were to the young fellow who had loved his own mother and sisters well a boon which he could hardly enjoy enough.

Winter was coming on, and, for the first time in their lives, the Wyndhams were obliged to try to make old answer for new in the matter of garments.

"Not a penny must be spent this season," declared Jessamy, sternly. "A year hence we may earn new clothes."

All the summer garments were laid away in the new divan. "Never throw away a winter thing in the spring, nor a summer thing in the fall," advised Ruth, that little woman wise in ways and means. "You cannot tell how anything looks out of its season, nor what you may want. Set up a scrap-box, and tuck everything into it; it's ten to one you'll be grateful for the very thing you thought least hopeful. Many a time I've all but hugged an old faded ribbon because its one bright part was found to be just the right shade and length to line a collar."

The scrap-box, therefore, was established, and easily filled from a stock not yet depleted. Jessamy's artistic talents developed in the direction of hats. Ruth taught her to take the long wrists of light suede gloves which were past wearing and stretch them over a frame for the crowns of especially pretty hats.

Jessamy made a hat apiece, with crowns of glove-wrists and rims of puffed velvet, trimmed with feathers and bows from the new scrap-box; each was different, yet each a "James Dandy," according to Tom's authoritative verdict.

Dressmaking was a more serious matter, but the three Wyndhams essayed it with the courage of ignorance. Ruth brought down mysterious paper patterns, "perforated to confuse the innocent," Bab said, and announced that she had come for a dress-parade. Her friends were still too unversed in being poor to realize that when she came thus Ruth was sacrificing her own good to theirs, since her time meant money, and little Ruth's pockets jingled only when she spent long days at her needle.

"Get out all last year's glories," commanded Ruth, perched on the foot-board of Jessamy and Phyllis's bed. "That's a pretty dark-blue cloth suit; whose is that?"

"Phyllis's; it was nice, but she tried it on the other day, and it's full in the skirt," said Jessamy.

"I wouldn't dare touch anything so tailor-made; if we ripped it we could never give it the same finish. But we could take out the gathers and lay a box-plait in the back; that will make it flatter—more in style," cried Ruth, with sudden illumination. "Now isn't it true that there's good blown to someone on all winds? If you hadn't stoves in your rooms you wouldn't have a place to heat irons, and don't I know the impossibility of getting irons from the lower regions when one is boarding?"

"What does 'lower regions' mean? It sounds doubtful," inquired Tom, from the doorway.

"Go away; this is a feminine occasion—no boys allowed," cried Ruth.

"Mysteries of Isis?" suggested Tom. "I only want a buttonhole sewed up; wouldn't the goddess allow that?"

"Yes," said Phyllis, holding out her hand for the collar Tom waved appealingly. "It is rather in the line of the service about to begin in this temple. We are going into dress-making."

"You'll succeed; you can do anything," said Tom, watching Phyllis's fingers as she twitched the thread in a scientific manner, drawing the gaping buttonhole together.

"Those laundry people apparently dry collars by hanging them on crowbars thrust through the buttonholes. Couldn't I help your dress-making? I know there are bones in waists; maybe I could set them."

The four girls groaned. "Such a pale, feeble little jokelet!" sighed Bab. "Take it to the hospital to be measured for crutches."

"Yes; here's your collar. Run away and play with the other little boys, we're busy. By and by, if you're good, we may let you take out bastings," said Phyllis.

"Jupiter! That sounds familiar," sighed Tom. "My mother used to say just that when I was seven. Much obliged for the collar. When you want me for the bastings, sing out. I'll pardon your impertinence in consideration of service rendered." And Tom disappeared.

"Phyl will do very well with the blue, then," said Ruth, resuming practicalities. "What are your prospects, Other Two?"

"Jessamy's gray with chinchilla is as good as new, but I spilled something on this brown of mine right down the front, and I haven't a smidge of the goods," said Bab, sadly.

"A what?" murmured Ruth, absently, wrinkling her brow over the problem. "I have it!" she cried, slipping to the floor from her perch with a triumphant little shout.

"Eureka, Miss Archimedes! What is it?" asked Phyllis.

"Braid!" cried Ruth. "We'll get the narrowest silk soutache; Jessamy shall draw a design; Bab, you shall braid the entire front breadth of your skirt, resolving at each stitch to be neater in future. And now for house wear," Ruth continued, while Bab made a wry face at the prospect before her.

"I thought perhaps we could make waists out of these skirts; they would be pretty with our cloth skirts," said Phyllis, doubtfully, turning over a heap of bright-colored fancy silks.

"Could! Of course we can; let's rip them now," said Ruth, whipping out her little scissors.

The eight hands made quick work of the ripping, and Ruth cut out three waists by the tissue-paper patterns she had brought, pinned and basted them together, and left her friends to carry out her instructions.

Phyllis proved adept at the new art, Jessamy succeeded fairly, but Bab had a hard time with her waist. Seams puckered and drew askew, because of her reckless way of sewing them up in various widths, and she felt aggrieved when the waist proved one-sided in trying on. As to sleeves, Bab's were bewitched. The poor child basted, tried on, ripped and tried again, refusing all help in her determination to be independent, till her cheeks were purple, and throwing the waist down, she cried forlornly.

Tom surprised her in this tempest, and laughed at her till she longed to flay him. Then, sincerely repentant for having aggravated her woes, he humbly begged her pardon, and took her for a walk with Nixie to calm her ruffled nerves. When she returned Phyllis had disregarded her wishes and basted in the refractory sleeves for her, which, like everything else, had yielded to Phyllis's charm and gone meekly into place.

There was real pleasure to the girls in using their wits for these things; there were compensations in poverty, they found. But the ugly side remained: the jealousy of three girls who wore photograph-buttons, and were the Wyndhams' opposites, at table as well as literally; the landlady's insinuations that she considered the rate of payment from the Wyndhams insufficient to remunerate her for the immense, though to them imperceptible, generosity with which she served them.

And Mrs. Wyndham was ailing, fretting her heart out over the present situation and her poor girls' future. But the most serious aspect of the anxieties closing in around the Wyndhams was that, in spite of all their prudence, money slipped away; laundry bills took on alarming proportions, and they had never dreamed how fast five-cent car-fares could swell into as many dollars. Although they had taken care to make their expenditures come well within their income, they saw that there was not going to be enough to meet an emergency, should it arise; and Jessamy and Phyllis talked till midnight many a night, discussing how they should put their young shoulders to the wheel and join the great army of wage-earners.

CHAPTER FIVE: PHYLLIS AND BARBARA ENTER THE LISTS

AUNT HENRIETTA ALWAYS stayed until November in her cottage near Marblehead. She said that she never enjoyed the ocean until she was alone with it, and Jessamy suggested afterward that it was a trifle hard on the ocean—a severe remark for Jessamy, whose genuinely high standards of good breeding forbade her unkind comments on others, even on Aunt Henrietta when she was most trying.

Immediately on her return to town Mrs. Hewlett came to look up "her fallen kindred," as Barbara said. That young lady went down to the parlor to conduct her great-aunt to her mother. "It would make a lovely title for an improving book for the young, wouldn't it?" she said, turning from the glass, where she had been inspecting the last faint trace of the mishap to her nose. "'Little Barbara's Upward Leading,' or 'Toward the Skies,' or 'Helped Upward,' or 'Mounting Heavenward,' or even simply 'Uplifted.'"

"Barbara, I am ashamed of you!" said her mother, as severely as she could, while trying not to laugh.

"Now, Bab, do be nice," pleaded Jessamy.

"Nice! I'd like to know what could be nicer than to plan moral little titles like those?" said Bab, in an injured voice. "But don't worry. I'll be a sweet morsel when I get down there."

"You look thinner," said Aunt Henrietta, when Barbara had delicately touched the unresponsive cheek offered her to kiss.

"I am thinner, aunt. We're none of us waxing fleshly. Sally's cooking was more comforting than our present fare," said Bab.

"H'm! Where under heavens are your rooms?" demanded Mrs. Hewlett.

"Just there, Aunt Henrietta—right under heavens, on the top floor," laughed Barbara.

"Do you mean to say you've taken your delicate mother up all those flights? You ought to be ashamed of yourselves!" said her great-aunt.

"What could we do, aunt?" asked Barbara, meekly, though her cheeks reddened. "We were not able to make any boarding-house-keeper give us better rooms at our price for mama's sake."

"Do? You ought to be earning money—three great healthy girls, and Phyllis only a niece-in-law of your mother's, besides! I came to talk to you about this," said Mrs. Hewlett.

"Please wait till we get upstairs. I fancy there are always ears about here," said Bab, and led the way to their own quarters.

"Excelsior is our motto, aunt," she said, pausing at the head of the second flight, and finding malicious pleasure in her relative's labored breathing.

"Well, Emily, the consequences of your imprudence are severe. I am sorry to find you thus. You don't look well," was Aunt Henrietta's greeting to Mrs. Wyndham. "Now, I want to get down to business without delay," she added, removing her splendid furs. "You are living wretchedly to keep these girls fine ladies. You always spoiled them, Emily, but your weakness should really have some limit. It is outrageous for you to climb all these stairs that a slender income may support four people. These girls should contribute to you, not be a drain upon you. You can't be poor and be fine ladies all at once."

"We hope that we can be, aunt," said Jessamy, "but you are mistaken if you think we wish to spare ourselves at our mother's expense."

Only Mrs. Wyndham's hand holding Bab's wrist tight kept that small torpedo from exploding. "This question has been discussed among us, aunt," said Mrs. Wyndham, quietly, though her voice trembled. "Jessamy has determined on her course. She has talent, and we think will do good book illustrations. She is going to fit herself for her work. From the first Jessamy has declared that she should prepare herself to do something well."

"Jessamy has sense," said Aunt Henrietta, surveying the girl with something like approbation. "She is so pretty that she will undoubtedly marry before she follows any occupation long. I only hope she will remember her necessities, and marry well."

"If you mean by well a good man whom she loves and trusts, I hope so too Aunt Henrietta," said Mrs. Wyndham, with heightened color. "My trouble would be bitter indeed if I thought it would lead one of my girls to marry for wealth or ambition."

"Sentimentality! You were never practical, Emily," said Aunt Henrietta, impatiently; but more pressing interests than merely possible marriage prevented her stopping to quarrel. "How about the other two?"

"I agree with Aunt Henrietta that I, at least, should be earning money," said Phyllis.

"Not you any more than me, Phyl," cried Bab, with more warmth than correctness.

"Well, I cut an advertisement from the morning paper for Barbara to answer," said Aunt Henrietta, producing a clipping. "Answer it now, and I'll post the letter when I go. It would probably be easy employment, and you are too flighty for most things."

"Thanks, Aunt Henrietta," commented Barbara, spearing the slip to the pincushion with a hat-pin. "I'll answer it; not just now, though."

"Oh, fancy my little Bab, my baby, going down to business every day!" cried Mrs. Wyndham.

"There's your foolish pride again, Emily," said Mrs. Hewlett, sternly. "Your daughters are no better than other people's daughters."

"It is not pride," said Mrs. Wyndham, stung to self-defense. "Unwomanly women are a misfortune to themselves and all the community, and it is impossible to knock about the world without losing something of that dear and delicate loveliness which is fast going out of fashion at best. If it can be avoided, I think no girl should be placed in the thick of the fight, striding through the world in fierce competition with men."

"If it can be avoided—precisely; but it cannot be avoided," said Aunt Henrietta, calmly; "for none of your relatives can afford to help you, Emily."

"Help! When did I ever dream of wanting or being willing to accept help, aunt?" cried Mrs. Wyndham, hysterically. "But if I prefer to practise stern self-denial to keep my girls sheltered until such time as they can help me in more feminine ways than going into business offices, is that wrong?"

"Not wrong," said Aunt Henrietta, with exasperating soothing in her voice, and entire conviction of being right, "but utterly foolish and impractical. Now, I have a proposition for Phyllis. I spoke of it when I first heard you were ruined. An acquaintance of mine is looking for some one to read French with her daughter and three of her young friends. She will pay a girl twenty-five dollars a month for two hours' reading every afternoon. Fortunately, Phyllis's French is perfect, and that is a feminine employment, and so ought to satisfy you, Emily."

Mrs. Wyndham twisted her handkerchief nervously.

This was bringing poverty home to her. She clung tenaciously, poor lady, to the hope of sheltering her little brood, and no amount of privation seemed to her like thrusting the burden on them as did their going out into the world to earn their living.

"I'll try it, aunt," said Phyllis.

"That is right," said Mrs. Hewlett, rising, well pleased at finding her grand-nieces so reasonable—"reasonable" meaning, to her mind, as to most others under like circumstances, ready to accept her advice. "I wrote this introductory line on the back of my visiting-card. You will find Mrs. Haines at that number East Forty-Fifth Street, just out of Fifth Avenue. You will do well to apply at once."

"You won't mind if Phyllis mentions that she is your niece in applying?" inquired Jessamy, with intent hidden under her gentle manner.

But satire was lost on Aunt Henrietta. "Not at all; you are only my grand-nieces, and nothing of the sort could affect my social position," she said. Then she went away, leaving a perturbed roomful behind her.

"Now, let me tell you, my dearest aunty-mother, that I'm glad to read the French," said Phyllis. "Twenty-five dollars a month will nearly pay my board, and I'd be happier to feel I were helping. It won't be the end of my career, I hope, but it will answer for a beginning. I honestly think our metallic great-aunt is right—that we ought to be bettering matters, rather than settle down satisfied to such a life as this."

Mrs. Wyndham was crying softly. "To think that if I had heeded Mr. Hurd we should have enough!" she moaned.

"If—if, madrina! What is the use of ifs now?" cried Barbara. "You did what you thought right, and we can't bear to have you reproach yourself. I'll answer that advertisement, and we'll try to enter the lists to fight for you like true knights—pity we're girls, for it spoils my fine simile."

"I think not, Babbie baby; a knightly spirit is quite as often in a girl's breast as in a boy's," said her mother, kissing her.

"The worst of it is that I feel so mean and selfish to let you both help while I idle," said Jessamy. "But I honestly believe I can do more by waiting and following my natural bent. You won't think I'm shirking? When even little Bab is trying to earn her living I feel guilty."

"'Even little Bab'—who is anything but even—is only a year younger than you, miss," said Bab; while Phyllis, putting her arms around Jessamy, kissed her and said: "No one would ever suspect you of not playing fair, my crystal cousin."

Phyllis went forth in her blue gown the next day "to secure the young ideas which in the end she would probably want to shoot," Bab said.

She found four foolish girls of fifteen and a newly rich woman, in the person of Mrs. Haines and her daughter and that daughter's friends. They were only too glad to secure a Miss Wyndham for their tutor, a fact even Phyllis's inexperience could not fail to perceive; the arrangement between them was made without loss of time.

"I am engaged, girls," said Phyllis, coming, with very red cheeks, into the room on her return. But she did not say how disagreeable she had found her recent encounter.

Barbara heard nothing from the answer she had made to the advertisement Aunt Henrietta had brought her, so she applied to Mr. Hurd for aid. The little lawyer obtained for her the position of cashier with a friend of his own, with whom the young girl would at least be secure from many of the drawbacks to a business career which her mother dreaded for her.

But, to Bab's unspeakable mortification, she found that she was incompetent to fill the position. She made change slowly, often wrongly, and at night her columns would not add up right, no matter how often she went over them, nor how carefully she counted her fingers. At the end of a week she came home crest-fallen, having been kindly dismissed, to be comforted and petted by her mother and the girls. Accomplishments she had, but practical knowledge, especially of arithmetic, she lacked. Phyllis had been right when in the beginning of their trouble she had said they were not able to compete with those they had thought inferiors, in doing the serious work of the world.

After this experiment Mr. Hurd placed Barbara in an office where she was to address envelopes. This she did well, for her fingers and brain were quick; but she was far from an expert, and her salary was but three dollars and a half a week. Fortunately, the office was within walking distance, so that no car-fare had to come from this magnificent result of six days' labor.

Jessamy worked hard at her drawing, and Phyllis went daily to her tutoring, saying so little of her experiences that her family concluded that they were not wholly pleasant. But one bright ray of hope shone out of the gloom for Phyllis. A little story which she had written was accepted by one of the large syndicates, and paid for—fifteen dollars. The sum was not large, though it was more than half of what she was paid monthly by Mrs. Haines; but the glory, and the hope it shed on the future, were invaluable. On the whole, Phyllis and Barbara found their entrance into the lists not easy, and the blows of the tourney hard, but they kept on with courage fine to see.

They all felt that in some way their skies would brighten when Mrs. Van Alyn returned; she was their "Lady from Philadelphia," and would be sure to find a way through their difficulties. But Mrs. Van Alyn had gone to England to stay until after the holidays, and in the meantime the Wyndhams struggled on.

CHAPTER SIX: MARK TAPLEY'S KIND OF DAYS

PHYLLIS WAS FINDING her occupation trying. The girls were too near her own age to be easily controlled by her; indeed, they had never been under control in their lives, and study was not part of their programme. They wished to learn only so much French as would serve them in a coming European trip, and this they seemed to expect their young instructor to get into their brains with no effort on their own part.

But the hardest thing about her new life to Phyllis was the insight it gave her to a manner of living which shocked and tortured her; for Phyllis was conscientious, and the first actual contact with the worldly side of the world is bitter to such as she. Although they were three years younger than Phyllis, and that at a time of life when a year's difference in age marks a wide divergence, they were far older than she in many ways. They discussed flirtations, theaters, trashy novels, while munching chocolates during their lesson, betraying the most sordid ambition, till innocent and honest Phyllis was horrified. She went home daily heavy in heart and foot, loathing the atmosphere from which she had come, and wondering if the world, from which she had hitherto been shielded, was actually governed by such standards as she heard advocated in the Haines household.

Tom, before long, saw that she was looking downhearted and ill, and he made it his business to come home her way and meet her, trying to cheer her into forgetfulness of the annoyances of which he only guessed, for Phyllis could not reconcile it with her idea of honor to talk to any one of what she saw in the home to which she had been admitted. Yet she longed to ask someone if all the world, save her own narrow one, was like this new one. Jessamy and Bab knew no better than she herself, and her aunt was too ill to be troubled. So one day, after an especially trying afternoon, Phyllis met Tom with a keen sensation of relief as well as of pleasure, he looked so manly and reliable that her troubles broke over their barriers almost in spite of herself.

"It's no use, Tom," she said; "I've been trying not to tell you, but I must. Is it I or the world that's out of joint?"

"On general principles, I can assure you that it's not you, Phyllis; you're all right. But, if I might, I should like to have something more explicit," said Tom, looking very kindly down on the flushed, earnest face.

Phyllis began at the beginning, and poured forth to Tom all the matters which had distressed her in the Haines household, ending with a conversation of that afternoon.

"Well, what do you want me to tell you, Phyllis?" asked Tom. "Surely you don't question whether you or heartless, flirting, worldly girls are right?"

"No, not that; right is right, and wrong is wrong—" began Phyllis.

"Always," broke in Tom.

"Yes, I know; but what makes me down-right sick is the fear that dear aunty has kept us shut away from a world that is full of this sort of thing—that it is all like this," cried Phyllis. "Are we different from the rest of the world? These months have frightened me."

"Not much wonder," said Tom, heartily. "Poor little soul! Now look here, Phyllis; you're not different from all the world, but you're different from lots of it. The best never gets run out, but it often runs low. You've been shown the highest standards in everything, and they can't be common. It's much easier to be bad than good for people who start crooked. You started straight, you and Jessamy and Bab. All you've got to do is to be yourself, and not worry. Keep your own ideas and steer by them, and let the rest go. Do you suppose I don't see heaps and piles of things I hate? More than you ever will, because a fellow runs up against the world as no girl does. I'd like to be able to tell you I see none but sweet, modest, true girls; but, honest, there are lots of worldly ones. Girls exasperate me, though I feel mean to say it; they wouldn't if I didn't think they were so much nicer than we are when they *are* nice. You see, Phyl, girls don't understand that the whole world is in their hands; we're all what women, young and old, make us. Now, you and I had good mothers and sisters. When I went away my oldest sister—she's past thirty—talked to me. 'Shut your eyes to the bold girls, Tom,' she said, 'and take none for a friend you would not like for your sisters' friend. Keep your ideals, and be sure there will always be sweet, wholesome girls in the world to save it.' So I have been shutting my eyes to the strong-minded sisterhood, and the giddy ones too, and just when I was getting too lonely, and needed you, the Wyndhams turned up, thank Heaven!

So you'll find it, Phyl; it's a queer, crooked old world, but there are straight folk in it. Keep your ideals, miss, as my sister told me, and 'gang your ways.' And don't take it too hard that there's wrong and injustice in the world; that's being morbid. You'll get used to it; it's the first plunge that costs; the world's like the ocean in that. There's heaps of good lying around, even mixed up with the bad, though that's what no young person sees at first. You know I'm ever so much older than you, because I've been out in the fray some time. Don't get to thinking it's a bad world; it's a good one. The Lord said so when he made it. Thus endeth my first lesson. I never talked so long in all my life, not at one stretch. I sha'n't do so again very soon. Come into this drug-store and have some hot coffee; you look fagged."

"You're such a comfort, Tom," said Phyllis. "I feel much better. There was no use in talking to the girls, because we all know no more and no less than one another, but I did want straightening out. And aunty looks so ill lately, don't you think so?"

Tom looked serious. "I think she is ill, Phyllis," he said. "There's nothing the matter with her except one of the worst things: she is exhausted, worn out with fret and trouble, and she doesn't get enough nourishment; she needs nursing."

"Oh, I see it, Tom," cried Phyllis, as they left the soda-fountain. "What can I do?"

"Take care of yourself, for one thing; you don't look right, either," said Tom.

"I feel dragging, that's the only word I know for it," said Phyllis.

"I'm going to fix you up some quinine and calisaya, with malt; I'm not pleased with you of late, Miss Phyllis," said Tom.

Four days later Phyllis trailed her weary way homeward. The end of her first month's labor had come; the twenty-five dollars she had earned lay in her pocket-book in four new bills. Her head ached, her knees felt strangely unreliable, her spine seemed to be someone else's, so burning and painful it felt in its present place, and her eyes played her tricks by showing her objects in false positions and sizes, occasionally flaring up and then darkening completely for a few dreadful seconds.

Jessamy met her at the door with an anxious face. "Mama has given out wholly, Phyl," she said. "She is in bed, and frightens me, she looks so weak, and her heart beats unevenly and feebly."

"That's bad," said Phyllis, so indifferently that Jessamy stared in amazement, then saw with utter sinking of her heart that Phyllis looked desperately ill herself. If Phyllis, the rock on which they all leaned, gave out now, what should she do?

"What is the matter, Phyl?" she asked, putting her arm around her cousin.

"I have no idea. My head aches unbearably; it is a headache that reaches to the soles of my feet," answered Phyllis, miserably. "I've twenty-five dollars in my purse;

that will pay for several visits, won't it? Send for Dr. Jerome, I mean," said Phyllis, uncertainly. She dropped her hat on the floor beside her, and pushed her hair back from her temples as she spoke, resting both elbows on her knees. "One of the girls is ill; the doctor thought it might be typhoid," she added.

"Is that contagious?" demanded Jessamy, her breath shortening.

"I don't know. Don't be afraid, Jessamy. I'm too full of pain for anything else to get in. I couldn't catch it," said Phyllis, with no intention of being humorous.

Jessamy waited to hear no more. Running across to Tom's room, she knocked impatiently.

"Oh, Tom, dear Tom, do come quick!" she cried. "Phyllis has come home so ill that I'm more frightened about her than about mama now."

They found Phyllis exactly as Jessamy had left her. Tom felt her pulse; her hands were burning, her pulses galloping. "She must wait till the doctor comes; I'll give her a sedative, but I'd rather not do anything more," said Tom, looking grave. "Get her to bed, and don't look so hopeless, dear girl. Phyllis is possibly going to have the grip—the real thing, not a cold under that name—and though it is a severe sickness, it does not need such a tragic face to meet it."

But Jessamy would not smile. "One of Phyllis's pupils has a fever; the doctor thinks it may be typhoid; is that contagious?" she asked.

For the life of him Tom could not repress a slight start; then he bethought himself, and answered cheerfully: "Not a bit; only infectious. Get Phyllis quiet in bed, and try not to borrow trouble."

But as he crossed the hall he shook his head like an old practitioner. "Not contagious, it is true; but Phyl has been in the same atmosphere as that girl, and may have contracted typhoid under the same conditions," he said, rubbing Nixie's head absent-mindedly as the little dog poked it into his hand, recognizing his master's troubled expression. "I don't like it, Nixie, old man; I confess I don't like it at all."

Dr. Jerome came. His verdict as to Mrs. Wyndham corroborated Tom's; she needed careful nursing, nourishing, complete rest, and cheer. And to insure the latter prescription there was Phyllis! On her case the doctor said it was far too early to decide, but—yes, it might be typhoid. He would do all he could to break it up, but Phyllis was seriously ill. There must be a nurse; even though Barbara gave up her employment to help Jessamy, they were both too inexperienced to undertake a case in which everything depended on the nursing.

Barbara came home into the trouble, very tired, and discouraged over her own uselessness. She who had felt so confident that she could do anything had thus far been able to earn only three dollars and a half for many hours' labor; in the old days she had spent that in a week on candies. Jessamy and she had a consultation, at which Tom assisted, as to the present situation. Tom undertook to procure a woman who had nursed in his family, and who, he felt sure, would serve him for less than the usual terms of a professional nurse. "The two patients must be separate, of course," he added. "You and Bab will use my room, and the nurse will take her share of rest where it suits her."

"And where will you sleep, you dear, generous boy?" cried Jessamy.

"I've a friend I can bunk with till you're through with the room," said Tom. "It won't trouble me a bit, so don't call me names, Princess."

Tom's good woman came; she was the kindest soul in the world, and no less competent than kind. Barbara gave up her envelopes to help Jessamy; with two patients she was needed, and even then there were hardly hands enough to render the service required. Tom ran in and out at all hours of the day and night: Jessamy felt that if she lived ninety-nine years she could never repay him for his help and cheer, though she devoted her life to trying to do so.

Mrs. Wyndham lay in that wearying state of feebleness peculiar to exhausted nerves—not in actual danger, except the danger of continued prostration. But Phyllis grew more ill; twice a day the old doctor came to watch her progress, which was steadily downward. Out of the five hundred dollars coming to the Wyndhams quarterly there was an excess over necessary expenditures of about ninety dollars; this was all the capital Jessamy had in hand to meet the present emergency, and underlying her other anxieties was the fear that she should be obliged to borrow of Aunt Henrietta to tide herself through the double illness which had come upon them. Her mother required all sorts of expensive food preparations, and Jessamy realized that her little fund would not carry them further on their hard road than three weeks' distance.

Christmas was coming—the Christmas they had dreaded at best to meet in a boarding-house, the first since they became homeless, but now what a Christmas it was!

Barbara, sitting, as she did every moment that the nurse would intrust Phyllis to her, close by her cousin's bed, thought with falling tears of what Phyllis had always said, that nothing mattered while they had one another. What if they were not always to have one another? What if Phyllis herself, dear, unselfish, sweet Phyllis, was to be the one to go away, leaving a void forever which no one could fill? Bab the light-hearted refused to fulfil her title, but sat stonily looking forward to Phyllis's death. Jessamy, more equable, kept up a little courage, but for her also hope was hard.

And so Christmas Eve dawned grimly enough upon the two poor girls, and on them only, for Mrs. Wyndham was too weak to give more than a sick woman's passing thought to the day, and for Phyllis in her delirium there was neither day nor night.

Dr. Jerome came that morning, and looked more anxious than ever. "Your mother is doing fairly," he said, "but this little girl does not mend; the typhoid symptoms increase, and I'm not heading it off yet. Nurse, if you will get your scissors, I think this heavy hair must come off."

"Oh, don't, please don't cut off Phyllis's beautiful hair!" cried Bab, while Jessamy clasped her hands in mute appeal.

"Nonsense, Bab; it will relieve her more than you can imagine," said Tom, sharply. He had followed the doctor into the room. "It would fall after such an illness; it is better for the hair to cut it: but if it weren't it would still have to be done. Pray be sensible."

The nurse brought the scissors, and with a few strokes the long, warm, dark masses of hair lay on the quilt.

"That's better," said the doctor, as Phyllis moved her head as though at once conscious of relief. He left a few additional directions for the nurse, and went away.

Phyllis's hair lay on a paper; the sunlight, resting on it, brought out its rich reddish tint. Tom lifted a tress tenderly. "Poor, sweet Phyllis!" he said.

Jessamy turned away to the window without a word, and Bab stifled a sob in the table-cover. What a Christmas Eve, indeed!

CHAPTER SEVEN: TAKING ARMS AGAINST A SEA OF TROUBLES

CHRISTMAS MORNING DAWNED clear and cold, with a few errant snowflakes drifting on the wind, as if to show New York that the great Northwest had not forgotten her, but had only delayed its Christmas box of winter weather for a little while.

It is hard wholly to escape the universal joy in the Christmas air, and, in spite of anxiety, Jessamy and Barbara felt more hopeful than they had the night before. Then little crumbs of comfort floated their way in the morning, as the snowflakes were floating without. Beautiful flowers came to Mrs. Wyndham from Mr. Hurd and other friends, and the expressman had left packages for the girls late the preceding night, which the chambermaid with the chronically dust-branded forehead brought up the first thing in the morning. Then the postman came, bringing Christmas greetings to the girls from several old friends, and a letter from Mrs. Van Alyn, with an ivy-leaf from Stratford-on-Avon for Phyllis, a photograph of Botticelli's beautiful little picture of the Nativity, from the National Gallery, for Jessamy, and for Bab an oak-leaf from the sleepy old English town whence the first ancestor of the Wyndhams had sailed away to America two hundred years before. But best and most wonderful of all, he brought a note from Aunt Henrietta, which Jessamy read aloud to Bab after they were upstairs.

"'MY DEAR NIECES,'" it ran: "'I am concerned to hear that your mother and Phyllis are ill, though it would be more becoming if you had acquainted me with the fact directly, rather than leave me to learn it circuitously through Mrs. Haines. I trust Phyllis is not going to have typhoid, like the Haines child. Also that your mother will try to overcome her natural weakness. It is a pity she has none of the Wyndham endurance—'"

"Yet dear papa died, not madrina," interrupted Bab.

"'I should have been to see you, '" continued Jessamy, "'but that I myself have been suffering. I have had a severe attack of bronchitis, and the doctor thought I should not escape appendicitis—'"

"Mercy! They're not much alike, except in that horrible long *i* sound!" exclaimed Bab, who grew what Tom called "Babbish" the moment pressure on her spirits was relaxed.

"Do be still, Babbie," cried Jessamy, and read on: "'Escape appendicitis; but the symptoms were caused, as you may conjecture, by acute indigestion. When I am able to be out I shall go to see you. In the meantime I send you each a small Christmas remembrance which may be useful to you in your present circumstances. Your affectionate aunt, HENRIETTA HEWLETT.'"

The "small Christmas remembrance" was a check for each member of the family for twenty-five dollars. Jessamy snatched them up greedily. No one knew how she had dreaded applying to Aunt Henrietta for a loan, and now Aunt Henrietta herself had precluded the necessity! A hundred dollars! It would carry them more than two weeks into the new year, when their interest came in; perhaps before this windfall was used they might be able to dispense with the nurse. It is difficult to be hopeful with money anxieties corroding the heart, and with these relieved Jessamy and Bab looked on their two dear patients for the first time with courage, pressing each other's waist with their encircling arms, feeling very grateful for the comfort Christmas had brought them, and something very like love for Aunt Henrietta, who, in spite of ways all her own, had done a generous thing.

Mrs. Black rose to the requirements of the festival, and gave her "guests" an unwonted feast; Mrs. Wyndham took little bits of the delicate meat around the turkey wishbone with more relish than she had shown for anything since her breaking down.

After dinner Ruth Wells came down, her basket on her arm, like a happy combination of Little Red Riding-Hood and Little Mabel, whose "willing mind" could not have been as ready to serve others as kindly Ruth's. Out of her basket she produced a veil-case for Jessamy, a handkerchief-case for Bab, a glove-case for Phyllis, all embroidered in tiny Dresden flowers on white linen—not in her spare moments, for Ruth had no spare moments, but in those she had pilfered from her work for her friends. And for the sick ones were clear jellies, and a mold of blanc-mange, with bits of holly stuck blithely on the top.

"Oh, Ruth, how could you make all these, and how did you get them down here?" cried Bab.

"That comes of having one's own flat and not boarding," laughed Ruth; "at least, as far as the making goes. As to getting them down, a little more or less, once you have a basket, doesn't matter. Your mother looks decidedly brighter."

"Yes; she ate with a little appetite today. But Phyllis doesn't improve. And oh, Ruth, they have cut off her hair!" said Jessamy.

"Well," said Ruth, stoutly, "what of it? You speak as though it were her head. I suppose it won't be like the raveled-yarn hair on the knit doll I had when I was a little tot; I cut that off when he was going to a party, and was dreadfully grieved that it never grew again. Phyllis's will, I suspect."

"Come and see her," said Jessamy. Ruth followed. She really was a wonderfully comforting girl. Not a shadow of regret could Jessamy and Bab, watching her closely, discover as she looked on poor shorn Phyllis, lying quietly just then. Instead Ruth said cheerily:

"It will probably grow out in little soft curls all over her head, and how pretty she will look!"

And, as if to reward Ruth for her goodness, Phyllis opened her eyes, smiled faintly, and said, in a hardly audible voice: "I'm lazy, Ruth."

It was the first sign of recognition she had given since she had become unconscious, and Jessamy and Bab clutched each other in speechless joy. To be sure, Phyllis said no more, but dropped away again into that mysterious space wherein the sick exist, and Tom had gone away to keep the holidays with his family, so there was no one to whom they could fly to ask just how good a symptom this might be. But the nurse told them that, though it might mean little, it was encouraging, and the eager girls resolved to take it at its highest valuation, to get all the joy they could out of a Christmas not too bright at best.

"Good-by, Ruthy; you are so heartening! I wish madrina could take you for a tonic; I'm sure I don't know any other equal to you," said Bab, as Ruth left them.

The last seven days of the year slipped by with alternations of hope and fear for Phyllis filling Jessamy and Barbara's moments—for Phyllis, because the question of whether she was to throw off the fever or settle down to long typhoid was determining, and Mrs. Wyndham's condition involved no present danger. On the whole, hope predominated; the times in which Phyllis had lucid moments grew more frequent and longer; Dr. Jerome looked more cheerful each day.

But finally, as if she knew that the time of good resolutions and amendment had come, on the closing night of the year Phyllis threw off the last trace of her fever, and lay white and weak, but smilingly conscious, to greet the New Year's dawn.

Tom and Nixie came back to hear the good news, bringing cheer with them. Altogether Jessamy felt that night, when she lay down to sleep, that her troubles were nearly over, and she saw light ahead. She had yet to learn that the long days of convalescence held trials greater than those she had borne.

In the first place, the January days fulfilled the old prophecy of increased cold with greater length, and the little stoves, to which she and Bab offered up holocausts of knuckles and finger-tips, tried them almost past endurance.

"It really isn't the stove that bothers me," said Bab, falling back on her heels as she knelt before it, and raising a discouraged and smutty face to Jessamy. "The stove is like the rest of us: It would behave better if it could get something to consume."

That was true; it took constant battling to keep coal on hand to replenish the fire. Mrs. Black's interest in the coal question was only to save it, and the result was that the swift-drawing cylinder-stoves were perilously low half the time.

The matter of getting food suitable to convalescents kept the poor girls' nerves quivering. They bought chops and gave them to Mrs. Black to be cooked, bribing the cook to do it well; but the meat that had looked so succulent and so tender when it was cut reappeared dry and blackened, with congealing fat around the edges of the plate, or else was so rare that Phyllis's big hungry eyes filled with tears at the mere sight of it.

Jessamy and Bab tried extracting beef-juice in glass jars with cold water and salt, as Mrs. Wells taught them to do, and they got a broiling-fork and cooked chops over their stoves until the irascible old man below them complained to the landlady of the odor of broiling. Jessamy began to have a little line between her eyes, and her sweet voice grew almost sharp from nervous strain, while Bab, though she really struggled hard "to be good," as she said, found her naturally quick temper roused beyond her ability to curb it in the effort to obtain justice, if not kindness, for her dear patients, whose recovery depended on proper care.

For a month these two poor little heroines struggled on in a daily round of petty annoyances—not petty, after all, when one considered what was involved.

"We're getting awful, Jessamy," said Bab, tearfully, one sad night. "We're getting sharp-tempered, nervous, hard; and I wonder where shall we end?"

"Come in here, girls," was heard in Phyllis's voice, still tremulous, from the next room. "And do bring Tom."

Tom and Nixie had resumed their old quarters since the nurse had gone, and now both the dog and his master came as readily as they always did when any one of the Wyndhams called them.

"I heard what you said, Babbie," said Phyllis, motioning Tom to the seat of honor, and welcoming Nixie to her side in the big chair. "I've been seeing what a hard time you were having, and I want to tell you both what we're going to do."

"It sounds rather solemn, Phyl, summoning us to a conclave like this. If we're going to do anything bad, don't tell us tonight," said Jessamy.

"What we're going to do—or what I'm going to do—is go to housekeeping," Phyllis said.

There was a shout of laughter from her audience, after a moment of surprised silence. "You look like housekeeping just now," said Bab.

"I look less like boarding," said Phyllis, stoutly. "Ruth Wells is perfectly right. We should be far better off in a little home of our own, 'be it ever so humble.' It takes strong—no, I mean tough people to get on without home comforts. You and Jessamy are getting utterly worn out, as nervous and fretted as you can be, and if you put half the strength it takes to live this way into healthy housework you would have everything you need, and not be tired, still less cross."

"Phyllis is right!" cried Tom. "It's a miserable way to live."

"Of course I'm right," said Phyllis. "Now I've been figuring. It costs us about six-teen hundred a year to live in this wretched way, and I don't know what you are spending besides for these nourishing things aunty and I are having."

"I do," said Jessamy, with a half-humorous, half-genuine sigh.

"I am sure you do, and that it is awful," said Phyllis. "Well, now listen. We are going to take a flat, the best we can find for the money, at forty dollars a month. We are going to have a woman come in two days each week to wash, iron, and sweep, at a dollar and a quarter a day, making about a hundred and twenty-six dollars a year. We are going to cook on gas—Ruth said so—seventy-two dollars more. And we're going to live plainly, but have nice, wholesome things to eat, and all we want, for six hundred a year—Ruth again, and she knows! And that makes a total of thirteen hundred dollars, allowing a little margin. That's three hundred dollars less than we spend now, and even if it were more, who wouldn't rather be in her own dear little home, with all scratchy, maddening things and people shut out?"

Phyllis stopped, breathless, and the others had listened in so much the same condition that it was a moment before anyone spoke. Then Bab leaped to her feet, and ran over to hug Phyllis in a rapture. "You dear, quiet, splendid old Phyllistine!" she cried. "It's just blissfully lovely! To think of you being the one to do it, when you're still so weak and forlorn!"

"Ask me to tea, have me up to help; let me catch the crumbs from your table," said Tom. "Phyllis, you're a trump, and you've saved the day."

"Crumbs from the table!" cried Jessamy, catching her breath. "That's just it. It's a dream, Phyl, but how in the world can we do it? There won't be any crumbs from the table, nor anything to eat. We can't do anything, any of us. I'm not sure mama understands cooking."

"Aunty can direct a cook," said Phyllis; "and I'm not afraid, with a good cook-book, and Ruth to ask. We can learn a few things, and do them every day, if necessary. It's better than this, at the worst, and we shall save money, too. If we failed, we could have one servant, and still spend no more than we do now. You and Bab go to look for flats tomorrow. You'll see I'm right."

Phyllis's last remark settled the question. If they could afford a servant in case of necessity, there could be no risk in the attempt. Barbara would not admit risk in any case. Tom was unselfishly enthusiastic over the scheme, though he said he dared not think of his loneliness if they left the "Blackboard." But Bab hospitably gave him the freedom of the new apartment, and before they separated for the night the place was rented, furnished, and they had moved in. And, best of all, Tom had promised Phyllis that she should own a kitten.

CHAPTER EIGHT: THE TURN OF THE LANE

JESSAMY AND BARBARA were ready for their expedition in search of peace by nine o'clock the next morning.

"Phyllis is rather like the centurion in the gospel: She tells one to go, and she goeth, and to another to do this, and she doeth it. That isn't irreverent, because the centurion was only a Roman soldier—not even a prophet," said Bab, as she toiled up the elevated-road steps at Thirty-third Street. "I wonder what it is in Phyl we all yield to?"

"She is very decided, with all her quietness, for one thing, and we have learned that she is generally right and pulls us out of difficulties, for another," said Jessamy. "Wait; I think I've two tickets."

"What does it matter? We shall need them when we've moved uptown," said Bab, airily, as she dashed ahead and deposited ten cents at the ticket-seller's window.

It was not a wholly attractive section of the city where they found themselves on their arrival at One Hundred and Fourth Street. Jessamy and Bab felt their ardor dampened after they had rung several janitors' bells in uniformly small vestibules decorated with stenciling on the ceilings and walls, and possessing too many little brass speaking-tubes and electric bells, and, in many cases, too many small children munching cookies and staring, round-eyed, at the strangers.

But Barbara said, "Where there's scope there's hope, and New York is large," and they kept on cheerfully. At last they discovered a house farther uptown, but still below the bend of the elevated road (around which they felt certain their mother would never travel), which looked attractive. The rosy-cheeked German janitor's wife showed them seven rooms, not large, but not as small as the others they had seen, looking on a quiet street, with the upper entrance to Central Park only two blocks away. The rent of the apartment, they were told, was forty-five dollars a month, but since it was February the janitor thought it could be had for forty. Jessamy and Barbara, unversed in landlords' ways, trembled lest someone should get their bargain before they had time to report it at home and secure it.

"Oh, girls," cried Phyllis, on their return, when she had heard of their success, "Mrs. Van Alyn has come; she's been here. She approves our plan, but she advises us to settle everything without speaking to aunty, for she thinks she is too weak to see anything but its disadvantages. And—and—oh, Jess! oh, Bab! I'm half crazy. She has some of our dearest things stored away for us, because she felt sure we should sometime have another home: uncle's chair, Bab's piano, our desks, tables, photographs, casts—oh, I don't know what!—out of our dear old home, all ready for this little new one!"

Bab turned white, then took a header into the pillows to smother the irrepressible cry of joy which her mother must not hear, while Jessamy, who had silently mourned her lost treasures more than either of the others, dropped into the rocking-chair, crying for happiness.

It was a great comfort that Mrs. Van Alyn approved the new plan; it made it better if it should go wrong: for Jessamy did not like to assume the entire responsibility of such a radical change of which her mother was to be ignorant. The flat was taken, and then the joy of furnishing began.

New papers, a soft gray-green in the parlor, a rich red, olive, and brown tapestry in the dining-room, with soft imitations of burlaps in the small bedrooms, completely altered the effect given by the ugly papers which had preceded them. Pretty denims, labor-saving as well, covered the bedroom floors, and the dining-room and parlor floors were stained for a border to their tasteful rugs. The three-foot hall running through the apartment was also stained, and black goatskin rugs, laid at intervals, softened the sound of feet; they were real of their kind, and Jessamy abhorred imitations.

Ruth was called into consultation for kitchen furnishing. She and Barbara spent a delightful morning in a hardware-shop, buying bright tins and fascinating japanned boxes, as pretty in the eyes of the homesick girls as art treasures. Jessamy, Phyllis, and Bab were so wild with delight during these last days they could hardly get through them, so impatient were they to take possession of their kingdom. Tom was not less excited than they; not a day passed without his bringing home some wonderful contribution to the cooperative housekeeping, in which cooperation he claimed his full share.

And at last, on the day before the Wyndhams were to move uptown, Mrs. Van Alyn carried Tom off with her to the apartment, forbidding the girls their own precincts, and with his help set in place the priceless treasures of old association

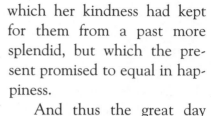

*The expedition in
search of peace*

which her kindness had kept for them from a past more splendid, but which the present promised to equal in happiness.

And thus the great day came. Mrs. Wyndham had been told but two days before of the home awaiting her, and received the news with rather more apprehension than pleasure. Phyllis gave up all thought of returning to Mrs. Haines; they hoped to save under the new arrangement more than she had earned there, and to do this her services were needed at home. Mrs. Van Alyn once more sent her carriage for her friend's use, Mrs. Black "assembled," as Tom said, to see her off, and Phyllis shared her aunt's drive, with refreshments for both invalids to sustain them until they got home. Home!—a word to conjure with, driving illness away. The coachman was bidden take them up through the park at an easy pace, and so, in the carriage in which she had been borne away from her first home, poor Mrs. Wyndham, full of the recollection, too ill and sad to share the girls' enthusiasm, rode away to her new one.

The trunks, and all Tom's mad contributions to the apartment, had gone away early, and as soon as the door had closed on their mother and Phyllis, Jessamy and Bab tore up the long flights to get their hats and jackets and hasten after them.

Bab seized Jessamy around the waist and waltzed her all over both empty rooms, singing at the top of her voice, while the chambermaid pushed her reddish pompadour out of her eyes to see better, and grinned sympathetically; she liked the Wyndhams, and would have rejoiced to get out of bondage herself.

"Come on, Jess! Don't stop for gloves; put them on in the train for once. Got everything? Oh, hurry! We must get there first, and I'm wild to see what Mrs. Van Alyn and that boy did yesterday! Don't stop for gloves, *please*—I'm going crazy!" cried Bab.

"You're crazy now," said Jessamy; but she tucked her gloves into her coat pocket, and her voice shook, her cheeks were crimson. "Come, then. Good-by, Nellie; I hope you will be well and happy. Good-by, old room; we might have left you sorrowful instead of rejoicing, and at least I may thank you for that."

Barbara was already half-way downstairs; Jessamy ran after her, and they reached the lower hall breathless, to find Mrs. Black waiting to say farewell.

"I wish you luck," she said, with an air that implied it was a hopeless desire for anyone mad enough to leave her sheltering roof. "You'll find housekeeping very different from having no cares and being free to enjoy yourselves. I hope you may be happy, and your ma won't break down under the strain; she can't stand much."

The ride to Harlem seemed endless to the two girls, but at last the tedious journey ended, and once they had turned east out of crowded Columbus Avenue, Jessamy and Bab fairly ran down the street on which their apartment waited them.

They let themselves into the house with their own latch-key. The janitor's wife was cleaning brasses, and said good morning pleasantly, but with no notion of what a great event was happening before her Swabian eyes. How could she have, poor soul, since people move in and out of apartments every day, and few of them are young exiles, hungry for home, come to take possession of the Land of Promise?

Jessamy's heart beat so that she could hardly get upstairs; but Bab honorably waited for her, and would not put the key into the lock—not the general lock of the outer door, solemn as that ceremony had been, but the sacred, blessed lock of their own private entrance. She threw the door open, clutched Jessamy's hand, who returned the pressure with interest, and together they entered.

They ran from room to room, calling each other, sobbing and laughing, and kissing the inanimate things like crazy girls. Phyllis's desk stood in her room, and beside her bed the little rocking-chair Bab loved best held out its arms to her. In the dining-room they found silver they had thought never to see again, and dishes which they knew would be equal to food, whether empty or full, to their mother.

They made their excited way back to the parlor, and Jessamy dropped, exhausted, into the window-seat, which was mysteriously draped in white lace, though they had made up their minds to self-denial in the matter of curtains. Her eyes rested on her father's chair, and her lips trembled with joy and gratitude. "Oh, the Lord bless that dear, dear Mrs. Van Alyn!" she said, though she usually found such expression impossible.

Barbara opened the piano and laid her hands on the keys. She struck two or three chords of "Home, Sweet Home," and laid her head down on the pretty case to cry the happiest tears she had ever shed.

It was fortunate that Jessamy and Barbara had more than half an hour to await the arrival of the invalids, for neither Phyllis nor their mother was strong enough to encounter them while their excitement was at its height. When they arrived the girls had calmed down enough to open the door quietly and say, with only a little tremor in the voice of each: "Welcome home, mama and Phyllis!"

Phyllis looked white after her drive, but the color rushed from her throat to her short hair at the sight that met her eyes. She did not attempt to go farther than the parlor sofa, where Bab led her, and lay still, in a trance of delight, looking from one dear picture to another, letting the soothing green tone of the room sink into her brain and rest her as if a cool hand had been laid on her throbbing nerves.

Mrs. Wyndham did not get beyond her husband's chair. She sank into it, laid her weary head against the cool leather, and burst into quiet tears. But even the inexperienced girls recognized them for tears that would restore her, standing for the breaking up of the apathy which had been the worst phase of her illness, and they felt certain they had done well in taking matters into their own hands and giving the frail little mother a home once more.

Oh, the joy of preparing that first dinner, to which Ruth and Tom came! Tom had camped out, and he insisted on cooking the steak; Ruth showed the girls how to boil potatoes so that they would neither crumble to bits nor emerge water-soaked from the operation. What bliss it was to Jessamy to make the tea by the venerable rule of one teaspoonful for each cup, and one for the pot! And the unutterable joy of peering into the fat little Japanese teapot later, with an air of experience, to see if it were drawn! And the still greater happiness of making cocoa for the invalids, in the alluring agate saucepan, brought forth from beneath the kitchen closet to be useful for the first time in its gray satin-finish life!

Bab was delirious—cut a slice of bread, and ran to hug her mother; set the cold water running, and then was saved by Jessamy from filling the pitcher from the hot-water faucet. Jessamy took her happiness in another way. She went about with an uplifted look on her lovely face; touched everything with a kind of reverence, brooding over the teacups and lifting the butter-jar as if they were little babies. She forgot nothing,

Tom insisted on cooking the steak.

left nothing undone, and when she went to call her mother and Phyllis to their first meal at home, though her voice would quaver, they were summoned to a perfect meal, thanks to her, and in spite of Bab's temporary craziness.

Nixie had a brilliant red bow, which he despised, on his collar for the occasion, and was fed in turn by everyone till he could eat no more, and retired to the front of the radiator to meditate on the advantages of house-keeping.

Mrs. Wyndham took her place at the head of her table, and showed such an improved appetite that Jessamy and Bab made their dinner chiefly of rapture, watching her and Phyllis enjoy the juicy steak.

"Now I've one more contribution to this mansion," said Tom, laying aside the gingham apron he had insisted on donning to help wash the dishes, when everything was once more in order. "I wanted to show you it before dinner, but I feared we'd get nothing to eat. Your mother has it in the parlor; it's for Phyllis."

Phyllis, guessing, jumped from the rocking-chair where she had been installed in range of the kitchen door to watch the dish-washing, and ran, as if she had never been ill, into the parlor. There sat her aunt, and in her lap lay curled up, like a powder-puff, the tiniest, whitest kitten ever seen! Phyllis had it cuddled in her neck in a moment.

"Oh, Tom, it's lovely! Oh, if you only knew how I'd been wanting a kitten! How did you find such a white one?" she cried rapturously.

"I've had it engaged for ten days; we've been waiting for it to learn to eat; it's only a month old," said Tom, looking very happy in Phyllis's pleasure. "Its mother is a white lady of most favorable record and perfect manners. They say her kittens are models in every way. Hope this one will do you and her credit."

"It shall be called 'Truce,' because we're at peace, and it's all white," said Phyllis.

"Truce isn't peace. However, it's a nice name," said Tom. "I called it 'Antiseptic Cotton'; it looks just like the packages of cotton we use in the hospitals; but I don't mind if you change the name—it is not quite convenient to call."

"Horrid!" said Bab, decidedly. "Truce is pretty. I think you might let someone else see just the tip of its tail, Phyl; we like kittens, too."

"This adds the very last touch of homeiness to everything," said Phyllis, generously handing her treasure to Bab. "Bless you, Tom, for getting it."

CHAPTER NINE: HOME-KEEPING HEARTS

THE WYNDHAMS HAD been "out of Egypt," as Phyllis called it, a month. Tom painted a highly decorative sign bearing the word "Canaan" in gold letters on a red ground, to be placed over the front door, because his friends were not only out of Egypt, but entered into the Land of Promise. Although it was not quite possible to hang the inscription in the front hall, Phyllis would not discard it, but placed it over the window in the dining-room; the flat was indeed the Land of Promise to them all, and each realized it in her own way.

Mrs. Wyndham was almost entirely well; her improvement had been rapid from the first, and she was far happier than she had been since the fatal day when Mr. Hurd had come to tell her of her loss—a day that was now nearly a year in the past.

Phyllis was completely recovered; she was too happy to be less than well. Her hair had grown out in soft rings of curls, as Ruth had prophesied it would, and she had never been half as pretty in her life as now, with present joy and hope for the future shining in her beautiful eyes. For Phyllis was dreaming and working; when household duties were done she spent certain hours of each day over her desk, and it was hard for her not to share Jessamy and Barbara's conviction that her little stories were one day to see the light.

The new plan was working triumphantly; the girls were so afraid of the failure prophesied for them that they dared not spend what they could honestly afford to spend, and their first month's bills were under the estimate; yet they had everything they needed for comfort as well as health. There were bad days, when everything went crossways from dawn till sunset—such days as will come to all households, even the best regulated. But when they came the girls treated them politely, pretending not to notice that they were crooked, as Phyllis suggested doing, and so those days came less often to them than to people who dwelt on their deficiencies.

Jessamy and Bab were making beds one morning, as usual, and Phyllis was out in the kitchen, clearing away the breakfast. Truce was on her shoulder; it was growing fast, but did not seem to find that a reason for abandoning its favorite perch. It was the most loving of small catkins, with golden eyes and a preternaturally long tail, and wore a scarlet ribbon on its scarlet leather collar to set off its pink-lined ears and pink nose and the snowy coat its devoted mistress kept spotless with soap and water. Truce never objected to anything Phyllis chose to do; indeed, Truce had what Bab called "reversed hydrophobia," for water had such an irresistible fascination for it that anything containing water was in danger from the meddlesome little white paws, whether it was the biggest water-pitcher or the daintiest vase.

Phyllis was singing, as usual. The two girls in the room nearby heard her chanting to a tune of her own:

> *"Stay, stay at home, my heart, and rest:*
> *Home-keeping hearts are happiest;*
> *For those that wander they know not where*
> *Are full of trouble and full of care;*
> *To stay at home is best."*

Then she apparently tired of Longfellow, for there were a few moments of silence, alternating with chatter to the kitten. Suddenly she began singing to a swinging, not particularly tuneful tune, like those sung by children in their games; this time it was a funny little song of her own:

> "Home-y and happy, cheery and bright,
> New tins to left of me, new tins to right;
> A little white kitten to pet and to cuddle,
> And purr back my peace when I get in a muddle;
> A getting-well mother, two girls, and a cat—
> My joys are so many they're crowding the flat."

"Look out, Truchi-ki, you'll fall!" And Jessamy and Bab heard a saucepan-cover drop, and guessed Phyllis had put up her hand to steady Truce on her shoulder.

"Copyrighted, Phyl?" called Bab, but Phyllis, on her knees looking at her cake

in the oven, did not hear, and Jessamy put her hand over her sister's lips. "Let her alone, Bab; listen; she may improvise again," she said. "Now she's beginning to sweep, and that usually inspires her."

Phyllis's broom flew, and Jessamy and Bab waited developments. Evidently Truce had dismounted and was ready for the frolic that sweeping always meant, for they heard Phyllis laugh, and cry: "Look out, Chuchi-ki! How do you expect me to sweep if you hold my broom? I'll spank you, kitten; you've never had one tiny, least spanking in all your life!" Phyllis always talked nonsense to Truce, whose name had developed through an Italian pronunciation of Truce, Truchi, Chuchi, and finally into the Japanese-sounding Chuchi-ki, which Phyllis said meant "Trucie ki-tten," but which Jessamy more correctly defined as meaning nonsensical affec-

"Look out, Truchi-ki, you'll fall!"

tion. Luckily for them, however, all the Wyndhams loved nonsense. To prove it, Phyllis began to sing once more—a long jumble of nonsense in one rhyme:

> *"Trouble found me where I sat,*
> *But I didn't care for that,*
> *Only learned my lesson pat;*
> *Then I took a heavy bat,*
> *And I hit old Trouble—spat!*
> *And I gave him tit for tat;*
> *Last, I drowned him in a vat.*
> *Now I've learned to make a hat,*
> *Wash a dish, and sweep a mat,*
> *And I think I'm getting fat*
> *In this blessed little flat,*
> *With my snowy Trucie—cat;*
> *I'm so very happy that*
> *I don't know where I am at!"*

This was too much for the audience; two peals of laughter rang out from the bedroom, echoed by Mrs. Wyndham from the hall.

"Going crazy, Phyl?" gasped Bab.

"I don't know; I don't see that it matters," returned Phyllis. "I'm brushing up our own kitchen, and everything I've sung is true; I'd like to know what consequence a little more or less sanity is under these circumstances? Oh, dear peoplekins, do you think we shall ever get used to this niceness? You needn't laugh at my inspirations; they're real hymns of praise in spirit, even if they sound crazy."

"I am the one to sing hymns of praise, dear little Phyllis," said Mrs. Wyndham, fondly. "No one was ever blessed with three happy, contented, true-hearted props in misfortune as I have been."

"I'll tell you a secret, mama," said Jessamy, emerging from under Phyllis's desk, where she had been picking up scraps of torn paper. "I suspect it isn't misfortune; I have a deep-seated suspicion that it is good luck that has come to us, and that if we had stayed rich we should have missed getting into the heart of things, and the real fun of living."

"Now be honest, Jessamy," said Bab. "I have entire confidence in Phyllis and myself enjoying makeshifts, but I have a horrid doubt that you may be making the best of it. Don't you wish you could go about, and have all the pretty things you love, and do no housework, only be beautiful all day long?"

Jessamy paused, her color heightened; she was too honest to answer equivocally.

"Sometimes," she said slowly, "I remember that, though we are rather simple girls, and like to stay girlish as long as we can, still we are growing up, and I'd like a bit more girlish fun, because we can't be young long. The pretty things I don't miss, because I have them—to make a bull. I mean our stock of pretty clothes is not used up; and our flat is simple, but it has the right look; thank fortune, beauty is not a matter of cost. I am very happy, and truly contented; your 'horrid doubt,' Bab, needn't come again. I think this year has done more for us than we realize, and I am honestly satisfied. But I do hope we may be able to better ourselves, if only my illustrating turns out something, I ask nothing more of fate."

"Hear, hear!—there's Ruth," Bab broke off suddenly, and ran to admit her friend.

Ruth had come to spend the day, and hem the ruffles of her new white dimity, for there were hints of spring in the air, and the willows near the northern entrance to Central Park had a filmy, yellow-green effect in the distance, as if the coming leaves were foreshadowed in a mist of sap.

The girls gathered in Phyllis's room, where the sewing-machine stood, with its top invitingly laid back ready for the "bee." The Wyndhams were to sew on spring garments, too, and they all had prepared for a pleasant day.

"If we had nothing to do but practise a little music, get through a little shopping, make and receive a few calls, we should miss this sort of pleasantness," said Jessamy, touching up a bow on the hat she was trimming, and holding it off to look at it in the glass in true artistic manner.

"Half the best things in life are not to be met on the highways; it's the byways which are loveliest, figuratively and literally," said Ruth, contentedly.

"That sounds like a poem condensed into prose," remarked Bab. "Are you going to drop into poetry?"

Ruth laughed. "All happy people are more or less poetical, I fancy," she said. "I wonder if Silas Wegg meant more than he knew when he talked about dropping into poetry in the light of a friend? If you're friendly toward life and people, then you get happy, then poetical; it's a clear sequence in my mind, only I haven't expressed it clearly."

"Not very, Ruthlet, and that's undeniable," laughed Phyllis. "I'm certain Mr. Wegg meant nothing so complex, even if he had a wooden leg. However, your idea is all right; I know from experience one becomes a poet under pressure of happiness."

"*One* does; the rest don't," said Jessamy. "Phyllis sings yards of rhymes when she's salubrious, but Bab and I remain prose copies. Oh, dear, there's the bell, just when we are so cozy!"

"Here is Mrs. Van Alyn, girls; she's coming in there," called Bab from the hall.

"I have come to be disagreeable and spoil all your plans," said Mrs. Van Alyn, kissing Phyllis and Jessamy. "Don't get up, dears, the end of the bed is all I want, for I mean to hurry off, and take Jessamy with me." And she pushed to one side the breadths of an organdie Jessamy was cutting.

"Oh, don't sit on Trucie!" cried Bab. "The kitten's somewhere there, asleep, after bothering our lives out."

"Dear me!" cried Mrs. Van Alyn, jumping up hastily. "Why, Barbara, you scamp, why did you startle me so? The kitten is rolled up in the pillow-sham. Where is your mother?"

"Mama went out to market, and to sit in the park awhile; she hasn't come in," said Bab.

"Then I can speak in ordinary tones; the worst of these dear little apartments is that the rooms are too close together to allow secrets," laughed Mrs. Van Alyn. "I would rather your mother should not know of my errand, lest it lead to hopes that would come to nothing. There is a young lawyer of my acquaintance—the son of very nice people I met in the Berkshires—who had a desk in Mr. Abbott's office over a year ago; he thinks he may be able to help Mr. Hurd prove that Abbott made over his property too late to have done so legally, in which case the law would recover part of your loss. I want to carry Jessamy off to lunch, and Mr. Lane, the young lawyer, will call to see her. It will save your mother possible disappointment, and you know enough of the matter to satisfy him, don't you, Jessamy?"

"I know more than when it happened, for then I knew nothing," said Jessamy, rising at once to get ready to go out; "I have tried to learn all about it since. Of course I will go. Dear Mrs. Van Alyn, you are always so good to us!"

"Nonsense, my dear! There is not much goodness in stealing one of you for a few hours; you are such busy bees nowadays I can hardly get a peep at you. Make haste, or such haste as can be made consistently with looking your prettiest. Old Peter is driving up and down, and I'm dreadfully afraid of him; he looks unutterable things if I have the horses out longer than he approves. I wish you girls could keep me here all day, instead of the exigencies of the law driving Jessamy and me away. There are never bright spots like this in my house." And Mrs. Van Alyn's sweet face clouded; her three little girls, who would have been the age of the Wyndhams, had been in their graves for more than ten long years.

"Ready, Jessamy sweet?" she asked, as Jessamy returned, looking lovely in her gray gown, with the blush roses nestling against her hair under the soft brim of her hat. "Goodby, Phyllida, Babette, and little Ruth, who manages to glean so much worth having. Tell your mother only that I carried Jessamy off to lunch, and will return her safely."

"Wouldn't it be nice if we could get some of our money back?" asked Bab, thoughtfully tickling Truce's nose with the end of his long tail, when she had come back from seeing Mrs. Van Alyn and Jessamy off.

"Nice! It would be glorious," cried Phyllis—"though that doesn't sound quite consistent with all we've been saying."

CHAPTER TEN: THE LITTLE BLIND GOD OPENS HIS EYES

THERE WAS GRIEF in the Wyndham apartment for Tom-Tom, who was as dear to them as one of themselves, and who had brightened their days of trial, as he had shared their recent pleasure. Tom and Nixie visited it no more. It was all the fault of Bab, and her mother and the girls were powerless to straighten out the dreadful tangle.

Tom had been gradually showing pretty plainly that, though all the Wyndhams were dear to him, the dearest was the small person who had fallen across his path, quite literally, nearly a year before—that for little Babbie he cherished a feeling different from the brotherly love he gave Jessamy and Phyllis.

Bab herself knew this perfectly well, and it turned her into a pocket-edition of Beatrice; she flouted poor Tom with more cruelty than "the dear Lady Disdain" bestowed on Benedick. For a time Tom bore her sarcasms and snubbing with pained surprise and patience; but that day was past. He had decided, apparently, that if Bab did not want him he would not inflict his presence upon her, and thus it was that "Canaan" was dreary for the lack of his cheery laugh, and to all the Wyndhams the loss was hard to bear. To all; for, though Bab betrayed her feeling on the subject by no word or sign, she grew thinner, and learned the habit of silence, which transformed her into a being unrecognizable to those who knew her best.

"She's Barbie, mama, not Babbie," said Jessamy, tears of impatience and regret in her eyes. "She has put a barbed-wire fence all around herself, and she's not only keeping out our happiness, but the worst of it is, I'm sure she's driving off her own happiness, too! And I feel so sorry for Tom that I can hardly keep from saying: 'Oh, Tom dear, just please be fond of me, and let that naughty girl go!'"

"That would be a singular performance on the part of my dignified elder daughter," her mother said, smiling. "I am quite as sorry as you are, my dear, and anxious; but I am trying to let matters take their course, and I think they may straighten themselves."

"They aren't taking their course," sighed Jessamy. "Bab is warping them all out of line. The dreadful part of it is that Babbie is evidently behaving so badly to Tom because she wants to treat him so particularly well. I wish I could straighten her out!"

"Don't try; wait," advised her mother. "Bab is very young. I believe I dread to see one of my girls with a lover, though it be such a dear boy as Tom."

While the Wyndhams had lost one friend, they had gained another—not one to fill the place Tom's absence left vacant, but one they enjoyed greatly. On the top floor of the house where the "Land of Canaan" apartment made the third lived a family whose youngest member, a girl of eleven, frequently held what Bab called "overflow meetings" with her dolls on the steps, for the family was large—as was the doll family, for that matter—and little Margery was forced, by lack of space, to the street, the playground of city children.

A friendship had sprung up between her and the Wyndhams, especially Bab, born of mutual admiration for Jumeau babies with spasmodic joints, and a little girl's unspeakable worship for an older one. Margery was a quaint child, given to the companionship of books and people beyond her age, and with the contradicting childishness and maturity of an only child in a family of adults.

Tom was included in her favor, both for his own and for Nixie's sake; once when Margery had a sore throat Tom cured her, and henceforth was brevetted "my doctor," a distinction he valued. As weeks went by Margery's sharp eyes noticed the estrangement and increasing coolness between "her doctor" and her dearest Bab, and finally that Tom came to the house no more. After long puzzling over it, Margery set her nimble wits to work to remedy the wrong she could not understand. Simple methods did not appeal to the queer little girl; at last, however, she hit upon a plan that suited her childish love of the theatrical and an unconfessed longing to be a heroine.

A rainy day came, and Margery, left alone with the servant, recognized her opportunity. Bab, alone too, as it chanced, was startled by a violent peal of the bell. Answering the summons, she faced the Hortons' maid, white under her freckles, who stood on the door-mat, wringing her hands, and crying at the sight of her: "Oh, Miss Wyndham, pl'ase do come up, for the love of Hiven! I do be alone wid Margery, an' she's took that bad she'll be dead ag'in' her mother comes back!"

"Dead! Margery!" gasped Bab, and flew up the stairs, in her alarm outstripping Norah.

There was cause for alarm, to the eyes of inexperienced Bab, as she looked at the little figure stretched on the bed, her face swollen out of all likeness to pretty Margery, or even to human features. A crimson face, cheeks, eyelids, lips puffed and distorted, lay on the pillow; crimson hands as shapely as tomatoes picked the quilt; while hollow groans issued from the purpling mouth.

"Oh, Margery!" cried Bab, in an agony of terror, "what has happened? Run, run, Norah, for Dr. Gilbert; I'll stay with her. It must be poison. Oh, what has she eaten?"

"Nothin', miss, but her lunch wid the rest of 'em," began Norah, while Margery moaned:

"Not Dr. Gilbert; I want my own Dr. Tom."

"Oh, Margery dear, Dr. Gilbert is so much older and wiser," Bab pleaded.

But Margery only burst into plaintive sobs. "I want my own doctor; I shouldn't think you'd be cruel to him now," she sighed.

"Then call Dr. Leighton, Norah," said Bab, blushing at this betrayal of Margery's observation. "Only hurry, hurry!"

It seemed hours before Tom came, though Norah met him in the street and returned within fifteen minutes. Bab spent the minutes bathing the still swelling face, soothing the poor little patient, and trying to control her own nerves. Margery grew more ill every moment; would Tom never come?

At last he came, and as he entered the room the relief was so great that Bab forgot to incase herself in the disguise she had worn so long. Her eyes were so full of love and joy as she raised them to Tom that he stopped short in amazement at the revelation, and a great flood of happiness rushed over him, too great for any circumstances to check.

"Oh, Tom, I'm so glad you've come! Now it will be all right," said Barbara, in a low voice of absolute trust. "Margery is dreadfully ill, but I am sure you will save her."

Tom did not answer; he walked straight to the bed, without looking at Barbara. His heart throbbed so joyfully that he had hard work to force his thoughts to duty.

"Margery, what have you eaten?" he demanded, having felt the child's pulse and looked closely under the almost closed eyelids.

"Nothing," murmured Margery.

"Margery, remember I am a doctor and know when I am told the truth; you must tell me what you have taken," said Tom, sternly.

Bab crept close to Tom, oblivious to all other considerations on hearing this hint confirming her fear of poison. Tom put one hand over the two little hands clasped imploringly on his shoulder, trying to remember only Margery and to forget that this was Bab coming to him thus voluntarily.

"I always tell the truth," said Margery, with all the dignity her strength allowed. "I haven't eaten anything, but I didn't say I hadn't taken anything. I took quinine, but it's much worse than the other time; I wouldn't tell you if I wasn't dying."

"Quinine! Ah, that's it! And worse than the other time? Has quinine made you ill in this way before?" asked Tom, comfortingly patting Bab's head, which had drooped on his shoulder at the word "dying."

"Once, but not so bad. I didn't think it would be so awful when I took it, though I did think I'd feel dreadfully. The doctor said I had an idiotsinkersy in me about taking quinine," groaned Margery.

"Did you take it purposely?" asked Tom, amazed, as he handed Norah a prescription and bade her hasten to get it filled. "That was certainly an idiot-syncrasy! Why have you done such a thing? Do you like to be ill, Margery?"

"No; but—oh, my mama won't like to find me dead!" And Margery burst into open wailing, in which Bab joined.

"You are not going to die," said Tom. "Bab dear, don't cry so; Margery will come out all right. But why, in the name of all that is wonderful, have you taken what you knew would make you ill, little lassie?"

"For your sake," said suffering Margery, as impressively as her swollen features permitted.

"For my sake!" echoed Tom, dumfounded.

"I knew that if I was awfully ill Miss Bab would be nice to you," murmured Margery.

"You dreadful child!" cried Bab, indignantly, springing away from Tom's side.

Margery turned away, hiding her swollen face, tears, and wounded heart silently in her pillow.

"She doesn't mean that, Margery," said Tom, gently. "You are hurting her, Bab; you know she adores you. Be just to the poor mite, and remember her motives were good, even if her methods are doubtful," he whispered hastily.

Bab knelt contritely by the bed, and took the queer, forlorn little figure in her arms. "No, of course I didn't mean that," she said. "Forgive me, Margery. What made you think of such a very strange thing to do?"

"I knew that if I was awfully ill Miss Bab would be nice to you," murmured Margery.

"The Bible says you ought to lay down your life for your friends, doesn't it?" sobbed Margery, drying her eyes on the ruffle on her nightgown sleeve, in default of a handkerchief.

"It says you can't prove greater love than by dying for them—yes," said Bab.

"Well, then, I thought I ought to be willing just to be sick for you, when all the books say how everyone forgives everyone else and foes make up around sick-beds and things. I couldn't bear to see you and my doctor getting worse foes all the time, so I took the quinine, though I knew I had an idiotsinkersy in me that made it poison me, and I'd be dreadfully sick. I thought you'd make up around my bed, and love me, and say how I'd saved you, and how you'd never forget me. And now you are friends around my bed, and I'm fearfully sick, but you only call me dreadful! Oh, why don't my mama come and take care of me?" And Margery wailed anew over the ingratitude of humankind.

What could Bab do less than express—though Tom was there—her gratitude to this martyr to her welfare?

"Dear little Margery, you're not dreadful; I am dreadful to have called you so, even though I didn't mean it. You are a dear, devoted little friend. Please forgive me, for you know I love you dearly," she said, kissing the sad, shapeless little face.

"And my doctor?" stipulated Margery, before according pardon.

"I think we shall be better friends; I won't be horrid to him anymore," whispered Barbara. And then Margery gave the kiss of peace.

Mrs. Horton returned at this opportune moment, and Tom escorted Bab downstairs, leaving Margery, already better, to her mother's care.

Barbara let herself into the apartment with her key, and for a few moments an awkward silence prevailed, broken at last by Tom.

"I think I shall adopt a Margery rampant, with a quinine capsule in the quartering, for my coat of arms," he said. "Our queer little friend with the constitutional idiosyncrasy against that drug has done me a great service. She has proved that you don't hate me after all, do you, Babbie?"

Bab was silent.

"Barbara Wyndham, don't waste any more time. You have treated me badly enough, Heaven knows, and I haven't enjoyed it. Tell me this instant that you love me," said Tom, in a tone which Bab might have resented had not her recent fright and humiliation subdued her.

"I love you, Tom," she repeated meekly, and straightway forgot all doubt, all fear, in perfect happiness.

When Jessamy came home, before her mother and Phyllis, she nearly dropped in the doorway, for there was Bab throned in the window, looking radiantly pretty with the joy and womanly tenderness which the events of the afternoon had called forth shining in her face. And beside her, on a low stool, sat Tom, looking entirely blissful and unusually humble. He sprang up at the sight of Jessamy. "Come to your brother, Jessamy!" he cried. "Bab has promised to marry me."

"Indeed, I have promised *not* to marry him," said Bab. "I have told him I will not so much as hear it mentioned for ages. As though I wanted to marry yet!"

But Jessamy waited to hear no more. She threw herself at Bab in some mysterious way, and hugged and kissed her sister, with a kiss for Tom too, in almost hysterical rapture.

"It was pretty rough on me to be treated as I have been lately," said Tom, as they tried to settle down to sanity. "But I ought to have known what it meant, for the very first time I ever saw Bab she threw herself at my feet, for me to take or leave, as I chose."

"Why, Thomas Leighton!" cried Bab, indignantly.

"Fact, and you know it," affirmed Tom. "Never mind, Babbie; 'some falls are means the happier to rise,' you know. That fall of yours on the Blackboard steps was one of them, for, my heart, aren't we happy?"

CHAPTER ELEVEN: THE LADY OF THE SCALES

THERE WAS MYSTERY in the air of the little apartment from the day on which Mrs. Van Alyn had carried Jessamy away to meet the young lawyer, Robert Lane—mystery from which Mrs. Wyndham felt herself excluded. Evidently the girls were in a conspiracy of some sort, but their mother did not give the matter much thought, knowing that when they were ready they would confide in her, and feeling quite certain she was excluded from their secrets for her own sake.

Robert Lane, whose possible connection with her fate was unknown to Mrs. Wyndham, became a frequent visitor; sometimes it seemed to her he, too, was concerned in the conspiracy with her girls, but she dismissed the thought as unlikely, since he was such a new acquaintance. Whatever was in the wind, it could be nothing bad, for they all were as blithe as birds, and Jessamy and Phyllis were as happy over their good fortune as Bab was in her engagement. For Phyllis had written three stories, which Jessamy had illustrated, and two out of the three had been accepted by a reputable magazine, and the editor had asked for more work from both the young aspirants. It seemed to the girls that fortune, fame, and happiness lay at the points of their pen and pencil.

"It is such a nice, quiet time now, mama, with no special work on hand, let's ask Aunt Henrietta to spend the day," said Jessamy, one morning.

Bab groaned, and even Phyllis looked downcast. "Oh, dear, it's awful to have a sense of duty," sighed Bab. "What does make you so dreadfully conscientious, Jessamy?"

"It isn't such a tremendous proof of conscientiousness—" Jessamy began; but her mother interrupted her:

"It is precisely what I have been meaning to suggest. We have scarcely seen our aunt lately, and we owe her attention; she is growing old."

"She isn't growing old, madrina; you know that: She was always old, but she doesn't mean to admit it, nor let it increase," said Bab. "Well, I suppose I can maintain my portion of family virtue. Write your note, Jessamy—Griselda, the patient and heroic!"

Aunt Henrietta accepted the invitation, which was for three days later, and appeared, in all the dignity of a stiff black silk, at half-past twelve, because she disapproved of the custom of arriving ten minutes before luncheon; half an hour was not too long, she declared, to rest after reaching one's destination before sitting down to the table.

"You've been getting a new rug for your dining-room," said Aunt Henrietta, in the tone of disapproval which she kept "for family use," as Bab said.

"Yes; that is Phyllis's contribution to our comfort: she bought it with the check from one of her stories," replied Mrs. Wyndham, mildly.

"So Barbara is the only drone!" said Aunt Henrietta. "No, no potatoes; you must know that my doctor forbids them. It is often the one who says most who does least."

"Barbara is far from a drone, aunt," said Phyllis, seeing Bab fold her lips with a look at once angry and hurt. "There must be one to help with the housekeeping, and she has all the care of providing. Bab is the most competent little person, and is so cheerful she keeps us all up to the mark."

"Humph!" ejaculated Aunt Henrietta, with a world of significance in the sound. "Take away that dreadful cat; I always detested cats! How people can want animals in such limited space I can't conceive. When are you to be married, Barbara?—or will that young man you are engaged to ever be able to support you?"

"Next fall, if Dr. Leighton has his wish," said Bab, while Phyllis gathered up Truce and bore him, surprised and indignant, from the room, where, as everywhere, he was used to being considered an acquisition. "Dr. Leighton would not have asked me to marry him if he could not support me." Barbara disdained reminding her aunt that Tom was heir to a good inheritance; it would have been unbearable if even Aunt Henrietta, for whose opinion in general she had little regard, looked on her marriage from a mercenary point of view.

"Very probably; he seems to be a very nice young man," said Aunt Henrietta, to Bab's surprise, for she had prepared to do battle for her lover.

The luncheon passed off with no further passage of arms, and Aunt Henrietta settled herself comfortably to slow knitting in the best chair in the parlor, and to conversation with Mrs. Wyndham. The girls were unmistakably "fidgety," as Aunt Henrietta protestingly remarked. A note had come for Jessamy during lunch; she had read it with quickened breath, and conveyed it to the other two slyly. The effect on them all had been disturbing. Bab slipped out for a few moments, and Mrs. Wyndham thought she caught a whisper from her to Phyllis containing the words "telephone," "Tom," and "Ruth." When Bab returned she flitted from room to room as if she could not keep still, and though Phyllis had greater control of her nerves, her answers to remarks were so wide of the mark that Aunt Henrietta commented on it, and her Aunt Wyndham kindly let her alone.

A bearer of good tidings

As to Jessamy, her cheeks were burning, her eyes so bright that Aunt Henrietta, scanning her attentively, prescribed: "Six drops of No. 3 syrup, in a half-glass of water, and take one teaspoonful every hour. You are certainly feverish, child," she added. Jessamy's great beauty had made her Aunt Henrietta's favorite from childhood.

At half-past four, just as Aunt Henrietta was rolling up her work preparatory to taking tea before setting out homeward—"You live at such an unearthly distance from civilization," she said, as reproachfully as though the Wyndhams were selfishly pursuing their own pleasure in going uptown for low rent—just at half-past four the bell rang—at the door was Robert Lane, looking so excited, entering with such a quick step and flashing eyes, that he brought an electric atmosphere with him.

"What has happened to you, Mr. Lane?" asked Mrs. Wyndham, rising to welcome him. "You know my aunt, Mrs. Hewlett? You look as though someone had made you heir to a fortune."

"Not a bad guess, Mrs. Wyndham," said Robert, taking the extended hand. "I have as good news as that to tell you; I honestly believe I like it better than a fortune for myself."

"Then it is all right? He has come to terms?" cried Bab, while Jessamy and Phyllis, knowing the answer before it was given, dropped, quite pale, on the sofa, their arms holding each other tight.

"All right, little lady; the check is here," cried Robert, jubilantly slapping himself on the breast.

Mrs. Wyndham turned pale; even Aunt Henrietta began to tremble.

"May we know what you are talking about, young man?" she said sternly. "Evidently the girls are in your counsels."

"My dear Mrs. Wyndham," Robert began, "it is rather a long story; the beginning dates from the winter before last, when I was first graduated from the law school, and had a desk in Mr. Abbott's outer office."

At the mention of that fateful name, Mrs. Wyndham sat erect, clasping tight the arms of her chair. "Mr. Abbott!" she whispered.

"Precisely; the Abbott who robbed you," said Robert, nodding emphatically. "At the time I was frequently asked to witness his signature to papers; among others there were three transfer deeds. The dates of those deeds I remember, owing to circumstances, and I saw enough of their contents to know they transferred a portion of Abbott's property to his wife. The first was signed on my own birthday, December 7; the second on January 3, the birthday of a chum of mine, on which we always dine together; the third on the eve of Washington's birthday, and I witnessed it with my coat on, ready to start out of town for the holiday—so I was prepared to swear to all three dates with absolute certainty. There were many things then which led me to suspect Mr. Abbott did not quite come up to one's idea of an honest man, and the following spring I heard of the failure of the Wyndham Iron Works, and that you had lost everything, while Abbott still prospered. Then I thought hard, and as a result of cogitating I went to Mr. Hurd and told him about those papers I had witnessed, and how that rascal had put property out of his hands when the company was already involved. Mr. Hurd jumped at the information. 'Young man,' he said, 'you maybe the very witness we need to establish what we all knew, but could not prove.' Then Mrs. Van Alyn let me meet Miss Jessamy, and she gave me information we lacked. Mr. Hurd did not have to disturb you, having your power of attorney, and they thought it better not to tell you about it until they were sure of success. Well, there were undoubtedly other transfers made besides those I witnessed, but those were all we could prove; still, they amounted to forty thousand dollars. We convinced Abbott we could prove that much rascality, and that if he didn't disgorge he would be sued, and made to give up not only that, but costs and reputation—what he has of it! The old scamp hated the alternative, but he's too sharp not to know it was the cheapest thing he could do, so he gave Mr. Hurd his check for forty thousand—it's certified—and as a reward for the little assistance I've been, Mr. Hurd let me bring it up to you.

"Mrs. Wyndham, here is a check for forty thousand dollars, and if you are as glad about it as I am, you are a happy woman."

So saying, and with a decided choke in his voice, Robert laid the certified check on Mrs. Wyndham's knee, and dropped quietly back in his chair.

Not a sound broke the stillness with which all present had listened to the long story. Then Aunt Henrietta electrified the company. Without a word, she arose to her full stately height, walked deliberately over to where Robert sat, put both arms around him, and kissed him soundly, with a kiss that resounded. "You are a second Daniel Webster," she said, and solemnly resumed her seat.

Nothing better could have happened; Aunt Henrietta had relieved the tension of a moment that was in danger of becoming overstrained. Following her aunt's example, though with a difference, Mrs. Wyndham took both of Robert's hands, tears of joy running down her cheeks. "I can't thank you, my dear," she said simply. "I know you are as glad as we are. But I shall never, never forget that we owe it to you that this portion of our property is restored. And to us, having been taught the lesson of economy so sharply, forty thousand dollars will be a far larger sum than it once would have seemed."

Jessamy, Phyllis, and Bab were crying, but their faces were flushed with joy, and they were smiling as they wept. "Oh, there's Tom!" cried Bab, running to the door to let him in, as she always did on hearing his peculiar signal.

"Hallo, Bob, old man; I see you've got it. Bab telephoned me," cried Tom, the instant he saw the April faces. "Talk about special providences, wasn't it about the neatest bit of good fortune that you should have witnessed those deeds? I tell you, Mother Wyndham, I'm tremendously glad! Now it's over, and you know the whole story, I don't mind acknowledging that my engagement to Bab depended on the recovery of that money; if it hadn't been captured I should have broken it off—I wouldn't have married a girl without a little fortune."

"She hasn't married you yet, sir, that girl-with-a-fortune, so you'd better not be too sure of her. I may take my share of the forty thousand and purchase a little Frenchman with a little French title," said Bab, saucily—so saucily that Aunt Henrietta said severely: "Barbara, such jests are not seemly."

Once more the bell rang, and Ruth dashed in like a whirlwind, and seized the entire family in her arms at once, apparently, so swift were her motions. "Oh, dear, dear girls, I am so glad!" she cried. "When you telephoned, Bab, I was out, but the moment I came in I turned right around and started over here. I couldn't be more gladder if it were my own money."

"Nor more mixed up in your comparatives," laughed Bab, returning Ruth's hug with vehemence. "I knew you'd be glad; you're that kind. You sympathized with our trouble, but it counts for even more to be glad of our joy. You are a trump, Miss Wells, and I call our lawyer, Mr. Lane, to witness I said so."

"Are you going to move, or do anything different now?" asked Ruth.

"Not we," said Jessamy. "This was our Land of Canaan, and we will not desert the dear little place because our income is doubled."

"We never could love any other little place so well," said Phyllis. "It is so much our very own home. I'm not sure, even, that I regret our dear old home now. It will be very nice to feel that our shoes no longer pinch; that will satisfy me."

"And still nicer, literally, to be able to get shoes that don't pinch whenever ours are shabby. My idea of happiness is not wealth, but just enough to feel luxurious in having necessities plentifully. I shall buy half a dozen gloves and three pairs of shoes the moment madrina cashes that check," said Bab, whose harmless vanity was her pretty hands and feet.

"I don't think I can get beyond rejoicing to know that each of the girls now can have a little fortune when I am no longer with them," said Mrs. Wyndham.

She looked dangerously near tears, and Tom had an inspiration.

"Put that check on the floor, right in the middle," he cried. "Now, hands all round. Come on, Mrs. Hewlett." And the bad boy forcibly pulled Aunt Henrietta from her dignified seat. "'Ain't I glad I'm out of the wilderness, out of the wilderness, out of the wilderness,'" he sang; and the girls and Robert joined in breathlessly, laughing and dancing joyfully as they sang.

Round and round the check reposing on the floor they danced, Nixie and Trucie, who were the best of friends, capering outside the circle, and regarding the whole thing as done for their personal entertainment.

In a few moments Mrs. Wyndham gasped out appeals for mercy, and the Indian dance of triumph ended.

"Now we can settle down to peaceful happiness," said Jessamy, fanning herself.

"A little fortune, and our stories and pictures to make it bigger, dear Princess—why, we are going to be wealthy!" said Phyllis, throwing her arms around Jessamy in an aftermath of delight.

Bab encircled them both impartially, standing on tiptoe to do it.

"The troubles of the Wyndham girls are over," she said. "They are the happiest three in the world, because 'Home-keeping hearts are happiest,' you know, and

"East or West, Home is Best!"

First published in the January 1902 edition of *St. Nicholas Magazine*

Bread and Jam

BY HENRY BACON

IT HAPPENED IN France. Two little girls were on their way to school one morning in the summer-time. These little girls lived with their mother on the boundary of the village, and their school was in the village, so they had a long walk along a solitary road between their home and the "Sister's" school, as it was called, for the teacher was a Sister of Charity.

Each of these little girls had a basket on her arm, and in each basket were large slices of white bread, stuck together with plum-jam.

They were very fond of white bread made of wheat flour, for the principal food at their home was black bread, which was made of buckwheat; and they considered white bread a luxury.

Later in the year, each would have had a big rosy apple to eat with the bread, instead of jam, but the apples were not ripe—as yet they were hardly larger than cherries. These little children were not sorry, however, for they liked plum-jam much better than an apple, even the ripest, rosiest apple. There was no danger the jam would soil their school-books; for they had none—their lessons were written by the Sister with chalk on a blackboard, and they had no need of books.

Hand in hand, these little girls were trudging along the solitary road, when, turning a corner, they saw before them a man sitting on a log, with his head buried in his hands. The children were not much frightened; why should they be, by a man resting upon the side of the road? No one had ever harmed them. They could not see the man's face, but, thinking he must be some one they knew, they went on fearlessly, stopping when they were opposite the stranger.

The man did not stir, and they looked at him in silence for some seconds.

"What is the matter?" asked Marie, the elder. The man raised his head slightly, and looked at the children. They could see his eyes shining through the long hair that hung about his face.

"Hungry," he answered in a voice between a whine and a growl.

Louise, the little sister, was frightened; the man's eyes reminded her of the wolf—the wolf that she had heard about, that met Little Red Riding Hood on the road as she was going to see her grandmother—and so she was frightened. Away she ran—scampering down the road toward the village as fast as she could. Marie also was frightened: not so much as her little sister, but she did not like being left alone with the stranger, and so she followed the younger sister, not looking behind her until they were again hand in hand. Then both looked back; the man had not stirred from his seat on the log.

"He is hungry," said Marie.

"Yes, he is hungry," repeated Louise.

"He must be very hungry," said Marie.

"Yes, he must be very hungry," repeated little Louise.

"It must be terrible to be so hungry," said Marie, standing motionless in the road, and still looking back.

"Yes, it must be terrible," Louise

They saw the man, sitting on the log.

repeated again, pulling hard at her sister to prevent her standing still.

"Suppose we give him some of our lunch," said Marie.

"And what would we do at noon?" asked Louise, opening her basket and looking in, to assure herself that her bread and jam were safe.

"Don't you remember, the Sister told us if we helped others, we would be provided for? Let us give the man some of our bread."

"But the plum-jam?" questioned Louise.

"Perhaps he likes jam," said her sister.

"So do I," half whimpered Louise.

"And then, the good Sister told us, the other day, about Saint Elizabeth. Don't you remember how, when she gave her best cloak to a beggar, she found another—a better one—hanging up in her room?"

"But the beggar did not eat up her cloak; it was not like bread and jam."

"No, but if we give our lunch to the beggar, perhaps—perhaps at noon we shall find a better lunch in our basket, just as Saint Elizabeth found a better cloak when her husband sent for her to come down and see the kings who had come to make them a visit."

"Are you *sure*, Marie?"

"No, not *sure*, but *perhaps*. Let us try."

"I wish you would say *sure*."

"Sure!" said Marie.

"Say it again!" exclaimed Louise.

"Sure!" repeated her sister.

"He shall have my lunch, then; but must we go back? Let us put it down here, and then run. He will find it, like the birds."

Marie was not willing to leave the lunch on the ground and then run, as her sister wished. She had listened to many wonderful stories, and wished that something wonderful might happen through her. Then, she thought, perhaps there might some day be another Saint Marie, and other little children would be told the story of this saint, and of her charities when a child. But it was not all vanity with this peasant child, for Marie's nature was kind and charitable. So, clinging to one another, back they went to feed the hungry.

"Did you say you were hungry?" asked Marie, when they had come nearer, but were still at a safe distance from the stranger.

"He is asleep," whispered Louise, for the man took no notice of the question.

"Here is something to eat," persisted Marie, thrusting her lunch almost into the man's face.

The man suddenly startled the children. With a low cry, he snatched the food, which he instantly began to devour like a wild animal. The children stood watching the hungry man, and as he stuffed the last morsel of Marie's bread and jam into his mouth, Louise held out her portion: "Now, mine."

The man, whose hunger was somewhat appeased, and whose mouth was too full to speak, shook his head.

"Now, mine," insisted Louise, looking disappointed at the refusal.

"No," said the man, as soon as he could, still refusing, for now he was no longer terribly hungry, he was somewhat ashamed of having taken the child's lunch.

"Now, mine," insisted Louise, thrusting her offering into the man's hands, and, as one child's lunch was not much for a hungry tramp, and she would not be denied, he took a large bite through both slices of the bread and jam. It almost brought tears to the eyes of Louise as she saw them going—still, Marie had said "*Sure!*" But suppose Marie should be mistaken?

When recess came, the Sister told her pupils they could get their baskets and eat their lunch in the school-yard, under the trees. Standing at the school-room door, the teacher watched over the children. Soon she noticed Marie and Louise sitting at the foot of one of the trees, their heads close together, Marie looking very sad, and Louise crying. They had made themselves comfortable on the ground before opening their baskets, confident they should find a good lunch—and both baskets were empty!

"Saint Elizabeth has forgotten us!" exclaimed Marie.

"But you said 'sure,' twice," whimpered Louise, and began to cry and say she was hungry.

"Why do you not eat your lunch?" asked the Sister.

"Saint Elizabeth has forgotten us," answered Marie.

"And Marie said '*sure*,' twice!"

It was with much difficulty that the Sister led the children to give an intelligible account of their attempt at charity. When at last she understood, she said:

"Wait; I will see. Perhaps you are not forgotten, after all," and she went into the house, leaving the children wondering. Soon, the teacher returned, holding in her hand a large piece of bread which she broke into halves, giving a piece to each of the sisters.

"There, children, you see you have been remembered," and so saying, she left them to enjoy their lunch.

"But Saint Elizabeth has forgotten the jam!" exclaimed Louise, after taking a bite and finding it was only dry bread.

"Perhaps she did not know there was jam on our bread."

"The good Sister ought to have told her."

"She could not," explained Marie, adding, "I never tasted such nice bread before."

But little Louise did not echo as usual, for, to her, dry bread without jam was simply dry bread, and it may have been Marie's imagination that helped her to enjoy her crust.

The adventure was told over again to the mother when the children went home from school.

"Was it not kind of Saint Elizabeth to have remembered us, after all, Mother?" asked Marie, when she had finished.

"She forgot the plum-jam," said Louise.

"But suppose Saint Elizabeth was obliged to go hungry!" exclaimed the practical peasant mother.

"Surely not Saint Elizabeth, mother?"

"Some one must have gone hungry; probably the Sister gave you what she had intended to eat herself."

"And was it not Saint Elizabeth?" asked Marie. "I was so sure it came from her."

"Not unless the good Sister is so named. No, my dear, when the Sister saw you were hungry, she gave to you out of her frugal store. My dears, it was very sweet of you, to wish to feed the hungry man. But remember, when you give, that you must not do so in the hope of being rewarded. That is not charity. Neither is it charity to give bread to one and take from the mouth of another. Probably the good Sister went hungry."

"I am so sorry," Marie said, disappointed and repentant, bursting into tears.

Louise only pouted and muttered to herself—"But she forgot the jam!"

First published in the July 1889 edition of *St. Nicholas Magazine*

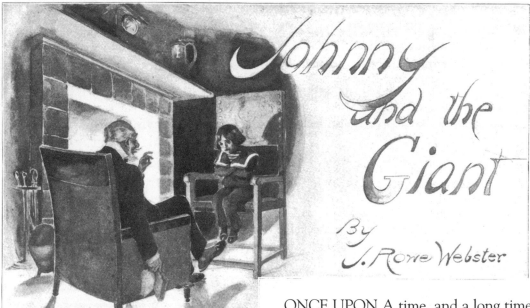

Johnny and the Giant

By J. Rowe Webster

ONCE UPON A time, and a long time ago, there lived near the town of Groton a mighty giant. He lived so many, many years ago that nobody who lives in the town now remembers any-thing about him. But the other day, when out walking, I met a very old man with white hair and a white beard, who said that his grandfather used to tell him stories about this giant when he himself was a very little boy indeed. When I heard the old man with white hair say this, you may be sure I asked him whether he couldn't remember some of the stories which his grandfather used to tell. At first he shook his head; but I kept on asking and asking, until finally he invited me into his little house, gave me a seat by the blazing fire, and told me what I am now about to tell you.

You must know that a long time ago there were not nearly so many buildings in Groton as there are now. There was no Groton school at all, and in the village there were only nine houses and no town hall. No, there wasn't even a railroad sta-tion for as there were no railroads then, of course no stations were needed. Do you want to know the names of the people who lived in the village?

Well, there was a Mr. Cobb who kept cows, and a Mr. Dobb who kept hens, and a Mr. Bobb who kept sheep. Then there was a Mr. Nagg who raised sweet-potatoes, a Mr. Bragg who raised strawberries, and a Mr. Gagg who didn't raise anything but a rumpus whenever he had the chance. There was also a Mr. Coon who had a fine big apple-orchard, a Mr. Moon who sold sweet-peas, and a Mr. Loon who couldn't walk because he could never make both his feet point the same way. On account of his inability to walk, Mr. Loon used to ride about in a wheelbarrow pulled by a big dog, in which he couldn't go very fast because the legs of the wheelbarrow were so near the ground that they used to bump into everything, or sometimes stick fast in the mud; and as the roads were always uneven and muddy, Mr. Loon had a hard time in getting anywhere.

And now, to sum it up, these were the names of the families in the village: The Cobbs, the Dobbs, and the Bobbs; the Naggs, the Braggs, and the Gaggs; the Coons, the Moons, and the Loons; and then, on the top of Gibbet Hill, half a mile away, lived somebody else. Who do you think it was? Why, it was the Giant himself, of course! He didn't have any name, though. People just called him "the Giant," and that was enough.

What a tremendous fellow he was!

His head was as big as a haystack—and, indeed, looked very like one, for his hair was stiff and of the color of straw. He never wore any hat.

His body was so big that his clothes had to be made of carpets cut out and sewed together, for no pieces of cloth were thick enough or big enough. His Sunday waistcoat was cut out of a Turkish rug. If he had laid his hand flat on the ground, you couldn't have jumped over one of his fingers. His legs were so long that he went rods at every step; and his feet were as big as freight-cars. On them he wore blue boots, which he polished up every day with bluing.

The Giant's principal food consisted of sweet-potatoes. He bought these from Mr. Nagg, who had acres and acres of land planted with nothing else. Every day the Giant would come down to Mr. Nagg's from his big stone house on Gibbet Hill with ten empty sacks, and when he went home again he carried back all the sacks full of sweet-potatoes.

Now, it happened one day that Johnny Nagg, the little six-year-old son of Mr. Nagg, had gone out walking alone, and had not come back again in time for dinner. What a time there was then in the village! Everybody thought that the little boy was lost, and all were out hunting for him. Mr. Nagg ran up and down the street, asking every teamster he met whether anything had been seen of Johnny. Mrs. Nagg was terribly anxious, and was sobbing as if her heart would break. Poor Mr. Moon wanted to be of some help, so he sent her a huge bunch of sweet-peas from his garden. When she received them Mrs. Nagg felt a little better, but not very much. Mr. Bragg stopped picking his strawberries and went to the big white church, where he began to ring the bell violently, in order that everybody might know that something terrible had happened. Mr. Dobb told Mr. Nagg that some of his hens had been crowing all day, so that he had felt sure that something was the matter. Mr. Cobb said that he had thought so too, for one of his cows had that morning neighed like a horse. Mr. Bobb said yes, and that three of his sheep had barked like dogs.

Mr. Gagg during all this time had been riding about on a large white horse and shouting, but what he said nobody could understand, since everybody else was shouting too. Mr. Loon—who, you remember, couldn't walk—came riding along in his wheelbarrow, pulled by his big black dog, and said he was willing to join in the hunt as best he could. After thanking him for his kindness, Mr. Nagg had to pull the legs of the wheelbarrow out of the mud in which they had stuck when the dog stopped.

At this the children would have laughed, had they been there to see; but they were all running about the streets, shouting, "Johnny, Johnny! where are you?" as loud as they could.

And in the midst of all the crying and the shouting and bell-ringing, the Giant came striding along. In his hand he carried a walking-stick made of a tall pine-tree with all the branches left on, and on his feet he wore his famous blue boots which he polished up with bluing every day. As he didn't seem to be troubled about anything at all, everyone stopped talking and looked at him, in the hope that he could give them some help. I have forgotten to say that this Groton Giant was a jolly and kind one, and was always ready to do all he could for everybody.

"How long has he been lost?" inquired the Giant.

He first looked down on the crowd in silence. Then he shouted out in a voice like thunder:

"What is the matter, and why are you all shouting and yelling and ringing that old church bell?"

"Oh, Mr. Giant!" cried out Johnny Nagg's father, "my little boy is lost, and nobody knows where to find him, and I don't know what in the world to do!"

"How long has he been lost?" inquired the Giant.

"Five hours," sobbed Mrs. Nagg, taking her handkerchief away from her eyes for just a few moments, and smelling of the bunch of sweet-peas.

"What direction was he going in when he was last seen?"

Nobody spoke for several moments, for nobody seemed to know. At last a little girl came out from among the rest of the children and said:

"Oh, Mr. Giant, I saw little Johnny Nagg early this morning. He was running across the fields as hard as he could go, over there"; and she pointed away toward a hill in the distance, far on the other side of the Giant's house.

"Aha, now I know where he is!" shouted the Giant, pounding the ground with his pine-tree staff, so that the earth shook for miles around—"now I know where he is!" and he strode off across the fields in the direction which the little girl had given.

All the people followed as fast as they could. The children ran screaming and whooping with delight. Mr. Nagg was at their head, and Mrs. Nagg, who had stopped crying, came along behind. Mr. Loon drove along as best he might in his wheelbarrow; but Mr. Coon, with his furry hair, and Mr. Moon, with his big round face, had to help him and his dog over fences and stone walls. Ahead of all still was Mr. Nagg riding his white horse—ahead of them all except the Giant, who, of course, could walk faster than any horse could trot. Stride after stride the Giant took, looking neither to the right nor to the left. He led them across the tops of high hills and down across valleys, over stone walls and through brooks, until everybody had become so wet and so tired that it seemed as if no one could go a step more. The Giant by this time was far in the lead. Last of all in the line following him were Mr. Loon, Mr. Coon, and Mr. Moon, who had all tried to ride together in the wheelbarrow, and had stuck fast in a swamp.

Finally the Giant stopped short, and waited until those who were running had come up to him; then he roared out, "Look over there!" and as he spoke pointed with his pine-tree.

Everybody looked, and far away in the distance they could see something like a big pole stuck into the ground. On its top was to be faintly made out a little figure that was waving its arms wildly.

"That's Johnny—that's Johnny! I am sure that's Johnny!" cried out Mrs. Nagg, so excited that she dropped her bunch of sweet-peas.

"Yes, that is Johnny," roared out the Giant, stooping and picking up the sweet-peas, which he handed to Mrs. Nagg with a bow.

"But what is he doing on top of that pole?" said Mr. Nagg anxiously. "It looks miles high, and I am afraid he'll fall."

"Pole? What pole, sir?" roared the Giant. "That isn't any pole, but a tall tower that I made years and years ago." And he set off again, as before, with everybody running after him. The nearer they came to the tower, the higher and higher it seemed to grow, until at last, when they reached its foot, it was found to be many times as high as the Giant himself.

"Oh, Johnny, Johnny," screamed Mrs. Nagg, "do be careful, and don't fall! And how in the world did you get up there?"

He led them over stone walls and brooks.

"A big bird flew away with me up here, and left me," shouted Johnny from the flat top of the tower, looking very glad to see his father and mother again.

"I know what big bird it was," said the Giant. "It was my pet eagle. He is always picking things up and leaving them on top of the tower; so I expected to find Johnny here."

"But how in the world is Johnny to get down?" asked Mr. Nagg.

True enough! There seemed to be no way either for him to get down from the Giant's tower, or for anybody else to get up.

"Just wait a minute!" roared the Giant; and he set off on the run toward his house.

Now, when a giant runs you may be sure that it does not take long for him to get anywhere; and although his stone house would have been a long way off for you or for me, the Giant was there and back again in a few seconds.

What do you suppose he brought back with him from his stone house?

A long ladder.

He put the ladder up against the tower, and all the children cheered. Then the ladder was seen to be not long enough, and everybody groaned.

"What's the matter?" roared the Giant; and everybody kept quiet.

The Giant now took his pine-tree staff and began to go up the ladder. He was so heavy that he had to go very slowly, for fear he would fall. When he reached the

He pointed the tree straight at her.

top rung of the ladder he stood still. Then, taking hold of the pine-tree by the butt-end, he pushed up the top with its branches to where Johnny was, and at last everybody on the ground saw what the Giant was going to do.

"Climb into the pine-tree and hold on tight," said the Giant, in a firm but pleasant voice.

Little Johnny obeyed. Although he was very much scared, he wanted to get back to his father and mother so much that he lost no time in climbing into the very top of the pine-tree, where he hung on for dear life.

Then the Giant slowly, slowly went down the ladder again. When he reached the ground he bowed to Mrs. Nagg, and said:

"Madam, I have the honor of returning to you a very nice little boy."

So speaking, he pointed the pine-tree straight at her. Little Johnny scrambled out of its top, and fell into his mother's arms. How he and his father and mother laughed and cried for joy! And how the throng of little children cheered!

When they were all so tired of hurrahing that they couldn't hurrah any more, the Giant roared out:

"Let's go home to dinner!"

And they all went.

First published in the January 1898 edition of *St. Nicholas Magazine*

LAETITIA AND THE REDCOATS

BY LILLIAN L. PRICE

DAME WRIGHT HAD just taken the last loaves from the oven, and was dusting off some ashes from the wooden bread-shovel before she replaced it in its corner. Clear spring sunlight streamed into the kitchen, warming the stone floor to a deep brown color, and touching the mugs and platters on the dresser, till they fairly winked back its brightness. A robin outside was whistling gaily, and a long branch of lilac buds peeped in at the wide-swung upper door, as if desirous of finishing its career in the blue and gold pitcher which stood on the dresser, even before it had attained to bloom on its own native bush. A patter of flying feet sounded outside, and the lower door was flung hastily open, revealing a little figure in a long, blue cloak, the hood of which, fallen back, discovered a head of short-cropped, curly hair. Laetitia's eyes were dilated with surprise and terror, and before the astonished dame could comment on her disheveled appearance, she gasped out:

"Oh, Grandmother, the British are crossing the valley, and Master Paxton saith they will camp here at nightfall! He saith thou and Grandfather must hasten to depart at once. Thou shalt have two of his horses, and accompany him to the huts on the mountain side!"

"Neighbor Paxton is a kindly man. Calm thyself, Laetitia. When thou hast thy breath, run to the mill, child, and bid thy grandfather come. Alas! for these troublous times when the aged and children fly before the march of strong men!"

With a sad, anxious face, she began instant preparations, while Laetitia, hurriedly pulling her hood over her curls, sped down the path toward the mill. She met her grandfather coming homeward. He was old, feeble, and bent, clad in homespun.

"Laetitia," he said, as she trotted along at his side, "vex not thy grandmother this day with foolish terrors, but lend thy help like the willing little handmaiden that thou art, and remember that all things come from the hand of the Lord."

Laetitia glanced up at his face.

"But will not the redcoats spoil the house of goods and furniture, perhaps burn thy dear home, Grandfather, and thou an old man without sons—and Grandmother, too, so old?"

"I know not, my daughter. So far, the Lord hath spared my gray hairs, though this war hath taken the five boys, my five brave lads!" His voice shook. "But thou must be brave, Laetitia. Thou art our one ewe lamb."

"I will, then, Grandfather. Not another tear will I shed."

They entered the yard, bright with violet-sprinkled grass, and found Dame Wright busily packing what she could into secret places, and piling up household treasures, for burial in the woods. Laetitia flitted hither and yon all day, her nimble little feet and clever head saving the old people much worry and fatigue. She was kneeling in a roomy closet upstairs, searching out her grandmother's camlet cloak, when her bright eyes fell on her grandfather's ink-horn and quill pen lying on some deep-blue paper. As she had gone about from room to room, up and down the old house, more and more the fear had grown upon her that it was for the last time. The thought of her grandparents homeless and desolate, of rough soldiers clanking about the house with devastating hands, filled the soft eyes with tears and caused her heart to throb. The ink and paper were a suggestion. She ran downstairs with the cloak, and finding that neither grandfather nor grandmother needed her at that instant, she returned to the closet and carefully prepared her writing materials.

The quill was new and the ink good. Slowly and thoughtfully the little fingers guided the goose-feather along the faint lines, first across one sheet, and then across another. When the task was finished, Laetitia raised her flushed face and surveyed the result with satisfaction, and no small degree of hope shone in her eyes. It ran:

To THE REDCOATS:
I am Laetitia Wright, aged fourteen, who live in this house with my grand-parents. They are old and feeble folk, gentle and peaceful to friend and foe. I pray you, dear Redcoats, spare their home to them, and do not burn nor ruin our house. Perhaps thou hast a little maid like me in England, and old parents. Thou couldst not burn the roof from over their heads, and in such pity and mercy, spare ours! We leave thee much to eat, and would leave thee more, were our store larger.

Signed, LAETITIA WRIGHT

This was neatly written on both papers, and Laetitia, tucking them into her pocket, slipped off to her duties with a lighter heart. The last preparations were soon made, and they started to join the little cavalcade already in line, to travel up the side of Orange Mountain to the log huts built there, in readiness for such invasions as this.

"Alas, my geese!" exclaimed Laetitia, when with tearful eyes they had turned their backs on the low, white house. "My geese are still in the pen, Grandmother! Let me hasten back and turn them loose."

Permission was given her, and away she darted across the brook, on its rough foot-log, and to the goose-pen. There were her snow-white geese and the gray gander. They were Laetitia's particular pride and care, and knew her well, but, only stopping to stroke one smooth back, she opened the wicket and drove them, honking and hissing, into the woods. Then she pulled the papers from her pocket, and hastily slipping one below the kitchen door, she fastened the other on the front-door knocker, and, rejoining her grandparents, was soon mounted behind her grandfather in the little procession which wound slowly up the rough mountain road to shelter and safety.

At sunset the British reached the village, and though but a small detachment, proceeded to occupy every available building. The peaceful quiet and exquisite neatness of the Wright homestead were rudely invaded by coarse laughter, loud shouts, and the tramp of heavy boots and chink of spurs.

One of the officers soon found and read the note of Laetitia's which was under the knocker, while a soldier, a stalwart, good-natured fellow, spelled out the other in the kitchen. Colonel Ross looked long and contemplatively at the crude, childish characters, and his stern face softened.

"Thou'rt a bold little lass," he muttered under his breath. "Thou must take us for fiends to destroy thy home after this." He glanced at the humble cottage so bravely pleaded for, and then across to the mountains, where a faint spring twilight was falling and the young moon shone out pale and clear.

The officer found and read Laetitia's note.

Insensibly his thoughts drifted

Laetitia sprang forward.

to his own English home, where that same moon would light up his little Cicely's casement. His own little lass! There was a heart under that terrible red jacket.

Striding into the kitchen, he found a knot of men commenting on the other letter, and his orders soon went forth that no pillage except for necessary food and fodder was to be indulged in throughout the village, and no damage was to be done to goods or furniture.

Just as the men, hungry and tired, were searching for supper, along the brook came Laetitia's geese toward their pen.

A shout welcomed them and they were quickly seized and dispatched. All but the gander. One young soldier had a knife raised to kill this squawking fowl, when he paused suddenly. "Mistress Laetitia, since this bird may be thine, I'll spare him out of courtesy," he said, gaily, as he popped the old gander into the open pen. "He will make thee a good roast, ere thou hast the wherewithal to refill thy empty larder." So the solitary gander escaped with his life.

Next night, at sunset, the bugles blew the marching-signal, and the sound echoed and re-echoed up the silent valley, penetrating to the little huts in the forest, where there was anxious watching for the red light of burning homes, and smoke of destroyed crops. But the night fell and waned, and not a glimmer shone to indicate such calamity to the fugitives. Early next morning the little band returned to the village. Instead of wailing and tears, shouts of joy and thanksgiving arose from every house. Dirt and disorder reigned supreme, but not one broken chair nor mutilated dish told of wanton recklessness. In a day or two all could be restored, except for the depopulated poultry roosts, and several pigs which were missing. The sown fields were not trampled, and the door-yard flowers still budded unharmed.

Laetitia's little heart beat with thankfulness, but she kept quite silent. As they dismounted before their own door she saw the disconsolate gander solemnly perambulating the green, like some self-imposed guardian. "Alas, for the rest of the flock!" cried Dame Wright. "But what has the fowl on its neck? Such a burden I never saw on gander before."

Laetitia sprang forward, and, kneeling down, detached a little bag and a slip of paper. The bag chinked with coin, and a dimpled smile broke over her hitherto anxious little face as she read the slip.

"Listen, Grandmother, and dear Grandfather!" she cried, gleefully. Evidently the soldier had written it.

> *"Sweet Mistress Wright, We bid you good-night,*
> *'Tis time for us soldiers to wander.*
> *We've paid for your geese, A penny apiece,*
> *And left the change with the gander.*
> *Though redcoats we be, You plainly will see,*
> *We know how to grant a petition.*
> *With rough soldier care, We've endeavored to spare*
> *Your homes in a decent condition."*

It was signed by the colonel and by a number of the soldiers. Then, in reply to her grandparents' astonished questions, she shyly told them about her petitions, and the daring with which she had left them at the doors.

Fervent were the blessings called down on her pretty, curly head when the news was spread abroad, but she only laughed merrily and escaped them when she could.

"It is as thou saidst, Grandfather," she declared, as she tossed some corn to the bereft gander. "The Lord's hand stayed that of the enemy, and perhaps," stopping to pick a violet while a sweet look came into her face, "the redcoats have hearts like ours." "Ay, and obedient daughters to touch them to good deeds," said Dame Wright, as she lovingly kissed Laetitia's upturned face.

First published in the July 1889 edition of *St. Nicholas Magazine*

The Rescue of a Red-coat

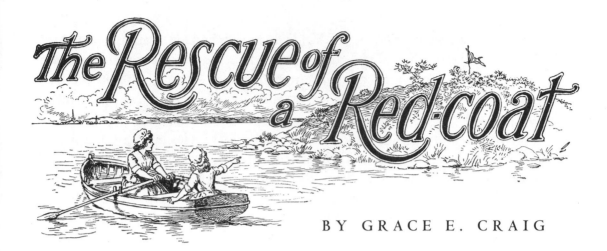

BY GRACE E. CRAIG

CHARITY MAY STEPPED briskly to and fro before the spinning-wheel which she had brought out to the door-stone of the gray farm-house on the hill. Occasionally she lifted her brown eyes from her work and gazed out over the rolling pastures of the fair island of Prudence or across the strip of bay to the Rhode Island shore.

"'Tis a fine day, Polly," she said at length, to the small girl who sat beside her sewing. "I think perhaps mother will let us go out in the boat when our work is finished."

"Oh, Charity! Does thee think she will?" chirped little Polly, in her excitement taking rather longer stitches than usual. "'Twill be beautiful on the bay this morning."

Charity studied the sea and sky intently.

"There's very little breeze stirring," she replied. "I am almost sure mother will say we may go for a while if we do our work particularly well. Take care of those stitches, Poll. The last ones had best come out. They will never earn thee a jaunt, but more like an extra long psalm."

Polly pouted, but in a moment laughed and pulled out the offending stitches, crooning softly to herself as she set them again with great care. Charity worked with a will, and her task was soon finished. She disappeared into the house, and in a few moments her voice rang merrily through the open door.

"Mother says 'yes,' Pollykins. Put up thy work for today."

Sweet Mother May followed her elder daughter to the door, and gazed lovingly after the two young figures.

Though Charity was Polly's senior by five years, the sisters were loving comrades. They were both very happy when their brother Ben built for them a boat. It was a rough craft but staunch and seaworthy. Charity had strong young arms, and soon became expert with the oars, and even eight-year-old Polly quickly learned to pull away gallantly.

This morning the boat lay on the sand where Ben had left it after a fishing trip the day before. Polly, with a joyful gurgle, climbed in, and took her seat in the stern. Charity pushed off with little difficulty, and they were soon floating on the wide bosom of Narragansett Bay. On this August morning the warm, blue haze made all distant points vague and indistinct.

Presently Charity dropped her oars and sat still with clasped hands, and even Polly for once was quiet, as the little boat drifted with the ebbing tide down toward Newport and the ocean.

"The French ships sailed out yesterday to meet Admiral Howe's squadron at sea, so Father was telling Ben last night," Charity said at last, breaking the long silence. "How *can* men fight and kill each other in this lovely summer weather?"

"Oh, Charity! Do they really do such dreadful things? Does thee think it can be really true?" and Polly lifted a horrified face from the water, in which she had been dabbling her dimpled fingers liberally bespattering her gray gown and white kerchief.

"I fear it is, lambkin," her sister answered with a shadow for a moment in her dark eyes. "Ben said he heard firing over in Portsmouth when he was out fishing yesterday."

A puff of wind coming over the water made Charity look up suddenly at the sun.

"'Tis past noonday, sis," she said, "and we are a long way from home. We must start at once or mother will worry."

Hastily picking up her oars she turned the boat away from the near-by Portsmouth shore, and headed for Prudence Island. As she settled herself for the long pull homeward, something on a point of land directly in front of her caught her eye. She held her oars suspended and looked again.

"That must be a signal of distress yonder," she finally said to her sister. "Turn about, Poll, and see what thee can make of it."

Polly screwed her body around, and gazed with wide, blue eyes.

"I see naught but a rag tied to a stick," she said. "How thee affrighted me, Charity!"

"Yes, but why should a rag be tied to a stick on that lonely point? Some poor creature must be in trouble. We will go and see."

"But, Charity," objected the little girl, "'Tis lonely there, as thee says. Some one may hurt us. And then, too, 'tis growing late, and the wind is rising. The bay is all white ruffles now. If we don't get home soon, I shall be afeared."

"Don't fear, little one," Charity soothed, "sister will take care of thee. Sit still now. We will be only a few moments, and then if we both row I think we can get home before three." And she turned the boat again toward Portsmouth.

Once on shore, she hesitated. Was she taking her little sister into peril?

"Would thee rather sit in the boat and wait for Charity?" she asked.

"No, no," and Polly scrambled hastily out and caught her hand. "I'll not be left. I will go with thee. We will take care of each other."

The two girls climbed the slope to the summit of a knoll, and there, a few feet away, was the little staff with its pitiful banner. They threaded their way through the tangle of bushes, stopping now and then to look and listen. All about the bayberry and sweet-fern had been crushed and trampled as by heavy feet, but nothing broke the stillness of the summer noontide save the bees buzzing over the flowers and the crickets chirping in the grass.

"There must have been a skirmish here yesterday," Charity said.

Suddenly she stumbled and almost fell over something, and stopped with an exclamation. There, in the shelter of a thicket of bayberry, lay a man in the uniform of a British officer.

Polly clung to her sister and began to cry loudly.

At the sound of her weeping the man moved slightly, and opened his eyes.

"Hush, little one," Charity whispered. "He cannot harm thee. He is badly injured. His leg is broken, I think."

At her sister's assurance, Polly took courage and stopped crying. Coming closer, she examined admiringly the scarlet coat with its trappings of gold. To the little Quaker lass, who had never before seen anything but sober garments, it seemed wonderful indeed.

But it was Charity's turn to look distressed.

"We must get him into the boat and take him home at once," she said.

"But how, Charity? He looks heavy," and Polly surveyed the prostrate man doubtfully.

"I don't know," answered her sister, "but we must find a way," and she gently touched the gold-braided sleeve. Again the soldier opened his eyes. Suddenly he made a weak effort to rise.

"Can thee not move a little way now, if we help thee?" Charity asked, looking out a bit anxiously across the wide strip of water to Prudence Island. A fresh westerly wind had sprung up, and Polly's "white ruffles" of an hour ago had become whole caps now.

Once more the soldier endeavored to rise, and this time, with the girls' help, succeeded.

"If thee can only get down to our boat," Charity urged, "we can take thee home, and then mother will care for thee."

"Come, poor soldier," Polly echoed. "Dear mother will make thee quite well."

A smile crossed the officer's pain-drawn face.

"Bless your dear heart, pretty one," he said.

*Limping painfully, he made
his way to the beach.*

Limping painfully with the stiffened leg dragging, he made his way to the beach, Charity just behind him, supporting him when he stopped to rest, and Polly by his side patting his red sleeve when she felt he needed encouragement. The man's breath came in gasps, but he smiled at his rescuers.

"You are good little Samaritans," he whispered.

Suddenly Polly cried out loudly, "Oh, Charity! Look, there's a storm coming!"

Sure enough. Over the high shoulder of Prudence Island, great masses of purple clouds were rolling heavily eastward. The wind was increasing almost to a gale, too. One of the sudden, violent storms of the region was approaching.

"We must get home before it breaks." Charity spoke calmly, but for a moment her heartbeats quickened. "There is no shelter hereabouts."

Making a last, supreme effort the soldier rolled into the boat and fainted.

"Never mind him, Polly," Charity commanded. "Thee must take the other pair of oars and pull for dear life."

A low growl of thunder in the west served to turn Polly's attention from their wounded passenger. She caught up her oars and rowed like the brave little woman she was.

"What time does thee think it is, Charity?" she inquired once.

"After three a good bit," her sister answered.

"Mother will be worrying," the little girl said, with a slight shiver.

"Yes, mother will be worrying," her sister repeated, looking over her shoulder at the approaching clouds. She fully realized what Polly only felt, that they were in a perilous position.

Wind and tide were both against them, but they made good progress for some little time. The young man at their feet moaned now and then and moved uneasily, but the two rowers pulled steadily on.

"Mother will care for him, once we reach home," Charity said, looking back again at the clouds, which had now rolled over the sun.

It grew suddenly dark on the bay, the wind died away slowly and the sea became oily. In the lull the rowers paused to rest.

Suddenly a vivid flash of lightning rent the darkened sky, followed by a crashing peal of thunder. The girls in the boat sat motionless, petrified with terror. For a blinding, deafening moment, sea and sky seemed to meet. Then the squall shrieked down upon them in all its fury.

Charity's cap blew off, and her dark hair waved wildly about her face, but she flung the whole weight of her slender body upon the oars, pulling valiantly, and shouting through the din for Polly to do the same.

One moment of hesitation on the part of either would have caused disaster, but, guided by the two pairs of oars, the little craft kept her nose pointed to the seas, and rode out the gale.

The worst of the blow was over in a few minutes, and then sheets of rain began to fall. Through the storm the young mariners rowed bravely on toward the home shore, and, after a half hour of hard work, pulled into the calm water inside the point.

When the storm clouds had all rolled over, leaving the western sky aflame with gold, and a rainbow spanned the bay, promising a beautiful tomorrow, Charity and Polly, once more in spotless caps and kerchiefs, were sitting on the old door-stone hand in hand.

"I'm glad we saved the young man," Polly remarked happily, "and I think his red coat is very pretty, even though 'tis wicked."

"Dear little Poll," Charity answered with a half smile. "'Tis not wicked for him to wear a red coat He wears red, the color of his king, just as we wear the gray of the Friends [Quakers]."

"I wish Friends wore red then, if 'tis not wicked. I like it," Polly said decisively.

"For shame, Polly," her sister admonished. "If Elder White should hear thee, he would say again that mother is not strict enough with us."

Upstairs the British officer, his injury having been found to be only a bad strain, lay in Mother May's lavender-scented best-room bed. He was now fairly comfortable and had told his story.

When the French ships had been lured from Newport harbor by the appearance of Admiral Howe's fleet, the British troops had marched out of the city, and succeeded in driving the Americans from the island, though not without severe loss. In the battle on the downs, he, Sir Hugh Grantham, major in his Majesty's Sixty-third Foot Regiment, met with an accident. His horse was shot, and fell instantly, pinning him beneath its body, and injuring his right leg.

With difficulty he crawled away from the scene of the combat, and, when the British retreated to the city, was left unnoticed in his place of refuge under the bushes. Next day, he succeeded in dragging himself nearer the shore and hoisting a signal of distress, a bit of his shirt-sleeve tied to a stick.

The young soldier improved steadily under the kindly care of the Quakers, and soon was able to limp down-stairs, and often joined the children in their favorite working-place on the old door-stone. He proved a merry companion, telling many stories of his home across the sea, the old red manor-house among the great oak-trees, where his mother lived with his little sister Marjory, whom he declared Charity strongly resembled. Polly rejoiced greatly when he once more donned the beautiful red and gold coat.

"It is so gay," she said, patting it often. "I do like it."

"Dear heart!" its wearer cried one day, catching her up, "I believe you are a little turncoat. I think you would really change your peaceful gray for warlike red. Is it not so?"

"Yes," and Polly struggled to be free. "I would. Does thee not think I could be as good a girl in a red coat as in a gray one?"

"Perhaps," he answered gravely; "but certainly you could not be a braver little maid."

At last the day came for Father May to take Major Grantham over to Newport, whence he was to sail for England with his regiment, and two very sorrowful little lasses in white caps and kerchiefs watched their father's boat out of sight.

They missed their friend sadly and they had not forgotten him, when, in the early spring, a boat came up from Newport bringing letters and a large box which had just arrived from over the sea. The letters were from the major and his mother, thanking the Mays once more for their kindness to the wounded "redcoat," praising the bravery of the little girls, and begging that the family accept the contents of the box with the heartfelt gratitude of the Granthams. Marjory sent many loving messages to Charity.

When the great box was opened, wonderful treasures were disclosed, beautiful things such as the simple New England Friends had seldom seen. Books for Father May and the boys, fine linen and delicate china for the mother, some heavy silver spoons for Charity's dower-chest, "just like Marjory's" the letters said, and, down in the very bottom something red. As Mother May drew it out, Polly began to dance.

"For me!" she cried, "is it not, mother dear?"

Her mother looked at the label a little doubtfully, and then suddenly smiled, as she saw her little girl's shining face. In another moment Polly was shaking out before the admiring eyes of the family a beautiful, long, scarlet cloak.

"May I wear it, mother? Will thee not say I may?" she begged.

And Mother May, wise woman that she was, still smiling answered gently, "Thee may wear it sometimes, my dear."

And Polly did wear it until the Friends in Providence City heard of the frivolous red cloak down on Prudence Island, and sent a stern letter of remonstrance to Mother May. Then it was laid carefully away and has been kept safely through many, many years, and Polly's great, great, grand-children treasure it still as a memento of their little Revolutionary ancestress.

First published in the July 1908 edition of *St. Nicholas Magazine*

BY ADELINE KNAPP

CHAPTER ONE: WHAT THE CHILDREN SAW FROM THE PLAY-GROUND ON THE PLATEAU

ONE SUNNY FORENOON in the month of May, more than six hundred years ago, a few boys and girls were playing under some gnarled, low trees that clustered in small groups here and there in a pleasant meadow on a high plateau. This meadow was part of a great table-land over-looking a wide stretch of country. The south side descended in a steep cliff, and up and down its slope the huts of a little village seemed to climb along the stony path that led to the plateau. Farther away lines of dark forest stretched off out of sight. On all sides were mountains, covered with trees or crowned with snow, from which, when the sun went down, the wind blew chill. Beyond the stream a highway climbed the valley, and the children could see, from their playground, the place where it issued from the edge of the wood and wound through a narrow pass among the hills.

Toward the north, and far overhead, rose the grim walls and towers of the great castle that watched the pass and sheltered the little village on the cliff-side. Those were rude, stern times, and the people in the village were often glad of the protection which the castle gave from attacks by stranger invaders; but they paid for their security from time to time when the defenders themselves sallied forth upon the hamlet and took toll from its flocks and herds.

It was "the evil time when there was no Emperor" in Germany. Of real rule there was none in the land, but every man held his life in his own charge. Knights sworn to deeds of mercy and bravery, returning from the holy war at Jerusalem, were undone by the lawlessness of the times, and, forgetful of all knightly vows, turned robbers and foes where they should have been warders and helpers. The lesser nobles and landholders were become freebooters and plunderers, while the common people, pillaged and oppressed by these, had few rights and less freedom.

The children under the oak-trees played at knights and robbers. Neighboring the meadow was the common pasture where tethered goats and sheep, and large, slow cattle, stood them as great flocks and caravans to sally out upon and harry. Now and again a party would break forth from one clump of trees to raid their playmates in a pretended village within another. Of storming castles, or of real knight's play, they knew naught; for they were of the common people, poor working-folk sunk to a state but little above thraldom, and they heard, in the guarded talk of their elders, stories only of the robber-knights' dark acts, never of deeds daring and true, such as belong to unspotted knighthood.

As the young folk lay in make-believe ambush among the shrubbery near the edge of the plateau, Ludovic, the oldest boy, suddenly called to them to look where, from the forest, a figure on horseback was coming out upon the highway.

"See!" Ludovic cried. "Yonder comes a sightly knight. Look, Hansei, at his shining armor and his glittering lance."

"He is none of hereabout," nodded Hansei, flashing his wide blue eyes upon the gleaming figure. "My lord's men-at-arms are none so shining fair. Whence may he be, Ludovic?"

"How should I know?" asked Ludovic, testily, with the older boy's vexation when a youngster asks him that which he cannot answer. "Small chance he bringeth good," added he, "wherever he be from; but, in any case, let us lie here until he passes."

"He weareth a long ruddy beard," said keen-eyed Gretel, as a slight bend in the road brought the knight full-facing the group.

"It is no long beard," said Hansei, who had been watching eagerly. "'Tis something that he bears before him at his saddle-peak."

This was, indeed, true. The shining stranger, as the children could now plainly see, held in front of him, on the saddle-peak, a good-sized burden, though what it was the young watchers could not, for the distance, make out. Nevertheless, they could see that it was no common burden; nor, in truth, was it any common figure that rode along the highway. He was still some distance off, but already the children began to hear the ring of the great horse's iron hoofs on the stones of the road, and the jangle of metal about the rider when sword and armor clashed out their music to the time of trotting hoofs. But as they watched and harkened, their delight and wonder ever growing, there came suddenly to their ears, when the knight had now drawn much closer, the tuneful winding of a horn.

The rider on the highway heard the sound as well; but, to the children's amazement, instead of pricking forward the faster, like a knight of hot courage, he drew rein and turned half-way about, as minded to seek shelter among the willows growing along stream. There was no shelter there, however, for man or horse, and on the other hand the narrowing valley shut the road in, with no footing up the wooded bluff. When the knight saw all this, he rode close into the thicket, and leaning from his saddle, dropped, with wondrous gentleness, his burden among the willows.

"'Tis some treasure," murmured Ludovic. "He fears the robber-knights may get it."

By now there showed, coming down the pass, another knight; but the second comer was no such goodly figure as the one below. His armor, instead of gleaming in the sunlight, was tarnished and stained. His helmet was black and unplumed, and upon his shield appeared the white cross of a Crusader. Nevertheless, albeit of no glistening splendor, he was of right knightly mien, and the horse he bestrode was a fine creature, whose springy step seemed to scorn the road he trod.

"'Tis a knight from the castle," the children said, and Hansei added, "Mighty Herr Banf it is, I know him by his white cross. Now there will be fighting!"

Down below, where the road widened a bit, winding with a bend of the stream, the shining stranger sat his horse, waiting, lance at rest, to see what the black knight would do. The moment the latter espied him he left the matter in no doubt, but couched his lance, and bore hard along the road, as minded to make an end of the stranger; whereupon the latter urged forward his own steed, and the two came together with a huge rush, so that the crash of armor against armor rang out fierce and clear up the pass, and both spears were shattered in the onset.

Then the two knights fought with their swords, dealing such blows as seemed to the children, watching, enough to fell forest trees. They wheeled their horses and dashed at each other again and again, until the air was filled with the din of fighting, and the young watchers were spellbound at the sight.

The shining stranger was a knight of valor, despite the unwillingness he first showed. He laid on stoutly with his blade, so that more than once his foe reeled in the saddle; but the black knight came back each time with greater fury, while the stranger and his horse were plainly weary.

Especially was this true of the horse. Still eagerly he wheeled and sprang forward to each fresh charge; but each time he dashed on more heavily, and more than once he stumbled, so that his rider missed a blow, and was like to have come to the ground through the empty swing of his sword.

At last the Crusader came on with mighty force, whereupon his foe charged again to meet him; but the weary horse stumbled, caught himself, staggered forward a pace or two, and came first to his knees, then shoulder down, upon the rough stones of the road. The shining knight pitched forward over his head and lay quite still in the highway, while the Crusader reined in beside him with threatening blade, and shout-

The two knights wheeled their horses and dashed at each other again and again.

ed to him to cry "quits." But the stranger neither moved nor spoke; so the other alighted from his horse, and bent over him to see his face.

When he had done this he drew back, and putting his horn to his lips, blew four great blasts, which he repeated again and again, waiting after each to listen.

Presently an answering horn sounded in the distance, and a little later a party of mounted men came dashing down the road from the castle. These clustered about the fallen knight, and when one, who seemed to be their leader, and whom the children knew for Baron Everhardt himself, saw the stranger's face, he turned to the victor and for very joy smote him between the iron-clad shoulders, from which the children thought that the new-comer could have been no friend of their baron.

Then the men stooped and, by main force, lifted the limp figure in its jangling armor, and set it astride the great horse that stood stupidly by as wondering what had befallen his master. The latter made no move, but lay forward on the good

Putting his horn to his lips, he blew four great blasts.

steed's neck, and so they made him fast, after doing which the whole party turned their faces upward, and rode along toward the castle.

Not until the last sound died away up the pass did the children come out from their amazement and great awe. They drew back from the edge of the cliff and looked wonderingly at one another, for it seemed to them as if years must have gone by since they had begun their play on the plateau. At last Ludovic spoke.

"The treasure is still among the willows," he said. "When night falls, Hansei, thou and I will slip down across the stream and find it. There may be great riches there. But no word about it; for if they knew it at the castle we should lose our pains."

Solemnly Hansei agreed to Ludovic's plan, and the children left the plateau, thinking of all that they had seen, and silently climbed down the path to their homes along the cliff.

CHAPTER TWO: HOW KARL THE ARMORER TOOK THE SHINING KNIGHT'S TREASURE FROM AMONG THE WILLOWS

THE CHILDREN HAD scarcely gone from the plateau when there came down the defile from the castle a tall, broad-shouldered man, clad in leather that was worn and creased, showing much hard wear. Over his left shoulder he carried two great swords in their scabbards, and his right hand gripped a long, stout staff. The face beneath his hood was brown and weather-beaten, of long and thoughtful mold, but turned from overmuch sternness by the steady, kindly gleam of his gray eyes.

Had the children still been upon the plateau they would have known the figure for Karl of the forge in the forest below the village. He had been, as was often his errand, to the castle, this time with a breastlet that he had wrought for the baron, and was returning with the very sword wherewith the Herr Banf had made end of the shining knight, and with that blade also which had been the stranger's own, to make good all hurts to their tempered edges and fit them for further service in battle.

He swung along the descending road until he came over against the place by the clump of willows, where the children had seen the knight drop his burden. There he suddenly stopped, and leaned to listen. He thought that he heard a faint cry from the green tangle; so he waited a little space, to learn if it would sound again. Sure enough, it came a second time—a feeble, piteous moan, as of some young creature in distress, and spent with long wailing.

He plunged in among the willows; but he had gone but a step or two when he started back in dismay, for he had nearly trodden upon a yellow-haired babe who sat among the willows. He reached up his arms, and Karl stooped and raised him to his broad chest.

"Now, what foul work is here?" he muttered to himself. "This is no chick from the village, nor from the castle either, or there would have been hue and cry ere this!"

He pressed back the little face that had been buried against his neck, and surveyed it sharply.

"What is thy name, little one?" he demanded.

At sound of the armorer's voice the child again looked at him, and seemed not to understand the question until Karl had several times repeated it, saying the words slowly and plainly, when at last the baby said, with a touch of impatience: "Wulf, Wulf," adding plaintively: "Wulf hungry."

Then he broke down and sobbed tiredly on Karl's big shoulder, so that the armorer was fain to hush him softly, comforting him with wonderful gentleness, while he drew from his own wallet a bit of coarse bread and gave it to the little fellow. The latter ate it with a sharp appetite, and afterward drank a deep draught from the leather cup which Karl filled from the stream. As he was drinking, a sound was heard, as of someone passing on the road, whereupon the boy became suddenly still, looking at Karl in a way that made the armorer understand that for some reason it had been taught him that unknown sounds were a signal for silence.

"Ay?" thought Karl. "That's naught like a baby. He has been with hunted men to learn that trick."

When the child had eaten and drunk all he would, he settled down again in

Karl's arms, asking no questions, if, indeed, he could talk enough to do so, a matter of which the armorer doubted; for the little chap was but three or four years old at most. He took it kindly when Karl settled him against his shoulder, throwing over him a sort of short cloak of travel-stained red stuff, in which he had been wrapped as he lay among the willows, and stepped out upon the road. He first made sure that no one was in sight; then he walked hurriedly forward, minded to leave the highway as soon as he reached a little foot-path he knew that led through the forest to his forge.

Good fortune favored him, and he gained the foot-path without meeting any one; so that, ere long, the two were passing through the deep, friendly wood, the baby fast asleep in Karl's arms. Karl stepped softly as any woman, lest his charge awaken.

Thus they fared, until at last they reached the forge and the hut where the armorer dwelt alone. Karl laid little Wulf upon a heap of skins just beyond the great chimney, and began to prepare food for himself and his charge.

CHAPTER THREE: HOW WULF FARED AT KARL THE ARMORER'S HUT

BIG KARL THE ARMORER was busy at his forge, next morning, long before his wee guest awakened. Working with deft lightness of hand at a small, long anvil close beside the forge, Karl had tempered and hammered the broken point of Herr Banf's sword until the stout blade was again ready for yeoman service, and then he turned to the stranger knight's blade, which was broken somewhat about the hilt and guard.

It was a good weapon, and as Karl traced his finger thoughtfully down its length, he turned it toward the open door, that the early sunlight might catch it. Then he suddenly gave a start, and hastily carried the sword out into the full daylight, where he stared it over closely from hilt to point, turning it this way and that, with knit brows and a look of deep sorrow on his browned visage. After that he strode into the smithy, and went over to where the boy lay, still fast asleep.

Turning him over upon the pelts, he studied the little face as sharply as he had done the sword, noting the broad white brow, the delicate round of the cheek, and the set of the chin, firm despite its baby curves; and as he did so a great sternness came over the face of the armorer.

"There's some awful work here," he said at last to himself. "Heaven be praised I came upon the little one! Would that I might have had a look at the face of that big knight."

Still musing, he turned and went to a cleverly hid cupboard in the wall beside the great chimney. Opening this, he disclosed an array of blades of many sorts and shapes, and from among these he took one that in general appearance seemed the fellow of the stranger's weapon, save that it had, to all look, seen but scant service in warfare.

Karl compared the two, and then set to a strange task. Hanging the service-battered sword naked within the cupboard, he took the new blade and began to ill-treat it upon his anvil: battering the hilt, taking a bit of metal from the guard, and putting nicks into the edge, only to beat and grind them very carefully out again. He took a bottle of acid from a shelf and spilled a few drops where blade met hilt, wiping it off again when it had

Little Wulf in the doorway of the armorer's forge

somewhat stained and roughened the steel. This roughness he afterward smoothed away, and worked at the sword until he had it looking like a badly used tool put in good order by a skilful smith.

This done, he sheathed it in the scabbard which the stranger had worn, and which was a fair sheath, wrought with gold ornaments cunningly devised. Karl looked at it with longing.

"I'd like well to save it for ye, youngster," he said; "but 'tis a fair risk as it stands. Let Herr Ritter Banf alone for having spied the gold o' this sheath; it must e'en go back to him." He laid the sheathed weapon away in a chest with Herr Banf's own until such time as he should make his next trip to the castle.

He had hardly done when, turning, he beheld the child watching him from the pile of skins, looking at the strange scene about him, but keeping quiet, though the tender lips quivered and the look in the blue eyes filled Karl with pity.

"There's naught to fear, little one," he said with gruff kindness, lifting the boy from the pile. And from out the coals of the forge he drew a pannikin, where it had been keeping warm some porridge.

Very gently he proceeded to give the porridge to the child, with some rich goat's milk to help it along. In truth, however, it needed not that to give the boy an appetite. He ate in a half-famished way that touched Karl's heart.

"In sooth, now," the latter said, watching him, "thou'st roughed it, little one, and much I marvel what it all may mean. But one thing sure, this is no time to be asking about the farings of any of *thy* breed, so thou shalt e'en bide here with old Karl till these evil days lighten, or Count Rudolph comes to help the land—if it be not past helping. It'll be hard fare for thee, my sweet, but there's no doing other. The castle yonder were worse for thee than the forge here with Karl."

"Karl?" The child spoke with the fearless ease of one wonted, even thus early, to question strangers and to be answered by them.

"Ay, Karl," replied the armorer. "Karl, who will be father and mother to thee till such time as God sends thee to thine own again."

"Good Karl," said the baby, when the man ceased speaking, and he reached out his hands to the armorer. The latter lifted him and carried him to the forge door.

"Thou 'rt a sturdy rascal," he said, nodding approval of the firm, well-knit little figure. "Sit thou there and finish the porridge."

The little fellow sat in the wide door of the smithy and ate his coarse food with a relish good to see. It was a rough place into which he had tumbled—how rough, he was too young as yet to realize; but much worse, even of outward things, might have fallen to his share.

Big Karl at his forge knew naught of books, and to him, in those evil days, had come much knowledge of the cruelty and wickedness of evil men. Nevertheless, safe within his strong nature dwelt the child-soul, unhurt by all these. It looked from his honest blue eyes, and put tenderness into the strength of his great hands when he touched the other child, and this child-soul was to be the boy's playmate through the years of childhood; a wholesome playmate it was, keeping Wulf company cleanly wise, and no harm came to him, but rather good.

Then, besides the ministering care of the gentle, manly big armorer, little Wulf had, through those years, the teaching and companionship of the great forest. It grew close up about the shop, so that its small wild life constantly came in at the open doors, or invited the youngster forth to play. Rabbits and squirrels peeped in at him; birds wandered in and built their nests in dark corners; and one winter a vixen fox took shelter with them, remaining until spring, and grew so tame that she would eat bread from Wulf's hand.

The great trees were his constant companions and friends, but one mighty oak that grew close beside the door, and sent out its huge arms completely over the shop, became, next to Karl, his chosen comrade. Whenever the armorer had to go to village or castle, Wulf used to take shelter in this tree, not so much from fear—for even in those evil days the armorer's grandson, as he grew to be regard-ed by those who came about the forge, was too insignificant to be molested—but because of his love for the great tree. As he became older he was able to climb higher and higher among its black arms, until at last he made him a nest in the very crown of the wood giant.

Every tree, throughout its life, stores up within its heart light and heat from the sun. It does this so well, because it is its appointed task in nature, that the very life and love that the sun stands for to us become a part of its being, knit up within its woody fiber. When we burn this wood in our stoves or our fireplaces the warmth and blaze that are thrown out are just this sunshine which the tree has caught in its heart from the time it was a tiny seedling till the ax was laid at its root. So, when we sit by the coal fire and enjoy its genial radiance, we are really warming ourselves by some of the same sunlight and warmth that sifted down through the leaves of great forest trees—perhaps thousands of years ago.

Into Wulf's sound young heart there crept, as the years went by, somewhat of the strength and the sunshine-storing quality of his forest comrade, until, long before he became a man, those who knew him grew to feel that here was a strong, warm heart of human sunshine, ready to be useful and comforting wherever use and comfort were needed.

At first faint memories haunted him; but as years went by, he learned to think of them as a part of one of Karl's stories, one that he always meant, sometime, to ask him to tell again. The years slipped away, however, and his childish impressions grew fainter and fainter, until at last they had quite faded into the far past.

CHAPTER FOUR: HOW WULF FIRST WENT TO THE CASTLE, AND WHAT BEFELL

FOR A MATTER of nine or ten years Wulf dwelt with Karl at the forge, and knew no other manner of life than if he had been indeed the armorer's own grandson. He was now a well-grown lad of perhaps fourteen years, not tall, but sturdy, strong of thigh and arm, and good to look at, with a ruddy color, fair hair, and steady eyes.

Karl had taught him to fence and thrust, and much of sword-play, in which the armorer was skilled, and while his play at these was that of a lad, the boy could fair-ly hold his own with cudgel and quarter-staff, and more than once had surprised Karl by a clever feint or twist or a stout blow, when, as was their wont on summer evenings, the two wrestled or sparred together on the short green grass under the great oak-tree.

He was happy, going about his work with the big armorer, or wandering up and down the forest, or, of long winter evenings, sitting beside the forge fire watching

Karl, who used to sit, knife in hand, deftly carving a long-handled wooden spoon, or a bowl. The women in the village were always glad to trade for these with fresh eggs, or a pat of butter, or a young fowl; for the armorer had as clever a knack with his knife as with his hammer.

It happened, at last, on a day when Karl was making ready to go to the castle with a corselet which he had mended for the baron himself, that the armorer met with an accident that changed Wulf's whole life. Karl was doing a bit of tinkering on the smaller anvil by the forge, when one support of the iron gave way, and it fell, crushing the great toe of one foot so that the stout fellow fairly rocked with the pain, while Wulf made haste to prepare a poultice of wormwood for the hurt member.

Despite all their skill, however, the toe continued to swell and to stiffen, until it was plain that all thought of Karl's climbing the mountain that day, or for many days to come, must be put aside.

"There's no help for it, lad," he said at last, as he sat on the big chest, scowling blackly at his foot in its rough swathings. "It's well on toward noon now, and the baron will pay me my wage on my own head if his corselet be not to hand today; for he rides tomorrow, with a company from the castle, on an errand beyond. Thou'lt need to take the castle road, boy, and speedily, if thou'rt to be back by night."

Nothing could have pleased Wulf more than such an errand; for although he often went with Karl on other matters about the country, and had even gone with him as far as the Convent of St. Ursula on the other side of the forest, the armorer, despite his entreaties, had never allowed him to go along when his way lay toward the Swartzburg. This had puzzled the boy greatly, for Karl steadfastly refused him any reason why it should be.

The boy made all haste, therefore, to get ready for the journey, lest Karl should repent of his plan. It was but the shortest of quarter-hours, in fact, before he was passing through the wood toward the road to the Swartzburg.

It was not so very long ere he had cleared the forest and was stepping up the rough stone road that climbed the mountain pass to the castle.

Up and up the stony way he trudged stoutly, until it became at last the merest bridle-path, descending to the open moat across which the bridge was thrown. On a tower above he descried the sentry, and below, beyond the bridge, the great gates into the castle courtyard stood open.

Doubting somewhat as to what he ought to do, he crossed the bridge and passed through the gloomy opening that pierced the thick wall. Once inside, he stood looking about him curiously, forgetful, in his wonder and delight at the scene, that Karl had told him to ask for Gotta Brent, Baron Everhardt's man-at-arms, and to deliver the corselet to him.

He was still without the inner wall of the castle, in a sort of courtyard of great size, the outer bailey of the stronghold. Beyond where he stood he could see a second wall with big gates, similar to the one through which he had just passed. Before these gates, in the outer court, two young men were fencing, while a third stood beside them, acting as a sort of umpire, or judge, of fence. The contestants were very equally matched, and Wulf watched them with keenest enjoyment. He had fenced with Karl, and once or twice a knight, while waiting at the forge, had deigned to pass the time in crossing blades with the boy, always to the latter's discomfiture; but he had never before stood by while two skilled men were at swordplay, and the sight held him spellbound.

Thanks to Karl, he was familiar with the mysteries of quart and tierce and all the rest, and followed with knowing delight each clever feint and thrust made with the grace and precision of good fence. He could watch forever, it seemed to him; but as he stood thus, following the beautiful play, out through the gate of the inner bailey came three children, a girl a year or two younger than he, and two boys about his own age.

He gave them but the briefest glance, for just at that moment the players began a new set-to that claimed his attention. A moment later, however, he felt a sharp buffet at the side of his head, and turning, saw that one of the boys had thrown the rind of a melon so as to strike him on the cheek. As Wulf looked around both the boys were laughing; but the little girl stood somewhat off from them, her eyes flashing and her cheeks aglow as with anger. She said no word, but looked with great scorn upon her companions.

"Well, tinker," called the boy who had thrown the melon-rind, "mind thy manners before the lady. Have off thy cap or thou'lt get this"; and he grasped the other half-rind of melon, which the second boy held.

"Nay, Conradt," the little maid cried, staying his hand. "The lad is a stranger, and come upon an errand. Do we treat such folk thus?"

Wulf's cap was by now in his hand, and, with crimson cheeks, he made a shy salutation to the little girl, who returned it courteously, while the boys still laughed.

"What dost thou next, tinker?" the one whom she had called Conradt said, strutting forward. "Faith, thy manners sorely need mending. What dost to me?"

"Fight thee," said Wulf, quick as a flash; and then drew back abashed, for as the boy came forward Wulf saw that he bore a great hump upon his twisted back, while one of his shoulders was higher than the other.

The deformed boy saw the motion, and his face grew dark with rage and hate.

"Thou'lt fight me?" he screamed, springing forward. "Ay, that thou shalt, and rue it after, tinker's varlet that thou art!" And with his hand he smote Wulf upon the mouth, whereupon Wulf dropped the corselet and clenched his fists, but could lay no blow on the pitiful creature before him. Seeing this, the other, half crazed with anger, drew a short sword which he wore, and made at Wulf, who raised the armorer's staff which he still held, and struck the little blade to the ground.

By now the two fencers and their umpire were drawn near to see the trouble, and one of them picked up the sword.

"Come, cockerel," he said, restoring it to Conradt, "put up thy spur and let be. Now, lad, what is the trouble?" and he turned sharp upon Wulf.

"'Tis the armorer's cub," he said to his companions as he made him out. "By the rood, lad, canst not come on a small errand for thy master without brawling in this fashion in the castle yard? Go do thy message, and get about home, and bid thy master teach thee what is due thy betters ere he sends thee hither again."

"Yon lad struck me," Wulf said stoutly. "I've spoken no word till now."

"Truly, Herr Werner," put in the little girl, earnestly, "it is as he says. Conradt has e'en gone far out of his way to show the boy an ill will, though he has done naught."

At this Herr Werner looked again upon Conradt. "So, cockerel," he said; "didst not get wisdom from the last pickle I pulled thee out of?"

"Why does the fellow hang about here, then?" demanded Conradt, sulkily. "Let him go to the stables, as he should, and leave his matter there."

"I was to see Gotta Brent," Wulf said, ignoring Conradt and speaking to the young knight.

"See him thou shalt," was the reply. But anything further that Herr Werner might have said was cut short by the sound of a great hue and cry of men, and a groom ran through the gate shouting:

"Back! Back for your lives! The foul fiend himself is loose here!"

At his heels came half a dozen men with stable-forks and poles, and two others who were hanging with all their weight upon the bridle-reins of a great horse that was doing his best to throw off their hold, rearing and plunging furiously, and now and again lashing out with his iron-shod hoofs.

There was a hurrying to shelter in the group about Wulf, who soon stood alone, staring at the horse. The latter finally struck one of the grooms, so that the fellow lay where he rolled, at one side of the court; and then began a battle royal between horse and men.

One after another, and all together, the men tried to lay hold upon the dangling rein, only to be bitten, or struck, or tossed aside, as the case might be, until at last the huge beast stood free in the middle of the court, while the grooms and stable-hangers made all haste to get out of the way, some limping, others rubbing heads or shoulders, and one nursing a badly bitten arm.

"Tinker," called the knight, from behind an abutment of the wall, "art clean daft? Get away before he makes a meal off thee! Gad! 'Twill take an arrow to save him now, and for that any man's life would be forfeit to Herr Banf."

There was a scream from the little girl, for the horse had spied Wulf, and came edging toward him, looking wild enough, with ears laid back and teeth showing, as minded to make an end to the boy, as doubtless he was. For the life of him Wulf could not have told why he was not afraid as he stood there alone, and with no weapon save the armorer's staff, which he had not time to raise ere the beast was upon him.

Then were all who looked on amazed at what they saw; for close beside Wulf the horse stopped, and began smelling the boy. Then he took to trembling in all his legs, and arched his neck and thrust his big head against Wulf's breast, until, half dazed, the boy raised a hand and began patting the broad neck and stroking the mane of the charger.

"By the rood," cried one of the grooms, "the tinker hath the horseman's word, and no mistake! The old imp knows it."

"See if thou canst take the halter, boy," called Herr Werner; and laying a hand upon the rein, Wulf stepped back a pace, whereupon the horse pressed close to him and whinnied eagerly, as if fearful that Wulf would leave him. He smelled him over again, thrusting his muzzle now into Wulf's hands, now against his face,

The boy began to pat the neck of the charger.

and putting up his nose to take the boy's breath, as horses do with those they love.

"By my forefathers!" cried Herr Werner. "Could Herr Banf see him now—aha!"

He paused, for, hurrying into the courtyard, followed by still another frightened groom, came a knight who, seeing Wulf and the horse, stood as if rooted in his tracks. Softly now the charger stepped about the boy, nickering under his breath, so low that his nostrils hardly stirred, stooping meekly, as one who loved a service he would do, and thus waited.

An instant Wulf stood dazed; then he passed his hand across his forehead, for a strange, troubled notion, as of some forgotten dream, passed through his brain. At last, obeying some impelling instinct that yet seemed to him like a memory, he laid a hand upon the horse's withers and sprang to his back.

Up then pranced the noble creature, and stepped about the courtyard, tossing his head and gently champing the bit, as a horse will when he is pleased.

"Ride him to the stables, boy, and I will have word with thee there," cried the older knight, who had come out last; and pressing the rein, though still wondering to himself how he knew what to do, Wulf turned the steed through the inner gate to the bailey, and letting him have his head, was carried proudly to the stables whence the throng of grooms and stable-boys had come rushing. They came to the group of outbuildings and offices that made up the stables, followed by all the men, Herr Banf in the lead, and the place, which had been quite deserted, was immediately thronged, attendants from the castle itself coming on a run as news spread of the wonderful thing that was happening.

Once within the stable-yard, the horse stood quiet, to let Wulf dismount; but not even Herr Banf himself would he let lay a hand upon him, though he stood meek as a sheep while the boy, instructed by the knight, took off the bridle and fastened on the halter. Then he led his charge into a stall that one of the lads pointed out to him, and made him fast before the manger. When this was done, the horse gave a rub of his head against Wulf, and then turned to eating his fodder quietly, as though he had never done otherwise.

Then Herr Banf took to questioning Wulf sharply; but very little could the boy tell him. Indeed, some instinct warned him against speaking even of the faint thoughts stirring within him. He was full of anxiety to get away to Karl and tell *him* of this wonderful new experience, and he could say naught to the knight save that he was Karl the armorer's grandson; that he had never had the care of horses, and in his life had mounted but few, chiefly those of the men-at-arms who rode with their masters to the forge when Karl's skill was needed. He was troubled, too, about Karl's hurt, of which he told Herr Banf, and begged to be allowed to hasten back to the smithy.

"Go, then," said Herr Banf, at last, "and I will see thy grandsire tomorrow. Thou'rt too promising a varlet to be left to grow up an armorer. We need thy kind elsewhere."

So, when he had given the nearly forgotten corselet to Gotta Brent, Wulf fared down the rocky way to the forge, where he told Karl all that had chanced to him that day.

"Let that remain with thee alone, boy," the armorer said, when the boy had told him of the strange memories that teemed in his brain. "These are no times to talk of such matters an thou'dst keep a head on thy shoulders. Thou'rt of my own raising, Wulf; but more than that I cannot tell thee, for I do not know." And there the lad was forced to let the matter rest.

"It is all one with my dreams," he said to himself, as he sought his bed of skins. "Mayhap other dreams will make it clearer."

But no dreams troubled his healthy boy's sleep that night, nor woke he until the morning sun streamed full in his upturned face.

CHAPTER FIVE: HOW WULF WENT TO THE SWARTZBURG, AND OF HIS BEGINNING THERE

IT WAS MAYBE a week after Wulf's visit to the Swartzburg that Herr Banf rode through the forest to the smithy. He was mounted upon the great stallion that had been so wild that day, and as he drew rein before the shop the horse gave a shrill neigh, for he smelled Wulf. Karl's foot was by so far mended that he was able to limp about the forge, and he and the boy were busy mending a wrought tunic of fine chain mail which the lady superior of St. Ursula had sent to them that morning.

"A fair day, friend Karl," the knight called out as he sat his horse under the big oak-tree. "Here am I come for that youngster of thine. He is too useful a scamp to be let spend his days tinkering here. Haply he has told thee how this big 'Siegfried' of mine took to him. I' faith, not a groom at the castle can handle the horse!"

"Ay?" said Karl, and he said no more, but stood with hands folded upon the top of his hammer, and looked steadily at Herr Banf. Wulf, meanwhile, had dropped the tongs that he held, and run out to the horse, who now stood nuzzling his neck and face in great delight.

"By the rood," cried Herr Banf, "'tis plain love at first sight! If any other came so near Siegfried's teeth, I'd look to see him eaten. I must have the boy, Karl!"

Now, that great horse was none other than the one which the shining knight had ridden on the day of his meeting with Herr Banf. The Crusader had taken the beast for his own charger, and a rare war-horse he was, but getting on in years by now, and turning wild at times, after the manner of his kind. Not a groom or stable-lad about the castle but had reason to know his temper; so that, because of their fear of him, the horse often lacked for care.

When Herr Banf had said that Wulf must come with him, Karl stood silent, watching the lad and Siegfried; but in a moment he said:

"In truth, they seem fast friends. Well, it shall be as the boy says."

"For what he says I will undertake," the knight said, laughing. "Wilt come to the castle, lad?"

Wulf looked from the horse to Karl and back again. It was easy to see where his desire lay.

"Shall I be able to see Grandsire Karl now and then?" he asked, turning to Herr Banf.

"As often as need be," said the knight.

"What shall I say?" Wulf turned to Karl.

"What thou wilt," the armorer nodded. "We have talked o' that."

So had they, and Wulf's question was but the last wavering of the boy's heart, loath to leave all it had yet known. In another moment his will regained its strength, and the matter ended in his taking again the climbing road up the Swartzburg pass, this time with a hand clinging to Herr Banf's stirrup-leather, while the great horse stepped gently, keeping pace with the boy's stride.

"Where didst thou learn to bewitch a horse, lad?" the knight asked as they journeyed. "What is thy 'horseman's word'?"

"I have none," was the reply. "The horse seemed to know me, and I him. I cannot tell how or other."

"By my forefathers, but beasts be hard to understand as men! What was't thou didst, by the way, to the little crooked cock at the castle?"

"Him they call Conradt, Herr Knight? I did naught."

"Well, he means to fight thee for it."

"Nay," replied Wulf, "that he'll not."

"How is that?"

"It would not be becoming for me to fight him."

"So," Herr Banf said grimly. "Thou'st a good idea of what is due thy betters."

"It is not that," explained Wulf, simply. "I am the better of us two; a whole man goes not against a weakling."

The knight looked keenly down at the lad, noting, as he had not done before, the easy movement of his body as he stepped lightly along, more like a soldier than like a peasant. He was alert and trim, with shapely shoulders and the head carried well up.

"A queer armorer's lad, this," thought Herr Banf, in some wonder. But by now they were before the castle watch-tower, and in a moment more, still with one hand at the knight's stirrup, Wulf again entered at the castle gate. There, in the outer bailey, Herr Banf lighted down, and bade Wulf take Siegfried to the stables for the night.

It was Hansei (now grown to young manhood) who at supper-time took him into the great hall where the household and its hangers-on gathered for meals, and got for him a trencher and food, though little cared Wulf for eating on that first night, when all was new and strange to him.

The hall was very large, and Wulf, looking up toward its lofty roof, could not see its timbers for the deep shadows there. At either end was a great fireplace, but the one at the upper end was the larger and finer. Near it, on a platform raised above the earthen floor, Baron Everhardt sat at board, with the knights of his train. Below them were the men-at-arms and lower officers of the castle, and seated upon benches about the walls were the fighting-men and general hangers-on of the place.

These sat not at board, but helped themselves to the food that was passed about among them after the tables were served, and ate, some from their hands, others from wooden trenchers which they had secured. Wulf and Hansei were among the lowliest of the lot, and the stable-boys did not sit down at all, but took their supper standing, leaning against the wall just inside the door, and farthest from the hearth, and they were among the last served.

But, as we have seen, Wulf cared little that night for food or drink, though his new friend pressed him to eat. Soon the great tankards began to pass from hand to hand; and the men drank long and deep, while loud jests and mighty laughter filled all the place, until only Wulf's sturdy boy's pride kept him from stealing out, through the darkness, back to Karl at the forge.

Presently, however, he began to notice faces among the company at the upper end of the hall. Two or three ladies were present, having come in by another door when the meal was well over, and these were sitting with the baron and Herr Banf. One of the ladies, Hansei told him, was the baron's lady, and with her, Wulf noticed, was the little girl whom he had seen at the time of his first visit to the castle.

"Who is she?" he asked.

"A ward of our baron's," Hansei answered, "and she is the Fräulein Elise von Hofenhoer. They say she is to be married, in good time, to young Conradt, the nephew of our baron; and that, methinks, is a sorry fate for any maiden."

"Conradt?"

"Yea; the crooked stick yonder, the baron's precious nephew."

Following Hansei's glance, Wulf descried the hunchback boy of his adventure, seated at board, drinking from a great mug of ale. With him was the other boy, who, Hansei told him, was Waldemar Guelder, and some kin to Herr Banf, in whose charge he was, to be trained as a knight.

"He's not such a bad one," the stable-boy said, "an it were not for Master Conradt, who would drag down the best that had to do with him."

Thus, one by one, Hansei pointed out knights and followers, squires and men, until in Wulf's tired brain all was a jumble of names and faces that he knew not. Glad indeed was he when at last his companion nodded to him, and slipping out from the hall, they made their way to the horse-barn, where, up under the rafters of a great hay-filled loft, the pair made their beds in the fragrant grasses, and slept soundly, until the stamping of horses below them, and the sunlight streaming into their faces through an open door of the loft, awakened them.

CHAPTER SIX: HOW CONRADT PLOTTED MISCHIEF, AND HOW WULF WON A FRIEND

IT WAS PERHAPS a matter of six weeks after Wulf's coming to the Swartzburg that he sat, one day, in a wing of the stables, cleaning and shining Herr Banf's horse-gear. He was alone at the time, for most of the castle-folk had ridden with the baron on a freebooting errand against a body of merchants known to be traveling that way with rich loads of goods and much money. Only Herr Werner, of all the knights, was at the castle.

Save for Hansei, who stood by him stoutly, Wulf had as yet made no friends among his fellow-workers; but full well had he shown himself able to take his own part, so that his bravery and prowess, and his heartiness to help whenever a lift or a hand was needed, had already won him a place and fair treatment among them. Moreover, his quick wit and craft with Siegfried, the terror of the stables, made the Master of Horse his powerful friend. And, again, Wulf was already growing well used to the ways of the place, so that it was with a right cheerful and contented mind that he sat, that day, scouring away upon a rusty stirrup-iron.

Presently it seemed to him that he heard a little noise from over by the stables, and peering along under the arch of the great saddle before him, he saw a puzzling thing. Crossing the stable floor with wary tread and watchful mien, as minded to do some deed privily, and fearful to be seen, was Conradt.

"Now, what may he be bent upon?" Wulf asked of his own thought. "No good, I'll lay wager"; and he sat very still, watching every movement of the little crooked fellow.

Down the long row of stalls went the hunchback, until he reached the large loose box where stood Siegfried. The stallion saw him, and laid back his ears, but made no further sign of noting the new-comer. Indeed, since Wulf had been his tender the old horse had grown much more governable, and for a month or more had given no trouble.

Conradt's face, however, as he drew nigh the stall, was of aspect so hateful and wicked that Wulf stilly, but with all speed, left his place and crept nearer, keeping in shelter behind the great racks of harness, to learn what might be toward. As he did so he was filled with amazement and wrath to see the hunchback, sword in hand, reach over the low wall of the stall and thrust at Siegfried. The horse shied over and avoided the blade, though, from the plunge he made, Wulf deemed that he had felt the point.

While the watcher stood dumfounded, wondering what the thing might mean, Conradt sneaked around to the other side, plainly minded to try that wickedness again, whereupon Wulf sprang forward, snatching up, on his way, a flail that lay to his hand, flung down by one of the men from the threshing-floor.

"Have done with you!" he called as he ran; and forgetting, in his wrath, both the rank and the weakness of the misdoer, he shrieked: "What is 'twouldst do? Out with it!" And he raised the flail.

Taken unaware though he was, Conradt, who was rare skilful at fence, guarded on the instant, and by a clever twist of his blade cut clean in twain the leather hinge that held together the two halves of the flail. 'Twas a master stroke whereat, angry as he was, Wulf wondered, nor could he withhold a swordsman's delight in the blow, albeit the sword's wielder was plain proven a ruffian.

He had small time to think, however, for by now Conradt let at him full drive, and he was sore put to it to fend himself from the onslaught, having no other weapon than the handle of the flail.

Evil was in the hunchback's eyes as he pressed up against his foe, as Wulf was not slow to be aware. The latter could do naught but fend and parry with his stick; but this he did with coolness and skill, as he stood back to wall against the stall, watching every move of that malignant being with whom he fought.

Up, down, in, out, thrust, parry, return! The sounds filled the barn. Wulf was the taller and equally skilled, but Conradt's weapon gave him an advantage that, but for the blindness of his hatred, would have won his way for him. But soon he was fair weary with fury, and Wulf began to think that he would soon make end of the trouble, when he felt a sharp prick, and something warm and wet began to trickle down his right arm, filling his hand. Conradt saw the stain and gave a joyful grunt.

"One for thee, tinker," he gasped, his breath nigh spent. "I'll let a little more of thy mongrel blood ere I quit."

"An thou dost," cried Wulf, stung to a fury he seldom felt, "save a drop for thyself. A little that's honest would not come amiss in the black stream in thy veins." And he guarded again as Conradt came on.

This the latter did with a rush, at which Wulf sprang aside, and ere his foe could whirl he came at him askance, catching his sword-hand just across the back of the wrist with the tip of his stick, so that, for an instant, Conradt's arm dropped, and the point of his blade touched the floor. 'Twas a trick in which Wulf felt little pride,

Wulf defends himself and the horse from Conradt.

though fair enough, and he did not follow up the advantage, knowing he had his enemy beaten for the time.

The hunchback stood glaring at Wulf, but ere he could move to attack again a voice cried: "Well done, tinker! An ye had a blade, our cockerel had crowed smaller, and I had missed a rare bit of sport."

On this both boys turned, for they knew that voice, and Herr Werner came forward, not laughing now, as mostly he was, but with a sterner look on his youthful face than even Conradt had ever seen.

"Now, then, how is this?" he demanded of Wulf. "What is this brawl about?"

The boy met Werner's eyes frankly. "He had best tell," he said, nodding toward Conradt.

"Suppose, then, thou dost," and Herr Werner looked at the hunchback, who, his eyes going down before the knight's, lied, as was his wont.

"He came at me with the flail, and," he added, unable to withhold bragging, "I clipped it for him."

"And what hadst thou done to make him come at thee?"

"I did but look at the horses, and stood to play with old Siegfried here. 'Tis become so that my uncle, the baron himself, may yet look to be called to account by this tinker's upstart."

The stern lines about Herr Werner's mouth grew deeper.

"Heed thou this, Conradt," he said with great earnestness. "Yonder was I, by the pillar, and saw this whole matter. What didst thou plan ill to the stallion for?"

"The truth is, not to have him hereabout," muttered Conradt, his face dark with fear and anger.

"These be my uncle's stables, and this great beast hath had tooth or hoof toll off everyone about the place."

"True, i' the main," Herr Werner said scornfully. "And for this, is it, that the baron thinketh to make thee Master of the Horse? Shall I tell him with what zeal thou followest thy duties?"

Conradt's face was fair distorted now. Fear of his uncle's wrath was the one thing that kept the wickedness of his evil nature in any sort of check, and well he knew how bitter would be his taste of that wrath should this thing come to the baron's ears.

So, too, knew Herr Werner, and, in less manner, Wulf; for his keen wit had taught him much during his six weeks' service at the castle.

"What shall I say to the baron of this?" demanded Herr Werner again, as he lowered above them.

"I care not," muttered Conradt, falsely.

But Wulf said: "Need aught be said, Herr Werner? I hold naught against him, save for Siegfried's sake"—with a loving glance over at the great horse—"and 'tis not likely he'll be at this mischief again."

"What say'st thou, my fine fellow?" asked the young knight of Conradt; but the latter said no word.

"Bah!" cried Herr Werner, at last. "In sooth, this tinker is at heart a truer man than thou on every showing. Get hence, that I waste on thee no more of the time that should go to his wound," he added; for Wulf, in moving his arm, had suddenly pinched, and his face was pale. In another moment Herr Werner had the hurt member in hand, and as he was, like most men of that rude time, somewhat skilled in caring for wounds, he had soon bandaged this one, which was of no great extent, but more painful than serious, and was quickly eased.

Meanwhile Conradt had moved off, leaving the two alone. Though it would never be set to his credit, his malice had wrought a good work; for in that hour our Wulf got himself a strong and true friend in the young knight, who was well won by the sterling stuff that showed in the lad.

"He hath more of knightliness in him, here in the stables," thought he, as he left Wulf, "than Conradt will ever know as lord of the castle; and, by my forefathers, he shall have what chance may be mine to give him!"

And that vow Herr Werner never forgot.

CHAPTER SEVEN: HOW WULF CLIMBED THE IVY TOWER, AND WHAT HE SAW AT THE BARRED WINDOW

GOOD AS HIS word had Herr Werner been in finding Wulf the chance to show that other stuff dwelt in him than might go to the making of a mere stable-lad. For the next three years he was under the young knight's helping protection, and, thanks to the latter's good offices in part, but in the end, as must always be the case with boy or man, thanks to his own efforts, he made so good use of his chance that his tinker origin was haply overlooked, if not forgotten, by those left behind him as he rose from height to height of the castle's life.

When all was said and done, 'twas hard to hold hatred of such a nature as his. The training of old Karl, and the forest, had done their work well with him, and he was still the simple, sunny-hearted Wulf of the forge, ever ready to help, and forgiving even where forgiveness was unsought. He was by now a sturdy, broad-chested young fellow, getting well on to manhood, noted for his strength and for his skill in all the games and feats of prowess and endurance that were a part of the training of boys in those days. Already had he ridden with Herr Werner in battle, and the baron himself had more than once taken note of the youth, and had on two occasions made him his messenger on errands both perilous and nice, calling for wit as well as bravery.

Only Conradt hated him still—Conradt, with the sorry, twisted soul, that held to hatred as surely as Wulf held to love. He was a year or two older than Wulf, and was already a candidate for knighthood; for, despite his crooked body, he was skilled beyond many who rode in his uncle's following in all play at arms. There was no better swordsman, even among the younger knights, and among the bowmen he had already a name.

Despite all this, however, the baron's nephew was held in light esteem, even among that train of robbers and bandits—for naught better were they, in truth, despite their knighthood and their gentlehood. They lived by foray and pillage and petty warfare with other bands like themselves, and in many a village were dark stories whispered of their wild raids.

Yet few even of his own followers would hold long or close fellowship with Conradt, albeit they dared not openly flout the baron's nephew.

Well knew the baron, overlord of all that district, of the doings of his doughty nephew; but for reasons of his own he saw fit to wink at them, save when some worse infamy than common was brought to his notice in such fashion that he could not pass it by. He were a brave man, however, who could dare the baron's wrath so far as to complain lightly to him of Conradt, so the fellow went for the most part scot-free of his misdeeds, save so far as he might feel the scorn and shunning of his equals.

It was on a bright autumn afternoon that a company of the boys and younger men of the Swartzburg were trying feats of strength and of athletic skill before the castle, in the inner bailey. From a little balcony overlooking the terrace the ladies of the household looked down upon the sports, to which their presence gave more than ordinary zest. Among the ladies was Elise, now grown a fair maiden of some fifteen years. Well was she known to be meant by the baron for the bride of his nephew; but this knowledge among the youths of the place did not hinder many a quick glance from wandering her way, and already had more than one young squire chosen her as the lady of his worship, for whose sake he pledged himself, as the manner of the time was, to deeds of bravery and high virtue.

The contestants in the courtyard had been wrestling and racing. There had been tilts with the spear, and bouts with the fists and of sword-play, when at last one of the number challenged his fellows to a climbing trial of the hardest sort.

Just where the massive square bulk of the keep raised its grim stories a great buttress thrust boldly out from the castle, running up beside the wall of the tower for a considerable distance. The two were just enough apart to be firmly touched on either side by a man who might stand between them, and it was a mighty test of courage and strength for a man to climb up between them, even a few yards, by hand and foot pressure only. It was the great feat to perform among the more ambitious knights and squires about the castle.

The challenger on this afternoon was young Waldemar Guelder, Herr Banf's ward, now grown a stalwart squire; and he raised himself, by sheer strength of grip and pressure of foot and open hand against the rough stones, up and up, until he reached the point, some thirty feet above ground, where the buttress bent in to the main wall again, and gave no further support to the climber, who was fain to come down quickly and by the same way as he went up.

Shouts of "Well done! Well done!" greeted Waldemar's deed when he reached the ground, panting, but flushed with pride, and looked up toward the balcony, whence came a clapping of fair hands and waving of white kerchiefs in token that his prowess had been noted.

Then one after another made trial of the feat; but none, not even Conradt, who was accounted among the skilfulest climbers, was able to reach the mark set by young Guelder, until, last of all, for he had given place time after time to his eagerer fellows, Wulf's turn came.

He, too, glanced up at the balcony as he began the ascent, and Elise, meeting his glance, smiled down upon him. These two were good friends, in a frank fashion little common in that time, when the merest youths deemed it their duty to throw a tinge of sentimentality into their relation with all maids.

Conradt noted their glances, and glowered at Wulf as the latter prepared to climb. No sneer of his had ever moved Elise to treat "the tinker" with scorn. Indeed, Conradt sometimes fancied that her friendship for Wulf was in despite of him, and of the mastership he often tried to assert over her. That, however, was impossible to an honest nature like Elise. She was Wulf's friend because of her hearty trust in him and liking for him, and so she leaned forward now, eager to see what he might do toward meeting Waldemar's feat.

Steadily Wulf set hands and feet to the stones, and braced himself for the work.

Reach by reach he raised himself higher, higher, until it was plain to all that he would find it no task to climb to where the champion had gone.

"He'll win to it!" cried one and then another of the watchers, and Waldemar himself shouted out encouragement to the climber when once he seemed to falter.

At last came a cry from Hansei: "He has it! Hurrah! Hurrah!" And a general shout went up. From the balcony, too, came the sound of applause as Wulf reached the top of the buttress.

"In truth, our tinker hath mounted in the world," sneered Conradt from the terrace. "Well, there's naught more certain than that he'll come down again."

Wulf heard the words, as Conradt meant he should, and caught, as well, the laugh that rose from some of the lower fellows. Then a murmur of surprise went through the company.

The walls of the keep were overgrown with ivy, so that only here and there a mere shadow showed where a staircase window pierced the stones. In the recess where the young men were wont to climb, the vines were torn down, but above the buttress, over both keep and castle, the great branches grew and clung, reaching clean to the top of the tower; and Wulf, unable to go farther between the walls, was now pulling himself up along the twisted ivy growth that covered the face of the tower.

On he went, minded to reach the top and scale the battlement. It was no such great feat, the lower wall once passed, but none of the watchers below had ever thought to try it, so were they surprised into the more admiration, while in the balcony was real fear for the adventurous climber.

He reached the top in safety, however, and passing along the parapet just below the battlement, turned a corner and was lost to their sight.

On the farther side of the keep he found, as he had deemed likely, that the ivy gave him safe and easy support to the ground, so lowering himself to the vines again, he began the descent.

He had gone but a little way when, feeling with his feet for a lower hold, he found none directly under him, but was forced to reach out toward the side to get it, from which he judged that he must be opposite a window, and lowering himself further, he came upon two upright iron bars set in a narrow casement nearly overgrown with ivy. Behind the bars all seemed dark; but as Wulf's eyes became wonted to the dimness, he became aware, first of a shadowy something that seemed to move, then of a face gaunt, white, and drawn, with great, unreasoning eyes that stared blankly into his own.

He felt his heart hammering at his ribs as he stared back. The piteous, vacant eyes seemed to draw his very soul, and a choking feeling came in his throat. For a full moment the two pairs of eyes gazed at each other, until Wulf felt as if his heart would break for sheer pity; then the white face behind the bars faded back into the darkness, and Wulf was ware once more of the world without, the yellow, autumnal sunshine, and the green ivy with its black ropes of twisted stems, that were all that kept him from dashing to death on the stones of the courtyard below.

So shaken was he by what he had seen that he could scarcely hold by his hands while he reached for foothold. Little by little, however, he gathered strength, and came to himself again, until by the time he reached the ground he was once more able to face his fellows, who gathered about, full of praise for his feat.

But little cared our Wulf for their acclaim when, glancing up toward the balcony, he caught the wave of a white hand. His heart nearly leaped from his throat, a second later, as he saw a little gleam of color, and was

Wulf climbs the ivy on the tower and makes a strange discovery.

ware that the hand held a bit of bright ribband which presently fluttered over the edge of the balcony and down toward the terrace.

It never touched earth. There was a rush toward it by all the young men, each eager to grasp the token; but Wulf, with a leap that carried his outstretched hand high above the others, laid hold upon the prize and bore it quickly from out the press.

"'Tis mine! mine! Yield it!" screamed Conradt, rushing after him.

"Nay; that thou must prove," laughed Wulf; and winning easily away from the hunchback, he ran through the inner bailey to his own quarters, whence, being busy about some matters of Herr Werner's, he came not forth until nightfall. At that time Conradt did not see him; for the baron had summoned his nephew to him about a matter of which we shall hear more.

CHAPTER EIGHT: HOW BARON EVERHARDT WAS OUTLAWED, AND HOW WULF HEARD OF THE BABY IN THE WILLOWS

ONE BRIGHT MORNING, not long after Wulf had climbed the ivy tower, there came to the Swartzburg a herald bearing a message whereat Baron Everhardt laughed long and loud. So, also, laughed the youngerlings of the place when the thing came to be noised among them; albeit two or three, and in especial Wulf and Hansei, who was now head groom, laughed not, but were sore troubled.

The baron had been declared an outlaw.

For an emperor now ruled in Germany, and good folk had begun to dare hope that the evil days might be drawing to a close. The new emperor was none other than Rudolf of Hapsburg, he who had been count of that name, and since coming to the throne he had bent his whole mind and strength to the task of bringing peace and good days to the land, and order and law within reach of the unhappy common folk whose lives were now passed in hardship and fear.

To this end the Emperor Rudolf had early sent to summon all of the barons and the lesser nobles of the land to come to his help against the rebel counts, Ulric and Eberhard of Würtemberg, who had joined with King Ottakar of Bohemia to defy the new ruler. The head of the Swartzburg had been summoned with the others; but, filled with contempt for "the poor Swiss count," as he dubbed the emperor, had defied him, and torn up the summons before the eyes of the herald who brought it.

Nevertheless, in spite of the refusal of nearly all the nobles to aid their emperor, the latter had, with his own men, gone against the two rebel counts and their kingly ally, and had beaten their armies and brought them to sue for peace. Now he was turning his attention to the larger task of putting fear of the law and of rightful authority into the hearts of the robber-nobles.

Of these a goodly number were already declared outlaws, and now the baron's turn had come. Moreover, one of the men of the Swartzburg, who had ridden beyond the mountains on a matter for Herr Banf, had ridden back with word that the emperor, with a strong army, was already out against the outlawed strongholds, and that he meant soon to call at the Swartzburg.

"And a warm welcome shall we give this new emperor of ours," boasted Conradt, on the castle terrace. "Emperor, forsooth! By the rood, Count Rudolf will have need of all his Swiss rabble, if he would bring the Swartzburg's men to knee before him!"

A chorus of assent greeted this speech. For once his hearers listened respectfully to the baron's nephew. Right eager were all the young men for the fray that was threatening; and so great was their contempt for the emperor that they could see for it but one outcome.

"But that his Austrians were in revolt and his army divided," declared one, "King Ottakar had never yielded to the Swiss. He of Hapsburg will find it a harder matter to yoke the German barons." And all his hearers nodded assent to the bragging speech.

What Baron Everhardt, at council with his knights, thought of the outlook, not even Conradt, among those on the terrace, rightly knew; but a few hours later, by orders sent out through the stewards and the masters of arms and horse, the routine of the castle was being put upon a war footing, to the joy of the eager young men. All were busy, each at his own line of duty, in the work of preparation for battle, and, to Wulf's delight, it fell to his lot to fare down the valley to the forge on an errand for Herr Werner.

It was weeks since Wulf had seen Karl, and glad was he now to be going to him; for in his own mind he was sore perplexed in this matter of the new emperor's proclamation of the baron, and he longed for the armorer's wise and honest thought about it all.

"Thou hast seen this emperor of ours?" he said, as he sat in the doorway of the smithy, whence he could look at will within at the forge, or without adown a long green aisle of the forest.

"Ay," said Karl, proudly; "his own man-at-arms was I during the Holy War. Served him have I, and gripped his hand—the hand of an honest man and a sore-needed one in this land today."

"Dost think he can master the barons?" the boy asked; and Karl looked troubled.

"These be ill times for thought, boy," he said, "and worse for speech; but if the emperor bring not order into our midst, then, in truth, are the scoffers wise, and God hath forgotten us up in heaven."

"Would I were of his train!" Wulf said, gazing with troubled eyes adown between the black trunks of the great trees. Karl, watching him, gathered rightly that he was worried as to his duty.

"If he be in truth the emperor by will of the people," Wulf added at last, "then are all true men, who love Germany, bound to come to his banner."

"Ay."

"But I am of the Swartzburg's men; and how may I be an honest one and fail at this moment when every blade is needed?"

"'Tis hard," Karl said, "and that only thine own heart can teach thee. No man may show another what his best action may be; but perhaps thou'rt nearer being the emperor's man than the baron's, were the truth known. If I guess rightly, 'twere ill faring if one of thy line raised blade against Rudolf of Hapsburg." The armorer muttered this half in his beard, nor looked at Wulf as he spoke.

"Nay, Karl," the boy cried sharply; "make me no more riddles, but speak out plainly, man to man. What is all this that thou hast ever held from me? What mean'st thou by 'any of my line'?"

"Alas!" said the armorer, sadly. "Naught know I, in truth, and there's the heart-break. 'Tis a chain of which some links are missing. Would to God I did know, that I might speak of a surety that which my heart is settled upon. But this that I do know shalt thou hear today." And coming over by the doorway, Karl took seat upon the great chest near by, and fell to telling Wulf of that which we already know—of his trip to the Swartzburg a dozen years before, and how he had taken him from the willows.

"Never saw I that knight, nor aught dared I ever ask of him; but slain was he by Herr Banf, and no noise was ever made of who he was. Only this I know: that the sword Herr Banf gave me to put in order had been that stranger's, and none other was it than one forged by these own hands for Count Wulfstanger of Hartsburg when he rode with Count Rudolf to Prussia, and he was our emperor's heart's friend. Three swords made I at that time, alike in temper and fashion, and one was for Count Wulfstanger; one was his who is now emperor; and one I kept and brought with me to this place—" Karl halted just here, but Wulf was too taken with the tale to note that.

"But thou knowest not that aught had I to do with that stranger knight," he urged, longing for Karl's answer.

"That do I not. But, lad, thou art as like the Count Otto von Wulfstanger as his own son might be; and how camest thou in the willows just at that time? Oh, I have worn thin my poor wits over this thing. But naught have I been able to learn or guess. I did what I might, and if ever thou comest to thine own, and thine own be what I think—ah, boy, thou'rt fit for it!" And the old armorer's face shone with loving pride as his eyes took in the figure in the doorway.

"Thanks to thee, good Karl, I can bear arms and sit a horse and hold mine honor clean," said Wulf, simply. "But oh, Karl, fain would I know the rights of this strange matter!"

He sighed, his thoughts going back to the castle, and to the memory of a fair small hand fluttering a ribband down over the heads of a rabble of scrambling youths. Truly, the tinker's lad, if such he was, was looking high.

"I wish that I might see that sword," he said at last.

"That thou shalt see."

The armorer arose from his seat on the chest and turned toward the cupboard; but just then there showed, riding out from the forest and up to the door of the forge, two or three riders whom Wulf knew to be from Conradt's mongrel band of thieves and cutthroats.

They had with them a matter of work that, he quickly saw, would keep Karl busy for an hour or two; so, mindful of his errand and of the need to get back to the Swartzburg, where so great things were going on, he arose from the doorway.

What of loyalty and duty his mind might fix upon at last, he knew not yet; but the thought of one who in the trouble to come might be in danger drew him like a magnet. So, bidding Karl good-by, he went his way.

His mind was full of confused thoughts as he fared through the forest. The weighty matters that pressed upon his brain kept mind and heart engaged while he journeyed; but his duty seemed no clearer to him, when he had reached the castle, than it had seemed at the forge with Karl.

CHAPTER NINE: OF THE ILL NEWS THAT THE BARON BROKE TO HIS MAIDEN WARD, AND OF HOW SHE TOOK THAT SAME

BARON EVERHARDT SAT beside a table in the great hall of the castle, scowling blackly at a pile of weighty-seeming papers that lay before him. The baron could himself neither read nor write, but Father Franz, his confessor and penman, had been with him all forenoon, and together they had gone over the parchments, one by one, and the warrior noble had, to all seeming, found enough to keep his mind busy with them since.

The parchments were none other than the deeds in the matters of the estate of the baron's ward, Fraulein Elise von Hofenhoer, regarding which estate the emperor had sent word that he should demand accounting after he had wrought order at the Swartzburg. The baron's face was not good to see when he recalled the words of the emperor's message.

"By the rood!" he muttered, bringing a clenched fist down on the table. "The poor Swiss count were wiser to busy himself with setting his own soul in order against coming to the Swartzburg."

He sprang from his chair and paced the floor wrathfully, when there entered to him his ward, whom he had sent to summon.

A stately slip of maidenhood was Elise—tall and fair, with fearless eyes of dark blue. She seemed older than her few years, and as she stood within the hall even the dark visage of the baron lightened at sight of her, and the growl of his voice softened in answering her greeting.

"There be many gruesome things in these hard days, Fraulein," he said, "and things that may easily work ill for a maid."

A startled look came into Elise's eyes, but naught said she, though the dread in her heart warned her what the baron's words might portend.

"Thou knowest," her guardian went on, "that thy father left thee in my care.

Our good Hofenhoer! May he be at greater peace than we are like to know for many a long year!"

There was an oily smoothness in the baron's tone that did not ease the fear in Elise's heart.

Never had she known him to speak of her father, whom she could not remember, and, indeed, never before had he spoken to her at such length; for the baron was more at home in the saddle, or at tilt and foray, than with the women of his household. But he grew bland as any lawyer as he went on, with a gesture toward the parchments:

"These be all the matters of what property thy father left, though little enough of it have I been able to save for thee—what with the wickedness of the times. And now this greedy thief of a robber-count who calls himself Emperor of Germany, forsooth, seems minded to take even that little—and thee into the bargain, belike—an we find not a way to hinder him."

"Take me?" Elise said, in some amazement, as the baron seemed waiting her word.

"Ay. The fellow hath proclaimed me outlaw, though, for that matter, do I as easily proclaim him interloper. So, doubtless, 'tis even." And the baron smiled grimly.

"But that is by the way," he added, his bland air coming back. "I've sent for thee on a weightier matter, Fraulein, for war and evil are all around us. I am none so young as once I was, and no man knows what may hap when this Swiss count comes hunting the nobles of the land as he might chase wild dogs. 'Tis plain thou must have a younger protector, and"—here the baron gave a snicker as he looked at Elise—"all maids be alike in this, I trow, that to none is a husband amiss. Is't not so?"

Elise was by now turned white as death, and her slim fingers gripped hard on the chair-arms.

"What mean'st thou, sir?" she asked faintly.

The baron's uneasy blandness slipped away before his readier frown, yet still he smiled in set fashion.

"Said I not," he cried, with clownish attempt at lightness, "that all maids are alike? Well knowest thou my meaning. Yet wouldst thou question and hedge, like all the others. Canst be ready for thy marriage by the day after tomorrow? We must needs have thee a sheltered wife ere the Swiss hawk pounce upon thee and leave thee plucked. Moreover, thy groom waxes impatient these days."

"And who is he?" Elise almost whispered with lips made stiff by dread.

"Who, indeed," snarled the baron, losing his scant self-mastery, "but my nephew, to whom, as well thou knowest, thou hast been betrothed since thou wert a child?"

The maiden sprang wildly to her feet, then cowered back in her chair and hid her face in her hands.

"Conradt? Oh, never, never!" she moaned.

"Come, come," her guardian said, not unkindly. "Conradt is no beauty, I grant. God hath dealt hardly with him in a way that might well win him a maiden's pity," he added with a sham piousness that made Elise shiver.

"Thou must have a husband's protection," the baron went on. "Naught else will avail in these times, and 'twas thy father's will."

"Nay, I believe not that," Elise cried, looking straight at him with flashing eyes. "Ne'er knew I my father, but 'twere not in any father's heart, my lord, to will so dreadful a thing for his one daughter. Not so will I dishonor that brave nobleman's memory as to believe that this was his will for me."

The baron sprang up, dashing the parchments aside.

"Heed thy words, girl!" he roared. "Thy father's will or not thy father's will—thou'lt wed my nephew on tomorrow's morrow."

Elise came a step nearer with a gesture of pleading.

"My lord," she said with earnest dignity, "ye cannot mean it! I am a poor, help-less maiden, with nor father nor brother to fend for me. Never canst thou mean to do me this wrong."

"'Tis needful, girl," the baron said, keeping his eyes lowered. "This is no time for thee to be unwed. Thou must have a legal protector other than I. Only a hus-band can hold thy property from the emperor's greed—and perhaps save thee from eviler straits."

"Nay, who cares for the wretched stuff?" cried she, impatiently. "Ah, my lord, let it go. Take it, all of it, an ye will, and let me enter a convent—rather than this."

But for this the baron had no mind. Already had he turned his ward's proper-ty to his own use, and her marriage with Conradt was planned but that he might hide his theft from the knowledge of others. Well knew he how stern an account-ing of his guardianship would be demanded, did Elise enter the shelter of a con-vent; but he only said:

"Thou art not of age. Thou canst not take so grave a step. The law will not let thee consent."

"Then how may I consent to this other?"

"To this I consent for thee, minx. Let that suffice, and go about thy preparations."

"I cannot! I cannot! Oh, Herr Baron, dost thou not fear God? As he lives, I will never do this thing!"

Then the baron gripped her by the arm.

"Now, miss," he said, his face close to hers, "enough of folly. Yet am I master at the Swartzburg, and two days of grace have I granted thee. But a word more, and Father Franz shall make thee a bride this night if thy thieving cur of a bridegroom show his face in the castle. See, now; naught canst thou gain by thy stubborn

Then the Baron gripped her by the arm.

unreason. I can have patience with a maid's whims, but if thou triest me too greatly, it will go hard but that I shall find a way to break thy stubborn will. Now get yonder and prepare thy bridal robes." And he strode away.

Elise turned and fled from that place, scarce noting whither she went. Not back to the women's chambers. She could not face the baroness and her ladies until she had faced this monstrous trouble alone.

Out she sped, then, to the castle garden, fleeing, poor, hunted fawn that she was, to the one spot of refuge she knew, the sheltering shade of a drooping elm, at whose foot welled up a little stream that, husbanded and led by careful gardening, wandered through the pleasance to water my lady's rose-garden beyond. There had ever been her favorite dreaming-place, and thither brought she this great woe wherewith she must wrestle. But ere she could cast herself down upon the welcoming moss at the roots of the tree, a figure started up from within the shadow of the great black trunk, and came toward her.

She started back with a startled cry, wondering, even then, that aught could cause her trouble or dismay beyond what was already hers. In the next instant, however, she recognized Wulf. He was passing through the garden, and had been minded to turn aside for a moment to sit beneath the elm where he knew the fair lily of the castle had her favorite nook. But he was even then departing, when he was aware of Elise coming toward him.

Then he saw her face, all distraught with pain and sorrow, and wrath filled him.

"Who hath harmed thee?" he cried. "'Twere an ill faring for him an I come nigh him."

"Wulf, Wulf!" moaned Elise, as soon as she knew him. "Surely Heaven hath sent thee to help me!" And standing there under the sheltering tree, she told him, as best she might for shame and woe and the maidenly wrath that were hers, the terrible doom fallen upon her.

And Wulf's face grew stern and white as he listened, and there fell off from it the boyish look of ease and light-heartedness that is the right of youth, and the look of a man came there instead.

Now and again, as Elise spoke, his hand sought the dagger at his belt, and his breath came thick from beneath his teeth; but no words wasted be in wrath, for his wit was working fast on the matter before them, which was the finding of a way of escape for the maiden.

"There is but one way for it," he said at last, "and that must be this very night, for this business of the emperor's coming makes every moment beyond the present one a thing of doubt. It cannot be before midnight, though, that I may help thee; for till then I guard the postern-gate, and I may not leave that which is intrusted me. But after that, do thou make shift to come to me here, and, God helping us, thou'lt be far from here ere daybreak."

"But whither can I go?" Elise cried, shrinking in terror from the bold step. "How may a maiden wander forth into the night?"

"That is a simple matter," said Wulf. "Where, indeed, but to the Convent of St. Ursula, beyond the wood? Thou'lt be safe there, for the lady superior is blood kin to the emperor, and already is the place under protection of his men. Even if he think to seek thee there, our wild baron would pause before going against those walls."

"'Tis a fair chance," said Elise, at last, "but if 'twere still worse, 'twere better worth trying, even to death, than to live unto tomorrow's morrow and what 'twill bring"; and a shudder shook her till she sobbed with grief.

The time was too short even for much planning, while many things remained to be done; so Elise sought her own little nest in the castle wing, there to make ready for flight, while Wulf took pains to show himself as usual about the tasks wherewith he was wont to fill his hours.

CHAPTER TEN: HOW WULF TOOK
ELISE FROM THE SWARTZBURG

IT WAS A little past midnight, and the air was black and soft as velvet, when two figures crept across the inner bailey and gained the outer court of the castle. Feeling by hand and foot along the walls, Wulf led, while Elise crept after him, holding fast by his sleeve, till at last they were at the postern-gate.

"Gotta Brent's son followed me on watch here," he whispered to Elise. "He is a sleepy fellow, and will not have got well settled to the tramp yet."

"Thou'lt not harm him, Wulf?" she breathed back anxiously. "Ne'er again could I be happy if any hurt comes to an innocent person through me."

"Nay, let thy heart be easy," replied Wulf. "I will but fix him in easy position for the sleep he loves. He were no fellow to be put on watch in time of danger."

Just then the clank of metal came to their ears, and they knew that the sentinel was drawing near on his beat.

Close back they pressed into the deep shadow of the bastion, while Elise put both hands over her heart in an instinct to muffle its wild beating.

Almost beside them, lantern in hand, the watch paused; but his body was between them and his light, and its rays did not shine into the bastion.

He bent toward them, and Wulf braced himself to spring upon him, when of a sudden a call rang out from the sentinel on the watch-tower far adown the wall.

"One hour past midnight, and all's well," it said; and the sentinel beside them took it up, bellowing out the words until they sounded fair awful coming out of the darkness. From elsewhere the watch-cry sounded again, and ere it had clean died away Wulf gave a forward spring, catching the sentinel just as he was turning to walk adown his beat.

"One hour past midnight, and all's well!"

In a flash the sleepy watchman had received a blow from his own staff that quieted him. Then, dashing out the lantern, Wulf, as best he could in the darkness, thrust a soft leathern gag into the man's mouth, making it fast by cords to the back of his head. Then he bound him hand and foot, and taking from the fellow's girdle the key of the postern, he grasped Elise's hand, and together they made out to open the gate and creep forth.

Between them and liberty there yet lay the ditch; but Wulf knew where the warden's boat was tied, and he managed to get Elise into the small craft. By now a few stars shone through the darkness, lighting them, feebly enough, to the other side, and presently the pair had clambered again ahead.

"Now for it," whispered Wulf. "Gird thy skirts well, for if we win away now, 'twill be by foot-fleetness."

Bravely Elise obeyed him, and taking her hand again, Wulf led off at a long, low run, none too hard for her prowess, yet getting well over the ground. Thus they began descending the defile. It was cruel work for a tender maid, but Elise was of such stuff as in years gone had made warrior queens; she neither moaned nor flinched, but kept steady pace at Wulf's side.

Thus they fared for a matter of two or three miles, and had gotten well away down the pass when they caught, on the still night air, an alarum of horns from the castle. Plainly something was astir, and that, most likely, the discovery that some one had come or gone by the postern-gate.

"The boat will soon tell them which 'tis," said Wulf, "and they'll be after us full soon."

They quickened pace, and sped down the stony road, Wulf with an arm about the maiden's waist, that he might lift her along, she with a hand on his shoulder, bravely keeping the pace.

By now they were beyond the steepest of the way, and near to where the stream that kept it company toward the valley widened over the plain for some miles in a sedgy, grass-tufted morass, with here and there clumps of wild bog-willow and tall reeds.

The noise of pursuit sounded loud and terrible behind them, till they could almost tell the different voices of the men. Then, without warning, over the crest of the mountains towering up on one side rose the late moon, full and lambent, flooding the whole scene with light.

"Quick, quick!" cried Wulf, and fairly lifting his companion, he swung down the rocks that edged the cliff, sliding, slipping, scrambling, still holding her safe, until, with a spring, they gained the shelter of the willows.

There they lay breathless for a moment, while above them a party of horsemen swept by in full cry.

"They will soon be back," said Wulf. "We must e'en pick our way over yonder, Elise."

"We can never!" gasped the girl, almost in despair.

"That were a long day," answered Wulf, easily. "I wot not if any other man from the castle can do it, but well know I how it can be done."

Stooping, he lifted Elise in his strong arms, and resting her light weight on shoulder and chest, went lightly forward, now stepping upon a ready islet of green just showing in the moonlight, now plunging almost waist-deep in water below which other trips had taught him was foothold, but never stopping until he drew near the other side. Then, sore wearied, he raised Elise that she might lay hold on some overhanging boughs and swing herself up among them, after which Wulf crawled ashore and lay panting, while Elise bent over him, calling him softly by name, and taking blame to herself for all his weariness.

He did but wait to get his breath, however; then, as they heard the hue and cry of the returning horsemen, he started up again. Freshened by their short rest, they plunged into the forest.

Well was it for them that Wulf knew, as some men today know their home cities, the wayless depths of that wood. With the sureness of a hiving bee, he led Elise through the great tree-aisles. Here and there, where boughs were thinner, the moon's rays sifted in, but for the most part it was fair dark, until, after long travel, as they came to a little bit of open where ancient forest fire had cleared the trees, they saw that the moonlight had given place to the first gray tint of dawn.

On they went for yet another hour, and now it was clear daylight, when, sounding through the woods, came again the noise of horsemen. Evidently the baron's men had skirted the stream and struck through the forest. For all the fugitives knew, they might show before them any moment now.

"Wulf," cried Elise, "do thou leave me here. I can go no further; but go thou on. I will stay to meet them. They dare not kill me—would they did!—but if I stay and go back with them to the castle, thou canst escape, and thy death will not be at my charge."

"Hush!" Wulf answered almost roughly. "Dost think I will do thy bidding in this? But here is no place to hide. We must get on, if we may, where the bush is thicker; so hearten thyself for one more trial."

His arm once more on her waist, they ran on, she sobbing with weariness and fear for him, through the forest.

But nearer and nearer, louder and more clear, came the noise of their pursuers, and still more feebly ran the tired pair, stumbling over fallen boughs and matted tangles of dead leaves.

"Wulf, I am like to die of weariness," gasped Elise, at last. "Go on alone, I beg thee."

"Hark!" Wulf interrupted, with a quick gesture. "What is that?"

They were at the edge of another open, which they were minded to skirt, fearful to cross it and risk discovery; but beyond it came the sound of still another body of horsemen crashing through the forest.

"Belike the party have divided," Wulf whispered, "the better to find us." But even as he spoke a squire rode from the bush into the open, bearing a banner that Wulf had never before seen. He shrank back into the thicket, keeping tight hold of

Elise's hand; but the newcomer had evidently ridden out by mistake from the body of his fellows, and retired again by the way he came. They could hear him going on through the brush.

"They are not Swartzburg riders," Wulf said; and then a mighty din arose among the trees. The woods rang on all sides with the cries of fighting-men and the clashing of weapons, and in another moment Wulf made out clearly the battle-cry of Baron Everhardt's men. But above it and all the din of fighting there rose another cry—"For God and the emperor!"—so that he knew that a party of Rudolf's men, if not his whole army, had fallen in with the pursuers, and his hot young blood stirred with longing to be in the fray.

Then he bethought him of the matter at hand.

"Now, now, Elise, this is our chance! We must be off. One more dash and we shall be well on our way to the convent."

He pressed to her lips an opened bottle filled with goat's milk, urging her to drink, and when she had done so, she looked up at him with fresh courage in her eyes.

"I am ready," she said, rising.

He stopped the bottle and secured it at his belt, and again they went on, dashing forward, unmindful of any noise they might make when all the wood was so full of direful sound. The new hope that had come to Elise gave her fresh strength, so that it seemed to her as if she had but just begun to run.

In this fashion they traveled on until at last Wulf halted in the deepest depth of the great forest.

"We shall be safe to rest here," he said, still speaking softly, "while we break our fast."

CHAPTER ELEVEN: HOW THE FUGITIVES CAME TO ST. URSULA AND MET THE EMPEROR

THE MILK WAS still sweet, and being young, wholesome creatures, the two made out to take the food and drink they needed, and were afterward able to go on their way, warily, but steadily, through the woods.

Nevertheless, it was close upon nightfall when the convent walls showed gray before them where the woods had been cleared away.

All was bustle and confusion there. The close was full of armed men, and about the stables and courtyards were many great war-horses, while grooms and men-at-arms ran to and fro on divers errands, or busied themselves about the horses and their gear. Altogether the scene was one of such liveliness as Wulf had never dreamed the convent could take on.

At the little barred window of the cloister gate where he knocked with Elise, a lay sister was in waiting, who told them the reason of all this business. The new emperor, with his train, was the convent's guest. That night he would bide there, awaiting the coming of the bulk of his army, wherewith later he meant to attack the Swartzburg. The sister admitted our travelers, and took Elise straight to the mother superior, leaving Wulf to find the way, which well he knew, to the kitchen.

The emperor and the mother superior were together in the latter's little reception-room when Elise was brought before them, trembling and shy, as a maiden might well be in the presence of royalty and of churchly dignity; but the mother superior, though she had never seen the little maid, called her by name, the lay sister having made it known, and turned with her to the emperor.

"This, sire," she said, "is the child of your old friend Von Hofenhoer, and sometime ward of our baron, who, I fear, is ill prepared to make accounting of his stewardship. But why she is here I know not yet, save that the sister tells me that she was brought here a refugee from the castle by the grandson of old Karl of the forge—he of whom you were asking but now."

The emperor was a tall, lean man, with eagle-like visage, clean-shaven and stern. His long, straight hair fell down on either side of his gaunt face, and his eyes were bright and keen. He was plainly, almost meanly dressed. Nevertheless, he was of right kingly aspect, and, moreover, despite his stern looks, he smiled kindly as he placed a hand on Elise's bowed head.

"Thy father was my good comrade, child," he said, "and sorry am I to see his daughter in such plight; but thou shalt tell us about it presently, and we shall see what is to be done."

The lay sister returned, bearing some wine and a plate of biscuits; and seating her in an arm-chair, the mother superior bade Elise partake of these, which she did gladly. When she had finished, the two dignitaries, who were own cousins and old friends, drew from her, little by little, the story of her flight from the castle, and of her reasons therefor.

As the emperor heard her tell of the baron's cruel demand, he paced up and down the little stone-floored room, now frowning sternly, now softening again as he looked upon the fair young maiden, so spent with fear and hardship.

"This is bad work," he said at last, "and well is it that we have come to clean out the jackal's nest. But this boy Wulf whom she speaks of, he must be here yet. Him I would see—and our good old Karl. Would he were here now!"

So Wulf was summoned before the great emperor, and came with swift-beating heart. Brought face to face with Rudolf, he fell upon one knee, cap in hand, and waited the monarch's will.

When the latter spoke it was with great kindliness; for well was he pleased with the goodly looking youth.

"Rise," he said, when he had glanced keenly over the kneeling figure. "And so thou'rt my old friend Karl's grandson. If there's aught in blood, thou shouldst be an honest man and a brave; for truer nor braver man ever lived, and well knows Rudolf of Hapsburg that."

A thousand thoughts and impulses surged through Wulf's brain while the emperor spoke, but the moment seemed none for speech, other than that with which he finally contented himself, saying simply:

"He brought me up, sire."

"And that is thy good fortune," cried the emperor. "But tell me when I may have speech of my friend; for there is a matter hath brought me hither that needeth his help, though I knew not that he were even alive until the mother superior here told me of his presence hereabout. Well knew she how Rudolf loved his ancient man-at-arms."

"If he knew what was afoot," Wulf said respectfully, "he would be here now to honor the emperor. Readily could I take him a message, your Majesty," he added.

"That were well done," began Rudolf. But Mother Ursula interrupted.

"Nay," she said; "the baron's men belike are even now scouring the country for the boy. 'Twere the price of his life to send him forth again, at least till the Swartzburg is taken."

"True enough," said the emperor. "In faith, my longing in this matter hath made me forgetful. Well, I must e'en seek another messenger."

"If I might go, sire," Wulf persisted, with manly modesty that still further won Rudolf's straightforward heart, "no messenger could go so quickly as I—by ways I know that are quite safe. I can fare back now, and be there by daylight." "By the rood, no!" cried the emperor. "Thou shalt rest some hours ere we think further of this. There's none too much such timber as thou in the land, that we should be in haste to fell it. Get thee now to refreshment and rest, and if we need thee thou shalt know it."

Thus dismissed, Wulf was fain to be content with retiring; and despite his anxiety to serve the emperor, who had won the boy's whole loyal heart, right glad was he, after a hearty supper, to go to bed. So, when he was shown, at last, into the traveler's dormitory, he threw himself down upon the hard cot spread for him, and fell at once into a deep sleep.

CHAPTER TWELVE: HOW WULF TOOK THE EMPEROR'S MESSAGE TO KARL OF THE FORGE

IT STILL WANTED an hour of daybreak when the convent porter bent over the pallet where Wulf lay and shook the boy into wakefulness.

Mother Ursula and the emperor were still talking when Wulf, having knocked at the door of the little reception-room, answered the former's call to enter. To all appearance, neither had taken any rest since Wulf had last seen them, and so eagerly was the emperor talking that neither paid any heed to the boy as he stood waiting their pleasure.

"He was known to have ridden hither," Rudolf was saying, "and to have brought the boy. He was minded to leave him with you, my lady, against his going again to Jerusalem; but no word ever came from either. Right gladly would I lay down the crown, that is proving overburdensome to my poor head, to set eyes upon the face of either."

The emperor paced the floor sadly, his stern, homely face drawn by emotion.

"He would have sought out Karl, had he known," Rudolf went on. "I must see the man. Ah, here is the boy!"

He turned, seeing the boy, who advanced and did knee service. Rudolf bade him rise.

"So," the emperor said, "we are going to use thy stout legs, boy. Make thou their best speed to thy grandsire, and tell him that Count Rudolf rides to the Swartzburg and would have him at hand. Canst do that?"

"Ay, sire."

"But stay," said Rudolf. "Haply he has grown too feeble for bearing arms?"

Wulf flushed with indignation for stalwart Karl.

"Nay," he said stoutly. "He will carry what weapon thou wilt, and enter the castle close behind thee."

"Sh!" cried Mother Ursula, shocked at the boy's speech. "Thou'rt speaking to the emperor, lad!"

Rudolf laughed. "Let the boy alone," he said. "One may speak freely to whom he will of a man like Karl. Now hasten," the emperor said kindly, "'tis time thou wast on the way—and God be with thee!"

And Wulf went forth.

As he passed through the refectory the porter handed him some food, which he put into his sack, and filling his leathern water-bottle at the fountain in the convent yard, he fastened it to his belt and swung out on his journey.

By now had come dawn, and the birds were beginning their earliest twitter among the trees. Later, squirrels and other small wood-creatures began to move about, and to chatter among the boughs and in the fallen leaves. The forest was full of pleasant sights and sounds, and the early morning breeze brought sweet, woodsy smells to his eager nostrils.

By and by a red fox stole across an opening with a plump hare flung back over his shoulder, and Wulf gave challenge for sheer joy of life and of the morning.

Reynard paused long enough to give him a slant glance out of one wise eye, then trotted on. Long pencils of early sunlight began to write cheery greetings on the mossy earth and on the tree-trunks. The witchery of the hour was upon everything, and Wulf felt boundlessly happy as he stepped along. All his thoughts were vague and sweet—of Elise safe at the convent, doubtless still sleeping; of the emperor's gracious kindness; of Karl's joy at the message he was bringing; even the sorry medley of half-knowledge about his own name and state had no power to make him unhappy that morning.

Not but that he longed to know the truth. He had never been ashamed to think of himself as Karl's grandson; but the bare idea of something other than that set his blood tingling, and caused such wild hopes to leap within him that but for the need to walk warily, on this errand so fraught with danger, he could have shouted and sung for joy.

He went on steadily, stopping but once, in the middle of the forenoon, to eat a bit of bread and to refill his water-bottle at a clear, pure stream which he crossed.

Traveling thus, bent now only upon his errand, he never saw the stealthy shadow that, mile after mile, kept pace with him beyond the thicket, dodging when he paused, moving when he moved, until, satisfied as to where he was going, the evil thing hurried back over the way to keep tryst with a master as evil, and to carry to Conradt the welcome news that the tinker had gone alone back to the forge, where quick work might surprise and catch him.

It was the middle of the afternoon when he reached the forge and found Karl, who stared at sight of him.

"I'd dreamed thou wast safe away, boy," he said, shaking him lovingly by the broad shoulders. "What madness is this? The baron's men have been here for thee, and thy life is worth naught if they find thee. Why art thou so foolhardy, son?"

"Count Rudolf is at St. Ursula's, and sends for thee," Wulf said, laughing at his fears.

Karl turned on the instant, and seized a great sword that lay on the anvil.

"Say'st so? And thou hast seen the count?—I mean the emperor? How looked he? What said he? And he remembered old Karl? Ah, his was ever a true heart!" The rough face was alight with loving, excited pride.

"Give me a bite to eat, and we'll fare back together," Wulf said; but Karl became anxious again.

"Nay," he said. "Thou'st escaped the baron's wolves this time, but by now they swarm the woods. Moreover, thou art tired out. Bide thee in hiding here. They will never dream that thou art simple enough to come aback to the forge at this time. Here is thy best refuge now. Rest, then, and by tomorrow the emperor's men will have harried them all back to the castle to defend the place."

To Wulf this word seemed wise, and fain was he to rest, being footsore and weary; so he busied himself with helping Karl make ready.

At last Karl went to the cupboard beside the forge, and opening it, lifted out the shining knight's sword.

"This is the blade I have told ye of, lad," he said—"the very one; for I gave Herr Banf mine own, that had never seen battle and kept this one for thee."

He ran his thumb along the keen edge. "Mayhap thou'st no claim on earth to it," he said, "yet no man hath showed a better, and thou'lt give it play for the emperor, whose service owns it. So take it, Wulf. But, lad, lad," he cried, "as thou lov'st God and this poor lost land, remember 'twas a brave and a true man first carried that sword 'gainst foe!"

"Ay, ay, Karl, I will remember," said Wulf, solemnly, taking the sword in hand. Karl had fitted it with a plain, strong scabbard, and it was ready for stout and worthy deeds.

A thrill went through the boy as he girt it to him, and silently, within his own mind, he vowed that blade to knightly and true service, and hid it high up behind the forge till the time should come for him to wield it.

Then Karl bade him good-by, and stepped forth through the woods to do the emperor's bidding.

CHAPTER THIRTEEN: HOW DANGER CAME TO WULF AT THE FORGE

ONCE KARL WAS gone, Wulf set to work to cook some food for himself over the forge fire, and when he had eaten he was about to throw himself down upon the armorer's pallet to seek the rest he so much needed, but suddenly his quick ear caught some slight noise in the forest.

He sprang up, and waited to hear further.

Sure enough; all too plainly, through the trees, but still far off, could be heard the sound of horsemen.

Softly closing the door behind him, Wulf sprang to the great oak, his friend and shelter in childhood and boyhood, now his haven in deadly peril. Easily he swung himself up, higher and higher, until he was safe among the thick foliage of the broad, spreading top. So huge were the branches, even here, that a man might stand beneath and look up at the very one where Wulf lay, yet never dream that aught were hidden there.

The baron himself was of the party who rode up around the smithy just as Wulf was settled in his place. Straight to the door he strode, and with the head of his battle-ax struck it a blow that sent it inward on its hinges.

One or two men bearing torches sprang into the house, and the single room became suddenly alight; but no one showed there. Hastily they searched the place, while the baron, from the doorway, roared forth his orders, sending one man here, another yonder, to be at the thicket and scour all the places. One even came under the great tree and held up his torch, throwing the light high aloft, but seeing naught of Wulf.

Then the baron laughed savagely.

"This be thy chase, nephew Conradt," he jeered. "Said I not he would never be here? The armorer's whelp is a hangman's rogue fast

The Baron struck the door with a blow that sent it inward.

enough, but no fool to blunder hither once he were safe away with the girl." And mounting, the company raced away from the place, so that soon not one remained, nor any sound from them came back upon the wind.

Nevertheless, Wulf deemed it best not to venture down, but lay along a great bough of the oak tree, and at last fell into a doze that lasted until daylight. Even then, when he would have descended, his quick ears caught the sound of passers at no great distance off; so he kept his hiding-place hour after hour, until at last, when the sun shining upon the tree-tops told him that the noon was close at hand, all seemed so still that he swung himself down, stiffly, for he was cramped and sore, and gained the ground.

But at that moment again came the sound of approaching men, and from all the openings about the clearing appeared horsemen and foot-soldiers, while from beyond rose the noise of horses and armor, and of men's voices.

Springing up aloft to gain his sword, and then to the door, Wulf stood at bay, blade in hand, meaning to sell his life dearly, rather than be taken, when a voice that he knew was raised, and Karl the armorer shouted:

"Nay, lad! an thou'rt a loyal German, give thine emperor better homage than that!" And, through all his weariness and daze, Wulf made out to come forward and kneel at the emperor's stirrup.

They were friends, not foes, who had come this time.

CHAPTER FOURTEEN: OF THE GREAT BATTLE THAT WAS FOUGHT, AND OF HOW WULF SAVED THE DAY

NOW WERE WULF'S anxieties well over; for this great company of riders and foot-soldiers were none other than the main part of the Emperor Rudolf's army, that had ridden on that day from St. Ursula's wood, and the emperor's will was that tomorrow should see the attack begun on the Swartzburg.

They were still an hour's march from the place set for resting that night, where would gather to them a smaller body that had come by another way, minded to meet with a company of riders from the castle, known to be thereabout. So, when he had spoken kindly to young Wulf, for whose sake, indeed, the troop had made their way lie past the forge, Rudolf of Hapsburg bade the boy fall in with the men, and the whole company again went forward.

Getting for himself a good bow and arrow from the smithy, Wulf fell in with the ranks of footmen, and then was he amazed to find that his right-hand neighbor was Hansei, from the Swartzburg.

Right pleased was he at the discovery, though well he wondered what it might mean, and he made haste to ask Hansei about the matter. Then did he hear how, two days before, a company of knights and others from the castle, riding in chase of Elise and himself, had fallen in with an outriding party of Rudolf's men, and there had been fighting.

"Ay," said Wulf, remembering, "and there at hand were we when that fighting began."

"Glad am I that we knew it not," Hansei cried, "for the most part of the emperor's men were slain or taken prisoner, and few escaped to carry word to the convent. But with them ran I, for I had small stomach to fight 'gainst the lawful rulers of this land, and thou a hunted man beside."

Then did Hansei ask Wulf of his faring in the woods, whereupon Wulf, as they marched, told him all the story.

So talking, the two kept pace with the marching company, until, by nightfall, they came up with the other party, and camp was made, well on the road toward the Swartzburg.

No fires were built, for Rudolf of Hapsburg was minded, if possible, to come close before the castle gates ere those within were aware; but every man cared for his own needs as best he might, and before long the whole host was sleeping, save for the watchers.

It was nigh upon daybreak when a wild alarum went through the camp. Every man sprang to his feet and grasped his weapon as he ran forward in the darkness to learn what the matter was. The cries of men, the clashing of weapons and armor, the shrill screams of wounded horses, came up on every side, while so dark was it that for a little time the emperor's soldiers scarce knew friend from foe as they pressed on, half dazed.

Soon, however, they made shift to form their array in some sort of order, and there in the forest began a mighty battle.

For the baron, filled with vanity and wrath, and made foolhardy by the easy victory his men had won over Rudolf's soldiers two days before, had planned this night attack, knowing, through Conradt's spies, where the emperor's army were lying, and had deemed that it would be a light matter to set upon that force in the darkness, and destroy it, man and horse.

But Baron Everhardt had believed that that smaller body which the spies had seen and brought him word of was the main army, and so the men of the Swartzburg had all unthinkingly walked into a trap where they had been minded to set one.

Sharp and grim, now, the fighting went on, sword meeting sword, pike striking spear, as knight met knight or common soldier alike in the confusion. Above all the din rang out the battle-cries of the two parties, the Swartzburg men ever meeting the royal war-cry, "God and the emperor!" with their own ringing watchword, "The Swartzburg and liberty!" until the whole wood seemed filled with the sound.

In the midst of the fray went Rudolf of Hapsburg, with his great two-handed sword, clearing a way for those behind him. No armor wore he, save a light shirt of chain mail, and no shield save his helmet; but beside him fought Karl the armorer, with a huge battle-ax, so that Wulf, catching glimpse of him in the press at day-dawn, felt a great joy fill his heart at sight of that good soldier.

Not long could he look, however, for he and Hansei were in the thick of it, well to the fore, where Rudolf's banner-bearer had his place. In the close quarters there was no work for the bowmen, so Wulf fought with the sword that Karl had given him the day before, and a goodly blade he found it, while Hansei wielded a great pike that he had wrested from one of the baron's men, and laid about him lustily wherever a foe showed.

Riding his great war-horse, and followed close by Karl, Rudolf cut a way throught the Swartzburg ranks.

So the hours passed; and many men were slain on either side, when it began to be felt by the emperor's soldiers that the Swartzburg men were slowly falling back toward the defile, to gain the castle.

"If they do that," Hansei gasped, as he met Wulf again, "a long and weary siege will we have to make; for thou well knowest the Swartzburg's strength, and well hath the baron made ready."

Then to Wulf came a right war-craftly notion, which he told to Hansei, whereupon the two set to gather to them some scores or more of the young men, and these fell back toward the edge of the battle, until they were out of the press, and hastened through the wood, as only Wulf knew how to lead them.

They came at last to the morass, not far from where he and Elise had crossed that night when they fled from the castle.

"There is never a crossing there!" Hansei cried, aghast, when he saw the place; but Wulf laughed.

"Crossing there is," he said lightly, "so that ye all follow me softly, stepping where I step. Mind ye do that, for beyond the willows and the pool yonder is quick-sand, and that means death, for no footing is there for any helper."

Thus warned, the young men looked at one another uneasily; but none fell back; so, unseen by the foe, and noting well each step that Wulf made, at last they won clear across that treacherous morass, and came safe a-land again among the willows, well up the pass toward the Swartzburg.

More than an hour they waited there, and by and by the sound of battle began swelling up the defile. The baron's men were in retreat, but fighting stoutly as they fell back, pressed close by the foe. Already had the baron wound his horn, loud and long, and cheerily was it answered from the watch-tower with a blast which told that the keepers there were in readiness, and that open gates and safe shelter awaited the retreating men—when out at their backs sprang Wulf and his fellows, and fell upon them, right and left.

Then wild confusion was on all. Those attacked at the rear pressed forward upon their comrades, who knew not what had happened, but drove them back again to meet the swords and pikes of those lusty young men, who made the most of the foes' surprise, and cut down many a seasoned warrior ere he could well learn how he was beset.

Then the baron sounded his horn again, and out from the castle came all of the Swartzburg's reserve to the rescue, and Wulf and his little band were in turn beset, and like to be destroyed had not Rudolf himself, now riding his great war-horse, and followed close by Karl, cut a way through the Swartzburg ranks to their aid.

By now the fighting was man to man, pell-mell, all up the pass, and so confused was that mass of battling soldiery that friend and foe of the Swartzburg pressed together across the draw and in through the castle gates, fighting as fight a pack of wolves when one is down.

Then above all the din sounded Herr Banf's voice, calling the men of the Swartzburg to the baron; and there, against the wall of the outer bailey, made they their last stand. Well had Baron Everhardt fought among his men, but at last a well-hurled spear thrown from one of the emperor's soldiers pierced his helmet as he was rallying his friends, and there he fell.

Quickly Herr Banf and Herr Werner took him up and bore him within the inner bailey, while without the fighting went on. But the castle's men fought half-heartedly now; for their leader was gone, and well knew they that they were battling against their lawful emperor. So, ere long, all resistance fell away, and the emperor and his men poured, unhindered, into the courtyard.

The Swartzburg was taken.

CHAPTER FIFTEEN: HOW THE SHINING KNIGHT'S TREASURE WAS BROUGHT TO LIGHT

IT WAS HIGH noon when the last of the knights of the Swartzburg had laid down his arms at the feet of the emperor and had sworn fealty to him. Of the castle's company Herr Banf alone was missing; for he had ridden forth, in the confusion that followed the entrance of Rudolf's men, to make his way through the woods and thence out from that land, minded rather to live an outlaw than to bend knee to the foe of his well-loved friend.

A wise ruler as well as a brave soldier was Rudolf of Hapsburg, and well knew he how to win, as well as to conquer. So, when all the knights had taken oath, to each was returned his arms, and then the emperor greeted him as friend.

Within the castle hall the dead master lay at rest, and beside him watched the baroness, a pale, broken-spirited lady, whose life had been one long season of fear of her liege lord, and who felt, now, as little sorrow as hope. The emperor had already visited her, to pay her respect and to assure her of protection, and now, with the two or three women of that stern and wild household of men-folk, she waited what might come.

Meanwhile, through castle and stables and offices the emperor's appointed searchers went, taking note of all things; but Rudolf of Hapsburg sat in the court-yard, in sight of his men, who were by now making shift to prepare themselves a meal; for the greater number had not tasted food that day.

To Wulf the whole changed scene seemed like a dream; so familiar the place, yet so strange—as one in dreams finds some well-known place puzzling him by some unwonted aspect. He stood watching the soldiers feeding here and there about the bailey, when there came two squires from the keep, leading between them a bent and piteous figure.

It was a man who cowed and blinked, and sought to cover his dazzled eyes from the unwonted light of day. Him the soldiers brought before the emperor, and on the moment Wulf knew that face to be the one which he had seen at the barred window of the keep on that day when he had climbed the tower.

"What is this?" demanded Rudolf, as he looked the woeful figure up and down. Scarce bore it likeness to a man, so unkempt and terrible was its aspect, so drawn and wan the face, wherein no light of reason showed.

"We know not, your Majesty," one of the squires replied; "but we found him in a cell high up in the keep, chained by the ankle to a stone bench, and I broke the fetter with a sledge."

By now the nobles and knights of Rudolf's army were gathered about; but none spoke, for pity. Then the emperor caused all the knights of the Swartzburg to be summoned, and he questioned them close, but not one of them knew who the man might be, or why he was a prisoner at the Swartzburg. Indeed, of all the company, only one or two knew that such a prisoner had been held in the keep. Of the two men who might have told his name, one lay dead in the great hall, and one, Herr Banf, was riding from the Swartzburg, an outlaw.

But the emperor was troubled.

A haunting something in that seemingly empty face drew his very heartstrings, and made him long to know the man's name. And then suddenly through the press of knights and nobles rushed forth Karl the armorer, and clasped the woeful figure in his arms, while Karl himself trembled and sobbed with wrath and sorrow.

"See, my lord!" he cried, bringing the man closer before Rudolf. "Look upon this man! Knowest thou not who 'tis?"

The emperor had grown very white, and he sighed as he passed one hand over his eyes.

"Nay," he said, "it is never—it cannot be—"

"Ah, my lord, my lord!" sobbed the armorer, his great chest heaving, and the tears streaming down from his unashamed eyes. "It is the count—Count Otto himself, thine old comrade, whom thou and I didst love. Look upon him, and thou wilt know him!"

So white now was the emperor that his face was like death, but the lines of it were set in fierce wrath, too, as, little by little, he began to see that Karl might be right. He bent forward and laid a hand on the man's shoulder.

"Otto, friend Otto!" he called loudly, that the dulled senses might take in his words. "Otto, dost know me?"

Slowly the other looked up; a dim light seemed to gather in his eyes.

"Ay, Rudolf," he whispered hoarsely; then the light went out, and he shrank back again.

"There is a tale I would have told your Majesty," Karl said, recovering himself, "if the herald had not come just as he did on the night before last." And then, seeing Wulf in the throng, he called him to come forward.

Wondering, the boy obeyed, while, with a hand on his arm, Karl told the emperor all that he had been able to tell Wulf that day at the forge—of the battle between the knights, of how he had thereafter found the stranger child in the willows, and how he had kept the blade that Herr Banf had won.

"Now know I of surety," he said at last, "that that knight was Count Otto von Wulfstanger, but who this boy may be I can only guess."

Now a voice spoke from amid the throng. Hansei, who had been edging nearer and nearer, could keep silence no longer.

"He must be the 'shining knight's' treasure! Well I remember it, your Majesty!" he cried.

"What meanest thou?" demanded Rudolf; and there, before them all, Hansei told what the children had seen from the playground on the plateau that day, so many years agone.

The emperor grew thoughtful. He looked at Wulf from under lowered brows.

"Ay," he said at last. "'Tis like to be true. Count Otto rode this way with his child, meaning to leave him with our cousin at St. Ursula; for his mother was dead, and he was off to the Holy Land. He must have missed the convent road and got on the wrong way. Thou art strongly like him in looks, lad."

His voice was shaking, but Wulf noted it not; for he had drawn near to Karl,

who was bending over the wan prisoner. The boy's heart was nearly broken with
pity.

Was this his father, this doleful figure now resting against Karl, wholly unable
to support itself? Gently Wulf pressed the armorer back and took the slight weight
in his strong young arms. "'Tis mine to have charge of him, if ye all speak truth,"
he said.

Few were the dry eyes in that company as Wulf clasped the frail body to him
and the weary head rested against his breast.

"See that he is cared for," the emperor said at last, and from the throng came
the noblest of those knights to carry the count into the castle. Wulf would have
gone with them, but just then the emperor called him back.

"Stand forth," he said, pointing to a spot just before him, and Wulf obeyed.

"Thou hast fought well today, boy," Rudolf went on. "But for thy ready wit, that
led thy fellows by a way to fall upon the foe from behind, this castle had been long
in the winning, and our work by that much hindered. Thou hast proved thy gentle blood by the knightly deed thou didst for the young maid, now our own ward,
and sure are we that thou art the son of our loved comrade Count Otto von
Wulfstanger. Kneel down."

Then, as Wulf knelt, fair dazed by the surging of his own blood in his ears, the
emperor laid his drawn sword across the youth's bowed shoulders.

"Rise, Herr Wulf von Wulfstanger," he said.

The young knight, trembling like any timid maid, got to his feet again, though
how he could not have told.

"He'll need thy nursing a bit, Karl," Rudolf of Hapsburg said, an amused smile
playing about his grim mouth, and our Wulf never knew that the old armorer more
carried than led him away to quiet and rest.

NOT ALL IN a day was order restored at the Swartzburg; for many and woeful had
been the deeds of the high-handed robber who had so long ruled within those grim
walls. They came to light little by little under the searching of the emperor's war-
dens; and when the parchments relating to the Swartzburg properties came to be
examined, it was found that not the baron, nor Conradt, his heir-at-law, had all
along been owner of the castle, but young Elise von Hofenhoer, whose guardian the
treacherous noble had been. There were other outlying lands, as well, from which
the baron had long collected the revenues, and it was to keep his hold on what he
had so wrongfully seized that he would have by force have married Elise to
Conradt, his wicked nephew and ready tool.

The emperor himself now became guardian to the maiden, who, happy in the
safe shelter of St. Ursula, was to remain there until such time as a husband might

claim the right to fend for her and hers, if need should come.

And now our Wulf of the forge and the forest abode in the hall of his father, Count Otto von Wulfstanger, and made bright that wronged one's days. Rudolf of Hapsburg had long been in charge of the estates of the lost nobleman, and a straight accounting made the honest soldier-emperor to Wulf, as his heir, of all that he had held in trust.

With old Karl for helper and adviser, Wulf, all doubt and mystery cleared, ruled in the hall of his fathers. Later he brought to that stately home his fair bride from St. Ursula, given into his keeping by the emperor

The emporer laid his sword across Wulf's shoulders.

himself, and there, the story tells, Baron Wulf von Wulfstanger and his lady lived long a life of usefulness and good deeds, whereby those hard times were made easier for many, and the sunshine, gathered through the years, made warmth and light for others, as must always be in this world when any life is lived for the sake of usefulness and helpfulness.

First published in the December 1901 edition of *St. Nicholas Magazine*

"Pigs Is Pigs"

BY ELLIS PARKER BUTLER

MIKE FLANNERY, THE Westcote agent of the Interurban Express Company, leaned over the counter of the express office and shook his fist. Mr. Morehouse, angry and red, stood on the other side of the counter, trembling with rage. The argument had been long and heated, and at last Mr. Morehouse had talked himself speechless. The cause of the trouble stood on the counter between the two men. It was a soap box across the top of which were nailed a number of strips, forming a rough but serviceable cage. In it two spotted guinea-pigs were greedily eating lettuce leaves.

"Do as you loike, then!" shouted Flannery, "pay for thim an' take thim, or don't pay for thim and leave thim be. Rules is rules, Misther Morehouse, an' Mike Flannery's not goin' to be called down fer breakin' of thim."

"But, you everlastingly stupid idiot!" shouted Mr. Morehouse, madly shaking a flimsy printed book beneath the agent's nose, "can't you read it here—in your own plain printed rates? 'Pets, domestic, Franklin to Westcote, if properly boxed, twenty-five cents each.'" He threw the book on the counter in disgust. "What more do you want? Aren't they pets? Aren't they domestic? Aren't they properly boxed? What?"

He turned and walked back and forth rapidly, frowning ferociously.

Suddenly he turned to Flannery, and forcing his voice to an artificial calmness spoke slowly but with intense sarcasm.

"Pets," he said "P-e-t-s! Twenty-five cents each. There are two of them. One! Two! Two times twenty-five are fifty! Can you understand that? I offer you fifty cents."

Flannery reached for the book. He ran his hand through the pages and stopped at page sixty-four.

"An' I don't take fifty cints," he whispered in mockery. "Here's the rule for ut. 'Whin the agint be in anny doubt regardin' which of two rates applies to a shipment, he shall charge the larger. The con-sign-ey may file a claim for the overcharge.' In this case, Misther Morehouse, I be in doubt. Pets thim animals may be, an' domestic they be, but pigs I'm blame sure they do be, an' me rules says plain as the nose on yer face, 'Pigs Franklin to Westcote, thirty cints each.' An' Mister Morehouse, by me arithmetical knowledge two times thurty comes to sixty cints."

Mr. Morehouse shook his head savagely. "Nonsense!" he shouted, "confounded nonsense, I tell you! Why, you poor ignorant foreigner, that rule means common pigs, domestic pigs, not guinea pigs!"

Flannery was stubborn.

"Pigs is pigs," he declared firmly. "Guinea-pigs, or French pigs or Irish pigs is all the same to the Interurban Express Company an' to Mike Flannery. Th' nationality of the pig creates no differentiality in the rate, Misther Morehouse! 'Twould be the same was they Dutch pigs or Rooshun pigs. Mike Flannery," he added, "is here to tind to the exprise business and not to hould conversation wid guinea-pigs in sivinteen languages fer to discover be they Chinese or Tipperary by birth an' nativity."

"Pets thim animals may be, an' domestic they be, but pigs I'm blame sure they do be."

Mr. Morehouse hesitated. He bit his lip and then flung out his arms wildly.

"Very well!" he shouted, "you shall hear of this! Your president shall hear of this! It is an outrage! I have offered you fifty cents. You refuse it! Keep the pigs until you are ready to take the fifty cents, but, by George, sir, if one hair of those pigs' heads is harmed I will have the law on you!"

He turned and stalked out, slamming the door. Flannery carefully lifted the soap box from the counter and placed it in a corner. He was not worried. He felt the peace that comes to a faithful servant who has done his duty and done it well.

Mr. Morehouse went home raging. His boy, who had been awaiting the guinea-pigs, knew better than to ask him for them. He was a normal boy and therefore always had a guilty conscience when his father was angry. So the boy slipped quietly around the house. There is nothing so soothing to a guilty conscience as to be out of the path of the avenger. Mr. Morehouse stormed into the house. "Where's the ink?" he shouted at his wife as soon as his foot was across the doorsill.

Mrs. Morehouse jumped, guiltily. She never used ink. She had not seen the ink, nor moved the ink, nor thought of the ink, but her husband's tone convicted her of the guilt of having borne and reared a boy, and she knew that whenever her husband wanted anything in a loud voice the boy had been at it.

"I'll find Sammy," she said meekly.

When the ink was found Mr. Morehouse wrote rapidly, and he read the completed letter and smiled a triumphant smile.

"That will settle that crazy Irishman!" he exclaimed. "When they get that letter he will hunt another job, all right!"

A week later Mr. Morehouse received a long official envelope with the card of the Interurban Express Company in the upper left corner. He tore it open eagerly and drew out a sheet of paper. At the top it bore the number A6754. The letter was short. "Subject—Rate on guinea-pigs," it said, "Dr. Sir—We are in receipt of your letter regarding rate on guinea-pigs between Franklin and Westcote addressed to the president of this company. All claims for overcharge should be addressed to the Claims Department."

Mr. Morehouse wrote to the Claims Department. He wrote six pages of choice sarcasm, vituperation, and argument, and sent them to the Claims Department.

A few weeks later he received a reply from the Claims Department. Attached to it was his last letter.

"Dr. Sir," said the reply. "Your letter of the 16th inst., addressed to this Department, subject rate on guinea-pigs from Franklin to Westcote, rec'd. We have taken up the matter with our agent at Westcote, and his reply is attached herewith. He informs us that you refused to receive the consignment or to pay the charges. You have therefore no claim against this company, and your letter regarding the proper rate on the consignment should be addressed to our Tariff Department."

Mr. Morehouse wrote to the Tariff Department. He stated his case clearly, and gave his arguments in full, quoting a page or two from the encyclopedia to prove that guinea-pigs were not common pigs.

With the care that characterizes corporations when they are systematically conducted, Mr. Morehouse's letter was numbered, O.K'd, and started through the regular channels. Duplicate copies of the bill of lading, manifest, Flannery's receipt for the package, and several other pertinent papers were pinned to the letter, and they were passed to the head of the Tariff Department.

The head of the Tariff Department put his feet on his desk and yawned. He looked through the papers carelessly.

"Miss Kane," he said to his stenographer, "take this letter. 'Agent, Westcote, N.J. Please advise why consignment referred to in attached papers was refused domestic pet rates.'"

Miss Kane made a series of curves and angles on her notebook and waited with pencil poised. The head of the department looked at the papers again.

"Huh! guinea-pigs!" he said. "Probably starved to death by this time! Add this to that letter: 'Give condition of consignment at present.'"

He tossed the papers onto the stenographer's desk, took his feet from his own desk, and went out to lunch.

When Mike Flannery received the letter he scratched his head.

"Give prisint condition," he repeated thoughtfully. "Now what do thim clerks be wantin' to know, I wonder! 'Prisint condition,' is ut? Thim pigs, praise St. Patrick, do be in good health, so far as I know, but I niver was no veternairy surgeon to guinea-pigs. Mebby thim clerks wants me to call in the pig docther an' have their pulses took. Wan thing I do know, howiver, which is they've glorious appytites for pigs of their soize. Ate? They'd ate the brass padlocks off of a barn door! If the paddy pig, by the same token, ate as hearty as these guinea-pigs do, there'd be a famine in Ireland."

To assure himself that his report would be up to date, Flannery went to the rear of the office and looked into the cage. The pigs had been transferred to a larger box—a dry goods box.

"Wan—two—t'ree—four—five—six—sivin—eight!" he counted. "Sivin spotted an' wan all black. All well an' hearty an' all eatin' loike ragin' hippypottymusses. He went back to his desk and wrote.

"Mr. Morgan, Head of Tariff Department," he wrote. "Why do I say guinea-pigs is pigs because they is pigs and will be til you say they ain't which is what the rule book says stop your jollying me you know it as well as I do. As to health they are all well and hoping you are the same. P. S. There are eight now the family increased all good eaters. P. S. I paid out so far two dollars for cabbage which they like shall I put in bill for same what?"

Morgan, head of the Tariff Department, when he received this letter, laughed. He read it again and became serious.

"By George!" he said, "Flannery is right, 'pigs is pigs.' I'll have to get authority on this thing. Meanwhile, Miss Kane, take this letter: Agent, Westcote, N.J. Regarding shipment guinea-pigs, File No. A6754. Rule 83, General Instruction to Agents, clearly states that agents shall collect from consignee all costs of provender, etc., etc., required for live stock while in transit or storage. You will proceed to collect same from consignee."

Flannery received this letter next morning, and when he read it he grinned.

"Proceed to collect," he said softly. "How thim clerks do loike to be talkin'! *Me* proceed to collect two dollars and twinty-foive cints off Misther Morehouse! I wonder do thim clerks *know* Misther Morehouse? I'll git it! Oh, yes! 'Misther Morehouse, two an' a quarter, plaze.' 'Cert'nly, me dear frind Flannery. Delighted!' *Not!*"

Flannery drove the express wagon to Mr. Morehouse's door. Mr. Morehouse answered the bell.

"Ah, ha!" he cried as soon as he saw it was Flannery. "So you've come to your senses at last, have you? I thought you would! Bring the box in."

"I hev no box," said Flannery coldly. "I hev a bill agin Misther John C. Morehouse for two dollars and twinty-foive cints for kebbages aten by his pigs. Wud you wish to pay ut?"

"Pay—Cabbages—!" gasped Mr. Morehouse. "Do you mean to say that two little guinea-pigs—"

"Eight!" said Flannery. "Papa an' mamma an' the six childer. Eight!"

"Flannery is right, 'pigs is pigs.'"

For answer Mr. Morehouse slammed the door in Flannery's face. Flannery looked at the door reproachfully.

"I take ut the con-*sign*-y don't want to pay for thim kebbages," he said. "If I know signs of refusal, the con-*sign*-y refuses to pay for wan dang kebbage leaf an' be hanged to me!"

Mr. Morgan, the head of the Tariff Department, consulted the president of the Interurban Express Company regarding guinea-pigs, as to whether they were pigs or not pigs. The president was inclined to treat the matter lightly.

"What is the rate on pigs and on pets?" he asked.

"Pigs thirty cents, pets twenty-five," said Morgan.

"Then of course guinea-pigs are pigs," said the president.

"Yes," agreed Morgan, "I look at it that way, too. A thing that can come under two rates is naturally due to be classed as the higher. But are guinea-pigs, pigs? Aren't they rabbits?"

"Come to think of it," said the president, "I believe they are more like rabbits. Sort of half-way station between pig and rabbit. I think the question is this—are guinea-pigs of the domestic pig family? I'll ask professor Gordon. He is authority on such things. Leave the papers with me."

The president put the papers on his desk and wrote a letter to Professor Gordon. Unfortunately the Professor was in South America collecting zoological specimens, and the letter was forwarded to him by his wife. As the Professor was in the highest Andes, where no white man had ever penetrated, the letter was many months in reaching him. The president forgot the guinea-pigs, Morgan forgot them, Mr. Morehouse forgot them, but Flannery did not. One-half of his time he gave to the duties of his agency; the other half was devoted to the guinea-pigs. Long before Professor Gordon received the president's letter Morgan received one from Flannery.

"About them pigs," it said, "what shall I do they are great in family life, no race suicide for them, there are thirty-two now shall I sell them do you take this express office for a menagerie, answer quick."

Morgan reached for a telegraph blank and wrote:

"Agent, Westcote. Don't sell pigs."

He then wrote Flannery a letter calling his attention to the fact that the pigs were not the property of the company but were merely being held during a settlement of a dispute regarding rates. He advised Flannery to take the best possible care of them.

Flannery, letter in hand, looked at the pigs and sighed. The dry-goods box cage had become too small. He boarded up twenty feet of the rear of the express office to make a large and airy home for them, and went about his business. He worked with feverish intensity when out on his rounds, for the pigs required attention and took most of his time. Some months later, in desperation, he seized a sheet of paper and wrote "160" across it and mailed it to Morgan. Morgan returned it asking for explanation. Flannery replied:

"There be now one hundred sixty of them guinea-pigs, for heavens sake let me sell off some, do you want me to go crazy, what."

"Sell no pigs," Morgan wired.

Not long after this the president of the express company received a letter from Professor Gordon. It was a long and scholarly letter, but the point was that the guinea-pig was the *Cavia aparoea* while the common pig was the genus *Sus* of the family *Suidae*. He remarked that they were prolific and multiplied rapidly.

"They are not pigs," said the president, decidedly, to Morgan. "The twenty-five cent rate applies."

Morgan made the proper notation on the papers that had accumulated in File A6754, and turned them over to the Audit Department. The Audit Department took some time to look the matter up, and after the usual delay wrote Flannery that as he had on hand one hundred and sixty guinea-pigs, the property of consignee, he should deliver them and collect charges at the rate of twenty-five cents each.

Flannery spent a day herding his charges through a narrow opening in their cage so that he might count them.

"Audit Dept." he wrote, when he had finished the count, "you are way off there may be was one hundred and sixty guinea-pigs once, but wake up don't be a back number. I've got even eight hundred, now shall I collect for eight hundred or what, how about sixty-four dollars I paid out for cabbages."

It required a great many letters back and forth before the Audit Department was able to understand why the error had been made of billing one hundred and sixty instead of eight hundred, and still more time for it to get the meaning of the "cabbages."

Flannery was crowded into a few feet at the extreme front of the office. The pigs had all the rest of the room and two boys were employed constantly attending to them. The

"Proceed to collect."

day after Flannery had counted the guinea-pigs there were eight more added to his drove, and by the time the Audit Department gave him authority to collect for eight hundred Flannery had given up all attempts to attend to the receipt or the delivery of goods. He was hastily building galleries around the express office, tier above tier. He had four thousand and sixty-four guinea-pigs to care for! More were arriving daily.

Immediately following its authorization the Audit Department sent another letter, but Flannery was too busy to open it. They wrote another and then they telegraphed:

"Error in guinea-pig bill. Collect for two guinea-pigs, fifty cents. Deliver all to consignee."

Flannery read the telegram and cheered up. He wrote out a bill as rapidly as his pencil could travel over paper and ran all the way to the Morehouse home. At the gate he stopped suddenly. The house stared at him with vacant eyes. The windows were bare of curtains and he could see into the empty rooms. A sign on the porch said, "To Let." Mr. Morehouse had moved! Flannery ran all the way back to the express office. Sixty-nine guinea-pigs had been born during his absence. He ran out again and made feverish inquiries in the village. Mr. Morehouse had not only moved, but he had left Westcote. Flannery returned to the express office and found that two hundred and six guinea-pigs had entered the world since he left it. He wrote a telegram to the Audit Department.

"Can't collect fifty cents for two pigs consignee has left town address unknown what shall I do? Flannery."

The telegram was handed to one of the clerks in the Audit Department, and as he read it he laughed.

"Flannery must be crazy. He ought to know that the thing to do is to return the consignment here," said the clerk. He telegraphed Flannery to send the pigs to the main office of the company at Franklin.

When Flannery received the telegram he set to work. The six boys he had engaged to help him also set to work. They worked with the haste of desperate men, making cages out of soap boxes, cracker boxes, and all kinds of boxes, and as fast as the cages were completed they filled them with guinea-pigs and expressed them to

Mr. Morehouse had moved!

Franklin. Day after day the cages of guinea-pigs flowed in a steady stream from Westcote to Franklin, and still Flannery and his six helpers ripped and nailed and packed—relentlessly and feverishly. At the end of the week they had shipped two hundred and eighty cases of guinea-pigs, and there were in the express office seven hundred and four more pigs than when they began packing them.

"Stop sending pigs. Warehouse full," came a telegram to Flannery. He stopped packing only long enough to wire back, "Can't stop," and kept on sending them. On the next train up from Franklin came one of the company's inspectors. He had instructions to stop the stream of guinea-pigs at all hazards. As his train drew up at Westcote station he saw a cattle car standing on the express company's siding. When he reached the express office he saw the express wagon backed up to the door. Six boys were carrying bushel baskets full of guinea-pigs from the office and dumping them into the wagon. Inside the room Flannery, with his coat and vest off, was shoveling guinea-pigs into bushel baskets with a coal scoop. He was winding up the guinea-pig episode.

Winding up the guinea-pig episode

He looked up at the inspector with a snort of anger.

"Wan wagonload more an' I'll be quit of thim, an' niver will ye catch Flannery wid no more foreign pigs on his hands. No, sur! They near was the death o' me. Nixt toime I'll know that pigs of whaiver nationality is domistic pets—an' go at the lowest rate."

He began shoveling again rapidly, speaking quickly between breaths.

"Rules may be rules, but you can't fool Mike Flannery twice wid the same thrick—whin ut comes to live stock, dang the rules. So long as Flannery runs this expriss office—pigs is pets—an' cows is pets—an' horses is pets—an' lions an' tigers an' Rocky Mountain goats is pets—an' the rate on thim is twinty-foive cints."

He paused long enough to let one of the boys put an empty basket in the place of the one he had just filled. There were only a few guinea-pigs left. As he noted their limited number his natural habit of looking on the bright side returned.

"Well, annyhow," he said cheerfully, "'tis not so bad as ut might be. What if thim pigs had been elephants!"

First published in the September 1905 edition of *The American Magazine*

Frieda's Doves

BY BLANCHE WILLIS HOWARD

FRIEDA GRIEVED MOST at leaving the cathedral. For Freiburg itself she cared little. She was only a lame child, who could not run about with her strong brothers, and sometimes, indeed, when her back was very weary, she could not even walk. But she was not unhappy, for Bäbele was always kind, and was so gentle on the days when the pain came that the touch of her rough, hard-working hands was as tender as an angel's, Frieda thought. And then Bäbele was so droll, and knew how to tell such delightful tales about the Höllenthal, the wild mountain pass near Freiburg, through which the boys often tramped to gather and bring home flowers for the little sister. "Here are your weeds, Frieda," they would shout, laughingly, and would almost bury the little girl under the fresh fragrant mass of blossoms. The brothers were rough sometimes with one another, but never to Frieda. Johann, the eldest, worked with his father in the picture department of a publishing house. Heinrich and Otto were still at school.

In the twilight, after the day's work was done and before it was quite dark enough to light the candle—for they were poor and thrifty people, who had to be careful not to waste anything—Bäbele used to take Frieda in her arms and tell her wonderful tales, not only of the wild Hollenthal, but of the Wildsee, the Mummelsee, the Murgthal, and many another spot in the Black Forest, as well as legends of the Rhine and the Hartz Mountains, and of the Thuringian Woods and the Wartburg; and the most astonishing thing was, there was never a day when the pain came that Bäbele, although she had been telling fairy tales all these years—and Frieda was nine years old now—did not have a perfectly marvelous story to tell, full of unheard-of adventures, and irresistible charm. And Frieda would listen entranced, until she forgot the poor little aching back that did not grow straight like other children's backs.

But it did not always ache, and Frieda was really a contented little girl, and merry, too, in her quiet way. She used to sit in her low chair and watch Bäbele at her work, and croon sweet solemn airs she heard in the cathedral, and help, too, whenever she could. Sometimes she could sew a button on Johann's shirt, or even darn a sock for restless little Otto, who wore everything out so fast; and she was always pleased to be useful.

At night, when the boys came home, they would tell her what had happened to them during the day, and she was clever enough to assist Heinrich and Otto with their lessons, for in her feeble body dwelt a sweet, strong, and helpful spirit. Then Johann would explain to her how they made pictures, until she understood the process almost as well as he. As for her papa, she saw little of him except during the dinner hour at noon; for he worked hard all day, and when evening came sat with his fellow-workmen smoking his pipe, and seldom came home until after the children were asleep. He did his best for his family, but he had never been the same man, Bäbele said, since his bright, cheery wife died, and that was a few months after Frieda was born. And these nine years Bäbele had staid on, and kept the house and the children clean, and toiled early and late, and all for love of Frieda; for it was little wages that she received, and the growing boys needed more and more every day, and Frieda's father would have been desperate and helpless without faithful Bäbele. When the neighbors remonstrated and told her she could get higher wages as servant in some grand house, she replied scornfully:

"A dress on my back, a roof over my head, and bread enough for the day—what more do I want? And I wouldn't live without Frieda, no, not in the King's palace and on the King's throne, and that's the beginning and the end of it."

The neighbors shook their heads and advised this and that, because neighbors like to seem wise and delight to give advice, but in their hearts they thought all the more of Bäbele for her devotion to Frieda.

So, though lame and motherless and poor, Frieda was not an unhappy child. She had many joys, and the greatest joy of all was the cathedral. They lived close by, almost in its shadow, and on her "well days" Bäbele used to lead Frieda over and leave her there alone for hours, knowing that no harm could come to her in that sacred place. The old beadle knew her well and was kind to her, and all the people who came regularly learned to look for the quiet little figure sitting alone by the great pillar, and to be glad of the gentle smile of greeting from the pale child with the large brown eyes and the heavy chestnut hair falling below her waist, concealing with its beautiful luxuriance the pitiful little hump between the shoulders.

Strangers often turned to wonder at the blessed, peaceful look the deformed child wore. But they need not have wondered. She knew only love at home, and lived always among beautiful thoughts. Why should she not be happy?

There she would sit by the hour watching the warm violet and rose lights from the stained-glass windows, gleaming and glowing here and there on the cold stone, now falling on the bowed head of a peasant woman kneeling with her heavy basket by her side, now lingering on the cheek and hair and soft rich draperies of a fair young girl. How Frieda loved the changing lights! How she loved all she saw there in the great, solemn, still cathedral. The massive shafts, the noble arches, the slanting rays of colored light, the many voices of the organ. She knew it all so well that she could see every line as clearly when her eyes were closed as when they were open.

The corner of the cathedral

Only once did anything ever happen to make her refuge seem less dear and safe. It was in summer, when Freiburg is full of strangers. Frieda was so used to them, she knew at a glance, when a party came into the church, whether they were people who really loved the noble lines as she did, or whether they were what she called the "tired ones" who looked too weary to love anything, or the business-like, loud-talking ones who always mentioned that they had "been in Milan and Cologne, and did not think much of this cathedral." Little did Frieda care for the unfavorable compari-son. It was her cathedral, her world. And little did people know how close an observer the still, fragile child was. She was too gentle to criticize, but she uncon-sciously made very clever distinctions. One day a gentleman and lady and a boy of ten or twelve entered the cathedral. "He is a tired one," thought Frieda, "and she has been in Milan and Cologne." The boy had small black eyes, quick move-ments, was richly dressed, and carried a little cane. As they passed, the lady gave the lonely little figure by the pillar a careless glance, and threw some pennies into her lap. This did not wound Frieda's gentle spirit. Such a thing had, indeed, hap-pened now and then, but only unthinking, careless people could possibly make the mistake of imagining that those restful, patient eyes were asking for charity. Frieda rose slowly, walked over to a poor-box, and dropped the pennies in. The lady and gentleman had gone on, and did not see her. The boy looked at her mockingly with his hard, bright eyes, and then said: "This is the way you go," at the same time dropping his chin on his breast, hunching his back, and walking with a slow, mincing step.

The English words Frieda did not understand, but the tone and the action were too brutally plain to mistake their meaning. Like a crushed flower the lame child sank drooping into her chair, and looked with wide, sorrowful eyes at the boy, who, with a grimace and a "Good-bye, Owl!" ran on to join his parents.

When Bäbele came to take Frieda home, the little girl was pale and very silent. Bäbele thought she was weary, but when the next day and the next and still another day came, and she said gently that she did not care to go to the cathedral, but preferred to stay with her good Bäbele, the faithful woman grew anxious.

"Is it the pain, my Frieda?"

"No, Bäbele, it's not the pain. At least, it's not *that* pain," the child said, gravely.

"Where is the pain, then?" asked Bäbele.

"Only here," said Frieda, pressing her slight hand against her heart. Then suddenly, for the first time in her life, she asked:

"Why didn't God make me straight, like the other children?"

And then poor Bäbele, whose love had so guarded the child that no harsh thing had ever disturbed her peace, knew that some strange hand had struck a blow, over which her darling had grieved many days; and, kneeling by Frieda's bed, she sobbed aloud, and taking the child in her strong arms, and covering her with kisses, said, in her warm, German fashion:

"Dearest, dear little heart, what makes the pain? What cruel thing has happened that my darling never wants to see the pretty lights or hear the grand organ any more? Tell thy Bäbele, little sweetheart."

"He had very black eyes and a velvet hat," murmured Frieda slowly, "and a crimson necktie, and a little walking-stick with an ivory dog's head. He did not mean any harm. He did not know it would make a pain in my heart to have him show me how I looked, and he made his pretty little straight back very ugly"—she was whispering now—"and I thought if I was like that, I must disturb people who come to see tall straight pillars, so I'd better stay away."

Bäbele trembled from head to foot. She saw it all now as if she had been present. Her darling, who had lived in a magic world of legendary lore and poetry and music, who had known all her life only the calm, solemn influences of the cathedral and the tender sweet influences of her simple home, had been wounded to the heart by this strange boy, and cruelly awakened to a consciousness of the deformity which separated her from other children.

"My lamb, my angel, I would give much to have saved thee this and to have kept the pain from thy heart," Bäbele exclaimed, adding fiercely, "and if I had that imp here I'd wring his neck and crush him in my two hands."

"Oh, no!" whispered Frieda, laying her gentle hand on Bäbele's lips. "The little strange boy did not know. He did not know how I love the straight pillars and high arches. He did not know I forgot to think of myself because I love them so—and I *am* crooked, Bäbele," she went on with a piteous sob——"I AM. He could not help seeing it."

"Dear heart," said Bäbele, kissing the frail hands again and again, "I am only an ignorant woman, and I don't know how to make things clear. Even the wise men can't make things clear always. But I know this much. Something is wanting everywhere. It must be best so, or it wouldn't be so. And thou, my angel, thy back is crooked, but thy spirit is straight—and the wicked boy who mocked thee, his back is straight, but his spirit is crooked—and oh, thou darling of my heart, perhaps no one loves him as thy old Bäbele loves thee!"

"No," said the child, thoughtfully, "his papa was too tired to love him, and his mamma was too busy. Poor little boy!"

There was a long, long silence. Then Frieda smiled again. Throwing her arms round Bäbele's neck, she said softly to her faithful guardian:

"Love is best!" and the next day she said, "Please take me over, Bäbele dear. I want my lights," and Bäbele could have wept for joy as she led her to the cathedral. If after that Frieda shrank a little behind her favorite pillar when she saw a certain kind of boy coming toward her, and if she breathed more freely when he had passed, and if her great deep eyes seemed to grow still larger, still more thoughtful than before, at least she never complained, and she kept her thoughts to herself.

Months passed by, and in time she was ten years old, and everybody was sad because her papa had died. Bäbele at first scarcely knew what to do with the four children. But she was, as usual, brave and patient, and help came. Frieda's uncle from Geneva said he would take Heinrich and Otto and send them to school, and Johann was seventeen now and a steady lad, and he must continue where he was and look out for himself. As to Frieda, here the uncle hesitated. His own family was large, his wife had many cares, and was not very patient. The boys would be out of the house most of the day, and they would not mind a hasty word now and then, but this pale, lame child, with the strange soft eyes—he shook his head doubtfully.

"*Ach*, I will take the blessed lamb!" cried Bäbele. "She would grieve so among strangers. Let me take her with me and I will make a home for her in my old home.

Indeed, she shall not want while I live—and she is like an angel in the house, she is so wise and so sweet. She brings a blessing with her wherever she goes."

So all was arranged. Johann was to stay in Freiburg. Heinrich and Otto were to go to Geneva, and Frieda was to go to Bäbele's old home. Frieda was very sad, for she dreaded leaving the boys. But Johann, Otto, and Heinrich perhaps could come to her some day, Bäbele said, and could write to her always. But the cathedral, thought Frieda, could neither come nor write, and so, in her childish way, she grieved most of all at leaving the cathedral.

FRIEDA KISSED HER brothers good-bye with a large lump in her throat, the day they went off with their uncle. She tied Otto's cravat with trembling fingers, and brushed Heinrich's hat in her motherly little fashion, but did not cry, for Bäbele had told her that the parting would be harder for the boys if she were not brave. After they were gone, and the house began to feel strangely still and empty, Bäbele led her into the cathedral and left her there for the last time in her old place. The poor little girl pressed her cheek against the cold pillar and sobbed as if her heart would break. At least, she need not restrain her tears out of consideration for the cathedral's feelings. That was a comfort. No one noticed her. The shadows were deepening around her. Still clinging to the pillar, she wept until she stopped out of pure weariness. She was so little, so troubled. The cathedral was so vast and tall and calm. She grew quieted in spite of herself. "Everybody must love Heinrich and Otto and be good to them, for they are good!" she said. "And I can always remember that I used to be here. Nothing can take that away," and the thought comforted her, though a great sob came with it. Then the organ began. Its thrilling tones seemed to be the voice of the great cathedral saying farewell to the pained little soul. She closed her eyes and sat motionless. Great waves of music surged round her. And above the mighty volume of tone soared a single pure melody, ever sweeter, ever higher, up into the vaulted roof, up to the skies, up to heaven itself. The tired child felt as if she were lying in strong and tender arms, and as if many murmuring voices were saying softly, "Be loving! Be brave! Farewell!" She smiled gently. "Farewell, little Frieda! Be brave, be brave!" said the voices.

When Bäbele came, she found Frieda fast asleep, her tear-stained but placid face pressed close against the pillar, her arms clasping it lovingly. The next day they left Freiburg. Frieda was quite calm. She looked at the cathedral spires as they passed.

"Wilt thou go in, once more, my lamb?" asked Bäbele, anxiously watching her face.

"No," answered the child, gravely. "We said good-bye to each other yesterday."

It was a short journey to Bäbele's old home, but long and hard for Frieda. She had never been in the cars, and they jarred and wearied her sadly, though Bäbele traveled slowly and gave her long rests, taking three days to do what she herself would have done in one, had she been alone. As they reached their destination, Bäbele was wild with delight.

"See, dear heart," she cried, "how it lies among the hills. It is like a warm nest in this great cold world. And out beyond, a long, long way, is our village. And there's the old castle and the tower and the great drooping trees of the park."

Now it was far too dark to see anything whatever, except the lighted streets of the new city, but Frieda strained her eyes and dutifully tried to look in all directions at once to please Bäbele, whom she had never before seen so excited and gay. Presently a stout, broad-waisted, rosy lass darted from among the crowd by the station with a hearty:

"Greeting! Greeting, Bäbele! Dost thou not remember thy cousin Rickele? Have I grown so old in ten long years?"

"*Ach was!* Thou art little Rickele! And thou wast such a wee bit of a thing!" And Bäbele laughed and cried for joy.

"And the mother greets thee, and she has chosen a good room for thee, as thou didst write, and I am to take thee there, but I cannot be spared long, for the mistress said I was to come back in an hour, and the mother bids thee and the little one welcome, and she will come to thee when she brings her butter and eggs to market next week; and the neighbors greet thee, Bäbele, and wish thee health and good days with thy homecoming; and Peter, the shoemaker, has taken the baker's Mariele, and the wedding is next month, and the dance will be at the 'Golden Lamb.'"

So the girl chattered on, telling all the news of the village, swinging the travelers' boxes and bags, answering Bäbele's eager questions and leading the way to the new home.

The chatter, the lights and buildings, together with her fatigue, made Frieda quite confused, but she looked up so sweetly at this great, strong, kind Rickele that the girl's heart was won in a moment. "I will carry thee, little one!" she exclaimed, as they reached a tall dark house in a narrow street, and swinging the child up like a feather, she bore her in triumph up four long steep flights of stairs to the little room awaiting them.

The room had a sloping ceiling and a dormer window. There were two narrow beds in it, a stove, a bare wooden table, a couple of chairs, a chest of drawers, a few shelves with plates, cups, a dish or two, and a pitcher on them, bright brass kitchen utensils hanging on the wall, and a pot of pinks on the window-sill. Poor as it all was, the bare white floor shone from its recent scouring, and the room was as neat and clean as strong arms and willing hearts could make it.

With a deep sigh of contentment, Bäbele surveyed her apartment. It was to be her home, and the home of the being she loved best on earth. To keep it, she must toil early and late. What mattered it? It was her own as long as she could pay for it, and she was once more among her kinfolk—she was among the hills she had climbed as a girl. The very air she breathed was dear to her.

"Ah! How happy we shall be in this nest, my Frieda!" she exclaimed. "How beautiful is the homecoming to the wanderer! But thou art weary, my lamb; thou must eat a bit and sleep." And she undressed the child and laid her in her bed, beneath the great red coverlet of feathers, which seemed like an enormous hen cheerfully spreading its warm wings over the tired little girl.

"Sleep soft, my treasure!"

"Good-night, dear Bäbele; good night, Rickele," murmured Frieda, drowsily, and she sank to sleep with the shafts of the cathedral rising before her eyes, and the organ pealing in her ears, above all the noise and bustle of the journey.

It was after nine the next morning when Frieda woke. Bäbele had already prepared their simple breakfast. The same joy still beamed from her honest face. She kissed Frieda again and again, and called her her sweet angel, as she helped her dress, then led her to one of the little windows in the roof. The child saw at first only sunshine and roofs; roofs near, roofs far, roofs everywhere. It was so high, so strange. At Freiburg they had no stairs to climb. They were on the ground-floor. Here they were as high as birds. Frieda threw open the casement. The fresh spring breezes touched her cheek and blew her long hair. The sun shone on steep, red roofs and quaint gables. Two white doves sat on the roof near by. Frieda laughed and threw them bread crumbs from her breakfast. A big cat was

The dormer window

solemnly blinking his eyes in a dormer window of the next house. Beyond the roofs rose the church tower; beyond the tower the fair, green hills.

"Oh, Bäbele, how happy I am!" cried Frieda. "When I shut my eyes, I see my cathedral; when I open them, here are the roofs and the doves."

And Bäbele looked at her with tears of joy.

This was the homecoming. It began kindly, with the welcome of friends and the heaven's sunshine. But long days of wearisome work followed. Bäbele could not go into service, because of the child; so she did washing and mending, and bravely earned each day the bread they ate. The days she washed at home, Frieda was contented as a kitten, and made the hours fly by with her sweet songs and quaint remarks. But the four days of the week, when Bäbele went off at day-break and Frieda was alone until toward evening, were very, very long for the little girl, and she spent them as best she might. With wide-open eyes she watched the doves, and the roofs, and the hills, then shut her eyes and saw the cathedral. She kept the wash accounts, and answered politely if anybody came to inquire about Bäbele Hartneck, the washerwoman, and when at last Bäbele returned, the two were happy as queens.

And Sundays! Ah, those were blessed days. Then Bäbele had time to take Frieda down the four steep flights and out, out into the spring-time, out among the lilies of the valley, and the yellow cowslips and crocuses and slender jonquils, and all the sweet flowers that grow on the Suabian hills. Sometimes she would even manage to get taken out to Bachsdorf, where her people lived, and where the irregular, queer little houses seemed to be gossiping together and nodding their heads till they almost touched over the narrow straggling village street, and where the peasants in their red waistcoats and silver buttons and knickerbockers would sit the whole afternoon, under the chestnut trees of the 'Golden Lamb' garden, and Bäbele would laugh as Frieda never heard her laugh in the old Freiburg days. The week was long and full of toil, but Sunday, under a fair sky, among kinsfolk and old friends, brought freedom, joy, and peace.

The two were quite happy—Bäbele could scarcely save a penny, but she was strong and brave and always had steady work. One day there was a great surprise for Frieda. She was alone. There came a heavy thumping at the door, and actually four men brought in a *pianino* into the small crowded room. Bäbele had discovered it among all sorts of rubbish, at a pawnbroker's shop, and hired it for a mere nothing.

"Art thou stark mad, Bäbele Hartneck," cried the other washerwoman on the same floor. "Do the Freiburg washerwomen scrub to the sound of music?" And all the neighbors standing in their door-ways with their hands on their hips, laughed loud and long at Bäbele's foolishness.

"Be easy, neighbor," replied Bäbele, stoutly. "Wash thine own skirts, and I will wash mine. Thou hast no angel in thy room. Angels in heaven have their harps. Mine shall have her sweet sounds. Let me go my way. I am no babe born yesterday." And the neighbors were silent and laughed no more; for they loved Frieda's gentle ways and earnest eyes.

After this bold deed of Bäbele's, Frieda never had one lonely moment. The tones of the piano were quavering, like those of a very old lady's voice, but like that, too, it retained a few sweet notes suggestive of a far-off youth, and Frieda knew how to bring out all its faint sweetness, and was so blessed, she did not mind its frequent wheezes. And what else did this wise, imprudent, loving, obstinate, dear Bäbele do? She found a hard-working young girl who gave music lessons, and, on the principle that exchange is no robbery, made a certain practical little arrangement with her, by which Bäbele had a couple of hours' extra work now and then, and Frieda, twice a week, a half-hour's instruction in music. Now, Frieda's life was quite full. Up in her nest among the roofs, far above the noise of the busy streets, she was at rest. Hour after hour she was alone, but not lonely. She was not strong enough to work hard at her music, but she loved it, and it loved her and lingered with her. Besides what her teacher taught her, fragments of old fugues and Masses she had heard in the cathedral found their way from her heart to her frail little fingers. And when she was weary, there were the open casement, the red roofs and gables, the doves, the tower, the hills.

"How beautiful and kind the world is!" thought the little lame child, who spent most of her days alone in the little room under the roof.

Two years passed in this quiet fashion. Things had scarcely changed at all. Bäbele worked on as steadily, as cheerily, as ever, managed to pay her way, and was thankful. One warm June day, Frieda stood at her casement. Bäbele would not return until five o'clock. The little girl had softly played an adagio of Beethoven's until she was weary. She had then fed her doves, who had fluttered about her, perched lovingly on her shoulder, and finally taken their position on the sunny roof below, cooing and pluming themselves.

"Pretty dears!" said Frieda, and carelessly taking up a wash-book from the table near by, and a stump of a pencil, half unconsciously she began to draw their softly curving heads. "Heads must have bodies," she said aloud, and presently the two doves from their beaks to their tails adorned a blank page of somebody's wash-book.

"Doves can't stand on nothing," murmured Frieda, and merely to give the doves a resting-place, she hastily sketched the roof, and then other roofs, the chimney, the curious little dormer windows, then, quite naturally, the old church tower, the lines of the distant hills, even the great masses of white clouds, where she saw all the heroes of the fairy tales she knew so well. It was all done to give the doves a place to perch upon, and a background.

"There, my dears. How do you like sitting for your portraits?" and she added a heavier line to Elsa's beak, and made Lohengrin's tail feathers more airy. At this moment, Dornroschen and the Prince happened to appear on the scene, and perched lower down on the same roof. "Dearie me, I must make you too or you'll be jealous as usual!" laughed Frieda, and Dornroschen and the Prince were added to the sketch.

It was really very curious. Frieda had never drawn anything in all her life. Her papa used to draw, and Johann too was quite clever with his pencil. But a little girl like her!—the idea had never occurred to her. Now, in this careless fashion, having finished her doves, she shut her eyes an instant in order to see better, and then with bold, clear strokes began to draw the picture that was imprinted on her soul—the shafts, the high arches, the rich window where the lovely lights streamed in—in short, the whole of her favorite corner in the cathedral. Swiftly, unhesitatingly the child's hand moved. Her cheeks flushed. The doves fluttered about her in vain. She heard no sounds rising from the street. She was back in the old days. Again she was listening to the organ, and to the high, clear, angel voice leading her soul far away. And when it was finished, she gave a sigh of relief, then closing the book, thought no more about it.

She might indeed have remembered her sketches and laughingly have shown them to Bäbele, had not a misfortune come to them which put such trifles quite out of her head. Poor Bäbele was brought home that very day with a badly sprained ankle. She had slipped on a wet floor and fallen, as she was moving a heavy tub.

She tried hard to be patient and not distress Frieda, but the prospect of long helpless days with her foot up in a chair was trying enough to the active woman, and more than that, she knew they needed her daily work for their daily bread. But how good everybody was! The baker round the corner sent some rolls the next day as soon as he heard of the accident, and the butcher a bit of good meat, and the rival washerwoman on the same floor came in to take home clothes that were finished and wash-books—and Bäbele rubbed her eyes and said, "It's all because of that blessed angel!"

It was Monday that she came home unfit for work. Thursday morning there was a violent knock at the door. Bäbele started instinctively, but lay back with a moan, as Frieda opened the door.

A gray-haired old gentleman with shaggy eyebrows, and looking quite cross, came in. In one hand he carried a cane, in the other something very like a wash-book.

He gave one sharp look at Bäbele with her foot up—another at Frieda, who thought he was more like an ogre than any being she had ever seen.

"Good-morning," he said, gruffly. "I wish to find the young man who made these things in my book." And he pointed a stern forefinger at Frieda's sketches.

She came timidly forward. "If you please, sir, it was I. I didn't mean any harm, sir. I was only making my doves at first. I am very sorry I scribbled in your book, sir."

The gentleman looked at her in blank amazement. "You!" was all he could ejaculate, glancing at the shy little figure before him.

"Yes, if you please, sir," said Frieda, now thoroughly alarmed.

"You, indeed!" said the gruff voice again and, taking out his handkerchief, this very strange old gentleman gave a loud and vehement blast.

"Yes, sir," said Frieda, great tears gathering in her eyes, "and I'm sure I'm very sorry, sir."

"H'm!" muttered the stranger, "if you did it, do it again now."

Frieda seized her stump of a pencil and obediently looked about for a sheet of paper.

"Take this," he said, abruptly, giving her the wash-book. With perfect simplicity the child took it and began. Leaning an elbow on the table, and resting her head on her left hand, her long hair falling over her face, steadily and firmly she did her work. She quite forgot the cross old gentleman's sharp eyes, and only saw the soft violet lights from the stained window, as the picture grew beneath her sure, rapid touch.

The gentleman stood near, watching her closely. He gave no sign of sympathy or encouragement, but Bäbele saw his eyes twinkle, and though she did not understand what it was all about, she felt that he meant no harm.

Presently, having completed her corner of the cathedral, Frieda, without a word, began to do the roofs and doves, calmly beginning as before with Elsa's head. At this the gentleman smiled, and then Bäbele was sure he meant only good.

Frieda gave him the book.

"H'm!" was his only acknowledgment. But he did not seem so fierce as he did at first Frieda thought him the most extraordinary person she had ever seen—to be so angry because she had spoiled a couple of pages in his wash-book, and to grow gentle when she did the same thing over.

"Who taught you?" he asked at length.

"Nobody," said Frieda, wonderingly.

"And you only wanted to make your doves?"

"Yes, sir," replied Frieda, meekly.

"And then you thought you'd fill up the opposite page?"

"Yes, sir," and Frieda began to feel quite anxious again.

"Well, my dear, you are a witch," remarked this strange old gentleman. And how it happened nobody could exactly tell, but Frieda found herself on his knee, and his eyes did not look ogreish at all, but quite mild and merry, behind his gold-bowed spectacles, and they were soon telling him all about the Freiburg days and the cathedral, and steady Johann, clever Heinrich, and fly-away Otto; and the more Bäbele and Frieda related of their simple life, the more this most delightful but very curious old gentleman sniffed and snorted and wiped his spectacles. Why —neither Bäbele nor Frieda could imagine, yet it seemed the most natural thing in the world to be telling him about it all. He did not ask many questions, but he soon knew as much about it as they themselves. He even discovered Bäbele's uneasiness, because she must be idle for so long. He shook her hand warmly when he rose to go, telling her not to be troubled; and she took heart of grace without knowing why.

That was certainly a day of wonderful experiences. In the first place, soon after the gentleman went, a great box came, filled with good things, enough to last for weeks, and on a card was written:

"To the little witch in the roof, from her devoted friend,
—Prof. Rudolph Reinwald

And when they were still rejoicing over good fortune, another knock came, and in walked a gentleman, who said he was Professor Reinwald's friend and physician, and the professor had sent him to look after Bäbele Hartneck's sprained ankle. And later, still, a comfortable reclining-chair made its appearance.

The excitement in the roof was really tremendous. The neighbors came in to wonder, rejoice, and sympathize, and Bäbele, bandaged, and extended in her comfortable chair, received her guests with the dignity of a queen.

The professor came again in a few days and after that frequently. Frieda used to watch eagerly for him, and grew so used to him, she quite forgot to be shy—and sang her little songs to him and played her sweet airs on the queer, cracked piano, and chattered to him about the heroes of her fairy tales, until the good man, who was an old bachelor and who knew nothing about children, really believed she was the most wonderful little being on the earth.

And as soon as Bäbele was well, he proposed that they should leave their home in the roof and come to him. He was a lonely, eccentric, cross old fellow, he told them, but that was all the more reason why he should be taken care of and improved, and he needed just such a faithful soul as Bäbele to look after his house, and just such a dear child as Frieda to make his home happy.

And so they came to him, and did indeed make him as happy as he had made them. It was a great house, where Bäbele had every opportunity to bustle about until everything shone to her heart's content. And Frieda had a garden with great shady trees and a hammock, a piano whose voice was not cracked, and best of all she studied systematically and learned to draw and to be helpful to her "other papa," as she called the professor. For he was an architect, devoted to his profession, and he had recognized, in spite of its childishness and imperfection, the real talent in Frieda's sketches of her dear roofs and her beloved arches.

She never grew tall nor strong, and there were days when the pain came just as it did when she was a child, but she was a happy, thankful soul. The boys did well in school, and came to visit her every vacation. The first thing Frieda did when she saw Otto was to tie his cravat, feeling sure it had been awry ever since he had left her.

She saw the cathedrals of many lands, but never loved any as she did the one that had taught her so much that was beautiful and good when she was a little lonely child in the old days. She saw famous pictures. She met distinguished men. But no features ever seemed so lovely to her as Bäbele's rough, adoring face, nobody so clever, so altogether admirable, as her "other papa."

In the professor's studio, directly by his desk, hang two small pencil sketches—a bit of a cathedral interior and a study of quaint steep gables, with doves pluming themselves in the sunshine. The lines are faint. The paper rough and curious. "And what may this be?" inquires a guest who is examining the professor's rare engravings.

"Ask my daughter Frieda," says the professor, turning with a tender smile to the lame girl with the happy face who sits quietly by his desk.

"Ask Bäbele, ask our house-angel, what the doves mean," says Frieda, as Bäbele comes to lead her from the room.

And Bäbele, who is a privileged character, tries to frown, then tugs violently at her apron, then asks appealingly, "Now, do I look much like doves, and angels, and such?"—

And she is right; she does not by any means—the dear, brave, true-hearted Bäbele.

First published in the August 1884 edition of *St. Nicholas Magazine*

Aunt 'Phroney's Boy

BY L. FRANK BAUM

THE BOY REALIZED he had made a mistake before he had driven the big tour-ing car a half-mile along this dreadful lane. The map had shown the road to Fennport clearly enough, but it was such a roundabout way that, when the boy came to this crossing, he decided to chance it, hoping it would get him to Fennport much quicker. The landscape was barren of interest, the farm-houses few and far between, and the cross-road seemed as promising as the main way. Meanwhile, at Fennport, the county fair was progressing, and there was no use wasting time on the road.

The promise faded after a short stretch; ruts and ditches appeared; rotten cul-verts and sandy hollows threatened the safety of the car. The boy frowned, but doggedly kept going. He must be fully half-way to another road by this time, and, if he could manage to keep on without breaking a spring or ripping a tire, it would be as well to continue as to turn back.

Suddenly the engines began muttering and hesitated in doing their duty. The boy caught the warning sound, and instantly divined the reason: he had forgotten to replenish the gasoline before starting, and the tank was about empty. Casting a quick, inquiring glance around, he saw the roof of a farm-house showing through the trees just ahead. That was a joyful sight, for he had scarcely dared hope to find a building upon this unused, seemingly abandoned lane. He adjusted the carbure-tor, and urged the engines to feed upon the last drops of the precious fluid they could absorb. Slowly, with staggering gait, the automobile pushed forward until just opposite the farm-house, when, with a final moan, the engines gave up the strug-gle, and the car stopped dead.

Then the boy turned and looked at the lonely dwelling. It was a small, primi-tive sort of building, ancient and weather-stained. There was a simple garden at the front, which faced the grove and not the lane, and farther along, stood a rickety, rambling barn that was considerably larger than the house.

Upon a tiny side porch of the dwelling, directly facing the road, sat an old woman with a battered tin pan full of rosy-cheeked apples in her lap. She was holding a knife in one hand and a half-pared apple in the other. Her mouth was wide open in amaze-ment, her spectacled eyes staring fixedly at the automobile—as if it had been a mag-ical apparition and the boy a weird necromancer who had conjured it up.

He laughed a little at the amusing expression of the old woman, for he was a good-humored boy in spite of his present vexations. Then, springing to the ground, he walked toward the porch and removed his cap, to make a graceful bow. She did not alter her pose, and, with eyes still fixed upon the car, she gasped:

"Laws-a-me! ef it ain't one o' them no-hoss keeridges."

"Nothing wonderful about that, is there?" asked the boy, smiling, as he reached the porch.

"Why not?" said she; "ain't they the mos' wunnerful things in all the world? Mart'n Luther's seen 'em in town, an' told me about 'em, but I never thought as I'd see one with my own eyes."

Her awe and interest were so intense that, as yet, she had not glanced once at the boy's face. He laughed, in his quiet way, as he leaned over the porch rail, but it occurred to him that there was something pathetic in the fact that the lonely old woman had never seen an automobile before.

"Don't you ever go to town yourself?" he asked curiously.

She shook her head. "Not often, though sometimes I do," she replied. "Went to Fennport a year ago las' June, an' put in a whole day there. But it tired me, the waggin jolts so. I'm too old now fer sech doin's, an' Mart'n Luther 'lows it ain't wuth payin' toll-gate both ways for. He has to go sometimes, you know, to sell truck an' buy groceries; he's there today, 'tendin' the county fair; but I've stayed home an' minded my own business 'til I hain't got much hankerin' fer travel any more."

During this speech, she reluctantly withdrew her eyes from the automobile and turned them upon the boy's face. He was regarding her placid features with a wonder almost equal to her own. It seemed so strange to find one so isolated and secluded from the world, and so resigned to such a fate.

"No near neighbors?" he said.

"The Bascomes live two miles north, but Mis' Bascome an' I don't git on well. She ain't never had religion."

"But you go to church?"

"Certain sure, boy! But our church ain't town way, you know; it's over to Hobbs' Corners. Ev'ry Sunday fer the las' year, I've been lookin' out fer them no-hoss waggins, thinkin' one might pass the Corners. But none ever did."

"This is a queer, forsaken corner of the world," the boy said reflectively, "and yet it's in the heart of one of the most populous and progressive states in the Union."

"You're right 'bout that," she agreed. "Silas Herrin's bought the lates' style thrash'n'-machine—all painted red—an' I guess the county fair at Fennport makes the rest o' the world open its eyes some. We're ahead of 'em all on progressin', as Mart'n Luther's said more 'n once."

"Who is Martin Luther?" asked the boy.

"He's my husband. His name's Mart'n Luther Sager, an' I'm Aunt 'Phroney Sager—the which my baptism name is *Sophroney*. Mart'n Luther were named fer the great Meth'dis' leader. He had a hankerin' to be a Baptis' in his young days, but he dasn't with such a name. So he j'ined the Meth'dists to make things harmoni'us, an' he's never regretted it."

The boy smiled in an amused way, but he did not laugh at her. There was something in her simple, homely speech, as well as in the expression of her face, that commanded respect. Her eyes were keen, yet gentle; her lips firm, yet smiling; her aged, wrinkled features complacent and confident, yet radiating a childlike innocence.

"Ain't ye 'fraid to run the thing?" she asked, reverting to the automobile.

"No; indeed. It's as simple as a sewing-machine—when you know how."

"I'd like to see it go. It come so sudden-like past the grove that when I looked up, you'd stopped short."

"I'd like to see it go myself, Aunt 'Phroney," the boy answered; "but it won't move a step unless you help it. Just think, ma'am, you've never seen a motor-car before, and yet the big machine can't move without your assistance!"

She knew he was joking, and returned his merry smile; but the speech puzzled her.

"As how, boy?" she inquired.

"The 'no-hoss keeridge' is a hungry monster, and has to be fed before he'll work. I hope you will feed him, Aunt 'Phroney."

"On what?"

"Gasoline. I forgot to fill up the tank before I started, and now the last drop is gone."

"Gasoline!" she exclaimed, with a startled look; "why, we don't keep gasoline, child. How on earth did you expect to find sech a thing in a farm-house?"

"Don't you cook with gasoline?" he asked.

"My, no! We use good chopped wood—splinters an' knots. Mis' Bascome had a gas'line stove once, but it busted an' set fire to the baby; so they buried it in the back yard."

"The baby?"

"No, boy; the stove. They managed to put the baby out."

The statement puzzled him, but his mind was more on the gasoline.

"Doesn't your husband use gasoline around the farm?" he inquired.

"No, 'ndeed."

"And you haven't any naphtha or benzine—just a little?"

"Not a drop."

"Nor alcohol?"

"Mercy, no!"

The boy's face fell. "Where is the nearest place I might get some gasoline?" he asked.

"Lemme see. Harpers' might have it—that's six mile' west—or Clark's store might have some, at Everdale. That's seven mile' off, but I ain't sure they keep it. The only place they're sure to have it is over to Fennport, which is 'leven mile' from here by the turnpike."

The boy considered all this seriously. "Can I borrow a horse from you—and a buggy?" he asked.

"Mart'n Luther's gone to town with the only team we own. We ain't had a buggy fer twenty-two years."

He sighed, and sat down on the steps, looking disconsolately toward the big touring car that was now so helpless. Aunt 'Phroney resumed her task of paring the apples, but now and then she also would glance admiringly at the automobile.

"Come far?" she presently inquired.

"From Durham."

"Today? Why, Durham's thirty mile' from here."

"I know; that's only an hour's run, with good roads."

"Mercy me!"

"But the roads are not good in this neighborhood. I wanted to run over to Fennport to see the fair. I thought there might be some fun there, and I'd jog over this morning and run back home tonight. That wouldn't have been any trick at all, if I hadn't forgotten the gasoline."

"Live in Durham?" she asked.

"Yes; Father has the bank there."

"Pretty big town, I've heard."

"Why, it's only a village. And a stupid, tiresome village at that. Lonely, too. That's why Father got this touring car; he said it would help to amuse me. May I have an apple?"

Aunt 'Phroney smiled indulgently, and handed him an apple from the pan. The idea of one who lived in the thriving, busy town of Durham becoming lonely filled her with amusement. For her part, she hadn't left the old farm-house, except to go to church, for nearly two years, and days at a time she never saw a human being other than her silent, morose husband. Yet she was not lonely—not really lonely—only at times did her isolation weigh upon her spirits.

"Got a mother, child?" she softly inquired.

He nodded, biting the apple.

"Mother's an invalid. She doesn't leave her own rooms, and keeps two trained nurses and a special cook, and she studies social science—and such things."

"What does that mean?"

"I don't know; it's only a name to Father and me. But Father has the bank to
interest him, and as I'm not ready for the bank yet, he lets me run the automobile."

Aunt 'Phroney gave him a pitying look.

"Guess I un'erstan' your hist'ry now," she said gently. "You needn't say no more
'bout it. Hev another apple?"

"I will, thank you. They're fine. Grow 'em here?"

"Yes. Mart'n Luther's entered a peck at the county fair, an' hopes to git the premium. It's two dollars, in cash. He's put up our Plymouth Rock rooster an' some
pertaters fer prizes, too, an' seein' he's entered 'em, it don't cost him anything to
get into the fair grounds—only the ten cents fer toll-gate."

"Why didn't you go with him?" asked the boy.

Aunt 'Phroney flushed a little. "That's some more hist'ry—the kind that's bet-
ter not studied," she remarked quietly. "Mart'n Luther took it from his pa, I guess.
His pa once cried like a baby when he lost four cents through a hole in his pocket.
After that, ev'ry penny was kep' strapped up in his leather pocket-book, which
were never unstrapped without a groan. Yes, Mart'n Luther's a' honest man, an'
God-fearin'; but I guess he takes after his pa."

The boy finished his apple.

"Come out and see our touring car," he said. "I'd like to show it to you,
although I can't take you to ride in it."

"Thank you," she eagerly replied. "I'll come in a minute. Let me git this apple-
sass started cookin' first."

She went into the kitchen with the apples, but soon came back, and with a
brisk air followed the boy across the patch of rank grass to the road.

"I can't walk six miles or more, you know," he remarked, "and lug a can of gasoline back with me; so I'll have to wait until your husband comes back tonight with
the team. You don't mind my staying with you, do you?"

"Of course not," she answered. "I like boys—boys like you, that is. We—we
never had no children of our own."

He showed her all the parts of the automobile, and explained how they worked
and what they were for, all in a simple way that enabled her readily to understand.
She was in a flutter of excitement at her close proximity to the wonderful inven-
tion, and the luxury of the seats and interior fittings filled her with awe. At first,
he could not induce Aunt 'Phroney to enter the car and sit down upon the soft
cushions, but, after much urging, she finally yielded, and was frankly delighted at
the experience.

"It must 'a' cost a lot o' money," she observed. "I guess your pa is pretty good
to you. Like enough *he* didn't take after anyone with a strapped pocket-book."

"No," laughed the boy; "Father is always kind to me. But I wish—I wish—"

"What, child?"

"I wish we lived together on a farm like this, where we could enjoy each other. All day he's at the bank, you know."

"If he worked the farm," said the woman, "you wouldn't see much of him then, either, 'cept at meal-time. Mart'n Luther gits up at daylight, works in the fields all day, an' goes to bed after supper. In heaven we may find time to enjoy the sassiety of our friends, but p'r'aps there'll be so much company there, it won't matter."

"I think," said the boy, solemnly, "we need a good deal more here than we shall need in heaven. Does anyone get what he needs, I wonder?"

"Some may, but not many," she rejoined cheerfully. "Some of us don't get even gasoline, you know. Funny, ain't it, how such a little thing'll spoil a great big creation like this? Why, in some ways, it beats Silas Herrin's new thrash'n'-machine; but it ain't so useful, 'cause the thrash'n'-machine runs along the road without horses to where it wants to go, an' then its injynes do the thrashin' better 'n hands can do it."

"I've never really examined one," he replied thoughtfully; "it must be very interesting."

"Come into the barn," she said, "an' I'll show you Silas Herrin's new one. He brought it here yest'day, but he an' all his crew are at the fair today, an' they won't begin thrashin' our crop till nex' Monday."

He followed her to the barn, willing to while away the time examining the big thresher. It filled nearly all the clear space on the barn floor, and towered half as high as the haymow. With its bright red body and diverse mechanical parts, the machine certainly presented an imposing appearance. The boy examined it with much curiosity.

"There are two distinct engines," he said musingly; "one a motor, I suppose, and one to do the work. The big one runs by steam, but this smaller one seems a gasoline engine."

"Perhaps it is," said the woman; "I never had it explained to me like you did your own machine."

"If it is," he suddenly exclaimed, "there must be some gasoline among Mr. Herrin's traps to run it with! If I can only find it, I'll borrow enough to get me to Fennport."

Eagerly, now, he began the search, the woman looking on with interest. In a short time, he drew out from the interior of the thresher a ten-gallon can, which proved to be filled with the fluid he sought.

"Hooray!" he cried joyfully. "We'll have our ride, after all. Aunt 'Phroney."

"It—it ain't stealin', is it?" she asked doubtfully. "This all b'longs to Silas Herrin, you know."

"It's a law of the road, ma'am, that any one needing gasoline has the right to help himself—if he pays for what he takes. I'll pay Silas Herrin a good price, and he'll have plenty left to run his engine with."

He got a bucket, measured out about three gallons, and placed a silver dollar on top of the can for payment. Then, when he had "fed" his automobile, an operation watched carefully by the old woman, the boy turned and said:

"Aunt 'Phroney, I've a proposition to make. Get on your things, and I'll take you to the fair at Fennport and give you a good time."

"Land sakes, boy!" she cried, holding up both hands; "I couldn't think of it."

"Why not?"

"There's the work to do."

"Cut it out for today. Martin Luther's having a holiday, and I'm sure you're entitled to one, too."

"He—he might be mad."

"I don't see why. It won't cost him a cent, you know, and perhaps we won't see him at all. We'll have a good dinner somewhere, see all the sights, have a fine auto ride, and I'll fetch you home in plenty of time to get supper for your husband."

The temptation was too strong to be resisted. Aunt 'Phroney's face broke into a beaming smile, and she hurried into the house to get on her "bes' bib an' tucker."

Her reappearance caused the boy's eyes to twinkle. She wore a plain, black gown, baggy and ill made, an old-fashioned "Peasley" shawl wrapped around her shoulders, and a wonderful hat that no milliner would have recognized as modern head-gear. But the boy did not mind. He helped her to the seat beside him, saw that she was comfortable, and started the engines slowly, so as not to alarm her.

The lane from the farm-house to the Fennport turnpike was in much better condition than the other end, which Aunt 'Phroney said was seldom used by anyone. They traversed it with merely a few bumps, and on reaching the turnpike glided along so smoothly, that the old woman was in an ecstasy of delight.

"I almos' hope Mart'n Luther will see us," she remarked, "Wouldn't he be s'prised, though, to see me in this stylish no-hoss keeridge?"

"I think he would," said the boy.

"An' jealous, too. Mart'n Luther says I take life easier ner he does, 'though my work's jus' as hard fer me as his is fer him. Only diff'rence is, I don't complain."

"Is—is your husband a poor man?" the boy hazarded.

"Goodness, no! Mart'n Luther's pretty well off, I'm told. Not by him, mind you. He only tells me what he can't afford. But our minister once said he wouldn't be s'prised if Mart'n Luther had a thousan' dollars laid up! It's a pretty good farm, an' he works it himself. An' he's so keerful o' spendin'."

"Doesn't he give you money for—for clothes and—and things?"

"Oh, yes; he's good 'bout that. We made an agreement, once, an' he's stuck to it like a man. Ev'ry New-Year's, he gives me five dollars for dresses an' hats, an' ev'ry Fourth o' July I git fifty cents an' no questions asked."

The boy's eyes grew big at this.

"Doesn't he spend anything on himself, either?" he inquired.

"A little, of course. He gits his clo's second-hand from the drug-store keeper, who's about the same size as Mart'n Luther, but some fatter, an' he puts five cents in the contribution box ev'ry Sunday, an'—an'—well, there's the toll-gate he has to pay for ev'ry time he goes to town. That toll-gate makes him orful mad. We're comin' to it pretty soon. *You* don't mind, do you?"

"Not at all," he cried, laughing merrily.

"Mart'n Luther's savin', an' no mistake," she continued musingly. "He wouldn't let me put him up no lunch today, 'cause he said Tom Dwyer would be sure to ask him to eat with him, an' if he didn't, he could easy get hold o' some fruit on exhibition. He said to save the food fer his supper tonight, an' he'd git along somehow."

"He ought to be worth several thousand dollars, at that rate," observed the boy, not without indignation. "But what good is his money to him, or to you, if he doesn't enjoy it? You ought to have a better allowance than you get, for you've certainly helped him to accumulate the money."

She heaved a little sigh.

"He says he can't afford any more," she replied, "an' I'm satisfied, as things be. I used to long to buy pretty things an' go 'round, once in a while, but I've got all over that now. I'm happy, an' the Lord takes keer o' me. Didn't He send you here today with the—this—orto—orto—machine o' yours?"

"I wonder if He did?" returned the boy, gravely.

"Oh, here's the dreadful toll-gate, Aunt 'Phroney."

It was nearly eleven o'clock when they entered the big gate of the fair grounds. The automobile attracted considerable attention, although there were two or three others in Fennport. As the boy assisted Aunt 'Phroney from the car, she was recognized by several acquaintances who frequented her church, and it was good to witness the old woman's pride and satisfaction at the looks of bewilderment that greeted her. She took the boy's arm and passed through the crowd with her chin well up, and presently they were in the main pavilion, where the largest part of the display was centered.

"Let's look at the fruits an' veg'tibles," she eagerly exclaimed. "I want to see if Mart'n Luther's won any prizes. Do you know, boy, he promised me all the money he won that come to over four dollars?"

"Did he really?"

"Yes, he were feelin' quite chirky this mornin', 'fore he left, so he promised it.

It was nearly eleven o'clock when they entered the fair grounds.

But if he won first prize on ev'rything, it'd be only five dollars altogether, so I guess he didn't risk much."

They found the fruits, but Martin Luther's red apples had no ribbon on them, either blue or red.

"They don't look as good here, longside the others, as they did to home," sighed Aunt 'Phroney; "so I guess the jedge was correc' in lett'n' 'em pass by. Let's see how the pertaters turned out."

Martin Luther's potatoes had failed to win. They lay just between the lots which had drawn the first and second prizes, and even the boy's inexperienced eyes could see they were inferior to the others.

"They bake well," murmured Aunt 'Phroney, "an' they bile jus' fine; but they ain't so pretty as them others, thet's a fact. I guess Mart'n Luther won't hev to give me any of his prize-money this year—'specially as he don't git any."

"Didn't you say you had a chicken in the show?" asked the boy.

"Yes, an' a mighty fine rooster he is, if I do say it. I've looked after him myself, ever since he were an egg, an' he's that high an' mighty, I named him 'The Bishop.' Seems to me he'll be hard to beat, but p'r'aps when he's compared to others, the Bishop'll be like the apples an' 'taters."

"Where is he?"

"The poultry show'll be in a tent somewheres."

"Let's find him," said the boy, almost as interested as his companion. They inquired the way, and, in passing through the grounds to the poultry tent, they passed a crowd surrounding one of those fakers so prominent at every country fair. Aunt 'Phroney wanted to see what was going on, so the boy drew her dexterously through the circle of spectators. As soon as they reached a place of observation, the old woman gave a violent start and grabbed her escort's arm. A lean, round-shouldered man with chin whiskers was tossing rings at a board filled with jack-knives of all sizes and shapes, in a vain endeavor to "ring" one of them. He failed, and the crowd jeered. Then he drew a leather wallet from his pocket, unstrapped it, and withdrew a coin with which he purchased more delusive rings. The boy felt Aunt 'Phroney trembling beside him.

"See that ol' feller yonder?" she asked.

"Yes," said he.

"That's Mart'n Luther!" They watched him with breathless interest, but not one of the rings he threw managed to capture a knife. Others tried them, undeterred by the failure of the old farmer, and, after watching them a short time, out came Martin Luther's leather pocket-book again.

"Come!" whispered the woman, in deep distress; "let's go afore I faint dead away! Who'd believe Mart'n Luther could be sech a spen'thrift an' prodigal? I didn't b'lieve 'twas in him."

The boy said nothing, but led her out of the crowd. To solace his companion's grief, he "treated" Aunt 'Phroney to pink lemonade, which had the effect of decidedly cheering her up. They found the poultry tent almost deserted, and, after a brief search, the woman recognized the Bishop. A man down the row of cages was even now judging the fowls and attaching ribbons to the winning birds as he went along.

"He'll come to the Plymouth Rocks in a minute," whispered Aunt 'Phroney; "let's wait an' see what happens."

It didn't take the judge very long to decide. Quite promptly he pinned a blue ribbon to the Bishop's cage, and Aunt 'Phroney exclaimed: "There! we've got a prize at last, boy!"

The judge looked up, saw the boy, and held out his hand with a smile of recognition.

"Why, how are you, Mr. Carroll?" he exclaimed cordially; "I thought I was the

"Come! Let's go before I faint dead away!"

only Durham man on the grounds. Did you drive your new car over?"

The boy nodded.

"They sent for me to judge this poultry show," continued the man, "but it's the poorest lot of alleged thoroughbreds I ever saw together. Not a really good bird in the show."

"That ought to make your task easier," said the boy.

"No, it makes it harder. For instance, there's the Sweepstakes Prize for the best bird of any sort on exhibition. Tell me, how am I to make such an award, where all are undeserving?"

"Very well, I'll tell you," returned the boy, audaciously. "If I were judging, I'd give this fellow"—pointing to the Bishop—"the Sweepstakes."

"Eh? This fellow?" muttered the judge, eying Aunt 'Phroney's pet critically. "Why, I don't know but you're right, Mr. Carroll. I had it in mind to give the Sweepstakes to that White Leghorn yonder, but this Plymouth Rock seems well set up and has good style."

The Bishop had recognized his mistress, and was strutting proudly and showing to excellent advantage. While the judge considered him, he flapped his wings and gave a lusty crow.

"I'll take back my statement," said the man. "Here is a really good bird. Guess

I'll follow your advice, Mr. Carroll"; and he pinned a bright yellow ribbon marked "Sweepstakes" next to the blue one on the Bishop's cage.

Aunt 'Phroney drew a long breath. Her eyes were sparkling.

"How much is the Sweepstakes, jedge?" she inquired.

"It's the largest money prize offered—twenty-five dollars—and there's a silver water-pitcher besides. I'm sorry such a liberal premium did not bring out a better display. But I must hurry and make my report, for I want to catch the two o'clock train home. Good day, Mr. Carroll."

As he bowed and left the tent, Aunt 'Phroney was staring proudly at the Bishop.

"Twenty-five dollars!" she gasped, "an' two dollars first prize for Plymouth Rocks! Twenty-seven dollars an' a silver pitcher! Boy, do you know what this means? It means I'll git twenty-three dollars—an' Mart'n Luther'll git jus' four."

"Will he keep his promise?" the boy asked.

"Yes. Mart'n Luther's a' honest man, an' God-fearin'—but he ain't got much jedgment 'bout ringin' jack-knives. Dear me, who'd ever think he'd turn out a squanderer?"

The boy took her away to the big dining-hall. It was divided into two sections by a rail. On one side was a sign reading: "Square Meal, 25¢." On the other side was the legend: "Regular Dinner, with Oysters and Ice-Cream, 50¢."

Disregarding his companion's protests, the boy led her into the latter section, which had few patrons compared with the cheaper one. No sooner had Aunt 'Phroney tucked her napkin under her chin than she grew pale and stared amazed across the rail. The boy's eyes followed hers and recognized Martin Luther seated at a table facing them, and eating with ravenous industry.

"Twenty-five cents gone—an' he might 'a' took the lunch I offered him!" wailed the old woman. Perhaps the magnetism of their combined gaze affected Martin Luther, for he raised his eyes and encountered his wife's horrified stare. The man was justified in being equally astonished. Motionless, with a piece of beef poised half-way to his mouth, he glared alternately at the strange boy and at Aunt 'Phroney. His face betokened bewilderment, shame at being discovered, and, at the last, an unreasoning panic. He slowly rose to his feet, turned his back, and ignominiously fled from the hall.

"Never mind," said the woman, her lips firmly set, "he'll know he's got somethin' to explain when he gits home; an' if Mart'n Luther ever hears the last o' them jack-knives an' his prodigal 'square meal,' my name ain't Sophroney Sager!"

After the dinner, with its accompanying luxuries of oysters and ice-cream, was over, they saw the balloon ascension and the races; and then, early in the afternoon, the boy put Aunt 'Phroney into the touring car and they drove to Fennport, where the tank was filled with gasoline. During this operation, the boy noticed that the old woman shivered slightly in the cool autumn weather, and drew her thin shawl more closely around her as she sat waiting in the car.

"You ought to have brought a heavy coat," he said.

"Why I haven't got any," she returned, smiling at him cheerfully.

"No coat! What do you wear in winter, when you go to church?" the boy asked.

"When it's real cold, I wrap a comforter 'round me on the way, an' then wear this shawl into church. Aunt Sally left it to me when she died. It's real Peasley."

"Get out of the car, please, Aunt 'Phroney," the boy said quietly.

"Why cert'nly, if you say so; but what for?"

"I had a birthday last week, and Father gave me a check. I want to buy a present for my best girl at this store, and I wish you to help me pick it out."

She went in, then, full of interest, and the boy whispered to the clerk, who began to display a collection of thick, warm coats in sober colors.

"Try this one on Aunt 'Phroney," urged the boy.

"Try this one on, Aunt 'Phroney," urged the boy.

Suddenly she became suspicious, and flushed like a school-girl.

"Boy," she began, "if you dare—"

"Hush, please!" he pleaded. "Do you want to shame me before all these strangers? And spoil my birthday? And prove that I haven't any best girl?"

The appeal was effective. The old woman meekly submitted to the "try-on," and presently he said to the clerk: "This one will do. Mrs. Sager will take it with her and wear it home, as the air is a bit chilly."

Before she could recover from her dazed condition, they were once more in the automobile and speeding down the turnpike toward the farm.

"Feel warm enough. Aunt 'Phroney?" asked the boy, turning a merry face toward her. Then he saw that her eyes were full of tears. She nestled closer to him and murmured softly: "You know, boy, we—we never had a chick or a child of our own!"

THAT EVENING FATHER and son were seated in the banker's library.

"I spent twenty dollars of my birthday money, today," said the boy.

"Indeed. In what way?"

"Trying to make an old country woman happy."

"Really, my son?"

"Really, Father; and I think—I'm quite sure—that I succeeded."

And then he told him the whole story.

First published in the December 1912 edition of *St. Nicholas Magazine*

Little Brother o' Dreams

BY ELAINE GOODALE EASTMAN

ONE OF HIS earliest recollections was of standing at a window, watching the big snowflakes sail out of a great, gray void, and settle like a flock of white birds upon the waiting earth.

Had he ever seen anything like that before? It seemed to him that he never had. This was the first snowfall of the year, and last winter was a long, long time ago.

Closer and closer he pressed against the cold window-pane, straining his eyes to pierce the dizzy emptiness of the upper air, following the mysterious birds in their swift, soundless flight, that seemed to bear them straight into his eager heart. Nearer and nearer they came, growing ever bigger and more beautiful.

At first he thought it had been so still, that first snowfall; not like the rain, that tapped on the glass with impatient fingers, or the wind that shook the windows angrily, and cried down the chimney. But when he had looked at the flying birds a long time, he was almost sure that he heard soft singing—not like the chorus of bird-song on spring mornings, but somehow muffled—a far-off, delicate chime, that made him so happy he could scarcely breathe. "Oh, mother, mother! Listen to the White Birds singing!"

His mother was busy putting supper on the table, moving about the kitchen with a tread that sounded heavy after that white hurrying dance out of doors and that song of the snow, that was so much finer and smaller and sweeter even than the purr of the back log in the big fireplace, or the lisp of the long grass in the meadow, or the heart-beat of the tiny brook under its thick armor of ice. Everybody could hear those, he decided, but everybody couldn't hear the White Birds, for his mother, when he called to her about them, only said:

"Come away from that window, child; you'll catch your death o' cold!"

And then when he asked Don, the hired man, who came in the next minute with the milk-pail, first stamping his feet and shaking himself like a big dog—when he went close up to Don and asked him quite low if he hadn't heard the White Birds, the big fellow looked at him hard a minute out of those clear blue, twinkling eyes of his, and all *he* said was:

"Been dreamin' again, sonny?"

Of course he hadn't been dreaming, for how can you dream when you're not asleep? and he had been quite wide awake all the time! But, to be sure, he hadn't heard them until he listened very close indeed, and mother and Don had so much

He was almost sure that he heard soft singing

work to do, they hardly ever had time to listen like that.

In silence he ate his supper of fresh bread and honey, not thinking much about it, except that the honey tasted of last summer, and wondering what flowers the bees liked best, but not wanting to ask, because his mother's face still looked a great way off, although she sat quite near him and helped him twice to honey, and filled up his tumbler with new milk. Eating was all very well, but not half so nice as the music, and he heard it again after he went to bed, where he lay with his eyes shut, thinking about the White Birds and seeing their radiant flight blot out the darkness until he really did fall asleep.

That was a memorable winter to Little Brother O' Dreams. It was a long, long winter, and bitter cold up there on Fray Mountain. It truly seemed sometimes as if the cold was like wolves, snarling and whining just outside the door, reaching in through every crack and cranny in the crazy little old house with their white fangs and their long, sharp claws that bit and tore. Out-of-Doors was so beautiful, but dangerous, like some glorious wild beast; and In-Doors was safe and warm enough, he thought—for his mother saw to that—but it was dingy and dull, and dark and lonesome—oh, so lonesome! There wasn't anybody to talk to. One couldn't talk to the chairs and the tables—they weren't alive like the trees and the brook. Sometimes you could talk to the fire, and sometimes to the pictures—there were two or three pictures—and beside these there was mother; but then mother didn't understand. It was hard when little boys had only mother, and she didn't understand. She hardly ever answered at all when one told her about things, and her eyes looked tired and sad, and far away. To be sure there was Don, too, sometimes, when he came in from doing the chores, and his eyes looked as if he did understand—a little—but he usually said: "What, dreamin' again, boy?" and that was nonsense, you know, when one hadn't even been asleep!

One night Little Brother told Don about being so lonesome, after a whole week of storm and bitter weather, such weather that he couldn't go with Don to the wood-lot on the bob-sled, nor to the mill with corn, and there were only the calves

and chickens in the barn, and they weren't so very
interesting—they always seemed to be thinking about something to eat!

"Why don't ye l'arn to read, sonny?" asked the big, blue-eyed fellow, quite sympathetically. "Wouldn't that be kind o' company for ye, now?"

"What is that—to learn to read?" Little Brother demanded, his pale, homely
little face lighting up marvelously as he spoke.

"Why, don't ye know?" said puzzled Don, carefully spreading the weekly paper
out on the table which had just been cleared of the supper dishes. "Look a-here,
these little marks all mean somethin'; you l'arn to figger out what they mean, and
then the paper'll talk to ye!"

"And will you tell me what they mean?" pleaded Little Brother, catching fire at
once.

"Wa'al, mebbe I can tell ye some on 'em—or mebbe your ma—" he paused in
red embarrassment and glanced toward the woman who stood with her back to
them, washing dishes; a woman whose face, hair, and dress all seemed of one color;
and as she spoke, in a low, monotonous voice, Little Brother thought with a dull
ache that her voice sounded just the same color, too.

"He's only five; I guess he don't need to learn to read just yet, 'n I've no time
to teach him. He'll have to go to school some day, when he's old enough. But
how—*how* am I to manage it?" She spoke the last words passionately, under her
breath, and threw a look of distress at the boy, whose cheeks by now were fairly
blazing, and his eyes like hot coals.

Twice he opened his mouth to speak, but the words wouldn't come; and as his
mother said nothing more and did not even seem to see him at all for the rest of
the evening, he snuggled up close to Don in the circle of yellow lamplight, and
began to pick out one by one the largest capital letters in the newspaper, and by
dint of whispered question and answer he had mastered half of them before bed-
time.

The next morning he got hold of the paper again;
and as his mother did not forbid him, and even told

him a letter or a word now and then, while Don helped sturdily of evenings, it was not many weeks before he graduated into the *Pilgrim's Progress*, one of the half dozen books on the high shelf beside the clock, and that was company indeed!

It was soon after this that he began to call himself "Little Brother."

"I like that name," he said, "because it makes me feel as if there were more of us. It isn't a lonesome name; it's a nice all-together sort of name!"

At last and at last the spring began to come, high up on Fray Mountain. Little Brother felt a good deal as he supposed the brook felt when it burst its icy armor and ran boisterously over the meadow, half laughing and half crying, and all but breaking its little heart for pure joy.

He ran all over the meadows, too; but when he came in with wet feet and a croak in his throat his mother put him right to bed with a hot soapstone, and made him take bad-tasting medicine. Happily, a pair of blue-birds flashed past the window on purpose to comfort him, he thought, and Don brought him a big bunch of skunk-cabbage, but his mother threw it out of doors because, she said, "it smelled so." To Little Brother it seemed, after all, a good, clean, growing smell!

In a few days he was out again, and beginning expectantly to haunt the remembered places, the warm, sunny nooks where, out of cozy nests of dry leaves, they had been used to lift up to his their tender faces—the first flowers of the year! As he knelt one day in a pale ecstasy with arms outspread, making a fence around one little clump of pinkish lavender bloom that he loved far too much to pick, or even to caress it, a song bubbled right up inside him, and he began to croon it over softly, scarcely knowing whether the flowers were singing it to him or he to the flowers. It was something like this:

> *Little children, little children*
> *Of the spring,*
> *Say, what greeting, happy greeting,*
> *Do you bring?*
> *Little sisters, little sisters,*
> *Do you hear?*
> *Is it love and is it hoping?*
> *Tell me, dear!*

Little Brother O' Dreams had never asked about a brother; but the idea of a sister had dawned upon him somehow, one scarcely knows how; and although it was not easy for him to speak out his heart's desire, he told his mother once how he would love to have a little sister. But she only said, with unusual sternness: "You will never have a sister; don't speak of it again!"

The tears filled Little Brother's eyes, but he winked them away. Although he was only six years old that summer, he never cried aloud except for real hard pain, and then it was not noisy crying, but a sort of musical wail that really sounded more like a sad singing. This time the tears kept coming faster and faster, and he kept on winking and rubbing his eyes and seeing things double, but he made no fuss that anybody noticed, and he did not speak of wanting a little sister again.

He thought of a sister, however, more and more earnestly, and wished for her in fairy rings and by wishing trees, until he really expected her to appear in some queer fashion—a real little sister, about as old as he was; for, as he argued with himself, there is so much magic in the world, and there isn't any "never"—that's only what grown-up people say, but it can't be, for everything happens some time!

There was always Don, who was so tall and straight and strong, and so good to look at, and had such a big soft heart, and who found time, with all his work, to be kinder than ever to Little Brother that summer. He used often to bring him flowers, "blows," he called them, from swamps and wild places where little boys couldn't go. Once it was a great bunch of very special trailing arbutus from high up on Fray Mountain; later on, an armful of the tallest lady's-slippers, clear pink and white; and then the purple rhodora, tremulous as a spray of royal butterflies. Little Brother didn't know their names, and he wouldn't have picked them himself for anything, it seemed as if it must hurt them; but he couldn't doubt Don's goodness; and they were oh, so beautiful!

It was one of the boy's simple pleasures to bring out his own cup to be filled at every milking-time, and he was always tenderly lifted to the swaying top of every sweet-smelling load of hay and down again, even when a shower threatened and Don was in a hurry. Mother had to come out into the field herself for the hay-making; and she would say: "Never mind about the boy this time, Don"; but, all the same, Little Brother never missed his ride to the barn behind the red oxen when he was on hand and ready for it.

The haying was scarcely over when a strange thing happened; something that had never happened before within the boy's remembrance. You see the small, stony farm, scarcely more than a rough clearing, away up on the shaggy side of the mountain, and the ancient, little unpainted house, blackened by the rains, and leaning slantwise like some old wind-buffeted tree, were quite off the highroad on a grass-grown cart-track, along which Don and the red oxen took their undisputed way to market or to mill. But on a hot day in midsummer there came through the unfrequented wood road, where the trees met overhead, straight to the half-ruined cottage smothered in a riot of cinnamon roses and coarse tawny lilies and straggling currant bushes with their strings of scarlet beads, a great mountain wagon, drawn by four horses and filled with visitors from another world! They drew up at the old

Poor Little Brother o' Dreams shrank back among the tall lilies

well-sweep, and called for water, and poor Little Brother O' Dreams shrank back among the tall lilies, vainly hoping himself unseen, for his great, asking eyes had fastened themselves instantly upon the fairylike vision of a little girl on one of the big seats—a little girl with tumbled nut-brown curls and delicately modeled features, and the softest, most soulful of brown eyes! All in white she was, dazzling as any fairy; and Little Brother caught his breath for sheer astonishment and delight; but the next instant the brown eyes had met the black ones, and there was that in them that fairly crushed the sensitive little heart.

It was Don who found him, half an hour later, sobbing almost soundlessly, face downward among the lilies.

"Why did she look at me so, Don? Why did she?" was all that he could say.

"There, there, sonny; don't take on so," comforted Don, patting the black head; helpless as a man must be, yet tender as a woman.

"She was so beautiful, and no bigger than me, Don; and she was so light on her feet, and straight—not like me! And she looked as if she were afraid—and—and—sorry for me, Don!" he sobbed.

It was the end of one chapter in the life of Little Brother O' Dreams.

OF COURSE, HE knew now that he was different from other children. He supposed that was why his mother hadn't sent him to school; at least, it must be part of the reason; and maybe it was why she looked so sad and tired and far away. She *couldn't* love him as much as she could have loved a little boy who was strong and beautiful; of that he was sure. Yes, he was *quite* sure of that!

But the trees loved him, and the flowers, and the sky; and the little people of the woods, the birds and squirrels, didn't mind his plain face and crooked little body; and Don was always good to him and never looked sorry for him, either! And then there were the sunsets on Fray Mountain!

"Oh, mother, mother! Is heaven on fire?" cried Little Brother one evening when he was five years old. "Will it all burn up, mother? And what will God do then?"

Two or three years later he made a poem about the two sunsets—the autumn, of day, you know, and the sunset of the year. It was like this:

> *On the castle of Night a red, red flag, that flies*
> *For the prince Tomorrow;*
> *In the face of the Cold a blazing world; and Hope*
> *At the door of Sorrow!*

You know most of us love the things that are near and can be touched and handled and understood. Little Brother was different. He loved best what was big and far off and mysterious, like the night and thunder-storms, and the shadowy pine wood where he dared not go alone, for that would be to disobey his mother. She had said that he might get lost. Not that he was at all afraid of getting lost; it seemed to him that to be lost in such a quiet, holy place would be like going to church and forgetting all about the rest of the world; and as he said to himself by way of argument—for he was fond of reasoning things out with himself—"She means that I might not know where I was or the way home; but God would know, and He would be sure to show me the way when it was time to go home!" However, his mother had forbidden him to go there alone, and he was an obedient child.

He had all sorts of strange fancies about Night. Oftenest she seemed to him a beautiful and grand woman with a great deal of long black hair, covering her all up but her eyes, which shone like stars. Afraid of the dark? He *loved* the dark; and yet his bedtime was at seven o'clock in winter and eight in summer, and he had never been out of doors at night in his whole life!

And then there was the majesty of a summer thunder-storm sweeping over Fray Mountain; how he shivered for pure joy in its approach, feeling to the ends of his fingers, and in every hair of his head, the electric thrill and tingle of it! The impulse to run out in the face of all that stir and secret turmoil, out and up to some high, open place where he could read every bit of the silver writing on the cloud and feel himself the center of the clash of elements and crash of worlds, was very strong in Little Brother O' Dreams.

Once it actually mastered him. The child slipped away unseen while his mother was hurrying to shut doors and windows against the heralding wind, and, flying up through the wood like a hunted thing, was standing alone on the bald, bare mountain summit when the floods were let loose out of heaven.

Half an hour afterward, a dripping, rain-beaten and altogether forlorn little figure appeared to his startled mother at the cottage door in the last throes of the storm, with a strange, uplifted look upon his pale wet face that made her draw him hastily within and chide in muttered undertones, harmless as the echoes of the departing thunder. He never remembered being punished for naughtiness; somehow it was impossible to punish Little Brother!

Now there were certain trees that come into the story, for they were very friendly to the boy. He loved all trees, of course; but there were some that stood up grand and noble, kissing the sky—trees that one would scarcely venture to speak to; and then again there were others whose branches bent over and caressed your face, whose aspect, homely, and almost human, invited your confidence.

One, in especial, was an old curly maple, knotted and gnarled, with a broad, low, comfortable seat near the ground; and hidden among a world of pointed, Gothic-shaped leaves in the lap of that old mother-maple, Little Brother told her many things. More than once or twice he had told her about the little girl—or the fairy, he wasn't quite sure which—who was so very beautiful, and yet whose loving brown eyes had hurt him so without meaning to do it. At first the hurt had been sharper even than his delight in her loveliness; but the more he thought about it the sweeter it was to think of so perfect a creature, and patiently as the tree herself takes a fresh wound right into her heart and surrounds it with living wood, he accepted the hurt, and covered it up and smoothed it over till nothing but a little scar was left—a scar that only Don noticed.

Not far from the old maple there was a brown brook that rippled in singing shallows over a pebbly bottom; and as this brook was so tiny that even the most anxious or careful mother could not conceive it to be a danger, Little Brother was allowed to play there, on the express condition that he must not wet his feet.

Since he did not know how to play like other children, fishing, and sailing boats, and since wading was forbidden, he usually lay flat on his face at the edge of the water, gazing downward into the clear, brown pools, which reflected his own face—and something more. And one long midsummer day while he lay thus, a whole year after the coming of the strangers to Fray Mountain, there came to his ears a pitiful little cry, like that of a lost or frightened bird—just one cry, and then silence.

Little Brother awoke from his dream of a sweet face looking up to meet his from the rounding ripples in the pool, and scrambling to his feet, he scurried along like a rabbit in the direction of the sound. The ground was rough, and in a little hollow there was a heap of something white, which he soon made out to be a little girl who had fallen and was frightened, or hurt, or perhaps both. She sat up as he came near, and he saw the tumbled brown curls and the brown eyes that, this time, met his with neither pity nor fear, but with a flash of pleased surprise.

"Oh, it is you, little boy!" she exclaimed joyfully.

"I'm not Little Boy," he replied at once. "I'm Little Brother!"

"Then if you're Little Brother, I must be Little Sister!"

The old, old wish had come true; he had found a sister at last!

A red blush of delight covered his whole face as he held out a small, frail hand to help the little maiden to her feet. But with a merry laugh, she sprang lightly up, and gamboled about him like a young fawn, as she exclaimed:

"I wasn't hurt a bit, not a bit, not a bit! I was running and I caught my foot in a vine, and I cried out because I was all alone!"

"But you won't be all alone now you have found me, Little Sister."

"No, of course I shan't, Little Brother! But what do you do here? Show me everything in this wood, and tell me all the stories you know!"

So he took her to the old mother-tree, the maple whose lap was so nice and wide and her arms so comforting, and who kept secrets so well. And there he told her several little stories.

Next, he took her to the lady birch, who seemed to be ever leaning forward as if she were listening, and trying to pull her one foot out of the ground, so that he thought she wanted to get away and go somewhere else—to the other side of the world, perhaps!

"And where is the other side of the world, Little Brother?"

"Why, it's over the mountain, where the sun goes when it sets," he answered.

And then he showed her the old man hemlock, shaggy-haired and silent and sober; but the birds and the squirrels were fond of him; there were ever so many foot-prints all around him in the wintertime.

"Do you live here in the winter, too?" He fancied that the little girl shivered a bit as she spoke.

"Why, yes. Don't you? But I think you must live on the other side of the world, Little Sister, where it is always summer, and you have the sun when there isn't any

He took her to the old Mother-tree, whose lap was so nice and wide

sun here; and that must be what makes your hair so beautiful—and your face—"

But she was dancing on before him; and they came to the tiny brook, and she said quite suddenly: "I must go home, now." And the next minute she was gone.

THE BROWN BROOK and the mother-maple were a long, long way from home, Little Brother thought. You see, he was only seven years old. It might have been half a mile, at the foot of the mowing; and his mother only let him go there when Don was in the field and had promised to "keep an eye on the little feller." Fortunately, haying had begun again, and so the very next day he went to the same spot and saw Little Sister again, as he had been quite sure he would. He had lain awake from happiness on his cot, and stared at the cracked and stained walls, where he had been used to fancy all sorts of pictures after he went to bed. But the only picture he saw that night was of an arch and lovely little face with eyes as brown as the clearest pool, looking out from a mass of tumbled curls.

As soon as she spied him again, Little Sister ran to meet him, crying happily: "I've come to hear the stories this time, Little Brother!"

"Well, I don't know any more stories; but I know poems, ever so many poems! Shall I say a poem for you?"

"Yes, do say a poem, Little Brother!"

Then they sat down side by side under a tree, and Little Brother began:

> *"I love sweet fairyland; I love the lovely flowers,*
> *Their faces smile upon me to lighten weary hours.*
> *I love the grass; I love the sky;*
> *From this latter place God looks down from high!"*

"That's nice," said the little girl. "Where do the poems come from?"

"Oh, they just *grow*," said Little Brother.

"They don't grow in this wood, do they?"

"They grow right up inside of me—just sing themselves to me. Whenever I'm happy, I make a poem about it, and when I'm sad I often make a poem about that, too."

"I like poems, whether they're sad or happy," said Little Sister. "But it's time for me to go home now. If your mother asks you anything, you can say you dreamed a sister in the wood. That's what I told them yesterday!"

"She never asks me anything, only if I got my feet wet, and if I want my dinner," said Little Brother.

"Well, they asked me where I had been, and I said in the wood. I said I played with my dream brother; and they just laughed; they don't think you are real, you see!"

"But I am real!" exclaimed Little Brother, in an anxious voice.

"Of course you are; but I call you my dream brother, because if they were to know about you, they wouldn't let me come here any more!"

At these words everything seemed to get dark and cold all at once, and he could only cry out pitifully:

"But you are coming again, *aren't you?*"

"Of course I am. Little Brother! I'm coming 'most every day, if I can! And I want you to say another poem for me, tomorrow!" And then she was gone.

The meetings went on for several days; not every day, but several days; and nobody knew anything about it, not even Don, who was greatly pressed just then with haying and harvest coming on, and only took time to notice that Little Brother was safe, and looking unusually well, for him. The pale little face actually got quite brown, and round with something of childish roundness, and a new expression crept into the big, black, speaking eyes.

As for the little fairy whose father had bought a great estate and built a summer castle on the other side of the wood, her pretty young mother was in heaven, and she had just then a thoughtless new nurse who was willing enough to be free for a part of the day, and who didn't see that the child could come to any harm, picking flowers by herself in the wood and roadside near by.

But one night when she spoke of her "Dream Brother," her grave-faced father took her on his knee, and gently and kindly began to question her more closely.

"Tell me some more about this Dream Brother of yours, little daughter," he said.

She gazed straight into his eyes. "He makes poems, father," she said.

"What sort of poems? Where does he get them?"

"They grow right up in his heart, he says. I can say one of them to you now." And she did.

"Hm, hm," said her father. "And what does he look like, daughter?"

"He looks—oh, he looks—different! And he is different; but he is my Little Brother and I'm his Little Sister that he had been looking for, ever and ever so long; and he says he'll die if I don't come any more; and I—shan't die, because I don't want to die, but you *will* let me go and listen to his poems—won't you, father dear!"

"Is my child a poet?" thought her father. "Or is there really some one in the wood?"

So the very next day when she slipped away from her nurse he followed. And the day after, he made some quiet inquiries about the tumbledown cottage on the mountain side, and heard about the young woman who had lived there with her boy ever since his father died; how the boy was dreadfully deformed, and, some said, not quite right in his mind; and they never called him by his name, but only "Little Brother." He heard about the faithful "hired man" who worked the tiny place on shares, and in this way kept the woman and her little boy from going to the poor-house.

When he had heard everything they knew, he called at the cottage, and there was a long talk between the rich man who had lost the wife of his heart, and whose hair was streaked with white, but not from years, and the woman whose youth and prettiness were quite gone, and whose life held nothing save poverty and toil and bitterness—and her poor frail boy with the twisted little body that it hurt her to look at, and with the poet soul that she could not understand. They talked a long time in low voices; but what they said I shall not tell you, and you may guess for yourselves how it came about that before Christmas Day Little Brother O' Dreams went to the other side of the world with his Little Sister.

First published in the December 1907 edition of *St. Nicholas Magazine*

The Sea-Horse of Grand Terre

BY CHARLES TENNEY JACKSON

ALLESJANDRO, THE SEINE-CAPTAIN, first told the men at Chinese Platforms that the light-keeper at Grand Terre Island was sick. One of the *Stephanie*'s crew had gone ashore for water, and reported that old Schumitz was "done beat out with feveh." The *Stephanie* had two hundred dollars' worth of shrimp which a few hours' delay under the Louisiana sun would spoil, so the lugger sailed for the drying plat-forms, where Allesjandro told Mr. West, the camp boss.

And the camp boss turned with simple confidence to his sturdy sixteen-year-old son, who, that morning, was idling in the shade of the commissary with his chum, George Fernald.

"Better go see to the old man, Paul. The *Tucker* is flying the catch-flag, and the launch is going to tow her in. Landry will put you ashore, and you can hike up the beach with some lemons and stuff. See if he needs the doctor."

And blazing hot as low-lying Grand Terre appeared in the September calm, the boys were eager to go. Schumitz was a friend of Paul's. In half an hour, they had the few delicacies and simple remedies which the camp possessed, and were on the launch speeding for the outlying reef.

For a week, black, majestic storm-clouds had swung about Barataria Bay, at intervals, for this was the time of the equinox, when the south coast had been swept time and again by the West Indian hurricanes. Still the shrimp luggers went out, and when the boys landed in the salt marsh, they saw the *Tucker*, limp-sailed and far on the gulf, aside the *Deb* and the *Anastasya*, but flying the red flag that told of a successful catch. The launch went on through Four Bayou Pass to meet her, while the lads turned up the six-mile beach to the lighthouse.

"Dad said that Gaspar, who takes care of the oyster-beds here and keeps an eye on our cattle, might round up a couple of horses for us," commented Paul. "But all the stock seems to be miles away, and Gaspar isn't around his shack."

They passed the tiny, palm-thatched hut perched on a ten-foot platform above the tides. The mud beneath was trampled where the stock sought refuge from the sun, and here Paul pointed out a great hoof-mark.

"That's Big King's, the stallion that Father turned loose here when he went into this experiment with stock on the salt marsh. He has never been able to recapture him since. Gaspar complains that the white stallion hates him, and chases him every time he goes ashore. The *Stephanie*'s crew say that they saw Big King follow Gaspar in his skiff away out in deep water, and that the Cajun was so scared that, finally, he dived over and swam to their boat. Gaspar sometimes declares he will shoot the horse or quit his job!"

"Must be a regular old sea-horse!" laughed George. "Is that him—that beautiful big white fellow over in the mangroves?"

"Yes," Paul whispered cautiously. "And don't provoke him to charge us—there isn't a place to escape him if he does!"

Two hundred yards away, the splendid creature stood, his eyes warily on the invaders. He snorted menacingly, his mane erect and tail spread, but he let them pass, and then charged magnificently down the wet sands to turn and watch them, with the surf breaking about his legs.

Big King followed Gaspar in his skiff away out in the deep water.

"What a grand old fellow he is!" cried Paul. "Father ought not to put him in charge of an oyster-digger like Gaspar—of course he'd hate him!"

It was dazzling noon when the weary lads reached the lighthouse. The oppressive calm made the heat in the marshy hollows intolerable, and they hailed with relief the sight of the keeper, whom they found lying on his airy platform. The keeper's eyes were feverish as he explained how, all the morning, he had watched them with his powerful glasses, which gave him the only diversion of his monotonous life. But he wasn't sick, he said—just a "touch o' sun," and he was chagrined to find that the *Stephanie* had reported him ill. "Lighthouse folks ain't no business gettin' sick, ever," he declared.

All the same, he was glad to get the lemons and other things the boys brought, and when they tried to make him a corn-starch pudding, the ensuing hilarity seemed to hearten him wonderfully. When they came out on the gallery, he declared all this "cuttin'-up had made him plumb well." But when the keeper gazed around, he fixed an intent look on the southeast.

"Your dad's goin' to have the launch at Four Bayou for you?" he asked. "Well, you boys better get off. The wind's scuddin' them clouds fast over there, and this is the hurricane month, remember. There's a sea running now, and—feel that? The air's twitching!"

And in fifteen minutes it was more than twitching. Out of the strange, calm oasis with the black clouds rolling up all about the horizon, there suddenly shot a squall from the southeast that tore the sand from under the boys' feet when they went down Mr. Schumitz's ladder. But they didn't mind the blow. They laughed, and shook Schumitz's hand, and promised to come the next day with the launch and make another pudding, and with raisins in it.

"Mebbe you will and mebbe you won't," shouted the old man. "It's time for a blow up from Cuby, and I reckon I'm better off here than you'll be on your dad's crazy platforms. You boys won't see old man Schumitz for a while, if a sou'east sea begins to pound over them marshes. In La Chenière storm, there wasn't a thing above water except this light, from here to upper Lafourche. And your dad's platform villages—pooh! wasn't stick or stump left of any of 'em!"

The boys talked of the dreaded gulf hurricanes as they tramped on the harder sand, as near to the water as they could. On their left, the sand was already blowing from the dunes, and when they reached a little bayou which they had crossed dryshod in the morning, they found the water pounding half a mile inland, and had to go around it. "The gulf is so shallow for miles out," explained Paul, "that the least little wind kicks up a quick sea."

But when they rounded the bayou and went over the low ridge, the wind was so fierce as to stagger them and whirl the loose sand around their feet.

Big King charged magnificently down the wet sands to turn and watch them.

"Whew!" cried George, "and just see how the water's rising, Paul! It's all through the grass there, and beyond—why, it's a lake!"

"Let's cut over on the bay side and see if the mangroves won't break the wind a bit," suggested Paul. "If it keeps on, we can't well walk against it." He reached a rise in the meadows and vainly stared at the pass which, two miles away, was hidden by the oncoming rain and scud. There was no boat in sight, and, northward, Barataria Bay was whipped to as furious a sea as was the outside water to the south. "It's there sure," Paul muttered, "but, if we *made* the launch, I don't think she'd live in that gale. But we can run to Grand Bank and put into that camp for the night."

He hastened on, not telling his friend all his fears. But from the highest dune they saw nothing except the oyster-guard's thatched hut, and, far off, near the mangrove clumps, a few of the cattle wandering with the storm.

"Ticklish business if we have to spend the night in this shack," George declared half an hour later, when, wet and tired, they reached the hut on the edge of the marsh and climbed the ladder to the door. Indeed, the sight was an evil one. The oyster-stakes had entirely disappeared, and the rising sea was pouring across the island in three places back on the way they had come. The pounding water against the piles made the shack reel, while every now and then portions of the thatched sides would be torn off, and go humming away in the gale. The boys went in and inspected the gaping roof; the sheets of rain reached every inch of the interior—they were as well off outside. Where Gaspar had gone they did not know; they concluded that he had abandoned his job—"Scared off by the big horse," said Paul.

"If the water keeps on rising, you'll lose all your stock," observed George. "But the launch—where do you suppose it is?"

Though night and darkness were coming on, they could see the pass enough to know it held no boat. What had happened was that the launch, early in the afternoon, had broken its propeller in towing the *Tucker*, and had then drifted until both boats grounded in the marsh, where the crew clung, half drowned, to the lugger's rigging through the night of the hurricane. The boys, huddled in what should have been the lee shelter of the thatch on the platform, noticed again how fast the shallow sea was rising. Grand Terre light was invisible in the storm, and it seemed that the whitecaps were speeding across the island everywhere except over the higher sand-ridge near them. Watching this, they saw the backs of the cattle moving through the mangroves, and then Mr. West's old bay mare. "The stock are coming back!" cried Paul. "The water's coming in from the pass now, and it's turned them." He looked apprehensively at his companion's face. "George, if it rises high enough to get a sweep at this shack over the bars, the platform won't last half the night."

"Your cattle are coming here, anyway. And look, the big horse is leading them!"

The stock had been accustomed to huddle in the shade of the platform hut, and now they were deserting the mangrove ridge to seek this bit of human companionship. The cows were mooing in a scared fashion as they waded, more than knee-deep, to the place. The two bay horses cast appealing looks up at the boys, and Paul called down encouragingly. Big King lunged about the piling and whinnied, watching off to the mainland. The frail structure trembled when the crowding cattle got under it.

"Better drive them out," George shouted above the wind. But this was impossible; and presently, as the darkness fell, the animals were quieter in the fierce rain, though the waves pounded over their backs, and the calves could hardly keep their footing.

Paul crawled back on the platform after an inspection of the base of the timbers. The sands were washing up badly, and the tramping hoofs assisted at the slow settling of the platform. Paul could touch the horses' necks from the floor, and once his fingers went lightly along the rough mane of the white stallion. The big brute turned about his fine, wary eyes at the boy. But he did not bite; he even seemed to crowd closer to his master's son. "Get over there—you!" Paul yelled; "don't crowd against that post!"

He reached down and slapped the great horse, and then dug him in the ribs ineffectually. King neither resented it nor obeyed. The boys laid out full-length on the boards to avoid the wind, and in the last light saw their dumb companions half buried in the waves. Although the rain was not cold, they were shivering with exhaustion from the pounding wind and water. For an hour, the dark was intense. Then it seemed as if the rising moon broke the gloom a trifle, though the storm did not abate.

"It's still rising!" commented Paul, after he had thrust a crab-net pole down by the piling; "and very fast, George. I wish it was daylight!"

Then, when he had crawled back to his wet comrade, there came a tremendous shock to the platform. They heard one of the calves bawl wildly, and felt a rush and stagger of the animals beneath them. Paul jumped up and ran to the other end of the reeling platform, where an entire side of the thatched wall fell out into the sea.

"It's a big tree!" he shouted back, as

"Look, the big horse is leading them!"

George groped for his hand. "I was afraid of that, whenever the tide got high enough to bring the drift off the gulf side. Now we're in for it! It tore out three of the piles, and it's dragging at another. Come, let's try to get it off!"

Thirty-five miles away, the Southwest Pass of the Mississippi poured all the flotsam of the mighty river into the gulf to be spread far along the sand-dunes by the tides, and every south-easter sent this wreckage charging over the marshes. In every great blow the platform dwellers of Barataria dreaded this invasion. The lads vainly hunted for poles to fend off the tree pounding under their shelter. Some of the cattle had been knocked down and others were scattered, and Paul saw one of the mares go swimming off in the whitecaps to certain death. Above the wind they heard the frightened stock struggling for foothold in the sand and the groaning of the timbers. There was nothing to do. The shack, trembling, twisting, finally settled slowly back; the big cypress-tree had gone on, luckily. But presently a smaller one was battering at the piling, and more of the cattle were scattered.

"The other end of the platform is sinking!" George shouted; "everything is gone there!"

They fought their way back just in time to see more than half the thatch hut tumble into the waves. Paul had saved a coil of half-inch rope from Gaspar's belongings, with the idea of tying fast some of the loose piles, but this was now useless.

"The rest of it will go sure!" he muttered. "George, when it does, jump clear of the cattle and head southwest—" he looked helplessly off in the dark—"if we can swim to the mangroves, maybe we can hold on a little longer."

But to reach the ridge, even if it was above the breakers, was an impossibility, for one would have to swim directly into the storm. And the boys had lost all sense of direction. The next big shock from the driftwood sent them to their feet in a wild effort to leap free of the animals, although how many of them there still were they did not know. The last log crashed through the midst of them and left the platform tilted at such an angle that the boys could no longer walk on it. Paul slipped and went over the side to his waist, but he still clung to his rope. As he kicked to recover his footing, while George reached down to help him, he slowly became aware that his legs were over the wet, heaving back of Big King. His hold on the boards was slipping; the entire platform seemed to be coming after him.

"It's all sinking!" George yelled at him. "Don't let it pin you under the water!"

But Paul was motioning wildly for his friend to slide after him. He was reaching around the slipping boards to drag the rope about the big stallion's neck.

"If it goes," he shouted, "hang to the rope; maybe Big King will drag us free of the stuff."

He was working busily at the rope about the horse's neck when George was thrown into the water beside him. The stallion was plunging about with Paul firmly astride his back and George fighting to grasp the rope. Another instant and the wrecked platform slid down upon them, striking Paul in the side and dealing the horse a savage blow on the flank, driving him out from under the piles where he had fought to the last against the sea. He plunged on madly, with the water breaking over his back, to which Paul clung while he tried to drag his friend up behind him. They never would have succeeded if King had been on dry land. But the water and the small drift impeded his struggles to shake off the rope and the burden, and now he dashed into a depression where his hoofs failed to find bottom, and the waves swept entirely over him.

The panting lads clung to the rope and to each other. Paul was dragged off the back of the swimming horse, and then they both were thrown against him and regained a hold on his tough and heavy mane. But the whitecaps were almost drowning them. Big King reached a ridge and drew himself up where the water was hardly to his breast; then he plunged on in the teeth of the storm, swimming again. He knew where he was going well enough. While the foolish cattle drifted with the waves out to the open bay, the lion-hearted stallion fought his way seaward and to the mangrove ridge.

The panting lads clung to the rope and to each other.

But before he gained it, the boys were all but washed off. Once, indeed, Paul felt his friend's hand slip from his. George went over the horse's flank and under the water, but he kept his grip on the rope. From his gasps, the rope was apparently all but strangling the stallion. When they reached another shallow, Paul leaned forward and loosened it. "Hold up, old fellow!" he muttered; "hold up, and we'll make it yet!"

And the big wild horse actually twisted his shaggy neck knowingly under the boy's fingers as he eased the line! Paul got George on the animal's back again, as they reached the mangrove ridge. The bushes, beaten by the hurricane, cut and pounded their faces, and the choppy seas broke through, churning the sands about them. But the water here was not more than three feet deep, and Big King fought through it.

Paul was anxious to stop him now. They were on the highest point, and no other refuge was possible. He began patting the horse and murmuring to him as one would to a pet colt, and, after a quarter of a mile of fruitless tramping, Big King suddenly rounded the thickest clump of mangrove and stopped, with his tail pointing into the gale.

"He knows!" whispered Paul, weakly, to his comrade. "It's the only shelter to be found. Now if he only lets us stay on his back!"

But apart from nervous and resentful starts and shakings, the horse did not stir. He seemed badly exhausted himself. The boys laid forward on his heaving back, Paul clinging to him, and George to Paul, and there the weary, dark hours passed. The sea was rising more slowly now.

At times, King struggled deeper into the bushes as the sand washed from under his feet. And how the wind did blow! It was as if the air above them was full of salt water, and even with their backs to it, the boys could not speak without strangling. The lashing mangroves skinned their legs painfully, and the salt added to their suffering. But their chief fear was the rising water. They measured it time and again during the long night, but could never tell whether it was coming up or whether their live refuge was slowly sinking. The stallion changed his position whenever his legs went in too deep. "Old boy," muttered Paul, "you can manage this much better than we can."

Somehow, in his heart, he felt a hot and almost tearful love and admiration for the dreaded horse of the Grand Terre meadows. "If we ever get out," Paul told George, "I'll take him back to New Orleans and ride him. He's the biggest, bravest horse in all the world!"

"*If* we get out!" retorted George. "And I do believe the rain is quitting!" And with the ceasing of the rain, a slow lightening came over the waters. Yet not for hours longer, while the long, tugging swells surged through the mangroves and kept the tired boys ever struggling to retain their place, did it become light enough to be really day. And then they saw nothing in any direction but gray sky over the stormy sea. For two hundred yards, the higher mangroves were above the flood. Of the palm-thatched hut and the platform not a stick remained, nor was a single one of the cattle or either of the two mares in sight.

"Nobody but Big King," muttered Paul, "and you and me, George! I'm going to get down and pet the old fellow!"

He swung off in water to his armpits and went about to King's head. The horse bared his teeth, and then slowly, with lessening pride, allowed the boy's hand to stroke his muzzle. "Old man," whispered Paul, "you weathered the blow for us, didn't you!"

And the strangest thing was that, when the boys were tired of standing in the water, the great creature allowed them to climb again on his back. At last the wind died out, and when the first glint of sun broke through, it could be seen that the sea was not rising further. Big King began nibbling at the mangroves, while the exhausted lads half dozed and watched the waters to the north. It was two hours before they could see anything two miles distant, and knew that the "hurricane-tide," so feared by the shrimpers, had turned again seaward. Drift and wreckage were going out through the flooded pass. And, finally, almost at noon, Paul made out the little gas steamer that ran from camp to camp, headed down from the direction of the platforms.

"It's looking for us, George!" he cried. "But Dad—he'll never dream we lived through it all!"

They watched the boat with weak yells of jubilation. A mile away, Big King's white flanks caught the attention of the steamer men. Then they saw the boys, and, fifteen minutes later, Paul and George were shaking hands with Paul's father. "Dad, your old sea-horse did it!" cried the son. "I'm going to get him off this island, for he deserves better things. He ought to get a life-saving medal!"

"I'll wager," laughed Mr. West, "you'll never lay hands on him again."

And the boys never did, though they made three trips to Grand Terre after the sea went down, first to attend to old man Schumitz, and then to tame the great white horse. Big King did not molest them; he even let Paul come close enough to reach out a loving finger to his nervous muzzle. But that was all; at sight of a halter or the motion of a hand to his neck, he was off, again charging magnificently down the wet sands to turn and watch them, with the surf breaking about his legs. To the end of his days he was the lonely and wild sea-horse of Grand Terre.

First published in the May 1914 edition of *St. Nicholas Magazine*

The Brownies' Garden

WRITTEN AND ILLUSTRATED BY PALMER COX

ONE night, as spring began to show
In buds above and blades below,
The Brownies reached a garden square
That seemed in need of proper care.
Said one, "Neglected ground like this
Must argue some one most remiss,
Or beds and paths would here be found
Instead of rubbish scattered 'round.
Old staves, and boots, and woolen strings,
With bottles, bones, and wire springs,

Are quite unsightly things to see
Where tender plants should sprouting be.
The crows are cawing on the limb,
The swallows o'er the meadows skim;
I heard the robin's merry note
This evening through the valley float,
While bluebirds flew around in quest
Of hollow stumps fit for a nest.
This work must be progressing soon,
If blossoms are to smile in June."

A second said, "Let all give heed:
On me depend to find the seed.
And neither village shop I'll raid,
Nor city store of larger trade;
For, thanks to my foreseeing mind,
To merchants' goods we're not confined.
Last autumn, when the leaves grew sere
And birds sought regions less severe,
One night through gardens fair I sped,
And gathered seeds from every bed;
Then placed them in a hollow tree,
Where still they rest. So trust to me
To bring supplies, while you prepare
The mellow garden-soil with care."
Another cried, "While some one goes
To find the shovels, rakes, and hoes,
That in the sheds are stowed away,
We'll use this plow as best we may.

Our arms, united at the chain,
Will not be exercised in vain,
But, as though colts were in the trace,
We'll make it dance around the place,
I know how deep the point should go,
And how the sods to overthrow.
So not a patch of ground the size
Of this old cap, when flat it lies,
But shall attentive care receive,
And be improved before we leave."

Then some to guide the plow began,
Others the walks and beds to plan.
And soon they gazed with anxious eyes
For those who ran for seed-supplies.
But, when they came, one had his say,
And thus explained the long delay:

"A woodchuck in the tree had made
His bed just where the seeds were laid,
We wasted half an hour at least
In striving to dislodge the beast;
Until at length he turned around,
Then, quick as thought, without a sound,
And ere he had his bearings got,
The rogue was half across the lot."

Then seed was sown in various styles,
In circles, squares, and single files;
While here and there, in central parts,
They fashioned diamonds, stars, and hearts,
Some using rake, some plying hoe,
Some making holes where seed should go;
While some laid garden tools aside
And to the soil their hands applied.

And be surprised to find each morn
New blossoms do each bed adorn.
And in their own peculiar screed
Will bless the hands that sowed the seed."

To stakes and racks more were assigned,
That climbing vines support might find.
Cried one, "Here, side by side, will stand
The fairest flowers in the land—

The stately hollyhock will tower
O'er many a sweet and modest flower.
Here, royal plants, all weighted down
With purple robe or golden crown,
Away their pomp and pride will fling
And to their nearest neighbor cling.

But morning broke (as break it will
Though one's awake or sleeping still),
And then the seeds on every side
The hurried Brownies scattered wide.

The thrifty bees for miles around
Ere long will seek this plot of ground,

Along the road and through the lane
They pattered on the ground like rain,
Where Brownies, as away they flew,
Both right and left full handfuls threw,
And children often halted there
To pick the blossoms, sweet and fair,
That sprung like daisies from the mead
Where fleeing Brownies flung the seed.

First published in the August 1889 edition of *St. Nicholas Magazine*

Tom Sawyer, Detective

AS TOLD BY HUCK FINN

BY MARK TWAIN

Strange as the incidents of this story are, they are not inventions, but facts—even to the public confession of the accused. I take them from an old-time Swedish criminal trial, change the actors, and transfer the scene to America. I have added some details, but only a couple of them are important ones.   *—M. T.*

CHAPTER ONE

WELL, IT WAS the next spring after me and Tom Sawyer set our old slave Jim free, the time he was chained up for a runaway slave down there on Tom's uncle Silas's farm in Arkansaw. The frost was working out of the ground, and out of the air too, and it was getting closer and closer onto barefoot time every day; and next it would be marble time, and next mumbletypeg, and next tops and hoops, and next kites, and then right away it would be summer and going in a-swimming. It just makes a boy homesick to look ahead like that and see how far off summer is. Yes, and it sets him to sighing and saddening around, and there's something the matter with him, he don't know what. But anyway, he gets out by himself and mopes and thinks; and mostly he hunts for a lonesome place high up on the hill in the edge of the woods, and sets there and looks away off on the big Mississippi down there a-reaching miles and miles around the points where the timber looks smoky and dim it's so far off and still, and everything's so solemn it seems like everybody you've loved is dead and gone, and you 'most wish you was dead and gone too, and done with it all.

Don't you know what that is? It's spring fever. That is what the name of it is. And when you've got it, you want—oh, you don't quite know what it is you *do* want, but it just fairly makes your heart ache, you want it so! It seems to you that mainly what you want is to get away; get away from the same old tedious things you're so used to seeing and so tired of, and see something new. That is the idea; you want to go and be a wanderer; you want to go wandering far away to strange countries where everything is mysterious and wonderful and romantic. And if you can't do that, you'll put up with considerable less; you'll go anywhere you *can* go, just so as to get away, and be thankful of the chance, too.

Well, me and Tom Sawyer had the spring-fever, and had it bad, too; but it warn't any use to think about Tom trying to get away, because, as he said, his aunt Polly wouldn't let him quit school and go traipsing off somers wasting time; so we was pretty blue. We was setting on the front steps one day about sundown talking this way, when out comes his aunt Polly with a letter in her hand and says—

"Tom, I reckon you've got to pack up and go down to Arkansaw—your aunt Sally wants you."

I 'most jumped out of my skin for joy. I reckoned Tom would fly at his aunt and hug her head off; but if you believe me he set there like a rock, and never said a word. It made me fit to cry to see him act so foolish, with such a noble chance as this opening up. Why, we might lose it if he didn't speak up and show he was thankful and grateful. But he set there and studied and studied till I was that distressed I didn't know what to do; then he says, very ca'm, and I could a shot him for it:

"Well," he says, "I'm right down sorry, Aunt Polly, but I reckon I got to be excused—for the present."

His aunt Polly was knocked so stupid and so mad at the cold impudence of it that she couldn't say a word for as much as a half a minute, and this give me a chance to nudge Tom and whisper:

"Ain't you got any sense? Sp'iling such a noble chance as this and throwing it away?"

But he warn't disturbed. He mumbled back:

"Huck Finn, do you want me to let her *see* how bad I want to go? Why, she'd begin to doubt, right away, and imagine a lot of sicknesses and dangers and objections, and first you know she'd take it all back. You lemme alone; I reckon I know how to work her."

Now I never would a thought of that. But he was right. Tom Sawyer was always right—the levelest head I ever see and always *at* himself and ready for anything you might spring on him. By this time his aunt Polly was all straight again, and she let fly. She says:

"You'll be excused! *You* will! Well, I never heard the like of it in all my days! The idea of you talking like that to *me!* Now take yourself off and pack your traps; and if I hear another word out of you about what you'll be excused from and what you won't, I lay *I'll* excuse you—with a hickory!"

She hit his head a thump with her thimble as we dodged by, and he let on to be whimpering as we struck for the stairs. Up in his room he hugged me, he was so out of his head for gladness because he was going travelling. And he says:

"Before we get away she'll wish she hadn't let me go, but she won't know anyway to get around it now. After what she's said, her pride won't let her take it back."

Tom was packed in ten minutes, all except what his aunt and Mary would finish up for him; then we waited ten more for her to get cooled down and sweet and gentle again; for Tom said it took her ten minutes to unruffle in times when half of her feathers was up, but twenty when they was all up, and this was one of the times when they was all up. Then we went down, being in a sweat to know what the letter said.

She was setting there in a brown study, with it laying in her lap. We set down and she says:

"They're in considerable trouble down there, and they think you and Huck'll be a kind of adversion for them—'comfort,' they say. Much of that they'll get out of you and Huck Finn, I reckon. There's a neighbor named Brace Dunlap that's been wanting to marry their Benny for three months, and at last they told him pine blank and once for all, he *couldn't*; so he has soured on them, and they're worried about it. I reckon he's somebody they think they better be on the good side of, for they've tried to please him by hiring his no-account brother to help on the farm when they can't hardly afford it, and don't want him around anyhow. Who are the Dunlaps?"

"They live about a mile from Uncle Silas's place, Aunt Polly—all the farmers live about a mile apart down there—and Brace Dunlap is a long sight richer than any of the others, and owns a whole grist of darkies. He's a widower, thirty-six years old, without any children, and is proud of his money and overbearing, and everybody is a little afraid of him. I judge he thought he could have any girl he wanted, just for the asking, and it

"I reckon I got to be excused."

must have set him back a good deal when he found he couldn't get Benny. Why, Benny's only half as old as he is, and just as sweet and lovely as—well, you've seen her. Poor old Uncle Silas—why, it's pitiful, him trying to curry favor that way—so hard pushed and poor, and yet hiring that useless Jubiter Dunlap to please his ornery brother."

"What a name—Jubiter! Where'd he get it?"

"It's only just a nickname. I reckon they've forgot his real name long before this. He's twenty-seven, now, and has had it ever since the first time he ever went in swimming. The school-teacher seen a round brown mole the size of a dime on his left leg above his knee, and four little bits of moles around it, when he was naked, and he said it minded him of Jubiter and his moons; and the children thought it was funny, and so they got to calling him Jubiter, and he's Jubiter yet. He's tall, and lazy, and sly, and sneaky, and ruther cowardly, too, but kind of good-natured, and wears long brown hair and no beard, and hasn't got a cent, and Brace boards him for nothing, and gives him his old clothes to wear, and despises him. Jubiter is a twin."

"What's t'other twin like?"

"Just exactly like Jubiter—so they say; used to was, anyway, but he hain't been seen for seven years. He got to robbing when he was nineteen or twenty, and they jailed him; but he broke jail and got away—up North here, somers. They used to hear about him robbing and burglaring now and then, but that was years ago. He's dead, now. At least that's what they say. They don't hear about him any more."

"What was his name?"

"Jake."

There wasn't anything more said for a considerable while; the old lady was thinking. At last she says:

"The thing that is mostly worrying your aunt Sally is the tempers that that man Jubiter gets your uncle into."

Tom was astonished, and so was I. Tom says:

"Tempers? Uncle Silas? Land, you must be joking! I didn't know he *had* any temper."

"Works him up into perfect rages, your aunt Sally says; says he acts as if he would really hit the man, sometimes."

"Aunt Polly, it beats anything I ever heard of. Why, he's just as gentle as mush."

"Well, she's worried, anyway. Says your uncle Silas is like a changed man, on account of all this quarrelling. And the neighbors talk about it, and lay all the blame on your uncle, of course, because he's a preacher and hain't got any business to quarrel. Your aunt Sally says he hates to go into the pulpit he's so ashamed; and the people have begun to cool towards him, and he ain't as popular now as he used to was."

"Well, ain't it strange? Why, Aunt Polly, he was always so good and kind and moony and absent-minded and chuckle-headed and lovable—why, he was just an angel! What *can* be the matter of him, do you reckon?"

CHAPTER TWO

WE HAD POWERFUL good luck; because we got a chance in a stern-wheeler from away North which was bound for one of them bayous or one-horse rivers away down Louisiana way, and so we could go all the way down the Upper Mississippi and all the way down the Lower Mississippi to that farm in Arkansaw without having to change steamboats at St. Louis: not so very much short of a thousand miles at one pull.

A pretty lonesome boat; there warn't but few passengers, and all old folks, that set around, wide apart, dozing, and was very quiet. We was four days getting out of the "upper river," because we got aground so much. But it warn't dull—couldn't be for boys that was travelling, of course.

From the very start me and Tom allowed that there was somebody sick in the stateroom next to ourn, because the meals was always toted in there by the waiters. By-and-by we asked about it—Tom did—and the waiter said it was a man, but he didn't look sick.

"Well, but *ain't* he sick?"

"I don't know; maybe he is, but 'pears to me he's just letting on."

"What makes you think that?"

"Because if he was sick he would pull his clothes off *some* time or other—don't you reckon he would? Well, this one don't. At least he don't ever pull off his boots, anyway."

"The mischief he don't! Not even when he goes to bed?"

It was always nuts for Tom Sawyer—a mystery was. If you'd lay out a mystery and a pie before me and him, you wouldn't have to say take your choice; it was a thing that would regulate itself. Because in my nature I have always run to pie, whilst in his nature he has always run to mystery. People are made different. And it is the best way. Tom says to the waiter:

"What's the man's name?"

"Phillips."

"Where'd he come aboard?"

"I think he got aboard at Elexandria, up on the Iowa line."

"What do you reckon he's a-playing?"

"I hain't any notion—I never thought of it."

I says to myself, here's another one that runs to pie.

"Anything peculiar about him?—the way he acts or talks?"

"No—nothing, except he seems so scary, and keeps his doors locked night and day both, and when you knock he won't let you in till he opens the door a crack and sees who it is."

"By jimminy, it's int'resting! I'd like to get a look at him. Say—the next time you're going in there, don't you reckon you could spread the door and—"

"No, indeedy! He's always behind it. He would block that game."

Tom studied over it, and then be says:

"Looky-here. You lend me your apern and let me take him his breakfast in the morning. I'll give you a quarter."

The boy was plenty willing enough, if the head steward wouldn't mind. Tom says that's all right, he reckoned he could fix it with the head steward; and he done it. He fixed it so as we could both go in with aperns on and toting vittles.

He didn't sleep much, he was in such a sweat to get in there and find out the mystery about Phillips; and moreover he done a lot of guessing about it all night, which warn't no use, for if you are going to find out the facts of a thing, what's the sense in guessing out what ain't the facts and wasting ammunition? I didn't lose no sleep. I wouldn't give a dern to know what's the matter of Phillips, I says to myself.

Well, in the morning we put on the aperns and got a couple of trays of truck, and Tom he knocked on the door. The man opened it a crack, and then he let us in and shut it quick. By Jackson, when we got a sight of him, we most dropped the trays! and Tom says:

"Why, Jubiter Dunlap, where'd *you* come from!"

Well, the man was astonished, of course; and first off he looked like he didn't know whether to be scared, or glad, or both, or which, but finally he settled down to being glad; and then his color come back, though at first his face had turned pretty white. So we got to talking together while he et his breakfast. And he says:

"But I ain't Jubiter Dunlap. I'd just as soon tell you who I am, though, if you'll swear to keep mum, for I ain't no Phillips, either."

Tom says:

"We'll keep mum, but there ain't any need to tell who you are if you ain't Jubiter Dunlap."

"Why?"

"Because if you ain't him you're t'other twin, Jake. You're the spit'n image of Jubiter."

"Well, I *am* Jake. But looky-here, how do you come to know us Dunlaps?"

Tom told about the adventures we'd had down there at his uncle Silas's last summer, and when he see that there warn't anything about his folks—or him either, for that matter—that we didn't know, he opened out and talked perfectly free and candid. He never made any bones about his own case; said he'd been a hard lot, was a hard lot yet, and reckoned he'd *be* a hard lot plumb to the end. He said of course it was a dangerous life, and—

He give a kind of gasp, and set his head like a person that's listening. We didn't say anything, and so it was very still for a second or so, and there warn't no sounds but the screaking of the wood-work and the chug-chugging of the machinery down below.

Then we got him comfortable again, telling him about his people, and how Brace's wife had been dead three years, and Brace wanted to marry Benny and she shook him, and Jubiter was working for Uncle Silas, and him and Uncle Silas quarrelling all the time—and then he let go and laughed.

"Land!" he says, "it's like old times to hear all this tittle-tattle, and does me good. It's been seven years and more since I heard any. How do they talk about me these days?"

"Who?"

"The farmers—and the family."

"Why, they don't talk about you at all—at least only just a mention, once in a long time."

"The nation!" he says, surprised; "why is that?"

"Because they think you are dead long ago."

"No! Are you speaking true?—honor bright, now." He jumped up, excited.

"Honor bright. There ain't anybody thinks you are alive."

"Then I'm saved, I'm saved, sure! Ill go home. They'll hide me and save my life. You keep mum. Swear you'll keep mum—swear you'll never, never tell on me. Oh, boys, be good to a poor devil that's being hunted day and night, and dasn't show his face! I've never done you any harm; I'll never do you any, as God is in the heavens; swear you'll be good to me and help me save my life."

We'd a swore it if he'd been a dog; and so we done it. Well, he couldn't love us enough for it or be grateful enough, poor cuss; it was all he could do to keep from hugging us.

We talked along, and he got out a little hand-bag and begun to open it, and told us to turn our backs. We done it, and when he told us to turn again he was perfectly different to what he was before. He had on blue goggles and the naturalest-looking long brown whiskers and mustashes you ever see. His own mother wouldn't a knowed him. He asked us if he looked like his brother Jubiter, now.

"No," Tom said; "there ain't anything left that's like him except the long hair."

"All right, I'll get that cropped close to my head before I get there; then him and Brace will keep my secret, and I'll live with them as being a stranger, and the neighbors won't ever guess me out. What do you think?"

"Swear you'll be good to me and help me save my life."

Tom he studied awhile, then he says:

"Well, of course me and Huck are going to keep mum there, but if you don't keep mum yourself there's going to be a little bit of a risk—it ain't much, maybe, but it's a little. I mean, if you talk, won't people notice that your voice is just like Jubiter's; and mightn't it make them think of the twin they reckoned was dead, but maybe after all was hid all this time under another name?"

"By George," he says, "you're a sharp one! You're perfectly right. I've got to play deef and dumb when there's a neighbor around. If I'd a struck for home and forgot that little detail— However, I wasn't striking for home. I was breaking for any place where I could get away from these fellows that are after me; then I was going to put on this disguise and get some different clothes, and—"

He jumped for the outside door and laid his ear against it and listened, pale and kind of panting. Presently he whispers:

"Sounded like cocking a gun! Lord, what a life to lead!"

Then he sunk down in a chair all limp and sick like, and wiped the sweat off of his face.

CHAPTER THREE

FROM THAT TIME out, we was with him 'most all the time, and one or t'other of us slept in his upper berth. He said he had been so lonesome and it was such a comfort to him to have company, and somebody to talk to in his troubles. We was in a sweat to find out what his secret was, but Tom said the best way was not to seem anxious, then likely he would drop into it himself in one of his talks, but if we got to asking questions he would get suspicious and shet up his shell. It turned out just so. It warn't no trouble to see that he *wanted* to talk about it, but always along at first he would scare away from it when he got on the very edge of it, and go to talking about something else. The way it come about was this: He got to asking us, kind of indifferent like, about the passengers down on deck. We told him about them. But he warn't satisfied; we warn't particular enough. He told us to describe them better. Tom done it. At last, when Tom was describing one of the roughest and raggedest ones, he gave a shiver and a gasp and says:

"Oh, lordy, that's one of them! They're aboard sure—I just knowed it. I sort of hoped I had got away, but I never believed it. Go on."

Presently when Tom was describing another mangy rough deck passenger, he give that shiver again and says—

"That's him!—that's the other one. If it would only come a good black stormy night and I could get ashore! You see, they've got spies on me. They've got a right to come up and buy drinks at the bar yonder forrard, and they take that chance to bribe somebody to keep watch on me—porter or boots or somebody. If I was to slip ashore without anybody seeing me, they would know it inside of an hour."

So then he got to wandering along, and pretty soon, sure enough, he was telling! He was poking along through his ups and downs, and when he come to that place he went right along. He says:

"It was a confidence game. We played it on a julery-shop in St. Louis. What we was after was a couple of noble big di'monds as big as hazelnuts, which everybody was running to see. We was dressed up fine, and we played it on them in broad daylight. We ordered the di'monds sent to the hotel for us to see if we wanted to buy, and when we was examining them we had paste counterfeits all ready, and *them* was the things that went back to the shop when we said the water wasn't quite fine enough for twelve thousand dollars."

"Sounded like cocking a gun!"

"Twelve—thousand—dollars!" Tom says. "Was they really worth all that money, do you reckon?"

"Every cent of it."

"And you fellows got away with them?"

"As easy as nothing. I don't reckon the julery people know they've been robbed yet. But it wouldn't be good sense to stay around St. Louis, of course, so we considered where we'd go. One was for going one way, one another, so we threwed up, heads or tails, and the Upper Mississippi won. We done up the di'monds in a paper and put our names on it and put it in the keep of the hotel clerk, and told him not to ever let either of us have it again without the others was on hand to see it done; then we went downtown, each by his own self—because I reckon maybe we all had the same notion. I don't know for certain, but I reckon maybe we had."

"What notion?" Tom says.

"To rob the others."

"What—one take everything, after all of you had helped to get it?"

"Cert'nly."

It disgusted Tom Sawyer, and he said it was the orneriest, low-downest thing he ever heard of. But Jake Dunlap said it warn't unusual in the profession. Said when a person was in that line of business he'd got to look out for his own intrust, there warn't nobody else going to do it for him. And then he went on. He says:

"You see, the trouble was, you couldn't divide up two di'monds amongst three. If there'd been three— But never mind about that, there *warn't* three. I loafed along the back streets studying and studying. And I says to myself, I'll hog them di'monds the first chance I get, and I'll have a disguise all ready and I'll give the boys the slip, and when I'm safe away I'll put it on, and then let them find me if they can. So I got the false whiskers and the goggles and this countrified suit of clothes, and fetched them along back in a hand-bag; and when I was passing a shop where they sell all sorts of things, I got a glimpse of one of my pals through the window. It was Bud Dixon. I was glad, you bet. I says to myself, I'll see what he buys. So I kept shady, and watched. Now what do you reckon it was he bought?"

"Whiskers?" said I.

"Goggles?"

"No."

"Oh, keep still, Huck Finn, can't you, you're only just hendering all you can. What *was* it he bought, Jake?"

"You'd never guess in the world. It was only just a screw-driver—just a wee little bit of a screw-driver."

"Well, I declare! What did he want with that?"

"That's what *I* thought. It was curious. It clean stumped me. I says to myself, what can he want with that thing? Well, when he come out I stood back out of sight, and then tracked him to a second-hand slop-shop and see him buy a red flannel shirt and some old ragged clothes—just the ones he's got on now, as you've described. Then I went down to the wharf and hid my things aboard the up-river boat that we had picked out, and then started back and had another streak of luck. I seen our other pal lay in *his* stock of old rusty second-handers. We got the di'monds and went aboard the boat.

"But now we was up a stump, for we couldn't go to bed. We had to set up and watch one another. Pity, that was; pity to put that kind of a strain on us, because there was bad blood between us from a couple of weeks back, and we was only friends in the way of business. Bad anyway, seeing there was only two di'monds betwixt three men. First we had supper, and then tramped up and down the deck together smoking till most midnight; then we went and set down in my state-room and locked the doors and looked in the piece of paper to see if the di'monds was all right, then laid it on the lower berth right in full sight; and there we set, and set, and by-and-by it got to be dreadful hard to keep awake. At last Bud Dixon dropped off. As soon as he was snoring a good regular gait that was likely to last, and had his chin on his breast and hooked permanent, Hal Clayton nodded towards the di'monds and then towards the outside door, and I understood. I reached and got the paper, and then we stood up and waited perfectly still; Bud never stirred; I turned the key of the outside door very soft and slow, then turned the knob the same way, and we went tiptoeing out onto the guard, and shut the door very soft and gentle.

"There warn't nobody stirring anywhere, and the boat was slipping along, swift and steady, through the big water in the smoky moonlight. We never said a word, but went straight up onto the hurricane-deck and plumb back aft, and set down on the end of the skylight. Both of us knowed what that meant, without having to explain to one another. Bud Dixon would wake up and miss the swag, and would come straight for us, for he ain't afeard of anything or anybody, that man ain't. He would come, and we would heave him overboard, or get killed trying. It made me shiver, because I ain't as brave as some people, but if I showed the white feather—well, I knowed better than do that. I kind of hoped the boat would land somers, and we could skip ashore and not have to run the risk of this row, I was so scared of Bud Dixon, but she was an upper-river tub and there warn't no real chance of that.

"Well, the time strung along and along, and that fellow never come! Why, it strung along till dawn begun to break, and still he never come. 'Thunder,' I says, 'what do you make out of this?—ain't it suspicious?' 'Land!' Hal says, 'do you reck-on he's playing us?—open the paper!' I done it, and by gracious there warn't any-thing in it but a couple of little pieces of loaf-sugar! *That's* the reason he could set

"We stood up and waited perfectly still."

there and snooze all night so comfortable. Smart? Well, I reckon! He had had them two papers all fixed and ready, and he had put one of them in place of t'other right under our noses.

"We felt pretty cheap. But the thing to do, straight off, was to make a plan; and we done it. We would do up the paper again, just as it was, and slip in, very elaborate and soft, and lay it on the bunk again, and let on *we* didn't know about any trick, and hadn't any idea he was a-laughing at us behind them bogus snares of his'n; and we would stick by him, and the first night we was ashore we would get him drunk and search him, and get the di'monds; and *do* for him, too, if it warn't too risky. If we got the swag, we'd *got* to do for him, or he would hunt us down and do for us, sure. But I didn't have no real hope. I knowed we could get him drunk—he was always ready for that—but what's the good of it? You might search him a year and never find—

"Well, right there I catched my breath and broke off my thought! For an idea went ripping through my head that tore my brains to rags—and land, but I felt gay and good! You see, I had had my boots off, to unswell my feet, and just then I took up one of them to put it on, and I catched a glimpse of the heel-bottom, and it just took my breath away. You remember about that puzzlesome little screw-driver?"

"You bet I do," says Tom, all excited.

"Well, when I catched that glimpse of that boot heel, the idea that went smashing through my head was, *I know where he's hid the di'monds!* You look at this boot heel, now. See, it's bottomed with a steel plate, and the plate is fastened on with little screws. Now there wasn't a screw about that feller anywhere but in his boot heels; so, if he needed a screw-driver, I reckoned I knowed why."

"Huck, ain't it bully!" says Tom.

"Well, I got my boots on, and we went down and slipped in and laid the paper of sugar on the berth, and sat down soft and sheepish and went to listening to Bud Dixon snore. Hal Clayton dropped off pretty soon, but I didn't; I wasn't ever so wide-awake in my life. I was spying out from under the shade of my hat brim, searching the floor for leather. It took me a long time, and I begun to think maybe my guess was wrong, but at last I struck it. It laid over by the bulkhead, and was nearly the color of the carpet. It was a little round plug about as thick as the end of your little finger, and I says to myself there's a di'mond in the nest you've come from. Before long I spied out the plug's mate.

"Think of the smartness and coolness of that blatherskite! He put up that scheme on us and reasoned out what we would do, and we went ahead and done it perfectly exact, like a couple of pudd'n-heads. He set there and took his own time to unscrew his heel-plates and cut out his plugs and stick in the di'monds and screw on his plates again. He allowed we would steal the bogus swag and wait all night for him to come up and get drownded, and by George it's just what we done! *I* think it was powerful smart."

"You bet your life it was!" says Tom, just full of admiration.

CHAPTER FOUR

"WELL, ALL DAY we went through the humbug of watching one another, and it was pretty sickly business for two of us and hard to act out, I can tell you. About night we landed at one of them little Missouri towns high up towards Iowa, and had supper at the tavern, and got a room upstairs with a cot and a double bed in it, but I dumped my bag under a deal table in the dark hall whilst we was moving along it to bed, single file, me last, and the landlord in the lead with a tallow candle. We had up a lot of whiskey, and went to playing high-low-jack for dimes, and as soon as the whiskey begun to take hold of Bud we stopped drinking, but we didn't let him stop. We loaded him till he fell out of his chair and laid there snoring.

"We was ready for business now. I said we better pull our boots off, and his'n too, and not make any noise, then we could pull him and haul him around and ransack him without any trouble. So we done it. I set my boots and Bud's side by side, where they'd be handy. Then we stripped him and searched his seams and his pockets and his socks and the inside of his boots, and everything, and searched his bundle. Never found any di'monds. We found the screw-driver, and Hal says, 'What do you reckon he wanted with that?' I said I didn't know; but when he wasn't looking I hooked it.

At last Hal he looked beat and discouraged, and said we'd got to give it up. That was what I was waiting for. I says:

"'There's one place we hain't searched.'

"'What place is that?' he says.

"'His stomach.'

"'By gracious, I never thought of that! *Now* we're on the homestretch, to a dead moral certainty. How'll we manage?'

"'Well,' I says, 'just stay by him till I turn out and hunt up a drug-store, and I reckon I'll fetch something that'll make them di'monds tired of the company they're keeping.'

They searched his seams and his pockets and his socks.

"He said that's the ticket, and with him looking straight at me I slid myself into Bud's boots instead of my own, and he never noticed. They was just a shade large for me, but that was considerable better than being too small. I got my bag as I went a-groping through the hall, and in about a minute I was out the back way and stretching up the river road at a five-mile gait.

"And not feeling so very bad, neither—walking on di'monds don't have no such effect. When I had gone fifteen minutes I says to myself, there's more'n a mile behind me, and everything quiet. Another five minutes and I says there's considerable more land behind me now, and there's a man back there that's begun to wonder what's the trouble. Another five and I says to myself he's getting real uneasy—he's walking the floor now. Another five, and I says to myself, there's two mile and a half behind me, and he's *awful* uneasy—beginning to cuss, I reckon. Pretty soon I says to myself, forty minutes gone—he *knows* there's something up! Fifty minutes—the truth's a-busting on him now! he is reckoning I my found the di'monds whilst we was searching, and shoved them in my pocket and and never let on—yes, and he's starting out to hunt for me. He'll hunt for new tracks in the dust, and they'll as likely send him down the river as up.

"Just then I see a man coming down on a mule, and before I thought I jumped into the bush. It was stupid! When he got abreast he stopped and waited a little for me to come out; then he rode on again. But I didn't feel gay any more. I says to myself I've botched my chances by that; I surely have, if he meets up with Hal Clayton.

"Well, about three in the morning I fetched Elexandria and see this stern-wheeler laying there, and was very glad, because I felt perfectly safe, now, you know. It was just daybreak. I went aboard and got this stateroom and put on these clothes and went up in the pilot-house—to watch, though I didn't reckon there was any need of it. I set there and played with my di'monds and waited and waited for the boat to start, but she didn't. You see, they was mending her machinery, but I didn't know anything about it, not being very much used to steamboats.

"Well, to cut the tale short, we never left there till plumb noon and long before that I was hid in this state-room; for before breakfast I see a man coming, away off, that had a gait like Hal Clayton's, and it made me just sick. I says to myself, if he finds out I'm aboard this boat, he's got me like a rat in a trap. All he's got to do is to have me watched, and wait—wait till I slip ashore, thinking he is a thousand miles away, then slip after me and dog me to a good place and make me give up the di'monds, and then he'll—oh, I know what he'll do! Ain't it awful—awful! And now to think the *other* one's aboard, too! Oh, ain't it hard luck, boys—ain't it hard! But you'll help save me, *won't* you?—oh, boys, be good to a poor devil that's being hunted to death, and save me—I'll worship the very ground you walk on!"

We turned in and soothed him down and told him we would plan for him and help him, and he needn't be so afeard; and so by-and-by he got to feeling kind of comfortable again, and unscrewed his heel-plates and held up his di'monds this way and that, admiring them and loving them; and when the light struck into them they *was* beautiful, sure; why, they seemed to kind of bust, and snap fire out all around. But all the same I judged he was a fool. If I had been him I would a handed the di'-monds to them pals and got them to go ashore and leave me alone. But he was made different. He said it was a whole fortune and he couldn't bear the idea.

Twice we stopped to fix the machinery and laid a good while, once in the night; but it wasn't dark enough, and he was afeard to skip. But the third time we had to fix it there was a better chance. We laid up at a country wood-yard about forty mile above Uncle Silas's place a little after one at night, and it was thickening up and going to storm. So Jake he laid for a chance to slide. We begun to take in wood. Pretty soon the rain come a-drenching down, and the wind blowed hard. Of course every boat-hand fixed a gunny sack and put it on like a bonnet, the way they do when they are toting wood, and we got one for Jake, and he slipped down aft with his hand-bag and come tramping forrard just like the rest, and walked ashore with them, and when we see him pass out of the light of the torch-basket and get swallowed up in the dark, we got our breath again and just felt grateful and splendid. But it wasn't for long. Somebody told, I reckon; for in about eight or ten minutes them two pals come tearing forrard as tight as they could jump and darted ashore and was gone. We waited plumb till dawn for them

He walked ashore.

to come back, and kept hoping they would, but they never did. We was awful sorry and low-spirited. All the hope we had was that Jake had got such a start that they couldn't get on his track, and he would get to his brother's and hide there and be safe.

He was going to take the river road, and told us to find out if Brace and Jubiter was to home and no strangers there, and then slip out about sundown and tell him. Said he would wait for us in a little bunch of sycamores right back of Tom's uncle Silas's tobacker-field on the river road, a lonesome place.

We set and talked a long time about his chances, and Torn said he was all right if the pals struck up the river instead of down, but it wasn't likely, because maybe they knowed where he was from; more likely they would go right, and dog him all day, him not suspecting, and kill him when it come dark, and take the boots. So we was pretty sorrowful.

CHAPTER FIVE

WE DIDN'T GET done tinkering the machinery till away late in the afternoon, and so it was so close to sundown when we got home that we never stopped on our road, but made a break for the sycamores as tight as we could go, to tell Jake what the delay was, and have him wait till we could go to Brace's and find out how things was there. It was getting pretty dim by the time we turned the corner of the woods, sweating and panting with that long run, and see the sycamores thirty yards ahead of us; and just then we see a couple of men run in to the bunch and heard two or three terrible screams for help. "Poor Jake is killed, sure," we says. We was scared through and through, and broke for the tobacker-field and hid there, trembling so our clothes would hardly stay on; and just as we skipped in there, a couple of men went tearing by, and into the bunch they went, and in a second out jumps four men and took out up the road as tight as they could go, two chasing two.

We laid down, kind of weak and sick, and listened for more sounds, but didn't hear none for a good while but just our hearts. We was thinking of that awful thing laying yonder in the sycamores, and it seemed like being that close to a ghost, and it give me the cold shudders. The moon come a-swelling up out of the ground, now, powerful big and round and bright, behind a comb of trees, like a face looking through prison bars, and the black shadders and white places begun to creep around, and it was miserable quiet and still and night-breezy and graveyardy and scary. All of a sudden Tom whispers: "Look!—what's that?"

"Don't!" I says. "Don't take a person by surprise that way. I'm 'most ready to die, anyway, without you doing that."

"Look, I tell you. It's something coming out of the sycamores."

"Don't, Tom!"

"It's terrible tall!"

"Oh, lordy-lordy! let's—"

"Keep still—it's a-coming this way."

He was so excited he could hardly get breath enough to whisper. I had to look. I couldn't help it. So now we was both on our knees with our chins on a fence-rail and gazing—yes, and gasping, too. It was coming down the road—coming in the shadder of the trees, and you couldn't see it good; not till it was pretty close to us; then it stepped into a bright splotch of moonlight and we sunk right down in our tracks—it was Jake Dunlap's ghost! That was what we said to ourselves.

We couldn't stir for a minute or two; then it was gone. We talked about it in low voices. Tom says:

"They're mostly dim and smoky, or like they're made out of fog, but this one wasn't."

Jake Dunlap's ghost

"No," I says; "I seen the goggles and the whiskers perfectly plain."

"Yes, and the very colors in them loud countrified Sunday clothes—plaid breeches, green and black—"

"Cotton-velvet westcot, fire-red and yaller squares—"

"Leather straps to the bottoms of the breeches legs and one of them hanging unbuttoned—"

"Yes, and that hat—"

"What a hat for a ghost to wear!"

You see it was the first season anybody wore that kind—a black stiff-brim stove-pipe, very high, and not smooth, with a round top—just like a sugar-loaf.

"Did you notice if its hair was the same, Huck?"

"No—seems to me I did, then again it seems to me I didn't."

"I didn't either; but it had its bag along, I noticed that."

"So did I. How can there be a ghost-bag, Tom?"

"Sho! I wouldn't be as ignorant as that if I was you, Huck Finn. Whatever a ghost has, turns to ghost-stuff. They've got to have their things, like anybody else. You see, yourself, that its clothes was turned to ghost-stuff. Well, then, what's to hender its bag from turning, too? Of course it done it."

That was reasonable. I couldn't find no fault with it. Bill Withers and his brother Jack come along by, talking, and Jack says:

"What do you reckon he was toting?"

"I dunno; but it was pretty heavy."

"Yes, all he could lug. Ole slave stealing corn from old Parson Silas, I judged."

"So did I. And so I allowed I wouldn't let on to see him."

"That's me, too!"

Then they both laughed, and went on out of hearing. It showed how unpopular old Uncle Silas had got to be, now. They wouldn't a let a darkie steal anybody else's corn and never done anything to him.

We heard some more voices mumbling along towards us and getting louder, and sometimes a cackle of a laugh. It was Lem Beebe and Jim Lane. Jim Lane says:

"Who?—Jubiter Dunlap?"

"Yes."

"Oh, I don't know. I reckon so. I seen him spading up some ground along about an hour ago, just before sundown—him and the parson. Said he guessed he wouldn't go tonight, but we could have his dog if we wanted him."

"Too tired, I reckon."

"Yes—works so hard!"

"Oh, you bet!"

They cackled at that, and went on by. Tom said we better jump out and tagalong after them, because they was going our way and it wouldn't be comfortable to run across the ghost all by ourselves. So we done it, and got home all right.

That night was the second of September—a Saturday. I sha'n't ever forget it. You'll see why, pretty soon.

CHAPTER SIX

WE TRAMPED ALONG behind Jim and Lem till we come to the back stile where old Jim's cabin was that he was captivated in, the time we set him free, and here come the dogs piling around us to say howdy, and there was the lights of the house, too; so we warn't afeard anymore, and was going to climb over, but Tom says:

"Hold on; set down here a minute. By George!"

"What's the matter?" says I.

"Matter enough!" he says. "Wasn't you expecting we would be the first to tell the family who it is that's been killed yonder in the sycamores, and all about them rapscallions that done it, and about the di'monds they've smouched off of the corpse, and paint it up fine, and have the glory of being the ones that knows a lot more about it than anybody else?"

"Why, of course. It wouldn't be you, Tom Sawyer, if you was to let such a chance go by. I reckon it ain't going to suffer none for lack of paint," I says, "when you start in to scollop the facts."

"Well, now," he says, perfectly ca'm, "what would you say if I was to tell you I ain't going to start in at all?"

I was astonished to hear him talk so. I says:

"I'd say it's a lie. You ain't in earnest, Tom Sawyer."

"You'll soon see. Was the ghost bare-footed?"

"No, it wasn't. What of it?"

"You wait—I'll show you what. Did it have its boots on?"

"Yes. I seen them plain."

"Swear it?"

"Yes, I swear it."

"Was the ghost bare-footed?"

"So do I. Now do you know what that means?"

"No. What does it mean?"

"Means that them thieves *didn't get the di'monds?*"

"Jimminy! What makes you think that?"

"I don't only think it, I know it. Didn't the breeches and goggles and whiskers and hand-bag and every blessed thing turn to ghost-stuff? Everything it had on turned, didn't it? It shows that the reason its boots turned too was because it still had them on after it started to go ha'nting around, and if that ain't proof that them blatherskites didn't get the boots, I'd like to know what you'd *call* proof."

Think of that, now. I never see such a head as that boy had. Why, *I* had eyes and I could see things, but they never meant nothing to me. But Tom Sawyer was different. When Tom Sawyer seen a thing it just got up on its hind legs and *talked* to him—told him everything it knowed. *I* never see such a head.

"Tom Sawyer," I says, "I'll say it again as I've said it a many a time before: I ain't fitten to black your boots. But that's all right—that's neither here nor there. God Almighty made us all, and some He gives eyes that's blind, and some He gives eyes that can see, and I reckon it ain't none of our lookout what He done it for; it's all right, or He'd afixed it some other way. Go on—I see the plenty plain enough, now, that them thieves didn't get away with the di'monds. Why didn't they, do you reckon?"

"Because they got chased away by them other two men before they could pull the boots off of the corpse."

"That's so! I see it now. But looky-here, Tom, why ain't we to go and tell about it?"

"Oh, shucks, Huck Finn, can't you see? Look at it. What's a-going to happen? There's going to be an inquest in the morning. Them two men will tell how they heard the yells and rushed there just in time to not save the stranger. Then the jury'll twaddle and twaddle and twaddle, and finally they'll fetch in a verdict that he got shot or stuck or busted over time head with something, and come to his death by the inspiration of God. And after they've buried him they'll auction off his things for to pay the expenses, and then's our chance."

"How, Tom?"

"Buy the boots for two dollars!"

Well, it 'most took my breath.

"My land! Why, Tom, *we'll* get the di'monds!"

"You bet. Some day there'll be a big reward offered for them—a thousand dollars, sure. That's our money! Now we'll trot in and see the folks. And mind you we don't know anything about any murder, or any di'monds, or any thieves—don't you forget that."

I had to sigh a little over the way he had got it fixed. *I'd a sold* them di'monds—yes, sir—for twelve thousand dollars; but I didn't say anything. It wouldn't done any good. I says:

"But what are we going to tell your aunt Sally has made us so long getting down here from the village, Tom?"

"Oh, I'll leave that to you," he says. "I reckon you can explain it somehow."

He was always just that strict and delicate. He never would tell a lie himself.

We struck across the big yard, noticing this, that, and t'other thing that was so familiar, and we so glad to see it again, and when we got to the roofed big passage way betwixt the double log house and the kitchen part, there was everything hanging on the wall just as it used to was, even to Uncle Silas's old faded green baize working-gown with the hood to it, and raggedy white patch between the shoulders that always looked like somebody had hit him with a snowball; and then we lifted the latch and walked in. Aunt Sally she was just a-ripping and a-tearing around, and the children was huddled in one corner, and the old man he was huddled in the other and praying for help in time of need. She jumped for us with joy and tears running down her face and give us a whacking box on the ear, and then hugged us and kissed us and boxed us again, and just couldn't seem to get enough of it, she was so glad to see us; and she says:

"Where *have* you been a-loafing to, you good-for-nothing trash! I've been that worried about you I didn't know what to do. Your traps has been here ever so long, and I've had supper cooked fresh about four times so as to have it hot and good when you come, till at last my patience is just plumb wore out, and I declare I—I—why I could skin you alive! You must be starving, poor things!—set down, set down, everybody; don't lose no more time."

It was good to be there again behind all that noble corn pone and spareribs, and everything that you could ever want in this world. Old Uncle Silas he peeled off one of his bulliest old-time blessings, with as many layers to it as an onion, and whilst the angels was hauling in the slack of it I was trying to study up what to say about what kept us so long. When our plates was all loadened and we'd got a-going, she asked me, and I says:

"Well, you see—er—Mizzes—"

"Huck Finn! Since when am I Mizzes to you? Have I ever been stingy of cuffs or kisses for you since the day you stood in this room and I took you for Tom Sawyer and blessed God for sending you to me, though you told me four thousand lies and I believed every one of them like a simpleton? Call me Aunt Sally—like you always done."

So I done it. And I says:

"Well, me and Tom allowed we would come along afoot and take a smell of the woods, and we run across Lem Beebe and Jim Lane, and they asked us to go with them blackberrying tonight, and said they could borrow Jubiter Dunlap's dog, because he had told them just that minute—"

"Where did they see him?" says the old man; and when I looked up to see how *he* come to take an intrust in a little thing like that, his eyes was just burning into me, he was that eager. It surprised me so it kind of throwed me off, but I pulled myself together again and says:

"It was when he was spading up some ground along with you, towards sundown or along there." He only said, "Um," in a kind of a disappointed way, and didn't take no more intrust. So I went on. I says; "Well, then, as I was a-saying—"

"That'll do, you needn't go no furder." It was Aunt Sally. She was boring right into me with her eyes, and very indignant. "Huck Finn," she says, "how'd them men come to talk about going a-blackberrying in September—in *this* region?"

I see I had slipped up, and I couldn't say a word. She waited, still a-gazing at me, then she says:

"And how'd they come to strike that idiot idea of going a-blackberrying in the night?"

"Well, m'm, they—er—they told us they had a lantern, and—"

"Oh, *shet* up—do! Looky-here; what was they going to do with a dog?—hunt blackberries with it?"

"I think, m'm, they—"

"Now, Tom Sawyer, what kind of a lie are you fixing *your* mouth to contribit to this mess of rubbage? Speak out—and I warn you before you begin, that I don't believe a word of it. You and Huck's been up to something you no business to—*I* know it perfectly well; *I* know you, *both* of you. Now you explain that dog, and them blackberries, and the lantern, and the rest of that rot—and mind you talk as straight as a string—do you hear?"

Tom he looked considerable hurt, and says, very dignified:

"It is a pity if Huck is to be talked to that away, just for making a little bit of a mistake that anybody could make."

"What mistake has he made?"

"Why, only the mistake of saying blackberries when of course he meant strawberries."

"Tom Sawyer, I lay if you aggravate me a little more, I'll—"

"Aunt Sally, without knowing it—and of course without intending it—you are in the wrong. If you'd a studied natural history the way you ought, you would know that all over the world except just here in Arkansaw they *always* hunt strawberries with a dog—and a lantern—"

But she busted in on him there and just piled into him and snowed him under. She was so mad she couldn't get the words out fast enough, and she gushed them out in one everlasting freshet. That was what Tom Sawyer was after. He allowed to work her up and get her started and then leave her alone and let her burn herself out. Then she would be so aggravated with that subject that she wouldn't say another word about it, nor let anybody else. Well, it happened just so. When she was tuckered out and had to hold up, he says, quite ca'm:

"And yet, all the same, Aunt Sally—"

"Shet up!" she says, "I don't want to hear another word out of you." So we was perfectly safe, then, and didn't have no more trouble about that delay. Tom done it elegant.

CHAPTER SEVEN

BENNY SHE WAS looking pretty sober, and she sighed some, now and then; but pretty soon she got to asking about Mary, and Sid, and Tom's aunt Polly, and their Aunt Sally's clouds cleared oft and she got in a good humor and joined in on the questions and was her lovingest best self, and so the rest of the supper went along gay and pleasant. But the old man he didn't take any hand hardly, and was absent-minded and restless, and done a considerable amount of sighing; and it was kind of heart-breaking to see him so sad and troubled and worried.

By-and-by, a spell after supper, come a man and knocked on the door and put his head in with his old straw hat in his hand bowing and scraping, and said his Marse Brace was out at the stile and wanted his brother, and was getting tired waiting supper for him, and would Marse Silas please tell him where he was? I never see Uncle Silas speak up so sharp and fractious before. He says:

"Am *I* his brother's keeper?" And then he kind of wilted together, and looked like he wished he hadn't spoken so, and then he says, very gentle: "But you needn't say that, Billy; I was took sudden and irritable, and I ain't very well these days, and not hardly responsible. Tell him he ain't here."

And when the man was gone he got up and walked the floor backwards and forwards, mumbling and muttering to himself and ploughing his hands through his hair. It was real pitiful to see him. Aunt Sally she whispered to us and told us not to take notice of him, it embarrassed him. She said he was always thinking and thinking, since these troubles come on, and she allowed he didn't more'n about half know what he was about when the thinking spells was on him; and she said he walked in his sleep considerable more now than he used to, and sometimes wandered around over the house and even outdoors in his sleep, and if we catched him at it we must let him alone and not disturb him. She said she reckoned it didn't do him no harm, and maybe it done him good. She said Benny was the only one that was much help to him these days. Said Benny appeared to know just when to try to soothe him and when to leave him alone.

So he kept on tramping up and down the floor and muttering, till by-and-by he begun to look pretty tired; then Benny she went and snuggled up to his side and put one hand in his and one arm around his waist and walked with him; and he smiled down on her, and reached down and kissed her; and so, little by little the trouble went out of his face and she persuaded him off to his room. They had very petting ways together, and it was uncommon pretty to see.

Aunt Sally she was busy getting the children ready for bed; so by-and-by it got dull and tedious, and me and Tom took a turn in the moonlight, and fetched up in the watermelon-patch and et one, and had a good deal of talk. And Tom said he'd bet the quarrelling was all Jubiter's fault, and he was going to be on hand the first time he got a chance, and see; and if it was so, he was going to do his level best to get Uncle Silas to turn him off.

And so we talked and smoked and stuffed watermelon as much as two hours, and then it was pretty late, and when we got back the house was quiet and dark, and everybody gone to bed. Tom he always seen everything, and now he see that the old green baize workgown was gone, and said it wasn't gone when we went out; and so we allowed it was curious, and then we went up to bed.

We could hear Benny stirring around in her room, which was next to ourn, and judged she was worried a good deal about her father and couldn't sleep. We found we couldn't, neither. So we set up a long time, and smoked and talked in a low voice, and felt pretty dull and down-hearted. We talked the murder and the ghost over and over again, and got so creepy and crawly we couldn't get sleepy no how and no way.

By-and-by, when it was away late in the night and all the sounds was late sounds and solemn, Tom nudged me and whispers to me to look, and I done it, and there we see a man poking around in the yard like he didn't know just what he wanted to do, but it was pretty dim and we couldn't see him good. Then he started for the stile, and as he went over it the moon came out strong, and he had a long-handled shovel over his shoulder, and we see the white patch on the old workgown. So Tom says:

"He's a-walking in his sleep. I wish we was allowed to follow him and see where he's going to. There, he's turned down by the tobacker-field. Out of sight now. It's a dreadful pity he can't rest no better."

We waited a long time, but he didn't come back anymore, or if he did he come around the other way; so at last we was tuckered out and went to sleep and had nightmares, a million of them. But before dawn we was awake again, because meantime a storm had come up and been raging, and the thunder and lightning was awful, and the wind was a-thrashing the trees around, and the rain was driving down in slanting sheets, and the gullies was running rivers. Tom says:

They smoked and ate watermelon.

"Looky-here, Huck, I'll tell you one thing that's mighty curious. Up to the time we went out, last night, the family hadn't heard about Jake Dunlap being murdered. Now the men that chased Hal Clayton and Bud Dixon away would spread the thing around in a half an hour, and every neighbor that heard it would slim out and fly around from one farm to t'other and try to be the first to tell the news. Land, they don't have such a big thing as that to tell twice in thirty year! Huck, it's mighty strange; I don't understand it."

So then he was in a fidget for the rain to let up, so we could turn out and run across some of the people and see if they would say anything about it to us. And he said if they did we must be horribly surprised and shocked.

We was out and gone the minute the rain stopped. It was just broad day, then. We loafed along up the road, and now and then met a person and stopped and said howdy, and told them when we come, and how we left the folks at home, and how long we was going to stay, and all that, but none of them said a word about that thing; which was just astonishing, and no mistake. Tom said he believed if we went to the sycamores we would find that body laying there solitary and alone, and not a soul around. Said he believed the men chased the thieves so far into the woods that the thieves prob'ly seen a good chance and turned on them at last, and maybe they all killed each other, and so there wasn't anybody left to tell.

First we knowed, gabbling along that away, we was right at the sycamores. The cold chills trickled down my back and I wouldn't budge another step, for all Tom's persuading. But he couldn't hold in; he'd *got* to see if the boots was safe on that body yet. So he crope in—and the time next minute out he come again with his eyes bulging he was so excited, and says: "Huck, it's gone!"

I *was* astonished! I says:

"Tom, you don't mean it."

"It's gone, sure. There ain't a sign of it. The ground is trampled some, but if there was any blood it's all washed away by the storm, for it's all puddles and slush in there."

At last I give in, and went and took a look myself; and it was just as Tom said—there wasn't a sign of a corpse.

"Dern it," I says, "the di'monds is gone. Don't you reckon the thieves slunk back and lugged him off, Tom?"

"Looks like it. It just does. Now where'd they hide him, do you reckon?"

"I don't know," I says, disgusted, and what's more I don't care. They've got the boots, and that's all *I* cared about. He'll lay around these woods a long time before *I* hunt him up."

Tom didn't feel no more intrust in him neither, only curiosity to know what

"Huck, it's gone!"

come of him; but he said we'd lay low and keep dark and it wouldn't be long till the dogs or somebody rousted him out.

We went back home to breakfast ever so bothered and put out and disappointed and swindled. I warn't ever so down on a corpse before.

CHAPTER EIGHT

IT WARN'T VERY cheerful at breakfast. Aunt Sally she looked old and tired, and let the children snarl and fuss at one another and didn't seem to notice it was going on, which wasn't her usual style; me and Tom had a plenty to think about without talking; Benny she looked like she hadn't much sleep, and whenever she'd lift her head a little and steal a look towards her father you could see there was tears in her eyes; and as for the old man his things staid on his plate and got cold without him knowing they was there, I reckon, for he was thinking and thinking all the time, and never said a word and never et a bite.

By-and-by when it was stillest, that darkie's head was poked in at the door again, and he said his Marse Brace was getting powerful uneasy about Marse Jubiter, which hadn't come home yet, and would Marse Silas please—

He was looking at Uncle Silas, and he stopped there, like the rest of his words was froze; for Uncle Silas he rose up shaky and steadied himself leaning his fingers on the table, and he was panting, and his eyes was set on the darkie, and he kept swallowing, and put his other hand up to his throat a couple of times, and at last he got his words started, and says:

"Does he—does he—think—*what* does he think! Tell him—tell him—" Then he sunk down in his chair limp and weak, and says, so as you could hardly hear him: "Go away—go away!"

The darkie looked scared, and cleared out, and we all felt—well, I don't know how we felt, but it was awful, with the old man panting there, and his eyes set and looking like a person that was dying. None of us could budge; but Benny she slid around soft, with her tears running down, and stood by his side, and nestled his old gray head up against her and begun to stroke it and pet it with her hands, and nodded to us to go away, and we done it, going out very quiet, like the dead was there.

Me and Tom struck out for the woods mighty solemn, and saying how different it was now to what it was last summer when we was here, and everything was so peaceful and happy and everybody thought so much of Uncle Silas, and he was so cheerful and simple-hearted and pudd'nheaded and good—and now look at him. If he hadn't lost his mind he wasn't much short of it. That was what we allowed.

It was a most lovely day, now, and bright and sunshiny; and the further and further we went over the hill towards the prairie the lovelier and lovelier the trees and

"What does he think!"

flowers got to be, and the more it seemed strange and somehow wrong that there had to be trouble in such a world as this. And then all of a sudden I catched my breath and grabbed Tom's arm and all my livers and lungs and things fell down into my legs.

"There it is!" I says. We jumped back behind a bush, shivering, and Tom says: "Sh!—don't make a noise."

It was setting on a log right in the edge of the little prairie, thinking. I tried to get Tom to come away, but he wouldn't, and I dasn't budge by myself. He said we mightn't ever get another chance to see one, and he was going to look his fill at this one if he died for it. So I looked too, though it give me the fantods to do it. Tom he *had* to talk, but he talked low. He says:

"Poor Jakey, it's got all its things on, just as he said he would. *Now* you see what we wasn't certain about—its hair. It's not long, now, the way it was; it's got it cropped close to its head, the way he said he would. Huck, I never see anything look any more naturaler than what *it* does."

"Nor I neither," I says; "I'd recognize it anywheres."

"So would I. It looks perfectly solid and genuwyne, just the way it done before it died."

So we kept a-gazing. Pretty soon Tom says:

"Huck, there's something mighty curious about this one, don't you know? *It oughtn't to be going around in the daytime.*"

"That's so, Tom—I never heard the like of it before."

"No, sir, they don't ever come out only at night—and then not till after twelve. There's something wrong about this one, now you mark my words. I don't believe it's got any right to be around in the daytime. But don't it look natural! Jake was going to play deef and dumb here, so the neighbors wouldn't know his voice. Do you reckon it would do that if we was to holler at it?"

"Lordy, Tom, don't talk so! If you was to holler at it I'd die in my tracks."

"Don't you worry, I ain't going to holler at it. Look, Huck, it's a-scratching its head—don't you see?"

"Well, what of it?"

"Why, this: What's the sense of it scratching its head? There ain't anything there to itch; its head is made out of fog or something like that, and *can't* itch. A fog can't itch; any fool knows that."

"Well, then, if it don't itch and can't itch, what in the nation is it scratching it for? Ain't it just habit, don't you reckon?"

"No, sir, I don't. I ain't a bit satisfied about the way this one acts. I've a blame good notion it's a bogus one—I have, as sure as I'm a-setting here. Because, if it—Huck!"

"Well, what's the matter now?"

"You can't see the bushes through it!"

"Why, Tom, it's so, sure! It's as solid as a cow. I sort of begin to think—"

"Huck, it's biting off a chaw of tobacker! By George, *they* don't chaw—they hain't got anything to chaw *with.* Huck!"

"I'm a—listening."

"It ain't a ghost at all. It's Jake Dunlap his own self!"

"Oh, your granny!" I says.

"Huck Finn, did we find any corpse in the sycamores?"

"No."

"Or any sign of one?"

"No."

"Mighty good reason. Hadn't ever been any corpse there."

"Why, Tom, you know we heard—"

"Yes, we did—heard a howl or two. Does that prove anybody was killed? Course it don't. And we seen four men run, then this one come walking out, and we took it for a ghost. No more ghost than you are. It was Jake Dunlap his own self, and it's Jake Dunlap now. He's been and got his hair cropped, the way he said he would, and he's playing himself for a stranger, just the same as he said he would. Ghost! Hum?—he's as sound as a nut."

Then I see it all, and how we had took too much for granted. I was powerful glad he didn't get killed, and so was Tom, and we wondered which he would like the best—for us to never let on to know him, or how? Tom reckoned the best way would be to go and ask him. So he started; but I kept a little behind, because I didn't know but it might be a ghost, after all. When Tom got to where he was, he says:

"Me and Huck's mighty glad to see you again, and you needn't be afeard we'll tell. And if you think it'll be safer for you if we don't let on to know you when we run across you, say the word, and you'll see you can depend on us, and would ruther cut our hands off than get you into the least little bit of danger."

First off he looked surprised to see us, and not very glad, either; but as Tom went on he looked pleasanter, and when he was done he smiled, and nodded his head several times, and made signs with his hands, and says:

"Goo-goo—goo-goo," the way deef and dummies does.

Just then we see some of Steve Nickerson's people coming that lived t'other side of the prairie, so Tom says:

"Goo-goo—goo-goo."

"You do it elegant; I never seen anybody do it better. You're right; play it on us, too; play it on us same as the others; it'll keep you in practice and prevent you making blunders. We'll keep away from you and let on we don't know you, but any time we can be any help, you just let us know."

Then we loafed along past the Nickersons, and of course they asked if that was the new stranger yonder, and where'd he come from, and what was his name, and which communion was he, Babtis' or

Methodis', and which politics, Whig or Democrat, and how long is he staying, and
all them other questions that humans always asks when a stranger comes, and animals does too. But Tom said he warn't able to make anything out of deef and dumb
signs, and the same with goo-gooing. Then we watched them go and bully-rag Jake;
because we was pretty uneasy for him. Tom said it would take him days to get so he
wouldn't forget he was a deef and dummy sometimes, and speak out before he
thought. When we had watched long enough to see that Jake was getting along all
right and working his signs very good, we loafed along again, allowing to strike the
school-house about recess time, which was a three-mile tramp.

I was so disappointed not to hear Jake tell about the row in the sycamores, and
how near he come to getting killed, that I couldn't seem to get over it, and Tom he
felt the same, but said if we was in Jake's fix we would want to go careful and keep
still, and not take any chances.

The boys and girls was all glad to see us again, and we had a real good time all
through recess. Coming to school the Henderson boys had come across the new deef
and dummy and told the rest; so all the scholars was chuck-full of him and couldn't
talk about anything else, and was in a sweat to get a sight of him because they had-
n't ever seen a deef and dummy in their lives, and it made a powerful excitement.

Tom said it was tough to have to keep mum now; said we would be heroes if we
could come out and tell all we knowed; but, after all, it was still more heroic to
keep mum; there warn't two boys in a million could do it. That was Tom Sawyer's
idea about it, and I reckoned there warn't anybody could better it.

CHAPTER NINE

IN THE NEXT two or three days Dummy he got to be powerful popular. He went
associating around with the neighbors, and they made much of him and was proud
to have such a rattling curiosity amongst them. They had him to breakfast, they
had him to dinner, they had him to supper; they kept him loaded up with hog and
hominy, and warn't ever tired staring at him and wondering over him, and wishing
they knowed more about him, he was so uncommon and romantic. His signs warn't
no good; people couldn' tunderstand them, and he prob'ly couldn't himself, but he
done a sight of goo-gooing, and so everybody was satisfied, and admired to hear
him go it. He toted apiece of slate around, and a pencil; and people wrote questions on it and he wrote answers; but there warn't anybody could read his writing
but Brace Dunlap. Brace said he couldn't read it very good, but he could manage
to dig out the meaning most of the time. He said Dummy said he belonged away
off somers, and used to be well off, but got busted by swindlers which he had trusted, and was poor now, and hadn't any way to make a living.

Everybody praised Brace Dunlap for being so good to that stranger. He let him have a little log cabin all to himself, and had his darkies take care of it, and fetch him all the vittles he wanted.

Dummy was at our house some, because old Uncle Silas was so afflicted himself, these days, that anybody else that was afflicted was a comfort to him. Me and Tom didn't let on that we had knowed him before, and he didn't let on that he had knowed us before. The family talked their troubles out before him the same as if he wasn't there, but we reckoned it wasn't any harm for him to hear what they said. Gener'ly he didn't seem to notice, but sometimes he did.

Well, two or three days went along, and everybody got to getting uneasy about Jubiter Dunlap. Everybody was asking everybody if they had any idea what had become of him. No, they hadn't, they said; and they shook their heads and said there was something powerful strange about it. Another and another day went by; then there was a report got around that praps he was murdered. You bet it made a big stir! Everybody's tongue was clacking away after that. Saturday two or three gangs turned out and hunted the woods to see if they could run across his remainders. Me and Tom helped, and it was noble good times and exciting. Tom he was so brim-full of it he couldn't eat nor rest. He said if we could find that corpse we would be celebrated, and more talked about than if we got drownded.

The others got tired and give it up; but not Tom Sawyer—that warn't his style. Saturday night he didn't sleep any, hardly, trying to think up a plan; and towards daylight in the morning he struck it. He snaked me out of bed and was all excited, and says—

"Quick, Huck, snatch on your clothes—I've got it! Blood-hound!"

In two minutes we was tearing up the river road in the dark towards the village. Old Jeff Hooker had a blood-hound, and Tom was going to borrow him. I says—

"The trail's too old, Tom—and besides, it's rained, you know."

"It don't make any difference, Huck. If the body's hid in the woods anywhere around, the hound will find it. If he's been murdered and buried, they wouldn't bury him deep, it ain't likely, and if the dog goes over the spot he'll scent him, sure. Huck, we're going to be celebrated, sure as you're born!"

He was just a-blazing; and whenever he got afire he was most likely to get afire all over. That was the way this time. In two minutes he had got it all ciphered out, and wasn't only just going to find the corpse—no, he was going to get on the track of that murderer and hunt *him* down, too; and not only that, but he was going to stick to him till—

"Well," I says, "you better find the corpse first; I reckon that's a plenty for today. For all we know, there *ain't* any corpse and nobody hain't been murdered. That cuss could a gone off somers and not been killed at all."

That gravelled him, and he says—

"Huck Finn, I never seen such a person as you to want to spoil everything. As long as *you* can't see anything hopeful in a thing, you won't let anybody else. What good can it do you to throw cold water on that corpse and get up that selfish theory that there hain't been any murder? None in the world. I don't see how you can act so. I wouldn't treat you like that and you know it. Here we've got a noble good opportunity to make a ruputation, and—"

"Oh, go ahead," I says, "I'm sorry and I take it all back. I didn't mean nothing. Fix it any way you want it. *He* ain't any consequence to me. If he's killed, I'm as glad of it as you are; and if he—"

"I never said anything about being glad; I only—"

"Well, then, I'm as *sorry* as you are. Any way you druther have it, that is the way *I* druther have it. He—"

"There ain't any druthers about it, Huck Finn; nobody said anything about druthers. And as for—"

He forgot he was talking, and went tramping along, studying. He begun to get excited again, and pretty soon he says—

"Huck. It'll be the bulliest thing that ever happened if we find the body after everybody else has quit looking, and then go ahead and hunt up the murderer. It won't only be an honor to us, but it'll be an honor to Uncle Silas because it was us that done it. It'll set him up again, you see if it don't."

But old Jeff Hooker he throwed cold water on the whole business when we got to his blacksmith shop and told him what we come for.

"You can take the dog," he says, "but you ain't a-going to find any corpse, because there ain't any corpse to find. Everybody's quit looking, and they're right. Soon as they come to think, they knowed there warn't no corpse. And I'll tell you for why. What does a person kill another person for, Tom Sawyer?—answer me that."

"Why, he—er—"

"Answer up! You ain't no fool. What does he kill him *for?*"

"Well, sometimes it's for revenge, and—"

"Wait. One thing at a time. Revenge, says you; and right you are. Now who ever had anything agin that poor trifling no-account? Who do you reckon would want to kill him?— that rabbit!"

Tom was stuck. I reckon he hadn't thought of a person having to have a reason for killing a person before, and now he see it warn't likely anybody would have that much of a grudge against a lamb like Jubiter Dunlap. The blacksmith says, by-and-by—

"The revenge idea won't work, you see. Well, then, what's next? Robbery? B'gosh that must a been it, Tom! Yes, sir-ree, I reckon we've struck it this time.

Some feller wanted his gallus-buckles, and so he—"

But it was so funny he busted out laughing, and just went *on* laughing and laughing and laughing till he was 'most dead, and Tom looked so put out and cheap that I knowed he was ashamed he had come and wished he hadn't. But old Hooker never let up on him. He raked up everything a person ever could want to kill another person about, and any fool could see they didn't any of them fit this case, and he just made no end of fun of the whole business, and of the people that had been hunting the body; and he said—

"If they'd had any sense they'd a knowed the lazy cuss slid out because he wanted a loafing spell after all this work. He'll come pottering back in a couple of weeks, and then how'll you fellers feel? But, laws bless you, take the dog and go and hunt his remainders. Do, Tom."

Then he busted out and had another of them forty-rod laughs of his'n. Tom couldn't back down after all this, so he said, "All right, unchain him," and the blacksmith done it, and we started home, and left that old man laughing yet.

It was a lovely dog. There ain't any dog that's got a lovelier disposition than a blood-hound, and this one knowed us and liked us. He capered and raced around ever so friendly, and was powerful glad to be free and have a holiday; but Tom was so cut up he couldn't take any intrust in him, and said he wished he'd stopped and thought a minute before he ever started on such a fool errand. He said old Jeff Hooker would tell everybody, and we'd never hear the last of it.

So we loafed along home down the back lanes, feeling pretty glum and not talking. When we was passing the far corner of our tobacker-field we heard the dog set up a long howl in there, and we went to the place, and he was scratching the ground with all his might, and every now and then canting up his head sideways and fetching another howl.

It was a long square the shape of a grave; the rain had made it sink down and show the shape. The minute we come and stood there we looked at one another and never said a word. When the dog had dug down only a few inches he grabbed something arid pulled it up, and it was an arm and a sleeve. Tom kind of gasped out and says—

"Come away, Huck—it's found."

I just felt awful. We struck for the road and fetched the first men that come along. They got a spade at the crib and dug out the body, and you never see such an excitement. You couldn't make anything out of the face, but you didn't need to. Everybody said—

"Poor Jubiter; it's his clothes, to the last rag!"

Some rushed off to spread the news and tell the justice of the peace and have an inquest, and me and Torn lit out for the house. Tom was all afire and 'most out

Fetching another howl

of breath when we come tearing in where Uncle Silas and Aunt Sally and Benny was. Tom sung out—

"Me and Huck's found Jubiter Dunlap's corpse all by ourselves with a bloodhound after everybody else had quit hunting and given it up; and if it hadn't a been for us it never *would* a been found; and he was murdered, too—they done it with a club or something like that; and I'm going to start in and find the murderer, next, and I bet I'll do it!"

Aunt Sally and Benny sprung up pale and astonished, but Uncle Silas fell right forward out of his chair onto the floor, and groans out—

"Oh, my God, you've found him *now!*"

CHAPTER TEN

THEM AWFUL WORDS froze us solid. We couldn't move hand or foot for as much as a half a minute. Then we kind of come to, and lifted the old man up and got him into his chair, and Benny petted him and kissed him and tried to comfort him, and poor old Aunt Sally she done the same; but, poor things, they was so broke up and scared and knocked out of their right minds that they didn't hardly know what they was about. With Tom it was awful; it 'most petrified him to think maybe he had got his uncle into a thousand times more trouble than ever, and maybe it wouldn't ever happened if he hadn't been so ambitious to get celebrated, and let the corpse alone the way the others done. But pretty soon he sort of come to himself again and says—

"Uncle Silas, don't you say another word like that. It's dangerous, and there ain't a shadder of truth in it."

Aunt Sally and Benny was thankful to hear him say that, and they said the same; but the old man he wagged his head sorrowful and hopeless, and the tears run down his face, and he says—

"No—I done it; poor Jubiter, I done it!"

It was dreadful to hear him say it. Then he went on and told about it, and said it happened the day me and Tom come—along about sundown. He said Jubiter pestered him and aggravated him till he was so mad he just sort of lost his mind and grabbed up a stick and hit him over the head with all his might, and Jubiter dropped in his tracks. Then he was scared and sorry, and got down on his knees and lifted his head up, and begged him to speak and say he wasn't dead; and before long he come to, and when he see who it was holding his head, he jumped like he was 'most scared to death, and cleared the fence and tore into the woods and was gone. So he hoped he wasn't hurt bad.

"But laws," he says, "it was only just fear that give him that last little spurt of strength, and of course it soon played out, and he laid down in the bush, and there wasn't anybody to help him, and he died."

Then the old man cried and grieved, and said he was a murderer and the mark of Cain was on him, and he had disgraced his family and was going to be found out and hung. Tom said—

"No, you ain't going to be found out. You *didn't* kill him. *One* lick wouldn't kill him. Somebody else done it."

"Oh, yes," he says, "I done it—nobody else. Who else had anything against him? Who else *could* have anything against him?"

He looked up kind of like he hoped some of us could mention somebody that could have a grudge against that harmless no-account, but of course it warn't no use—he *had* us; we couldn't say a word. He noticed that, and he saddened down again, and I never see a face so miserable and so pitiful to see. Tom had a sudden idea, and says—

"But hold on!—somebody *buried* him. Now who—"

He shut off sudden. I knowed the reason. It give me the cold shudders when he said them words, because right away I remembered about us seeing Uncle Silas prowling around with a long-handled shovel away in the night that night. And I knowed Benny seen him too, because she was talking about it one day. The minute Tom shut off he changed the subject and went to begging Uncle Silas to keep mum, and the rest of us done the same, and said he *must*, and said it wasn't his business to tell on himself, and if he kept mum nobody would ever know, but if it was found out and any harm come to him it would break the family's hearts and kill them, and yet never do anybody any good. So at last he promised. We was all of us more comfortable then, and went to work to cheer up the old man. We told him all he'd got to do was to keep still and it wouldn't be long till the whole thing would blow over and be forgot. We all said there wouldn't anybody ever suspect Uncle Silas, nor ever dream of such a thing, he being so good and kind and having such a good character; and Tom says, cordial and hearty, he says—

"Why, just look at it a minute; just consider. Here is Uncle Silas, all these years a preacher—at his own expense; all these years doing good with all his might and every way he can think of—at his own expense, all the time; always been loved by everybody, and respected; always been peaceable and minding his own business, the very last man in this whole deestrict to touch a person, and everybody knows it. Suspect *him?* Why, it ain't any more possible than—"

"By authority of the State of Arkansaw—I arrest you for the murder of Jubiter Dunlap!" shouts the sheriff at the door.

It was awful. Aunt Sally and Benny flung themselves at Uncle Silas, screaming and crying, and hugged him and hung to him, and Aunt Sally said go away, she wouldn't ever give him up, they shouldn't have him, and the darkies they come crowding and crying to the door, and—well, I couldn't stand it; it was enough to break a person's heart; so I got out.

They took him up to the little one-horse jail in the village, and we all went along to tell him good-by, and Tom was feeling elegant, and says to me, "We'll have a most noble good time and heaps of danger some dark night, getting him out of there, Huck, and it'll be talked about everywheres and we will be celebrated"; but the old man busted that scheme up the minute he whispered to him about it. He said no, it was his duty to stand whatever the law done to him, and he would stick to the jail plumb through to the end, even if there warn't no door to it. It disappointed Tom, and gravelled him a good deal, but he had to put up with it.

But he felt responsible and bound to get his Uncle Silas free; and he told Aunt Sally, the last thing, not to worry, because he was going to turn in and work night and day and beat this game and fetch Uncle Silas out innocent; and she was very loving to him and thanked him and said she knowed he would do his very best.

And she told us to help Benny take care of the house and the children, and then we had a good-by cry all around and went back to the farm, and left her there to live with the jailer's wife a month till the trial in October.

CHAPTER ELEVEN

WELL, THAT WAS a hard month on us all. Poor Benny, she kept up the best she could, and me and Tom tried to keep things cheerful there at the house, but it kind of went for nothing, as you may say. It was the same up at the jail. We went up every day to see the old people, but it was awful dreary, because the old man warn't sleeping much, and was walking in his sleep considerable, and so he got to looking fagged and miserable, and his mind got shaky, and we all got afraid his troubles would break him down and kill him. And whenever we tried to persuade him to feel cheerfuler, he only shook his head and said if we only knowed what it was to carry around a murderer's load on your heart we wouldn't talk that way. Tom and all of us kept telling him it *wasn't* murder, but just accidental killing, but it never made any difference—it was murder, and he wouldn't have it any other way. He actuly begun to come out plain and square towards trial-time and acknowledge that he *tried* to kill the man. Why, that was awful, you know. It made things seem fifty times as dreadful, and there warn't no more comfort for Aunt Sally and Benny. But he promised he wouldn't say a word about his murder when others was around, and we was glad of that.

He kept me up 'most all night.

Tom Sawyer racked the head off of himself all that month trying to plan some way out for Uncle Silas, and many's the night he kept me up 'most all night with this kind of tiresome work, but he couldn't seem to get on the right track no way. As for me, I reckoned a body might as well give it up, it all looked so blue and I was so downhearted; but he wouldn't. He stuck to the business right along, and went on planning and thinking and ransacking his head.

So at last the trial come on, towards the middle of October, and we was all in the court. The place was jammed, of course. Poor old Uncle Silas, he looked more like a dead person than a live one, his eyes was so hollow and he looked so thin and so mournful. Benny she set on one side of him and Aunt Sally on the other, and they had veils on, and was full of trouble. But Tom he set by our lawyer, and had his finger in everywheres, of course. The lawyer let him, and the judge let him. He 'most took the business out of the lawyer's hands sometimes; which was well enough, because that was only a mud-turtle of a back-settlement lawyer, and didn't know enough to come in when it rains, as the saying is.

They swore in the jury, and then the lawyer for the prostitution got up and begun. He made a terrible speech against the old man, that made him moan and groan, and made Benny and Aunt Sally cry. The way *he* told about the murder kind of knocked us all stupid, it was so different from the old man's tale. He said he was going to prove that Uncle Silas was seen to kill Jubiter Dunlap, by two good witnesses, and done it deliberate, and *said* he was going to kill him the very minute he hit him with the club: and they seen him hide Jubiter in the bushes and they seen that Jubiter was stone-dead. And said Uncle Silas come later and lugged Jubiter down into the tobacker-field, and two men seen him do it. And said Uncle Silas turned out, away in the night, and buried Jubiter, and a man seen him at it.

I says to myself, poor old Uncle Silas has been lying about it because he reckoned nobody seen him and he couldn't bear to break Aunt Sally's heart and Benny's; and right he was: as for me, I would a lied the same way, and so would anybody that had any feeling, to save them such misery and sorrow which *they* warn't no ways responsible for. Well, it made our lawyer look pretty sick; and it knocked Tom silly too, for a little spell; but then he braced up and let on that he warn't worried—but I knowed he *was*, all the same. And the people—my, but it made a stir amongst them!

And when that lawyer was done telling the jury what he was going to prove, he set down and begun to work his witnesses.

First, he called a lot of them to show that there was bad blood betwixt Uncle Silas and the diseased; and they told how they had heard Uncle Silas threaten the diseased, at one time and another, and how it got worse and worse, and everybody was talking about it, and how diseased got afraid of his life, and told two or three of them he was certain Uncle Silas would up and kill him some time or another.

Tom and our lawyer asked them some questions, but it warn't no use, they stuck to what they said.

Next, they called up Lem Beebe, and he took the stand. It come into my mind, then, how Lem and Jim Lane had come along talking, that time, about borrowing a dog or something from Jubiter Dunlap; and that brought up the blackberries and the lantern; and that brought up Bill and Jack Withers, and how *they* passed by, talking about a darkie stealing Uncle Silas's corn; and that fetched up our old ghost that come along about the same time and scared us so—and here *he* was, too, and a privileged character, on accounts of his being deef and dumb and a stranger, and they had fixed him a chair inside the railing, where he could cross his legs and be comfortable, whilst the other people was all in a jam so they couldn't hardly breathe. So it all come back to me just the way it was that day; and it made me mournful to think how pleasant it was up to then, and how miserable ever since.

Lem Beebe sworn, said: "I was a-coming along, that day, second of September, and Jim Lane was with me, and it was towards sundown, and we heard loud talk, like quarrelling, and we was very close, only the hazel bushes between (that's along the fence); and we heard a voice say: 'I've told you more'n once I'd kill you,' and knowed it was this prisoner's voice; and then we see a club come up above the bushes and down out of sight again, and heard a smashing thump, and then a groan or two; and then we crope soft to where we could see, and there laid Jubiter Dunlap dead, and this prisoner standing over him with the club; and the next he hauled the dead man into a clump of bushes and hid him, and then we stooped low, to be out of sight, and got away.

Well, it was awful. It kind of froze everybody's blood to hear it, and the house was 'most as still whilst he was telling it as if there warn't nobody in it. And when he was done, you could hear them gasp and sigh, all over the house and look at one another the same as to say, "Ain't it perfectly terrible—ain't it awful!"

Now happened a thing that astonished me. All the time the first witnesses was proving the bad blood and the threats and all that, Torn Sawyer was alive and laying for them; and the minute they was through, he went for them, and done his level best to catch them in lies and spile their testimony. But now, how different! When Lem first begun to talk, and never said anything about speaking to Jubiter or trying to borrow a dog off of him, he was all alive and laying for Lem, and you could see he was getting ready to cross-question him to death pretty soon, and then I judged him and he would go on the stand by-and-by and tell what we heard him and Jim Lane say. But the next time I looked at Tom I got the cold shivers. Why, he was in the brownest study you ever see—miles and miles away. He warn't hearing a word Lem Beebe was saying; and when he got through he was still in that brown study, just the same. Our lawyer joggled him, and then he looked up startled, and says, "Take the witness if you want him. Lemme alone—I want to think."

Well, that beat me. I couldn't understand it. And Benny and her mother—oh, they looked sick, they was so troubled. They shoved their veils to one side and tried to get his eye, but it warn't any use, and I couldn't get his eye either. So the mud-turtle he tackled the witness, but it didn't amount to nothing; and he made a mess of it.

Then they called up Jim Lane, and he told the very same story over again, exact. Tom never listened to this one at all, but set there thinking and thinking, miles and miles away. So the mud-turtle went in alone again, and come out just as flat as he done before. The lawyer for the prostitution looked very comfortable, but the judge looked disgusted. You see, Tom was just the same as a regular lawyer, nearly, because it was Arkansaw law for a prisoner to choose anybody he wanted to help his lawyer, and Tom had had Uncle Silas shove him into the case, and now he was botching it, and you could see the judge didn't like it much.

All that the mud-turtle got out of Lem and Jim was this: he asked them—

"Why didn't you go and tell what you saw?"

"We was afraid we would get mixed up in it ourselves. And we was just starting down the river a-hunting for all the week besides; but as soon as we come back we found out they'd been searching for the body, so then we went and told Brace Dunlap all about it."

"When was that?"

"Saturday night, September 9th."

The judge he spoke up and says—

"Mr. Sheriff, arrest these two witnesses on suspicions of being accessionary after the fact to the murder."

The lawyer for the prostitution jumps up all excited, and says—

"Your Honor! I protest against this extraordi—"

"Set down!" says the judge, pulling his bowie and laying it on his pulpit. "I beg you to respect the Court."

So he done it. Then he called Bill Withers.

Bill Withers, sworn, said: "I was coming along about sundown, Saturday, September 2d, by the prisoner's field, and my brother Jack was with me, and we seen a man toting off something heavy on his back, and allowed it was a darkie stealing corn; we couldn't see distinct; next we made out that it was one man carrying another; and the way it hung, so kind of limp, we judged it

"Set down!"

was somebody that was drunk; and by the man's walk we said it was Parson Silas, and we judged he had found Sam Cooper drunk in the road, which he was always trying to reform him, and was toting him out of danger."

It made the people shiver to think of poor old Uncle Silas toting off the diseased down to the place in his tobacker-field where the dog dug up the body, but there warn't much sympathy around amongst the faces, and I heard one cuss say, "'Tis the coldest-blooded work I ever struck, lugging a murdered man around like that, and going to bury him like a animal, and him a preacher at that."

Tom he went on thinking, and never took no notice; so our lawyer took the witness and done the best he could, and it was plenty poor enough.

Then Jack Withers he come on the stand and told the same tale, just like Bill done.

And after him comes Brace Dunlap, and he was looking very mournful, and 'most crying; and there was a rustle and a stir all around, and everybody got ready to listen, and lots of the women folks said "Poor cretur, poor cretur," and you could see a many of them wiping their eyes.

> *Brace Dunlap*, sworn, said: "I was in considerable trouble a long time about my poor brother, but I reckoned things warn't near so bad as he made out, and I couldn't make myself believe anybody would have the heart to hurt a poor harmless cretur like that"—(by jings, I was sure I seen Tom give a kind of a faint little start, and then look disappointed again)—"and you know I *couldn't* think a preacher would hurt him—it warn't natural to think such an on likely thing—so I never paid much attention, and now I sha'n't ever, ever forgive myself; for if I had a-done different, my poor brother would be with me this day, and not laying yonder murdered, and him so harmless." He kind of broke down there and choked up, and waited to get his voice; and people all around said the most pitiful things, and women cried; and it was very still in there, and solemn, and old Uncle Silas, poor thing, he give a groan right out so everybody heard him. Then Brace he went on: "Saturday, September 2d, he didn't come home to supper. By-and-by I got a little uneasy, and one of my muggers went over to this prisoner's place, but come back and said he warn't there. So I got uneasier and uneasier, and couldn't rest. I went to bed, but I couldn't sleep; and turned out, away late in the night, and went wandering over to this prisoner's place and all around about there a good while, hoping I would run across my poor brother, and never knowing he was out of his troubles and gone to a better shore—" So he broke down and choked up again, and most all the women was crying now. Pretty soon he got another start and says: "But it warn't no use; so at last I went home and tried to get some sleep, but could-

n't. Well, in a day or two everybody was uneasy, and they got to talking about this prisoner's threats, and took to the idea, which I didn't take no stock in, that my brother was murdered; so they hunted around and tried to find his body, but couldn't, and give it up. And so I reckoned he was gone off somers to have a little peace, and would come back to us when his troubles was kind of healed. But late Saturday night, the 9th, Lem Beebe and Jim Lane come to my house and told me all—told me the whole awful 'sassination, and my heart was broke. And *then* I remembered something that hadn't took no hold of me at the time, because reports said this prisoner had took to walking in his sleep and doing all kind of things of no consequence, not knowing what he was about. I will tell you what that thing was that come back into my memory. Away late that awful Saturday night when I was wandering around about this prisoner's place, grieving and troubled, I was down by the coiner of the tobacker-field and I heard a sound like digging in a gritty soil; and I crope nearer and peeped through the vines that hung on the rail fence and seen this prisoner *shoveling*—shoveling with a long-handled shovel—heaving earth into a big hole that was most filled up; his back was to me, but it was bright moonlight arid I knowed him by his old green baize work-gown with a splattery white patch in the middle of the back like somebody had hit him with a snowball. *He was burying the man he'd murdered!*"

And he slumped down in his chair crying and sobbing, and 'most everybody in the house busted out wailing, and crying, and saying "Oh, it's awful—awful—horrible!" and there was a most tremenduous excitement, and you couldn't hear yourself think; and right in the midst of it up jumps old Uncle Silas, white as a sheet, and sings out—

"*It's true every word—I murdered him in cold blood!*"

By Jackson, it petrified them! People rose up wild all over the house, straining and staring for a better look at him, and the judge was hammering with his mallet, and the sheriff yelling "Order—order in the court—order!"

And all the while the old man stood there a-quaking and his eyes a-burning, and not looking at his wife and daughter, which was clinging to him and begging him to keep still, but pawing them off with his hands and saying he *would* clear his black soul from crime, he *would* heave off this load that was more than he could bear, and he *wouldn't* bear it another hour! And then he raged right along with his awful tale, everybody a-staring and gasping, judge, jury, lawyers, and everybody, and Benny and Aunt Sally crying their hearts out. And by George, Tom Sawyer never looked at him once! Never once—just set there gazing with all his eyes at something else, I couldn't tell what. And so the old man raged right along, pouring his words out like a stream of fire:

"I killed him! I am guilty! But I never had the notion in my life to hurt or harm him, spite of all them lies about my threatening him, till the very minute I raised the club—then my heart went cold!—then the pity all went out of it, and I struck to kill! In that one moment all my wrongs come into my mind; all the insults that that man and the scoundrel his brother, there, had put upon me, and how they had laid in together to ruin me with the people, and take away my good name, and *drive* me to some deed that would destroy me and my family that hadn't ever done *them* no harm, so help me God! And they done it in a mean revenge—for why? Because my innocent pure girl here at my side wouldn't marry that rich, insolent, ignorant coward, Brace Dunlap, who's been snivelling here over a brother he never cared a brass farthing for"—(I see Tom give a jump and look glad *this* time, to a dead certainty)—"and in that moment I've told you about, I forgot my God and remembered only my heart's bitterness—God forgive me!—and I struck to kill. In one second I was miserably sorry—oh, filled with remorse; but I thought of my poor family, and I *must* hide what I'd done for their sakes; and I did hide that corpse in the bushes; and presently I carried it to the tobacker-field; and in the deep night I went with my shovel and buried it where—"

Up jumps Tom and shouts—

"*Now*, I've got it!" and waves his hand, oh, ever so fine and starchy, towards the old man, and says—

"Set down! A murder *was* done, but you never had no hand in it!"

Well, sir, you could a heard a pin drop. And the old man he sunk down kind of bewildered in his seat, and Aunt Sally and Benny didn't know it, because they was so astonished and staring at Tom with their mouths open and not knowing what they was about. And the whole house the same. *I* never seen people look so helpless and tangled up, and I hain't ever seen eyes bug out and gaze without a blink the way theirn did. Tom says, perfectly ca'm—

"Your Honor, may I speak?"

"For God's sake, yes—go on!" says the judge, so astonished and mixed up he didn't know what he was about hardly.

Then Tom he stood there and waited a second or two—that was for to work up an "effect," as he calls it—then he started in just as ca'm as ever, and says:

"For about two weeks, now, there's been a little bill sticking on the front of this court-house offering two thousand dollars reward for a couple of big di'monds—stole at St. Louis. Them di'monds is worth twelve thousand dollars. But never mind about that till I get to it. Now about this murder. I will tell you all about it—how it happened—who done it—every *detail*."

You could see everybody nestle, now, and begin to listen for all they was worth.

"This man here, Brace Dunlap, that's been snivelling so about his dead broth-

"I struck to kill."

er that *you* know he never cared a straw for, wanted to marry that young girl there, and she wouldn't have him. So he told Uncle Silas he would make him sorry. Uncle Silas knowed how powerful he was, and how little chance he had against such a man, and he was scared and worried, and done everything he could think of to smooth him over and get him to be good to him; he even took his no-account brother Jubiter on the farm and give him wages, and stinted his own family to pay them; and Jubiter done everything his brother could contrive to insult Uncle Silas. And fret and worry him, and try to drive Uncle Silas into doing him a hurt, so as to injure Uncle Silas with the people. And it done it. Everybody turned against him and said the meanest kind of things about him, and it graduly broke his heart—yes, and he was so worried and distressed that often he warn't hardly in his right mind.

"Well, on that Saturday that we've had so much trouble about, two of these witnesses here, Lem Beebe and Jim Lane come along by where Uncle Silas and Jubiter Dunlap was at work—and that much of what they've said is true, the rest is lies. They didn't hear Uncle Silas say he would kill Jubiter; they didn't hear no blow struck; they didn't see no dead man, and they didn't see Uncle Silas hide anything in the bushes. Look at them now—how they set there, wishing they hadn't been so handy with their tongues; anyway, they'll wish it before I get done.

"That same Saturday evening, Bill and Jack Withers *did* see one man lugging off another one. That much of what they said is true, and the rest is lies. First off they thought it was a darkie stealing Uncle Silas's corn—you notice it makes them look silly, now, to find out somebody overheard them say that. That's because they found out by-and-by who it was that was doing the lugging, and *they* know best why they swore here that they took it for Uncle Silas by the gait—which it *wasn't*, and they knowed it when they swore to that lie.

"A man out in the moonlight *did* see a murdered person put underground in the tobacker-field—but it wasn't Uncle Silas that done the burying. He was in his bed at that very time.

"Now, then, before I go on, I want to ask you if you've ever noticed this: that people, when they're thinking deep, or when they're worried, are most always doing something with their hands, and they don't know it and don't notice what it is their hands are doing. Some stroke their chins; some stroke their noses; some stroke up *under* their chin with their hand; some twirl a chain, some fumble a button, then there's some that draws a figure or a letter with their finger on their cheek, or under their chin, or on their under lip. That's *my* way. When I'm restless, or worried, or thinking hard, I draw capital V's on my cheek or on my under lip or under my chin, and never anything *but* capital V's—and half the time I don't notice it and don't know I'm doing it."

That was odd. That is just what I do; only I make an O. And I could see people nodding to one another, same as they do when they mean "*that's* so."

"Now, then, I'll go on. That same Saturday—no it was the night before—there was a steamboat laying at Flagler's Landing, forty miles above here, and it was raining and storming like the nation. And there was a thief aboard, and he had them two big di'monds that's advertised out hereon this court-house door; and he slipped ashore with his hand-bag and struck out into the dark and the storm, and he was a-hoping he could get to this town all right and be safe. But he had two pals aboard the boat, hiding, and he knowed they was going to kill him the first chance they got and take the di'monds; because all three stole them and then this fellow he got hold of them and skipped.

"Well, he hadn't been gone more'n ten minutes before his pals found it out, and they jumped ashore and lit out after him. Prob'ly they burnt matches and found his tracks. Anyway, they dogged along after him all day Saturday and kept out of his sight; and towards sundown he come to the bunch of sycamores down by Uncle

Silas's field, and he went in there to get a disguise
out of his hand-bag and put it on before he
showed himself here in the town—and mind
you he done that just a little after the time
that Uncle Silas was hitting Jubiter
Dunlap over the head with a
club—for he *did* hit him.

"But the minute the pals see that
thief slide into the bunch of sycamores,
they jumped out of the bushes and slid in
after him.

"They fell on him and clubbed him to
death."

"Yes, for all he screamed and howled so, they
never had no mercy on him, but clubbed him to
death. And two men that was running along the
road heard him yelling that way, and they made a

"A murder was *done!"*

rush into the sycamore bunch—which was where they was bound for,
anyway—and when the pals saw them they lit out, and the two new men after
them a-chasing them as tight as they could go. But only a minute or two—then
these two new men slipped back very quiet into the sycamores.

"*Then* what did they do? I will tell you what they done. They found where the
thief had got his disguise out of his carpet-sack to put on; so one of them strips and
puts on that disguise."

Tom waited a little here, for some more "effect"—then he says, very deliberate—

"The man that put on that dead man's disguise was—*Jubiter Dunlap!*"

"Great Scott!" everybody shouted, all over the house, and old Uncle Silas he
looked perfectly astonished.

"Yes, it was Jubiter Dunlap. Not dead, you see. Then they pulled off the dead
man's boots and put Jubiter Dunlap's old ragged shoes on the corpse and put the
corpse's boots on Jubiter Dunlap. Then Jubiter Dunlap staid where he was, and the
other man lugged the dead body off in the twilight; and after midnight he went to
Uncle Silas's house, and took his old green work-robe off of the peg where it always
hangs in the passage betwixt the house and the kitchen and put it on, and stole the
long-handled shovel and went off down into the tobacker-field and buried the murdered man."

He stopped, and stood a half a minute. Then—

"And who do you reckon the murdered man was? It was—*Jake* Dunlap, the
long-lost burglar!"

"Great Scott!"

"And the man that buried him was—*Brace* Dunlap, his brother!"

"Great Scott!"

And who do you reckon is this mowing idiot here that's letting on all these weeks to be a deef and dumb stranger? It's—*Jubiter* Dunlap!"

My land, they all busted out in a howl, and you never see the like of that excitement since the day you was born. And Tom he made a jump for Jubiter, and snaked off his goggles and his false whiskers, and there was the murdered man, sure enough, just as alive as anybody! And Aunt Sally and Benny they went to hugging and crying and kissing and smothering, old Uncle Silas to that degree he was more muddled and confused and mushed up in his mind than he ever was before, and that is saying considerable. And next, people begun to yell—

"Tom Sawyer! Tom Sawyer! Shut up everybody, and let him go on! Go on, Tom Sawyer!"

Which made him feel uncommon bully, for it was nuts for Tom Sawyer to be a public character thataway, and a hero, as he calls it. So when it was all quiet, he says—

"There ain't much left, only this: When that man there, Brace Dunlap, had most worried the life and sense out of Uncle Silas till at last he plumb lost his mind and hit this other blatherskite his brother with a club, I reckon he seen his

There was the murdered man.

chance. Jubiter broke for the woods to hide, and I reckon the game was for him to slide out in the night and leave the country. Then Brace would make everybody believe Uncle Silas killed him and hid his body somers; and that would ruin Uncle Silas and drive *him* out of the country—hang him, maybe; I dunno. But when they found their dead brother in the sycamores without knowing him, because he was so battered up, they see they had a better thing: disguise *both* and bury Jake and dig him up presently all dressed up in Jubiter's clothes, and hire Jim Lane and Bill Withers and the

others to swear to some handy lies—which they done. And
there they set, now, and I told them they would be looking sick before I got done, and that is the way they're
looking now.

"Well, me and Huck Finn here, we come down
on the boat with the thieves, and the dead one
told us all about the di'monds, and said the others would murder him if they got the chance;
and we was going to help him all we could.
We was bound for the sycamores when we
heard them killing him in there; but we was in
there in the early morning after the storm and
allowed nobody hadn't been killed, after all. And
when we see Jubiter Dunlap here spreading
around in the very same disguise Jake told us *he* was
going to wear, we thought it was Jake his own
self—and he was goo-gooing deef and dumb, and *that*
was according to agreement.

He felt uncommon bully.

"Well, me and Huck went on hunting for the corpse after the others quit,
and we found it. And was proud, too; but Uncle Silas he knocked us crazy by
telling us *he* killed the man. So we was mighty sorry we found the body, and was
bound to save Uncle Silas's neck if we could; and it was going to be tough work,
too, because he wouldn't let us break him out of prison the way we done with
our old Jim.

"I done everything I could the whole month to think up some way to save
Uncle Silas, but I couldn't strike a thing. So when we come into court today I come
empty, and couldn't see no chance anywheres. But by-and-by I had a glimpse of
something that set me thinking—just a little wee glimpse—only that, and not
enough to make sure; but it set me thinking hard—and *watching*, when I was only
letting on to think; and by-and-by, sure enough, when Uncle Silas was piling out
that stuff about *him* killing Jubiter Dunlap, I catched that glimpse again, and this
time I jumped up and shut down the proceedings, because I *knowed* Jubiter Dunlap
was a-setting here before me. I knowed him by a thing which I seen him do—and
I remembered it. I'd seen him do it when I was here a year ago."

He stopped then, and studied a minute—laying for an "effect"—I knowed it
perfectly well. Then he turned off like he was going to leave the platform, and says,
kind of lazy and indifferent—

"Well, I believe that is all."

Why, you never heard such a howl—and it come from the whole house:

"What *was* it you seen him do? Stay where you are, you little devil! You think you are going to work a body up till his mouth's a-watering and stopt here? What *was* it he done?"

That was it, you see—he just done it to get an "effect"; you couldn't a pulled him off of that platform with a yoke of oxen.

"Oh, it wasn't anything much," he says. "I seen him looking a little excited when he found Uncle Silas was actuly fixing to hang himself for a murder that warn't ever done; and he got more and more nervous and worried, I a-watching him sharp but not seeming to look at him—and all of a sudden his hands begun to work and fidget, and pretty soon his left crept up and his *finger drawed a cross on his cheek*, and then I *had* him!"

Well, then they ripped and howled and stomped and clapped their hands till Tom Sawyer was that proud and happy he didn't know what to do with himself. And then the judge he looked down over his pulpit and says—

"My boy, did you *see* all the various details of this strange conspiracy and tragedy that you've been describing?"

"No, your Honor, I didn't see any of them."

"Didn't see any of them! Why, you've told the whole history straight through, just the same as if you'd seen it with your eyes. How did you manage that?"

Tom says, kind of easy and comfortable—

"Oh, just noticing the evidence and piecing this and that together, your Honor; just an ordinary little bit of detective work; anybody could a done it."

"Nothing of the kind! Not two in a million could a done it. You are a very remarkable boy."

Then they let go and give Tom another smashing round, and he—well, he wouldn't a sold out for a silver-mine. Then the judge says—

"But are you certain you've got this curious history straight?"

"Perfectly, your Honor. Here is Brace Dunlap—let him deny his share of it if he wants to take the chance: I'll engage to make him wish he hadn't said anything. . . . Well, you see *he's* pretty quiet. And his brother's pretty quiet; and them four witnesses that lied so and got paid for it, they're pretty quiet. And as for Uncle Silas, it ain't any use for him to put in his oar, I wouldn't believe him under oath!"

Well, sir, that fairly made them shout; and even the judge he let go and laughed. Tom he was just feeling like a rainbow. When they was done laughing he looks up at the judge and says—

"Your Honor, there's a thief in this house."

"A thief?"

"Yes, sir. And he's got them twelve-thousand-dollar di'monds on him."

By gracious, but it made a stir! Everybody went shouting—

"Which is him? which is him? Pint him out!" And the judge says—

"Point him out, my lad. Sheriff, you will arrest him. Which one is it?"

Tom says—

"This late dead man here—Jubiter Dunlap."

Then there was another thundering let-go of astonishment and excitement; but Jubiter, which was astonished enough before, was just fairly putrefied with astonishment this time. And he spoke up, about half crying, and says—

"Now *that's* a lie! Your Honor, it ain't fair; I'm plenty bad enough, without that. I done the other things—Brace he put me up to it, and persuaded me, and promised he'd make me rich, some day, and I done it, and I'm sorry I done it, and I wish't I hadn't; but I hain't stole no di'monds. and I hain't *got* no di'monds; I wish't I may never stir if it ain't so. The sheriff can search me and see."

Tom says—

"Your Honor, it wasn't right to call him a thief, and I'll let up on that a little. He did steal the di'monds, but he didn't know it. He stole them from his brother Jake when he was laying dead, after Jake had stole them from the other thieves; but Jubiter didn't know he was stealing them; and he's been swelling around here with them a month; yes, sir, twelve thousand dollars' worth of di'monds on him—all that riches, and going around here every day just like a poor man. Yes, your Honor, he's got them on him now."

The judge spoke up and says—

"Search him, sheriff."

Well, sir, the sheriff he ransacked him high and low, and everywhere; searched his hat, socks, seams, boots, everything—and Tom he stood there quiet, laying for another of them effects of his'n. Finally the sheriff he give it up, and everybody looked disappointed, and Jubiter says—

"There now! What'd I tell you?"

And the judge says—

"It appears you were mistaken this time, my boy."

Then Tom he took an attitude and let on to be studying with all his might, and scratching his head. Then all of a sudden he glanced up chipper and says—

"Oh, now I've got it! I'd forgot."

Which was a lie, and I knowed it. Then he says—

"Will somebody be good enough to lend me a little small screw-driver? There was one in your brother's hand-bag that you smouched, Jubiter, but I reckon you didn't fetch it with you."

"No, I didn't. I didn't want it, and I give it away."

"That was because you didn't know what it was for."

Jubiter had his boots on again by now, and when the thing Tom wanted was passed over the people's heads till it got to him, he says to Jubiter—

"Put up your foot on this chair" and he kneeled down and begun to unscrew the heel-plate, everybody watching; and when he got that big di'mond out of that boot heel and held it up and let it flash and blaze and squirt sunlight ever-which away, it just took everybody's breath; and Jubiter he looked so sick and sorry you never see the like of it. And when Tom held up the other di'mond he looked sorrier than ever. Land! he was thinking how he would a skipped out and been rich and independent in a foreign land if he'd only had the luck to guess what the screw-driver was in the carpet-bag for. Well, it was a most exciting time, take it all around, and Tom got cords of glory. The judge took the di'monds, and stood up in his pulpit, and shoved his spectacles back on his head, and cleared his throat, and says—

"I'll keep them and notify the owners; and when they send for them it will be a real pleasure to me to hand you the two thousand dollars, for you've earned the money—yes, and you've earned the deepest and most sincerest thanks of this community besides, for lifting a wronged and innocent family out of ruin and shame, and saving a good and honorable man from a felon's death, and for exposing to infamy and the punishment of the law a cruel and odious scoundrel and his miserable creatures."

Well, sir, if there'd been a brass band to bust out some music, then, it woulda been just the perfectest thing I ever see, and Tom Sawyer he said the same. Then the sheriff he nabbed Brace Dunlap and his crowd, and by-and-by next month the judge had them up for trial and jailed the whole lot. And everybody crowded back to Uncle Silas's little old church, and was ever so loving and kind to him and the family, and couldn't do enough for them; and Uncle Silas he preached them the blamedest, jambledest, idiotic sermons you ever struck, and would tangle you up so you couldn't find your way home in daylight; but the people never let on but what they thought it was the clearest and brightest and elegantest sermons that ever was; and they would set there and cry, for love and pity; but, by George, they give me the jimjams and the fantods and caked up what brains I had, and turned them solid; but by-and-by they loved the old man's intellects back into him again and he was as sound in his skull as ever he was, which ain't no flattery, I reckon. And so the whole family was as happy as birds, and nobody could be gratefuler and lovinger than what they was to Tom Sawyer; and the same to me, though I hadn't done nothing. And when the two thousand dollars come, Tom give half of it to me, and never told anybody so, which didn't surprise me, because I knowed him.

First published in the August and September 1896
editions of *Harper's New Monthly Magazine*

The Creature with No Claws

BY JOEL CHANDLER HARRIS

"W'EN YOU GIT a leetle bit older dan w'at you is, honey," said Uncle Remus to the little boy, "you'll know lots mo' dan you does now."

The old man had a pile of white oak splits by his side and these he was weaving into a chair-bottom. He was an expert in the art of "bottoming chairs," and he earned many a silver quarter in this way. The little boy seemed to be much interested in the process.

"Hit's des like I tell you," the old man went on; "I done had de speunce un it. I done got so now dat I don't b'lieve w'at I see, much less w'at I year. It got ter be whar I kin put my han' on it en fumble wid it. Folks kin fool deyse'f lots wuss dan yuther folks kin fool um, en ef you don't b'lieve w'at I'm a-tellin' un you, you kin des ax Brer Wolf de nex' time you meet 'im in de big road."

"What about Brother Wolf, Uncle Remus?" the little boy asked, as the old man paused to refill his pipe.

"Well, honey, 'tain't no great long rigamarole; hit's des one er deze yer tales w'at goes in a gallop twel it gits ter de jumpin'-off place.

"One time Brer Wolf wuz gwine long de big road feelin' mighty proud en high-strung. He wuz a mighty high-up man in dem days, Brer Wolf wuz, en 'mos' all de yuther creeturs wuz feard un 'im. Well, he wuz gwine 'long lickin' his chops en walkin' sorter stiff-kneed, w'en he happen ter look down 'pon de groun' en dar he seed a track in de san'. Brer Wolf stop, he did, en look at it, en den he low:

"'Heyo! w'at kind er creetur dish yer? Brer Dog ain't make dat track, en need-er is Brer Fox. Hit's one er deze yer kind er creeturs w'at ain't got no claws. I'll des 'bout foller 'im up, en ef I ketch 'im he'll sholy be my meat.'

"Dat de way Brer Wolf talk. He followed 'long atter de track, he did, en he look at it close, but he ain't see no print er no claw. Bimeby de track tuck 'n tu'n out de road en go up a dreen whar de rain done wash out. De track wuz plain dar in de wet san', but Brer Wolf ain't see no sign er no claws.

"He foller en foller, Brer Wolf did, en de track git fresher en fresher, but still he ain't see no print er no claw. Bimeby he come in sight er de creetur, en Brer Wolf stop, he did, en look at 'im. He stop stock-still and look. De creetur wuz mighty quare-lookin', en he wuz cuttin' up some mighty quare capers. He had big head, sharp nose, en bob tail; en he wuz walkin' roun' en roun' a big dog-wood tree, rubbin' his sides ag'in it. Brer Wolf watch 'im a right smart while, he act so quare, en den he 'low:

"'Shoo! dat creetur done bin in a fight en los' de bos' part er he tail; en w'at make he scratch hisse'f dat away? I lay I'll let 'im know who he foolin' 'long wid.'

"Atter 'while, Brer Wolf went up a leetle nigher de creetur, en holler out:

"'Heyo, dar! w'at you doin' scratchin' yo' scaly hide on my tree, en tryin' fer ter break hit down?'

"De creetur ain't make no answer. He des walk 'roun' en 'roun' de tree scratchin' he sides en back. Brer Wolf holler out:

"'I lay I'll make you year me ef I hatter come dar whar you is!'

"De creetur des walk 'roun' en 'roun' de tree, en ain't make no answer. Den Brer Wolf hail 'im ag'in, en talk like he mighty mad:

"'Ain't you gwine ter min' me, you imperdent scoundul? Ain't you gwine ter mozey outer my woods en let my tree 'lone?'

"Wid dat, Brer Wolf march todes de creetur des like he gwine ter squ'sh 'im in de groun'. De creetur rub hisse'f ag'in de tree en look like he feel mighty good. Brer Wolf keep on gwine todes 'im, en bimeby w'en he git sorter close de creetur tuck 'n sot up on his behime legs des like you see squir'ls do. Den Brer Wolf, he 'low, he did:

"'Ah-yi! you beggin', is you? But 'tain't gwine ter do you no good. I mout er let you off ef you'd a-minded me w'en I fus' holler atter you, but I ain't gwine ter let you off now. I'm a-gwine ter l'arn you a lesson dat'll stick by you.'

"Den de creetur sorter wrinkle up he face en mouf, en Brer Wolf 'low:

"'Oh, you nee'n'ter swell up en cry, you 'ceitful vilyun. I'm a-gwine ter gi' you a frailin' dat I boun' you won't forgit.'

"Brer Wolf make like he gwine tor hit de creetur, en den——"

Here Uncle Remus paused and looked all around the room and up at the rafters. When he began again his voice was very solemn.

—"Well, suh, dat creetur des fotch one swipe dis away, en 'n'er swipe dat away, en mos' 'fo' you can wink yo' eye-balls, Brer Wolf hide wuz mighty nigh teetotally tor'd off'n 'im. Atter dat de creetur sa'ntered off in de woods, en 'gun ter rub hisse'f on 'n'er tree."

"What kind of a creature was it, Uncle Remus?" asked the little boy.

"Well, honey," replied the old man in a confidential whisper, "hit want nobody on de top-side er de yeth but ole Brer Wildcat."

First published in the October 1888 edition of *St. Nicholas Magazine*

The Persian Columbus

A Fantasy of the Orient

BY JACK BENNETT

ONE SULTRY SUMMER evening in the eight hundred and seventieth year of the Mohammedan era, the renowned Caliph Haroun Al Huck-El-Berri, of Baghdad, sat frowning amid his magnificence.

The royal divan was fashioned of ruddy gold, thick-studded with virgin pearls. Overhead was an exquisite carved dome of ivory and ebony, radiant with the rosy glow of swaying brazen lamps and tall wax candles. Rich carpets of silk and velvet were scattered over the jasper floor, which reflected the alabaster columns. Tables inlaid with mother-of-pearl were spread with rare and aromatic viands, while the shimmering breezes were cooled and faintly perfumed by fountains of rose-water.

But, in spite of all this surrounding splendor, the Caliph of Baghdad was unmistakably as cross as two sticks, and champed his teeth savagely.

Through the open windows stole the silvery song of the nightingale and the sleepy trill of the belated bulbul in the orange-grove beyond the courtyard; and from the high gallery entrancing strains of music swept, above which arose the mellow snore of the Grand Vizir, snoozing among the damask cushions, with a copy of the Baghdad Herald over his face.

And yet, with a fierce frown upon his pale brow, the Caliph pored over the dog-eared pages of his primary geography.

Suddenly he closed the book with a bang.

"By the six white hairs upon the tail of the Prophet's mule!" quoth he, "these be strange tales indeed that the unlettered infidels of the West are telling the wise men of the East! Can it be possible that the whole Persian system of eclectic geography is in error? I must investigate this matter. Selim!" he cried imperiously to the Grand Vizir, who scrambled to his sleepy feet with a frightened start, "summon the Seven Sages of Baghdad and the Commissioner of Public Schools!"

The Sages were summoned instantly.

"Bah! You high-salaried indolents!" sternly hissed the Caliph, "I've a great notion to discharge you all! Aren't you ashamed to let the pale-faced Franks of Spain get ahead of you?"

"Illustrious Sun of the Noonday!" faltered the oldest among them, "what means this sudden tempest out of a clear sky? The Frankish philosophers do not know even the things that we have forgotten. They are but followers in our footsteps. We have taught them all they know."

"Oh, have you?" roared the Caliph. "Perhaps, then, ye knew that the world is round?"

"Oh, your Majesty!" gasped the Sages in chorus, hurriedly endeavoring to restore their paralyzed faculties with their smelling-salts, "what sort of a fairy-tale is this?"

"Fairy-tale!" roared the Caliph.

"Come now! Don't ye ever read the newspapers? Have ye not heard that there has arisen in the West a wild, strange, white-haired man who saith that the world is round like an orange or a ball? If ye did not know it, why have ye not found it out long ago? And if ye did know it, why have ye not told me of it before this? Tell me," cried the Caliph in an awful, blood-curdling tone, "tell me, ye ignoramuses, is the world round or flat?"

The Sages fell prostrate upon the gleaming floor, and bumped their aged heads against the tiles in despair. This riddle was too much for them; they had to give it up.

With a cruel glitter in his eagle eye the Caliph cried to the Chief Chamberlain: "Hassan, lock these gentlemen up in the pantry instantly, and be very careful that not one escapes. I will give them fifteen minutes in which to tell

"Tell me, ye ignoramuses," said the Caliph, "is the world round or flat?"

me positively whether the world be round or flat, or give some immediately prac-
ticable method of finding out."

The massive, burnished copper door closed with a dismal clang upon the
unfortunate and despairing Sages; while the School Commissioner, arriving just in
time to hear the latter part of the conversation from the hall-door, took to his
heels, and did not stop until he was three miles beyond the city limits and hidden
under a haystack.

Then the court waited in ominous silence, as the sand in the hour-glass trickled out the swiftly passing moments. The horizon began to look very squally for the
Seven Sages of Baghdad.

The Caliph sat sullenly upon the divan, playing with an orange. Suddenly he
gave a start, and an immense white smile illuminated his swarthy features. "Selim!"
he called, "look here, my boy! If this world be indeed round, as this imaginative
mariner from Genoa declares, it will not be so difficult to prove, methinks."

The Vizir eyed the Caliph with suspicion.

"If I begin here," continued the Caliph, placing his index finger upon the
orange, "and move onward, my finger soon passes completely around the orange
and returns to the point whence it started. Dost thou see?"

"Verily, your majesty, I am not blind!" said the Vizir, warily refusing to commit
himself further. "I see clearly."

"Well then?" said the Caliph, expectantly, looking at Selim.

"Well then?" said Selim, dubiously, looking at the Caliph, and edging toward
the door.

"Pshaw! Thou dolt! Dost thou not see that if this world be indeed round like
this orange, a man may ride around it and return whence he started? Bismillah! I
have solved the problem myself! Aha! I will fool these laggard, hesitating Franks;
and while the Spanish King Ferdinand hesitates to furnish funds for a fleet, I will
show this audacious Christopher Columbus that he is but a semicolon after all. I
will ride about the world myself, this very night, and thou shalt go with me, Selim;
thou shalt go with me, and we will ride around the world! Make haste, and call up
the camels. Hurrah! We are going around the world!"

"Oh, we are, are we?" muttered Selim, with chattering teeth, as he hurriedly
shuffled down the back stairs to the stable, to harness up the royal equipage.
"Around the world, indeed? Who wants to fall over the edge into nothing? Not
Selim! Well, I should say not! Not if Selim knows it!"

Then followed a scene of wild excitement, some hurrying hither and thither,
some scurrying backward and forward, some running round and round, and some
running nowhere at all, while hoarse voices shouted, camels snorted, horses
neighed, and countless dogs barked until the whole city was in an uproar.

"If the world be indeed round, a man may ride around it!"

Drums beat, spears swayed madly overhead, standards flapped frantically upon their swaying staves, dark faces gleamed with savage excitement from under snowy turbans. And then came a wilder clang from the deafening cymbals, a louder fanfare from the brazen-throated trumpets, and a mighty shout from the throats of the excited populace. "Hail to the Caliph! Hail, all hail! For he is going around the world!"

The royal band then struck up "Marching Through Persia," the small boys turned cart-wheels along the gutter, and the procession moved on through the streets of Baghdad.

Beyond the city gates the caravan halted.

"Your royal highness," asked Selim the Vizir, "which way shall we start-north, east, south, or west?"

"Hum—m—m!" mused the Caliph, stroking his beard thoughtfully, and getting out his railroad map of the Eastern Hemisphere.

"Hum—m—m!" resumed the Caliph, after a short study, "we will not go to the west; for Ferdinand and Isabella would be sure to see us marching past their house, and I want to surprise them by getting all the way around before they know anything about it. And we will not go to the east, because we should get too close to the sun when it rises in the morning, and might perhaps be sunstruck. And if we go to the south we shall have to ford the Indian Ocean. But I don't like to wade, and the stones hurt my bare feet, so I think we won't go south. Hum—m—m! That leaves only one other direction to go! Well then, we will go in that direction."

"Ho, Gaifar!" he called with a ringing voice to the drum-major at the head of the procession, "March straight for the North Star!"

Then he went sound asleep, as Gaifar tossed his baton high in the air, caught it as it fell, gave a triple flip-flap to the right, a double flub-dub to the left, and thirteen twirls around his little finger.

The band struck up, and the cavalcade headed across the broad, sandy plain, straight for the North Star.

As the hills along the horizon drew nearer and nearer, the Grand Vizir broke into a cold perspiration. As he stood erect, craning his long neck above the clouds of dust, he could see the far sky curve down, down, down on the other side of those purple mountain-peaks. "Ugh—h—h!" he gasped, with a shudder of terror. "Something must be done, and right away, too! There is the end of the world, and we'll all fall off and be smashed, sure!"

Galloping in palpitating haste to the side of the drum-major, he whispered with terrible impressiveness, "Gaifar, what do you know about astronomy?"

"I? Nothing!" said Gaifar, surprised.

"Oo—oo—ooh!" groaned the Vizir, pulling a long face, "I should not like to be in your shoes when the Caliph wakes!"

"Why not?" cried Gaifar, anxiously.

But the crafty Vizir made no reply.

"Gaifar," he whispered sepulchrally again, "did you ever study bacteriology?"

"N—no," gasped Gaifar, with startled eyes. The Vizir groaned again in such an awful tone that it chilled the very marrow of the poor drum-major's bones.

"Oo-oo-oo-ooh!" groaned the Vizir, until Gaifar fairly shook in his buckled

The Vizir waved the baton aloft.

shoes. "You will never be able to keep us all from falling off the under side of earth into nowhere when we go over the edge!"

"What can I do?" moaned Gaifar, piteously.

"Humph!" chuckled the Vizir. "Just give me your baton, and go climb up into the band-wagon and help beat the bass-drum. I will lead this procession myself."

With a sigh of relief Gaifar slunk out of sight, and the Vizir waved the baton aloft with a crafty look in his eye. Tramp, tramp, tramp, went the horses' hoofs. Puff, puff, puff, strode the cushioned camels through the sand. But the Caliph slept like a top through it all. He was not going to let a little thing like riding around the world interfere with his regular sleep. Not he!

But the sly Vizir, ever wildly waving his baton, shouting, "Onward, march!" and inciting haste, until every one behind him in the procession was utterly blinded by the choking dust, swept out of the beaten track in a great curve, round and round, so gradually, so very gradually, that not one noticed it—round and round until, after describing an immense semicircle through the plain, the caravan again faced the North Star—from the other side of the city.

It was actually marching straight back into Baghdad!

At this juncture the first-cornet player of the band stubbed his toe. In his excitement he blew a blast so loud, so shrill, and so discordant that it pierced the ears of the Caliph. Waking with a start, he looked about him, dazed. Then perceiving the minarets of the city, he called furiously for the Grand Vizir, who answered on a gallop.

"Thou dog, why hast thou dared to disobey my command?" thundered the Caliph.

"Disobey thy command, Sire? What dost thou mean?" exclaimed the Vizir, with well-simulated amazement.

"What do I mean? What do I mean?" screamed the Caliph. "Why are we marching toward Baghdad, you villain?"

"Baghdad? Baghdad?" said the Vizir, looking at the Caliph as if in great surprise at the question. "Why, your royal highness, we sighted Baghdad a good three hours ago. We must be pretty nearly around the world!"

"Goodness gracious me!" cried the Caliph, in a fever of excitement. "You don't say so? Why didn't you wake me up when we were down on the under side? I might have fallen and disarranged some of the stars!

"Why, Selim," he exclaimed enthusiastically, looking at his watch, "we shall be back to Baghdad in time for breakfast!"

"Indeed?" said the Vizir, with a smile that meant as much as four ordinary smiles. "Why, that is so! Even now, methinks, I hear the Baghdad town-clock striking four o'clock in the morning."

The return to Baghdad

As he spoke the far-away boom of the great bell tolled across the plain, and the roosters began to crow in the barn-yards along the way.

Just as day dawned in the East the head of the procession entered the great gate of Baghdad in triumph, the Caliph and the Grand Vizir riding in state, behind snow-white palfreys, while far in advance ran heralds shouting in stentorian voices, "Make way for the Caliph! For the world is round, and he has ridden around it! Way for the Caliph!"

And the townspeople, wakened out of their sound slumbers by the sound of the shouting, plunged into their trousers in fright, threw up their windows, hurled back the shutters, and asked where the fire was, until, learning the cause of the uproar, all Baghdad joined in a mighty shout of acclaim, "Hail to the Caliph! Hail! For the world is round, and he has ridden around it!"

Instantly, upon reaching the palace, the Caliph in exultation called for his swiftest messengers and despatched them to the geography publishers with the amazing tidings. "Tell them," said he, "that the world is round and ridgy like a muskmelon; and that Persia runs completely around it in one direction, and pretty nearly around it in the other!"

"Now," sighed the Caliph, with a satisfied smile, "we will have our breakfast."

"And, your royal highness," murmured the Vizir, "perhaps it might not be a bad idea, as a celebration of your achievement, to let the Seven Sages out of the pantry, so that they may hear that the world is round."

First published in the December 1892 edition of *St. Nicholas Magazine*